NE능률 영어교과서

대한민국 고등학생 10명 중
4.7 명이 보는 교과서

영어 고등 교과서 점유율 1위
(7차, 2007 개정, 2009 개정, 2015 개정)

능률보카

그동안 판매된
능률VOCA 1,100만 부

대한민국 박스오피스
천만명을 넘은 영화
단 28개

리딩튜터

그동안 판매된
리딩튜터 1,900만 부
차곡차곡 쌓으면 19만 미터

에베레스트
21배 높이

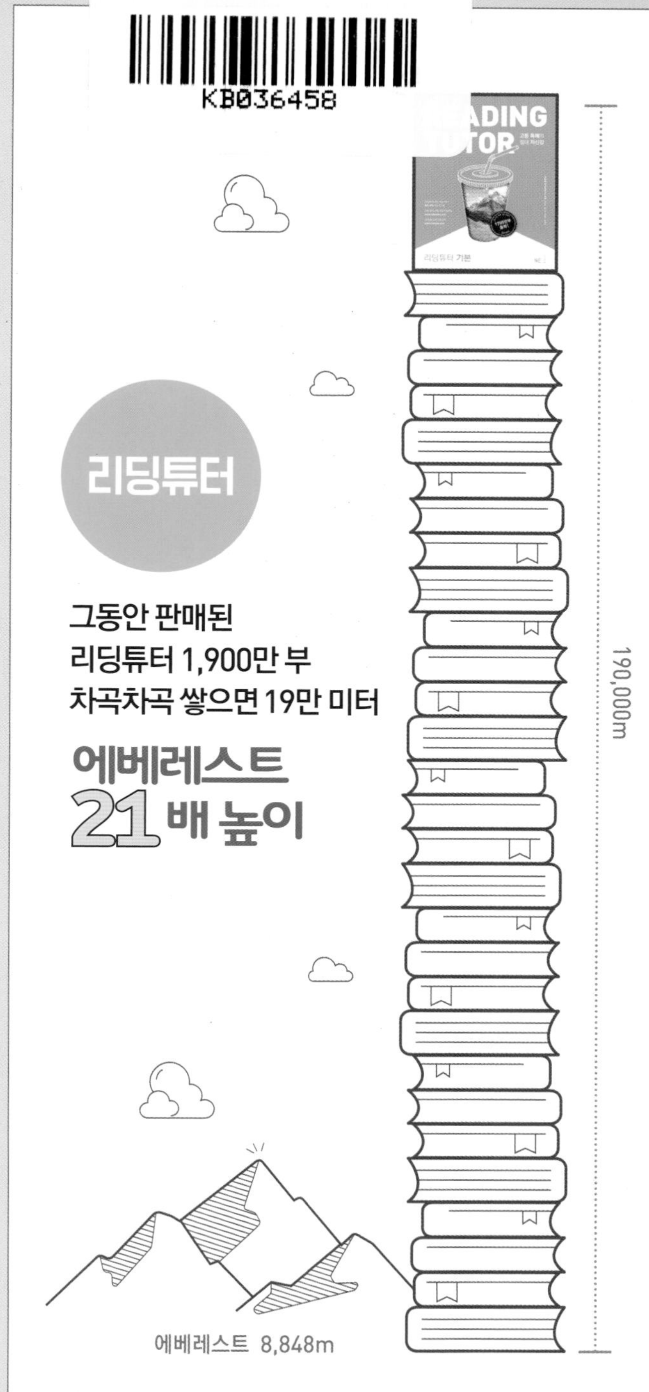

그래머존

그동안 판매된 450만 부의 그래머존을 바닥에 쭉 ~ 깔면
1000km 서울-부산 왕복가능

수능만만 기본

영어듣기 35+5회

지은이 NE능률 영어교육연구소
선임연구원 신유승
연구원 노지희
영문교열 MyAn Thi Le Patrick Ferraro August Niederhaus Caitlin Schmitt
디자인 민유화 김연주
내지 일러스트 박응식
맥편집 김미진
영업 한기영 이경구 박인규 정철교 김남준 이우현
마케팅 박혜선 남경진 이지원 김여진

NE능률이
미래를
창조합니다.

건강한 배움의 고객가치를 제공하겠다는 꿈을 실현하기 위해
40년이 넘는 시간 동안 열심히 달려왔습니다.

앞으로도 끊임없는 연구와 노력을 통해
당연한 것을 멈추지 않고

고객, 기업, 직원 모두가 함께 성장하는 NE능률이 되겠습니다.

만만한
수능영어

영어듣기
35+5회

구성과 특징

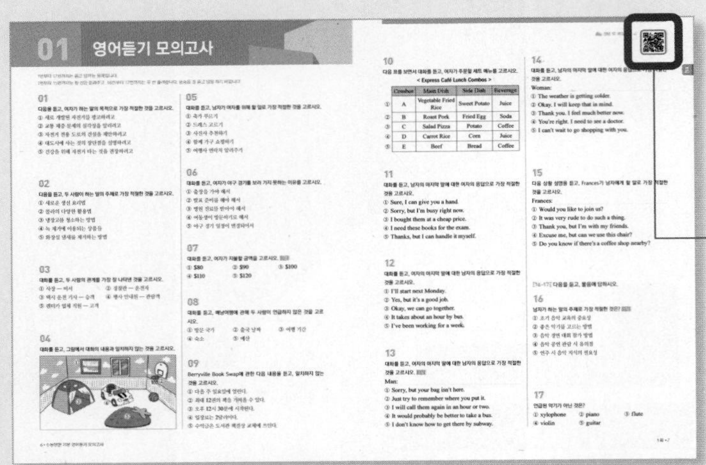

영어듣기 모의고사

- 최신 수능과 학력평가를 철저히 분석하여 문제 유형, 소재, 배치 등을 수능 및 학력평가와 동일하게 구성하였습니다.
- QR 코드를 스캔하면 바로 MP3를 청취할 수 있도록 하여 영어듣기 학습 편리성과 효율성을 높였습니다.

DICTATION

- 매 회 모의고사 뒤에 DICTATION 코너를 배치했습니다. 모의고사를 다시 듣고 잘 들리지 않은 연음, 중요한 표현을 받아쓰기하며 놓친 부분을 꼼꼼히 학습할 수 있습니다.

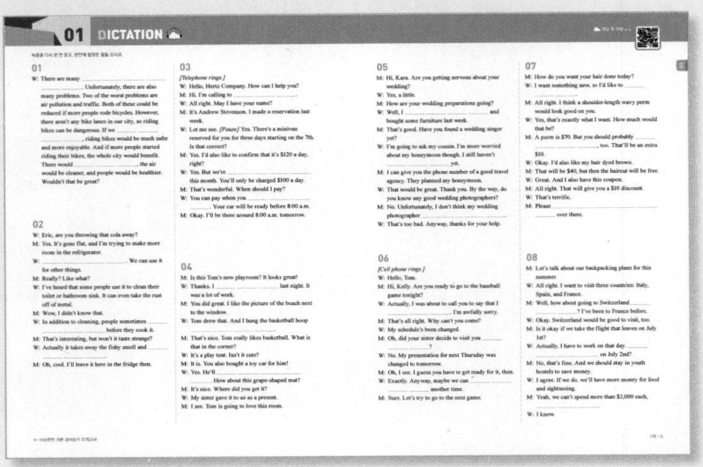

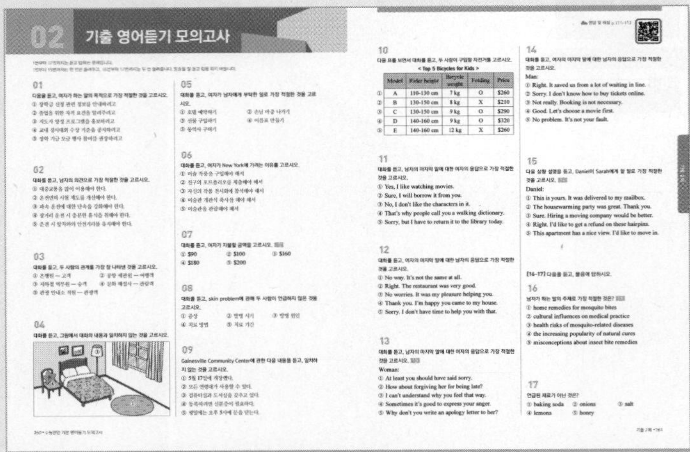

Words & Expressions

- 매 회 마지막 페이지에 모의고사 문제의 주요 어휘와 표현들을 정리했습니다. 꼼꼼히 확인하고 외우며 어휘 및 표현 실력을 높일 수 있습니다.

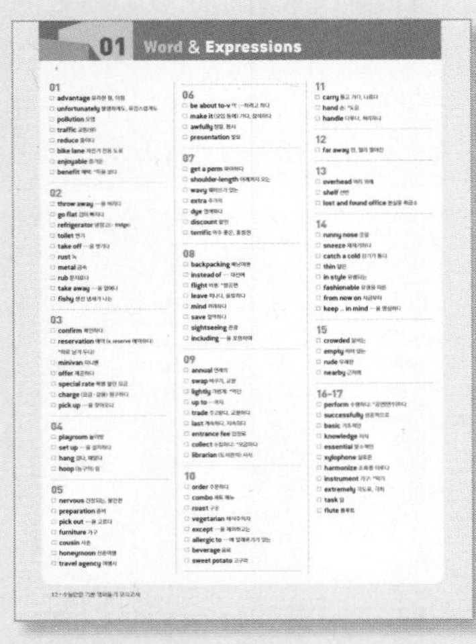

기출 영어듣기 모의고사

- 학력평가 기출 문항을 선별하여 모의고사 5회분을 수록하였습니다. 문제를 풀어보며 최신 학력평가의 경향을 파악하고 실전 감각을 높일 수 있습니다.

목차

수능만만
기 본

영어듣기 모의고사

—

01회 -35회

01 영어듣기 모의고사

1번부터 17번까지는 듣고 답하는 문제입니다.
1번부터 15번까지는 한 번만 들려주고, 16번부터 17번까지는 두 번 들려줍니다. 방송을 잘 듣고 답을 하기 바랍니다.

01

다음을 듣고, 여자가 하는 말의 목적으로 가장 적절한 것을 고르시오.

① 새로 개발된 자전거를 광고하려고
② 교통 체증 문제의 심각성을 알리려고
③ 자전거 전용 도로의 건설을 제안하려고
④ 대도시에 사는 것의 장단점을 설명하려고
⑤ 건강을 위해 자전거 타는 것을 권장하려고

02

다음을 듣고, 두 사람이 하는 말의 주제로 가장 적절한 것을 고르시오.

① 새로운 생선 요리법
② 콜라의 다양한 활용법
③ 냉장고를 청소하는 방법
④ 녹 제거에 이용되는 상품들
⑤ 화장실 냄새를 제거하는 방법

03

대화를 듣고, 두 사람의 관계를 가장 잘 나타낸 것을 고르시오.

① 사장 — 비서 ② 경찰관 — 운전자
③ 택시 운전 기사 — 승객 ④ 행사 안내원 — 관람객
⑤ 렌터카 업체 직원 — 고객

04

대화를 듣고, 그림에서 대화의 내용과 일치하지 않는 것을 고르시오.

05

대화를 듣고, 남자가 여자를 위해 할 일로 가장 적절한 것을 고르시오.

① 축가 부르기
② 드레스 고르기
③ 사진사 추천하기
④ 함께 가구 쇼핑하기
⑤ 여행사 연락처 알려주기

06

대화를 듣고, 여자가 야구 경기를 보러 가지 못하는 이유를 고르시오.

① 출장을 가야 해서
② 발표 준비를 해야 해서
③ 병원 진료를 받아야 해서
④ 여동생이 방문하기로 해서
⑤ 야구 경기 일정이 변경되어서

07

대화를 듣고, 여자가 지불할 금액을 고르시오. 3점

① \$80 ② \$90 ③ \$100
④ \$110 ⑤ \$120

08

대화를 듣고, 배낭여행에 관해 두 사람이 언급하지 않은 것을 고르시오.

① 방문 국가 ② 출국 날짜 ③ 여행 기간
④ 숙소 ⑤ 예산

09

Berryville Book Swap에 관한 다음 내용을 듣고, 일치하지 않는 것을 고르시오.

① 다음 주 일요일에 열린다.
② 최대 12권의 책을 가져올 수 있다.
③ 오후 12시 30분에 시작된다.
④ 입장료는 2달러이다.
⑤ 수익금은 도서관 책걸상 교체에 쓰인다.

10

다음 표를 보면서 대화를 듣고, 여자가 주문할 세트 메뉴를 고르시오.

< Express Café Lunch Combos >

	Combos	Main Dish	Side Dish	Beverage
①	A	Vegetable Fried Rice	Sweet Potato	Juice
②	B	Roast Pork	Fried Egg	Soda
③	C	Salad Pizza	Potato	Coffee
④	D	Carrot Rice	Corn	Juice
⑤	E	Beef	Bread	Coffee

11

대화를 듣고, 남자의 마지막 말에 대한 여자의 응답으로 가장 적절한 것을 고르시오.

① Sure, I can give you a hand.
② Sorry, but I'm busy right now.
③ I bought them at a cheap price.
④ I need these books for the exam.
⑤ Thanks, but I can handle it myself.

12

대화를 듣고, 여자의 마지막 말에 대한 남자의 응답으로 가장 적절한 것을 고르시오.

① I'll start next Monday.
② Yes, but it's a good job.
③ Okay, we can go together.
④ It takes about an hour by bus.
⑤ I've been working for a week.

13

대화를 듣고, 여자의 마지막 말에 대한 남자의 응답으로 가장 적절한 것을 고르시오. 3점

Man: ______________________

① Sorry, but your bag isn't here.
② Just try to remember where you put it.
③ I will call them again in an hour or two.
④ It would probably be better to take a bus.
⑤ I don't know how to get there by subway.

14

대화를 듣고, 남자의 마지막 말에 대한 여자의 응답으로 가장 적절한 것을 고르시오.

Woman: ______________________

① The weather is getting colder.
② Okay. I will keep that in mind.
③ Thank you. I feel much better now.
④ You're right. I need to see a doctor.
⑤ I can't wait to go shopping with you.

15

다음 상황 설명을 듣고, Frances가 남자에게 할 말로 가장 적절한 것을 고르시오.

Frances: ______________________

① Would you like to join us?
② It was very rude to do such a thing.
③ Thank you, but I'm with my friends.
④ Excuse me, but can we use this chair?
⑤ Do you know if there's a coffee shop nearby?

[16-17] 다음을 듣고, 물음에 답하시오.

16

남자가 하는 말의 주제로 가장 적절한 것은? 3점

① 조기 음악 교육의 중요성
② 좋은 악기를 고르는 방법
③ 음악 경연 대회 참가 방법
④ 음악 공연 관람 시 유의점
⑤ 연주 시 음악 지식의 필요성

17

언급된 악기가 아닌 것은?

① xylophone ② piano ③ flute
④ violin ⑤ guitar

01 DICTATION

녹음을 다시 한 번 듣고, 빈칸에 알맞은 말을 쓰시오.

01

W: There are many _______ _______ _______ _______ _______ _______. Unfortunately, there are also many problems. Two of the worst problems are air pollution and traffic. Both of these could be reduced if more people rode bicycles. However, there aren't any bike lanes in our city, so riding bikes can be dangerous. If we _______ _______ _______ _______, riding bikes would be much safer and more enjoyable. And if more people started riding their bikes, the whole city would benefit. There would _______ _______ _______, the air would be cleaner, and people would be healthier. Wouldn't that be great?

02

W: Eric, are you throwing that cola away?

M: Yes. It's gone flat, and I'm trying to make more room in the refrigerator.

W: _______ _______ _______ _______. We can use it for other things.

M: Really? Like what?

W: I've heard that some people use it to clean their toilet or bathroom sink. It can even take the rust off of metal.

M: Wow, I didn't know that.

W: In addition to cleaning, people sometimes _______ _______ _______ _______ before they cook it.

M: That's interesting, but won't it taste strange?

W: Actually it takes away the fishy smell and _______ _______ _______ _______.

M: Oh, cool. I'll leave it here in the fridge then.

03

[Telephone rings.]

W: Hello, Hertz Company. How can I help you?

M: Hi. I'm calling to _______ _______ _______.

W: All right. May I have your name?

M: It's Andrew Stevenson. I made a reservation last week.

W: Let me see. *[Pause]* Yes. There's a minivan reserved for you for three days starting on the 7th. Is that correct?

M: Yes. I'd also like to confirm that it's $120 a day, right?

W: Yes. But we're _______ _______ _______ _______ this month. You'll only be charged $100 a day.

M: That's wonderful. When should I pay?

W: You can pay when you _______ _______ _______ _______. Your car will be ready before 8:00 a.m.

M: Okay. I'll be there around 8:00 a.m. tomorrow.

04

M: Is this Tom's new playroom? It looks great!

W: Thanks. I _______ _______ _______ last night. It was a lot of work.

M: You did great. I like the picture of the beach next to the window.

W: Tom drew that. And I hung the basketball hoop _______ _______ _______ _______.

M: That's nice. Tom really likes basketball. What is that in the corner?

W: It's a play tent. Isn't it cute?

M: It is. You also bought a toy car for him!

W: Yes. He'll _______ _______ _______ _______ _______. How about this grape-shaped mat?

M: It's nice. Where did you get it?

W: My sister gave it to us as a present.

M: I see. Tom is going to love this room.

05

M: Hi, Kara. Are you getting nervous about your wedding?
W: Yes, a little.
M: How are your wedding preparations going?
W: Well, I _______ _______ _______ _______ and bought some furniture last week.
M: That's good. Have you found a wedding singer yet?
W: I'm going to ask my cousin. I'm more worried about my honeymoon though. I still haven't _______ _______ _______ yet.
M: I can give you the phone number of a good travel agency. They planned my honeymoon.
W: That would be great. Thank you. By the way, do you know any good wedding photographers?
M: No. Unfortunately, I don't think my wedding photographer _______ _______ _______ _______.
W: That's too bad. Anyway, thanks for your help.

06

[Cell phone rings.]
W: Hello, Tom.
M: Hi, Kelly. Are you ready to go to the baseball game tonight?
W: Actually, I was about to call you to say that I _______ _______ _______. I'm awfully sorry.
M: That's all right. Why can't you come?
W: My schedule's been changed.
M: Oh, did your sister decide to visit you _______ _______ _______?
W: No. My presentation for next Thursday was changed to tomorrow.
M: Oh, I see. I guess you have to get ready for it, then.
W: Exactly. Anyway, maybe we can _______ _______ _______ _______ another time.
M: Sure. Let's try to go to the next game.

07

M: How do you want your hair done today?
W: I want something new, so I'd like to _______ _______ _______.
M: All right. I think a shoulder-length wavy perm would look good on you.
W: Yes, that's exactly what I want. How much would that be?
M: A perm is $70. But you should probably _______ _______ _______ _______, too. That'll be an extra $10.
W: Okay. I'd also like my hair dyed brown.
M: That will be $40, but then the haircut will be free.
W: Great. And I also have this coupon.
M: All right. That will give you a $10 discount.
W: That's terrific.
M: Please _______ _______ _______ _______ _______ _______ over there.

08

M: Let's talk about our backpacking plans for this summer.
W: All right. I want to visit three countries: Italy, Spain, and France.
M: Well, how about going to Switzerland _______ _______ _______? I've been to France before.
W: Okay. Switzerland would be good to visit, too.
M: Is it okay if we take the flight that leaves on July 1st?
W: Actually, I have to work on that day. _______ _______ _______ _______ on July 2nd?
M: No, that's fine. And we should stay in youth hostels to save money.
W: I agree. If we do, we'll have more money for food and sightseeing.
M: Yeah, we can't spend more than $3,000 each, _______ _______ _______.
W: I know.

09

M: Hello, everyone! The first annual Berryville Book Swap will _______ _______ _______ _______ at the Hansontown Library. Please bring lightly used books that are still in good condition. You can _______ _______ _______ _______ _______ and trade them with others. The event starts at 12:30 p.m. and will last until four o'clock. Book trading is free, but there is a two-dollar entrance fee. The money collected will be used to _______ _______ _______ for the library. There will also be free snacks and drinks for everyone who attends. For more information, please speak with one of the librarians. We hope to see you all next week!

10

M: Welcome to Express Café. What can I get you today?

W: I'd like to order one of your lunch combos, but I'm not sure _______ _______ _______ _______.

M: How about the roast pork? It's the most popular combo.

W: Actually, I don't eat meat. I'm a vegetarian.

M: I see. We also have some vegetarian combos available. Which side dish _______ _______ _______?

W: I like everything except corn. I'm allergic to it.

M: Okay. Then which of these two combos would you like?

W: Let's see. Well, I don't drink coffee, so I'll _______ _______ _______.

M: Okay. Please have a seat, and I'll let you know when your order is ready.

11

M: Hi, Lisa. What are you carrying?

W: Hi, Mark. It's a box with some books I bought online yesterday.

M: It looks heavy. Do you _______ _______ _______ _______ _______?

W: (Thanks, but I can handle it myself.)

12

W: I heard you're starting a new job next week. Are you excited?

M: Yes, I can't wait! But the office is pretty far away.

W: Oh, is it? How long does it _______ _______ _______ _______?

M: (It takes about an hour by bus.)

13

W: Hi, Oliver. How are you today?

M: Not good. I _______ _______ _______ on the subway. I usually don't forget things like that.

W: Really? Are you sure you left it there?

M: Yes, I remember I put it on the overhead shelf before I sat down.

W: Then you should call the lost and found office. They _______ _______ _______.

M: I already did that. They said no one has brought in any bags today.

W: That's too bad. When were you on the subway?

M: Just thirty minutes ago.

W: In that case, maybe someone found it but _______ _______ _______ to the office yet.

M: (I will call them again in an hour or two.)

14

M: Jennifer, are you okay? You don't look so good.

W: I ________ ________ ________ ________, Dad.

M: What's wrong?

W: I have a runny nose, and I keep sneezing.

M: It sounds like you ________ ________ ________.

W: I think so, too. It's because of the cold weather these days.

M: I think the clothes you are wearing these days are too thin.

W: But they're really in style now. I want to look fashionable.

M: ________ ________ ________ ________ ________. Your health is the most important thing.

W: I guess you're right. I don't want to be sick.

M: You should wear warmer clothes and a scarf from now on.

W: (Okay. I will keep that in mind.)

15

W: Frances is a college student. One day, she and two of her friends decide to meet for coffee. When they arrive at the coffee shop, it ________ ________ ________. After getting their drinks, they find a free table, but there are only two chairs at that table. They look around the shop and see a man ________ ________ at a table. There is an empty chair next to him, but he doesn't seem to be waiting for anyone. Frances wants to ________ ________ ________ ________ ________ ________. In this situation, what would Frances most likely say to the man?

Frances: (Excuse me, but can we use this chair?)

16-17

M: What do you think is needed if you want to perform a song successfully? Well, a basic knowledge of music is essential. Here's ________ ________ ________ ________ ________. Imagine that you're a member of a music club at your school. Your club is going to perform the song "Do-Re-Mi" at your school festival. It ________ ________ ________ ________ ________ to play, but actually it's not. You will perform this song with four other students. Two of them will play the xylophone, and another student will play the piano. One other student will play the violin, and you're going to play the guitar. If you want to make the song sound good, your guitar ________ ________ ________ ________ each different instrument. Therefore, you need to understand how each instrument sounds. Without basic musical knowledge, that could be an extremely difficult task!

01 Word & Expressions

01
- □ **advantage** 유리한 점, 이점
- □ **unfortunately** 불행하게도, 유감스럽게도
- □ **pollution** 오염
- □ **traffic** 교통(량)
- □ **reduce** 줄이다
- □ **bike lane** 자전거 전용 도로
- □ **enjoyable** 즐거운
- □ **benefit** 혜택; *득을 보다

02
- □ **throw away** …을 버리다
- □ **go flat** 김이 빠지다
- □ **refrigerator** 냉장고(= fridge)
- □ **toilet** 변기
- □ **take off** …을 벗기다
- □ **rust** 녹
- □ **metal** 금속
- □ **rub** 문지르다
- □ **take away** …을 없애다
- □ **fishy** 생선 냄새가 나는

03
- □ **confirm** 확인하다
- □ **reservation** 예약 (v. reserve 예약하다; *따로 남겨 두다)
- □ **minivan** 미니밴
- □ **offer** 제공하다
- □ **special rate** 특별 할인 요금
- □ **charge** (요금 · 값을) 청구하다
- □ **pick up** …을 찾아오다

04
- □ **playroom** 놀이방
- □ **set up** …을 설치하다
- □ **hang** 걸다, 매달다
- □ **hoop** (농구의) 링

05
- □ **nervous** 긴장되는, 불안한
- □ **preparation** 준비
- □ **pick out** …을 고르다
- □ **furniture** 가구
- □ **cousin** 사촌
- □ **honeymoon** 신혼여행
- □ **travel agency** 여행사

06
- □ **be about to-v** 막 …하려고 하다
- □ **make it** (모임 등에) 가다, 참석하다
- □ **awfully** 정말, 몹시
- □ **presentation** 발표

07
- □ **get a perm** 파마하다
- □ **shoulder-length** 어깨까지 오는
- □ **wavy** 웨이브가 있는
- □ **extra** 추가의
- □ **dye** 염색하다
- □ **discount** 할인
- □ **terrific** 아주 좋은, 훌륭한

08
- □ **backpacking** 배낭여행
- □ **instead of** … 대신에
- □ **flight** 비행; *항공편
- □ **leave** 떠나다, 출발하다
- □ **mind** 꺼려하다
- □ **save** 절약하다
- □ **sightseeing** 관광
- □ **including** …을 포함하여

09
- □ **annual** 연례의
- □ **swap** 바꾸기, 교환
- □ **lightly** 가볍게; *약간
- □ **up to** …까지
- □ **trade** 주고받다, 교환하다
- □ **last** 계속하다, 지속되다
- □ **entrance fee** 입장료
- □ **collect** 수집하다; *모금하다
- □ **librarian** (도서관의) 사서

10
- □ **order** 주문하다
- □ **combo** 세트 메뉴
- □ **roast** 구운
- □ **vegetarian** 채식주의자
- □ **except** …을 제외하고는
- □ **allergic to** …에 알레르기가 있는
- □ **beverage** 음료
- □ **sweet potato** 고구마

11
- □ **carry** 들고 가다, 나르다
- □ **hand** 손; *도움
- □ **handle** 다루다, 처리하다

12
- □ **far away** 먼, 멀리 떨어진

13
- □ **overhead** 머리 위에
- □ **shelf** 선반
- □ **lost and found office** 분실물 취급소

14
- □ **runny nose** 콧물
- □ **sneeze** 재채기하다
- □ **catch a cold** 감기가 들다
- □ **thin** 얇은
- □ **in style** 유행되는
- □ **fashionable** 유행을 따른
- □ **from now on** 지금부터
- □ **keep ... in mind** …을 명심하다

15
- □ **crowded** 붐비는
- □ **empty** 비어 있는
- □ **rude** 무례한
- □ **nearby** 근처에

16-17
- □ **perform** 수행하다; *공연[연주]하다
- □ **successfully** 성공적으로
- □ **basic** 기초적인
- □ **knowledge** 지식
- □ **essential** 필수적인
- □ **xylophone** 실로폰
- □ **harmonize** 조화를 이루다
- □ **instrument** 기구; *악기
- □ **extremely** 극도로, 극히
- □ **task** 일
- □ **flute** 플루트

02 영어듣기 모의고사

정답 및 해설 p.5-7

1번부터 17번까지는 듣고 답하는 문제입니다.
1번부터 15번까지는 한 번만 들려주고, 16번부터 17번까지는 두 번 들려줍니다. 방송을 잘 듣고 답을 하기 바랍니다.

01

다음을 듣고, 여자가 하는 말의 목적으로 가장 적절한 것을 고르시오.

① 웃음의 긍정적인 효과를 강조하려고
② 공연 관람 시 주의사항을 공지하려고
③ 근육을 이완시키는 방법을 설명하려고
④ 집중력을 향상시키는 방법을 소개하려고
⑤ 무대 공포증을 극복하는 방법을 알리려고

02

대화를 듣고, 여자의 의견으로 가장 적절한 것을 고르시오.

① 게시판을 추가로 설치해야 한다.
② 지정된 장소에만 포스터를 붙여야 한다.
③ 포스터를 부착하려면 허가를 받아야 한다.
④ 게시판의 공지 사항을 자주 확인해야 한다.
⑤ 효과적인 홍보를 위해 포스터를 제작해야 한다.

03

대화를 듣고, 두 사람의 관계를 가장 잘 나타낸 것을 고르시오.

① 버스 기사 — 승객　② 여행사 직원 — 고객
③ 호텔 직원 — 투숙객　④ 항공사 직원 — 탑승객
⑤ 여행안내원 — 관광객

04

대화를 듣고, 그림에서 대화의 내용과 일치하지 않는 것을 고르시오.

05

대화를 듣고, 남자가 여자를 위해 할 일로 가장 적절한 것을 고르시오.

① 물건 반품하기
② 택배 상품 받기
③ 티셔츠 골라주기
④ 우편물 찾아오기
⑤ 여행 계획 세우기

06

대화를 듣고, 여자가 화가 난 이유를 고르시오.

① 미용실 대기 손님이 많아서
② 미용실 위치를 잘못 알려줘서
③ 미용실 직원이 친절하지 않아서
④ 머리 모양이 마음에 들지 않아서
⑤ 미용실 예약이 되어 있지 않아서

07

대화를 듣고, 여자가 지불할 금액을 고르시오. 3점

① $28　② $30　③ $45
④ $46　⑤ $50

08

대화를 듣고, 책에 관해 두 사람이 언급하지 않은 것을 고르시오.

① 작가　② 시대 배경
③ 첫 출간 연도　④ 인기 이유
⑤ 주인공의 직업

09

특별 전통 시장에 관한 다음 내용을 듣고, 일치하지 않는 것을 고르시오.

① 7월 한 달간 진행된다.
② 시청 앞에서 열릴 것이다.
③ 판매원들은 전통 의상을 착용할 것이다.
④ 전통 음식을 시식할 수 있다.
⑤ 주말을 제외하고 매일 열린다.

10

다음 표를 보면서 대화를 듣고, 남자가 구입할 태블릿 컴퓨터를 고르시오. 3점

< List of Tablet Computers >

	Model	Screen Size	Price	Storage
①	A	10 inch	$450	16 GB
②	B	12 inch	$460	16 GB
③	C	10 inch	$550	32 GB
④	D	7 inch	$250	8 GB
⑤	E	8 inch	$300	8 GB

11

대화를 듣고, 여자의 마지막 말에 대한 남자의 응답으로 가장 적절한 것을 고르시오.

① Don't worry. I can help you.
② I hope you will recover soon.
③ I'm sorry, but I can't join you.
④ Yes, he's feeling much better now.
⑤ It was a great time with my family.

12

대화를 듣고, 남자의 마지막 말에 대한 여자의 응답으로 가장 적절한 것을 고르시오.

① I go at least twice a month.
② I usually go there by subway.
③ I like romantic comedies the most.
④ I usually read books in my free time.
⑤ Why don't you see a movie this weekend?

13

대화를 듣고, 남자의 마지막 말에 대한 여자의 응답으로 가장 적절한 것을 고르시오. 3점

Woman: ____________________

① Then I'll email you our digital brochure.
② I think the Mediterranean cruise is better.
③ The information will be sent by mail, then.
④ When are you going on your business trip?
⑤ How about taking a more adventurous trip?

14

대화를 듣고, 여자의 마지막 말에 대한 남자의 응답으로 가장 적절한 것을 고르시오. 3점

Man: ____________________

① I'll pick a better topic next time.
② No, I submitted the report on time.
③ Don't worry. I can give you a hand.
④ Right. I've learned my lesson this time.
⑤ I don't think so. I usually do it in advance.

15

다음 상황 설명을 듣고, Gloria가 소방관에게 할 말로 가장 적절한 것을 고르시오.

Gloria: ____________________

① My leg got stuck between some rocks.
② Thank you for helping me find my lost cat.
③ A fire broke out in the park near my house.
④ I found someone who fell down in the park.
⑤ Can you come to the park to rescue this cat?

[16-17] 다음을 듣고, 물음에 답하시오.

16

남자가 하는 말의 목적으로 가장 적절한 것은?

① 음악 축제를 홍보하려고
② 축제 일정 변경을 공지하려고
③ 축제 표 예매 방법을 알리려고
④ 다양한 재활용 방법을 설명하려고
⑤ 축제 참여에 편리한 교통편을 소개하려고

17

표를 할인받을 수 있는 방법으로 언급되지 않은 것은?

① 기부할 옷 가져오기
② 재활용할 건전지 가져오기
③ 녹색 의상 착용하기
④ 대중 교통 이용하기
⑤ 소식지 신청하기

정답 및 해설 p.7

녹음을 다시 한 번 듣고, 빈칸에 알맞은 말을 쓰시오.

01

W: Some of you may feel nervous about giving a presentation or performance in front of many people. This anxiety is called "stage fright," and ________ ________ ________ ________. Fortunately, there are some things you can do to control it. First, take a few deep breaths. Next, sit or stand comfortably so that your muscles can relax. Then try to make the audience laugh to relieve some of the pressure. Finally, ________ ________ ________ what you need to do. Don't worry about what other people are going to think. These simple things can help you ________ ________ ________ ________ and get the best possible result.

02

M: Hi, Kate! What are you doing here?

W: Hi, Jack. I'm just putting up posters for the drama club. We're looking for new members.

M: I see. Did you ________ ________ ________ ________ ________?

W: Yes, I did.

M: Okay. But I don't think you can put the poster here.

W: Why not? It's the perfect place. Every student will see this poster ________ ________ ________ ________ the cafeteria.

M: But you're not allowed to hang it here. It has to go on the bulletin board.

W: I already checked the board. It's full.

M: Unfortunately, that's the only place for posters.

W: The school should make another board. That way, students can ________ ________ ________.

M: I agree.

03

W: Good evening, sir. How can I help you?

M: I'm just wondering what time the airport shuttle bus leaves tomorrow.

W: It ________ ________ ________ from 6:00 a.m. to 8:00 p.m.

M: Great. Thank you.

W: Is there anything else you want to ask?

M: Yes, one more thing. What time do I ________ ________ ________ ________ tomorrow?

W: Checkout is at 11:00 a.m.

M: It's a bit early. Is there any way I can check out three hours later?

W: I'm sorry, sir. There are no exceptions. But we can ________ ________ ________ at the front desk, and you can pick it up later.

M: Oh, that would be great.

04

M: The tent is all set up. Come on in.

W: Wow, it looks great. You put the table ________ ________ ________ ________ the tent.

M: Yes. I also put two chairs at the table. We can eat dinner there.

W: Excellent! Is this a heater?

M: Yes, I put a small heater to the right of the table. We can ________ ________ ________ when it gets cold.

W: Good job. And a lantern is hanging above the table. We can read books or play games at night.

M: Right. I also put up a small Christmas tree to celebrate Christmas Eve today.

W: Yeah. I see it to the left of the table.

M: This is going to be ________ ________ ________ ________.

05

M: Hi, Mary. I heard you're going to Florida for spring break.

W: Yeah. I'm leaving tomorrow, and I'll stay there ______ ______ ______.

M: You must be excited. It's the best time to visit there.

W: I think so, too. But could you ______ ______ ______ ______ while I'm gone?

M: Sure. What would you like me to do?

W: I have something I need to return by mail. I bought a T-shirt, but it doesn't fit.

M: That's too bad. Will the delivery man come to the office to pick it up?

W: Yes, he will visit the office tomorrow morning.

M: I see. ______ ______ ______ it. I'll give it to him.

W: Thanks a lot.

06

M: Welcome to BT Salon!

W: Hi. I ______ ______ ______ for two o'clock. My name is Susan Burns.

M: Susan Burns? There seems to be a problem.

W: It's all right if I have to wait for a few minutes.

M: Actually, I don't see your name. We have an appointment for another person at two o'clock.

W: But I called yesterday to confirm.

M: Sorry, ma'am. Would you like to ______ ______ ______ ______ ______?

W: No, I don't have any time this week except right now.

M: I'm sorry, but there are no available times until this evening.

W: I don't understand ______ ______ ______.

M: Again, I'm really sorry, but there's nothing I can do about it.

07

W: Hi. I would like to purchase some meal tickets for the cafeteria.

M: Okay. Each ticket is $2.

W: Is there a discount if I buy ______ ______ ______ ______?

M: Yes. Ten tickets are $18, and twenty tickets are $35.

W: Then I will buy twenty tickets.

M: Okay. Would you like to buy some café coupons, too? ______ ______ ______ $1 and is good for a cup of coffee from the library café.

W: Can't I just use cash there?

M: Yes, but if you purchase ten café coupons, we will ______ ______ ______ ______ ______.

W: Oh, that sounds like a good deal. I'll buy ten café coupons now, too.

08

W: Hi, Eric. What are you reading?

M: Hi, Samantha. I'm reading *A Farewell to Arms* by Ernest Hemingway.

W: Oh, I haven't read that book yet. What's it about?

M: It's a love story that ______ ______ ______ Italy during World War I.

W: Oh, that sounds interesting. When was it written?

M: It ______ ______ ______ in 1929, and it's been popular ever since.

W: I didn't know that. But I know that Hemingway is an American writer. Are the main characters American, too?

M: No, the main male character is an American soldier. The main female character is a British nurse.

W: I see. Maybe I'll ______ ______ ______ from the library later.

09

M: During July, there will be a fun month-long event in Seoul. We will set up a special market in front of City Hall. Sellers will be dressed _______ _______ _______, and they will sell many interesting items. Tourists can buy souvenirs while experiencing _______ _______ _______ of a traditional market. They will also enjoy sampling various traditional foods. The market will be open every day from 10:00 a.m. to 7:00 p.m. On the weekends, there will also be traditional music and dance performances! I hope many of you will _______ _______ _______ _______.

10

W: Hi. Can I help you?
M: Yes, I would like to buy a tablet computer.
W: Great. We _______ _______ _______ _______. Will you use it mainly for work or fun?
M: I'll mostly use it to watch movies and TV shows.
W: In that case, I recommend getting one with at least an eight-inch screen.
M: Okay, but I don't want to _______ _______ _______ $500.
W: No problem. Take a look at these. Would eight gigabytes be enough storage for you?
M: No, I need more storage.
W: Then we have _______ _______ _______.
M: I think I'll choose the one with the larger screen.
W: Okay, that's a great choice.

11

W: Matthew, did you have a good weekend?
M: No, I didn't. My father was sick, so I had to _______ _______ _______ _______.
W: Oh, I'm sorry to hear that. Has he recovered?
M: (Yes, he's feeling much better now.)

12

M: Jenny, what do you usually _______ _______ _______ _______ _______?
W: I really like going to the movies.
M: Oh, really? How often do you go to the movies?
W: (I go at least twice a month.)

13

[Telephone rings.]
W: Hello, Globe Travel Agency. How can I help you?
M: Hi. I'd like to _______ _______ _______ on your vacation packages this summer.
W: Great. Would you like something adventurous or relaxing?
M: Just something relaxing, please.
W: Then, which one would you like? The beach spa package or the cruise package?
M: The cruise package _______ _______ _______ _______.
W: Okay. We have luxury cruises in both the Mediterranean and the Caribbean.
M: Those sound nice. Could you send me some more information?
W: Of course. I can mail you a brochure today. Can I get your address?
M: Actually, I'm _______ _______ _______ _______ at the moment, so I can't get my mail.
W: (Then I'll email you our digital brochure.)

14

W: Did you finish your history report, Brian?

M: Yes, but I couldn't submit it today.

W: What? Then you might get an F on the report!

M: Yes, I know. I'm feeling really stressed out.

W: I'm sorry to hear that. Why didn't you _______ _______ _______ on time?

M: I was hurrying to finish the report this morning. And then I _______ _______ _______ it to school.

W: That's probably because you were rushing. Why didn't you work on it in advance?

M: I just kept putting it off. I usually start working right _______ _______ _______ anyway.

W: That sounds like a bad habit. This will keep happening if you don't start your work earlier.

M: (Right. I've learned my lesson this time.)

15

W: Gloria is _______ _______ _______ _______ from school in the afternoon. As she walks through the park near her house, she finds a cat stuck between some rocks. It _______ _______ _______ _______, and it is trembling. It looks very frightened. Gloria thinks the cat has probably been stuck there for a long time. However, she _______ _______ _______ _______ _______ _______ the cat because she cannot move the rocks. Therefore, she calls the fire station for help. In this situation, what would Gloria most likely say to the firefighter?

Gloria: (Can you come to the park to rescue this cat?)

16-17

M: May I have your attention, please? I would like to tell you about this year's Go-Green Music Festival. Last year's festival was lots of fun, as you know. So I hope that you all _______ _______ _______ this year to enjoy the music and fun activities. This year more singers and bands will participate in the festival. Plus, you can get a special discount on tickets by doing the following. Bring your old clothes to donate and used batteries to recycle, wear something green, or simply _______ _______ _______ _______ _______. Now, since parking is often a problem, please use public transportation. It will make your getting here easier, and it will be better for the environment. Finally, bring a garbage bag _______ _______ _______ _______. I'm looking forward to seeing you at Green Park on April 20th.

02 Word & Expressions

01
- □ performance 공연
- □ stage fright 무대 공포증
- □ completely 완전히
- □ control 통제하다; *막다
- □ take a deep breath 심호흡하다
- □ audience 청중
- □ relieve 덜어 주다
- □ pressure 압박감
- □ focus on …에 집중하다
- □ result 결과, 결실

02
- □ put up …을 세우다; *…을 게시하다
- □ permission 허가, 허락
- □ cafeteria 구내식당
- □ bulletin board 게시판
- □ share 공유하다

03
- □ wonder 궁금하다
- □ check out (호텔에서) 나가다, 체크아웃하다(n. checkout 체크아웃)
- □ exception 예외
- □ luggage 짐
- □ front desk 안내 데스크
- □ pick up …을 집다; …을 찾아오다

04
- □ set up …을 설치하다
- □ heater 난방기, 히터
- □ lantern 랜턴, 손전등
- □ hang 걸리다, 매달리다
- □ celebrate 기념하다

05
- □ do ... a favor …의 부탁을 들어주다
- □ by mail 우편으로
- □ fit 맞다
- □ delivery man 배달원

06
- □ appointment 약속, 예약
- □ confirm 확인하다
- □ reschedule 일정을 변경하다
- □ except 제외하고는
- □ available 이용할 수 있는

07
- □ purchase 구입하다
- □ at once 한꺼번에
- □ cash 현금
- □ deal 거래

08
- □ farewell 작별
- □ take place 일어나다, 발생하다
- □ publish 출판[출간]하다
- □ ever since 그 이래 줄곧
- □ main character 주인공
- □ male 남자의
- □ female 여자의
- □ check out (도서관 등에서) …을 대출하다

09
- □ traditional 전통적인
- □ clothing 옷, 의복
- □ souvenir 기념품
- □ unique 독특한
- □ atmosphere 분위기
- □ sample 시식하다
- □ various 다양한
- □ participate in …에 참가하다

10
- □ option 선택(권)
- □ mainly 주로, 대개
- □ recommend 추천하다
- □ storage 저장; *저장량

11
- □ take care of …을 돌보다
- □ recover (건강이) 회복되다

12
- □ at least 적어도

13
- □ package 꾸러미; *패키지여행
- □ adventurous 모험적인
- □ relaxing 마음을 느긋하게 해 주는
- □ luxury 호화로운
- □ cruise 유람선 여행
- □ brochure (안내) 책자, 브로셔
- □ business trip 출장

14
- □ submit 제출하다
- □ stressed out 스트레스를 받는
- □ hand in …을 제출하다
- □ on time 제때에
- □ rush (너무 급히) 서두르다
- □ in advance 미리
- □ put off …을 미루다
- □ deadline 기한, 마감 시간
- □ lesson 수업; *교훈

15
- □ stick (…에 끼여) 꼼짝하지 않다
- □ mud 진흙
- □ tremble 떨다
- □ frightened 겁먹은
- □ break out (화재 등이) 발생하다
- □ fall down 쓰러지다, 넘어지다
- □ rescue 구조하다

16-17
- □ attention 주의 집중, 주목
- □ following 다음 (사항)
- □ donate 기부하다
- □ recycle 재활용하다
- □ sign up for …을 신청하다
- □ newsletter (조직의) 소식지
- □ public transportation 대중교통
- □ environment 환경
- □ garbage bag 쓰레기봉투
- □ personal 개인적인
- □ trash 쓰레기
- □ look forward to …을 고대하다

03 영어듣기 모의고사

1번부터 17번까지는 듣고 답하는 문제입니다.
1번부터 15번까지는 한 번만 들려주고, 16번부터 17번까지는 두 번 들려줍니다. 방송을 잘 듣고 답을 하기 바랍니다.

01

다음을 듣고, 여자가 하는 말의 목적으로 가장 적절한 것을 고르시오.

① 상품의 품절을 알리려고
② 매장 오픈을 광고하려고
③ 특별 할인 행사를 공지하려고
④ 새로 나온 가방을 소개하려고
⑤ 상품 불량에 대해 사과하려고

02

대화를 듣고, 두 사람이 하는 말의 주제로 가장 적절한 것을 고르시오.

① 정전 사태의 원인
② 전기를 절약하는 방법
③ 외출 시 확인해야 할 사항
④ 전기세 부과 방식의 문제점
⑤ 전자제품 구입 시 유의할 점

03

대화를 듣고, 두 사람의 관계를 가장 잘 나타낸 것을 고르시오.

① 사육사 — 수의사　② 고객 — 서점 직원
③ 수강생 — 미술 교사　④ 출판사 직원 — 삽화가
⑤ 고객 — 인테리어 업자

04

대화를 듣고, 그림에서 대화의 내용과 일치하지 않는 것을 고르시오.

05

대화를 듣고, 여자가 남자를 위해 할 일로 가장 적절한 것을 고르시오.

① 호텔 예약하기
② 항공권 구입하기
③ 여행 계획 세우기
④ 여권 재발급 도와주기
⑤ 스페인어 가르쳐주기

06

대화를 듣고, 남자가 노트북 컴퓨터를 새로 구입하려는 이유를 고르시오.

① 고장이 나서
② 켜지지 않아서
③ 신제품이 출시돼서
④ 휴대하기 불편해서
⑤ 속도가 너무 느려서

07

대화를 듣고, 남자가 지불할 금액을 고르시오. 3점

① $9　② $14　③ $15
④ $17　⑤ $20

08

대화를 듣고, toy block tower에 관해 두 사람이 언급하지 않은 것을 고르시오.

① 만든 사람　② 높이　③ 사용한 블록 수
④ 만든 이유　⑤ 만든 시기

09

prairie dog에 관한 다음 내용을 듣고, 일치하지 않는 것을 고르시오. 3점

① 다람쥐의 한 종류이다.
② 풀과 작은 곤충을 먹고 산다.
③ 땅 밑에서 산다.
④ 서너 마리씩 작은 무리를 지어 산다.
⑤ 큰 소리를 내어 위험을 알린다.

정답 및 해설 p.8-10

10

다음 표를 보면서 대화를 듣고, 두 사람이 선택할 프로그램을 고르시오.

< Summer Camp Programs >

	Program	Subject	Number of Field Trips	Price
①	A	English	2	$30
②	B	Art	3	$45
③	C	History	2	$40
④	D	Science	3	$50
⑤	E	Math	4	$55

11

대화를 듣고, 여자의 마지막 말에 대한 남자의 응답으로 가장 적절한 것을 고르시오.

① I'm sorry, but those are our rules.
② Neither of those are very healthy.
③ All guests must show their ticket.
④ You can buy a ticket at the counter.
⑤ Those are the only snacks we sell here.

12

대화를 듣고, 남자의 마지막 말에 대한 여자의 응답으로 가장 적절한 것을 고르시오.

① I'm so sleepy right now.
② My neighbors are so noisy.
③ You need to go to bed early.
④ Getting enough sleep is important.
⑤ I'm used to being in an apartment.

13

대화를 듣고, 남자의 마지막 말에 대한 여자의 응답으로 가장 적절한 것을 고르시오.

Woman: ______________________

① Yeah, I'll take more vitamins.
② Is there anything else you need today?
③ Then why don't you try some samples?
④ There is no difference between the two.
⑤ I think that you've made the right decision.

14

대화를 듣고, 여자의 마지막 말에 대한 남자의 응답으로 가장 적절한 것을 고르시오.

Man: ______________________

① I didn't like the first book.
② I just want to buy the DVD.
③ Then I'll buy the whole series.
④ I really enjoyed the book series.
⑤ Let me know when they go on sale.

15

다음 상황 설명을 듣고, Amanda가 상점 직원에게 할 말로 가장 적절한 것을 고르시오.

Amanda: ______________________

① The package was delivered too late.
② The blouse that I ordered was white.
③ The blouse you sent me arrived dirty.
④ I thought that this blouse was on sale.
⑤ You sent me the blouse in the wrong size.

[16-17] 다음을 듣고, 물음에 답하시오.

16

남자가 하는 말의 목적으로 가장 적절한 것은?

① 노화 예방법을 소개하려고
② 비타민 섭취의 필요성을 강조하려고
③ 신선한 사과 선별 방법을 설명하려고
④ 아침 식사로 좋은 음식을 추천하려고
⑤ 사과를 먹는 다양한 방법을 알리려고

17

언급된 효능이 아닌 것은?

① 콜레스테롤 저하
② 심장병 예방
③ 암 예방
④ 뇌 기능 향상
⑤ 피부 노화 예방

03 DICTATION

녹음을 다시 한 번 듣고, 빈칸에 알맞은 말을 쓰시오.

01

W: Good evening, shoppers. We hope you are all enjoying our annual backpack sale. We have received a fantastic response from our customers regarding the sale. As a result, one of the backpack models is _______ _______ _______. The Hello Puppy backpacks, which were shown in our poster ads, are no longer available. Unfortunately, we cannot order any more of that item. We _______ _______ _______ _______. However, there are still many backpacks that are on sale from 30 to 60% off. I'm sure we have another backpack that's just right for you. Thank you for choosing Super Mart, and enjoy _______ _______ _______ your shopping.

02

W: Have you seen this month's electric bill?

M: Yeah. It's really high, isn't it?

W: Yes, it is. We need to _______ _______ _______.

M: But we've tried hard already. Is there anything more we can do?

W: I'm sure there is.

M: How? We always turn off the appliances _______ _______ _______ _______.

W: That's great, but they're still using electricity even when they're plugged in.

M: Okay. Let's try to remember to unplug them when we're not using them.

W: And we should stop using the air conditioner.

M: But it's still hot during the day.

W: We can use the fan _______ _______ _______ _______ _______.

M: Okay, I'm willing to try. Let's start doing that.

03

[Telephone rings.]

M: Hello?

W: Hi, Jeff. This is Wendy calling about the illustration for my book.

M: Hi, Wendy. I've just finished it.

W: That's good. I just _______ _______ _______ _______ it's correct. In the illustration, the man riding in front is looking back, right?

M: That's right. And he is wearing boots with pointed toes.

W: I see. Is he wearing a hat on his head?

M: Oh, sorry. I forgot that. I've already _______ _______ _______, so I have to sketch a new one.

W: I see. Will it take long to sketch and color it?

M: Not really, I think I need three hours.

W: Okay, so when can you send all your work to me?

M: I can _______ _______ _______ by tonight.

04

M: What a nice photo! Did you go swimming at the local pool?

W: Yes, I went there with my family last week.

M: The boy _______ _______ _______ _______ with his arms in the air looks happy.

W: That's my little brother, and that's me floating in a tube.

M: Who are the boys throwing the ball?

W: They're my cousins. The woman wearing sunglasses and _______ _______ _______ _______ is my aunt.

M: I see. Is the man on the other side of the pool her husband?

W: The one standing _______ _______ _______ _______ _______ _______? No. That's the lifeguard.

M: Oh, is it? Anyway, it looks like you had fun.

W: Yes, I did.

05

W: Mike, I heard you're going to Spain next month.
M: Yeah. _______ _______ _______!
W: Did you check when your passport expires?
M: Yes, I did. There are still a few years left.
W: How about the plane tickets? Have you bought them yet?
M: Yes, I bought them last month. I also _______ _______ _______ and planned out my schedule.
W: Wow! It sounds like you're all ready to go.
M: Yes, but I'm worried about my Spanish. I can't speak it at all.
W: Don't worry. I can help you with that. You know, I majored in Spanish.
M: That's great! _______ _______ _______ _______ some basic expressions?
W: Sure. Let's meet here tomorrow afternoon.

06

W: Hi, Eric. Do you _______ _______ _______ _______ _______ today?
M: Hi, Jessica. I'm going to the electronics store to buy a new laptop.
W: Don't you already have a laptop? Is yours broken?
M: No, it isn't. But it's very old. I bought it seven years ago.
W: Oh, you've used it for a long time. But if it works well, why do you want to buy a new one?
M: Well, it's very slow, _______ _______ _______.
W: Have you taken it to the service center before?
M: Of course, but they said there was nothing they could do to _______ _______.
W: I see. I hope you find something nice then.
M: Thanks.

07

M: Elaine, what movie would you like to watch tonight?
W: How about *Summer Love* at 6:00 p.m.?
M: Okay. I'll buy the tickets for us at the counter.
W: Oh, wait. I have this 30% off coupon.
M: Great. The tickets are $10 each, so it will _______ _______ _______ _______ _______.
W: Plus, this movie theater gives a five-dollar discount off the total price when we pay using a Global Rewards card.
M: _______ _______ _______ _______. I have that card.
W: Wait. I just noticed that this coupon cannot be used for 3D movies. The movie we're going to watch is 3D.
M: Oh, well. _______ _______ we'll still get the card discount.

08

W: Have you heard about the tallest toy block tower in the world?
M: No, I haven't. Tell me about it.
W: It _______ _______ _______ American students at a few schools in the state of Delaware.
M: How tall was it?
W: It was 112 feet. That's about the height of a building with 11 floors.
M: Wow! They must have used thousands of toy block pieces.
W: It was actually _______ _______ _______ about half a million toy blocks.
M: I wish I could have seen it.
W: Me, too. It's too bad that it was taken down a few days after it was built.
M: I guess the students just built it in order to _______ _______ _______ _______.
W: That's right.

09

M: If you've ever traveled across the central United States, you may have seen prairie dogs. _______ _______ _______ their name, they aren't related to dogs. They're actually a kind of squirrel. They are about 40 centimeters long, and they eat grass and small insects. Prairie dogs _______ _______ _______ North America, and they live underground. They form large communities that can spread for miles and include thousands of members. These communities help protect prairie dogs from predators like coyotes and eagles. When one prairie dog sees a dangerous animal approaching, it _______ _______ _______ _______ that tells all the others to get underground for safety.

10

W: Can you come here and look at this, honey?

M: Oh, are these the summer camp programs that Olivia's school is offering?

W: That's right. _______ _______ do you think she would like?

M: Well, she did science camp last month, so she'd probably like to try another subject.

W: I see. Then there are _______ _______ _______ _______ _______.

M: How many field trips do you think she'd like to go on?

W: Well, she really likes them, so at least three.

M: I think so, too. That leaves two choices.

W: But I don't want to pay more than $50.

M: Neither do I. So there is one option left.

W: Right. Let's _______ _______ _______ now.

11

W: Here is my ticket for the musical. Can I go in now?

M: Sorry, but _______ _______ _______ _______ snacks or drinks.

W: Really? But it's just popcorn and a soft drink.

M: (I'm sorry, but those are our rules.)

12

M: Mary, are you happy with your new apartment?

W: Not really. I _______ _______ _______ _______ these days.

M: Why? Is there something wrong?

W: (My neighbors are so noisy.)

13

W: Hello, sir. What are you looking for?

M: My hands are very dry. Could you recommend a good hand cream?

W: Well, we have several choices, but _______ _______ _______.

M: Oh, I don't mind the price. I only care if it works or not.

W: Okay. These are two of our best. They're both expensive but very _______ _______ _______ _______.

M: Hmm... What's the difference between these two?

W: Well, this one has more vitamins, but that one is for anti-aging.

M: My hands are very sensitive. Are they fragrance free?

W: Yes, they are.

M: _______ _______ _______ _______. I'm not sure which one will be better.

W: (Then why don't you try some samples?)

14

M: Excuse me. I'm ________ ________ ________ a book. Could you help me please?

W: Of course. What is it?

M: I'm looking for the *Fantasy World* book series.

W: Okay, ________ ________ ________. *[Pause]* Here it is. They are on the third shelf of this bookcase.

M: Oh, thank you. How much is the first book in the series?

W: Each book in the series is $9. Do you want to buy the first book?

M: I'd like to buy the whole series. How many books are there in total?

W: There are five books in the series.

M: Can I ________ ________ ________ if I buy all the books at once?

W: Yes. You can get a 20% discount.

M: (Then I'll buy the whole series.)

15

W: Amanda ________ ________ ________, and she sees a white blouse that is very pretty. She orders it and waits several days for its delivery. Finally, a package arrives at Amanda's house. She opens it, and takes out the blouse. At first, it looks perfect. But when she ________ ________ ________, it's too small. She checks the tag and realizes that the store sent her the wrong size. She decides to call the online store to tell them that they ________ ________ ________. In this situation, what would Amanda most likely say to the store's staff?

Amanda: (You sent me the blouse in the wrong size.)

16-17

M: You've probably heard the expression "An apple a day ________ ________ ________ ________." It's true that apples provide many benefits to the human body. Eating apples can help lower your cholesterol and keep you safe from heart disease. Apples even prevent certain types of cancers and signs of aging. But it might be a bit boring to just eat a plain apple every day. So here are ________ ________ ________ ways to use apples in some delicious dishes. First, I'd like to recommend a very simple snack. Just slice apples and add them to any salad. Second, you can make your own apple jam, which is delicious on toast. And who can forget apple pie? This dessert ________ ________ ________ ________! Just make sure to use less butter and sugar when you bake this sweet treat!

03 Word & Expressions

01
- □ **annual** 매년의, 연례의
- □ **backpack** 배낭
- □ **response** 반응
- □ **regarding** …에 관하여
- □ **as a result** 결과적으로
- □ **available** 이용 가능한, 구할 수 있는
- □ **apologize** 사과하다
- □ **inconvenience** 불편
- □ **rest** 나머지

02
- □ **electric bill** 전기요금 고지서
- □ **electricity** 전기
- □ **turn off** (전기·가스 등을) 끄다
- □ **appliance** (가정용) 기기
- □ **plug in** …의 플러그를 꽂다
- □ **rather than** …보다는

03
- □ **illustration** 삽화
- □ **pointed** 뾰족한
- □ **toe** 발가락; *(신발의) 발가락 부분
- □ **color** 색칠[채색]하다

04
- □ **local** 지역의
- □ **slide** 미끄러지다; *미끄럼틀
- □ **float** (물 위에) 뜨다
- □ **cousin** 사촌
- □ **waist** 허리
- □ **lifeguard** 안전요원

05
- □ **passport** 여권
- □ **expire** (기한이) 만료되다
- □ **book** 예약하다
- □ **plan out** …의 계획을 세우다
- □ **major in** …을 전공하다
- □ **expression** 표현

06
- □ **electronics store** 전자제품 매장
- □ **laptop** 휴대용[노트북] 컴퓨터
- □ **broken** 깨진, 고장 난
- □ **annoy** 짜증 나게 하다

07
- □ **save** 절약하다
- □ **notice** 알아차리다
- □ **at least** 적어도

08
- □ **height** 높이
- □ **be made up of** …로 구성되다
- □ **million** 백만
- □ **take down** (구조물을 해체하여) 치우다
- □ **in order to-v** …하기 위하여
- □ **set a record** 기록을 세우다

09
- □ **central** 중앙의
- □ **in spite of** …에도 불구하고
- □ **be related to** …와 관련이 있다
- □ **squirrel** 다람쥐
- □ **native to** … 원산[토종]의
- □ **underground** 지하에
- □ **community** 공동체
- □ **protect** 보호하다
- □ **predator** 포식자
- □ **approach** 접근하다

10
- □ **offer** 제공하다
- □ **subject** 과목
- □ **field trip** 현장 학습
- □ **at least** 최소한
- □ **choice** 선택; *선택 가능한 것
- □ **option** 선택(권)
- □ **sign up** …을 등록시키다

11
- □ **soft drink** 청량음료
- □ **rule** 규칙
- □ **neither** (둘 중) 어느 것도 … 아니다
- □ **guest** 손님

12
- □ **sleepy** 졸린
- □ **neighbor** 이웃
- □ **noisy** 시끄러운
- □ **be used to v-ing** …하는 데 익숙하다

13
- □ **several** 몇몇의
- □ **vary** 서로 다르다
- □ **work** 일하다; *효과가 나다[있다]
- □ **content** 함유량
- □ **anti-aging** 노화 방지
- □ **fragrance** 향
- □ **make a decision** 결정하다

14
- □ **have trouble v-ing** …하는 데 어려움을 겪다
- □ **fantasy** 공상, 환상
- □ **series** 연속; *시리즈
- □ **in total** 전체로서, 통틀어
- □ **get a discount** 할인을 받다
- □ **on sale** 할인 중인

15
- □ **delivery** 배송
- □ **try on** …을 입어보다
- □ **tag** 꼬리표, 가격표
- □ **make a mistake** 실수하다
- □ **staff** (전체) 직원

16-17
- □ **keep away** …을 멀리하다
- □ **benefit** 이익, 혜택
- □ **lower** 낮추다
- □ **cholesterol** 콜레스테롤
- □ **heart disease** 심장병
- □ **cancer** 암
- □ **sign** 징후, 조짐
- □ **aging** 노화
- □ **plain** 평범한
- □ **suggestion** 제안
- □ **bake** 굽다
- □ **sweet treat** 사탕, 과자 등의 단 음식

04 영어듣기 모의고사

정답 및 해설 p.11-13

1번부터 17번까지는 듣고 답하는 문제입니다.
1번부터 15번까지는 한 번만 들려주고, 16번부터 17번까지는 두 번 들려줍니다. 방송을 잘 듣고 답을 하기 바랍니다.

01

다음을 듣고, 여자가 하는 말의 목적으로 가장 적절한 것을 고르시오.

① 학교 신문 발간을 공지하려고
② 학교 신문 기자를 모집하려고
③ 신문 기사를 잘 쓰는 법을 설명하려고
④ 학교 게시판 이용 시 주의사항을 알리려고
⑤ 학교 신문 동아리 행사 참여를 권장하려고

02

대화를 듣고, 두 사람이 하는 말의 주제로 가장 적절한 것을 고르시오.

① 녹차의 부작용
② 물의 건강상 이점
③ 카페인 섭취를 줄이는 방법
④ 칼슘 수치가 낮아지는 원인
⑤ 사람들이 차를 마시는 이유

03

대화를 듣고, 두 사람의 관계를 가장 잘 나타낸 것을 고르시오.

① 경찰관 — 운전자
② 방문객 — 경비원
③ 자동차 수리공 — 고객
④ 자동차 판매원 — 고객
⑤ 행사 안내원 — 관람객

04

대화를 듣고, 그림에서 대화의 내용과 일치하지 않는 것을 고르시오.

05

대화를 듣고, 남자가 여자에게 부탁한 일로 가장 적절한 것을 고르시오.

① 약 사다 주기
② 책 대신 반납하기
③ 발표 준비 도와주기
④ 보고서 대신 제출하기
⑤ 인터넷으로 자료 찾아주기

06

대화를 듣고, 여자가 불안해하는 이유를 고르시오.

① 면접시험에 불합격해서
② 면접시험 준비를 못 해서
③ 회사 업무에 적응을 못 해서
④ 면접 시험장에 지각할 것 같아서
⑤ 면접 결과 발표를 기다리고 있어서

07

대화를 듣고, 여자가 환불받을 금액을 고르시오. 3점

① $180　② $200　③ $360
④ $380　⑤ $400

08

대화를 듣고, 새 식당에 관해 두 사람이 언급하지 않은 것을 고르시오.

① 위치　② 서비스 평가
③ 특선 요리　④ 분위기
⑤ 음식 가격대

09

수영 경기에 관한 다음 내용을 듣고, 일치하지 않는 것을 고르시오. 3점

① 8월 15일에 개최된다.
② 1km와 5km 두 개의 경기가 있다.
③ 18세 이상만 참가할 수 있다.
④ 프로 수영 선수는 참가할 수 없다.
⑤ 참가비는 15달러이다.

10

다음 표를 보면서 대화를 듣고, 남자가 선택할 영화를 고르시오.

< Box Office Startlight Theaters >

	Movie	Genre	Rating	2D/3D
①	A	Comedy	12+	3D
②	B	Romance	12+	2D
③	C	Comedy	12+	2D
④	D	Romance	15+	2D
⑤	E	Comedy	15+	3D

11

대화를 듣고, 여자의 마지막 말에 대한 남자의 응답으로 가장 적절한 것을 고르시오.

① It was held at the library.
② Yes, I've read his books before.
③ I spoke well and didn't get nervous.
④ It was excellent. I was very impressed.
⑤ I want to learn how to give a good speech.

12

대화를 듣고, 남자의 마지막 말에 대한 여자의 응답으로 가장 적절한 것을 고르시오.

① I took the subway.
② No, I live far from here.
③ I didn't buy anything yet.
④ I'm visiting my grandmother.
⑤ I saw you on the street yesterday.

13

대화를 듣고, 여자의 마지막 말에 대한 남자의 응답으로 가장 적절한 것을 고르시오.

Man: ______________________

① I think your chef is good at cooking.
② That's too bad. He'll find a job soon.
③ Then please ask him to come to see me.
④ No problem. I hired a good waiter yesterday.
⑤ Sorry, but I don't want to have seafood tonight.

14

대화를 듣고, 남자의 마지막 말에 대한 여자의 응답으로 가장 적절한 것을 고르시오.

Woman: ______________________

① It's the travel agent's mistake.
② Don't worry. I'll help you pack.
③ Thanks. I'll see a doctor tomorrow.
④ Did you decide on which country to visit?
⑤ Yes, I confirmed the reservation yesterday.

15

다음 상황 설명을 듣고, Hal이 Julie에게 할 말로 가장 적절한 것을 고르시오.

Hal: ______________________

① Thank you for your kind advice.
② I think I will be better next week.
③ Would you mind if I join your team?
④ Which chapter did we cover in class?
⑤ Could you email the project plan to me?

[16-17] 다음을 듣고, 물음에 답하시오.

16

남자가 하는 말의 목적으로 가장 적절한 것은?

① 새 호텔 완공을 알리려고
② 호텔 보수 공사 계획을 공지하려고
③ 호텔 이용 시 문제점을 불평하려고
④ 호텔 특별 할인 행사를 홍보하려고
⑤ 숙박 예약 시스템의 이용 방법을 설명하려고

17

언급된 호텔 시설이 아닌 것은?

① 객실 ② 옥상 수영장
③ 식당 ④ 커피숍
⑤ 주차장

정답 및 해설 p.13

녹음을 다시 한 번 듣고, 빈칸에 알맞은 말을 쓰시오.

01

W: Hello, everyone! I'm Lauren Cooper, the head editor of the school newspaper. Recently our school's fourth newspaper of the year was published. I hope all of you enjoyed reading it. We are now ________ ________ ________ that will write articles for the newspaper. If you want to apply to be a reporter, please submit two articles. Each article should be about school life. ________ ________, each should be around 500 words. The deadline is June 15th. The senior reporters will read your articles and evaluate them. The results will ________ ________ ________ the school bulletin board on June 22th. Thank you for your time!

02

M: Hey, Cindy. You've been drinking a lot of green tea lately.

W: Hi, Logan. Yes, I have. It has so many health benefits, so I don't even drink water these days.

M: You know, too much of a good thing ________ ________ ________.

W: What do you mean? I feel great. I hardly ever feel tired.

M: I know. That's because green tea contains caffeine. It's not good to consume too much of it.

W: Really? I didn't know that.

M: It can also reduce your calcium levels and ________ ________ ________.

W: Wow, that's surprising.

M: So you should be careful about drinking green tea.

W: Okay, I'll try to drink less of it ________ ________ ________.

03

W: Excuse me. Where can I park my car?

M: What is ________ ________ ________ ________ ________?

W: I'm just here to meet my friend for a few hours.

M: Then you need to get a parking pass from me.

W: Do I really need one? I'll only be here ________ ________ ________ ________.

M: Yes, it's for safety reasons. We need to have a record of every guest that enters the building.

W: I understand.

M: Just write down your name and your host's apartment number. I will ________ ________ the rest of the form.

W: Okay. *[Pause]* Here you go.

M: Great. Now please put this pass in your car, and park in the underground guest parking lot.

W: No problem. Thank you.

04

M: Did you visit the city garden with your friend yesterday?

W: Yes, I did. It was beautiful.

M: I heard there's a tall windmill ________ ________ ________ ________ the garden.

W: That's right. And there's a round pond behind the windmill.

M: Were there any tulips? They're my favorite flower.

W: Yes, there were some tulips ________ ________ ________ the windmill.

M: It sounds really nice. Did you have lunch there?

W: Yes. We had lunch in front of a heart-shaped sculpture to the left of the windmill.

M: That sounds great.

W: I also played on a swing. It ________ ________ ________ ________ to the right of the windmill.

M: That must have been fun!

05

W: Patrick, you look exhausted. What's wrong?

M: Hi, Amy. I didn't sleep at all last night.

W: Why not? Were you sick?

M: No. I have an art essay _______ _______. I worked on it all night.

W: So did you finish it?

M: No, I didn't. I still have to search for more information online.

W: You should _______ _______ _______ as soon as you finish the essay.

M: I wish I could. But I also have a history class presentation the day after tomorrow.

W: You're really busy. Is there anything I can help you with?

M: Actually, yes. Can you _______ _______ _______ to the library for me?

W: Sure, no problem.

06

M: Hey, Angela! How did your interview go?

W: Actually, _______ _______ _______, but I could have done better.

M: Well, you really prepared a lot for it for weeks. I'm sure your efforts will pay off.

W: Thanks. I hope you're right.

M: You don't look happy. Are you nervous about it?

W: Well, I really want the job, but I haven't heard anything from them yet.

M: When will they _______ _______ _______?

W: They said they'd tell us by the end of the week. I think I was rejected.

M: Relax. It's only Thursday. I'm sure you'll _______ _______ _______.

W: Thanks, Robert.

07

M: Hello. May I help you?

W: Yes, please. I'd like to _______ _______ _______ _______.

M: All right, but there is a cancellation fee, ma'am.

W: How much is it?

M: It's 5% of the ticket price if you cancel 72 hours _______ _______ and 10% if you cancel later.

W: I see. I still want to cancel it.

M: Okay. Do you know the reservation number?

W: Yes, it's KA50501.

M: Wait a minute, please. *[Pause]* Yes, Ms. Jolson. You made a reservation for two tickets to Chicago, correct?

W: Yes. The flight _______ _______ _______ at 9:00.

M: Right. Each ticket was $200.

W: Yes. Please cancel my reservation.

08

M: How about eating out at the new Italian restaurant tonight?

W: Do you mean Jessie's Kitchen _______ _______ _______ _______?

M: That's right. Look! I just found some reviews of that restaurant on a blog.

W: What do they say?

M: Most visitors _______ _______ _______ _______ the excellent service and delicious food.

W: Great. What is their specialty?

M: Their specialty is garlic cream pasta.

W: I love that. How are the prices?

M: The most expensive dish is less than 10 dollars.

W: That's quite reasonable. _______ _______ _______ _______ from home?

M: It will take only five minutes to walk there from our place.

W: Perfect! Let's go!

09

M: Good afternoon! I'm here to tell you about an exciting event. There will be an open-water race at Newport Harbor on August 15th. There will be a one-kilometer race and a five-kilometer race. All swimmers who are _______ _______ _______ _______ are welcome to participate. The winners of each race will receive a one-year membership to the Newport Fitness Club. Professional swimmers may participate but do not _______ _______ _______. There is a $15 entrance fee, and you can _______ _______ online. For more information, visit our website!

10

[Telephone rings.]

W: Starlight Theaters. How can I help you?

M: Hi. I'm calling to _______ _______ _______ _______ for a student group.

W: Okay. Which movie would you like to see?

M: I think the students would _______ _______ _______. Are there any comedies showing now?

W: Yes, there are a few you can choose from. How old are the students?

M: They're fourteen years old.

W: Okay. There are still _______ _______ _______. Would you like to watch it in 3D or 2D?

M: I think the students would enjoy watching something in 3D.

W: Then I think this one would be the best choice for you.

M: Okay, I'll choose that one.

11

W: What did you do last weekend, Kevin?

M: I _______ _______ _______ _______ by the author John Wiltshire.

W: How was his presentation?

M: (It was excellent. I was very impressed.)

12

M: Hi, Julia. I haven't seen you in a long time! How have you been?

W: Hi, Alfred! Not bad. You live on this street, right?

M: Yes, I do. _______ _______ _______ _______?

W: (I'm visiting my grandmother.)

13

W: What are you doing, Brad?

M: I need a new employee, so I'm writing a help-wanted ad.

W: For your restaurant? Are you hiring another chef?

M: No. One of my part-time waiters said he wanted to quit. I need to _______ _______.

W: Really? You know, my cousin is looking for a part-time job.

M: You mean Jake? He's a student, isn't he? I need someone who can work _______ _______ _______.

W: That's perfect. He's only taking night classes this semester.

M: Does he have any experience working at a restaurant? I want _______ _______ _______ _______.

W: As far as I know, he worked at a seafood restaurant for two years.

M: (Then please ask him to come to see me.)

14

W: I'm so excited for our trip! How about you?

M: Me, too. I can't believe we're going to be in Africa next week.

W: _______ _______ _______ we're completely ready.

M: We finished packing our clothes, and I put some emergency medicine in the bag.

W: That's good. We might need it if we get sick there.

M: I agree. And did you get your international driver's license issued?

W: Yes. I did it last week.

M: Great. You also _______ _______ _______, right?

W: Yes, I did. I have the South African money in my wallet.

M: Great. And we've _______ _______ _______, right?

W: (Yes, I confirmed the reservation yesterday.)

15

W: Hal _______ _______ _______ because he was sick. Later, his classmate Julie calls him because she is worried about him. She tells him which chapter the class covered, and she explains that the class has been _______ _______ _______ for a project. They are in the same group. The rest of the group members have already made a plan for the project without him. Hal wants her to send more information about the plan _______. In this situation, what would Hal most likely say to Julie?

Hal: (Could you email the project plan to me?)

16-17

M: Hello, everyone! We'd like to inform you of some exciting changes coming soon to North Lake Inn. Since 1980, North Lake Inn has become one of the city's most popular resorts. This year, we plan to _______ _______ _______, including guest rooms. You will be able to have a more comfortable and exciting time thanks to these upgrades. Construction will begin on March 1st. Our grand reopening will be October 1st. Our rooms will be bigger and more modern, and our building will include a new rooftop pool. We will also _______ _______ _______ _______ and build a 24-hour coffee shop in the resort's lobby. We are very sorry that you won't be able to use our resort during the renovations. But this autumn, you will _______ _______ _______ _______ all the changes. As always, thank you for your interest, and we'll see you in October!

04 Word & Expressions

01
- □ **head editor** 편집장
- □ **publish** 출판[출간]하다
- □ **reporter** 기자
- □ **article** 기사
- □ **submit** 제출하다
- □ **deadline** 마감일
- □ **senior** 선임자, 선배
- □ **evaluate** 평가하다
- □ **bulletin board** 게시판

02
- □ **benefit** 혜택, 이득
- □ **harmful** 해로운, 유해한
- □ **hardly** 거의 …아니다[않다]
- □ **contain** 포함하다
- □ **consume** 소모하다; *먹다, 마시다
- □ **calcium** 칼슘
- □ **level** 정도, 수준
- □ **careful** 조심하는, 주의 깊은

03
- □ **purpose** 목적
- □ **pass** 통과, *출입증, 통행증
- □ **safety** 안전
- □ **host** (손님을 초대한) 주인
- □ **fill in** (서식을) 작성하다
- □ **form** 양식
- □ **parking lot** 주차장

04
- □ **windmill** 풍차
- □ **pond** 연못
- □ **sculpture** 조각상
- □ **swing** 그네
- □ **hang** 걸다; *걸리다, 매달리다

05
- □ **exhausted** 기진맥진한, 탈진한
- □ **essay** 과제물, 리포트
- □ **due** …하기로 되어 있는, 예정된
- □ **search for** …을 찾다
- □ **get some rest** 휴식을 취하다
- □ **as soon as** …하자마자
- □ **the day after tomorrow** 모레
- □ **return** 반납하다

06
- □ **interview** 면접(시험)
- □ **go well** 잘되어 가다
- □ **effort** 노력
- □ **pay off** 성공하다, 결실을 맺다
- □ **announce** 발표하다, 알리다
- □ **reject** 거부[거절]하다; *불합격시키다

07
- □ **cancel** 취소하다(n. cancellation 취소)
- □ **flight** 항공편
- □ **reservation** 예약
- □ **fee** 수수료
- □ **departure** 출발(v. depart 출발하다)

08
- □ **eat out** 외식하다
- □ **review** 후기, 논평
- □ **be satisfied with** …에 만족하다
- □ **excellent** 훌륭한, 탁월한
- □ **specialty** 전공; *특제품, 특선품
- □ **reasonable** (가격이) 적당한, 비싸지 않은

09
- □ **harbor** 항구
- □ **participate** 참가하다
- □ **professional** 전문적인
- □ **qualify** …할 자격이 있다
- □ **entrance fee** 입장료
- □ **register** 등록하다
- □ **beforehand** 사전에

10
- □ **reserve** 예약하다
- □ **available** 이용할 수 있는
- □ **rating** (영화의) 등급

11
- □ **speech** 연설, 담화
- □ **author** 작가
- □ **presentation** 발표
- □ **impressed** 감명[감동]을 받은

13
- □ **employee** 직원
- □ **help-wanted ad** 구인 광고
- □ **hire** 고용하다
- □ **chef** 요리사
- □ **quit** 그만두다
- □ **replace** 대체하다
- □ **semester** 학기
- □ **experience** 경험, 경력

14
- □ **completely** 완전히
- □ **emergency medicine** 구급약
- □ **international** 국제적인
- □ **driver's license** 운전면허 자격증
- □ **issue** 발행하다
- □ **exchange** 환전하다
- □ **book** 예약하다
- □ **travel agent** 여행사 직원
- □ **confirm** 확인하다

15
- □ **miss** 놓치다
- □ **cover** 덮다; *다루다
- □ **divide A into B** A를 B로 나누다

16-17
- □ **inn** 여관, (작은) 호텔
- □ **improve** 개선하다
- □ **facility** (*pl.*) 시설
- □ **including** …을 포함하여(v. include 포함하다)
- □ **upgrade** 상승, 향상
- □ **construction** 공사
- □ **grand** 성대한
- □ **modern** 현대적인
- □ **rooftop** 옥상
- □ **renovate** 보수하다(n. renovation 수리)
- □ **interest** 관심, 흥미

05 영어듣기 모의고사

1번부터 17번까지는 듣고 답하는 문제입니다.
1번부터 15번까지는 한 번만 들려주고, 16번부터 17번까지는 두 번 들려줍니다. 방송을 잘 듣고 답을 하기 바랍니다.

01

다음을 듣고, 여자가 하는 말의 목적으로 가장 적절한 것을 고르시오.

① 학교 식당 건설을 요청하려고
② 오래된 학교 식당을 불평하려고
③ 다양해진 급식 메뉴를 소개하려고
④ 학교 식당 이용 규칙을 설명하려고
⑤ 학교 식당의 보수 공사를 공지하려고

02

대화를 듣고, 남자의 의견으로 가장 적절한 것을 고르시오. 3점

① 쓰레기 배출 공간을 넓혀야 한다.
② 재활용 쓰레기를 분리 배출해야 한다.
③ 재활용 쓰레기 배출 시간을 늘려야 한다.
④ 건물 주위 환경을 위해 쓰레기를 줄여야 한다.
⑤ 쓰레기 배출에 관한 건물 내 규칙을 따라야 한다.

03

대화를 듣고, 두 사람의 관계를 가장 잘 나타낸 것을 고르시오.

① 의사 — 환자 ② 엄마 — 아들
③ 축구팀 감독 — 선수 ④ 양호 선생님 — 학생
⑤ 체육 선생님 — 학생

04

대화를 듣고, 그림에서 대화의 내용과 일치하지 않는 것을 고르시오.

05

대화를 듣고, 여자가 할 일로 가장 적절한 것을 고르시오.

① 영화관에 전화하기 ② 다른 영화관 찾아보기
③ 주차장에 안내판 붙이기 ④ 홈페이지에 항의 글 쓰기
⑤ 영화 할인 티켓 출력하기

06

대화를 듣고, 여자가 남자에게 화가 난 이유를 고르시오.

① 귀가 시간을 지키지 않아서
② 휴대전화를 다시 잃어버려서
③ 지하철 노선을 잘못 알려줘서
④ 문자에 빨리 답을 하지 않아서
⑤ 휴대전화 여분 배터리를 챙기지 않아서

07

대화를 듣고, 남자가 지불할 금액을 고르시오. 3점

① $10 ② $13 ③ $14
④ $16 ⑤ $20

08

대화를 듣고, 미술 전시회에 관해 두 사람이 언급하지 않은 것을 고르시오.

① 작품 수 ② 작품 종류 ③ 날짜
④ 장소 ⑤ 입장료

09

sausage tree에 관한 다음 내용을 듣고, 일치하지 않는 것을 고르시오. 3점

① 아프리카의 열대 지역에서 자란다.
② 연중 비가 내리는 곳에서 늘 푸르다.
③ 해가 질 때 빨간색 꽃이 핀다.
④ 열매는 소시지를 닮았고 먹을 수 있다.
⑤ 피부 질환을 치료하는 데 열매를 이용한다.

정답 및 해설 p.14-16

10

다음 표를 보면서 대화를 듣고, 여자가 등록할 컴퓨터 강의를 고르시오.

< Marathon Computer Academy Classes >

	Class	Subject	Day	Time
①	A	Word + Excel	Sat.	8 - 10 p.m.
②	B	Word + PowerPoint	Tue. & Thu.	7 - 8 p.m.
③	C	Word + Excel + PowerPoint	Mon. & Wed.	8 - 9 p.m.
④	D	PowerPoint + Photoshop	Wed. & Sun.	7 - 8 p.m.
⑤	E	Excel + PowerPoint +Photoshop	Tue. & Fri.	5 - 6 p.m.

11

대화를 듣고, 여자의 마지막 말에 대한 남자의 응답으로 가장 적절한 것을 고르시오.

① Go ahead and try it on.
② Then how about this blue one?
③ I don't think the design suits me.
④ Thanks for shopping at our store.
⑤ Sorry, but the red one is sold out.

12

대화를 듣고, 남자의 마지막 말에 대한 여자의 응답으로 가장 적절한 것을 고르시오.

① Yes, I usually feel stressed out.
② That makes sense. It's very hard.
③ Things are really relaxing at work.
④ I think my computer stopped crashing.
⑤ Yes, someone is coming after lunch today.

13

대화를 듣고, 여자의 마지막 말에 대한 남자의 응답으로 가장 적절한 것을 고르시오.

Man: ______________________________

① Then could you lend it to me?
② I think the rain will stop soon.
③ I cannot trust the forecast any more.
④ How about going to the store with me?
⑤ You should buy an umbrella right now.

14

대화를 듣고, 남자의 마지막 말에 대한 여자의 응답으로 가장 적절한 것을 고르시오.

Woman: ______________________________

① Sure. Are you free this Sunday?
② You should keep practicing more.
③ No, I have never played the guitar.
④ Yes, I know a lot of great teachers.
⑤ I can help you choose a good guitar.

15

다음 상황 설명을 듣고, Justin이 계산대 점원에게 할 말로 가장 적절한 것을 고르시오.

Justin: ______________________________

① Can I pay by credit card?
② I have a coupon for 50% off.
③ Do you think this shirt suits me?
④ Does the shirt come in other colors?
⑤ I think there is a mistake with the price.

[16-17] 다음을 듣고, 물음에 답하시오.

16

남자가 하는 말의 목적으로 가장 적절한 것은?

① 교환 학생 프로그램을 안내하려고
② 외국어 학습의 필요성을 설명하려고
③ 해외여행 시 주의 사항을 당부하려고
④ 외국어 학습 동아리 가입을 권유하려고
⑤ 새로 개설된 외국어 강좌를 소개하려고

17

언급된 나라가 아닌 것은?

① 캐나다　② 프랑스　③ 중국
④ 일본　⑤ 독일

녹음을 다시 한 번 듣고, 빈칸에 알맞은 말을 쓰시오.

01

W: Good morning, students. It's Mrs. Hernandez, your vice principal. Today I have something to tell you. Many students _______ _______ _______ the school's old cafeteria. Fortunately, we have decided to renovate the school cafeteria. Students will not be able to use it for a month starting next Monday. The room will _______ _______ _______, and new tables and chairs will be added. Glass windows will be installed in front of the kitchen so you can see inside it. Not only the cafeteria's appearance, but the menu will also be changed. Please _______ _______ _______ _______ the new and improved cafeteria soon. Thank you.

02

M: Why did you bring the recycling back, honey?

W: The building manager said I can't _______ _______ _______ now.

M: Why not? It's Monday, which is recycling day.

W: He said it's only from 6:00 to 9:00 p.m. on Monday. I'm an hour late.

M: Only three hours? That's very short! What if we _______ _______ _______ by that time?

W: I don't know. It's just one of the rules at this apartment building.

M: I don't understand. All this garbage will pile up and make the whole house smell bad.

W: I know, but they want the trash area to stay as nice as possible.

M: Well, I think the time _______ _______ _______, though.

03

W: Hi. What's the problem?

M: My knees are bleeding.

W: Oh, let me see them. How did it happen?

M: _______ _______ _______ while I was kicking the ball during the soccer game.

W: Was it on the school playground?

M: Yes, it was. I missed the goal.

W: Sorry to hear that. Does it hurt a lot?

M: No, it's just a little sore.

W: Fortunately, it doesn't look so serious. Let me clean the wounds. I'll _______ _______ _______ _______, too. *[Pause]* Does that feel better?

M: It does. Thank you. I'll go back to class now.

W: _______ _______ _______ _______ the wound with dirty hands.

M: I will. Thank you.

04

W: Paul, I visited Luigi's Restaurant today. It _______ _______ _______.

M: Oh, really? How has it changed?

W: Well, they replaced the striped wallpaper with floral wallpaper.

M: That's good. Did they change the old rectangular tables as well?

W: They did. They have new round tables _______ _______ rectangular ones now.

M: Do they still have a vase on each table?

W: No, each table has a little candle instead.

M: How nice! How about the old chairs? They didn't have backs before.

W: Now they have regular _______ _______ _______.

M: That must be much nicer.

W: The only thing they didn't change was the ball-shaped light on the ceiling.

05

M: You look down. What's wrong?

W: I went to a movie at Western Shopping Center this afternoon.

M: _______ _______ _______ there?

W: Yes. I parked in the garage, and they charged me $40.

M: You paid $40? That's a lot. They give a discount if you show a movie ticket, don't they?

W: I showed it to them, but they said they stopped the service.

M: So you had to _______ _______ _______?

W: Yes. They should have notified customers about their change in policy.

M: Why don't you call them or go to their website? Tell them how you feel.

W: I will _______ _______ _______ _______. Then maybe they'll at least post a sign.

06

W: Why didn't you answer my messages while you were on your picnic, Dan?

M: I'm sorry, Mom. I couldn't.

W: Why not? Did your phone battery die?

M: No. Actually, I _______ _______ _______ _______.

W: Again? You lost your cell phone a few months ago, too. Where did you lose it this time?

M: Maybe on the subway _______ _______ _______ _______ the park. I remember using my cell phone on the subway. But I couldn't find it after getting off.

W: Did you _______ _______ _______ _______?

M: Yes, but they said they couldn't find it.

W: Oh, no! I can't believe that you've lost your cell phone again.

07

W: Welcome to Ice World. How can I help you, sir?

M: Hi. I need three tickets. One adult and two children, please.

W: Okay, adults are $6, and children are $4. Did you bring your skates?

M: No. I'll need to _______ _______ _______ _______ _______, too.

W: All skate rentals are $2, so that'll be $6 for the skates.

M: That sounds fine. Here's my credit card.

W: Oh! If you _______ _______ _______ _______ _______, you can get a 50% discount on the tickets.

M: That's a great deal.

W: Just to be clear, it's not a discount _______ _______ _______ _______. It's only the tickets, I mean.

M: I see.

08

M: Jane, would you like to _______ _______ _______ _______ _______ at a gallery next week?

W: Oh, yes. I love art. What kind of exhibition is it?

M: They are going to display more than 100 pieces of artwork by postmodern artists.

W: What kind of art will be exhibited there?

M: There will be paintings and sculptures.

W: That sounds great. When is the exhibition?

M: It _______ _______ _______ from July 10th through July 20th. How about going together next Friday afternoon?

W: That sounds good.

M: It's at the Western Art Museum downtown.

W: I know that place. It's really big.

M: Right. _______ _______ _______ downtown and then go to the exhibition.

09

M: Hello, everyone. Today we're going to learn about the sausage tree. It grows in the tropical parts of Africa. In places where it rains _______ _______ _______, the sausage tree stays green. It's often grown for decoration because of its flowers and unusual fruit. The tree's red flowers bloom _______ _______ _______ _______. And when the flowers fall to the ground, fruit grows in their place. The fruit is very big, about 30 to 100 cm long and 18 cm wide, and it _______ _______ a sausage. But you can't eat it. Local people use it to heal skin diseases. This tree is full of surprises, isn't it?

10

M: Welcome to Marathon Computer Academy. How can I help you?

W: Hi. I'd like to _______ _______ _______ a computer class.

M: We have many classes. What kind are you looking for?

W: I want to learn some programs for my job. But I need to learn more about Excel.

M: Many of our classes include instruction on the Excel program.

W: That's good. Also I can only _______ _______ _______ _______.

M: Then these are your choices.

W: I see. Well, I have to work until 6:00 p.m., so nothing before that time is possible.

M: Then this class would _______ _______ _______ _______.

W: Oh, that would be great. I can start next month.

11

W: Hi. I need a new hat. Can you show me some popular ones?

M: Why don't you _______ _______ _______? It's the most popular these days.

W: Well, the design is good, but I don't like red.

M: (Then how about this blue one?)

12

M: You look stressed out. Is everything okay?

W: No, my computer keeps crashing.

M: Is someone going to come to _______ _______ _______ soon?

W: (Yes, someone is coming after lunch today.)

13

M: Oh, no! It's raining!

W: I checked the weather forecast this morning, but they didn't say anything about rain.

M: Right. I didn't bring my umbrella when I _______ _______ _______.

W: The rain's not likely going to stop soon.

M: I agree. Do you have an umbrella?

W: Actually, I always keep one in the office.

M: You are very prepared. I have to _______ _______ _______ _______ to buy one.

W: Don't you have other umbrellas at home?

M: I do, but what other choice do I have? Unless I buy one now, I'll get completely wet on my way home.

W: Wait! I just remembered I _______ _______ _______ _______ in my drawer.

M: (Then could you lend it to me?)

14

M: Kelly, what do you usually do _______ _______ _______ _______?

W: Well, I play the guitar. It's one of my favorite hobbies.

M: Oh, really? I didn't know that you could play the guitar. How long have you been playing?

W: I've been playing since I was a little kid. My father _______ _______ _______.

M: Wow! You must be a good guitarist!

W: Not really. I still have a lot to learn.

M: Actually, I've always been interested in learning how to play the guitar.

W: It's fun, but it's also _______ _______ _______ _______ _______.

M: That's okay. Do you think you could teach me sometime?

W: (Sure. Are you free this Sunday?)

15

W: Justin is shopping at a clothing store. He finds a nice shirt. _______ _______ _______ it is $50. Then he finds a sticker on the tag that says it is 50% off. Justin thinks $25 is a good price to _______ _______ _______ _______, so he decides to buy it. He takes the shirt to the counter and the cashier scans it. She tells him the price is $50. Justin is confused and thinks there _______ _______ _______ _______. In this situation, what would Justin most likely say to the cashier?

Justin: (I think there is a mistake with the price.)

16-17

M: Attention all students! Want to improve your foreign language skills? One of the best ways to _______ _______ _______ _______ is to spend time in another country. This can be difficult and expensive. However, there is an easy solution—our overseas student exchange program. You can study in another country and immerse yourself in their culture. Plus, the cost is reasonable. Students can choose from schools in four countries: Canada, France, China, and Japan. To apply, visit the Student Center and _______ _______ _______ _______. You will be asked to choose a country and whether you'd prefer to stay at a dormitory or with a host family. Students must have a 3.0 GPA or higher and _______ _______ _______ _______ successfully to be a part of the program. The application deadline is May 15th. For more information, please read the announcement on the school homepage.

05 Word & Expressions

01
- □ **vice principal** 교감
- □ **complain** 불평하다
- □ **cafeteria** 구내식당
- □ **renovate** 보수[개조]하다
- □ **install** 설치하다
- □ **appearance** 겉모습, 외관

02
- □ **recycling** 재활용
- □ **throw away** …을 버리다
- □ **garbage** 쓰레기
- □ **pile up** 쌓이다
- □ **extend** 연장하다

03
- □ **knee** 무릎
- □ **bleed** 피가 흐르다
- □ **fall over** 넘어지다
- □ **goal** 골문; *골, 득점
- □ **sore** 아픈, 쓰린
- □ **wound** 상처
- □ **bandage** 붕대

04
- □ **replace** 교체하다
- □ **striped** 줄무늬가 있는
- □ **wallpaper** 벽지
- □ **floral** 꽃무늬의
- □ **rectangular** 직사각형의
- □ **vase** 꽃병
- □ **candle** 양초
- □ **back** (의자의) 등받이
- □ **ceiling** 천장

05
- □ **garage** 차고, 주차장
- □ **charge** (요금을) 청구하다
- □ **notify** (공식적으로) 알리다, 통고하다
- □ **policy** 정책, 방침
- □ **at least** 적어도
- □ **post** (안내문 등을) 게시하다
- □ **sign** 징후; *표지판

06
- □ **get off** 하차하다, 내리다
- □ **contact** 연락하다

07
- □ **rent** 임대하다; *빌리다
- □ **rental** 임대료, 대여료

08
- □ **exhibition** 전시회(v. exhibit 전시하다)
- □ **display** 전시하다
- □ **artwork** 미술품(= art)
- □ **postmodern** 포스트모던의
- □ **sculpture** 조각품
- □ **downtown** 시내에

09
- □ **tropical** 열대의
- □ **throughout** … 동안 죽, … 내내
- □ **decoration** 장식
- □ **unusual** 특이한
- □ **bloom** 꽃이 피다
- □ **set** (해·달이) 지다
- □ **local** 현지의
- □ **heal** 치유하다
- □ **skin disease** 피부병

10
- □ **sign up for** …을 신청하다
- □ **instruction** 지시; *교육
- □ **weekday** 평일

11
- □ **popular** 인기 있는
- □ **try on** (옷 등을) 입어보다
- □ **suit** (옷 등이) 어울리다
- □ **sold out** 품절된

12
- □ **stressed out** 스트레스를 받는
- □ **crash** 충돌하다; *(컴퓨터가) 갑자기 멈추다
- □ **fix** (문제를) 해결하다
- □ **make sense** 의미가 통하다, 이해가 되다

13
- □ **weather forecast** 일기 예보
- □ **likely** 아마
- □ **stop by** …에 잠시 들르다
- □ **get wet** 물에 젖다
- □ **completely** 완전히, 전적으로
- □ **drawer** 서랍

14
- □ **hobby** 취미

15
- □ **tag** 꼬리표, 가격표
- □ **cashier** (은행·상점의) 출납원, 계산원
- □ **confused** 혼란스러운
- □ **error** 오류
- □ **suit** (옷 등이) 어울리다
- □ **mistake** 실수; *(숫자 등의) 오류

16-17
- □ **foreign language** 외국어
- □ **overseas** 해외의
- □ **exchange** 교환
- □ **immerse** …에 몰두하게 만들다
- □ **reasonable** (가격이) 적정한, 비싸지 않은
- □ **fill out** …을 기입하다, …을 작성하다
- □ **application** 신청(서)
- □ **dormitory** 기숙사
- □ **host family** 민박 가정
- □ **part** 일부; *일원, 구성원
- □ **announcement** 공고, 발표

06 영어듣기 모의고사

정답 및 해설 p.17-19

1번부터 17번까지는 듣고 답하는 문제입니다.
1번부터 15번까지는 한 번만 들려주고, 16번부터 17번까지는 두 번 들려줍니다. 방송을 잘 듣고 답을 하기 바랍니다.

01

다음을 듣고, 여자가 하는 말의 목적으로 가장 적절한 것을 고르시오.

① 소방 훈련을 공지하려고
② 화재 예방을 당부하려고
③ 주방 화재 사건을 신고하려고
④ 화재경보기 오작동을 알리려고
⑤ 화재 발생 시 대처 방법을 설명하려고

02

대화를 듣고, 두 사람이 하는 말의 주제로 가장 적절한 것을 고르시오.

① 침대 이용의 장단점
② 허리 근육 강화에 좋은 운동
③ 올바른 수면 자세가 중요한 이유
④ 매트리스를 교체하는 적절한 시기
⑤ 자신에게 맞는 매트리스 고르는 법

03

대화를 듣고, 두 사람의 관계를 가장 잘 나타낸 것을 고르시오.

① 기자 — 편집장 ② 학생 — 선생님
③ 작가 — 출판 업자 ④ 손님 — 컴퓨터 수리공
⑤ 이용객 — 도서관 사서

04

대화를 듣고, 그림에서 대화의 내용과 일치하지 않는 것을 고르시오.

05

대화를 듣고, 여자가 남자에게 부탁한 일로 가장 적절한 것을 고르시오.

① 약 사다 주기 ② 체온 측정하기
③ 일찍 퇴근하기 ④ 과일 사다 주기
⑤ 병원에 태워주기

06

대화를 듣고, 여자가 밤에 숙면을 취하지 못하는 이유를 고르시오.

① 선풍기가 고장 나서
② 밤에 집안이 무더워서
③ 무서운 꿈을 많이 꿔서
④ 다음 주 시험이 걱정돼서
⑤ 이웃이 시끄럽게 떠들어서

07

대화를 듣고, 남자가 지불할 금액을 고르시오. 3점

① $80 ② $133 ③ $140
④ $152 ⑤ $160

08

대화를 듣고, 학생회장 선거에 관해 두 사람이 언급하지 않은 것을 고르시오.

① 날짜 ② 후보자 ③ 시간
④ 공약 ⑤ 장소

09

마라톤 경기에 관한 다음 내용을 듣고, 일치하지 않는 것을 고르시오.

① 희귀병 환자들을 위한 모금이 목적이다.
② 도서관 앞에서 경기가 끝난다.
③ 모든 참가자에게 무료로 티셔츠를 제공한다.
④ 참가비는 무료이다.
⑤ 참가하려면 온라인으로 등록을 해야 한다.

10

다음 표를 보면서 대화를 듣고, 남자가 예약할 숙소를 고르시오.

< Phuket Beach Houses >

	Beach House	Bedrooms	Option	Price (1 night)
①	A	1	Barbeque	$260
②	B	2	Pool	$280
③	C	2	Pool	$320
④	D	3	Barbeque	$300
⑤	E	1	Pool	$270

11

대화를 듣고, 여자의 마지막 말에 대한 남자의 응답으로 가장 적절한 것을 고르시오.

① Last time was much better.
② I think they got a new chef.
③ Thanks, but I'm already full.
④ It's all thanks to my new recipe.
⑤ I won't visit this restaurant anymore.

12

대화를 듣고, 남자의 마지막 말에 대한 여자의 응답으로 가장 적절한 것을 고르시오.

① You can send it by email.
② No, we didn't post anything.
③ We have many positions available.
④ We already found the right person.
⑤ You have to submit it by tomorrow.

13

대화를 듣고, 여자의 마지막 말에 대한 남자의 응답으로 가장 적절한 것을 고르시오. 3점

Man: ______________________

① I've never heard you sing yet.
② Please teach me how to sing well.
③ That's why you always need practice.
④ I'm glad that you have a positive attitude.
⑤ Cheer up! You'll have other opportunities.

14

대화를 듣고, 남자의 마지막 말에 대한 여자의 응답으로 가장 적절한 것을 고르시오. 3점

Woman: ______________________

① Right. I should use less electricity.
② Then can I get my money back today?
③ Thanks for calling me about the problem.
④ Sorry. Now I remember not paying for April.
⑤ Please don't make the same mistake next time.

15

다음 상황 설명을 듣고, Sam이 여자에게 할 말로 가장 적절한 것을 고르시오.

Sam: Excuse me, but ______________________

① is this the train to Chicago?
② where is the ticket machine?
③ I think you're sitting in my seat.
④ do you mind if I sit next to you?
⑤ could you call the train conductor?

[16-17] 다음을 듣고, 물음에 답하시오.

16

남자가 하는 말의 목적으로 가장 적절한 것은?

① 올바른 약물 복용법을 설명하려고
② 독성이 있는 음식 섭취를 경고하려고
③ 가정 내 안전 사고 예방법을 알리려고
④ 아동 안전 교육 프로그램을 홍보하려고
⑤ 가정용 화학제품 사용 시 주의점을 안내하려고

17

독성이 있는 것으로 언급되지 않은 것은?

① 의약품 ② 살충제 ③ 세정액
④ 화장품 ⑤ 버섯

정답 및 해설 p.19

녹음을 다시 한 번 듣고, 빈칸에 알맞은 말을 쓰시오.

01

W: Hello, everyone. Thank you for your cooperation this afternoon. The fire department has _______ _______ _______ _______ _______, and they said that luckily there was no fire. The fire alarm rang, but it _______ _______ _______. They think that some smoke from the kitchen on the fifth floor probably set the alarm off. But we're not sure yet. We will continue to test the alarm system to see what the problem was. The sudden confusion probably surprised you, but you _______ _______ _______ _______ _______. Thank you for your help and understanding once again.

02

M: Hi, Amy. Why are you walking like that?

W: Actually, my back _______ _______ _______ _______ since this morning.

M: Maybe your mattress is the problem.

W: You're right. It's too old. I should buy a new one. Could you recommend a good brand?

M: I don't think the brand is the most important thing.

W: How can I find out which mattress is _______ _______ _______ then?

M: It's easy. When you go to the store, you can just lie on the mattresses in your usual sleeping position.

W: Aha.

M: Spend about five to ten minutes lying on each mattress. Then you can _______ _______ if it's comfortable or not.

W: Okay. Thanks, Jack.

03

W: Hi, Mr. Anderson. Can I ask you a favor?

M: Sure, Cindy. What is it?

W: Could you _______ _______ _______ _______ on the report?

M: But it's due today. Were you confused about the due date?

W: I knew it, but I just didn't have time to finish it.

M: That's not a good excuse. If you needed more time, you _______ _______ _______ _______ _______ earlier.

W: Actually, my computer broke, so I couldn't type it.

M: Is that so?

W: Yes. Then I tried to write it all by hand, but it's about 10 pages. That's why I couldn't finish it in time.

M: In that case, you can turn it in tomorrow.

W: Thank you! I promise I'll _______ _______ _______ by then.

04

[Cell phone rings.]

M: Hi, honey. How's your business trip?

W: Oh, hi. It's fine. I'm sorry I _______ _______ _______ things into the new house.

M: That's okay. Everything looks great. I put the table and the two chairs in front of the window.

W: Nice. Did you install the television?

M: Yes. It's on the wall to the left of the window.

W: Okay. How about the clock?

M: It's _______ _______ _______.

W: I like it.

M: But I couldn't spread the new square rug on the floor. It's too big, so I used the round one from the last house.

W: That's fine. Where did you put the bike machine?

M: It's _______ _______ _______. We can exercise while watching TV.

W: Great idea.

05

[Cell phone rings.]

W: Hello?

M: Hi, dear. I just noticed that you had called me.

W: Where are you now?

M: I'm _______ _______ _______ _______ from work. I stopped at the supermarket to buy some fresh fruit.

W: That's nice. Anyway, I called to ask if you would _______ _______ _______ _______ for me on your way home.

M: Of course. Are you feeling sick?

W: Yes. I haven't been feeling well all day, and now I _______ _______.

M: Why don't I take you to the doctor?

W: Well, my temperature isn't that high, so I think simply taking medicine is enough.

M: All right. I'll be home soon.

06

M: You look exhausted, Sarah.

W: Yeah, I'm tired. I haven't been sleeping well at all these days.

M: _______ _______ _______ _______ because of the test next week?

W: Not really. I studied a lot, and I'm pretty well-prepared for the test.

M: Is it because of your neighbors then? Are they still _______ _______ _______ _______ _______ at night?

W: They aren't noisy anymore. I think it's just the weather.

M: Really? It's nice and cool at night at my house.

W: That's because you live near a mountain. At my house, even when I _______ _______ _______ _______, it's still too hot.

M: Oh, that's too bad. I hope you feel better soon.

07

M: Hi. I'd like to _______ _______ _______ of the same running shoes for my parents.

W: Sure. How about these gray ones here? They are very popular.

M: Those look good. How much are they?

W: These are $70 per pair.

M: Do you have them _______ _______ _______ 240 and a size 280?

W: Actually, we don't have any of this style in 280.

M: Then how about those other gray ones?

W: These cost $10 more because they're the newest model. But we do have them in both sizes.

M: _______ _______ _______ then. By the way, I can get 5% off with my membership card, right?

W: That's right.

08

W: Hey, Greg. Our school's student president election is March 25th.

M: Right! Did you decide who you'll vote for between the two candidates?

W: I'm not sure yet, but I'm thinking of voting for Kate. She _______ _______ _______ a new garden at the school.

M: That would be nice. But I like the other candidate, Richard.

W: He promised to extend lunchtime, didn't he?

M: That's correct. I really want to have a longer lunchtime.

W: That's good, but I think that promise will be _______ _______ _______ _______.

M: Maybe. Anyway, I didn't decide yet.

W: Then think some more about it. And _______ _______ _______ cast your vote in the cafeteria on Friday.

M: Sure.

09

M: Hi, everyone. I would like to announce that the Springfield Athletic Club is going to _______ _______ _______ on November 10th. The purpose of the event is to raise money for patients with rare diseases. The marathon will start downtown at City Hall and pass through the hills of east Springfield. It will end downtown _______ _______ _______ Springfield Library. All participants will receive a free T-shirt, and the winner will receive $500! Anyone fifteen years or older can participate with a $10 entry fee. If you would like to _______ _______ _______, please register on our website by November 1st.

10

[Telephone rings.]

W: Hello. Phuket Seaside Travel Agency.

M: Hi. I'd like to _______ _______ _______ _______ for next weekend.

W: Wonderful. There are still many beach houses available. How many bedrooms do you need?

M: There are four people including me, so I need at least two bedrooms.

W: Great. _______ _______ _______ the optional pool or barbeque?

M: Well, I'll be bringing my children, so I'd like a pool. They'll like that.

W: Okay. And what's your budget?

M: Hmm... I don't want to _______ _______ _______ $300 a night.

W: Then this beach house will be perfect for you.

M: Good. I'll reserve that one right now.

11

W: This restaurant's food tastes good, doesn't it?

M: Yes, it does. It's _______ _______ _______ the last time we visited.

W: The food improved a lot. I wonder what changed.

M: (I think they got a new chef.)

12

M: Excuse me. Is the job that you posted still open?

W: Yes. The position is still available.

M: Great. How can I _______ _______ _______?

W: (You can send it by email.)

13

M: Hi, Vanessa. You _______ _______ _______. Is something wrong?

W: Hi, Eric. Well, I had an audition for a role in the school musical.

M: That sounds like fun! What's the problem?

W: I _______ _______ _______ in the audition but failed to get a role.

M: Oh, I'm very sorry to hear that.

W: I practiced a lot, but I guess I'm just not a good singer.

M: That's not true. I've heard you sing before, and you have a great voice!

W: Thanks for saying so. But I've _______ _______ _______ in myself.

M: (Cheer up! You'll have other opportunities.)

14

[Telephone rings.]

M: Hi. This is Capital Electric. How may I help you?

W: Hi. There _______ _______ _______ _______ _______ with my home electric bill.

M: Could you tell me what the problem is?

W: I _______ _______ _______ _______ on last month's bill. I live alone, so I don't think I use as much electricity as it said.

M: I see. May I have your name and address?

W: Jodie Smith. And I live at 52 San Francisco Avenue.

M: Please wait a second. *[Pause]* Oh, you didn't pay the bill the month before last.

W: Oh, you mean this bill is _______ _______ _______?

M: Yes. It is for April and May.

W: (Sorry. Now I remember not paying for April.)

15

W: Sam is going home to Chicago to visit his family for winter vacation. When he gets to the train station, he _______ _______ _______ _______ the ticket machine because it's his first time. Eventually he is able to buy his ticket. He _______ _______ _______ _______ and begins looking for his seat. He soon finds it, but _______ _______ _______, there is already a woman sitting there. He double checks his ticket, and it's the correct seat. In this situation, what would Sam most likely say to the woman?

Sam: Excuse me, but (I think you're sitting in my seat.)

16-17

M: Good morning, listeners! Thank you for _______ _______ _______ 89.1 for all your favorite songs! But first, I'd like to share this important safety reminder. Accidents and injuries can happen anywhere. Even when you're at home, you should always be careful. So how can you keep yourself and your family safe? First of all, fires are one of _______ _______ _______ _______ _______ in the home. Make sure that you have a fire extinguisher, a working smoke alarm, and a family escape plan. Another danger at home, especially for young children, is poisoning. Medicines, cleaning solutions, and cosmetics _______ _______ _______ _______. Be sure that all of these things are out of your children's reach. Even your garden can be a dangerous place. Mushrooms and various other plants in your garden might actually be poisonous. Keep these things in mind so you can make your home safer.

06 Word & Expressions

01
- □ cooperation 협조
- □ fire department 소방서
- □ fire alarm 화재경보기
- □ improperly 부적절하게
- □ set off (경보장치를) 울리다
- □ sudden 갑작스러운
- □ confusion 혼란
- □ anxious 불안해하는

02
- □ in pain 아픈
- □ recommend 추천하다
- □ mattress (침대의) 매트리스
- □ lie 거짓말하다; *눕다
- □ usual 평상시의
- □ comfortable 편안한

03
- □ extension 확대; *(기간의) 연장
- □ confused 혼동한
- □ due date 마감일
- □ excuse 변명, 구실
- □ turn[hand] in …을 제출하다

04
- □ business trip 출장
- □ install 설치하다
- □ spread 펼치다, 펴다
- □ square 정사각형 모양의
- □ rug 깔개, 양탄자
- □ beside … 옆에

05
- □ notice 알아차리다
- □ stop 멈추다; *(잠시) 머무르다
- □ pick up …을 사다
- □ fever 열
- □ temperature 기온; *체온

06
- □ exhausted 지친, 기진맥진한
- □ stressed out 스트레스를 받는
- □ well-prepared 잘 준비된
- □ make (a) noise 떠들다, 소란을 피우다
- □ noisy 시끄러운
- □ fan 선풍기

07
- □ purchase 구입하다
- □ running shoes 운동화
- □ gray 회색의
- □ per …당[마다]

08
- □ president 회장
- □ election 선거
- □ vote for …에게 투표하다
- □ candidate 후보자
- □ promise 공약하다; 공약
- □ extend 연장하다, 늘리다
- □ carry out …을 수행하다
- □ cast one's vote 투표하다

09
- □ announce 발표하다, 알리다
- □ athletic 운동의, 경기의
- □ raise 올리다; *(자금 등을) 모으다
- □ rare 희귀한
- □ participant 참가자 (v. participate 참가하다)
- □ entry fee 참가비
- □ register 등록하다

10
- □ travel agency 여행사
- □ reserve 예약하다
- □ including …을 포함하여
- □ optional 선택적인

11
- □ improve 개선되다
- □ thanks to … 덕분에
- □ recipe 조리법

12
- □ post 게시하다
- □ position 위치; *일자리, 직위
- □ available 이용할[구할] 수 있는
- □ submit 제출하다
- □ application 지원서

13
- □ down 아래로; *우울한
- □ role 역할, 배역
- □ do one's best 최선을 다하다
- □ practice 연습하다; *연습
- □ confidence 자신감
- □ positive 긍정적인
- □ attitude 태도
- □ opportunity 기회

14
- □ electric bill 전기요금 고지서
- □ charge (요금을) 청구하다
- □ electricity 전기
- □ avenue (도시의) 거리, …가
- □ make a mistake 실수하다

15
- □ have trouble v-ing …하는 데 어려움을 겪다
- □ ticket machine 승차권 발매기
- □ eventually 결국
- □ get on …에 타다
- □ to one's surprise 놀랍게도
- □ double check 다시 확인하다, 재확인하다
- □ train conductor (기차의) 차장

16-17
- □ tune in to (라디오·TV 채널을) …에 맞추다
- □ safety 안전
- □ reminder 상기시키는 것
- □ injury 부상
- □ cause 원인
- □ fire extinguisher 소화기
- □ escape 탈출
- □ poisoning 중독
- □ cleaning solution 세정액
- □ cosmetic (*pl.*) 화장품
- □ poisonous 독이 있는
- □ out of reach 손이 닿지 않는 곳에
- □ mushroom 버섯

07 영어듣기 모의고사

1번부터 17번까지는 듣고 답하는 문제입니다.
1번부터 15번까지는 한 번만 들려주고, 16번부터 17번까지는 두 번 들려줍니다. 방송을 잘 듣고 답을 하기 바랍니다.

01

다음을 듣고, 여자가 하는 말의 목적으로 가장 적절한 것을 고르시오.

① 체육 대회 참여를 독려하려고
② 새로운 운동 방법을 소개하려고
③ 게임 중독의 위험성을 경고하려고
④ 어린이 비만 연구 결과를 설명하려고
⑤ 어린이 운동 시간 증가를 권유하려고

02

대화를 듣고, 두 사람이 하는 말의 주제로 가장 적절한 것을 고르시오.

① 보험 사기를 피하는 방법
② 여행자 보험금 신청 방법
③ 여행자 보험 가입의 중요성
④ 외국 여행시 주의해야 할 사항
⑤ 외국 여행 중 범죄 발생 시 대처법

03

대화를 듣고, 두 사람의 관계를 가장 잘 나타낸 것을 고르시오.

① 매니저 — 가수 ② 편집자 — 작가
③ 사진작가 — 모델 ④ 기자 — 영화감독
⑤ 팬 — 뮤지컬 배우

04

대화를 듣고, 그림에서 대화의 내용과 일치하지 않는 것을 고르시오.

05

대화를 듣고, 여자가 남자에게 부탁한 일로 가장 적절한 것을 고르시오.

① 자전거 빌려주기
② 친구에게 연락하기
③ 인터넷 쇼핑몰 추천하기
④ 자전거로 학교에 태워주기
⑤ 자전거 타는 법 가르쳐주기

06

대화를 듣고, 여자가 생일 파티에 가지 못하는 이유를 고르시오.

① 시험공부를 해야 해서
② 공연을 보러 가야 해서
③ 아르바이트를 해야 해서
④ 연극 리허설을 해야 해서
⑤ 도서관 행사에 참여해야 해서

07

대화를 듣고, 두 사람이 지불할 금액을 고르시오. 3점

① $36 ② $38 ③ $40
④ $42 ⑤ $44

08

대화를 듣고, 도서 대출에 관해 두 사람이 언급하지 않은 것을 고르시오.

① 대출 조건 ② 대출 기간
③ 연체료 ④ 대출 가능 권수
⑤ 대출 가능 시간

09

Okapi에 관한 다음 내용을 듣고, 일치하지 않는 것을 고르시오. 3점

① 중앙아프리카 우림 지역에 서식한다.
② 다리에 줄무늬가 있다.
③ 혀가 길고 유연하다.
④ 청각이 둔한 편이다.
⑤ 콩고의 화폐에 등장한다.

정답 및 해설 p.20-22

10

다음 표를 보면서 대화를 듣고, 두 사람이 예약할 호텔을 고르시오.

< Hotels in Guam >

	Hotel	Location	Breakfast	Charge (per night)
①	A	Seaside	X	$80
②	B	Downtown	O	$85
③	C	Seaside	O	$90
④	D	Downtown	X	$75
⑤	E	Seaside	O	$100

11

대화를 듣고, 여자의 마지막 말에 대한 남자의 응답으로 가장 적절한 것을 고르시오.

① I decided to stay here.
② I will study in Canada.
③ The plan was canceled.
④ I just want to take a break.
⑤ I'll go in March of next year.

12

대화를 듣고, 남자의 마지막 말에 대한 여자의 응답으로 가장 적절한 것을 고르시오.

① You are good at cooking.
② Can I take your order, please?
③ Sorry, but I already had lunch.
④ Yeah, they update it every week.
⑤ He posted his picture on the website.

13

대화를 듣고, 여자의 마지막 말에 대한 남자의 응답으로 가장 적절한 것을 고르시오.

Man: ______________________

① I'm sorry, but I can't be there.
② I will go to the meeting on time.
③ Let's make the video for him together.
④ I think my daughter will be very happy.
⑤ Okay. I'll try to get there as soon as possible.

14

대화를 듣고, 남자의 마지막 말에 대한 여자의 응답으로 가장 적절한 것을 고르시오. 3점

Woman: ______________________

① Yes, too many cooks spoil the broth.
② I wouldn't give everyone the same grade.
③ I promise I will work harder on the project.
④ I will try doing that next time with my group.
⑤ Now I see why you couldn't solve the problem.

15

다음 상황 설명을 듣고, Jane이 남자에게 할 말로 가장 적절한 것을 고르시오.

Jane: ______________________

① Where can I go to pay for these items?
② Can you go to the supermarket for me?
③ Excuse me, but you're in the wrong line.
④ It's not fair to cut in front of other people.
⑤ I'm sorry, but I didn't see you standing there.

[16-17] 다음을 듣고, 물음에 답하시오.

16

남자가 하는 말의 목적으로 가장 적절한 것은?

① 시험 일정을 공지하려고
② 새 학기 강의를 소개하려고
③ 수업의 적극적인 참여를 부탁하려고
④ 학생들에게 철학 전공을 권유하려고
⑤ 학생들의 성적 평가 기준을 알리려고

17

성적에 반영되는 요소로 언급되지 않은 것은?

① 에세이 ② 중간고사
③ 기말고사 ④ 출석
⑤ 수업 참여도

녹음을 다시 한 번 듣고, 빈칸에 알맞은 말을 쓰시오.

01

W: These days, children spend too much time sitting at their desks studying or playing on the computer. Because of this, they do not _______ _______ _______. According to a recent study, many young kids only exercise for 15 minutes a day. This is unhealthy and can cause them to become overweight. Doctors say that kids between the ages of 5 and 12 should exercise for _______ _______ _______ _______ each day. Therefore, we need to change the way kids spend their time. They should spend less time playing computer games and more time _______ _______.

02

W: Hi, Mark. How was your trip to Europe?

M: It was fun. But I _______ _______ _______ _______.

W: Oh, what happened?

M: Near the end of my trip, someone stole my backpack. I lost my camera and laptop.

W: That's terrible. So did you report it to the local police and get a police report?

M: No, I didn't. Why do I need a police report?

W: You could _______ _______ _______ _______ if you submit it to your insurance company.

M: Actually, I didn't have insurance. I didn't think I would need it.

W: What a shame! You should always get traveler's insurance when you go abroad.

M: Well, next time I go abroad, I'll _______ _______ _______ _______.

03

W: It is so nice to finally _______ _______ _______ _______!

M: Thank you for coming to see me.

W: Your performance today was fantastic. I loved your singing!

M: Thank you very much. Did you know today was my last time performing in this production?

W: Oh, really? Well, I'd love to see you on stage again. What are you going to do next?

M: Actually, I'm going to be in *Mamma Mia* next year. I'll _______ _______ next month.

W: How exciting! That's one of my favorite musicals.

M: Oh, is it? Then you should come and see it.

W: Definitely. By the way, can I _______ _______ _______?

M: Of course.

04

[Cell phone rings.]

M: Hello?

W: Hi, Steven. This is Carol Jones. I'm calling to ask how the renovations are _______ _______.

M: Oh, hi, Carol. Actually, we've just finished. We just installed your new sink on the left wall.

W: All right. Is there a mirror above it?

M: Yes, and the bathtub is in the back right corner, just _______ _______ _______.

W: Perfect. What about the towel rack?

M: It's on the wall next to the bathtub.

W: Okay, and did you install the shower curtain?

M: Yes. The curtain is _______ _______ _______ the bathtub.

W: Well, everything sounds great. I can't wait to see my new bathroom!

M: You should come and see it yourself!

05

M: Hey, Jessica! What are you doing?

W: Hi, Nathan. I'm _______ _______ _______ a good bicycle.

M: Oh, are you going to buy one?

W: Yes, because I've decided to bike to school every morning.

M: That sounds good. It will improve your health and save money.

W: But I cannot find _______ _______ _______ online. Do you know any website that sells cheap bikes?

M: Not really, but I have a friend who wants to sell his bicycle.

W: Really? How old is it? I don't want one that is too old.

M: He purchased it this year, so it looks great.

W: Good! Could you _______ _______ _______ _______ if he still wants to sell it?

M: Sure.

06

M: Are you going to Kelly's birthday party this weekend?

W: I'd really love to go, _______ _______ _______.

M: Why not? Do you have to work part-time at the library?

W: No, I only work during the week, after school.

M: Let me guess. You have an exam, right?

W: No, my drama club has a performance soon. I'm _______ _______ _______ _______ this weekend.

M: Oh, yes. That's right. How's that going?

W: It's a lot of fun! Anyway, I can't go because I have to be at rehearsal.

M: Can you stop by afterwards?

W: I'm not sure if I can. Rehearsal might _______ _______ _______.

M: Sorry to hear that. Anyway, I'll make sure to come to your play!

07

W: That was delicious. Are you ready to go?

M: Yes. Let's _______ _______ _______ _______. We had a salad, which was $5.

W: We also had the pasta and the pizza, which cost $15 and $18.

M: And the drinks were $2 each.

W: Oh, I have a "buy one, _______ _______ _______" drink coupon.

M: Great. Then we only have to pay for one.

W: I also have a membership card. Can we use the coupon and membership discount together?

M: Let's see. *[Pause]* The coupon says that it _______ _______ _______ _______ the membership card.

W: That's great. Then we can get a 10% discount as well.

M: Great!

08

W: Hi, could you tell me where the circulation desk is?

M: It's over here. Is it your first time in this library?

W: Yes, I'm a freshman.

M: Oh, then do you have a student ID? You need it _______ _______ _______ _______.

W: Fortunately, I got it yesterday. Here it is.

M: Great. Then you're fine.

W: I see. How long can I keep the books?

M: _______ _______ _______ _______. If anything is overdue, it's 25 cents a day for each book.

W: Okay. Also, how long is the library open?

M: It's open from 8:00 a.m. to 10:00 p.m. _______ _______ _______ _______. But you can only borrow books before 9:00 p.m.

W: Okay. Thanks for all your help!

7회

09

M: Have you ever heard of the okapi? The okapi is an animal that can be found _______ _______ _______ in central Africa. Because of the black and white stripes on its legs, you might think it is closely related to the zebra. However, it is actually more closely related to the giraffe. Like a giraffe, it has a long and flexible tongue. The okapi can even use it to clean its eyelids! They also have big ears, which can _______ _______ _______ and help the animal detect predators. The okapi is considered _______ _______ _______ _______ the Democratic Republic of the Congo and is printed on their money.

10

W: Honey, here is the list of hotels in Guam.

M: Oh, thanks. Which hotel should we choose?

W: I think we need to decide on the location first. Do you prefer seaside or downtown hotels?

M: I'd like to stay in a hotel _______ _______ _______. I want to enjoy the view.

W: Me, too. And I don't think we need breakfast.

M: Actually, I want one that offers breakfast because it's _______ _______.

W: Hmm... You're right. It would be better to choose one that offers breakfast.

M: Yes. Then we have two options left.

W: In that case, _______ _______ _______ is better. We can save some money to enjoy other things.

M: I think so, too. Let's reserve a room right now!

11

W: Paul, I heard you're planning to study abroad next year.

M: Yeah, I'm really excited about it.

W: Did you decide _______ _______ _______ _______ _______?

M: (I will study in Canada.)

12

M: What are you doing, Hailey?

W: I'm looking for the lunch menu today on the school website.

M: On the website? I didn't know that _______ _______ _______ there.

W: (Yeah, they update it every week.)

13

[Cell phone rings.]

W: Hi, Nick. How's it going?

M: Not bad, but I _______ _______ _______ to tonight's dinner on time.

W: But it's Matthew's birthday party. You'll miss the video we made for him.

M: I know. I wanted to go right after work, but _______ _______ _______.

W: What happened?

M: I completely forgot that today is "Fathers' Visiting Day" at my daughter's school.

W: Oh, I understand. You shouldn't miss that. It's _______ _______ _______ _______ you and your daughter.

M: Right. But as soon as the event ends, I'll go to Matthew's birthday party.

W: I hope you won't be too late.

M: (Okay. I'll try to get there as soon as possible.)

14

M: Sally, you _______ _______ _______. What's wrong?

W: It's because of the group work Mr. Sheridan gave us.

M: Why? Is it too difficult?

W: No, but some people in my group aren't doing any of the work.

M: I know what you mean. There are always some people like that.

W: Then they get the same grade as the people who worked hard. _______ _______ _______.

M: I had a similar problem with a group project last year.

W: How did you solve it?

M: We gave each member a different role for the group work. So everyone had to _______ _______ _______ _______ the work.

W: (I will try doing that next time with my group.)

15

W: Jane's mother is cooking dinner. She asks Jane to run to the store to _______ _______ a few ingredients. At the supermarket, Jane gets three items. When she goes to pay for them, she waits _______ _______ _______ _______ for people with five items or fewer. But she notices that the man in front of her has more than five items. In fact, he has about 15. Jane is _______ _______ _______ and doesn't want to wait longer. In this situation, what would Jane most likely say to the man?

Jane: (Excuse me, but you're in the wrong line.)

16-17

M: Welcome, students. My name is Andy Wilson, and I will be teaching Introduction to Western Philosophy this semester. The goal of this class is to give you _______ _______ _______ of Western philosophy. We will meet in this room every Tuesday and Friday from 3:00 p.m. to 4:30 p.m. For our textbook, we will be using *The History of Western Philosophy*. I will also post some additional reading materials online. Your grade will be determined _______ _______ _______ _______ that you will write throughout the semester. Of course, your final exam will affect your grade. I'll also look at your attendance and class participation. I _______ _______ _______ _______ you this semester. If you have any questions, you may contact me at any time through email.

7회

07 Word & Expressions

01
- □ **according to** …에 따르면
- □ **recent** 최근의
- □ **cause ... to-v** …가 ~하는 것을 초래하다
- □ **overweight** 과체중의, 비만의
- □ **active** 활동적인

02
- □ **report** 신고하다
- □ **local** 지역의, 현지의
- □ **police report** 조서
- □ **submit** 제출하다
- □ **insurance** 보험
- □ **keep ... in mind** …을 명심하다

03
- □ **in person** 직접
- □ **performance** 공연(v. perform 공연하다)
- □ **production** 생산; *(예술 등의) 작품
- □ **definitely** 분명히, 틀림없이
- □ **autograph** (유명인의) 사인

04
- □ **renovation** 수리
- □ **come along** (원하는 대로) 되어가다
- □ **install** 설치하다
- □ **sink** 싱크대; *세면대
- □ **bathtub** 욕조
- □ **request** 요청하다
- □ **towel rack** 수건걸이

05
- □ **search for** …을 찾다
- □ **bike** 자전거를 타다; 자전거
- □ **improve** 개선하다, 향상시키다
- □ **affordable** (가격이) 알맞은
- □ **purchase** 구입하다

06
- □ **rehearse** 리허설[예행연습]을 하다 (n. rehearsal 리허설)
- □ **stop by** 잠시 들르다
- □ **afterwards** 나중에, 그 뒤에

07
- □ **check** 계산서
- □ **as well** (…뿐만 아니라) …도

08
- □ **circulation desk** 대출대
- □ **freshman** 신입생
- □ **student ID** 학생증
- □ **borrow** 빌리다
- □ **up to** …까지
- □ **overdue** 기한이 지난
- □ **except** …을 제외하고

09
- □ **rainforest** 열대 우림
- □ **central** 중앙의
- □ **stripe** 줄무늬, 줄
- □ **be related to** …와 관계가 있다
- □ **flexible** 유연한
- □ **tongue** 혀
- □ **eyelid** 눈꺼풀
- □ **detect** 발견하다, 감지하다
- □ **predator** 포식 동물
- □ **symbol** 상징(물)
- □ **democratic** 민주주의의
- □ **republic** 공화국

10
- □ **location** 위치
- □ **seaside** 해변
- □ **downtown** 시내에 있는
- □ **overlooking** 내려다보는
- □ **offer** 제의하다; *제공하다
- □ **convenient** 편리한
- □ **save** 절약하다, 아끼다
- □ **reserve** 예약하다
- □ **charge** 요금

11
- □ **abroad** 해외에(서)
- □ **cancel** 취소하다
- □ **take a break** 휴식을 취하다

12
- □ **post** 게시하다
- □ **take one's order** 주문을 받다
- □ **update** 갱신하다, 새롭게 하다

13
- □ **make it** (모임 등에) 가다, 참석하다
- □ **on time** 정각에, 제때에
- □ **miss** 놓치다
- □ **completely** 완전히
- □ **as soon as possible** 가능한 한 빨리

14
- □ **stressed out** 스트레스를 받는
- □ **grade** 성적
- □ **fair** 타당한; *공평한
- □ **similar** 비슷한
- □ **involve** 관련시키다, 참여시키다
- □ **cook** 요리사
- □ **spoil** 망치다
- □ **broth** 수프, 죽

15
- □ **ingredient** 재료
- □ **item** 물품
- □ **notice** 알아차리다
- □ **in a rush** 아주 바쁘게

16-17
- □ **introduction** 입문
- □ **philosophy** 철학
- □ **semester** 학기
- □ **overview** 개요, 개관
- □ **post** 게시하다
- □ **additional** 부가의, 추가의
- □ **material** 재료; *자료
- □ **based on** …에 근거하여
- □ **attendance** 출석
- □ **participation** 참여
- □ **look forward to** …을 고대[기대]하다

08 영어듣기 모의고사

정답 및 해설 p.23-25

1번부터 17번까지는 듣고 답하는 문제입니다.
1번부터 15번까지는 한 번만 들려주고, 16번부터 17번까지는 두 번 들려줍니다. 방송을 잘 듣고 답을 하기 바랍니다.

01

다음을 듣고, 여자가 하는 말의 목적으로 가장 적절한 것을 고르시오.

① 새로 개설된 강의를 안내하려고
② 새 물리학 박물관을 홍보하려고
③ 과학 학습 온라인 사이트를 소개하려고
④ 실생활 속 물리학의 중요성을 설명하려고
⑤ 수업 시간에 졸음을 없애는 법을 알리려고

02

대화를 듣고, 여자의 의견으로 가장 적절한 것을 고르시오.

① 타인의 과제를 대신 해주면 안 된다.
② 맡은 일에 책임감을 가지고 임해야 한다.
③ 서둘러서 일을 하면 오히려 망칠 수 있다.
④ 함께 공부하는 것은 학습의 효율을 높인다.
⑤ 때로는 타인의 부탁을 거절하는 것이 필요하다.

03

대화를 듣고 두 사람의 관계를 가장 잘 나타낸 것을 고르시오.

① 교수 — 학생
② 미술관 관장 — 공예가
③ 접수원 — 대회 응모자
④ 판매상 — 재료 구입자
⑤ 디자이너 — 거래처 직원

04

대화를 듣고, 그림에서 대화의 내용과 일치하지 않는 것을 고르시오.

05

대화를 듣고, 남자가 할 일로 가장 적절한 것을 고르시오. 3점

① 설거지하기
② 세탁물 찾기
③ 꽃에 물 주기
④ 새 모이 주기
⑤ 식료품 사오기

06

대화를 듣고, 남자가 여자에게 화가 난 이유를 고르시오.

① 약속을 또 잊어버려서
② 쇼핑을 너무 자주 해서
③ 과학 숙제를 하지 않아서
④ 중요한 메모를 하지 않아서
⑤ 야구 경기 볼 것을 고집해서

07

대화를 듣고, 여자가 지불할 금액을 고르시오. 3점

① \$36
② \$40
③ \$44
④ \$48
⑤ \$52

08

대화를 듣고, 축제에 진행될 행사가 아닌 것을 고르시오.

① 쿠키 판매
② 연극 공연
③ 밴드 공연
④ 미술 전시회
⑤ 캐리커처 그리기

09

Mount Roraima에 관한 다음 내용을 듣고, 일치하지 않는 것을 고르시오. 3점

① 산 정상이 평평하다.
② 절벽으로 둘러싸여 있다.
③ 매우 높은 폭포들이 있다.
④ 식물이 자라기에 적합한 진흙 지역이 있다.
⑤ 오후 2시 이후에만 도보 여행이 허용된다.

10

다음 표를 보면서 대화를 듣고, 남자가 탈 버스를 고르시오.

< Bus Timetable >

	Bus	Departure Time	Number of Stops	Seat Type
①	A	7:30 a.m.	0	Comfort
②	B	9:15 a.m.	3	Economy
③	C	11:45 a.m.	2	Comfort
④	D	2:00 p.m.	0	Comfort
⑤	E	3:15 p.m.	4	Economy

11

대화를 듣고, 남자의 마지막 말에 대한 여자의 응답으로 가장 적절한 것을 고르시오.

① Where is the fitting room?
② Thank you, but I ordered one online.
③ No. I don't need one in a smaller size.
④ That's expensive. I can't spend that much.
⑤ That would be great. I don't mind waiting.

12

대화를 듣고, 여자의 마지막 말에 대한 남자의 응답으로 가장 적절한 것을 고르시오.

① I like taking the cable car.
② I don't like to walk up hills.
③ We wanted to walk for exercise.
④ Unfortunately, I don't have a car.
⑤ Actually, the subway was closed.

13

대화를 듣고, 여자의 마지막 말에 대한 남자의 응답으로 가장 적절한 것을 고르시오.

Man: ______________________________

① That will be 30 dollars in total.
② You should take one pill twice a day.
③ You should be careful of what you eat.
④ Don't forget to take your vitamin B pills.
⑤ You really shouldn't take iron supplements.

14

대화를 듣고, 남자의 마지막 말에 대한 여자의 응답으로 가장 적절한 것을 고르시오.

Woman: ______________________________

① I can fax the contract today.
② You can visit me anytime you want.
③ I forgot to ask my assistant to do that.
④ No, the repairman will come tomorrow.
⑤ Yes, I will be at your office around 7:00 p.m.

15

다음 상황 설명을 듣고, 상담 선생님이 Ryan에게 할 말로 가장 적절한 것을 고르시오.

Counselor: ______________________________

① Why don't you talk to your teacher?
② You should drink less coffee each day.
③ You need to try to stay awake during class.
④ If I were you, I wouldn't play so many games.
⑤ Don't play music when you are trying to sleep.

[16-17] 다음을 듣고, 물음에 답하시오.

16

남자가 하는 말의 목적으로 가장 적절한 것은?

① 아파트 거주의 장단점을 소개하려고
② 살기 좋은 집을 고르는 법을 알리려고
③ 이웃을 배려하는 것의 중요성을 강조하려고
④ 자녀들을 훈육하는 방법에 관해 조언하려고
⑤ 층간 소음을 줄이는 방법에 대해 설명하려고

17

언급된 방법이 아닌 것은?

① 두꺼운 카펫 깔기
② 슬리퍼 신고 걷기
③ 밤에 텔레비전 음량 낮추기
④ 밤늦게 샤워하지 않기
⑤ 밤늦게 청소기 사용하지 않기

정답 및 해설 p.25

녹음을 다시 한 번 듣고, 빈칸에 알맞은 말을 쓰시오.

01

W: Do you think physics is a difficult subject? Do you ________ ________ ________ ________ in physics class? Well, if you visit our new museum, you can find out how interesting physics is. This Friday, our museum will finally be open to the public. We want to show you that physics is fun, engaging, and exciting. Unlike in other museums, you ________ ________ ________ touch and interact with everything. Everyone can enjoy our fun activities. We will be open from 10:00 a.m. to 6:00 p.m., but we will ________ ________ every Tuesday. If you would like more information, please visit our website, www.funphysics.com.

02

W: Hi, Robert. What are you reading?

M: I'm reading my sister's essay for French class. She asked me to ________ ________ ________.

W: Are you done with your history assignment?

M: No, not yet. I was also supposed to help a friend study for a math test.

W: I think you should finish your own schoolwork first.

M: I just find it very ________ ________ ________ ________ to people who need help. I don't want to disappoint anyone.

W: I know. But sometimes you need to ________ ________ ________. They will understand.

M: You're right. I'll try to finish my work first from now on.

W: I think that would be a good idea.

03

M: How can I help you?

W: I'm here to submit my design portfolio to the design contest.

M: Oh, I'm sorry, but we can't accept any ________ ________ ________ ________.

W: What? I thought today was the last day to submit designs.

M: Actually, they were due yesterday.

W: But I've been ________ ________ ________ ________ for months.

M: There are very strict rules that we follow regarding the submission deadline.

W: It was an honest mistake. All of my designs were finished yesterday.

M: I feel really bad, but there's nothing I can do.

W: Can't you ________ ________ ________ just this once?

M: Sorry, but we have to treat all of the participants fairly.

04

W: Can you come over here and look at this, honey?

M: Sure. What is it?

W: I just ________ ________ the kitchen cabinet.

M: Did you put the tea and coffee on the middle shelf?

W: Yes, and I put the fruit juices on the bottom left shelf.

M: Okay, and the noodles are all together on the top right shelf. But why is the jar of honey ________ ________ ________ ________? That could be dangerous.

W: We don't use it often, so I think it'll be okay.

M: Oh, I see.

W: And I put the coffee machine, which ________ ________ ________, on top of the cabinet.

M: That's good. I like the way you organized everything.

05

W: What are you doing this afternoon, Tommy?

M: I have to go to my English class at two o'clock.

W: Well, _______ _______ _______ _______ grocery shopping. Can you do something for me?

M: Sure. What do you need me to do, Mom?

W: Can you feed the birds and water the flowers before going to class?

M: Sarah already did that this morning.

W: Okay. Well, I also need someone to _______ _______ _______ and pick up your father's dry cleaning. Can you do one of those things?

M: I'll _______ _______ the dry cleaning on my way home from class.

W: All right. I'll ask Sarah to do the dishes then.

M: Okay.

06

[Cell phone rings.]

W: Hi, Mike. What's up?

M: Hi, Ann. Where are you now?

W: I'm at the mall. Why do you ask?

M: Did you forget? We _______ _______ _______ _______ in the library to work on our science project!

W: Oh, I'm really sorry! I totally forgot about that.

M: This isn't the first time you've forgotten something like this. Last week, you didn't _______ _______ for the baseball game either.

W: I'm sorry. I promise I won't forget next time.

M: How are you going to remember?

W: I'm not sure. I always forget things.

M: I think you should _______ _______ _______ you need to do in a planner.

W: Okay, I'll try to do that.

07

M: Welcome to the National Art Museum. Can I help you?

W: Yes. I'd like to buy tickets. How much are they?

M: It's $12 _______ _______ and $6 for children under 13.

W: Then I'll take two adult tickets and two child tickets, please.

M: Okay. We also have an audio guide service. Do you want to use it?

W: Oh, I've never heard of that. What is it?

M: It's a service that _______ _______ _______ information about the artwork through headphones.

W: That sounds great. It will help us understand the artwork better.

M: Certainly.

W: How much does it cost?

M: It's only $2 per person.

W: Okay. I'll _______ _______ _______ _______. Here's my credit card.

08

W: Roger, the school festival is next weekend!

M: Yes! Are you going to _______ _______ _______ _______?

W: Yes, I'm selling cookies for the Hamilton Animal Shelter.

M: Great! Are you going to watch *Dan and Kate*? It's the play that the school's drama club _______ _______ _______.

W: Yes, I will. After the play, I'll go to the band concert because my best friend is playing the drums.

M: Oh, I can't go to that. I have an art exhibition during that time.

W: Really? I didn't know that. I'm sorry I can't go to your exhibition.

M: That's okay. By the way, I heard that the artist who did caricatures last year _______ _______ _______ this year.

W: Oh, no. I was looking forward to that.

09

M: Hello, everyone. Today I will talk about Mount Roraima in South America. The top of the mountain is _______ _______ _______ _______. It has 400-meter-tall cliffs on all sides. It rains nearly every day on top of the mountain. That means there are _______ _______ _______ _______. Most of its surface is just bare sandstone. But there are a few wet, muddy areas on the mountain where some plants can grow properly. Best of all, Mount Roraima is great for hiking. However, hikers _______ _______ _______ _______ begin hiking after 2:00 p.m.

10

[Telephone rings.]

W: Newtown Bus Terminal. How may I help you?

M: Hi. I need a bus ticket from here to Springfield for tomorrow.

W: What time would you like to leave? There are several options.

M: I need to leave in the morning. _______ _______ _______ will be fine.

W: That leaves three choices. You could go non-stop, but it's more expensive.

M: Oh, I don't mind stopping. I would _______ _______ _______ _______.

W: Okay. There are two buses leaving tomorrow morning, with stops.

M: Does one of them have bigger seats?

W: Yes, but comfort seating is more expensive.

M: Then I'll _______ _______ _______ _______.

W: Okay. That'll be $25.

11

M: How may I help you?

W: I'd like to buy this jacket. Do you have this in a size six?

M: Oh, we're out of that size now, but I can _______ _______ _______ _______.

W: (That would be great. I don't mind waiting.)

12

W: Did you do anything special last weekend?

M: Yes, I walked up to N Seoul Tower with my sister.

W: That sounds hard. _______ _______ _______ _______ the cable car?

M: (We wanted to walk for exercise.)

13

M: How may I help you, ma'am?

W: I feel very tired these days. I think I need to take some vitamin supplements.

M: I see. Do you have _______ _______ _______ _______?

W: No. Can you recommend some vitamins for me?

M: How about this vitamin B supplement? It's _______ _______ _______ tiredness.

W: That sounds good. Should I take it every day?

M: Yes, you should take two pills after breakfast.

W: Okay. Do you have anything else to recommend?

M: Try this iron supplement, too. It helps keep your immune system strong.

W: Okay. _______ _______ _______ _______ take it?

M: (You should take one pill twice a day.)

14

[Telephone rings.]

W: Hello. This is Darcy Wilson at City International. How can I help you?

M: Hi, Darcy. This is Tom Green.

W: Oh. Hi, Tom. How's everything going?

M: _______ _______ _______ _______, but I just wanted to check something.

W: What's that?

M: Your assistant _______ _______ _______ _______ me the new contract yesterday, but I never received it.

W: Actually, there have been problems with our fax machine all week.

M: I see. But we need that contract _______ _______ _______ _______.

W: Then I will personally deliver it to you this evening after work.

M: That's great. But are you sure you can do that by 8:00 p.m.?

W: (Yes, I will be at your office around 7:00 p.m.)

15

W: Ryan _______ _______ _______ at night lately. This is a huge problem because he always feels tired, and sometimes he even falls asleep in class. Moreover, his grades are going down. His teacher is worried about him, so she _______ _______ _______ _______ _______ the school counselor. The counselor listens to Ryan and finds out that he drinks three or four cups of coffee a day. She believes that the caffeine in the coffee is _______ _______ _______ falling asleep at night. In this situation, what would the counselor most likely say to Ryan?

Counselor: (You should drink less coffee each day.)

16-17

M: Good morning, residents. We've _______ _______ _______ about noise at night lately, so we'd like to share some tips with you. If you don't want your neighbors to complain, please try these tips to _______ _______ _______. First, put down a thick carpet. This will absorb most of the sounds that your family may make. In addition, you can get slippers to prevent your family members from making too much noise when they walk around. You should also _______ _______ _______ _______ at night so that you don't disturb your neighbors' sleep. Finally, avoid taking a shower too late at night. If you take a shower when people are trying to sleep, the sound of the water could be very annoying. Please keep these things in mind and try to be more careful. Thank you for your time.

08 Word & Expressions

01
- □ physics 물리학
- □ subject 과목
- □ public 대중
- □ engaging 호감이 가는, 매력적인
- □ be allowed to-v …하는 것이 허용되다
- □ interact with …와 상호 작용하다

02
- □ essay 과제물, 리포트
- □ assignment 과제
- □ be supposed to-v …하기로 되어있다, …해야 하다
- □ disappoint 실망시키다
- □ refuse 거절하다
- □ request 요구, 부탁

03
- □ portfolio 작품집, 포트폴리오
- □ accept 받아들이다
- □ due date 마감일
- □ submit 제출하다(n. submission 제안, 제출)
- □ strict 엄격한
- □ honest mistake 명백한 착오
- □ exception 예외
- □ fairly 공정하게

04
- □ organize 정리하다
- □ cabinet 장식장, 진열장
- □ shelf 선반; *(책장 등의) 칸
- □ jar 병, 단지
- □ rarely 좀처럼 …하지 않는

05
- □ be about to-v 막 …하려고 하다
- □ grocery shopping 장보기
- □ feed 먹이를 주다
- □ water 물을 주다
- □ do the dishes 설거지하다
- □ dry cleaning 드라이 클리닝한 세탁물

06
- □ totally 완전히
- □ show up 나타나다
- □ write down …을 적다
- □ planner 일정 계획표

08
- □ participate in …에 참여하다
- □ shelter 대피처; *보호소
- □ play 연극; (악기, 음악을) 연주하다
- □ exhibition 전시회

09
- □ flat 평평한
- □ cliff 절벽
- □ nearly 거의
- □ waterfall 폭포
- □ surface 표면
- □ bare 헐벗은
- □ sandstone 사암
- □ muddy 진흙의
- □ properly 제대로, 적절히
- □ permit 허락[허용]하다

10
- □ non-stop 직행의
- □ comfort 안락, 편안
- □ seating 좌석, 자리
- □ economy 경제적인; *보통석의
- □ departure 출발

11
- □ out of …이 떨어진[동난]
- □ order 주문하다
- □ fitting room 탈의실
- □ mind 언짢아하다, 상관하다

13
- □ supplement 보충물
- □ overcome 극복하다
- □ tiredness 피로
- □ pill 알약
- □ iron 철분
- □ immune system 면역 체계

14
- □ assistant 조수
- □ contract 계약서
- □ personally 직접, 개인적으로
- □ repairman 수리공

15
- □ have trouble v-ing …하는 데 어려움을 겪다
- □ fall asleep 잠들다
- □ counselor 상담가
- □ prevent A from v-ing A가 …하는 것을 막다

16-17
- □ complaint 불평, 항의(v. complain 불평하다)
- □ noise 소음
- □ reduce 줄이다
- □ absorb 흡수하다
- □ turn down (소리 · 온도 등을) 낮추다
- □ disturb 방해하다
- □ avoid 피하다
- □ annoying 짜증스러운

09 영어듣기 모의고사

1번부터 17번까지는 듣고 답하는 문제입니다.
1번부터 15번까지는 한 번만 들려주고, 16번부터 17번까지는 두 번 들려줍니다. 방송을 잘 듣고 답을 하기 바랍니다.

01

다음을 듣고, 여자가 하는 말의 목적으로 가장 적절한 것을 고르시오.

① 영어학과를 소개하려고
② 세미나 개최를 안내하려고
③ 토론의 필요성을 강조하려고
④ 새로 나온 연극을 홍보하려고
⑤ 올바른 연극 감상법을 설명하려고

02

대화를 듣고, 두 사람이 하는 말의 주제로 가장 적절한 것을 고르시오. 3점

① 오프라인 쇼핑의 장점
② 온라인 쇼핑 시 고려 사항
③ 쇼핑 중독을 극복하는 방법
④ 제품 환불 및 교환 시 유의점
⑤ 상황에 맞는 옷차림의 중요성

03

대화를 듣고, 두 사람의 관계를 가장 잘 나타낸 것을 고르시오.

① 아빠 — 딸
② 코치 — 수영 선수
③ 기자 — 메달리스트
④ 미술 선생님 — 학생
⑤ 코치 — 달리기 선수

04

대화를 듣고, 그림에서 대화의 내용과 일치하지 않는 것을 고르시오.

05

대화를 듣고, 여자가 남자에게 부탁한 일로 가장 적절한 것을 고르시오.

① 배터리 충전하기
② 회의 시간 늦추기
③ 발표 자료 준비하기
④ 노트북 컴퓨터 빌려주기
⑤ 서비스 센터 위치 알려주기

06

대화를 듣고, 남자가 책을 선택한 이유를 고르시오.

① 신간이라서
② 서평이 좋아서
③ 베스트셀러라서
④ 회사 업무에 필요해서
⑤ 유명 작가가 집필해서

07

대화를 듣고, 남자가 지불할 금액을 고르시오. 3점

① \$105 ② \$150 ③ \$165
④ \$180 ⑤ \$195

08

대화를 듣고, 뮤지컬 공연에 관해 두 사람이 언급하지 않은 것을 고르시오.

① 공연일 ② 공연자 ③ 줄거리
④ 표 가격 ⑤ 표 수령 장소

09

Friendship Day 행사에 관한 다음 내용을 듣고, 일치하지 않는 것을 고르시오.

① 오늘 오후 3시에 개최된다.
② 학교 도서관에서 진행된다.
③ 카드와 색연필이 준비된다.
④ 도서 목록에서 책을 골라야 한다.
⑤ 오늘 책이 배달될 것이다.

정답 및 해설 p.26-28

10

다음 표를 보면서 대화를 듣고, 여자가 지원할 식당을 고르시오.

< Part-Time Jobs >

	Restaurant	Working Hours (per day)	Required Experience	Pay (per hour)
①	A	3	5 months	$8
②	B	4	3 months	$12
③	C	4	6 months	$10
④	D	7	5 months	$7
⑤	E	8	1 months	$10

11

대화를 듣고, 남자의 마지막 말에 대한 여자의 응답으로 가장 적절한 것을 고르시오.

① Yes, you can pick me up now.
② Could you drive me to the office?
③ I'll return your umbrella tomorrow.
④ Sure, I'll be there in thirty minutes.
⑤ We need to cancel our appointment.

12

대화를 듣고, 여자의 마지막 말에 대한 남자의 응답으로 가장 적절한 것을 고르시오.

① Right, but I failed the road test.
② It's a pity you didn't pass both tests.
③ Well, I think you're good at driving.
④ I'll take a written test for the job soon.
⑤ I got a driver's license a few years ago.

13

대화를 듣고, 남자의 마지막 말에 대한 여자의 응답으로 가장 적절한 것을 고르시오.

Woman: ______________________________

① No. I didn't check my pockets.
② I think I left it in the car yesterday.
③ Don't worry. I'll lend you some money.
④ My sister gave it to me for my birthday.
⑤ You'd better try to stay more organized.

14

대화를 듣고, 여자의 마지막 말에 대한 남자의 응답으로 가장 적절한 것을 고르시오.

Man: ______________________________

① Sorry, I can't. I've never been there.
② Don't worry. I'll join and guide you.
③ Sure. I'll send you some sites by email.
④ You should be careful when you go there.
⑤ I agree that there are many attractive areas.

15

다음 상황 설명을 듣고, Ben이 Kimberly에게 할 말로 가장 적절한 것을 고르시오. 3점

Ben: ______________________________

① Try to make stronger eye contact.
② You'll pass the audition next time.
③ Why don't you take a short break?
④ You need to speak louder and clearer.
⑤ I'm sorry to hear that you failed again.

[16-17] 다음을 듣고, 물음에 답하시오.

16

남자가 하는 말의 목적으로 가장 적절한 것은?

① 과제를 안내하려고
② 시험에 관해 공지하려고
③ 발표 수업을 예고하려고
④ 학습한 내용을 정리하려고
⑤ 역사의 중요성을 강조하려고

17

포함되어야 할 내용으로 언급되지 않은 것은?

① 위치 ② 기후 ③ 크기
④ 인구 ⑤ 역사

녹음을 다시 한 번 듣고, 빈칸에 알맞은 말을 쓰시오.

01

W: Do you like Shakespeare? If so, listen carefully. The English department will have a one-day seminar on Shakespeare's plays. The seminar _______ _______ _______ in Lincoln Hall on October 18th. During the seminar, participants will discuss some of the writer's most famous plays, such as *Romeo and Juliet* and *Hamlet*. _______ _______ is interested in the topic is welcome. The entry fee is $20, and you can sign up at the desk in front of the hall _______ _______ _______ _______ that day. If you want to learn more about the seminar, please visit our website.

02

M: Hey Gina, what are you doing?

W: I'm shopping _______ _______ _______ _______.

M: What do you need a new dress for?

W: There will be a dance party next month. I want a nice dress for the party.

M: I see. Did you decide on a dress?

W: Almost. But the dress I want is on sale on several websites.

M: Then, you should check all the websites to _______ _______ _______ _______.

W: Yeah, I'm comparing prices now. Different online stores offer the same item at different prices.

M: Don't forget about delivery fees, too!

W: Of course. I'm checking which stores offer free delivery. I'm also checking if I can _______ _______ _______ or exchange.

M: You're right. That's also important.

03

M: Way to go, Beth! That was a great race.

W: Thanks.

M: You _______ _______ _______ _______! You're going to get the silver medal!

W: Yeah, I guess that's okay.

M: It's okay? What are you talking about? It's wonderful!

W: I could have _______ _______ _______ if I had kept my pace. I don't know why I started falling behind at the end.

M: You started making short strokes halfway through the race, which slowed you down. Make sure you're fully extending your arms out on every stroke.

W: Yes, sir. I'll keep practicing so that I'll do better _______ _______ _______ _______.

M: Good. Don't be too hard on yourself.

04

W: The charity bazaar is tomorrow! How should we _______ _______ _______ in the booth?

M: Well, we have two tables, a shelf, and hangers. First, let's put the rectangular table in the middle and place the dolls on it.

W: Good idea. How about these caps?

M: Let's put them _______ _______ _______ _______.

W: Okay. And we can put the round table in front of the rectangular one. I'd like to put the ties on it.

M: Great. What about the scarves? Should we put them on the shelf on the wall?

W: Yes. Then people can find them easily.

M: Okay. And finally, let's hang these clothes on the hangers and _______ _______ _______ _______ _______.

W: Perfect!

05

W: Oh, no! My new laptop has stopped working.

M: It's probably because of the battery. It doesn't ________ ________ ________.

W: But I charged it this morning. I haven't used it much since then.

M: Do you think it's broken?

W: I'm not sure. I think I need to take it to the service center.

M: That's a good idea. There's one downtown, ________ ________ ________ ________ ________.

W: Right, but I need a laptop for a meeting this afternoon. Can I use yours?

M: Sure. I'm going hiking today, so I don't need it.

W: Great. I can return it right after the meeting.

M: No problem. Just ________ ________ ________ to me tonight.

W: Thanks a lot.

06

W: Hi, Tom. What's that book in your hand?

M: It's a novel that I ________ ________ ________ ________.

W: Oh, what's it called?

M: *Twelve Days*. I can't wait to start reading it.

W: Aren't you busy these days? Do you ________ ________ ________ ________?

M: Well, I think I can read it for thirty minutes each night before I go to bed.

W: Is it a best-seller?

M: No, but all the reviews have been great, so I chose it without hesitation.

W: Who wrote it?

M: Douglas Kennedy. Though I'm not familiar with the name, I expect this novel will ________ ________ ________.

W: I see. I hope you enjoy the book.

07

W: Welcome to Jeju Rental Car. How can I help you?

M: I need to ________ ________ ________ for three days.

W: Great. We have five-seater and seven-seater cars.

M: How much are they per day?

W: Five-seater cars are $30 per day, and seven-seater cars are $50.

M: ________ ________ ________ ________ in my family. I want a seven-seater car.

W: All right. Is an old model okay? There is an extra $10 fee per day if you'd like the latest model.

M: Well, I don't need the new model.

W: Okay, and would you like insurance?

M: How much ________ ________ ________?

W: That's an extra $5 per day.

M: Yes, please.

08

W: Did you hear that the auditorium is reopening on February 20th?

M: Really? But the damage from the snowstorm was quite serious. Has everything been fixed?

W: Yes, everything ________ ________ ________ ________.

M: That's great news!

W: Right. And on opening day, there will be a performance of the musical *The Lions*.

M: Oh, cool. Who is going to be performing?

W: It will ________ ________ ________ the school drama club.

M: How much do tickets cost?

W: Actually, they're free.

M: That's great. Where can I get a ticket?

W: You can ________ ________ ________ at the student center tomorrow.

M: Okay. I can't wait to see the show!

09

M: Hello, everyone. I want to _______ _______ _______ a special event this afternoon. As you were already informed, we're going to have a Friendship Day event at 3:00 p.m. It'll _______ _______ _______ the school library. There will be desks with cards, colored pencils, and book lists. You can pick a friend and write a card to him or her. After that, you can choose a book that you want to _______ _______ your friend from the book list. We'll deliver the book with the card to your friend this Friday. I hope you'll take this chance to show your friendship!

10

M: Hi, Julie. _______ _______ _______ _______?

W: Hi, Mr. Olson. I'm looking for a part-time job as a waitress. Can you help me?

M: Sure, that's my job. Let's see... *[Typing sound]* There are many restaurants looking for a waitress. How many hours do you want to work?

W: I don't want to work _______ _______ _______ _______ a day.

M: I see. Do you have any experience working in a restaurant?

W: Yes, I worked as a waitress for five months last year.

M: Then you have two options to choose from.

W: Well, I'd like to _______ _______ _______ _______ that pays more.

M: Okay. I'll give you the restaurant's contact information.

W: Thank you!

11

[Cell phone rings.]

M: Hello, honey. Are you on your way home?

W: No, I'm already home. It's raining outside. Did you bring an umbrella?

M: Unfortunately, no. Could you come _______ _______ _______ at the office?

W: (Sure, I'll be there in thirty minutes.)

12

W: Charlie, you look down today. Is there something wrong?

M: Actually, I failed my driver's license test this morning.

W: You said you _______ _______ _______ _______, didn't you?

M: (Right, but I failed the road test.)

13

M: Are you ready to go?

W: Wait. _______ _______ _______ _______ _______.

M: Again? The last time you lost it, we looked everywhere in the house, and you finally found it in your coat pocket.

W: I remembered that, so I checked all of my pockets.

M: You should always put things in the same place so that you don't lose them.

W: You're right. I'll try to _______ _______ _______ _______.

M: Anyway, think about everything you did this morning, and try to remember the last time you had it.

W: Let me think... *[Pause]* Oh! _______ _______ _______!

M: Do you remember?

W: (I think I left it in the car yesterday.)

14

M: Sarah, do you have any plans for this winter vacation?

W: Yeah! I'm _______ _______ _______ _______ to New Zealand for two weeks.

M: Wow! That sounds great. I'm sure you'll have a wonderful time there.

W: Oh, didn't you say you had been there before? Were you just there for a trip?

M: Actually, I _______ _______ _______ _______ in Wellington studying English.

W: Oh, I'm going there. How's the weather in that city?

M: The climate is mild. It's very windy, though.

W: What did you like best in that country?

M: Probably the scenery. Everywhere I went, it was really beautiful.

W: Cool! Can you _______ _______ _______ to visit?

M: (Sure. I'll send you some sites by email.)

15

W: Kimberly wants to act in a movie, so she goes to many auditions. However, _______ _______ _______. She guesses it's because her acting isn't good enough. But she doesn't know what the exact problem is. She decides to ask her friend Ben _______ _______ because he is a good actor. Ben tells her to perform a monologue. When he watches her perform, he notices her problem. Her voice is very quiet and her pronunciation is unclear, so he can't understand _______ _______ _______. In this situation, what would Ben most likely say to Kimberly?

Ben: (You need to speak louder and clearer.)

16-17

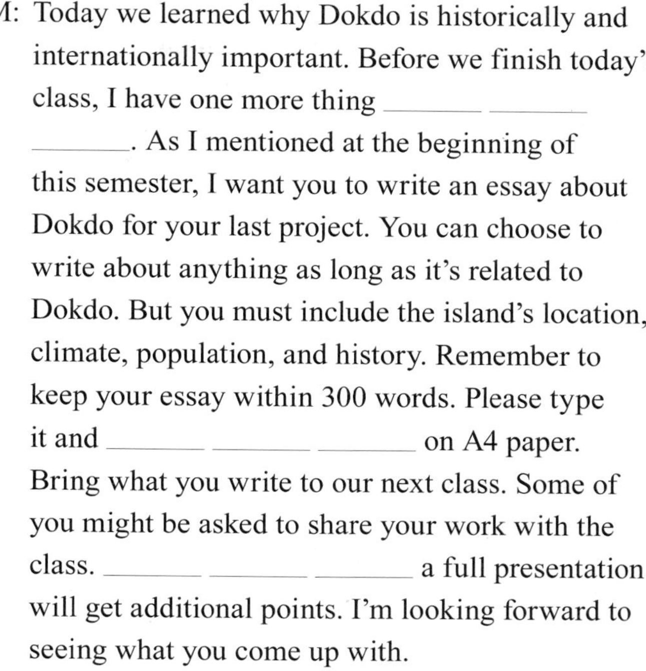

M: Today we learned why Dokdo is historically and internationally important. Before we finish today's class, I have one more thing _______ _______ _______. As I mentioned at the beginning of this semester, I want you to write an essay about Dokdo for your last project. You can choose to write about anything as long as it's related to Dokdo. But you must include the island's location, climate, population, and history. Remember to keep your essay within 300 words. Please type it and _______ _______ _______ on A4 paper. Bring what you write to our next class. Some of you might be asked to share your work with the class. _______ _______ _______ a full presentation will get additional points. I'm looking forward to seeing what you come up with.

9회

09 Word & Expressions

01
□ **carefully** 주의하여
□ **play** 놀이; *희곡
□ **hall** 복도; *홀, 회관
□ **participant** 참가자
□ **discuss** 의논하다
□ **entry fee** 참가비
□ **sign up** 등록하다

02
□ **several** 몇몇의
□ **best price** 최저 가격
□ **compare** 비교하다
□ **delivery** 배달
□ **fee** 요금
□ **refund** 환불
□ **exchange** 교환

03
□ **get first place** 1등을 하다
□ **pace** 속도
□ **fall behind** 뒤처지다
□ **stroke** (수영에서) 팔을 젓기
□ **slow down** (속도를) 늦추다
□ **extend** (길이를) 연장하다; *(팔을) 뻗다
□ **competition** 대회

04
□ **charity** 자선
□ **bazaar** 바자회
□ **arrange** 정리하다, 배열하다
□ **booth** (칸막이를 한) 점포, 전시장
□ **hanger** 옷걸이
□ **rectangular** 직사각형의
□ **cap** (챙이 달린) 모자
□ **scarf** 스카프

05
□ **last** 지속되다
□ **charge** 충전하다
□ **across from** …의 맞은편에

06
□ **order** 주문하다
□ **review** 검토; *서평
□ **hesitation** 망설임, 주저
□ **be familiar with** …에 익숙하다
□ **worth** …할 가치가 있는, …해 볼 만한

07
□ **rent** 대여하다
□ **seater** …인승
□ **extra** 추가의
□ **latest** 최신의
□ **insurance** 보험

08
□ **auditorium** 강당
□ **damage** 피해
□ **snowstorm** 눈보라, 폭설
□ **repair** 수리하다
□ **performance** 공연 (v. perform 공연하다)

09
□ **remind A of B** A에게 B를 상기시키다
□ **inform** (특히 공식적으로) 알리다
□ **colored pencil** 색연필
□ **share** 공유하다
□ **deliver** 배달하다

10
□ **experience** 경험
□ **apply** 지원하다
□ **contact information** 연락처
□ **required** 요구되는

11
□ **pick up** …을 (차에) 태우러 가다
□ **return** 돌려주다
□ **cancel** 취소하다
□ **appointment** 약속

12
□ **down** 우울한
□ **driver's license** 운전면허(증)
□ **written test** 필기시험
□ **road test** 도로주행 시험
□ **pity** 동정; *유감

13
□ **wallet** 지갑
□ **keep ... in mind** …을 명심하다
□ **organized** 정리된, 체계적인

14
□ **climate** 기후
□ **mild** 온화한
□ **windy** 바람이 많이 부는
□ **scenery** 경치, 풍경
□ **site** 장소
□ **attractive** 매력적인, 멋진

15
□ **act** 행동하다; *(영화 등에서) 연기하다
□ **audition** 오디션
□ **exact** 정확한
□ **monologue** (연극 등에서의) 독백
□ **notice** 알아차리다
□ **pronunciation** 발음
□ **unclear** 불확실한, 불명확한
□ **eye contact** 시선 맞추기

16-17
□ **historically** 역사적으로
□ **internationally** 국제적으로
□ **mention** 말하다, 언급하다
□ **beginning** 초(반), 시작
□ **semester** 학기
□ **as long as** …하는 한
□ **be related to** …와 관계가 있다
□ **location** 위치
□ **population** 인구
□ **print out** …을 출력하다
□ **additional** 추가의
□ **come up with** …을 생각하다, …을 제출하다

10 영어듣기 모의고사

정답 및 해설 p.29-31

1번부터 17번까지는 듣고 답하는 문제입니다.
1번부터 15번까지는 한 번만 들려주고, 16번부터 17번까지는 두 번 들려줍니다. 방송을 잘 듣고 답을 하기 바랍니다.

01

다음을 듣고, 여자가 하는 말의 목적으로 가장 적절한 것을 고르시오.

① 댄스 공연 관람을 권하려고
② 설문조사 참여를 부탁하려고
③ 무료 공연 초대장을 배포하려고
④ 공연장 시설의 문제점을 지적하려고
⑤ 공연장 보수 공사 기간을 공지하려고

02

대화를 듣고, 두 사람이 하는 말의 주제로 가장 적절한 것을 고르시오.

① 피부 노화의 원인
② 겨울철 피부 관리 방법
③ 비타민C 섭취의 필요성
④ 난방 기구의 올바른 사용법
⑤ 충분한 수분 섭취의 중요성

03

대화를 듣고, 두 사람의 관계를 가장 잘 나타낸 것을 고르시오.

① 팬 — 배우　　② 리포터 — 가수
③ 평론가 — 작곡가　　④ 사진작가 — 모델
⑤ 공연 기획가 — 매니저

04

대화를 듣고, 그림에서 대화의 내용과 일치하지 않는 것을 고르시오.

05

대화를 듣고, 남자가 여자에게 부탁한 일로 가장 적절한 것을 고르시오.

① 휴가 신청하기　　② 팩스 보내주기
③ 기념품 사오기　　④ 본사에 연락하기
⑤ 팩스 번호 알려주기

06

대화를 듣고, 남자가 호텔 지배인에 지원하지 못하는 이유를 고르시오.

① 경력이 부족해서
② 중국어를 못해서
③ 기숙사 생활을 해야 해서
④ 호텔 경영을 전공하지 않아서
⑤ 다음 달에 근무를 시작해야 해서

07

대화를 듣고, 여자가 지불할 금액을 고르시오. 3점

① $25　　② $30　　③ $35
④ $40　　⑤ $50

08

대화를 듣고, 여자가 구입한 선물로 언급되지 않은 것을 고르시오.

① 찻잔 세트　　② 녹차　　③ CD
④ 인형　　⑤ 전통 탈

09

새로 개장한 수영장에 관한 다음 내용을 듣고, 일치하지 않는 것을 고르시오. 3점

① 총 10개의 레인이 있다.
② 샤워장과 탈의실을 확장했다.
③ 사물함을 더 큰 것으로 교체했다.
④ 기존 회원은 다음 달 요금을 할인받을 수 있다.
⑤ 오전 6시부터 저녁 9시까지 개장한다.

10

다음 표를 보면서 대화를 듣고, 두 사람이 볼 연극을 고르시오.

< Number One Theater >

	Title	Time	Genre
①	Ms. Jessica	1:30 - 3:00 p.m.	Comedy
②	Fantastic World	12:00 - 1:30 p.m.	Romance
③	The Past	3:00 - 4:30 p.m.	History
④	Fantastic World	5:00 - 6:30 p.m.	Romance
⑤	The Past	12:30 - 2:00 p.m.	History

11

대화를 듣고, 남자의 마지막 말에 대한 여자의 응답으로 가장 적절한 것을 고르시오.

① We are closed every Monday.
② This one has already sold out.
③ I'm afraid those are not for sale.
④ Our leather sofas are 10% off now.
⑤ We have some other furniture as well.

12

대화를 듣고, 여자의 마지막 말에 대한 남자의 응답으로 가장 적절한 것을 고르시오.

① I had a horrible stomachache.
② Why don't you go see a doctor?
③ Be careful when you cross the street.
④ I didn't make any vacation plans yet.
⑤ He is in the hospital for an operation.

13

대화를 듣고, 여자의 마지막 말에 대한 남자의 응답으로 가장 적절한 것을 고르시오.

Man: ______________________________

① You can study with your smartphone.
② Yes, smartphones have many benefits.
③ I think you should stop using it so often.
④ I think you change your phones too often.
⑤ Many teenagers are addicted to smartphones.

14

대화를 듣고, 남자의 마지막 말에 대한 여자의 응답으로 가장 적절한 것을 고르시오.

Woman: ______________________________

① Oh, how did you find out about it?
② I'd like to travel with you to Jeju Island.
③ Thank you. I'll sign up for the race now.
④ Can I get more information on the event?
⑤ It's okay. Let's run a race together some other time.

15

다음 상황 설명을 듣고, Alice가 John에게 할 말로 가장 적절한 것을 고르시오.

Alice: ______________________________

① Which bus goes to our school?
② Where does the school bus stop?
③ When will our school bus arrive here?
④ How long does it take to get to school?
⑤ Can you lend me some money for the bus?

[16-17] 다음을 듣고, 물음에 답하시오.

16

남자가 하는 말의 주제로 가장 적절한 것은?

① 안전한 먹거리 조리법
② 크리스마스 전통 음식
③ 인상적인 손님 접대의 중요성
④ 독특한 크리스마스트리 장식품
⑤ 크리스마스트리를 장식하는 이유

17

언급된 음식이 아닌 것은?

① 쿠키 ② 사탕 ③ 초콜릿
④ 견과 ⑤ 말린 과일

정답 및 해설 p.31

녹음을 다시 한 번 듣고, 빈칸에 알맞은 말을 쓰시오.

01

W: Attention, please. Thank you for coming to our dance show. We hope all of you enjoy it. Before the show begins, we'd like to _______ _______ _______ _______. Please read the paper we gave you, and answer the questions on it. We have plans to renovate our dance theater soon. So we want your ideas on how we should renovate it. Your opinions _______ _______ _______ in our renovation plans. The survey will only take a couple of minutes to complete. Please _______ _______ _______ the paper in the box when you leave. Thank you and enjoy the show!

02

M: It's getting cold outside. Winter is around the corner.

W: Oh, no! My skin is always dry in winter.

M: Yeah, being indoors with the heater on _______ _______ _______ _______ _______.

W: But your skin looks so good. What's your secret?

M: Well, I try to drink about 2 liters of water _______ _______ _______.

W: That's a good idea.

M: I also sometimes put used green tea bags or cucumber slices on my skin.

W: Oh, I've heard vitamin C is great for our skin.

M: Yes, eating lots of fruits and vegetables will help you get plenty of it.

W: Thanks for your tips. I'll try to use them to _______ _______ _______ _______!

03

W: Hello. I'm Kate Smith.

M: Nice to meet you, Kate.

W: Nice to meet you, too. _______ _______ _______ _______ I ask you a few questions?

M: Not at all. What would you like to know?

W: You successfully finished your concert tour. How do you feel about that?

M: I feel very satisfied. And I'm thankful for my fans and everyone who has helped me.

W: They must be very happy. Do you have any plans for a new album?

M: Yes, it _______ _______ _______ on Christmas Eve.

W: Can you tell me more about the album?

M: Sure. Most of the songs will be love ballads.

W: I'm sure your fans _______ _______ _______ _______ them. Thank you for your time.

04

[Telephone rings.]

W: Hello. This is Ace Design.

M: Hi, Ms. Murphy. This is Max. Have you finished remodeling the kid's café?

W: Sure, I finished it this afternoon.

M: Did you _______ _______ _______ in the corner?

W: Yes, I placed it in the left back corner. And I also put a big ball pool on the left side of the café.

M: That sounds good. What about the toy cars?

W: I put them in the middle _______ _______ _______.

M: Great. Then there'll be enough space for the cars to drive. Where did you install the toy train track?

W: I installed it in the right back corner.

M: All right. Is there a place for the kids to sit down and eat?

W: There are _______ _______ _______ in front of the toy train track.

05

[Telephone rings.]

W: Hello. IT department. This is Cassie.

M: Cassie, it's John. Can you help me?

W: Of course. But aren't you _______ _______ in Hawaii?

M: I am, but I need help. Has a fax from the head office arrived?

W: Let me check. *[Pause]* Oh, yes. There is a fax for you here. What do you want me to do?

M: Could you _______ _______ _______ Mr. Jones for me? His fax number is on my desk.

W: You just want the same fax sent to him?

M: Yes. Anytime today before you leave would be great.

W: I can do that. _______ _______, could you get me a souvenir? *[Laughs]*

M: Sure. Thanks for your help!

06

W: Did you see the ad about the Star Hotel in Seoul? They're _______ _______ _______ _______ _______.

M: No, I didn't see it. Could you tell me more about the job?

W: Sure. You have to start next month.

M: I can do that. Anything else?

W: They are looking for a person _______ _______ _______ hotel management.

M: Oh, that was my major.

W: And you need at least five years of experience as a manager.

M: I worked at two different hotels for a total of 8 years.

W: The last requirement is that you need to _______ _______ _______ _______.

M: Really? I can't speak Chinese at all.

W: Oh, then I guess this isn't the right position for you.

07

W: Hi. I would like to buy some amusement park tickets.

M: Okay. Adult tickets are $15 each, and children _______ _______ _______ _______ _______ are $5 each. How many tickets do you want?

W: I need one adult ticket and two children's tickets.

M: Okay. Wait a second, please.

W: By the way, are _______ _______ _______ _______ _______ in the ticket?

M: Most are, but you have to pay $5 more for each person to ride the Devil's Spine.

W: Oh, it's a bit expensive.

M: But that would include a free lunch coupon at one of our cafés.

W: Free lunch? That sounds great! I'll _______ _______ _______ for Devil's Spine for all of us, then.

08

W: Hey, Jerry! I didn't expect to see you here.

M: Oh. Hi, Betty! What brings you here?

W: I came here to _______ _______ _______ for my family.

M: That's nice of you. What did you buy?

W: I got a set of teacups for my mother.

M: What about your father?

W: I bought some Korean green tea for him.

M: Your parents will definitely like your presents. What about your sister?

W: She's _______ _______ _______ _______ Korean pop music, so I bought some CDs for her.

M: Oh, I'm sure she'll love them. Did you also buy something for your brother?

W: Of course. _______ _______ _______ Korean culture, so I bought him a traditional Korean mask.

09

M: Hello, valued members of North Star Fitness Center. The remodeling of our pool has finally finished. _______ _______ _______ _______, you can use the new swimming pool. We added three lanes, so there are ten lanes now. Also, we expanded the shower area and the changing rooms. And we _______ _______ _______ _______ with bigger ones. We invite our current members to use the pool _______ _______ next month. Just show your membership card, and you can enter. The new pool is open from 6:00 a.m. to 9:00 p.m. Please come and enjoy all these great new features!

10

M: Jennifer, I just found the play schedule online. _______ _______ _______ to see tomorrow.

W: Okay. Which one do you want to see?

M: Any of them is fine if it starts after 1:00 p.m. I have to go to the gym tomorrow morning.

W: All right. Why don't we see *Ms. Jessica*? My sister said it was really interesting.

M: Actually, I saw that last week.

W: In that case, we _______ _______ _______ _______.

M: Yeah. Is there any genre you don't like? I like every genre.

W: Well, I don't want to see a romance play.

M: Really? Then there is _______ _______ _______ _______.

W: Okay. Let's buy the tickets.

11

M: Hi. I'm interested in buying a new sofa.

W: Great. Do you have anything specific in mind?

M: Not really. Is there _______ _______ _______?

W: (Our leather sofas are 10% off now.)

12

W: Hi, Andy! Long time no see. Were you on vacation?

M: No, I _______ _______ _______ _______ for three days.

W: I'm sorry to hear that. What happened?

M: (I had a horrible stomachache.)

13

M: I can't imagine a world without smartphones.

W: I agree. I use mine _______ _______ _______ these days.

M: Really? What do you usually use it for?

W: I use it for things such as checking my email, _______ _______ _______, playing games, and a lot more.

M: How many hours do you think you use it per day?

W: I use it all day long.

M: That's too much. It sounds like _______ _______ _______ your smartphone!

W: Maybe I am. I even start to feel nervous if I don't have it with me.

M: (I think you should stop using it so often.)

10회

14

W: What are you doing on the Internet, Gary?

M: I'm _______ _______ an application form. I'm signing up for a race.

W: Are you running a marathon? That's amazing!

M: No, I'm just running the 10-kilometer race.

W: That's still great. When is it?

M: It's on June 8th. _______ _______ _______ _______ _______?

W: I'm afraid I can't. I'll be in Jeju Island on that day.

M: Wow. Are you going on vacation there?

W: No, it's not a vacation. I have to _______ _______ _______ a seminar.

M: I see. I'm sorry you can't join the event.

W: (It's okay. Let's run a race together some other time.)

15

W: Alice gets up late and misses the school bus, so she decides to _______ _______ _______ _______ instead. She runs to the bus stop and gets there just before the bus arrives. However, she realizes that she _______ _______ _______ on her desk. She is frustrated because she doesn't have time to go back home and get her wallet. Just then, her classmate John comes toward her and says, "Hi." She wants to _______ _______ _______ for the bus fare from him. In this situation, what would Alice most likely say to John?

Alice: (Can you lend me some money for the bus?)

16-17

M: What does your Christmas tree look like this year? Does it just have the same lights and ornaments as last year? Christmas Day is approaching, and many houses _______ _______ _______ their Christmas trees. Every year people decorate Christmas trees with the same things. But if you want to have a special and memorable Christmas this year, try something different. How about decorating your tree with food items? The items should be things that _______ _______ _______ _______. They can be anything such as cookies, candies, nuts, and dried fruits. Put them in a small colored box and hang them on the tree. After your Christmas party, you can share the food with your family and friends. They will surely like it. _______ _______ _______ _______ _______ will enjoy the experience. So why don't you start this new, delicious Christmas tradition in your home?

10 Word & Expressions

01
- □ ask ... a favor …에게 부탁하다
- □ renovate 보수하다 (n. renovation 보수)
- □ opinion 의견
- □ reflect 반영하다
- □ survey 설문조사
- □ complete 완료하다; *기입[작성]하다

02
- □ around the corner 목전에 있는, 코앞에 있는
- □ indoors 실내에서
- □ extremely 극도로
- □ secret 비밀; *비결
- □ cucumber 오이
- □ slice 얇게 썬 조각
- □ plenty 풍부한 양

03
- □ successfully 성공적으로
- □ release 풀어 주다; *공개하다, 발표하다

04
- □ slide 미끄럼틀
- □ place 놓다, 두다; 장소
- □ request 요청하다
- □ space 공간
- □ install 설치하다
- □ track (기차) 선로

05
- □ department 부서
- □ be on vacation 휴가 중이다
- □ head office 본사
- □ in return 보답으로
- □ souvenir 기념품

06
- □ major in …을 전공하다
- □ management 경영
- □ requirement 요구 조건
- □ fluent 유창한

07
- □ amusement park 놀이공원
- □ ride 놀이기구; (탈 것에) 타다
- □ include 포함시키다

08
- □ expect 기대하다
- □ pick up …을 사다
- □ definitely 분명히
- □ curious 호기심이 많은
- □ traditional 전통적인
- □ mask 가면, 탈

09
- □ valued 귀중한, 소중한
- □ as of …일 자로
- □ lane 길; *(수영 대회 등의) 레인
- □ expand 확장하다
- □ changing room 탈의실
- □ replace 교체하다
- □ locker 사물함
- □ current 현재의
- □ feature 특징, 특색

10
- □ schedule 일정
- □ genre (예술작품의) 장르

11
- □ specific 특정한
- □ on sale 판매되는; *할인 중인
- □ for sale 팔려고 내놓은
- □ leather 가죽
- □ as well (…뿐만 아니라) …도

12
- □ on vacation 휴가 중인
- □ be in the hospital 입원 중이다
- □ horrible 지긋지긋한, 끔찍한
- □ stomachache 복통
- □ operation 수술

13
- □ imagine 상상하다
- □ all the time 항상
- □ be addicted to …에 중독되다
- □ nervous 불안해하는
- □ benefit 이익

14
- □ fill out …을 기입하다, …을 작성하다
- □ application form 신청서
- □ sign up for …을 신청하다
- □ take part in …에 참가하다
- □ find out 알아내다
- □ run a race 경주하다

15
- □ public 대중의, 일반의
- □ instead 대신에
- □ realize 깨닫다
- □ wallet 지갑
- □ frustrated 좌절감을 느끼는
- □ borrow 빌리다
- □ lend 빌려주다

16-17
- □ ornament 장식물
- □ approach 다가오다
- □ decorate 장식하다
- □ memorable 기억할 만한
- □ go bad (음식 등이) 상하다
- □ nut 견과
- □ hang 매달다
- □ A as well as B B뿐만 아니라 A도
- □ tradition 전통

11 영어듣기 모의고사

1번부터 17번까지는 듣고 답하는 문제입니다.
1번부터 15번까지는 한 번만 들려주고, 16번부터 17번까지는 두 번 들려줍니다. 방송을 잘 듣고 답을 하기 바랍니다.

01

다음을 듣고, 여자가 하는 말의 목적으로 가장 적절한 것을 고르시오.

① 전화 영어 수업을 홍보하려고
② 폭우에 대한 대비를 당부하려고
③ 수강료 환불 방법을 설명하려고
④ 수업이 취소되었음을 공지하려고
⑤ 일시적인 정전의 원인을 알리려고

02

대화를 듣고, 여자의 의견으로 가장 적절한 것을 고르시오.

① 밤늦게 먹는 것은 건강에 해롭다.
② 건강을 위해서 근력 운동을 해야 한다.
③ 근무 중 시간을 효율적으로 활용해야 한다.
④ 체중 감량을 위해서 규칙적으로 운동해야 한다.
⑤ 식사량을 줄이는 것이 다이어트에 가장 중요하다.

03

대화를 듣고, 두 사람의 관계를 가장 잘 나타낸 것을 고르시오.

① 시민 — 경찰관
② 투숙객 — 호텔 직원
③ 손님 — 부동산 중개인
④ 손님 — 이불가게 점원
⑤ 건물 관리인 — 청소부

04

대화를 듣고, 그림에서 대화의 내용과 일치하지 않는 것을 고르시오.

05

대화를 듣고, 여자가 남자에게 부탁한 일로 가장 적절한 것을 고르시오.

① 일자리 소개하기
② 이력서 수정하기
③ 면접 대비 질문하기
④ 긴장 푸는 법 알려주기
⑤ 회사에 관한 정보 검색하기

06

대화를 듣고, 남자가 전화를 건 이유를 고르시오.

① 주문한 물건이 도착하지 않아서
② 환불받은 금액이 잘못 입금되어서
③ 쇼핑몰 사이트에 접속이 되지 않아서
④ 구입한 스마트폰이 파손되어 도착해서
⑤ 수리받은 물건이 제대로 작동하지 않아서

07

대화를 듣고, 남자가 지불할 금액을 고르시오. 3점

① $540 ② $600 ③ $720 ④ $800 ⑤ $900

08

대화를 듣고, 유치원에 관해 두 사람이 언급하지 않은 것을 고르시오.

① 교사의 경력
② 학급당 학생 수
③ 원생 연령
④ 특별 수업의 종류
⑤ 셔틀버스 운행 여부

09

Planting Trees Campaign에 관한 다음 내용을 듣고, 일치하지 않는 것을 고르시오.

① 지금부터 이번 달 말까지 진행된다.
② 백화점 판매액의 1%가 기부된다.
③ 중국의 사막 지역에 나무를 심는다.
④ 5,000그루가 넘는 나무를 심을 계획이다.
⑤ 각 층 엘리베이터 옆에 모금함이 놓여 있다.

정답 및 해설 p.32-34 

10

다음 표를 보면서 대화를 듣고, 여자가 구입할 태블릿 컴퓨터를 고르시오.

< Tablet Computers >

	Model	Memory	Screen	Price
①	A	32GB	11 inches	$600
②	B	32GB	7 inches	$700
③	C	64GB	7 inches	$750
④	D	64GB	11 inches	$800
⑤	E	128GB	11 inches	$900

11

대화를 듣고, 여자의 마지막 말에 대한 남자의 응답으로 가장 적절한 것을 고르시오.

① I'll let him know you said that.
② He needed surgery on his left knee.
③ He will go to the hospital tomorrow.
④ Thank you. I recovered very quickly.
⑤ Then let's meet there at three o'clock.

12

대화를 듣고, 남자의 마지막 말에 대한 여자의 응답으로 가장 적절한 것을 고르시오.

① I'll rent it for three days.
② I bought the latest model.
③ I'm looking for a full-size van.
④ May I see your driver's license?
⑤ You should return the car by Tuesday.

13

대화를 듣고, 남자의 마지막 말에 대한 여자의 응답으로 가장 적절한 것을 고르시오.

Woman: ______________________

① Yes, it was in my inbox all along.
② Oh, I'll check that folder right now.
③ I'll let you know when I make a folder.
④ I'm sorry. I just don't need car insurance.
⑤ Don't worry. I'll send you a copy by email.

14

대화를 듣고, 여자의 마지막 말에 대한 남자의 응답으로 가장 적절한 것을 고르시오.

Man: ______________________

① No, just use the Internet next time.
② I'm sorry, but that wouldn't be fair.
③ Let me have a second chance, please.
④ I'm afraid you can't make an extra copy.
⑤ You should've found information on the Web.

15

다음 상황 설명을 듣고, Hailey가 남자에게 할 말로 가장 적절한 것을 고르시오.

Hailey: ______________________

① I think you dropped your wallet!
② Excuse me, where are you going?
③ Have you seen my wallet anywhere?
④ Do you know where the shopping mall is?
⑤ Please help me put these bags in the trunk.

[16-17] 다음을 듣고, 물음에 답하시오.

16

남자가 하는 말의 목적으로 가장 적절한 것은? 3점

① 역할 분담 계획을 공지하려고
② 연기를 잘하는 법을 알리려고
③ 팀 활동의 장점을 설명하려고
④ 글 잘 쓰는 방법을 소개하려고
⑤ 연극 동아리 가입을 권유하려고

17

관여한 작업으로 언급되지 않은 것은?

① 대본 쓰기 ② 연기 ③ 연출
④ 분장 ⑤ 의상 디자인

녹음을 다시 한 번 듣고, 빈칸에 알맞은 말을 쓰시오.

01

W: Good morning. As you may have heard on the news, there was _______ _______ _______ _______ here in Los Angeles over the weekend. Many areas near our office are temporarily without electricity. Also, some roads need to be cleared. As a result, some of the teachers in our phone-English program can't come to the office today. Therefore, some classes _______ _______ _______. Students whose classes are canceled will receive a text message beforehand. Makeup classes will be scheduled _______ _______ _______ _______. We apologize for the inconvenience. Thank you.

02

W: You look worried. Is there a problem?

M: I've _______ _______ _______. It's probably because I've been eating late at night.

W: Oh, that's too bad. Have you been trying to lose weight?

M: Yes. I'm trying not to eat snacks, especially at night.

W: That sounds like a good start. Do you exercise, too?

M: Not really. I _______ _______ _______ _______ to do that. I just do weight training sometimes.

W: Why don't you have time? Regular exercise is one of the best ways to lose weight.

M: I usually work at the office until late at night.

W: Still, you should find some time to exercise regularly. _______ _______ _______ has its limits.

M: That's true. I'll try to make time.

03

M: Excuse me.

W: Yes, sir. How can I help you?

M: Well, I _______ _______ _______.

W: I'm so sorry to hear that. What seems to be the problem?

M: I'm not satisfied with my room. There are stains on the bed sheets.

W: Oh, I apologize. The maid _______ _______ _______ _______ _______ them.

M: It also smells like someone has been smoking in there.

W: I will send someone to clean the room right away.

M: Well, I really don't want to wait for it to be cleaned. Can I just _______ _______ _______ _______ _______?

W: Of course we can do that. I'm really sorry again for the inconvenience.

M: It's okay. Thanks for your help.

04

W: Hi. How can I help you?

M: I'd like to order a birthday cake for my wife.

W: Great. Do you have any special cake in mind?

M: Well, I want a three-layer cake with hearts on the bottom layer.

W: Okay, and how about the middle layer?

M: Please just _______ _______ _______ around it.

W: I see.

M: But I'm not sure _______ _______ _______ the top layer.

W: Well, what about small dots?

M: Oh, that sounds good. Also, could you place a star-shaped decoration on the top of the cake?

W: Sure. That'll look great. And why don't you _______ _______ _______ around the bottom layer?

M: Yeah, that would be wonderful!

정답 및 해설 p.34

05

M: Hi, Wendy. You're looking for a new job, right?

W: That's right, Bob. Actually, I have an interview tomorrow.

M: Wow! I hope _______ _______ _______ _______.

W: Well, I'm not sure. I'm really nervous about the interview.

M: Just relax. I'll help you look up some information about the company. You can _______ _______ _______ with the information.

W: Thanks, but I've already done a lot of research.

M: Then how about I help you practice for the interview?

W: That's a great idea! Could you _______ _______ _______ _______ _______ they might ask?

M: Sure. Let's start right now.

W: Thanks. That way I'll be a lot less nervous.

06

[Telephone rings.]

W: Good morning. EZ Electronics Customer Service.

M: Hello. This is Kevin Taylor. I ordered a smartphone from your website last week.

W: Yes, Mr. Taylor. Didn't you _______ _______ _______ yet?

M: Yes, I got it yesterday. But there's a problem.

W: Oh, what's the problem?

M: _______ _______ _______ when I opened it.

W: I'm so sorry to hear that. How is it damaged?

M: The screen of the smartphone was broken.

W: I see. Would you like to exchange it for a new one?

M: No, _______ _______ _______ _______.

W: Okay. Then please send it back to us. When it arrives, we'll refund the money to your account. Again, I'm so sorry.

07

W: Hello. How can I help you?

M: I'd like to rent a hall for my company's New Year's party.

W: Okay. When is the party?

M: It's December 31st. There will be 45 people.

W: Then the Rose Hall _______ _______ from 3:00 p.m. to 8:00 p.m. that day.

M: I'd like to rent the hall from 3:00 p.m. to 7:00 p.m.

W: Fantastic. _______ _______ _______ is $150 an hour. But it's an extra $50 an hour for the sound system.

M: We need the sound system, too.

W: Okay, I'll prepare it. Since you have more than 40 people, you can _______ _______ _______ _______. It's 10% off the total price.

M: That's great.

08

[Telephone rings.]

W: Hello. Happy Times Kindergarten.

M: Hi. I'm thinking of _______ _______ _______ at this school, so I have some questions.

W: Sure. What would you like to know?

M: Do your teachers have teaching experience?

W: Yes. They all have at least three years of teaching experience.

M: That's good. _______ _______ _______ are in one class?

W: Each class has fifteen to eighteen students.

M: I see. And are there any special classes?

W: Yes. There are ballet and taekwondo classes.

M: Okay, and one last thing. Is there _______ _______ _______ to the kindergarten?

W: Yes, of course. You can use the bus if you live near here.

M: Great. Thanks for the information.

09

M: Good afternoon, shoppers. Thanks for shopping at Hearst Department Store. Today, I'd like to _______ _______ _______ about our special program. From now until the end of this month, we will be having the Planting Trees Campaign. During this time, 1% of all sales will go toward the planting of trees. We will use this money to plant trees _______ _______ _______ in China. We plan to plant more than 5,000 trees. There is also a donation box at the main entrance on the first floor. Any customers can donate money. You may donate _______ _______ _______ _______ _______. We thank you for shopping here. Please enjoy your day.

10

M: Good afternoon. What can I do for you?

W: I'm _______ _______ a tablet computer.

M: Okay, please come this way. *[Pause]* These are the tablet computers we have.

W: I see. Is there something with 64 GB or more? I need a model with a lot of memory.

M: Of course. You can _______ _______ _______ _______ _______. How about the screen size?

W: I'd like to watch videos with my tablet computer. I want something with a big screen.

M: In that case, something with an 11-inch screen will be fine. Do you have a certain price in mind?

W: Yes, I need the tablet computer _______ _______ _______ _______ $850.

M: Then this is the right one for you.

W: All right. I'll take it.

11

W: Hi, Gary. Did you hear that Tony got surgery last week?

M: Yes. I'm going to the hospital to visit him now.

W: Then tell him I hope _______ _______ _______.

M: (I'll let him know you said that.)

12

M: Welcome to Driving World. May I help you?

W: Yes. I'd like to _______ _______ _______ for the next two days.

M: Okay. What kind of car do you want?

W: (I'm looking for a full-size van.)

13

[Telephone rings.]

M: Hello! This is Bob from Life Saver Insurance. What can I do for you?

W: Hi, I'd like to know when I can expect to receive _______ _______ _______ my car insurance policy.

M: Sure. Could you tell me your name please?

W: My name is Jennifer Smith. I asked a different person to _______ _______ _______ _______ yesterday.

M: Let me check. *[Pause]* Yes, it says here that it was emailed to you yesterday. Could you check your email again?

W: I just checked it, but _______ _______ _______.

M: Have you received emails from us before?

W: No, I haven't.

M: Sometimes our emails go into people's spam folders.

W: (Oh, I'll check that folder right now.)

14

W: Mr. Harrison, do you have a minute?

M: Sure. What brings you here?

W: I wanted to ask you why I got a D on my report.

M: Well, I found that you _______ _______ _______ from the Internet. You didn't even change a single word.

W: But it was only a few sentences, Mr. Harrison.

M: You needed to write everything _______ _______ _______ _______, Rachel. I explained that in class.

W: What if I rewrite it again?

M: Everyone had the same amount of time to finish this assignment, Rachel.

W: Can I please _______ _______ _______ _______? I'll do it again right away.

M: (I'm sorry, but that wouldn't be fair.)

15

W: Hailey is walking to her car after _______ _______ _______ _______. When she gets to her car, she starts to put what she bought into the trunk of her car. At that time, a man walks by her, and his wallet _______ _______ _______ _______ _______ and falls onto the ground. He doesn't even seem to notice and keeps walking. Hailey is worried that someone else might pick it up and take it. She wants to _______ _______ _______ _______ about it. In this situation, what would Hailey most likely say to the man?

Hailey: (I think you dropped your wallet!)

16-17

M: If you have worked as part of a team, you know that _______ _______ _______ has its benefits. That's what I learned when I joined my school's drama club. The best part of working together was that we could make a more creative script. Because there were 20 people in the club, we had lots of ideas to choose from. Also, the work _______ _______ _______ all of us, so it wasn't too stressful. Although I mainly acted, I would sometimes give suggestions on makeup and costume designs. In addition, we gave each other advice when we would rehearse. As a result, we won first prize in our local drama contest and _______ _______ _______ _______ _______ in the National Drama Competition. I think we achieved these great results thanks to our teamwork.

11 Word & Expressions

01
□ **storm** 폭풍
□ **temporarily** 일시적으로
□ **electricity** 전기
□ **clear** (장애물을) 제거하다, 처리하다
□ **cancel** 취소하다
□ **beforehand** 사전에
□ **apologize** 사과하다
□ **inconvenience** 불편

02
□ **gain[lose] weight** 체중이 늘다[줄다]
□ **weight training** 웨이트[근력] 트레이닝
□ **regular** 규칙적인(adv. regularly 규칙적으로)
□ **control** 조절하다
□ **diet** 식사, 음식
□ **limit** 한계

03
□ **complaint** 불만
□ **be satisfied with** …에 만족하다
□ **stain** 얼룩
□ **maid** 하녀, 청소부

04
□ **layer** 층
□ **bottom** 맨 아래
□ **stripe** 줄무늬
□ **decorate** 장식하다(n. decoration 장식품)
□ **dot** 점

05
□ **nervous** 불안해하는, 긴장되는
□ **relax** 긴장을 풀다
□ **look up** …을 찾아보다
□ **impress** 깊은 인상을 주다
□ **interviewer** 면접관
□ **do research** 조사를 하다

06
□ **electronics** 전자제품
□ **shipment** 수송(품)
□ **damage** 손상을 주다
□ **exchange** 교환하다
□ **refund** 환불; 환불하다
□ **account** 계좌

07
□ **available** 이용 가능한
□ **rental fee** 대여료
□ **extra** 추가의

08
□ **kindergarten** 유치원
□ **enroll** 등록시키다
□ **ballet** 발레

09
□ **department store** 백화점
□ **plant** (나무 등을) 심다
□ **go toward** …에 도움되다
□ **desert** 사막
□ **donation** 기부(v. donate 기부하다)
□ **entrance** 출입구, 문

11
□ **surgery** 수술
□ **recover** 회복하다

12
□ **rent** 대여하다
□ **latest** 최신의
□ **full-size van** 승합차
□ **driver's license** 운전 면허증

13
□ **insurance** 보험
□ **policy** 보험 증권
□ **copy** *복사본; 복사하다, 베끼다
□ **spam** 스팸 메일
□ **inbox** 받은편지함
□ **all along** 내내, 계속

14
□ **copy** 복사하다, 베끼다
□ **rewrite** 다시 쓰다
□ **assignment** 과제
□ **chance** 기회
□ **fair** 공정한

15
□ **trunk** (나무의) 몸통; *(자동차의) 트렁크
□ **walk by** …을 지나가다
□ **slip** 미끄러지다, 빠져나가다
□ **notice** 알아차리다
□ **drop** 떨어뜨리다

16-17
□ **part** 부분; *일원, 구성원
□ **benefit** 이점
□ **creative** 창의적인
□ **script** 대본, 원고
□ **divide** 나누다
□ **stressful** 스트레스가 많은
□ **suggestion** 제안, 의견
□ **costume** 의상
□ **local** 지역의
□ **national** 전국적인
□ **competition** 대회
□ **achieve** 달성하다, 성취하다
□ **thanks to** … 덕분에

12 영어듣기 모의고사

정답 및 해설 p.35-37

1번부터 17번까지는 듣고 답하는 문제입니다.
1번부터 15번까지는 한 번만 들려주고, 16번부터 17번까지는 두 번 들려줍니다. 방송을 잘 듣고 답을 하기 바랍니다.

01

다음을 듣고, 여자가 하는 말의 목적으로 가장 적절한 것을 고르시오.

① 전국적인 태풍 예보를 전하려고
② 태풍에 대비한 교실 관리법을 안내하려고
③ 태풍 피해 복구 자원봉사자를 모집하려고
④ 태풍주의보에 따른 임시 휴교를 공지하려고
⑤ 태풍으로 인해 파손된 창문 교체를 알리려고

02

대화를 듣고, 두 사람이 하는 말의 주제로 가장 적절한 것을 고르시오.

① 규칙적인 수면의 필요성
② 밤에 숙면을 취하는 방법
③ 운동이 건강에 미치는 영향
④ 독서가 뇌 발달에 좋은 이유
⑤ 자신에 맞는 올바른 수면 자세

03

대화를 듣고, 두 사람의 관계를 가장 잘 나타낸 것을 고르시오.

① 요리사 — 수강생　② 기자 — 유명인사
③ 비서 — 취업 지원자　④ 이벤트 담당자 — 응모자
⑤ 잡지 편집자 — 식당 주인

04

대화를 듣고, 그림에서 대화의 내용과 일치하지 않는 것을 고르시오.

You're Invited! ②
①
Saturday, October 8th
③ 12:00-2:00 p.m.
Nick's House
④
⑤ *Phone number: 060-907-2875

05

대화를 듣고, 남자가 여자를 위해 할 일로 가장 적절한 것을 고르시오.

① 이메일 보내기
② 지도 출력하기
③ 프린터 수리하기
④ 세미나 함께 가기
⑤ 세미나 장소 변경하기

06

대화를 듣고, 여자가 이사하려는 이유를 고르시오.

① 집이 좁아서
② 집세가 비싸서
③ 경치가 좋지 않아서
④ 1층에 위치해 있어서
⑤ 직장과 거리가 멀어서

07

대화를 듣고, 여자가 지불할 금액을 고르시오. 3점

① \$3.50　② \$4.05　③ \$4.50
④ \$5.00　⑤ \$5.50

08

대화를 듣고, 장난감 대여점에 관해 두 사람이 언급하지 않은 것을 고르시오.

① 대여 기간　② 대여료　③ 연체료
④ 회원 가입 방법　⑤ 영업시간

09

방과 후 수업에 관한 다음 내용을 듣고, 일치하지 않는 것을 고르시오. 3점

① 최대 3개까지 신청할 수 있다.
② 수업료는 각각 5달러이다.
③ 홈페이지에 수업이 사진과 함께 소개되어 있다.
④ 등록하려면 부모님 동의서를 제출해야 한다.
⑤ 등록은 다음 주 수요일에 시작한다.

12회

10

다음 표를 보면서 대화를 듣고, 두 사람이 탑승할 기차를 고르시오. 3점

< Train Schedule: To Paris >

	Train Number	Express/ Local	Arrives in Paris	Dining Car
①	182	Local	8:30 a.m.	Yes
②	199	Express	8:45 a.m.	No
③	304	Express	9:00 a.m.	Yes
④	729	Express	9:35 a.m.	No
⑤	912	Local	10:15 a.m.	No

11

대화를 듣고, 여자의 마지막 말에 대한 남자의 응답으로 가장 적절한 것을 고르시오.

① I've just arrived at the airport.
② My mom gave me a ride yesterday.
③ All right. I'd be happy to drive you.
④ Let's meet at the airport at 5:00 p.m.
⑤ That's okay. I can take the airport shuttle.

12

대화를 듣고, 남자의 마지막 말에 대한 여자의 응답으로 가장 적절한 것을 고르시오.

① Yes, we should save more money.
② In that case, I'll just get half a box.
③ I know. It's not easy to grow oranges.
④ Exactly. You can use the peels as well.
⑤ Okay, we should have fruit more often.

13

대화를 듣고, 남자의 마지막 말에 대한 여자의 응답으로 가장 적절한 것을 고르시오.

Woman: ______________________

① No. I used to be bad at history.
② Maybe. You need an easier topic.
③ Yes. There isn't any way to avoid it.
④ Sorry. I don't have enough time to help you.
⑤ Sure. Practice helps you make fewer mistakes.

14

대화를 듣고, 여자의 마지막 말에 대한 남자의 응답으로 가장 적절한 것을 고르시오.

Man: ______________________

① I'm afraid I can't join you.
② Oh, thanks for reserving the cabin.
③ Well, I think we'd better change the place.
④ If you let me know the website, I'll book one right away.
⑤ We should pack some warm clothes and food just in case.

15

다음 상황 설명을 듣고, Todd가 어머니에게 할 말로 가장 적절한 것을 고르시오.

Todd: Mom, ______________________

① I found a good free online lecture.
② can I take one more class after school?
③ I think I need to quit some of my classes.
④ I'll take a science class with my classmates.
⑤ would you mind driving me to my academy?

[16-17] 다음을 듣고, 물음에 답하시오.

16

남자가 하는 말의 주제로 가장 적절한 것은?

① 성장기 운동의 중요성
② 아동기 뼈의 구조와 기능
③ 아동 성장을 촉진하는 법
④ 아동기 뼈 강화를 위한 방법
⑤ 비타민과 칼슘 섭취의 필요성

17

언급된 음식이 아닌 것은?

① 콩 ② 우유 ③ 계란
④ 버섯 ⑤ 생선

정답 및 해설 p.37

녹음을 다시 한 번 듣고, 빈칸에 알맞은 말을 쓰시오.

01

W: Good afternoon! This is your principal, Ms. Johns, speaking. _______ _______ _______ _______ _______, a strong typhoon is coming tonight. So I'd like to tell you what you should do to protect your classroom. First, _______ _______ _______ _______ all of the windows before you leave your classroom today. It'll stop the typhoon from damaging your computers and TVs. Secondly, closing the curtains is also important. If the typhoon breaks the windows, the curtains can prevent the pieces of glass from scattering all over the classroom. Please check that _______ _______ _______ _______ before you leave school. Thank you.

02

W: You look tired, Mark. Are you okay?

M: I just haven't been sleeping well lately, but I'm not sure why.

W: Well, _______ _______ _______ is really important for your health. Do you exercise much?

M: Just a little bit. Why? Is exercise good for sleep?

W: Sure. Proper exercise will help you get better and deeper sleep.

M: I see.

W: It's also important to take a shower with warm water before bedtime. It _______ _______ _______.

M: Okay. What about reading books? I heard that makes it easier to fall asleep.

W: That's not true. Reading actually keeps your brain awake when you're _______ _______ _______ _______.

M: Oh, I didn't know that.

03

[Telephone rings.]

W: Hello, Food Network. How may I help you?

M: Hello, I entered an event for a chance to participate in a cooking class with famous chef Nigel Sparks. I'd like to know if _______ _______ _______ _______ yet.

W: Sure. Could you please tell me your name?

M: Yes. My name is Edward James.

W: Let me check. *[Pause]* Congratulations! You're _______ _______ _______ _______ _______ that will participate in this cooking class.

M: That's amazing! I heard that thousands of people entered this event.

W: Yes, we always get a lot of entries since this event is only offered _______ _______ _______.

M: Thank you so much. I'm so grateful for this opportunity.

W: Congratulations once again, Mr. James.

04

M: I'm making an invitation for my birthday party. Can you help me?

W: Sure. Why don't you _______ _______ _______ on it? It's your birthday!

M: All right. I'll put it on the left. But I don't know what to write at the top of the card.

W: I think "You're Invited!" is fine.

M: Okay. Now where should I put the date, time, and location?

W: How about writing all that _______ _______ _______ _______?

M: Okay, but what should we put at the bottom?

W: How about drawing something?

M: I think stars would be great.

W: That would be nice. _______ _______ _______ _______ your phone number.

M: I'll put it right under the stars.

05

M: Hi, Vanessa. Did you hear that the location of tomorrow's seminar was changed?

W: No, I didn't. Why was it changed?

M: I guess there wasn't enough seating for everyone.

W: I see. Is there anything else that was changed?

M: No, that was it. But the new location is _______ _______. So we need to leave earlier than we planned.

W: Oh, do you know where the new place is?

M: Yes. They emailed everyone a map.

W: Really? _______ _______ _______ _______ me a copy?

M: Not at all. Let's go up to my office, and I'll print it.

W: Excellent. I'm glad you told me the new information. I _______ _______ _______ _______ the wrong place!

06

M: Amy, I think I saw you downtown yesterday.

W: Oh, really? I was _______ _______ _______ in that area. I'm thinking of moving to another place.

M: But didn't you just move into your current place?

W: Yes, and I really like my apartment, too. It's big and it _______ _______ _______ _______.

M: Then why are you moving? Is it too expensive?

W: No, the rent's fine. I just didn't realize how inconvenient the transportation is. It takes me nearly two hours to _______ _______ _______ _______.

M: I see. So did you see any nice places?

W: No. They were all on the first floor. I want a place that's higher up.

M: I'm sure you'll find one soon.

07

M: Hi, and welcome to Coffee King. What _______ _______ _______ _______ today?

W: Hi, how much are your Americanos?

M: A regular Americano is $2, and a large one is $3.

W: I'd like a large Americano, please.

M: Would you like that hot or iced? Iced drinks cost _______ _______ _______.

W: Iced, please. And I'll take one of those banana muffins. They look delicious.

M: Okay. They're $1.50, but you can get two for just $2.

W: I'll just have one. And here's my discount card.

M: All right. That gives you 10% _______ _______ _______ _______.

W: Thanks.

08

W: Hello. Is this the shop where you can rent children's toys?

M: Yes. We have lots of toys for children _______ _______ _______ _______ years old.

W: That's good. I need toys for my three-year-old son.

M: Then please look at these. Young children love to play with these toys.

W: How long can I rent them?

M: Toys _______ _______ _______ for two weeks.

W: I see. How much is the rental fee?

M: All toys are $3 each.

W: If I can't bring it back in two weeks, what happens?

M: Then we will _______ _______ _______ _______ of $1 a day.

W: Okay. What are your hours?

M: We're open every day, except Sunday, from 9:00 a.m. to 8:00 p.m.

W: Great.

09

M: Good morning, students. The new semester has just started, and the time to sign up for after-school classes is coming. Students may join _______ _______ _______ _______, and all students have to attend at least one class. Each class is $5. On the school website, the classes are introduced with some pictures. _______ _______ _______ signing up is 6:00 p.m. next Wednesday. In order to sign up, you need a permission slip signed by a parent. The permission slips are in the back of each classroom. The sign-up period _______ _______ _______. If you have any questions, please ask your teachers. Thank you!

10

W: Here is the train schedule. Let's decide on the train we will take.

M: Okay. We need to catch a morning train to Paris tomorrow.

W: Let's _______ _______ _______ _______. It only takes thirty minutes.

M: Great. What time do we need to be there?

W: The meeting starts at ten, so it's okay if we arrive before 9:30 a.m.

M: Right, but if we take an earlier train, we'll have _______ _______ _______ _______ before the meeting.

W: Oh, I agree. But we can take a dining car for that.

M: Well, I don't want to eat on the train. Also, the trains with dining cars are _______ _______.

W: I see. Let's have breakfast in Paris.

M: All right. Let's take this one, then.

11

W: You need to be at the airport soon, don't you?

M: Yes. My flight leaves at 6:00 p.m., so I'd better leave now.

W: I can _______ _______ _______ _______ if you want.

M: (That's okay. I can take the airport shuttle.)

12

M: Mom, how many oranges should we buy?

W: There are 30 of them in one box. Let's get a whole box.

M: But I think _______ _______ _______. We can't eat them all.

W: (In that case, I'll just get half a box.)

13

M: I have to _______ _______ _______ in history class tomorrow.

W: Oh, really? What's the topic?

M: I'm going to talk about Korea's Joseon dynasty.

W: That's great. You know a lot about Asian history, don't you?

M: Yes, I do. And I _______ _______ _______ _______ _______.

W: Good. You'll do great!

M: I'm not worried about that. But I hate talking in front of the whole class.

W: Why? Do you get nervous?

M: Very. I'm afraid I'm going to forget what to say.

W: Just repeat your presentation to yourself _______ _______ _______ _______ tonight.

M: Do you think that will be helpful?

W: (Sure. Practice helps you make fewer mistakes.)

14

W: Colin, do you have any plans for summer vacation?

M: Not really. But I want to do something special this summer.

W: Then _______ _______ _______ _______ _______?

M: That's a good idea. Where shall we go?

W: Let's go to Seorak Mountain. I know a nice hiking trail.

M: That sounds fantastic! I really want to _______ _______ _______ _______ _______. How long should we stay?

W: About two days would be great. We can spend the night in a mountain cabin.

M: How exciting! I can't wait to go.

W: One more thing. We need to _______ _______ _______ online. Can you do that?

M: (If you let me know the website, I'll book one right away.)

15

W: Todd goes to six academies these days because his mom wants him to. He studies math, English, Korean, history, science, and Chinese. He likes studying them, but he's starting to _______ _______ _______. He does not have enough time to do all of his homework. He thinks he should stop going to some of his academies. Besides, _______ _______ _______ _______ Korean, history, and science, he thinks he can study by himself. He wants to tell his mom _______ _______ _______. In this situation, what would Todd most likely say to his mother?

Todd: Mom, (I think I need to quit some of my classes.)

16-17

M: The human body contains _______ _______ _______. They can't be seen from the outside, but they are very important. And if they do not develop well during childhood, children can't grow properly. Surprisingly, some studies have shown that children's bones are very weak these days. So they need to develop healthy habits to _______ _______ _______ _______ _______. First, kids need to eat foods that have plenty of calcium, such as beans and milk. Second, vitamin D is also essential for growing healthy bones. Red meat, eggs, and oily fish are good sources of vitamin D, so it's important to eat those foods often. In addition, spending 10 to 15 minutes outside in the sun every day also provides the body with vitamin D. Lastly, it's always _______ _______ _______ _______. Even doing light exercise helps bones get stronger.

12 Word & Expressions

01
- □ principal 교장
- □ according to …에 따르면
- □ weather forecast 일기 예보
- □ typhoon 태풍
- □ protect 보호하다
- □ damage 파손시키다
- □ prevent A from v-ing A가 …하는 것을 막다
- □ scatter 흩어지다

02
- □ lately 최근에
- □ proper 적절한
- □ bedtime 취침 시간
- □ relax 긴장을 풀어주다
- □ fall asleep 잠이 들다
- □ awake 깨어있는

03
- □ enter 들어가다; *응시[응모]하다
- □ participate 참가하다
- □ chef 요리사
- □ entry 입장; *응모
- □ grateful 고마워하는
- □ opportunity 기회

04
- □ invitation 초대; *초대장(v. invite 초대하다)
- □ location 장소, 위치

05
- □ seating 좌석, 자리
- □ farther 더 멀리

06
- □ current 현재의
- □ view 전망, 조망
- □ rent 집세, 방세
- □ inconvenient 불편한
- □ transportation 수송, 교통
- □ nearly 거의

07
- □ regular (크기가) 보통의
- □ muffin 머핀

08
- □ rental fee 대여료
- □ charge 부과하다, 청구하다
- □ late fee 연체료
- □ except …을 제외하고는

09
- □ semester 학기
- □ sign up for …을 신청하다
- □ up to …까지
- □ at least 적어도
- □ deadline 마감일
- □ permission 허락, 허가
- □ slip 미끄러지다; *(작은 종이) 조각, 쪽지
- □ period 기간

10
- □ catch 잡다; *(기차 등을) 타다
- □ express 급행의
- □ dining car 식당차
- □ local 현지의; *(열차 등이) 완행의

11
- □ flight 비행; *항공편, 항공기
- □ give ... a ride …을 태워주다

12
- □ whole 전체의, 전부의
- □ exactly 정확히; *맞아, 바로 그거야
- □ peel 껍질

13
- □ presentation 발표
- □ dynasty 왕조
- □ do research 조사를 하다
- □ repeat 반복하다
- □ over and over (again) 반복해서
- □ used to-v …하곤 했다
- □ avoid 피하다

14
- □ hiking trail 하이킹 코스
- □ peak 산봉우리, 정상
- □ mountain cabin 산장
- □ reserve 예약하다
- □ book 예약하다
- □ pack 포장하다, 싸다
- □ just in case 만약을 위해서

15
- □ academy 학교, 학원
- □ when it comes to …에 관한 한
- □ free 무료의
- □ lecture 강의
- □ quit 그만두다

16-17
- □ contain …이 들어 있다
- □ develop 성장[발달]하다
- □ properly 제대로
- □ plenty of 많은
- □ calcium 칼슘
- □ essential 필수적인
- □ oily 기름기가 많은
- □ provide A with B A에게 B를 제공하다
- □ regularly 규칙적으로

13 영어듣기 모의고사

1번부터 17번까지는 듣고 답하는 문제입니다.
1번부터 15번까지는 한 번만 들려주고, 16번부터 17번까지는 두 번 들려줍니다. 방송을 잘 듣고 답을 하기 바랍니다.

01

다음을 듣고, 여자가 하는 말의 목적으로 가장 적절한 것을 고르시오. 3점

① 기숙사 신청 방법을 안내하려고
② 기숙사 내 생활 수칙을 알리려고
③ 기숙사 증축에 관한 의견을 물으려고
④ 기숙사 이용 시 불편 사항을 항의하려고
⑤ 공사 중 기숙사에 머물 수 없음을 공지하려고

02

대화를 듣고, 두 사람이 하는 말의 주제로 가장 적절한 것을 고르시오.

① 최근 유행하는 노래
② 이어폰 사용의 위험성
③ 최고의 음악 감상 방법
④ 주기적인 청력 검사의 필요성
⑤ 대중교통을 이용해야 하는 이유

03

대화를 듣고, 두 사람의 관계를 가장 잘 나타낸 것을 고르시오.

① 승무원 — 승객
② 매장 점원 — 사장
③ 향수 가게 점원 — 고객
④ 피부과 의사 — 환자
⑤ 화장품 가게 점원 — 고객

04

대화를 듣고, 그림에서 대화의 내용과 일치하지 않는 것을 고르시오.

05

대화를 듣고, 여자가 남자를 위해 할 일로 가장 적절한 것을 고르시오.

① 집 정리하기
② 식료품 사러 가기
③ 음식 배달 주문하기
④ 저녁 식사 준비하기
⑤ 이사할 집 찾아주기

06

대화를 듣고, 여자가 스페인 여행을 가지 못하는 이유를 고르시오.

① 몸이 좋지 않아서
② 출장을 가야 해서
③ 이사를 해야 해서
④ 날씨가 좋지 않아서
⑤ 다른 곳을 여행하고 싶어서

07

대화를 듣고, 여자가 시카고에 도착할 시간을 고르시오.

① 3:00 p.m.
② 5:00 p.m.
③ 6:00 p.m.
④ 7:00 p.m.
⑤ 8:00 p.m.

08

대화를 듣고, 코트에 관해 두 사람이 언급하지 않은 것을 고르시오.

① 색상
② 소재
③ 무게
④ 사이즈
⑤ 가격

09

Central-Mid-Levels Escalator에 관한 다음 내용을 듣고, 일치하지 않는 것을 고르시오. 3점

① 세계에서 가장 긴 야외 에스컬레이터이다.
② 통근을 목적으로 건설되었다.
③ 저녁에는 내리막 방향으로 움직인다.
④ 무료로 탑승할 수 있다.
⑤ 편도로 약 25분이 소요된다.

정답 및 해설 p.38-40

10

다음 표를 보면서 대화를 듣고, 남자가 구입할 약을 고르시오.

< Medicine for Headache >

	Product	Strength	Type	Price
①	A	Mild	Pill	$8
②	B	Strong	Pill	$10
③	C	Mild	Pill	$10
④	D	Strong	Liquid	$12
⑤	E	Mild	Liquid	$12

11

대화를 듣고, 여자의 마지막 말에 대한 남자의 응답으로 가장 적절한 것을 고르시오.

① You can send me a text message.
② I will get a new smartphone next month.
③ I can't remember where I left my smartphone.
④ I already paid the bill through Internet banking.
⑤ Oh, I forgot that I bought a game through my phone.

12

대화를 듣고, 남자의 마지막 말에 대한 여자의 응답으로 가장 적절한 것을 고르시오.

① There could be a virus in your file.
② I reviewed your report. It's perfect.
③ That's okay. I was able to open the file.
④ You need to submit your report by Tuesday.
⑤ I'll send you the email again from my laptop.

13

대화를 듣고, 남자의 마지막 말에 대한 여자의 응답으로 가장 적절한 것을 고르시오.

Woman: ______________________________

① That sounds great. How can I sign up?
② I don't think you can run faster than me.
③ Running races is very good for your health.
④ Let's meet at the hospital tomorrow morning.
⑤ I will not run a marathon unless it's for charity.

14

대화를 듣고, 여자의 마지막 말에 대한 남자의 응답으로 가장 적절한 것을 고르시오.

Man: ______________________________

① Take medicine to relieve your pain.
② Okay, I'll go pick it up this afternoon.
③ The pain should go away in a few hours.
④ Sure. Let me give you my email address.
⑤ Yes, I'll make an appointment tomorrow.

15

다음 상황 설명을 듣고, Smith 씨가 Amy에게 할 말로 가장 적절한 것을 고르시오.

Mr. Smith: ______________________________

① Where did you say your friend's house is?
② I think you should stay home this evening.
③ I will give you a ride to your friend's house.
④ Please check the weather forecast for tomorrow.
⑤ Why don't you take the subway instead of driving?

[16-17] 다음을 듣고, 물음에 답하시오.

16

남자가 하는 말의 주제로 가장 적절한 것은?

① 녹차의 부작용
② 녹차를 이용한 요리법
③ 녹차 섭취의 다양한 이점
④ 녹차를 이용한 피부 관리법
⑤ 녹차 티백을 재활용하는 방법

17

언급된 녹차의 효능이 아닌 것은?

① 암 예방　　② 충치 예방
③ 심장병 예방　　④ 노화 방지
⑤ 체중 감량

13 DICTATION

녹음을 다시 한 번 듣고, 빈칸에 알맞은 말을 쓰시오.

01

W: Can I have your attention, please? As you all know, some parts of this dormitory building are _______ _______ _______ _______. There are several leaking pipes that need to be fixed immediately. Also, the worn carpets need to be replaced. This work will _______ _______ _______ _______ _______, and during that time, all of the residents must stay elsewhere. You may enter the dormitory after 5:00 p.m. on Sunday. If you have no place to stay, talk to the dorm leader, and he will _______ _______ _______ in another dormitory. We apologize for the inconvenience.

02

M: Hey, Janet! Janet, can you hear me?

W: Oh. Hey, Ralph. Sorry, I was wearing my earphones.

M: I know. I could hear your music.

W: Oh, I guess it was _______ _______ _______ _______.

M: Yeah, you should consider lowering the volume. Loud sound can damage your hearing.

W: I know, but I can't hear anything if I don't _______ _______ _______ _______.

M: Still, you should try to protect your ears. Also you shouldn't wear earphones while you're walking around.

W: Why is that?

M: Because you might not notice that a car or bike is _______ _______ _______. You could get hurt.

W: That's true. I'll try to be more careful.

03

W: Hello! How can I help you?

M: My skin has been _______ _______ _______ recently. Especially my face.

W: That's a common problem in winter. The cold, dry air can be bad for our skin.

M: Could you recommend anything that might help?

W: Of course! This cream here is a very strong moisturizer. It's one of our top sellers.

M: Hmm... It _______ _______ _______ _______, though. Is there anything else that doesn't smell so strong?

W: Yes. How about this one? It doesn't have any fragrance, but it will definitely keep your skin soft and smooth.

M: That seems nice. I'll _______ _______ _______ _______ this one.

W: Okay. Here you are.

04

W: Christmas is coming! I can't wait to see all of the beautiful decorations.

M: Oh, I saw a beautiful Christmas tree at the mall yesterday.

W: Did you? What did it look like?

M: Well, it was very tall, and it had _______ _______ _______ at the top.

W: Wow! Were there any other ornaments on it?

M: Yes. There was a big ribbon below the star. And they put _______ _______ _______ under that.

W: That sounds pretty. Was there anything else?

M: There were some small bells hanging from the bottom of the tree.

W: Were there any presents under the tree?

M: Yes, there were _______ _______ _______!

W: It sounds nice. I'd like to see it!

05

[Knock on door]

M: Come in!

W: Hi, David. Are you unpacking?

M: Yes, I'm _______ _______. Just a few things left.

W: Is there anything I can help you with?

M: I'm fine. You found this house for me, so you've already helped me more than enough.

W: That was nothing. I just saw the ad in the newspaper and let you know.

M: Well, thanks again. Anyway, I have to _______ _______ _______ _______ to make dinner soon.

W: You must be tired from unpacking all day. How about we order Chinese food?

M: Oh, but I don't know anything about this area yet. Do you know any good restaurants?

W: Yes, I know the phone number. _______ _______ _______.

06

M: Hi, Sally. Are you still interested in going with us to Spain next month?

W: Unfortunately, I _______ _______ _______ _______ for a while.

M: Really? Why? Are you not feeling well?

W: I'm fine. I just have a very tight schedule.

M: Oh, right. I forgot that you're moving into a new apartment next month.

W: Actually, that's not the problem. I was just told that my business trip is at _______ _______ _______ _______ your trip to Spain.

M: Oh, that's a shame. That's the perfect time to go to Spain!

W: I know. I really wanted to go.

M: Don't worry. You can go there another time.

W: Right. Anyway, _______ _______!

07

[Cell phone rings.]

M: Jane, where are you? Are you in Chicago now?

W: I'm still at the airport back home.

M: Why? I thought you would already be here by now.

W: My flight _______ _______ _______ _______ at noon, but it's been delayed because of the snowstorm.

M: Oh, that's too bad. When will the flight depart then?

W: At 3:00 p.m. I have to _______ _______ _______ _______ in Washington, D.C.

M: How long does it take to get to Washington, D.C?

W: Two hours. Plus, I have to wait another two hours there before transferring.

M: I see. After that, you'll take an hour flight from there to Chicago, right?

W: That's right.

M: All right. I'll _______ _______ _______ _______our schedule.

08

W: Let's look around in this store. I need to buy a new coat.

M: Sure. How about this one here? I like the design.

W: Me, too. And the yellow color really _______ _______. It matches the design perfectly.

M: I think so, too. And it says on the tag that it's made of high-quality wool.

W: Yeah. That's really important. It'll _______ _______ _______.

M: And it seems to be lightweight.

W: Right. It says it weighs less than 200 g.

M: But it's a bit expensive. For a coat, $320 is a lot.

W: That's okay. I already expected to _______ _______ _______ after searching on the Internet.

M: In that case, you should get it.

13회

09

M: If you're _______ _______ _______ _______ Hong Kong, you should visit the Central-Mid-Levels Escalator. It is one of the city's most unique attractions. It's the longest outdoor covered escalator system in the world. It _______ _______ _______ in 1993 to help people go between their homes and their offices in Central Hong Kong. Now, over 60,000 people use the escalator every day. From 6:00 a.m. to 10:00 a.m., the escalator moves downhill. Then from 10:30 a.m. to midnight, it moves uphill. It's _______ _______ _______ and it takes about twenty-five minutes each way. It's a fun experience that you won't easily forget!

10

M: Excuse me, could you help me?

W: Of course, sir. What can I do for you?

M: I have a headache, but I'm not sure _______ _______ _______ _______.

W: Okay. These are all the headache medicines we have. You can choose one of these.

M: Which one would you recommend?

W: Let's see. How bad is the pain?

M: Not too bad, so I don't think I need anything strong.

W: All right. Then _______ _______ _______ _______ taking liquid medicine?

M: I prefer pills because I don't like the taste of liquid medicine.

W: Okay. Here are two kinds. There is a small _______ _______ _______.

M: I'd like the cheaper one, please.

11

W: Kevin, did you use your phone a lot last month?

M: No, I didn't. Is something wrong?

W: This month's phone bill is _______ _______ _______.

M: (Oh, I forgot that I bought a game through my phone.)

12

M: Did you read the report I emailed you?

W: No, I _______ _______ _______ _______.

M: Other people also said the same thing. I don't know what the problem is.

W: (There could be a virus in your file.)

13

W: Do you have any plans for Children's Day?

M: Yes, _______ _______ _______ _______ in a ten-kilometer race.

W: Wow! I didn't know you were a runner.

M: I'm not really. But the race is for a good cause, so I decided to join.

W: Oh, for what?

M: It's to _______ _______ _______ _______. The money is for children at the local hospital who have cancer.

W: That's great! How have you been preparing for this race?

M: I've been running for an hour every evening. Do you want to join me?

W: I really wish I could, but I've never run that far before.

M: There's also a five-kilometer race _______ _______.

W: (That sounds great. How can I sign up?)

14

[Telephone rings.]

W: Hello. This is White Teeth Clinic.

M: Hi. My name is Harvey Bloom, and I _______ _______ _______ _______ yesterday.

W: Yes, I remember. Is there a problem?

M: Well, I was in a lot of pain after the operation.

W: That's normal. It might last for about two to three days. _______ _______ _______ _______ right now?

M: Just a little bit. But I'm worried that it could get worse at any time.

W: Did you take the pain reliever that your doctor prescribed? It should help.

M: I see. Also, my doctor told me to avoid eating certain things, but I can't remember.

W: We have a written manual for patients. Would you like me to _______ _______ _______ _______?

M: (Sure. Let me give you my email address.)

15

W: Amy will go to her best friend's housewarming party this evening. Her friend's house _______ _______ _______ _______, and Amy is going to drive there. Amy's father, Mr. Smith, listens to the local weather forecast on the radio. It says that there is going to be heavy rain, and he thinks his daughter _______ _______ _______ _______ in such bad weather. There is a subway station near Amy's friend's house, so Mr. Smith wants Amy to _______ _______ _______ there. In this situation, what would Mr. Smith most likely say to Amy?

Mr. Smith: (Why don't you take the subway instead of driving?)

16-17

M: Everyone knows green tea _______ _______ _______ _______. It can prevent cancer and heart disease. Also, it helps prevent the signs of aging and encourages weight loss. Therefore, a lot of people enjoy drinking green tea. But what should people do after drinking it? Normally, people just throw the tea bags away. But the tea bags themselves have many uses. For example, _______ _______ _______ _______ _______ by taking a bath with some used tea bags. Or if you have some potted plants, put some tea bags on the holes at the bottom of the pot. The pot will lose water more slowly, and the nutrients from the tea bags will go into the soil. You can even use a tea bag to clean dark leather shoes. So from now on, be sure to _______ _______ _______ _______ after drinking green tea.

13 Word & Expressions

01
- □ **dormitory** 기숙사
- □ **be in need of** …이 필요하다
- □ **repair** 수리, 보수
- □ **leak** (액체·기체가) 새다
- □ **fix** 수리하다
- □ **worn** 낡은
- □ **replace** 교체하다
- □ **take place** 일어나다, 발생하다
- □ **resident** 거주자
- □ **elsewhere** 다른 곳에서
- □ **arrange** 준비하다
- □ **inconvenience** 불편

02
- □ **lower** 낮추다
- □ **volume** (라디오 등의) 음량, 볼륨
- □ **damage** 손상을 주다
- □ **hearing** 청력, 청각
- □ **turn up** (소리 등을) 높이다, 올리다
- □ **protect** 보호하다

03
- □ **common** 흔한
- □ **moisturizer** 보습제
- □ **scent** 향기, 냄새
- □ **fragrance** 향기
- □ **definitely** 분명히

04
- □ **decoration** 장식품
- □ **ornament** 장식품
- □ **stocking** 스타킹; *크리스마스 양말

05
- □ **unpack** (짐을) 풀다
- □ **ad** 광고(= advertisement)
- □ **grocery** (*pl.*) 식료품

06
- □ **tight** (여유가 없이) 빡빡한
- □ **schedule** 일정
- □ **business trip** 출장
- □ **shame** 애석한[아쉬운] 일

07
- □ **flight** 비행; 항공편
- □ **be supposed to-v** …하기로 되어 있다
- □ **depart** 출발하다
- □ **delay** 지연시키다
- □ **snowstorm** 눈보라
- □ **transfer** 갈아타다

08
- □ **stand out** 두드러지다, 쉽게 눈에 띄다
- □ **match** 어울리다, 맞다
- □ **tag** 꼬리표, 가격표
- □ **be made of** …로 구성되다
- □ **high-quality** 고급의
- □ **wool** 모직, 울
- □ **lightweight** 가벼운
- □ **weigh** 무게가 …이다

09
- □ **unique** 독특한
- □ **attraction** 매력; *관광 명소
- □ **originally** 원래
- □ **downhill** 내리막 아래로
- □ **midnight** 자정
- □ **uphill** 오르막길로

10
- □ **pain** 고통, 통증
- □ **liquid** 액체의
- □ **pill** 알약

11
- □ **bill** 고지서, 청구서
- □ **than usual** 평소보다

12
- □ **review** 검토하다
- □ **submit** 제출하다

13
- □ **cause** 원인; *대의, 목적
- □ **raise** 올리다; *(자금 등을) 모으다
- □ **charity** 자선 단체
- □ **local** 지역의, 현지의
- □ **cancer** 암
- □ **beginner** 초보자
- □ **sign up** 신청하다

14
- □ **operation** 수술
- □ **normal** 보통의, 정상적인
- □ **last** 지속되다
- □ **pain reliever** 진통제
- □ **avoid** 피하다
- □ **manual** 설명서, 안내서
- □ **relieve** (고통 등을) 덜어주다
- □ **make an appointment** 약속하다, 예약하다

15
- □ **housewarming party** 집들이
- □ **weather forecast** 일기 예보
- □ **give … a ride** …을 태워주다
- □ **instead of** … 대신에

16-17
- □ **benefit** 이익, 이점
- □ **prevent** 예방하다
- □ **sign** 표지판; *징후, 조짐
- □ **aging** 노화
- □ **encourage** 격려하다; *촉진하다
- □ **loss** 손실, 줄임
- □ **throw away** 버리다
- □ **use** 용도, 쓰임새; 사용하다
- □ **soften** 부드럽게 하다
- □ **potted** 화분에 심은 (n. pot 화분)
- □ **nutrient** 영양분
- □ **soil** 흙
- □ **leather** 가죽

14 영어듣기 모의고사

정답 및 해설 p.41-43

1번부터 17번까지는 듣고 답하는 문제입니다.
1번부터 15번까지는 한 번만 들려주고, 16번부터 17번까지는 두 번 들려줍니다. 방송을 잘 듣고 답을 하기 바랍니다.

01

다음을 듣고, 여자가 하는 말의 목적으로 가장 적절한 것을 고르시오.

① 법을 개정해야 할 필요성을 강조하려고
② 문화 교육의 새로운 접근법을 소개하려고
③ 자신의 시장 출마에 대한 지지를 호소하려고
④ 다문화 가정에 대한 경제적 지원을 촉구하려고
⑤ 다문화 교육 센터 설립을 위한 도움을 요청하려고

02

대화를 듣고, 여자의 의견으로 가장 적절한 것을 고르시오.

① 새로운 룸메이트를 찾아야 한다.
② 룸메이트의 생활 방식을 이해해야 한다.
③ 전자레인지 내부를 자주 청소해야 한다.
④ 룸메이트와 마음을 터놓고 대화해야 한다.
⑤ 타인의 감정을 상하게 하는 말은 하면 안 된다.

03

대화를 듣고 두 사람의 관계를 가장 잘 나타낸 것을 고르시오.

① 안내원 — 관광객 ② 경비원 — 입주자
③ 인사 담당자 — 구직자 ④ 은행 창구 직원 — 고객
⑤ 부동산 중개업자 — 고객

04

대화를 듣고, 그림에서 대화의 내용과 일치하지 않는 것을 고르시오.

05

대화를 듣고, 남자가 여자에게 부탁한 일로 가장 적절한 것을 고르시오.

① 바닥 쓸기
② 설거지하기
③ 분리수거하기
④ 장식품 치우기
⑤ 남은 음식 치우기

06

대화를 듣고, 남자가 인터넷 뱅킹을 이용할 수 없었던 이유를 고르시오.

① 계좌가 해킹을 당해서
② 전산상 장애가 있어서
③ 비밀번호를 잘못 입력해서
④ 컴퓨터 사양이 맞지 않아서
⑤ 보안 카드를 등록하지 않아서

07

대화를 듣고, 여자가 추가로 지불할 금액을 고르시오. 3점

① $60 ② $200 ③ $260
④ $300 ⑤ $500

08

대화를 듣고, 여자가 산 물건이 아닌 것을 고르시오.

① 카펫 ② 스카프 ③ 손거울
④ 애플티 ⑤ 접시

09

대회의 규칙에 관한 다음 내용을 듣고, 일치하지 않는 것을 고르시오.

① 두 가지 주제 중 하나를 선택하면 된다.
② 단어 수 제한이 있다.
③ 답안지에 메모를 하면 안 된다.
④ 제목을 반드시 써야 한다.
⑤ 제한 시간은 1시간이다.

10

다음 표를 보면서 대화를 듣고, 남자가 구입할 제품을 고르시오.

< Electric Fans for Sale >

	Model	Remote Control	Size	Speed	Price
①	A	Yes	Mid-size	3 speeds	$32
②	B	No	Compact	2 speeds	$25
③	C	No	Mid-size	1 speeds	$20
④	D	Yes	Full-size	2 speeds	$46
⑤	E	No	Compact	3 speeds	$40

11

대화를 듣고, 여자의 마지막 말에 대한 남자의 응답으로 가장 적절한 것을 고르시오.

① I did, but they weren't there.
② Can you clear the kitchen table?
③ That's true. I left them in the car.
④ I don't think I can move the table.
⑤ I'd like to help you, but I have to go.

12

대화를 듣고, 남자의 마지막 말에 대한 여자의 응답으로 가장 적절한 것을 고르시오.

① Please try it on first now.
② I don't need a new jacket.
③ I bought it on the Internet.
④ Sorry, but it's not my style.
⑤ You're right. I'll buy it online.

13

대화를 듣고, 여자의 마지막 말에 대한 남자의 응답으로 가장 적절한 것을 고르시오.

Man: ______________________________

① I asked him several questions.
② The pianist is getting better now.
③ We are ready for the competition.
④ I'm not good at playing the piano.
⑤ Oh, thanks. I'll call him right now.

14

대화를 듣고, 남자의 마지막 말에 대한 여자의 응답으로 가장 적절한 것을 고르시오. 3점

Woman: ______________________________

① The presentation time is too short.
② Well, you should submit it on time.
③ Why don't you take a deep breath?
④ I think you should use some charts.
⑤ I am very impressed with your work.

15

다음 상황 설명을 듣고, Mike가 고객 서비스 직원에게 할 말로 가장 적절한 것을 고르시오. 3점

Mike: ______________________________

① I want to get a refund.
② Please cancel my order.
③ I'll pay it with my credit card.
④ Can you send it to my account?
⑤ There was an error on your website.

[16-17] 다음을 듣고, 물음에 답하시오.

16

남자가 하는 말의 목적으로 가장 적절한 것은?

① 특이한 식재료를 홍보하려고
② 냉장고 냄새 제거법을 알리려고
③ 새로 나온 화학 세정제를 광고하려고
④ 천연 세정제 사용의 이점을 설명하려고
⑤ 식료품의 여러 가지 용도를 소개하려고

17

언급된 식료품이 아닌 것은?

① 베이킹소다　② 우유
③ 오렌지　④ 콜라
⑤ 양파

정답 및 해설 p.43

녹음을 다시 한 번 듣고, 빈칸에 알맞은 말을 쓰시오.

01

W: Good evening, everyone. Thank you for coming to today's meeting. As you know, our city is becoming ________ ________ ________ ________ these days. As a result, you can meet many people from other countries anywhere and anytime. Therefore, it's important not only to welcome new members into our city ________ ________ ________ ________ their cultures. That's why it is necessary to build a multicultural education center. I have already written a letter asking to build such a center. Before I send it to the city government, I ________ ________ ________. If you agree, please come forward and sign this letter. Thank you.

02

W: Peter, you look upset.
M: I am. I'm just ________ ________ ________ my roommate.
W: What's going on?
M: He never cleans up the kitchen after using it.
W: Oh, I see.
M: I can't even use the microwave now. The inside of it has pieces of food all over it.
W: He might not know how you feel. Why don't you tell him to ________ ________ ________?
M: I don't know what to say to him. I don't want to hurt his feelings.
W: The two of you need to have a heart-to-heart talk. You should tell him ________ ________ ________.
M: You're probably right.
W: Then he will hopefully change.

03

M: Welcome! Please have a seat.
W: Thank you.
M: Now, how can I help you?
W: Well, I just changed jobs, so I am looking for a new apartment.
M: Okay. Do you have ________ ________ ________ in mind?
W: It would be great if I could find something near City Hall.
M: How much can you ________ ________ ________?
W: I don't want to pay more than $500.
M: Hmm... It will be difficult to find an apartment around City Hall ________ ________ ________.
W: Then how about Memorial Park?
M: I think that is okay. Why don't we look at some apartments in that area?
W: That would be great.

04

W: I just finished ________ ________ ________ for the debate.
M: Wow. It looks really good.
W: Thanks a lot. Do you like the "DEBATE CONTEST" banner I hung on the wall?
M: Yeah. ________ ________ ________.
W: What about the rectangular table? I thought it would be better than a round one.
M: You're right. And that's a good idea to have those four water bottles ready.
W: Thanks. I thought the contestants might get thirsty.
M: What is that thing that ________ ________ ________ ________ on the table?
W: It's a clock. And how about the round sign that says "PROS" and "CONS" at the front?
M: It looks perfect. You did a great job.

05

W: That was a great housewarming party, wasn't it?

M: Yeah, it looks like everyone had a good time.

W: There is _______ _______ _______ _______ _______, though. It may take a while.

M: Let's start right now. I'll put the leftover food in the refrigerator.

W: Then I'll wash the dishes. Will you gather the plates and bring them to the sink?

M: That's all right. I'll wash them after I put the food away.

W: Then I'll start sweeping the floor.

M: Why don't you _______ _______ _______ instead? Put the plastic and glass by the door.

W: All right. But who's going to take down the decorations?

M: _______ _______ _______. I'll do that tomorrow.

W: Okay.

06

[Telephone rings.]

W: LTG Bank. How can I help you?

M: I'm having trouble _______ _______ _______ Internet banking. Is there any problem with your system?

W: I don't believe so. Can you tell me your name and _______ _______?

M: My name is Brian Smith. My account number is 46890.

W: Thank you. One moment please. *[Typing sound]* I see the problem now.

M: What's happening?

W: You didn't _______ _______ _______ _______ we gave you at your last visit.

M: Oh, I didn't know that was necessary. Can I do it over the phone right now?

W: No, sir. You need to register the card online.

M: Oh, I see. Thank you for your help.

07

[Telephone rings.]

M: Hello. Red Wings Travel. How can I help you?

W: Hi, I'd like to _______ _______ _______ _______ a flight that I booked.

M: Okay. What is your booking number?

W: TS003507.

M: Please wait a moment. *[Typing sound]* I see that it was _______ _______ _______. You paid $300 for the flight.

W: Yes. Is that a problem?

M: For tickets like this, we charge 20% of what you paid.

W: That's fine. I'd like to change the date to August 5th. How much is the cheapest flight on that day?

M: It's $500. So you must pay the difference in price, _______ _______ _______ the rebooking fee. Is that okay with you?

W: Well, I have no choice.

08

M: Hi, Jennifer! How was your trip to Turkey?

W: It was fantastic. _______ _______ _______ a lot of interesting souvenirs.

M: Oh, what did you buy?

W: I bought a carpet with a beautiful pattern.

M: That sounds nice. What else did you get?

W: I also bought several scarves and a few hand mirrors _______ _______ _______ _______ as gifts.

M: That was thoughtful of you. How about apple tea? You said you wanted to try that.

W: Oh, yes. It was really good, so I bought some for myself.

M: Sounds great. By the way, I heard Turkey's plates are beautiful. Did you buy any of them?

W: No, they would have been _______ _______ _______ _______.

09

M: Welcome to the Global Essay Competition. Before we start, let me first explain the rules of this competition. You will be given _______ _______ _______ about global issues. Choose one and write an essay about it. We ask you to limit your essay to 600 to 700 words. Don't write any notes _______ _______ _______ _______. If you want, use the space on the sheet where the topics are listed. Also, don't forget to write your name and the title of your essay on the answer sheet. You have two hours to _______ _______ _______. Do you have any questions?

10

M: Hello. I'm here to buy a fan. Can you show me all the electric fans you have?

W: Sure. Please follow me. *[Pause]* These are your options. Do you need a fan _______ _______ _______ _______?

M: I don't think so. I'm going to put it on my desk.

W: On your desk? Then a compact or mid-size fan would be good.

M: Yes, but I would _______ _______ _______ _______.

W: Okay. This one here is our best seller. It has three speeds.

M: That's great, but $40 is too much. I'd like to get the cheapest one possible.

W: Then _______ _______ _______ _______? It's cheaper, and it has two speeds.

M: That sounds perfect. I'll get that one.

W: You've made a good choice.

11

W: What are you looking for?

M: My car keys. _______ _______ _______, but I can't find them.

W: Did you look on the kitchen table? You often leave them there.

M: (I did, but they weren't there.)

12

M: This jacket looks great on you.

W: Yes, I really like it. But it's a little expensive.

M: Then how about trying to _______ _______ _______ _______ _______? It's usually cheaper.

W: (You're right. I'll buy it online.)

13

W: How are you today, Jimmy?

M: I'm very nervous about the chorus competition next week.

W: Don't worry. I'm sure you'll do great. How is practicing going?

M: Actually, there's a big problem. The pianist was in a car accident yesterday. So she'll _______ _______ _______ _______ for a couple weeks.

W: Sorry to hear that. Then she can't play the piano on that day.

M: Right. I don't know what to do.

W: You should _______ _______ _______!

M: But I don't know anyone else who can play the piano.

W: Hmm... You know, Tom _______ _______ _______ _______ the piano. Why don't you ask him?

M: (Oh, thanks. I'll call him right now.)

14

W: Hi, Patrick, have you _______ _______ _______ _______ for your science project?

M: Not yet. I'm still working on it.

W: When is it due?

M: This Thursday. But I'm worried about the 10-minute time limit.

W: Why? You don't think you can talk for that long?

M: No, I don't think I can finish the presentation within that time.

W: Is it okay if I _______ _______ _______ _______ the material?

M: Definitely. *[Pause]* What do you think?

W: Well, there's too much information. It seems _______ _______ _______. I think you need to make it simpler.

M: Oh, how do you think I can make it easier to understand?

W: (I think you should use some charts.)

15

W: Mike needs a new memory card for his digital camera, so he _______ _______ _______ on the Internet. He finds a suitable one and buys it using his Internet banking account. After sending the money, however, he realizes he _______ _______ _______. It cost $23 but he sent $33. He wants to tell the store to transfer $10 back into his account. He calls the store's customer service center and explains the problem. Then the customer service employee asks Mike how he'd like to _______ _______ _______ _______. In this situation, what would Mike most likely say to the customer service employee?

Mike: (Can you send it to my account?)

16-17

M: Good morning, listeners! Today, I'm going to talk about food. People usually think food is only for eating. But they don't know foods can be used _______ _______ _______ as well. For example, baking soda is used for making the baked goods you see at the bakery. However, it can also remove odors from clothes. You can also put a bowl of milk in your refrigerator to _______ _______ _______ smells. If you like eating oranges, keep the peels and rub them over your skin. This will help keep mosquitoes away. Even cola has an unexpected use. Just scrub your rusty bicycle with cola and you can watch the rust disappear! By remembering these simple tips, you can _______ _______ _______ foods in other ways. Next time, I'll be back with other helpful tips.

14 Word & Expressions

01
- □ **multicultural** 다문화의
- □ **not only A but also B** A뿐만 아니라 B도
- □ **necessary** 필요한, 필수적인
- □ **government** 정부
- □ **support** 지지

02
- □ **upset** 화난
- □ **microwave** 전자레인지
- □ **heart-to-heart** 털어놓고, 숨김없이
- □ **hopefully** 바라건대, 아마

03
- □ **certain** 특정한
- □ **location** 위치, 장소
- □ **city hall** 시청
- □ **memorial** 기념의, 추도의

04
- □ **organize** 준비[조직]하다
- □ **debate** 토론
- □ **contest** 대회
- □ **banner** 현수막
- □ **stand out** 두드러지다, 눈에 띄다
- □ **rectangular** 직사각형의, 사각의
- □ **contestant** 참가자, 논쟁자
- □ **pro** 찬성자, 찬성론
- □ **con** 반대자, 반대론

05
- □ **housewarming party** 집들이
- □ **leftover** 남은
- □ **plate** 접시
- □ **put away** …을 치우다
- □ **sweep** 쓸다, 청소하다
- □ **separate** 분리하다
- □ **trash** 쓰레기
- □ **take down** (구조물을 해체하여) 치우다
- □ **urgent** 긴급한

06
- □ **have trouble v-ing** …하는 데 어려움을 겪다
- □ **transfer** 옮기다
- □ **account** 계좌
- □ **register** 등록하다
- □ **security** 보안
- □ **necessary** 필요한, 필수적인

07
- □ **book** 예약하다
- □ **special deal** 특가 상품
- □ **charge** 청구하다
- □ **in addition to** …에 더하여, …뿐만 아니라

08
- □ **bring back** …을 가지고 오다
- □ **souvenir** 기념품
- □ **pattern** 무늬
- □ **several** 몇몇의
- □ **traditional** 전통의
- □ **thoughtful** 사려 깊은

09
- □ **global** 세계적인
- □ **competition** 경쟁, 대회
- □ **issue** 쟁점, 사안
- □ **limit** 제한하다
- □ **space** 공간
- □ **list** 목록을 작성하다, 열거하다
- □ **complete** 완료하다

10
- □ **(electric) fan** 선풍기
- □ **remote control** 리모컨
- □ **compact** 소형의

11
- □ **clear** 치우다

12
- □ **try on** (옷 등을) 입어보다

13
- □ **chorus** 합창단
- □ **car accident** 자동차사고
- □ **be in the hospital** 병원에 입원 중이다

14
- □ **presentation** 발표
- □ **material** 자료
- □ **complicated** 복잡한
- □ **submit** 제출하다
- □ **on time** 정각에, 제시간에
- □ **take a deep breath** 심호흡하다
- □ **impressed** 감명을 받은

15
- □ **suitable** 적절한, 적당한
- □ **make a mistake** 실수하다
- □ **employee** 직원
- □ **refund** 환불
- □ **cancel** 취소하다

16-17
- □ **purpose** 목적
- □ **remove** 제거하다
- □ **odor** 냄새, 악취
- □ **bowl** (움푹한) 그릇
- □ **get rid of** …을 제거하다
- □ **peel** 껍질
- □ **rub** 문지르다
- □ **keep away** …을 멀리하다
- □ **mosquito** 모기
- □ **unexpected** 예상 밖의
- □ **scrub** 문질러 씻다
- □ **rusty** 녹슨 (n. rust 녹)
- □ **make use of** …을 이용[활용]하다

15 영어듣기 모의고사

1번부터 17번까지는 듣고 답하는 문제입니다.
1번부터 15번까지는 한 번만 들려주고, 16번부터 17번까지는 두 번 들려줍니다. 방송을 잘 듣고 답을 하기 바랍니다.

01

다음을 듣고, 여자가 하는 말의 목적으로 가장 적절한 것을 고르시오.

① 쌀 소비를 권장하려고
② 쌀 섭취의 장점을 설명하려고
③ 쌀을 활용한 요리를 소개하려고
④ 아침 식사의 중요성을 강조하려고
⑤ 잘못된 식습관의 문제점을 알리려고

02

대화를 듣고, 두 사람이 하는 말의 주제로 가장 적절한 것을 고르시오.

① 환경 보호의 필요성
② 깨끗한 공기의 중요성
③ 환경 파괴 문제의 심각성
④ 나무가 주는 긍정적인 영향
⑤ 행사의 참여율이 저조한 이유

03

대화를 듣고, 두 사람의 관계를 가장 잘 나타낸 것을 고르시오.

① 아들 — 엄마　② 사장 — 비서
③ 교장 — 교사　④ 선생님 — 학생
⑤ 미화원 — 회사원

04

대화를 듣고, 그림에서 대화의 내용과 일치하지 않는 것을 고르시오.

05

대화를 듣고, 남자가 여자에게 부탁한 일로 가장 적절한 것을 고르시오.

① 자료 찾아주기
② 설문조사해주기
③ 설문지에 답하기
④ 보고서 검토해주기
⑤ 설문 항목 작성하기

06

대화를 듣고, 남자가 지원할 수 없는 이유를 고르시오. 3점

① 경력이 5년이 되지 않아서
② 근무 시작일이 맞지 않아서
③ 이력서 제출 마감일이 지나서
④ 축구를 지도한 경험이 없어서
⑤ 이번 주 금요일에 면접을 볼 수 없어서

07

대화를 듣고, 남자가 지불할 금액을 고르시오.

① \$160　② \$170　③ \$180
④ \$200　⑤ \$220

08

대화를 듣고, glass frog에 관해 두 사람이 언급하지 않은 것을 고르시오.

① 색상　② 서식지　③ 최초 발견 시기
④ 먹이　⑤ 크기

09

까페에 관한 다음 내용을 듣고, 일치하지 않는 것을 고르시오.

① 음료와 샌드위치를 판매한다.
② 수입금은 도서관의 책 구입을 위해 쓰인다.
③ 학교 정문 앞에 위치한다.
④ 자원봉사자를 모집하고 있다.
⑤ 오전 11시부터 오후 3시까지 운영한다.

정답 및 해설 p.44-46

10

다음 표를 보면서 대화를 듣고, 여자가 구입할 자전거를 고르시오.

< Bicycles for Sale >

	Product	Size of Wheel	Weight	Price
①	A	16 inches	7 kg	$169
②	B	16 inches	6 kg	$185
③	C	18 inches	7 kg	$179
④	D	20 inches	6 kg	$225
⑤	E	20 inches	8 kg	$210

11

대화를 듣고, 남자의 마지막 말에 대한 여자의 응답으로 가장 적절한 것을 고르시오.

① I always sit in the front row.
② I don't want to go out today.
③ I saw two movies last month.
④ Sorry, but I don't like scary films.
⑤ I'm reading a horror story these days.

12

대화를 듣고, 여자의 마지막 말에 대한 남자의 응답으로 가장 적절한 것을 고르시오.

① The food was great.
② I should have been there.
③ I'll be at the party on time.
④ I'm sorry that you missed it.
⑤ Your party was very enjoyable.

13

대화를 듣고, 여자의 마지막 말에 대한 남자의 응답으로 가장 적절한 것을 고르시오.

Man: ________________

① Thanks a lot. I'll see you later.
② I've never taken that class before.
③ Where did you buy the textbook?
④ Good luck with your history class.
⑤ How about using my book? I still have it.

14

대화를 듣고, 남자의 마지막 말에 대한 여자의 응답으로 가장 적절한 것을 고르시오. 3점

Woman: ________________

① Traveling abroad is always exciting.
② Me, too. That's the best way to do it.
③ It's good that you planned in advance.
④ Okay. I'll reserve a hotel room for you.
⑤ Then you should take a good travel book.

15

다음 상황 설명을 듣고, Betsy가 Tom에게 할 말로 가장 적절한 것을 고르시오.

Betsy: ________________

① I think I will quit my job.
② Let's split the chores fairly.
③ Take a break if you are tired.
④ We should buy a robot cleaner.
⑤ I hired someone to do the housework.

[16-17] 다음을 듣고, 물음에 답하시오.

16

남자가 하는 말의 목적으로 가장 적절한 것은?

① 음식 배달원을 모집하려고
② 패스트푸드의 단점을 알리려고
③ 새로 개업한 식당을 광고하려고
④ 음식 배달 서비스를 홍보하려고
⑤ 새로 문을 연 파티 장소를 소개하려고

17

언급된 음식이 아닌 것은?

① steak ② pasta ③ chicken salad
④ soup ⑤ fried rice

15회

녹음을 다시 한 번 듣고, 빈칸에 알맞은 말을 쓰시오.

01

W: Do you prefer to eat bread or rice? Nowadays, many people like to eat bread because it is convenient. And last year, we _______ _______ _______ _______ ever before. Because of this, farmers in our country are facing economic difficulties. However, we can help farmers by doing a few small things. Eating rice for breakfast _______ _______ _______ is a big help. You can also give rice cakes as gifts to celebrate holidays and anniversaries. There are many other ways to use rice and help farmers, too. Let's make sure we eat rice _______ _______ _______ _______ _______!

02

W: Hi, Justin. Did you see the poster on the town bulletin board?

M: Do you mean the poster about the tree-planting event?

W: Yes. _______ _______ _______ _______ _______ next week near our school.

M: Actually, I already signed up. Have you signed up yet?

W: I will soon! I think having more trees will _______ _______ _______ _______ and give us cleaner air.

M: Right. Then it will make our town more pleasant to live in!

W: And it will help the ecosystem, too. The trees will provide homes for birds and other small animals.

M: Wow! You're right. I'm really glad we're participating.

W: Me, too. I hope more students _______ _______ _______.

03

M: Thank you for arranging my new desk for me, Ms. Newton.

W: _______ _______ _______ _______, sir. Is it okay to put your printer next to your computer?

M: Yes. It's more convenient to use.

W: I'm happy you like it.

M: Thanks again. Could you show me my afternoon schedule?

W: No problem, sir. Hmm... You _______ _______ _______ at 2 p.m. with Mr. Jones.

M: Okay. Do I have any other appointments this afternoon?

W: No. But you're supposed to have dinner with Mr. Smith at 7 p.m.

M: Oh, I almost forgot.

W: _______ _______ _______ _______ you want to know, sir?

M: That's it. I'll call you when I need you.

04

[Cell phone rings.]

W: Hello?

M: Hi, honey. Did you finish preparing for our daughter's birthday party?

W: Yes. I set up a long rectangular table _______ _______ _______ _______.

M: How about a banner? You said you bought one.

W: It's in front of the table. It says "Happy Birthday."

M: That's nice. And did you _______ _______ _______?

W: Yes, it's a two-layer cake, and I put it in the center of the table.

M: How about gifts?

W: I wrapped the three gifts we got her and put them on the right side of the table.

M: That sounds good!

W: Also, there are pictures of her _______ _______ _______ _______.

M: I can't wait to see them. I'll be there soon.

05

W: How's your paper going, Sam?

M: I still need to ________ ________ ________ ________ ________.

W: Really? I finished my research and started writing.

M: I need to start writing, too. I'm ________ ________ ________.

W: Do you need help with your survey?

M: Yes, I need thirty people to take my survey. Could you help me?

W: Sure. I can ask my classmates. Do I need to read the survey questions to them?

M: No, you can just ________ ________ ________ ________ to them. It'll take about three to five minutes to complete.

W: And then I need to collect and return the surveys to you, right?

M: Exactly.

06

[Telephone rings.]

W: Forest Elementary School. This is Jane Smith.

M: Hi. I heard that you're looking for a PE teacher. I want to ________ ________ ________ ________.

W: Yes, we are. Please send us your résumé by this Friday.

M: I will. Are there any special programs that the PE teacher has to teach?

W: Yes. The PE teacher will coach the after-school soccer program.

M: Great! I ________ ________ ________ ________.

W: That's perfect. How many years have you taught?

M: I taught for three years after graduation.

W: Oh, I'm sorry. We're looking for someone who has ________ ________ ________ ________ of experience.

M: I see. Thank you for letting me know. And thank you for your time.

W: You're welcome, sir. Have a nice day.

07

W: How may I help you, sir?

M: I need to ________ ________ ________ for my family.

W: All right. How many people are there in your family?

M: Two adults and two kids.

W: Okay. What items would you like to rent?

M: Well, we need to rent everything. We'll also need day passes.

W: Then, ________ ________ ________ would be best for you. It includes skis, poles, boots, and a day pass.

M: That's great. How much is it?

W: It's $50 each for adults and $30 each for children.

M: Do you have ski clothes as well?

W: Yes. ________ ________ ________ ________ is $10 per person.

M: Then I'll rent clothes for all of us, too.

08

W: Shawn, have you done the homework for science class?

M: I'm almost done. I'm writing about glass frogs.

W: Glass frogs? I've ________ ________ ________ them.

M: They're usually green like most frogs. However, you can see their insides through the clear skin on their belly.

W: Wow, so that's why ________ ________ ________ glass frogs. Where do they live?

M: They live along rivers, where it is hard for people to find them.

W: When were they first discovered?

M: They ________ ________ ________ in 1872.

W: How big are they?

M: Around one to three inches long.

W: That's quite small. They sound like interesting animals.

09

M: Good morning, students. Our school festival starts next week. During the festival, we'll set up a café to sell drinks and sandwiches. All of the money that is raised will _______ _______ _______ _______ more books for the school library. The café will be in front of the main gate of the school. Currently, we are looking for student volunteers. _______ _______ _______, please talk to Mrs. Garcia. If you can't help out, then please _______ _______ _______ _______ during the festival. We hope lots of students come by. It will be open from 11:00 a.m. to 4:00 p.m. I hope to see you then.

10

W: Excuse me. I'm looking for a bike for my son.

M: What kind of bike are you looking for? We have many different options.

W: Well, I think he _______ _______ _______.

M: How old is your son?

W: He is nine years old.

M: Then wheels over 17 inches will be good for him.

W: Okay. Also, he needs to be able to lift the bike, so I want it _______ _______ _______, too.

M: I bet something 7 kg or less would be fine. That leaves us with these two choices.

W: They look very nice. Which one is cheaper?

M: This one is. It's also _______ _______ _______ _______ _______.

W: Excellent. I'll take it.

11

M: Kate, how about going to the movies tonight?

W: _______ _______ _______ _______. What do you want to see?

M: There's a new horror movie out today.

W: (Sorry, but I don't like scary films.)

12

W: Tim, why didn't you come to my housewarming party?

M: I'm sorry, but I was busy that day. How was it?

W: Many people came and _______ _______ _______.

M: (I should have been there.)

13

M: Becky, you look down. Are you okay?

W: I'm just _______ _______ _______ _______ about geography class.

M: Oh, are you in Mr. Baker's class?

W: Yes. Today was the first class of the semester, but it seems too hard.

M: Don't worry. I'm sure it'll be fun.

W: But _______ _______ _______ geography and there's a lot to study.

M: If you need help, you can ask me. I took his class last semester.

W: Great! I might ask a lot of questions, though.

M: That's fine. What are friends for?

W: Thanks. By the way, I'm _______ _______ _______ _______ the bookstore to get the textbook now.

M: (How about using my book? I still have it.)

14

W: You said you were going on a trip soon, right? Are you ready for it?

M: Well, I _______ _______ _______ for my trip.

W: Are you sure? Why don't you double check?

M: Don't worry. I already did.

W: How about your schedule for the trip? _______ _______ _______ _______?

M: No, I only booked my plane tickets and a hotel room.

W: What are you going to do each day then?

M: I don't know yet. I'll make plans every morning.

W: That's not bad. But it's _______ _______ _______ _______ before you go.

M: I know, but I don't have enough time to search for information now.

W: (Then you should take a good travel book.)

15

W: Tom and Betsy are a married couple. They both go to work every morning and come back home around 6:00 p.m. When they _______ _______ _______ _______, Betsy starts doing the housework and takes care of the children. However, Tom just sits down on the sofa and watches TV. Betsy thinks _______ _______ _______. He rarely does the household chores or takes care of the children. He always says that he's tired. Betsy thinks it would be better if Tom would _______ _______ _______ like her. In this situation, what would Betsy most likely say to Tom?

Betsy: (Let's split the chores fairly.)

16-17

M: Most people feel burdened when they have to prepare a lot of food for a party. Many may think that reserving a party room is the best way to _______ _______ _______ _______. But now you can stop being afraid to have a party in your own home. Order to Your Door is a cheap and convenient meal service that you can use for any party. With Order to Your Door, you can buy food online and _______ _______ _______ to your home. Simply choose the meal you want and the number of people you will be serving. You can enjoy steak, pasta, chicken salad, fried rice, and much more. Then we'll deliver your order on time directly to your door. Just _______ _______ _______ at least two days in advance. Order to Your Door is the best way to make your party easier.

15회

15 Word & Expressions

01
- □ **convenient** 편리한
- □ **face** 직면하다
- □ **economic** 경제적인
- □ **instead of** … 대신에
- □ **celebrate** 기념하다, 축하하다
- □ **anniversary** 기념일

02
- □ **bulletin board** 게시판
- □ **take place** 발생하다
- □ **sign up** 신청하다
- □ **pleasant** 쾌적한
- □ **ecosystem** 생태계
- □ **participate** 참가하다

03
- □ **arrange** 정리하다
- □ **appointment** 약속
- □ **be supposed to-v** …하기로 되어 있다

04
- □ **set up** …을 세우다, …을 설치하다
- □ **rectangular** 직사각형의
- □ **checkered** 체크무늬의
- □ **tablecloth** 테이블보
- □ **banner** 현수막
- □ **layer** 층, 단
- □ **wrap** 싸다, 포장하다

05
- □ **do research** 조사를 하다
- □ **run behind** …보다 뒤지다
- □ **survey** (설문) 조사
- □ **hand out** …을 나누어 주다
- □ **complete** 완료하다; *기입하다[작성하다]

06
- □ **PE** 체육(= physical education)
- □ **apply for** …에 지원하다
- □ **résumé** 이력서
- □ **graduation** 졸업
- □ **at least** 적어도

07
- □ **rent** 대여하다
- □ **equipment** 기구, 장비
- □ **day pass** 1일 이용권
- □ **standard** 일반적인, 보통의
- □ **clothing** 옷
- □ **rental fee** 대여료

08
- □ **inside** 내부
- □ **clear** 투명한
- □ **belly** 배
- □ **discover** 발견하다

09
- □ **raise** 올리다; *(자금 등을) 모으다
- □ **currently** 현재
- □ **volunteer** 자원봉사자
- □ **help out** 도와주다
- □ **stop[come] by** 잠시 들르다

10
- □ **wheel** 바퀴
- □ **lift** 들어 올리다
- □ **light** 가벼운
- □ **bet** (…이) 틀림없다[분명하다]
- □ **best seller** 잘 팔리는 상품

11
- □ **row** 줄, 열
- □ **scary** 무서운

12
- □ **housewarming party** 집들이
- □ **on time** 정각에, 제때에
- □ **miss** 놓치다
- □ **enjoyable** 즐거운

13
- □ **stressed out** 스트레스를 받는
- □ **geography** 지리학
- □ **semester** 학기
- □ **What are friends for?** 친구 좋다는 게 뭐겠니?
- □ **textbook** 교과서

14
- □ **pack** (짐을) 싸다
- □ **arrange** 정하다, 준비하다
- □ **book** 예약하다
- □ **search for** …을 찾다
- □ **abroad** 해외로
- □ **in advance** 미리
- □ **reserve** 예약하다

15
- □ **housework** 가사, 집안일
- □ **take care of** …을 돌보다
- □ **unfair** 불공평한
- □ **rarely** 좀처럼 …하지 않는
- □ **chore** (가정의) 잡일
- □ **quit** 그만두다
- □ **split** (몫 등을) 나누다
- □ **fairly** 공정하게
- □ **hire** 고용하다

16-17
- □ **burden** 부담을 지우다
- □ **deal with** …을 처리하다
- □ **convenient** 편리한
- □ **directly** 곧장, 바로
- □ **door** 문; *집
- □ **place an order** 주문하다

16 영어듣기 모의고사

정답 및 해설 p.47-49

1번부터 17번까지는 듣고 답하는 문제입니다.
1번부터 15번까지는 한 번만 들려주고, 16번부터 17번까지는 두 번 들려줍니다. 방송을 잘 듣고 답을 하기 바랍니다.

01

다음을 듣고, 여자가 하는 말의 목적으로 가장 적절한 것을 고르시오. 3점

① 정기적인 실내 환기를 권고하려고
② 가습기 사용 시 유의사항을 알리려고
③ 적정한 습도 유지의 중요성을 강조하려고
④ 겨울철 에너지 절약 캠페인을 홍보하려고
⑤ 잘못된 가습기 사용으로 인한 피해를 공유하려고

02

대화를 듣고, 두 사람이 하는 말의 주제로 가장 적절한 것을 고르시오. 3점

① 영양제 섭취의 필요성
② 영양제의 올바른 섭취 방법
③ 몸이 비타민을 흡수하는 과정
④ 비타민과 함께 먹으면 좋은 음식
⑤ 자신에게 맞는 영양제 고르는 법

03

대화를 듣고, 두 사람의 관계를 가장 잘 나타낸 것을 고르시오.

① 환자 — 간호사
② 방문객 — 경비원
③ 손님 — 서점 직원
④ 학생 — 도서관 사서
⑤ 관객 — 극장 매표소 직원

04

대화를 듣고, 그림에서 대화의 내용과 일치하지 않는 것을 고르시오.

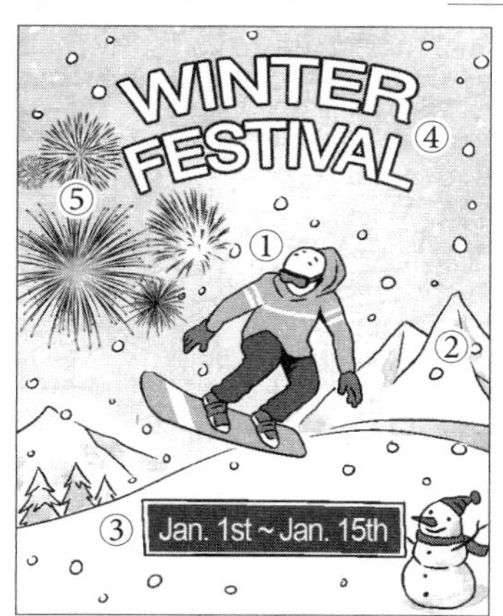

05

대화를 듣고, 남자가 여자에게 부탁한 일로 가장 적절한 것을 고르시오.

① 사진 찍어주기
② 자리 잡아주기
③ 춤 가르쳐주기
④ 동아리 가입하기
⑤ 카메라 빌려주기

06

대화를 듣고, 남자가 기뻐하는 이유를 고르시오

① 시험 성적이 좋아서
② 테니스 경기에서 이겨서
③ 부상이 완전히 회복되어서
④ 유명한 테니스 선수를 만나서
⑤ 테니스 경기에 출전할 수 있어서

07

대화를 듣고, 여자가 지불할 금액을 고르시오.

① $70 ② $100 ③ $140
④ $170 ⑤ $200

08

대화를 듣고, 하와이에 관해 두 사람이 언급하지 않은 것을 고르시오.

① 날씨 ② 위치 ③ 섬 개수
④ 관광명소 ⑤ 인구

09

할인 판매에 관한 다음 내용을 듣고, 일치하지 않는 것을 고르시오.

① 모든 노트북 컴퓨터와 태블릿 컴퓨터를 할인한다.
② 3일 동안만 진행된다.
③ 회원 카드가 있어야 할인을 받을 수 있다.
④ 전국 매장에서 동시에 진행된다.
⑤ 행사 기간 동안은 평소보다 늦게 문을 닫는다.

16회

10

다음 표를 보면서 대화를 듣고, 남자가 임대할 아파트를 고르시오.
3점

< Sunny Hill Tower >

	Apartment	Bedroom	Rent	Available
①	104	3	$800	From May 20th
②	201	1	$600	From June 15th
③	203	2	$850	From June 1st
④	205	1	$650	From June 1st
⑤	601	2	$755	From May 20th

11

대화를 듣고, 남자의 마지막 말에 대한 여자의 응답으로 가장 적절한 것을 고르시오.

① You need to speak up.
② Why don't we study together?
③ It's okay. I can hear you clearly.
④ Then I'll put on my headphones.
⑤ I'll ask him to lower the volume.

12

대화를 듣고, 여자의 마지막 말에 대한 남자의 응답으로 가장 적절한 것을 고르시오.

① Yes, it was a very exciting game.
② Go straight and turn left at the corner.
③ No, I'm not interested in baseball games.
④ I waited for you at the stadium for a long time.
⑤ I'd love to, but I have to visit my grandmother.

13

대화를 듣고, 남자의 마지막 말에 대한 여자의 응답으로 가장 적절한 것을 고르시오.

Woman: ______________________

① I should ask for a bigger allowance.
② In my opinion, it's a waste of money.
③ Great, but I already have a smartphone.
④ No, it was difficult to use that application.
⑤ That's right. I will download one right now.

14

대화를 듣고, 여자의 마지막 말에 대한 남자의 응답으로 가장 적절한 것을 고르시오.

Man: ______________________

① Yes, it was really exciting.
② Actually, I was too busy that day.
③ Great! I'll see you this afternoon!
④ I can't make it. How about Sunday?
⑤ I won't. I'll write it down on the calendar.

15

다음 상황 설명을 듣고, Michelle이 도서관 사서에게 할 말로 가장 적절한 것을 고르시오.

Michelle: ______________________

① Are there any new books today?
② How many books can I check out?
③ I don't know where I lost the book.
④ Is there an extra umbrella I can borrow?
⑤ This book is damaged. What should I do?

[16-17] 다음을 듣고, 물음에 답하시오.

16

남자가 하는 말의 목적으로 가장 적절한 것은?

① 두통약의 위험성을 경고하려고
② 새로 나온 두통약을 광고하려고
③ 건강 관리 프로그램을 홍보하려고
④ 두통의 다양한 원인을 설명하려고
⑤ 두통을 줄일 수 있는 방법을 알리려고

17

언급된 두통의 원인이 아닌 것은?

① 스트레스
② 수면 부족
③ 굶주림
④ 운동 부족
⑤ 수면 과다

정답 및 해설 p.49

녹음을 다시 한 번 듣고, 빈칸에 알맞은 말을 쓰시오.

01

W: As winters get colder, people _______ _______ _______ heaters. Although these heaters keep the house warm, they also dry out the air. Therefore, people start to use humidifiers. But these can also cause problems if you're not careful. _______ _______ _______ _______, you should first keep the humidifier clean. Clean both the outside and inside of the humidifier to prevent bacteria from growing. And be sure to replace the water every day. It's best to use water that you boil and cool first. Finally, make sure the air in your house doesn't get too humid. This can _______ _______ _______ _______.

02

M: Hey, Gwen. Are you taking medicine?

W: Hi, Shawn. Actually, these are multivitamins and calcium supplements. Do you want some?

M: I'm fine, thanks. But are you _______ _______ _______?

W: Yes. Is there a problem?

M: Actually, you shouldn't take them _______ _______ _______ _______.

W: Why is that?

M: Calcium makes it hard for your body to absorb the iron in the multivitamin. _______ _______ _______ take them at different times of the day.

W: Really? I didn't know that.

M: Yeah. And you should also take the multivitamin with some food.

W: Oh, I see. Thanks for telling me!

03

W: Excuse me. Can you help me?

M: Certainly. What can I do for you?

W: I want to see *Happy Holidays*, but I don't see it on the list.

M: That _______ _______ _______ next week.

W: I think I misread the schedule. Can you recommend another movie? I love romantic comedies.

M: We have another romantic comedy playing at 6:00 p.m.

W: Oh, really? What is it called?

M: *We Are in Love*. It's one of _______ _______ _______ _______ these days.

W: Hmm... I'll see that movie then. Can I get a ticket for a seat in the middle of the theater, please?

M: You're so lucky. _______ _______ _______ _______ _______ in the premium seating area.

W: That's great.

04

M: Janet, did you finish the winter festival poster?

W: Yes, I did. What do you think of it?

M: Wow, the snowboarder in the middle looks very nice.

W: Thanks. I added him because he makes the poster _______ _______ _______.

M: You put mountains covered with snow in the background, too.

W: Right, they give the poster more of a winter feeling. I also wrote the dates, January 1st to January 15th, next to the snowman.

M: Yeah. They are _______ _______ _______!

W: Definitely.

M: Most of all, I like the way "WINTER FESTIVAL" is written above the snowboarder.

W: And I didn't forget to put fireworks _______ _______ _______ _______ _______.

M: Yeah, they look cool.

05

M: Are you busy Saturday afternoon, Anne?

W: No, I don't have _______ _______ _______. Why do you ask?

M: Well, do you remember that I joined the school dance club?

W: Yes, you told me. Is there an event on Saturday?

M: Yes, we _______ _______ _______ in the school gym. All the club members will participate in the event.

W: That's great. You must be excited.

M: I am. But I want somebody to _______ _______ _______ me. Can you do that?

W: Sure. You know I bought a brand-new camera last month. What time does it start?

M: At 3:00 p.m. But I hope you'll come earlier than that in order to get a good spot.

W: All right. No problem.

06

W: Well, Mr. Taylor, I just got your test results.

M: So, how's my ankle? It feels much better than last week.

W: Yes, the broken bone _______ _______ _______.

M: Almost? How long will it take for a full recovery?

W: It will take about two more weeks. You should be fine by then.

M: Really? I'm glad to hear that.

W: Do you have any plans?

M: Actually there's a big tennis competition _______ _______ _______ _______ _______. I want to play in it.

W: I see. Well, I believe you'll be able to participate in that.

M: That's great news. I think I have _______ _______ _______ _______ _______ winning it!

W: Good for you. You can start light workouts in two weeks.

07

M: May I help you?

W: Yes, I need to _______ _______ _______ _______. The screen is broken.

M: Okay. Let me see it. *[Pause]* Hmm... Both the outer and inner screens are broken. Well, I think you need to _______ _______ _______ _______.

W: Is it that serious? How much will it cost?

M: It'll cost $100 to replace each screen.

W: Oh, that'll be expensive if I pay for both of them.

M: When did you get this phone? If it's less than a year old, we'll give you a 30% discount.

W: Oh, that's good. I bought it six months ago.

M: Then you can _______ _______ _______.

08

W: Look at this amazing picture of Hawaii!

M: Isn't it lovely? Actually, I lived in Hawaii for a year to study English.

W: Really? I would love to travel there someday.

M: You should. It is warm all year long, so it is _______ _______ _______ _______ _______.

W: That sounds great. Where is it?

M: It's southwest of mainland United States.

W: I see. Is it just one island?

M: Actually, _______ _______ _______ eight big islands and more than one hundred small islands.

W: There are so many of them. How many people live there?

M: I heard about 1.4 million people live there.

W: Oh, it has a small population.

M: That's right. So _______ _______ _______, and it's a good place to relax.

09

M: International Electronics is having a special summer sale. All of our laptops and tablet computers will _______ _______ _______ starting next week. All of these items will be sold at 25% off the original price. This sale will last for three days only, from July 7th to 9th. However, you must have our store membership card to receive the special sale prices. Also, this sale will _______ _______ _______ _______ our downtown location. Our other stores will not have this event. We'll be opening as usual but _______ _______ _______ _______ than we do on normal days. Don't miss this great chance!

10

W: Hello. How can I help you?

M: Hi. I want to rent an apartment. Can you help me find an appropriate one?

W: Okay. _______ _______ _______ are you looking for?

M: I live alone, so one or two bedrooms would be enough.

W: All right. And can I ask what your monthly budget is?

M: I _______ _______ _______ _______ $800 per month.

W: Okay. We have three apartments that fit your needs.

M: That's good. And _______ _______ _______ soon, so I need to move in as soon as possible.

W: Oh, when do you need to move in by?

M: May 21st.

W: Then this is the one you should rent.

11

M: Your music is too loud. I can hear it all the way in my room.

W: I'm sorry. I'll turn it down.

M: It's still too loud. I can't _______ _______ _______ _______.

W: (Then I'll put on my headphones.)

12

W: I can't wait to see this Saturday's big baseball game!

M: I'm so jealous. I love baseball!

W: Then _______ _______ _______ _______ to the stadium with us?

M: (I'd love to, but I have to visit my grandmother.)

13

M: Would you like to go to Smoothie World with me?

W: I wish I could, but I don't have any money right now.

M: Again? Did you spend all your allowance already?

W: Yeah. It just _______ _______ _______. I don't even remember where I spent my money.

M: That's terrible. I think you should start writing down everything you buy.

W: Actually, I've tried to do that, but it's hard to remember.

M: How about _______ _______ _______ on your smartphone? It'll be easier to record your expenses.

W: Oh, I hadn't thought of that. What a good idea!

M: Yeah, it will _______ _______ because you always have your phone with you.

W: (That's right. I will download one right now.)

16회

14

[Cell phone rings.]

W: Hi, Patrick. Where shall we meet today?

M: What do you mean? Do we have plans today?

W: Did you forget? We were going to _______ _______ _______ _______.

M: Oh, I'm so sorry. I completely forgot about it. I'm on my way to visit my cousins now.

W: Really? When _______ _______ _______ _______?

M: I'll be there for the whole weekend. But I'll be back Sunday night.

W: Well, that's disappointing. But I hope you have fun. See you _______ _______ _______ _______.

M: I'm really sorry. Can we make plans for next Saturday?

W: Okay. Don't forget this time!

M: (I won't. I'll write it down on the calendar.)

15

W: Michelle has to write a report for her history project, so she goes to the library and borrows five books. _______ _______ _______ _______, it suddenly starts to rain, but she doesn't have an umbrella. She decides to run home through the rain _______ _______ _______ _______ _______. When she arrives home, she finds that one of the books is so wet that its cover has been seriously damaged. The next day, she _______ _______ _______ the library to ask what she can do. In this situation, what would Michelle most likely say to the librarian?

Michelle: (This book is damaged. What should I do?)

16-17

M: Many people suffer from headaches. There are various causes for headaches, such as stress and lack of sleep. They can also be caused by hunger or even getting too much sleep. Usually people take medicine to _______ _______ _______ because it is an easy and quick way to solve the problem. But taking medicine is not always good because it can have some side effects. Therefore, if your headaches are not severe, you can try other ways to fight them first. Placing a cold pack of ice on your head can relieve some of the pain. _______ _______ _______ _______ can also help to relax you. There are also things you can do before the headache even happens. Always drink enough water throughout the day, and _______ _______ _______ _______. These tips can help you to relieve your headaches.

16 Word & Expressions

01
- □ **depend on** …에 의존하다
- □ **heater** 난방기
- □ **humidifier** 가습기
- □ **prevent** 막다, 예방하다
- □ **bacteria** (*pl.*) 세균
- □ **replace** 교체하다
- □ **boil** 끓이다
- □ **humid** 습한, 축축한
- □ **mold** 곰팡이

02
- □ **multivitamin** 종합비타민
- □ **calcium** 칼슘
- □ **supplement** 보충물[제]
- □ **absorb** 흡수하다
- □ **iron** 철분

03
- □ **misread** 잘못 읽다
- □ **premium** 아주 좋은
- □ **seating** 좌석, 자리

04
- □ **snowboarder** 스노보드를 타는 사람
- □ **covered with** …로 덮인
- □ **background** 배경
- □ **noticeable** 눈에 띄는
- □ **definitely** 분명히, 틀림없이
- □ **firework** 불꽃놀이

05
- □ **performance** 공연
- □ **gym** 체육관
- □ **participate in** …에 참가하다
- □ **brand-new** 완전 새것인
- □ **spot** (특정한) 장소, 자리

06
- □ **ankle** 발목
- □ **bone** 뼈
- □ **heal** 치유하다
- □ **recovery** 회복
- □ **competition** 대회
- □ **have a chance of** …의 가능성이 있다
- □ **workout** 운동

07
- □ **repair** 수리하다
- □ **both A and B** A와 B 둘 다
- □ **outer** 바깥쪽의
- □ **inner** 안쪽의
- □ **serious** 심각한

08
- □ **all year long** 일 년 내내
- □ **mainland** 본토
- □ **consist of** …로 구성되다
- □ **population** 인구
- □ **crowded** (사람들이) 붐비는, 혼잡한
- □ **relax** 휴식을 취하다

09
- □ **original** 원래의
- □ **last** 계속되다, 지속되다
- □ **take place** 일어나다, 발생하다
- □ **location** 위치, 장소
- □ **as usual** 평소대로
- □ **normal** 보통의, 평범한

10
- □ **rent** 세 내다, 임차하다; 방세, 임차료
- □ **appropriate** 적절한
- □ **budget** 예산
- □ **fit** 꼭 맞다, 적합하다
- □ **lease** 임대차 계약
- □ **expire** 만료되다
- □ **move in** 이사를 들다
- □ **available** 이용할 수 있는

11
- □ **all the way** 내내[시종]
- □ **focus on** …에 초점을 맞추다
- □ **speak up** 더 크게 말하다
- □ **clearly** 또렷하게
- □ **lower** 낮추다

12
- □ **jealous** 질투하는, 부러워하는
- □ **stadium** 경기장
- □ **corner** 모퉁이

13
- □ **allowance** 용돈
- □ **disappear** 사라지다
- □ **terrible** 끔찍한; *심한
- □ **application** 지원(서); *응용 프로그램
- □ **expense** (어떤 일에 드는) 돈, 비용

14
- □ **completely** 완전히
- □ **disappointing** 실망스러운
- □ **make it** (모임 등에) 가다
- □ **write down** …을 적다

15
- □ **suddenly** 갑자기
- □ **cover** 표지
- □ **seriously** 심각하게
- □ **damage** 손상을 주다, 훼손하다
- □ **librarian** 도서관 사서
- □ **check out** (책을) 대출하다
- □ **extra** 여분의, 남는

16-17
- □ **suffer from** …로 고통받다
- □ **various** 다양한
- □ **cause** 원인; 유발하다
- □ **such as** …와 같은
- □ **lack** 부족, 결핍
- □ **hunger** 굶주림
- □ **relieve** 덜어 주다
- □ **side effect** 부작용
- □ **severe** 극심한
- □ **regularly** 규칙적으로

17 영어듣기 모의고사

1번부터 17번까지는 듣고 답하는 문제입니다.
1번부터 15번까지는 한 번만 들려주고, 16번부터 17번까지는 두 번 들려줍니다. 방송을 잘 듣고 답을 하기 바랍니다.

01

다음을 듣고, 여자가 하는 말의 목적으로 가장 적절한 것을 고르시오.

① 눈길 안전 운전법을 알리려고
② 즉각적인 제설 작업을 요청하려고
③ 차 고장 시 위기 대처법을 설명하려고
④ 운전면허 시험 합격 비결을 공유하려고
⑤ 전국적인 폭설로 인한 피해를 보고하려고

02

대화를 듣고, 남자의 의견으로 가장 적절한 것을 고르시오.

① 주차 요금을 인하해야 한다.
② 지상 주차 공간을 늘려야 한다.
③ 불법 주차 단속을 실시해야 한다.
④ 낙후된 주차장 시설을 보수해야 한다.
⑤ 장애인 주차 구역에 주차하면 안 된다.

03

대화를 듣고, 두 사람의 관계를 가장 잘 나타낸 것을 고르시오.

① 요리사 — 심사위원
② 제과점 직원 — 고객
③ 옷 가게 직원 — 고객
④ 꽃꽂이 강사 — 수강생
⑤ 백화점 관리자 — 식료품 직원

04

대화를 듣고, 그림에서 대화의 내용과 일치하지 않는 것을 고르시오.

05

대화를 듣고, 남자가 여자에게 부탁한 일로 가장 적절한 것을 고르시오.

① 화가 소개해주기
② 영화 표 확인하기
③ 휴대전화 빌려주기
④ 휴대전화 수리 맡기기
⑤ 주말에 볼 영화 고르기

06

대화를 듣고, 여자가 직장을 그만둔 이유를 고르시오.

① 업무가 많아서
② 보수가 적어서
③ 소설가가 되고 싶어서
④ 스트레스를 많이 받아서
⑤ 동료와 사이가 안 좋아서

07

대화를 듣고, 남자가 지불할 금액을 고르시오.

① $12 ② $14 ③ $16 ④ $18 ⑤ $20

08

대화를 듣고, 도쿄 타워에 관해 두 사람이 언급하지 않은 것을 고르시오.

① 주요 기능 ② 무게 ③ 재료 ④ 설계자 ⑤ 개장 연도

09

도서 전시회에 관한 다음 내용을 듣고, 일치하지 않는 것을 고르시오. 3점

① 8월 9일부터 11일까지 개최된다.
② 소규모 출판사들의 새 책들을 읽을 수 있다.
③ 발표와 독서 토론회가 있을 것이다.
④ 12세 이하 어린이는 무료로 입장할 수 있다.
⑤ 수익금은 신인 작가들을 지원하는 데 쓰일 것이다.

10

다음 표를 보면서 대화를 듣고, 여자가 구입할 배드민턴 라켓을 고르시오.

< Badminton Rackets >

	Model	Weight	Grip Size	Price
①	A	75 g	3.0 inches	$23
②	B	77 g	4.0 inches	$17
③	C	82 g	3.5 inches	$15
④	D	79 g	3.0 inches	$21
⑤	E	85 g	4.5 inches	$13

11

대화를 듣고, 여자의 마지막 말에 대한 남자의 응답으로 가장 적절한 것을 고르시오.

① I already took this medicine.
② Fortunately, I don't have a fever.
③ I'm glad you're feeling better now.
④ I know a clinic that's open on Sundays.
⑤ It's a good thing you visited the doctor.

12

대화를 듣고, 남자의 마지막 말에 대한 여자의 응답으로 가장 적절한 것을 고르시오.

① I like the color very much.
② Actually, the jacket is sold out.
③ Yes. I found a small hole in the back.
④ Nothing. Everything is perfectly fine.
⑤ I'm sorry that you're not satisfied with it.

13

대화를 듣고, 남자의 마지막 말에 대한 여자의 응답으로 가장 적절한 것을 고르시오.

Woman: ______________________

① I didn't write a review on my blog.
② But I'm satisfied with their service.
③ Please tell me how to cook that food.
④ We shouldn't believe everything online.
⑤ Of course. Let's visit the restaurant again.

14

대화를 듣고, 여자의 마지막 말에 대한 남자의 응답으로 가장 적절한 것을 고르시오. 3점

Man: ______________________

① There is no reason to be angry.
② You need to stop lying. It's bad.
③ How about apologizing in a letter?
④ Don't worry. You can borrow my bag.
⑤ I think she wants to talk to me directly.

15

다음 상황 설명을 듣고, Susan이 세관원에게 할 말로 가장 적절한 것을 고르시오.

Susan: ______________________

① Those are not mine!
② How much do I have to pay?
③ Why can't I bring those items?
④ I ate some of them on the flight.
⑤ I'm sorry, but I totally forgot about it!

[16-17] 다음을 듣고, 물음에 답하시오.

16

남자가 하는 말의 주제로 가장 적절한 것은?

① 에너지 음료의 부작용
② 집중력을 유지하는 방법
③ 카페인과 건강의 상관관계
④ 에너지 음료를 마시는 이유
⑤ 설탕이 건강에 미치는 악영향

17

언급된 증상이 아닌 것은? 3점

① 불면증
② 불규칙한 심장박동
③ 충치
④ 체중 증가
⑤ 복통

녹음을 다시 한 번 듣고, 빈칸에 알맞은 말을 쓰시오.

01

W: Good morning, everyone. As you know, it will snow all across the country starting tomorrow morning. The snow _______ _______ _______ be heavy, so you should be especially careful when driving in this weather. It takes much longer than normal to stop your car on icy roads. Please _______ _______. Furthermore, keep your distance from the car in front of you. Plus, don't apply the brakes too suddenly, either. That might make your car slide. Also, _______ _______ _______ _______ _______ your headlights, even in the daytime. This helps other drivers see you through the snow.

02

M: Oh, look! The building is right there.

W: Good. But _______ _______ _______. The meeting starts in a few minutes.

M: You're right. But first we need to park the car in the underground parking lot.

W: Well, how about just parking in front of the building? The meeting won't be long.

M: No, we can't park there.

W: Why not? We _______ _______ _______ if we park there.

M: There is a "Disabled Parking" sign. Can you see it?

W: Oh, I see it now. But I don't think they'll check our car.

M: Even so, we _______ _______ _______. If we park there and someone actually needs it, they won't be able to use it.

W: Okay, you're right.

03

M: Welcome!

W: Hi. It smells really nice in here.

M: Thank you. Is there _______ _______ _______ that you're looking for today?

W: I haven't decided yet. I'll look around first.

M: Okay. Let me know if you have any questions.

W: Is everything here fresh?

M: Yes, everything _______ _______ _______ each morning.

W: Great. Do you use organic ingredients?

M: Yes. The flour and all of the other ingredients are 100% organic.

W: I'm glad to hear that. Which is your best seller?

M: This wheat one right here is the most popular kind. And if you buy one loaf, _______ _______ _______ _______.

W: Great! I'll take one.

04

M: I've finished decorating the back wall of the classroom.

W: Really? Tell me about it.

M: Well, I _______ _______ _______ _______ at the top.

W: Did you also put up the class motto?

M: Yes, the motto "Always Smile!" is _______ _______ _______ _______.

W: How about the timetable I made?

M: I put it on the left side of the board. Right next to it are our classmates' pictures.

W: That's great! By the way, did you put the list of classroom rules up as well? Our teacher wanted to add it.

M: Yes, I put it right next to the pictures.

W: Great. I hope she will _______ _______ _______ it.

05

M: Hey, Amy, how about seeing a movie this weekend?

W: That sounds great! Which one do you want to see?

M: What about *Now You See My Eyes*? It's a romance.

W: Isn't that the one about the painters who _______ _______ _______?

M: That's right. Have you heard about it?

W: Yes, my friend said it was touching. I really want to see it.

M: Great. I'll check if _______ _______ _______ _______ this weekend using my phone. *[Pause]* Oh, I don't think I can.

W: What's wrong?

M: My phone is dead. I _______ _______ _______ it last night. Could you check for the tickets on yours?

W: Sure. Wait a second.

M: Thanks.

06

M: Hi, Melissa. What are you doing here? Shouldn't you be at work?

W: Oh, hi, Peter. No, I quit last month.

M: Why? Was there too much to do?

W: No, it wasn't that busy. I could _______ _______ _______.

M: Then was it because you didn't like your coworkers?

W: No, I liked them. The people I worked with were very nice. I just wanted more time to think about my future.

M: Oh, I see. You must have _______ _______ _______ from your work.

W: That wasn't a problem. I just want to work toward my dream.

M: Oh. What's your dream?

W: I _______ _______ _______ _______ _______.

M: Wow! That sounds great. Good luck!

07

W: Can I help you with something, sir?

M: Yes, please. How much is the chicken?

W: A whole chicken is $10. If you want to _______ _______ _______, it's an extra $2.

M: Please cut up a chicken for me, then. I also need some carrots and onions.

W: Carrots are $2 each, and onions are $1 each. _______ _______ _______ _______ _______?

M: One carrot and two onions, please.

W: All right. Can I get you anything else?

M: Yes. I _______ _______ _______.

W: Okay. Potatoes are $2 each. Is that all?

M: Yes. Now I have everything to make chicken soup. Thanks.

W: You're welcome.

08

M: The next stop on our tour will be Tokyo Tower.

W: Is that an office building?

M: No. It's actually more like the Eiffel Tower. It mainly functions as a communications tower.

W: I see. How tall is it? It's _______ _______ _______ the Eiffel Tower, right?

M: Yes. It's about 10 meters taller, though. It also weighs about 4,000 tons.

W: Wow! That's a heavy structure.

M: Yes, you're right. Actually, _______ _______ _______ _______.

W: That makes sense. Does it get a lot of visitors?

M: It does. More than 150 million people have visited it since it opened in 1958.

W: Well, I'm _______ _______ _______ _______ it!

09

M: Hello, ladies and gentlemen. The annual State Book Fair _______ _______ _______ from August 9th to 11th in the City Convention Center. A lot of publishers from different companies will be there. You can read some new books from small publishing companies. Also, you'll be able to catch some interesting presentations and _______ _______ _______ book discussions. Admission to the fair is $15, but it's free for children twelve and under. Furthermore, the money made at the fair will _______ _______ _______ charities that support children's education. Thank you for your time.

10

M: How can I help you?

W: I need a badminton racket.

M: Well, these are our best aluminum rackets. They're really nice.

W: They look great, but I don't want _______ _______ _______.

M: If you want a light one, something weighing under 80 g will be good. Do you care about grip size, too?

W: Yes. I have small hands, so a big grip size _______ _______ _______.

M: Let me see your hands. *[Pause]* I think a grip less than 3.5 inches will fit you. You can choose one of these two. Which one do you prefer?

W: I'd like to _______ _______ _______ _______.

M: Then this is the one you want.

W: Great!

11

W: I'm not feeling very well. I have a headache and a fever.

M: Oh, really? Why don't you _______ _______ _______ _______ _______?

W: But today is Sunday. The doctor's office is closed.

M: (I know a clinic that's open on Sundays.)

12

M: How may I help you?

W: I bought this jacket yesterday, but _______ _______ _______ _______ _______.

M: Okay. May I ask what's wrong?

W: (Yes. I found a small hole in the back.)

13

W: What did you think of the restaurant?

M: _______ _______ _______!

W: Yeah, but I never thought it would be that bad. I guess my expectations were just too high.

M: I had very high expectations, too. But the food didn't taste good at all.

W: We wasted so much money on such bad food.

M: Right. We should have gone to another restaurant.

W: And the service was terrible.

M: I definitely _______ _______ _______ _______ there again. Didn't you say it's quite popular?

W: Yes, and there were a lot of good blog reviews.

M: They must be _______ _______ _______ _______ written by the restaurant.

W: (We shouldn't believe everything online.)

14

M: What's wrong, Jane? You look upset.

W: My sister, May, is angry at me. I don't know what to do.

M: Really? What happened?

W: I borrowed her bag, but I _______ _______ _______ _______ _______. I washed it, but it still has a stain.

M: What kind of bag is it? Is it a new one?

W: It's not new, but it's the bag that she likes the most.

M: Well, I can understand why she's angry.

W: I know. I _______ _______ _______ it.

M: We all make mistakes. You just need to tell her how sorry you are.

W: How can I do that? She _______ _______ _______ to me.

M: (How about apologizing in a letter?)

15

W: Susan flies from Canada to Australia for a vacation. When she lands, she _______ _______ _______ a customs officer. He asks if she has any fruit, vegetables, or meat in her suitcase. She says, "No," but when he opens her suitcase, there is _______ _______ _______ _______. She is surprised and embarrassed because she had completely forgotten about it. The officer tells her that she has to pay a fine, and it costs her $340! Susan wants to apologize and say that _______ _______ _______ _______. In this situation, what would Susan most likely say to the officer?

Susan: (I'm sorry, but I totally forgot about it!)

16-17

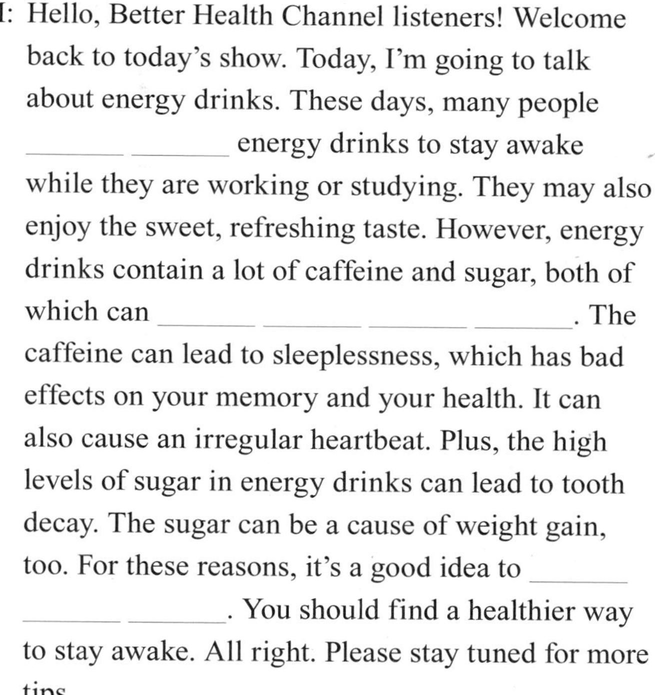

M: Hello, Better Health Channel listeners! Welcome back to today's show. Today, I'm going to talk about energy drinks. These days, many people _______ _______ energy drinks to stay awake while they are working or studying. They may also enjoy the sweet, refreshing taste. However, energy drinks contain a lot of caffeine and sugar, both of which can _______ _______ _______ _______. The caffeine can lead to sleeplessness, which has bad effects on your memory and your health. It can also cause an irregular heartbeat. Plus, the high levels of sugar in energy drinks can lead to tooth decay. The sugar can be a cause of weight gain, too. For these reasons, it's a good idea to _______ _______ _______. You should find a healthier way to stay awake. All right. Please stay tuned for more tips.

17 Word & Expressions

01
- □ **heavy** 무거운; *많은, 심한
- □ **normal** 보통, 평균
- □ **icy** 얼음으로 덮인
- □ **furthermore** 더욱이
- □ **distance** 거리
- □ **apply** 적용하다; *누르다, 힘을 가하다
- □ **suddenly** 갑자기
- □ **slide** 미끄러지다
- □ **headlight** 전조등, 헤드라이트
- □ **daytime** 낮, 주간

02
- □ **underground** 지하의
- □ **parking lot** 주차장
- □ **disabled** 장애를 가진
- □ **sign** 표지판, 간판

03
- □ **in particular** 특별히, 특별한
- □ **freshly** 갓[막] …한
- □ **organic** 유기농의
- □ **ingredient** 재료
- □ **flour** 밀가루
- □ **loaf** 한 덩어리의 빵

04
- □ **decorate** 장식하다
- □ **put up** …을 내붙이다, …을 게시하다
- □ **motto** 좌우명, 모토
- □ **be pleased with** …이 마음에 들다

05
- □ **painter** 화가
- □ **fall in love** 사랑에 빠지다
- □ **available** 이용할[구할] 수 있는
- □ **charge** 충전하다

06
- □ **quit** 그만두다
- □ **handle** 다루다
- □ **coworker** 동료
- □ **stressed out** 스트레스를 받는
- □ **novelist** 소설가

07
- □ **cut up** …을 잘게 자르다
- □ **extra** 여분의, 추가의

08
- □ **function** 기능하다
- □ **communication** (*pl.*) 정보 통신
- □ **weigh** 무게가 …이다
- □ **structure** 구조물
- □ **be made of** …로 만들어지다
- □ **steel** 강철
- □ **make sense** 의미가 통하다, 이해가 되다
- □ **look forward to v-ing** …을 기대하다

09
- □ **annual** 연례의, 매년의
- □ **book fair** 도서 전시회
- □ **publisher** 출판사
- □ **publishing company** 출판사
- □ **take part in** …에 참가하다
- □ **discussion** 토론, 논의
- □ **admission** 입장; *입장료
- □ **donate** 기부하다
- □ **charity** 자선 단체
- □ **support** 지원하다, 후원하다

10
- □ **racket** 라켓
- □ **weigh** 무게가 …이다
- □ **grip** 움켜쥠; *손잡이
- □ **fit** 꼭 맞다, 적합하다

11
- □ **see a doctor** 진찰을 받다
- □ **fortunately** 다행스럽게도
- □ **clinic** (전문 분야) 병원

12
- □ **hole** 구멍
- □ **be satisfied with** …에 만족하다

13
- □ **awful** 끔찍한
- □ **expectation** 기대
- □ **terrible** 끔찍한; 기분이 안 좋은; *형편없는
- □ **definitely** 분명히, 절대로
- □ **advertisement** 광고

14
- □ **upset** 속상한
- □ **spill** (액체 등을) 엎지르다
- □ **stain** 얼룩
- □ **refuse** 거절[거부]하다
- □ **apologize** 사과하다
- □ **directly** 직접적으로

15
- □ **land** 착륙하다
- □ **customs** 세관
- □ **suitcase** 여행 가방
- □ **embarrassed** 당황스러운
- □ **fine** 벌금

16-17
- □ **rely on** …에 의존하다
- □ **stay awake** 깨어있다
- □ **refreshing** 신선한, 상쾌한
- □ **contain** …이 들어있다
- □ **cause** 야기[초래]하다; 원인
- □ **side effect** 부작용
- □ **lead to** …을 유발[초래]하다
- □ **sleeplessness** 불면증
- □ **irregular** 불규칙적인
- □ **heartbeat** 심장박동
- □ **tooth decay** 충치

18 영어듣기 모의고사

정답 및 해설 p.53-55

1번부터 17번까지는 듣고 답하는 문제입니다.
1번부터 15번까지는 한 번만 들려주고, 16번부터 17번까지는 두 번 들려줍니다. 방송을 잘 듣고 답을 하기 바랍니다.

01

다음을 듣고, 여자가 하는 말의 목적으로 가장 적절한 것을 고르시오.

① 미술관 보수 공사를 알리려고
② 새 미술관 개관을 홍보하려고
③ 미술관 최신 시설을 소개하려고
④ 미술관 에어컨 고장을 불평하려고
⑤ 미술관 보수에 필요한 기금을 마련하려고

02

대화를 듣고, 두 사람이 하는 말의 주제로 가장 적절한 것을 고르시오.

① 이직 시 고려 사항
② 이력서를 잘 쓰는 방법
③ 직장 내 의사소통의 중요성
④ 구직 면접 시 주의해야 할 점
⑤ 적성에 맞는 직업을 구해야 하는 이유

03

대화를 듣고, 두 사람의 관계를 가장 잘 나타낸 것을 고르시오.

① 임대인 — 세입자
② 호텔 직원 — 투숙객
③ 아파트 관리인 — 입주민
④ 렌터카 회사 직원 — 고객
⑤ 부동산 중개업자 — 임대인

04

대화를 듣고, 그림에서 대화의 내용과 일치하지 않는 것을 고르시오.

05

대화를 듣고, 여자가 남자에게 부탁한 일로 가장 적절한 것을 고르시오.

① to book a wedding hall
② to reserve a hotel room
③ to buy party decorations
④ to invite friends to a party
⑤ to choose a wedding dress

06

대화를 듣고, 여자가 새로운 카드로 바꾸고 싶어 하는 이유를 고르시오. 3점

① 연회비가 비싸서
② 할인 혜택이 줄어서
③ 할부 수수료가 높아서
④ 주유 할인 혜택이 없어서
⑤ 고객 서비스가 안 좋아서

07

대화를 듣고, 남자가 지불할 금액을 고르시오.

① $18　② $20　③ $25
④ $27　⑤ $30

08

대화를 듣고, 시드니 하버 브리지에 관해 두 사람이 언급하지 않은 것을 고르시오.

① 재료　② 길이　③ 무게
④ 모양　⑤ 준공 기간

09

Boyana 교회에 관한 다음 내용을 듣고, 일치하지 않는 것을 고르시오. 3점

① 총 세 개의 건물로 구성되어 있다.
② 첫 번째 건물은 10세기에 지어졌다.
③ 두 번째 건물에는 많은 벽화가 있다.
④ 유네스코 세계 문화유산으로 지정되었다.
⑤ 세 번째 건물은 19세기 말에 지어졌다.

18회

10

다음 표를 보면서 대화를 듣고, 여자가 구입할 매트리스를 고르시오.

	Model	Size	Soft / Firm	Price
①	A	Single	Firm	$450
②	B	Double	Soft	$600
③	C	Single	Soft	$400
④	D	Double	Firm	$500
⑤	E	Single	Firm	$550

11

대화를 듣고, 여자의 마지막 말에 대한 남자의 응답으로 가장 적절한 것을 고르시오.

① Then I'll check the GPS.
② Please leave your address here.
③ No problem. I know where it is.
④ The library is closed at this time.
⑤ All library books must be returned today.

12

대화를 듣고, 남자의 마지막 말에 대한 여자의 응답으로 가장 적절한 것을 고르시오.

① The play starts at 6:30.
② It's called *The Lost World*.
③ It'll be performed at Grace Hall.
④ It was one of the best plays ever.
⑤ I'm going to a play with my mother.

13

대화를 듣고, 남자의 마지막 말에 대한 여자의 응답으로 가장 적절한 것을 고르시오.

Woman: ______________________________

① Take this pill after meals.
② Just a few minutes at most.
③ My headaches got even worse.
④ I've been waiting for a long time.
⑤ He had another appointment yesterday.

14

대화를 듣고, 여자의 마지막 말에 대한 남자의 응답으로 가장 적절한 것을 고르시오.

Man: ______________________________

① Thanks! I can see well now.
② I want to change the frames, too.
③ They'll be ready by four o'clock.
④ You don't need to replace the lenses.
⑤ You picked them up a few weeks ago.

15

다음 상황 설명을 듣고, Diana가 Nick에게 할 말로 가장 적절한 것을 고르시오. 3점

Diana: ______________________________

① I'm not good at math, either.
② Tell me how to improve my grades.
③ You'll do better on your final exam.
④ Why don't you take an online course?
⑤ You should concentrate in math class.

[16-17] 다음을 듣고, 물음에 답하시오.

16

남자가 하는 말의 목적으로 가장 적절한 것은?

① 쇼핑몰 할인 행사를 안내하려고
② 새로운 쇼핑몰 개장을 알리려고
③ 온라인 쇼핑몰 사이트를 광고하려고
④ 쇼핑몰 이용의 불편함을 항의하려고
⑤ 쇼핑몰을 개선할 방법을 제안하려고

17

쇼핑몰에 관해 언급되지 <u>않은</u> 것은?

① 매장 수　② 주차장　③ 옥상 정원
④ 교통편　⑤ 폐장 시간

정답 및 해설 p.55

녹음을 다시 한 번 듣고, 빈칸에 알맞은 말을 쓰시오.

01

W: Good morning, everyone. Thank you for visiting the California Art Museum. I have something to tell you today. We will _______ _______ starting next Monday. The renovations will last one month. The museum's air-conditioning is currently _______ _______ _______ in some rooms. It will be replaced. There will also be touchscreen displays with video explanations of our artwork on the first and second floors. Unfortunately, during this time, all floors under renovation will be closed. However, you can still see displays on the other floors. The museum will _______ _______ _______ _______, from 10:00 a.m. to 5:00 p.m., during the renovation. Thank you.

02

M: Hi, Sarah. I heard _______ _______ _______ _______ at a construction company. Congratulations!

W: Thanks, Doug. I started working there last month.

M: I hope I can get a job soon, too.

W: Have you _______ _______ _______ _______ recently?

M: Yes, I have. But I haven't received any interview requests yet.

W: Don't worry. I'm sure you'll get one if you keep trying.

M: Do you know what I can do to increase my chances of getting a job interview?

W: Well, try to make your résumé sound as impressive as possible. Don't make it too long.

M: What do you mean?

W: _______ _______ your work experience, and show that you are ready for the work.

M: Okay. Thanks for your advice!

03

W: Hi. Can I help you?

M: Yes. I want to talk to you about a room.

W: All right. We have _______ _______ _______ _______. What exactly are you looking for?

M: Well, actually, I have a room in my apartment for rent.

W: Oh, I see. You want to rent out a room. I can help you with that, too.

M: Great. What do I need to do?

W: First, _______ _______ _______ _______. It describes your room and how much rent you plan to charge.

M: All right. What else should I do?

W: Actually, that's it. We'll contact you if we find someone _______ _______ _______ _______ _______.

M: Okay. I'll wait for your call.

04

M: Wow, look out the window. What an amazing view!

W: Yeah! Look at those two birds _______ _______ _______ _______!

M: It's beautiful! That small boat near the beach looks nice, too.

W: It sure does. This scenery almost looks like a painting.

M: You're right. Look at that sandcastle. Maybe it was built by some children.

W: Yeah, I _______ _______ _______ _______ when I was young.

M: Me, too. Let's go to the beach after breakfast.

W: Good idea. We can sit on the two beach chairs under that big palm tree.

M: Yeah, and then shall we go to the café _______ _______ _______ on top of the hill?

W: Sure.

05

M: What are you doing, Amanda?

W: I'm _______ _______ _______ for my friend Amy's bridal shower.

M: What's a bridal shower?

W: It's a party for the bride before the wedding. Friends give her gifts and fun things like that.

M: I see. Where are you going to have it?

W: I'm not sure yet. I need to _______ _______ _______ _______.

M: How about a hotel room?

W: A hotel room? Wouldn't that be expensive?

M: Well, my father works at a hotel, so I can get a family discount. If you want, I can book a room for you.

W: Really? Then could you _______ _______ _______ for me? I'd love to have the bridal shower there.

M: Sure.

06

W: Dan, can I ask you a question?

M: Sure, what is it?

W: What kind of credit card do you use?

M: I use a Trust Bank credit card. Why do you ask?

W: Well, I'm _______ _______ _______ credit cards.

M: Oh, are your annual fees too high?

W: Not really. But I spend a lot of money on gas, and my card _______ _______ _______ _______.

M: Why don't you go to Trust Bank? They have a card that gives a 5% discount at gas stations.

W: That sounds good.

M: They also _______ _______ _______ _______. You can call them any time if you have any problems.

W: Great. I'll visit them today.

07

W: Welcome to Marley Stadium! How can I help you?

M: I'd like to buy tickets _______ _______ _______ _______.

W: Okay. But only tickets for the blue and red stands are left.

M: How much do they cost?

W: Blue stand tickets are $15, and red stand tickets are $10.

M: Why are the blue stands _______ _______?

W: The seats there are much closer to the field.

M: In that case, please give me two tickets for the blue stands. Are there _______ _______ _______?

W: You can get a 10% discount if you have a membership card.

M: Great. Here is my membership card and cash.

W: Here are your two tickets.

08

M: How was your trip to Australia, Ashley?

W: It was great! I finally saw the Sydney Harbour Bridge.

M: Cool. How was it?

W: As you may know, it's one of the world's largest steel bridges, and _______ _______ _______ is 3,770 feet. It was amazing to see.

M: I bet it was.

W: Did you know that its nickname is "The Coat Hanger"?

M: No, but I can guess why. Is it because of its arch shape?

W: Yes. It must have been _______ _______ _______. I read that it took almost ten years to construct.

M: Wow! That's a long time.

W: I climbed to the top of the bridge, too. That's _______ _______ _______ from the trip.

M: Sounds like you had a great time.

09

M: Let's move on to Boyana Church. It is located near Sofia, the capital of Bulgaria. It _______ _______ _______ _______. The first building was built in the 10th century. At the beginning of the 13th century, the second, two-story building was added. This second building has many paintings on its walls. They are _______ _______ _______ _______ _______ of eastern European medieval art. Because of the paintings, Boyana Church has even been named a UNESCO World Heritage Site. The church's third building was constructed in the early 19th century. _______ _______ _______ _______, we'll only be able to look at them for 15 minutes. I hope you enjoy them.

10

M: Hello. Can I help you find something?

W: Yes, I would like to buy a new mattress.

M: Okay, you've come to the right place. We have many great mattresses. What size do you want?

W: I'm just looking for _______ _______ _______.

M: How about this one? It is soft and feels really comfortable.

W: It looks nice. But I've been _______ _______ _______ recently, so I want a firm mattress.

M: Oh, then two of them would suit your needs.

W: I see. Is there any _______ _______ _______ between them?

M: Yes, one of them is $100 cheaper.

W: Then I'll take the cheaper one.

11

W: Hi. Please take me to the Applewood Public Library.

M: I've _______ _______ _______ _______. Where is it?

W: I don't know, either. I am new here.

M: (Then I'll check the GPS.)

12

M: How are you, Rebecca? You look excited.

W: Hi, John. Actually, I'm going to see a play this evening.

M: Wow. What's _______ _______ _______ _______ _______?

W: (It's called *The Lost World*.)

13

M: Hi. My name is Harry Rose.

W: Hello, Mr. Rose. Do you _______ _______ _______ with Dr. Kaine today?

M: Yes, I do. I called you yesterday.

W: Oh, yes. I remember now. Can you tell me what your problem is?

M: I have a bad headache. I started _______ _______ yesterday, and it's still bothering me.

W: Have you experienced similar symptoms before?

M: No, this is the first time. I'm usually quite healthy.

W: I see. Please _______ _______ _______ _______ and then take a seat in the waiting room.

M: All right. How long will I have to wait to see him?

W: (Just a few minutes at most.)

14

M: Good morning! How can I help you today?

W: Hello. I bought these glasses here about two months ago.

M: Ah, yes. Those are some of our _______ _______ _______. Is there anything wrong with them?

W: Well, I dropped them several times recently, and now I can't see well. I think the lenses _______ _______.

M: Let me see. *[Pause]* There are many scratches on the surface of your lenses. Would you like to replace them?

W: Yes, please. How much will that cost?

M: It will be $50.

W: That sounds reasonable. When can I _______ _______ _______?

M: (They'll be ready by four o'clock.)

15

W: Diana is _______ _______ _______ _______ of high school. She used to struggle in math class and feel stressed out about her grades. However, she is doing much better now. She improved because she _______ _______ _______ _______ _______ for six months. Today, she and her classmates received their midterm exam grades, and Diana got an A. However, her best friend, Nick, looks very disappointed. He got a very low score. He asks Diana for help to improve his math. Diana wants to _______ _______ _______ _______ what she did. In this situation, what would Diana most likely say to Nick?

Diana: (Why don't you take an online course?)

16-17

M: Here's some good news for you. These days, many people like to shop online because it is cheap and convenient. However, shopping at a nice mall can _______ _______ _______ _______. That's why you should visit the newly-opened Western Mall. This mall offers quality items at cheap prices. It _______ _______ _______ _______ _______ customers can move around all its 50 stores easily. And there are plenty of parking spaces in the mall's large parking garage. In addition, it has a rooftop garden where you can relax. The number 17 bus stops right across from the mall. The mall will open for the first time this Sunday at 9:00 a.m. On that day, you can get special gifts just for visiting the mall. So take a trip downtown and _______ _______ _______ _______ _______ with your friends.

18 Word & Expressions

01
- □ undergo 겪다
- □ renovation 보수, 개조
- □ last 지속되다
- □ currently 현재
- □ out of order 고장 난
- □ replace 교체하다
- □ artwork 예술품
- □ maintain 유지하다
- □ regular hours 정상 영업시간

02
- □ construction 건축, 건설
- □ apply for …에 지원하다
- □ request 요청
- □ résumé 이력서
- □ impressive 인상적인
- □ focus on …에 초점을 맞추다

03
- □ plenty of 많은
- □ available 이용할[구할] 수 있는
- □ rent out …을 임대하다
- □ fill out (서식을) 작성하다
- □ charge (요금·값을) 청구하다
- □ contact 연락하다

04
- □ scenery 경치, 풍경
- □ sandcastle 모래성
- □ used to-v …하곤 했다
- □ palm tree 야자수
- □ flag 깃발

05
- □ decoration 장식품
- □ bridal shower 신부를 위한 축하 파티
- □ bride 신부
- □ book 예약하다
- □ make a reservation 예약하다

06
- □ annual fee 연회비
- □ gas 휘발유
- □ gas station 주유소
- □ excellent 훌륭한, 탁월한

07
- □ stand 서다; *(경기장의) 관중석
- □ field 들판; *경기장

08
- □ steel 강철
- □ length 길이
- □ bet 확신하다
- □ coat hanger 옷걸이
- □ arch 아치형의
- □ construct 건설하다

09
- □ located …에 위치한
- □ capital 수도
- □ consist of …로 구성되다
- □ story 이야기; *층
- □ example 예; *(대표적인) 본보기, 전형
- □ medieval 중세의
- □ heritage 유산
- □ protect 보호하다

10
- □ comfortable 편안한
- □ back 허리
- □ pain (육체의) 아픔, 통증
- □ firm 딱딱한, 단단한
- □ suit 맞다, 적합하다

12
- □ play 연극
- □ perform 공연하다

13
- □ appointment 약속, 예약
- □ dizzy 어지러운
- □ bother 귀찮게 하다, 성가시게 하다
- □ symptom 증상
- □ pill 알약
- □ at most 기껏해야

14
- □ frame 테
- □ drop 떨어뜨리다
- □ scratch 긁다; 긁힌 자국
- □ surface 표면
- □ reasonable (가격이) 적정한
- □ pick up …을 찾다[찾아오다]

15
- □ struggle 분투[고투]하다, 애쓰다
- □ improve 나아지다, 향상시키다
- □ disappointed 실망한
- □ concentrate 집중하다

16-17
- □ convenient 편리한
- □ enjoyable 즐거운
- □ quality 질; *고급의
- □ parking garage 주차장
- □ rooftop 옥상

19 영어듣기 모의고사

1번부터 17번까지는 듣고 답하는 문제입니다.
1번부터 15번까지는 한 번만 들려주고, 16번부터 17번까지는 두 번 들려줍니다. 방송을 잘 듣고 답을 하기 바랍니다.

01

다음을 듣고, 여자가 하는 말의 목적으로 가장 적절한 것을 고르시오.

① 캠프장을 홍보하려고
② 캠핑의 장점을 설명하려고
③ 입장 시간 변경을 공지하려고
④ 주변 관광 명소를 소개하려고
⑤ 다양한 야외 활동을 추천하려고

02

대화를 듣고, 두 사람이 하는 말의 주제로 가장 적절한 것을 고르시오.

① 환경 오염의 주요 원인
② 쓰레기 분리수거 방법
③ 저렴한 셔츠 구입 요령
④ 다양한 업사이클링 상품
⑤ 환경 오염을 줄이는 생활 습관

03

대화를 듣고, 두 사람의 관계를 가장 잘 나타낸 것을 고르시오.

① 매표원 — 관람객 ② 경찰관 — 용의자
③ 극장 직원 — 입장객 ④ 공항 직원 — 탑승객
⑤ 관광 가이드 — 관광객

04

대화를 듣고, 그림에서 대화의 내용과 일치하지 않는 것을 고르시오.

05

대화를 듣고, 여자가 남자에게 부탁한 일로 가장 적절한 것을 고르시오.

① to call people to come early
② to get his friend to the party
③ to play badminton with his friend
④ to reserve a table at the restaurant
⑤ to hang up balloons and decorations

06

대화를 듣고, 남자가 전공을 바꾸려는 이유를 고르시오.

① 적성에 맞지 않아서
② 전공과목이 어려워서
③ 부모님이 바꾸기를 원해서
④ 미래에 대한 불확실성 때문에
⑤ 컴퓨터 공학을 전공하고 싶어서

07

대화를 듣고, 여자가 현금으로 지불할 금액을 고르시오. 3점

① $5 ② $10 ③ $20
④ $25 ⑤ $35

08

대화를 듣고, 초콜릿에 관해 두 사람이 언급하지 않은 것을 고르시오.

① 주원료 ② 첨가물 ③ 유래
④ 건강상 이점 ⑤ 요리법

09

오케스트라 단원 모집에 관한 다음 내용을 듣고, 일치하지 않는 것을 고르시오. 3점

① 바이올린 연주자를 모집한다.
② 지원자는 3년 이상의 경력이 있어야 한다.
③ 최근 연주 영상을 제출해야 한다.
④ 모든 참가자들에게 오디션 기회가 주어진다.
⑤ 접수 마감일은 8월 22일이다.

정답 및 해설 p.56-58

10

다음 표를 보면서 대화를 듣고, 여자가 구입할 카메라 모델을 고르시오.

< Types of DSLR Cameras >

	Model	Weight	Color	Battery Type	Price
①	A	300 g	black	disposable	$250
②	B	350 g	white	disposable	$500
③	C	450 g	white	rechargeable	$550
④	D	500 g	black	rechargeable	$600
⑤	E	700 g	white	rechargeable	$650

11

대화를 듣고, 여자의 마지막 말에 대한 남자의 응답으로 가장 적절한 것을 고르시오.

① Good idea. I'll call him right now.
② I already know what to buy for him.
③ I'm sure he'll love what you bought him.
④ I need to get a new pair of pants tomorrow.
⑤ I didn't give him a present on his birthday last year.

12

대화를 듣고, 남자의 마지막 말에 대한 여자의 응답으로 가장 적절한 것을 고르시오.

① When I finish it, I'll call you.
② That novel is one of my favorite books.
③ You should return the book in two weeks.
④ I'm sorry, but I cannot give you a discount.
⑤ One of them should be returned tomorrow.

13

대화를 듣고, 남자의 마지막 말에 대한 여자의 응답으로 가장 적절한 것을 고르시오.

Woman: ______________________

① Strange sleeping habits can be very scary.
② I'm glad you're an expert on sleepwalking.
③ I'll make an appointment with a doctor soon.
④ You must have dreamed about baseball, then.
⑤ I'm glad to know others talk in their sleep, too.

14

대화를 듣고, 여자의 마지막 말에 대한 남자의 응답으로 가장 적절한 것을 고르시오. 3점

Man: ______________________

① Store all your information on a smartphone.
② Don't surf the Internet too much on the road.
③ Buy electronic devices with larger memories.
④ Study a variety of topics instead of one thing.
⑤ Try to depend less on your electronic devices.

15

다음 상황 설명을 듣고, Angela가 고객 서비스 상담원에게 할 말로 가장 적절한 것을 고르시오.

Angela: ______________________

① Can you help me pick out a new phone?
② May I use your phone to call the airport?
③ Thank you so much for finding my phone.
④ Do you know where I can buy a travel bag?
⑤ Did you find a lost phone in one of your taxis?

[16-17] 다음을 듣고, 물음에 답하시오.

16

남자가 하는 말의 주제로 가장 적절한 것은?

① the best tasting fruit peels
② tools for peeling fruit easily
③ health benefits of fruit peels
④ ways to make use of fruit peels
⑤ how to get rid of smells in the kitchen

17

언급된 과일이 아닌 것은?

① orange ② banana ③ grape
④ pear ⑤ pineapple

녹음을 다시 한 번 듣고, 빈칸에 알맞은 말을 쓰시오.

01

W: Relaxing in nature is a great way to _______ _______ _______, and Rock Creek Campsite is a great place to do it. It is located just one hour outside of the city, and it has enough space for more than 50 tents. Our facilities include bathrooms, a swimming pool and a picnic area where you can barbecue. You can also _______ _______ _______ or rent a canoe to explore the nearby lake. However, you must make a reservation at least one week in advance. Give us a call today and start _______ _______ _______ for a weekend of fresh air and fun.

02

W: That shirt's interesting, Troy. Where did you get it?

M: Actually, I made it by upcycling.

W: Upcycling? What's that?

M: Upcycling is taking something old and turning it into something new. It's _______ _______ _______.

W: So you made this new shirt out of some old ones, right? Wow. That's cool.

M: Yeah, and it's a great way to help the earth. I'm always looking for new ways to protect the environment.

W: So am I. I _______ _______ _______ when I'm not using them. And I reduce waste by drinking from a mug instead of paper cups.

M: Those are good ways to help, too.

W: Thanks. I agree. We can _______ _______ _______ by not wasting what we have.

M: Exactly.

03

M: Excuse me, ma'am, but I can't let you go through the gate yet.

W: Why not? I have my ticket and my passport.

M: It's just a security check. I need to _______ _______ _______ _______.

W: Oh, okay. Here it is.

M: Do you have any bottles of liquid that are over 100 ml?

W: No, I put all the liquids in my checked baggage.

M: How about sharp objects, like a pocket knife? You can't fly with anything like that.

W: No, _______ _______ _______. I have a wallet, a digital camera, and a cell phone in my bag.

M: Okay. *[Pause]* Yes, it looks good. Now you can pass through the scanning equipment.

W: Okay.

M: Thank you _______ _______ _______. Have a nice trip!

04

W: Jeremy, is this your poster for the Healthy Lifestyles contest?

M: Yes, it is. I wrote the title "Walk and Bike to School!" at the top.

W: I see. It's near the sun, which is _______ _______ _______ a cloud.

M: Right. I wanted it to look real.

W: It does. And the tree on the left looks good too. I can see some apples on it.

M: Thanks. The school's big clock was the hardest part to draw.

W: It looks great! It's exactly _______ _______ _______ the real one.

M: What do you think of the two students? One is walking, and the other is riding a bike.

W: They're perfect. I'm sure you'll _______ _______ _______.

M: I hope so!

05

M: How are the preparations for Tom's birthday party going, Kate?

W: Good. You told everyone to come to the restaurant early, right?

M: Yes. Can I help you with anything? I can _______ _______ _______ or blow up balloons.

W: No, we've already taken care of those things.

M: I guess I will just come by the restaurant later then.

W: Actually, can you do something else?

M: Sure, what is it?

W: I _______ _______ _______ _______ Tom to the restaurant at six. But you need to trick him.

M: Okay. I'll play badminton with him after school. Then we'll _______ _______ _______ _______ for dinner at six.

W: Sounds like a good plan!

06

M: Jessica, your major is computer engineering, right?

W: Yes. It was the perfect choice.

M: I wish I could _______ _______ _______ _______ my major.

W: Oh, I'm sorry. Your major is philosophy, right? You don't like it?

M: Actually, my parents recommended it, and I love it. But I've been thinking about changing my major.

W: What's the problem? Is it too difficult?

M: Well, it's challenging, but not too hard. But I'm _______ _______ _______ _______.

W: Oh, I see. I guess it's not a great major for starting a career.

M: Exactly. I think I need to major in something more useful.

W: Well, how about computer engineering?

M: No, thanks! I don't like anything _______ _______ _______.

07

M: May I help you?

W: Yes. I'd like to exchange this coffee mug.

M: Is there a problem with it?

W: Not really. I got it _______ _______ _______, but I want a stainless steel one. This one is plastic.

M: All right. Here are the stainless steel ones. We have two different sizes.

W: I think the smaller size would be fine. Oh, this is a nice one. How much is it?

M: Well, that one is _______ _______ _______ the one you brought in. It's $35.

W: That's fine. I'll take it.

M: Okay. Your plastic mug was $20.

W: I have this $10 gift card. Can I use that and _______ _______ _______ _______ _______?

M: Of course you can.

08

M: This is where the chocolate is made.

W: Wow. So cacao beans are _______ _______ _______, right?

M: Yes, but sugar, milk, and artificial flavors are added.

W: I see. But where does chocolate come from originally?

M: _______ _______ _______ Central America. The Spanish learned how to make it from the Aztecs.

W: That's interesting. By the way, chocolate is generally unhealthy, isn't it?

M: Actually, it is. But dark chocolate _______ _______ _______ _______. It lowers blood pressure and stress.

W: I didn't know that.

M: It's true. We'll visit the gift shop next. You can purchase some chocolate there.

W: Sounds great.

19회

09

M: The Portsmouth City Orchestra is looking for a new violinist. Applicants must have _______ _______ _______ _______ of experience playing in an orchestra. A degree in music performance is preferred. Please send us a résumé, a cover letter, and a video of a recent performance. After _______ _______ _______, we will contact the top applicants. Auditions will be scheduled for early September. If necessary, a second round of auditions will be held shortly after. We expect to _______ _______ _______ _______ by September 15th. Please send your application by August 22nd. If you have any questions, you can email us at hiring@pco.org.

10

M: Hello, how may I help you?

W: I'm looking for a camera. _______ _______ _______ DSLR cameras.

M: Of course. Do you have a specific model in mind?

W: Not really, but I want a lighter one. I want to _______ _______ _______.

M: I think cameras under 500 g are convenient to carry.

W: Yeah, that sounds good. Oh, I heard that there is a white DSLR camera now.

M: That's right. The white ones were released just a year ago.

W: I want a white one _______ _______ _______ _______.

M: Okay. This camera would be perfect for you, but it's more than $500.

W: That's okay. I'll take that one.

11

W: Rob, did you buy a birthday present for Eric?

M: Not yet. I can't think of what to buy.

W: Neither can I. _______ _______ _______ _______ him what he needs?

M: (Good idea. I'll call him right now.)

12

M: Excuse me. Do you have *Great Expectations* by Charles Dickens?

W: Sorry. All of our copies are checked out right now.

M: I see. When can I _______ _______ _______?

W: (One of them should be returned tomorrow.)

13

M: Hi, Julia. Why the long face?

W: My sister said I _______ _______ _______ _______ again last night, but I can't remember anything.

M: That's interesting. Do you do it often?

W: Unfortunately, yes. She says I do it about three or four times a week.

M: That's quite often. What did you say last night?

W: She told me I was talking about a baseball game. _______ _______ _______ _______ about what I might say next time.

M: Well, I don't think it's dangerous.

W: I guess not. But it might cause a problem eventually. I'd like to know how to stop it.

M: Then you'd better _______ _______ _______ _______.

W: (I'll make an appointment with a doctor soon.)

14

W: Oh, no! I _______ _______ _______ again.

M: Does this happen a lot these days?

W: Yes, and I can't remember phone numbers.

M: I think I know the problem. You must have digital dementia.

W: Isn't that the disease that _______ _______ _______ _______ things?

M: It's something different. It means we forget things like passwords because we store them on electronic devices.

W: I see. So relying on phones and computers instead of memorizing things is bad for us?

M: Yes. If we keep doing it, our computers, phones, and tablet computers will become our memories.

W: That's terrible. _______ _______ _______ _______?

M: (Try to depend less on your electronic devices.)

15

W: After traveling in Australia, Angela _______ _______ _______ to Canada. When she arrives at the airport, she decides to take a taxi because she has a lot of luggage. She picks it up in a hurry and takes a taxi home. However, when she arrives at her house, she finds that _______ _______ _______ _______. She thinks about it and is sure that she had her phone when she got in the taxi. She _______ _______ _______ of the taxi company's customer service from her home phone. In this situation, what would Angela most likely say to the customer service representative?

Angela: (Did you find a lost phone in one of your taxis?)

16-17

M: Welcome to Earth News Today. You probably already know that fruit _______ _______ _______ _______ _______. But that's not all it's good for. After you've finished eating a piece of fruit, there are lots of things you can do with the peel. Orange peels, for example, can be mixed together with salt and used to clean your dirty pots and pans. And most of the stains on your shoes _______ _______ _______ _______ _______ with a banana peel. Also, grape skins are perfect for removing the smell of garlic from dishes and bowls. Finally, don't forget about pineapples. Their rough peels can be used to remove dirt and stains from stoves and microwaves. So the next time you're enjoying some fruit, _______ _______ _______ throwing the peel into the trash. There's probably something else you can do with it.

19 Word & Expressions

01
- □ **campsite** 야영지, 캠프장
- □ **located** …에 위치한
- □ **facility** 시설
- □ **barbecue** 바비큐하다
- □ **make a reservation** 예약하다
- □ **in advance** 미리

02
- □ **similar** 비슷한, 유사한
- □ **protect** 보호하다
- □ **turn off** (전원을) 끄다
- □ **electronics** 전자 기기
- □ **instead of** … 대신에
- □ **waste** 낭비하다

03
- □ **security** 보안
- □ **liquid** 액체
- □ **checked baggage** 위탁 수하물
- □ **sharp** 날카로운
- □ **pocket knife** 주머니칼
- □ **scanning equipment** 탐지기
- □ **cooperation** 협조

04
- □ **lifestyle** 생활 방식
- □ **partly** 부분적으로
- □ **prize** 상

05
- □ **preparation** 준비
- □ **hang up** …을 매달다
- □ **decoration** 장식품
- □ **take care of** …을 처리하다
- □ **come by** …에 들르다
- □ **trick** 속이다
- □ **reserve** 예약하다

06
- □ **major** 전공
- □ **computer engineering** 컴퓨터 공학
- □ **philosophy** 철학
- □ **recommend** 추천하다
- □ **challenging** 도전적인
- □ **career** 직업, 직장 생활
- □ **major in** …을 전공하다
- □ **useful** 유용한, 쓸모있는
- □ **related to** …와 관련이 있는

07
- □ **exchange** 교환하다
- □ **stainless steel** 스테인리스강(鋼)
- □ **bring in** …을 가져오다, …을 들여오다
- □ **rest** (어떤 것의) 나머지
- □ **in cash** 현금으로

08
- □ **ingredient** 원료, 재료
- □ **artificial flavor** 인공 향미료
- □ **come from** …에서 나오다[생산되다]
- □ **originally** 원래, 본래
- □ **benefit** 혜택, 이득
- □ **blood pressure** 혈압
- □ **purchase** 구매하다

09
- □ **applicant** 지원자
- □ **degree** 정도; *학위
- □ **résumé** 이력서
- □ **cover letter** 자기소개서
- □ **review** 검토하다
- □ **application** 지원서
- □ **contact** 연락하다
- □ **necessary** 필요한, 필수적인
- □ **round** 한 차례[회]

10
- □ **specific** 특정한
- □ **convenient** 편리한
- □ **release** 출시하다
- □ **rechargeable** 충전식인
- □ **disposable** 일회용의

12
- □ **copy** 복사; *한 부
- □ **check out** (책 등을) 대출하다

13
- □ **long face** 시무룩한 얼굴
- □ **talk in one's sleep** 잠꼬대를 하다
- □ **cause** 야기하다
- □ **expert** 전문가
- □ **sleepwalking** 몽유병

14
- □ **password** 비밀번호
- □ **dementia** 치매
- □ **store** 저장하다
- □ **electronic device** 전자 기기
- □ **rely on** …에 의존하다
- □ **memorize** 암기하다
- □ **surf** 인터넷을 검색하다
- □ **depend on** …에 의존하다

15
- □ **luggage** 짐
- □ **in a hurry** 서둘러
- □ **missing** 없어진, 실종된
- □ **dial** 전화를 걸다
- □ **representative** 대표, 대리인
- □ **lost** 길을 잃은; *분실된

16-17
- □ **peel** (과일 등의) 껍질; 껍질을 벗기다[깎다]
- □ **mix** 섞다
- □ **pot** 냄비
- □ **stain** 얼룩
- □ **wipe away** …을 닦아내다
- □ **remove** 제거하다
- □ **rough** 거친
- □ **stove** 가스레인지
- □ **microwave** 전자레인지
- □ **benefit** 이점
- □ **make use of** …을 이용하다
- □ **get rid of** …을 제거하다

20 영어듣기 모의고사

정답 및 해설 p.59-61

1번부터 17번까지는 듣고 답하는 문제입니다.
1번부터 15번까지는 한 번만 들려주고, 16번부터 17번까지는 두 번 들려줍니다. 방송을 잘 듣고 답을 하기 바랍니다.

01

다음을 듣고, 여자가 하는 말의 목적으로 가장 적절한 것을 고르시오. 3점

① 출입문 비밀번호 변경을 알리려고
② CCTV 설치의 필요성을 강조하려고
③ 건물 보안 시스템 교체를 요청하려고
④ 도난 사고 방지를 위한 회의를 공지하려고
⑤ 아파트 외부인 출입의 문제점을 설명하려고

02

대화를 듣고, 여자의 의견으로 가장 적절한 것을 고르시오.

① 휴식을 취하는 여행을 해야 한다.
② 지역 관광 명소를 방문해야 한다.
③ 해외여행은 피로감을 증가시킨다.
④ 여행 전에 미리 계획을 세워야 한다.
⑤ 여행 중 다양한 스포츠 활동을 해야 한다.

03

대화를 듣고, 두 사람의 관계를 가장 잘 나타낸 것을 고르시오.

① 고객 — 수리공
② 세입자 — 집주인
③ 고객 — 부동산 중개인
④ 투숙객 — 호텔 종업원
⑤ 건축 설계사 — 관리소 직원

04

대화를 듣고, 그림에서 대화의 내용과 일치하지 않는 것을 고르시오.

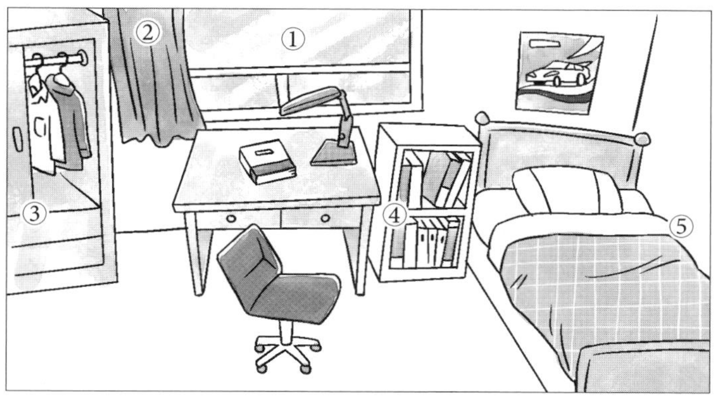

05

대화를 듣고, 남자가 할 일로 가장 적절한 것을 고르시오.

① 식당 예약하기
② 저녁 메뉴 정하기
③ 식당 위치 검색하기
④ 블로그에 후기 올리기
⑤ 휴대전화 배터리 충전하기

06

대화를 듣고, 여자가 입주자 회의에 참석하지 못하는 이유를 고르시오.

① 몸이 안 좋아서
② 휴가를 갈 예정이라서
③ 고객과 약속이 있어서
④ 차량 등록을 해야 해서
⑤ 자동차를 수리해야 해서

07

대화를 듣고, 남자가 지불할 금액을 고르시오. 3점

① \$400 ② \$410 ③ \$420 ④ \$540 ⑤ \$600

08

대화를 듣고, 벼룩시장에 관해 두 사람이 언급하지 않은 것을 고르시오.

① 개최 시기 ② 판매 물품 ③ 판매 가격 ④ 개최 목적 ⑤ 개최 장소

09

Atacama 사막에 관한 다음 내용을 듣고, 일치하지 않는 것을 고르시오. 3점

① 연평균 강우량은 약 15mm이다.
② 비가 전혀 내리지 않는 곳도 있다.
③ 칠레의 내륙에 위치해 있다.
④ 낮에는 기온이 30도 이상 올라간다.
⑤ 영화 촬영지로 이용된 적이 있다.

10

다음 표를 보면서 대화를 듣고, 여자가 예약할 호텔을 고르시오.

< Hotels around Shoreville >

	Hotel	Price (a night)	Location	Breakfast
①	A	$100	Beach	Included
②	B	$140	Beach	Not included
③	C	$120	Mountain	Included
④	D	$130	City	Included
⑤	E	$175	City	Not included

11

대화를 듣고, 남자의 마지막 말에 대한 여자의 응답으로 가장 적절한 것을 고르시오.

① The train will not be delayed.
② You're at the wrong platform.
③ I have been waiting for too long.
④ It takes two hours to get to London.
⑤ The train is running 30 minutes late.

12

대화를 듣고, 여자의 마지막 말에 대한 남자의 응답으로 가장 적절한 것을 고르시오.

① I hope your presentation goes well.
② I took some medicine 20 minutes ago.
③ When do you think you'll be finished?
④ Then you should go home and get some sleep.
⑤ I was really tired during her presentation, too.

13

대화를 듣고, 여자의 마지막 말에 대한 남자의 응답으로 가장 적절한 것을 고르시오.

Man: ______________________________

① I did my best. Please don't be upset.
② There's no excuse for your behavior.
③ I just hope your dog will be all right.
④ Let's meet somewhere else tomorrow.
⑤ No problem. You're just doing your job.

14

대화를 듣고, 남자의 마지막 말에 대한 여자의 응답으로 가장 적절한 것을 고르시오.

Woman: ______________________________

① I am pleased that you got good grades.
② The same thing will happen next time.
③ You are naturally good at giving speeches.
④ Contests are never a waste of time if you win.
⑤ This experience will help you improve in the future.

15

다음 상황 설명을 듣고, James가 Amy에게 할 말로 가장 적절한 것을 고르시오.

James: ______________________________

① I'll bring some sandwiches for lunch.
② Sorry, but can we postpone our plans?
③ You should see a doctor as soon as possible.
④ I will be a little bit late, so could you wait for me?
⑤ Let's go somewhere else instead of the amusement park.

[16-17] 다음을 듣고, 물음에 답하시오.

16

남자가 하는 말의 목적으로 가장 적절한 것은?

① to announce changes to a school trip
② to review a school volunteering event
③ to recruit students for a volunteer program
④ to explain why it is important to help other people
⑤ to introduce various activities available during vacation

17

언급된 활동이 아닌 것은?

① 약품 제공하기
② 음식 제공하기
③ 교실 짓기
④ TV 설치하기
⑤ 영어 가르치기

정답 및 해설 p.61

녹음을 다시 한 번 듣고, 빈칸에 알맞은 말을 쓰시오.

01

W: Attention, Tower Manor residents. As some of you already know, a resident on the first floor was robbed. After reviewing the CCTV recordings, we were able to identify a suspect. To _______ _______ _______, we decided to make some immediate changes. We are placing tighter controls on outsider access. A stronger security system _______ _______ _______ our gates. It is protected by a new password that can be found in the management office. Please visit the office to get the new access code, and please _______ _______ _______. If you have any questions, please feel free to contact the management office. Thank you.

02

M: Jessie, have you made plans for our trip to Hawaii?
W: Not yet. _______ _______ _______ _______ to do?
M: I want to do lots of outdoor activities, such as hiking, swimming, surfing, and scuba diving.
W: Do you really want to try everything?
M: Um... _______ _______ _______ you don't like my idea.
W: I don't think we can do that many activities. We'll be there only for three days.
M: Then what would you like to do?
W: _______ _______ _______ the time at the beach relaxing and enjoying the sunshine.
M: That sounds a bit boring to me.
W: Well, I don't want to come back from vacation more tired than I am now.
M: Okay. Maybe we can just do one or two activities.

03

[Cell phone rings.]
W: Hello?
M: Hi, Mrs. Johnson. It's Harry Goldman. I received your message this morning. What can I do for you?
W: Oh, thank you for returning my call. There's a problem with the house.
M: What is it?
W: _______ _______ _______ _______ a leak in the ceiling of the storage room.
M: I just had the ceiling repaired last summer. Are you sure?
W: Yes. When it rained, _______ _______ _______. Everything I put there got wet.
M: I'm sorry to hear that. Why don't I come by this afternoon and take a look?
W: That would be great.
M: If I can't _______ _______ _______, I will call a repairman to come and do it.
W: Thank you.

04

W: Joe, have you finished moving into the dormitory?
M: Yeah. I really like my room.
W: Cool! Did you say it is a single room?
M: Yes. _______ _______ _______ _______, but there is a big window that lets in a lot of natural light.
W: Oh, that's great.
M: It also has a thick curtain, so I can sleep _______ _______ _______ _______ _______.
W: That's good. What else is in the room?
M: There's a large closet next to the window.
W: Nice. How about a bookshelf?
M: There is _______ _______ _______ _______ right next to my desk.
W: Good. Do you think you'll sleep well there?
M: Yes. There's a nice comfortable bed in the right corner.

05

M: Amanda, do you have any suggestions for dinner tonight?

W: Actually, there is a new restaurant that I really want to try.

M: Oh. _______ _______ _______ _______?

W: It's called Pasta Heaven.

M: I've heard of it. It sounds like the food is really delicious. But it might be _______ _______ _______ _______ _______ there.

W: You're right, and they don't take reservations.

M: Then why don't we leave right now?

W: Okay. But I don't know the exact location, and _______ _______ _______ _______ _______.

M: It's not a big deal. I can look it up on my phone.

W: That would be great. See if you can find it.

M: All right. I'll try now.

06

M: Honey, you look upset. What's wrong?

W: Well, _______ _______ _______ _______ _______, so I took it to the mechanic.

M: Really? What happened to it?

W: Someone hit it while it was parked in the parking lot and just drove away.

M: That's terrible. Maybe a security camera filmed the license plate.

W: Unfortunately, there isn't a camera _______ _______ _______ _______ we park.

M: You're kidding! We need to complain about this at the residents' meeting on Wednesday.

W: Well, _______ _______ _______ _______. I have an appointment with a customer on Wednesday.

M: That's okay. I'll go alone and insist that they install more security cameras.

W: Thanks, honey. That would be great.

07

W: Welcome to Fitness Zone. How may I help you?

M: I'm thinking of purchasing a membership.

W: Great. _______ _______ _______ would you like to register for?

M: I'm undecided. How much is it for one month?

W: One month costs $100.

M: Can I get a discount if I _______ _______ _______ _______ _______?

W: Yes. If you resister for three to five months, you get a 10% discount. For six months or more, the discount is 30%.

M: I'll sign up for six months then. Also, I have a 10% off coupon.

W: Sorry, this coupon is expired. But you can still get $10 off _______ _______ _______ _______.

M: That's great. Thanks for the help.

08

M: Tina, did you _______ _______ _______ on the local bulletin board?

W: No. What did it say?

M: There is going to be a flea market next weekend.

W: How exciting! _______ _______ _______ _______ will be sold?

M: I've heard there will be a lot of arts and crafts—paintings, furniture, pottery, and other things.

W: That sounds interesting. Is there any special reason for it?

M: It _______ _______ _______ _______ the work of local artists in our town.

W: What a good idea! I'd love to go and see what local artists are making.

M: Why don't we go together? It's going to be held in City Square.

W: Perfect. I can't wait to go.

09

M: Our next destination is the Atacama Desert in Chile. It is _______ _______ _______ _______ _______ on earth. Its average rainfall is only about 15 mm per year. There are even places there where it has never rained. This is surprising, since the desert lies right alongside Chile's coast, near the Pacific Ocean. And because of its high altitude, it can become very cold at night. But temperatures can _______ _______ _______ 30°C in the daytime. Due to its extreme environment, the Atacama Desert has been compared to the planet Mars. It's even _______ _______ _______ a filming location for movies about Mars.

10

[Telephone rings.]

M: Five-Star Travel Agency. How can I help you?

W: I'm going to Shoreville next month, and I'd like to _______ _______ _______ _______ for two nights.

M: Great. Do you have any particular place in mind?

W: Not really, but my budget won't allow any more than $150 a night.

M: Okay. We have hotels on the beach, near the mountains, and in the city. _______ _______ _______ _______?

W: I'd like to stay anywhere except near the mountains.

M: I see. Would you like to have breakfast included or not?

W: I usually don't eat in the morning, so it's not necessary.

M: Then I think I have found a hotel that _______ _______ _______.

11

M: Pardon me, but is this the right platform for the train to London?

W: Yes, but the train _______ _______ _______.

M: Do you know how long the delay will be?

W: (The train is running 30 minutes late.)

12

W: I _______ _______ _______ _______ preparing a presentation for today.

M: You did? Did you give the presentation yet?

W: Yes. The class just ended. I'm really exhausted.

M: (Then you should go home and get some sleep.)

13

W: Good morning. Welcome to Greenstone National Park.

M: Thank you. I'm just here to _______ _______ _______ _______ my dog.

W: Oh, I'm sorry, sir. You can't bring pets into the park.

M: Really? Why not?

W: It's a park rule. Your pet could hurt or kill small animals in the park.

M: Oh, I didn't think about that.

W: We also don't allow pets because they could cause damage.

M: _______ _______ _______ _______?

W: Well, they could dig up the grass or flowers.

M: Oh, now I understand. In that case, I'll bring my dog home and _______ _______ _______ _______ _______.

W: I'm very sorry for the inconvenience.

M: (No problem. You're just doing your job.)

20회

14

M: Mom, I'm home.

W: Oh, hi, Ted. How was the speech contest?

M: _______ _______ _______ _______, Mom. It was terrible.

W: Uh-oh. Did something go wrong?

M: Yes. I was extremely nervous, and I totally forgot my speech.

W: _______ _______ _______ _______ _______ you spoke in front of so many people. It's no wonder you felt nervous.

M: I don't know... Now I feel like I've wasted my time on something useless.

W: Do you think it was useless?

M: Yes. I _______ _______ _______ _______ for my upcoming exams instead.

W: I don't think so.

M: Why not? Now I might get bad grades on my exams, too.

W: (This experience will help you improve in the future.)

15

W: James is _______ _______ _______ going on a date with his girlfriend, Amy, this afternoon. They have made plans to visit a newly opened amusement park that looks like a lot of fun. _______ _______ _______, James feels hungry, so he eats a sandwich. Just as he is about to leave his house, though, his stomach starts to hurt. He takes some medicine, but it just _______ _______. He begins to worry that he is really sick. He gives Amy a phone call to let her know he wants to meet her some other time. In this situation, what would James most likely say to Amy?

James: (Sorry, but can we postpone our plans?)

16-17

M: Do you have any special plans for this summer vacation? Why don't you _______ _______ _______ a great program that will allow you to travel while helping others? This year, Jameson High School's Volunteer Club is taking a trip to Myanmar. We will spend two weeks there providing medication and food _______ _______ _______ _______. You will also help build a new classroom at a school and teach English to children. Any students who are interested in this program can apply. Please submit a one-page essay on why you want to go and what skills you have. Applications are due April 30th, and you can turn them in at the school's activities office. If you have any questions, please _______ _______ _______ come up to the office and ask us. Thank you for your time.

20 Word & Expressions

01
- □ resident 거주자
- □ rob 털다, 도둑질하다
- □ identify 찾다, 발견하다
- □ suspect 용의자
- □ guarantee 보장하다
- □ immediate 즉각적인
- □ control 통제
- □ outsider 외부인
- □ access 접근
- □ security system 보안 장치
- □ install 설치하다
- □ management office 관리사무실
- □ private 사적인, 비공개의

02
- □ outdoor activity 야외 활동
- □ surfing 파도타기
- □ scuba diving 스쿠버 다이빙

03
- □ leak 누수
- □ ceiling 천장
- □ storage room 창고
- □ patch 때우다, 덧대다
- □ repairman 수리공

04
- □ dormitory 기숙사
- □ let in …을 들어오게 하다
- □ natural sunlight 자연광
- □ closet 옷장

05
- □ suggestion 제안
- □ reservation 예약
- □ exact 정확한
- □ location 위치
- □ look up …을 찾아보다

06
- □ mechanic 정비공
- □ parking lot 주차장
- □ security 보안
- □ film 촬영하다
- □ license plate 차량 번호판
- □ make it (모임 등에) 참석하다
- □ insist 주장하다

07
- □ membership 회원권
- □ register 등록하다
- □ undecided 결정하지 못한
- □ sign up 등록하다
- □ expire 만료되다

08
- □ notice 주목; *공고문
- □ flea market 벼룩시장
- □ item 물품, 품목
- □ craft 공예품
- □ pottery 도자기
- □ be supposed to-v …하기로 되어 있다
- □ promote 홍보하다

09
- □ destination 목적지
- □ rainfall 강우(량)
- □ alongside … 옆에, …와 나란히
- □ altitude 고도
- □ extreme 극단적인
- □ compare to …와 비교하다
- □ Mars 화성

10
- □ particular 특별한
- □ budget 예산
- □ allow 허락[허용]하다
- □ except …을 제외하고
- □ included 포함된
- □ necessary 필요한, 필수적인

11
- □ platform (기차역의) 플랫폼
- □ delay 지연시키다; 지연, 지체
- □ run 달리다; *운행하다

12
- □ stay up 깨어있다
- □ presentation 발표
- □ exhausted 진이 다 빠진

13
- □ take a walk 산책하다
- □ damage 손상, 피해
- □ dig up …을 파헤치다
- □ inconvenience 불편
- □ excuse 변명

14
- □ bring up (화제를) 꺼내다
- □ extremely 극도로
- □ totally 완전히
- □ speech 연설
- □ waste 낭비하다
- □ useless 쓸모없는
- □ upcoming 다가오는
- □ naturally 선천적으로
- □ improve 향상시키다

15
- □ go on a date 데이트하러 가다
- □ some other time 나중에 다시
- □ postpone 연기하다

16-17
- □ take part in …에 참가하다
- □ medication 약품
- □ in need 어려움에 처한
- □ submit 제출하다
- □ application 지원서
- □ turn in …을 제출하다
- □ recruit 모집하다

21 영어듣기 모의고사

1번부터 17번까지는 듣고 답하는 문제입니다.
1번부터 15번까지는 한 번만 들려주고, 16번부터 17번까지는 두 번 들려줍니다. 방송을 잘 듣고 답을 하기 바랍니다.

01

다음을 듣고, 여자가 하는 말의 목적으로 가장 적절한 것을 고르시오.

① 유학 생활의 장단점을 설명하려고
② 인기 있는 학습 프로그램을 홍보하려고
③ 교환 학생 프로그램 지원 방법을 소개하려고
④ 교환 학생 프로그램의 변경 사항을 공지하려고
⑤ 폐강 과목 선정 기준의 문제점에 대해 항의하려고

02

대화를 듣고, 두 사람이 하는 말의 주제로 가장 적절한 것을 고르시오.

① 흔한 이름의 단점
② 친구를 사귀는 방법
③ 좋은 성적을 받는 비법
④ 이름을 잘 기억하는 방법
⑤ 수학 시험을 잘 못 본 이유

03

대화를 듣고, 두 사람의 관계를 가장 잘 나타낸 것을 고르시오.

① 의사 — 환자
② 경찰관 — 운전자
③ 간호사 — 영업자
④ 보험사 직원 — 고객
⑤ 운전자 — 사고 피해자

04

대화를 듣고, 그림에서 대화의 내용과 일치하지 않는 것을 고르시오.

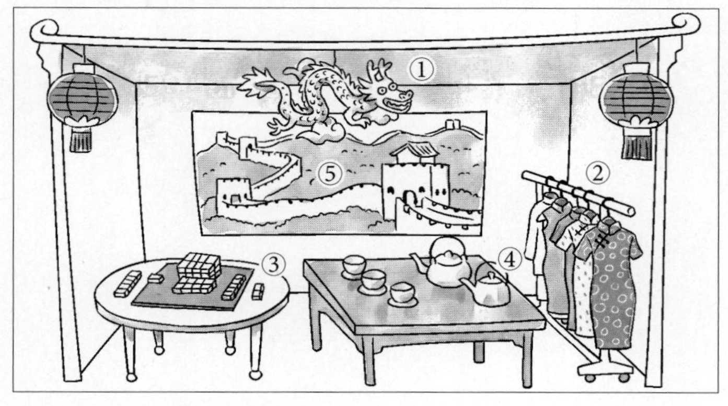

05

대화를 듣고, 여자가 남자에게 부탁한 일로 가장 적절한 것을 고르시오.

① to find a job website
② to show her his résumé
③ to give her honest answers
④ to share more interview tips
⑤ to recommend an internship

06

대화를 듣고, 여자가 가게 문을 닫는 이유를 고르시오.

① 여행을 가야 해서
② 딸을 간호해야 해서
③ 교육을 들으러 가야 해서
④ 본인이 수술을 받아야 해서
⑤ 가게의 인테리어 공사를 해서

07

대화를 듣고, 남자가 지불할 금액을 고르시오.

① $16 ② $24 ③ $30 ④ $48 ⑤ $60

08

대화를 듣고, 우쿨렐레에 관해 두 사람이 언급하지 않은 것을 고르시오.

① 유래 ② 모양 ③ 현의 수 ④ 음색 ⑤ 가격

09

영화 개봉 행사에 관한 다음 내용을 듣고, 일치하지 않는 것을 고르시오. 3점

① 액션 영화가 상영될 예정이다.
② 영화에 출연한 배우들이 참석할 것이다.
③ 영화 관람 후 사인회가 진행될 것이다.
④ 12월 1일까지 참가 신청을 해야 한다.
⑤ 선착순 50명에게 무료 티켓이 제공된다.

정답 및 해설 p.62-64

10

다음 표를 보면서 대화를 듣고, 여자가 예약할 리조트를 고르시오.

< Types of Resorts >

	Resort	Price (a night)	Swimming Pool	Kitchen	Breakfast
①	A	$100	Yes	No	No
②	B	$140	Yes	Yes	Yes
③	C	$120	No	Yes	Yes
④	D	$130	Yes	Yes	No
⑤	E	$175	No	No	No

11

대화를 듣고, 남자의 마지막 말에 대한 여자의 응답으로 가장 적절한 것을 고르시오.

① That's great. I'm very happy for you!
② Sorry. I don't have time this afternoon.
③ That sounds good. I love to learn science.
④ No, thanks. Actually, I don't like to exercise.
⑤ I heard the soccer club is already full, though.

12

대화를 듣고, 여자의 마지막 말에 대한 남자의 응답으로 가장 적절한 것을 고르시오.

① I think you should give it a try.
② Thank you for telling me the truth.
③ That's the reason why I like it, too.
④ They should have invited you camping.
⑤ Maybe we can change the schedule for you.

13

대화를 듣고, 여자의 마지막 말에 대한 남자의 응답으로 가장 적절한 것을 고르시오. 3점

Man: ______________________________

① I hope that relieves some of the pressure.
② I'm glad to hear they will be coming back.
③ Why do you want to apply for that position?
④ You're right. I'm moving to another city soon.
⑤ Give me a hand. I can't deal with this by myself.

14

대화를 듣고, 남자의 마지막 말에 대한 여자의 응답으로 가장 적절한 것을 고르시오.

Woman: ______________________________

① Okay, I'll keep that in mind.
② It was scary being all alone there.
③ My trip is scheduled for mid-July.
④ I would like to try some local food.
⑤ I want to go to Brazil with my friends.

15

다음 상황 설명을 듣고, Greg이 Jenny에게 할 말로 가장 적절한 것을 고르시오. 3점

Greg: ______________________________

① You should let me make my own decisions.
② My friend told me that these jeans are in style.
③ I'm not overweight, and I'll eat whatever I want.
④ You are the one who shouldn't eat unhealthy food.
⑤ I trust your judgment, so I don't think I'll buy them.

[16-17] 다음을 듣고, 물음에 답하시오.

16

남자가 하는 말의 목적으로 가장 적절한 것은?

① to promote a multicultural event
② to announce a school celebration
③ to describe festivals around the world
④ to introduce the idea of multiculturalism
⑤ to explain why different cultures are mixing

17

행사에 관해 언급되지 않은 것은?

① 개최 이유　② 참여 인원
③ 장소　④ 기념품
⑤ 입장권 가격

녹음을 다시 한 번 듣고, 빈칸에 알맞은 말을 쓰시오.

01

W: Our university has been _______ _______ _______ for international exchange students for many years. Today, we have some important announcements for students interested in our exchange programs. Most of our usual study programs will be offered this year. However, fewer than five students _______ _______ _______ the special science exchange program last year. Therefore, it will no longer be offered. Also, the application deadline for all our programs will be changed from October 30th to October 15th. _______ _______ _______ _______ _______, though—the cost of our programs has been reduced by 10%. If you have any questions, talk to an international exchange advisor at your school.

02

W: Hi, John. I heard your bad news. Are you okay?
M: Bad news? What are you talking about?
W: I heard that you _______ _______ _______ _______.
M: Oh. That wasn't me, Mary.
W: Really? But I heard it from the teaching assistant.
M: Actually, there is another person named "John" in my class. The teacher accidentally _______ _______ _______ on our math exams!
W: So that is what happened. I've had a similar problem. My best friend's name is also "Mary."
M: That _______ _______ _______.
W: Yeah, whenever someone says, "Hey Mary," we always have to say, "Which Mary?"
M: I guess that's the trouble with names like ours.
W: I wish I had a more unique name!

03

[Telephone rings.]
M: Hi, can I help you?
W: Yes, I need to _______ _______ _______.
M: Okay. Would you please tell me your name?
W: Yes, it's Jessica Morgan.
M: One moment. *[Typing sound]* All right. I see you've _______ _______ _______ _______ us for several years.
W: That's right.
M: So may I ask what happened?
W: Yes. Last week, I got hit by a car and _______ _______ _______ _______ for three days.
M: I'm sorry to hear that. Did you need surgery?
W: No, I didn't. But they put a cast on my left leg.
M: Well, I have good news—you're completely covered. Send us your hospital bill and we'll pay it.
W: That's great! Thank you.

04

W: Chen, did you _______ _______ _______ the Chinese booth for International Day?
M: Yes. I've just hung a round lantern on either side of it.
W: They look pretty. Oh, is that a dragon lantern in the middle?
M: Yes. Dragons are very special in China.
W: I see. You've got a lot of traditional Chinese clothes, too.
M: Yeah. Visitors can _______ _______ _______ on the hangers.
W: Sounds interesting. Is that a Chinese board game on the round table?
M: Yes. And there are some Chinese teapots and cups _______ _______ _______ _______.
W: Oh, there is a picture of pandas in the back. How cute!
M: Yes. Isn't it eye-catching? Chinese people love pandas.
W: Everything looks great!

05

W: Kevin, how did you find your internship?
M: I just looked on a job-seeking website and _______ _______ one that looked interesting.
W: I need to do that. But I'm too nervous.
M: What are you nervous about?
W: I don't like interviews. I never know what to say.
M: Just be friendly and confident, and answer all of the questions honestly.
W: _______ _______ _______ _______. By the way, did they ask for your résumé?
M: Yes. It's very important that it's written well.
W: I don't even have one yet. Can I _______ _______ _______ _______ _______?
M: Sure, I'll email you a copy of it tonight.
W: Thanks. Hopefully, I can find an internship soon.

06

M: Hey, Jenny. I heard that your coffee shop has free coffee classes.
W: Yes, it does.
M: Can I _______ _______ _______ next Friday?
W: Unfortunately, the class is canceled next week. The shop will be closed for a week starting Monday.
M: Why? Are you changing the store's interior? Or are you traveling somewhere?
W: No. Actually, my daughter will _______ _______ _______ next Monday.
M: Oh, no! Is it serious?
W: Not really. It's a simple operation, but I have to be with her while she recovers.
M: Well, I hope she _______ _______ _______ _______.
W: Thanks, Frank. The shop will be open again soon.

07

W: Good morning, sir. Do you need some help?
M: Yes. I need to print some photos from this USB flash drive.
W: No problem. _______ _______ _______ would you like? You can choose between standard and large.
M: What's the difference in price?
W: Standard size prints are one dollar each, and large ones are three dollars each.
M: Then I'll go with 15 standard photos and five large photos.
W: All right. By the way, if you're a student at Springfield College, you can get 20% off the total.
M: Is that so? I go to Springfield College.
W: Would you please _______ _______ _______ _______ _______?
M: Sure. Here you are.
W: Thank you. Your photos will _______ _______ _______ _______ _______.

08

M: What is that, Miri? It looks like a small guitar.
W: It's a ukulele.
M: Oh! It's a Hawaiian instrument, isn't it?
W: Yes, but Portuguese immigrants actually _______ _______ _______ Hawaii in the 19th century.
M: I see. I've seen one shaped like a pineapple before.
W: Yes, there are many shapes. Some are shaped like guitars, but others are oval or square.
M: That's interesting. Do they all _______ _______ _______ like yours?
W: Most do, but they can also have six or eight.
M: I see. I'd like to learn _______ _______ _______ _______. How much do they cost?
W: They can be as cheap as $20, but I saw one that was being sold for $4,000.
M: Wow, that's a wide price range!

21회

09

M: I'm pleased to announce a special premiere event. _______ _______ _______ of the action movie *Disaster Train* will take place at Circle Theater on December 10th. Since much of the film was shot in our town, the director has decided to hold the event here. Many of the actors and actresses in the movie will _______ _______ _______. After seeing the movie, there will be a signing event with the director and stars. If you'd like to attend this once-in-a-lifetime event, stop by the town hall by December 1st and sign up. We will have a drawing and randomly select 50 winners who will _______ _______ _______ _______ to attend. Don't miss this opportunity.

10

M: Welcome to the Sunny Travel Agency. Can I help you?

W: Yes. I'd like to _______ _______ _______ in a resort near Yellow Lake for next weekend.

M: Okay. There are several nice resorts in that area. Can I ask your budget?

W: I don't want to pay more than $150 per night.

M: There are a few resorts _______ _______ _______ _______. But the cheapest one doesn't have a swimming pool.

W: No, that's not good. I definitely need a place with a swimming pool.

M: All right. Well, what about a kitchen? Is that necessary?

W: Yes. I'm going to cook for myself, so I don't need breakfast service either.

M: Then I think this place _______ _______ _______ _______ _______.

11

M: Have you joined any after-school clubs yet?

W: Not yet. I don't know which one to join.

M: I will _______ _______ _______ _______. You could join it, too!

W: (No, thanks. Actually, I don't like to exercise.)

12

W: My friends are going camping next week, but I'm not.

M: Why not? Don't you like going camping?

W: _______ _______ _______, I've never gone before. I don't know anything about it.

M: (I think you should give it a try.)

13

W: Hey, Dan. You look tired.

M: Yeah. I have a lot of _______ _______ _______ _______ these days.

W: Yes, I heard two of your coworkers quit.

M: That's right. Helen and Laura left the company to go back to school.

W: I see. That's good for them at least.

M: I agree, but I have to work _______ _______ _______ _______. I'm kind of stressed out, to be honest.

W: Don't feel bad. I have some good news for you.

M: What is it?

W: I heard that the company is planning to _______ _______ _______ _______ for your team.

M: Oh, really? That is exactly what I've been waiting to hear.

W: Yeah. The new workers will start at the beginning of next month.

M: (I hope that relieves some of the pressure.)

14

M: Hey Abby, do you have any summer vacation plans?

W: Yes. I'm planning a trip to Brazil.

M: Oh, are you going with your friends?

W: No, I'll be traveling alone. I want to be free to ________ ________ ________ ________.

M: Good idea. That way, if you like a place, you can stay there as long as you want.

W: That's right. Also, I can meet new people and make friends ________ ________ ________ ________.

M: That's true. Those things are harder to do when you're traveling in a group.

W: Exactly. ________ ________ ________ ________, I can eat whatever food I like. I love to try local food.

M: That sounds great. Just be sure to avoid dangerous places when you're alone.

W: (Okay, I'll keep that in mind.)

15

W: Greg is often annoyed when he is with his older sister, Jenny. That's because she always ________ ________ ________ ________ ________. One day, they eat lunch together, but Greg is still hungry after eating. So he wants to order another cheeseburger. However, his sister tells him that he ________ ________ ________ ________, and she makes him order a salad instead. Now they are shopping for clothes. Greg finds a nice pair of jeans, but his sister says they aren't in style, so he shouldn't buy them. He is ________ ________ ________. He doesn't like his sister telling him what to do. In this situation, what would Greg most likely say to Jenny?

Greg: (You should let me make my own decisions.)

16-17

M: Our city is becoming more and more international every day. As more people from around the world move here, different cultures are mixing together. Many of us might not ________ ________ ________ ________. So, to help residents learn more about our new multicultural society, we will be holding our annual World Harmony Day this month. Each year, more than 500 people gather at Riverview Park to ________ ________ ________ ________. There will be free music and food from more than 20 different countries, along with fireworks and other fun events. At just $5 per ticket, this is ________ ________ ________ ________ ________ around. It will be held on Sunday, July 27th this year, starting at noon and continuing into the night. If you have any questions, you can call City Hall at 518-9211. We look forward to seeing you soon!

21회

21 Word & Expressions

01
- □ **destination** 목적지
- □ **exchange student** 교환 학생
- □ **announcement** 발표
- □ **offer** 제안하다; *제공하다
- □ **sign up for** …을 신청하다
- □ **application** 지원
- □ **deadline** 기한, 마감 시간
- □ **advisor** 고문

02
- □ **fail** 실패하다; *(시험에) 떨어지다, 낙제하다
- □ **teaching assistant** 보조 교사
- □ **accidentally** 우연히; *잘못하여
- □ **switch** 바꾸다
- □ **similar** 비슷한, 유사한
- □ **confusing** 혼란스러운
- □ **unique** 독특한

03
- □ **claim** 주장; *(보상금 등에 대한) 청구[신청]
- □ **policy** 정책; *보험 증권[증서]
- □ **surgery** 수술
- □ **cast** 깁스
- □ **completely** 완전히
- □ **cover** (보험으로) 보장하다
- □ **hospital bill** 병원비 영수증

04
- □ **set up** …을 설치하다
- □ **booth** (칸막이를 한) 작은 공간, 부스
- □ **dragon** 용
- □ **lantern** 랜턴, 등
- □ **try on** (옷 따위를) 입어[신어] 보다
- □ **teapot** 찻주전자
- □ **eye-catching** 눈길을 끄는

05
- □ **internship** 인턴직
- □ **job-seeking** 구직의
- □ **apply for** …에 지원하다
- □ **confident** 자신감 있는
- □ **honestly** 솔직하게(adj. honest 솔직한, 정직한)
- □ **résumé** 이력서

06
- □ **attend** 참석하다
- □ **cancel** 취소하다
- □ **interior** 인테리어, 실내 장식
- □ **operation** 수술
- □ **recover** 회복하다(n. recovery 회복)

07
- □ **print** 인쇄하다; (필름을 인화한) 사진
- □ **standard** 표준 규격의
- □ **student ID** 학생증

08
- □ **instrument** 도구; *악기
- □ **immigrant** 이민자
- □ **oval** 타원형의
- □ **square** 정사각형의
- □ **string** (악기의) 현
- □ **price range** 가격대

09
- □ **premiere** (영화의) 개봉
- □ **disaster** 재난, 참사
- □ **shoot** 쏘다; *촬영하다
- □ **director** (영화의) 감독
- □ **be in attendance** 참석하다
- □ **once-in-a-lifetime** 일생에 한 번의
- □ **drawing** 추첨
- □ **randomly** 무작위로
- □ **opportunity** 기회

10
- □ **travel agency** 여행사
- □ **budget** 예산, 경비
- □ **definitely** 분명히, 틀림없이
- □ **necessary** 필요한
- □ **fit** 꼭 맞다, 적합하다
- □ **need** 필요; *요구

12
- □ **to be honest** 솔직히 말하자면
- □ **give it a try** 시도하다

13
- □ **deal with** …을 처리하다
- □ **coworker** (직장) 동료
- □ **quit** 그만두다
- □ **employee** 직원
- □ **relieve** 없애[덜어]주다
- □ **pressure** 압박감

14
- □ **by oneself** 홀로
- □ **on top of that** 게다가, 뿐만 아니라
- □ **local** 현지의
- □ **avoid** 피하다
- □ **keep ... in mind** …을 명심하다

15
- □ **annoyed** 짜증이 난
- □ **in style** 유행하는
- □ **get upset** 화나다
- □ **overweight** 과체중의
- □ **judgment** 판단

16-17
- □ **be accustomed to** …에 익숙해지다
- □ **resident** 거주자, 주민
- □ **multicultural** 다문화의 (n. multiculturalism 다문화주의)
- □ **annual** 연례의
- □ **along with** …와 함께
- □ **firework** (*pl.*) 불꽃놀이
- □ **bargain** (정상가보다) 싸게 사는 물건
- □ **continue** 계속되다
- □ **celebration** 기념행사

22 영어듣기 모의고사

정답 및 해설 p.65-67

1번부터 17번까지는 듣고 답하는 문제입니다.
1번부터 15번까지는 한 번만 들려주고, 16번부터 17번까지는 두 번 들려줍니다. 방송을 잘 듣고 답을 하기 바랍니다.

01

다음을 듣고, 여자가 하는 말의 목적으로 가장 적절한 것을 고르시오.

① 비행기 승무원에 지원하려고
② 비행기 연착에 관해 안내하려고
③ 기내식을 개선할 것을 요구하려고
④ 항공사의 운영 방식을 칭찬하려고
⑤ 항공사의 서비스에 대해 항의하려고

02

대화를 듣고, 두 사람이 하는 말의 주제로 가장 적절한 것을 고르시오.

① 캠핑하기에 좋은 계절
② 겨울 캠핑을 위한 준비
③ 겨울철 방한 의류의 중요성
④ 여름과 겨울 야외 활동의 차이점
⑤ 여행 시 일기 예보 확인의 필요성

03

대화를 듣고, 두 사람의 관계를 가장 잘 나타낸 것을 고르시오.

① 집주인 — 수리공
② 웨이터 — 요리사
③ 손님 — 식당 지배인
④ 방문객 — 접수 담당자
⑤ 사진사 — 푸드 스타일리스트

04

대화를 듣고, 그림에서 대화의 내용과 일치하지 않는 것을 고르시오.

05

대화를 듣고, 여자가 남자에게 부탁한 일로 가장 적절한 것을 고르시오.

① 새 차 사주기
② 중고차 반값에 팔기
③ 함께 중고차 고르러 가기
④ 중고차 구입에 필요한 정보 찾기
⑤ 믿을 만한 중고차 판매업자 소개하기

06

대화를 듣고, 남자가 우유를 마시지 않는 이유를 고르시오.

① 다이어트 중이라서
② 주스를 더 좋아해서
③ 목이 마르지 않아서
④ 유제품 알레르기가 있어서
⑤ 우유를 먹으면 배가 아파서

07

대화를 듣고, 남자가 지불할 금액을 고르시오.

① $240　② $300　③ $320
④ $360　⑤ $400

08

대화를 듣고, Margherita 피자에 관해 두 사람이 언급하지 않은 것을 고르시오.

① 재료　② 최초 개발 연도　③ 이름 유래
④ 가격　⑤ 개발한 사람

09

해파리 호수에 관한 다음 내용을 듣고, 일치하지 않는 것을 고르시오.

① Palau의 작은 섬에 위치해 있다.
② 약 12,000년 전에 바다와 연결이 끊겼다.
③ 천적이 없어 해파리 개체 수가 급격히 증가했다.
④ 낮에 해파리들은 태양 빛을 따라 움직인다.
⑤ 해파리에게 쏘일 수 있어 수영은 금지되어 있다.

22회

10

다음 표를 보면서 대화를 듣고, 여자가 들을 수업을 고르시오. 3점

< Music Academy Summer Specials >

	Package	Features	Schedule	Monthly Fee
①	A	jazz piano, free practice room use	Mon., Thur. / 10-11 a.m.	$50
②	B	acoustic guitar, jazz piano	Tue., Thur. / 9-11 a.m.	$70
③	C	vocals, drums, free practice room use	Wed. / 2-4 p.m.	$110
④	D	vocals, free practice room use	Sat. / 12-2 p.m.	$80
⑤	E	drums, electric guitar	Mon., Thur. / 3-5 p.m.	$120

11

대화를 듣고, 여자의 마지막 말에 대한 남자의 응답으로 가장 적절한 것을 고르시오.

① I have plenty to read on the plane.
② The airport is just 30 minutes away.
③ His flight left at seven this morning.
④ It takes about ten hours to get to Italy.
⑤ It takes off in three hours, so I should leave now.

12

대화를 듣고, 남자의 마지막 말에 대한 여자의 응답으로 가장 적절한 것을 고르시오.

① No, thanks. I don't eat meat.
② Then I'll just have two steaks.
③ A friend of mine recommended the wine.
④ Would this wine match well with the steak?
⑤ Yes, but let me look at the menu first, please.

13

대화를 듣고, 여자의 마지막 말에 대한 남자의 응답으로 가장 적절한 것을 고르시오.

Man: ______________________

① Huge lunches always make me sleepy.
② I'd like to have a tuna sandwich for lunch.
③ I usually have milk and cereal for breakfast.
④ I need to find a way to increase my appetite.
⑤ You're right. I'll have breakfast before I leave.

14

대화를 듣고, 남자의 마지막 말에 대한 여자의 응답으로 가장 적절한 것을 고르시오. 3점

Woman: ______________________

① Please help Liam finish his homework.
② I don't think you need to come to our class.
③ Yes, I will have some free time next month.
④ Sure. Just let me know when you are available.
⑤ I will pick up your uniform from the dry cleaner's.

15

다음 상황 설명을 듣고, Ethan이 학생들에게 할 말로 가장 적절한 것을 고르시오.

Ethan: ______________________

① Let's drink some juice at the table.
② Would you please lend me some money?
③ I'm sorry, but I don't have any money right now.
④ Excuse me, did any of you see a brown wallet here?
⑤ I'll help you look for your wallet on the playground.

[16-17] 다음을 듣고, 물음에 답하시오.

16

남자가 하는 말의 목적으로 가장 적절한 것은? 3점

① to explain how to feed dogs
② to advertise a new dog chocolate
③ to show the downside of having a dog
④ to warn against feeding chocolate to dogs
⑤ to show why fruit is good for a dog's health

17

언급된 증상이 아닌 것은?

① 초조하게 걷기 ② 구토 ③ 갈증
④ 불규칙한 심장 박동 ⑤ 혼수상태

정답 및 해설 p.68

녹음을 다시 한 번 듣고, 빈칸에 알맞은 말을 쓰시오.

01

W: My name is Tanya Parker. I've flown with your airline for years, and I've always _______ _______ _______ your service. But recently I had an unpleasant experience. My flight from Chicago to Bali on July 19th was delayed due to bad weathers. I fully understood the situation, but I had to wait several hours on the plane with no air conditioning. Furthermore, the crew did not _______ _______ _______ _______ the passengers. When I asked for water, the flight attendant told me to wait and did nothing. Overall, the service was very disappointing. I hope you _______ _______ _______ in the future.

02

W: I don't like winter. I wish I could _______ _______ _______.

M: How about going camping with me?

W: It's too cold to go camping these days.

M: Well, summer is _______ _______ _______ _______ _______. But if you bring the right supplies, camping in the winter can be fun as well.

W: Is that so? Hmm... What would we need?

M: We have to wear warm, waterproof clothes. And we need _______ _______ _______ _______ _______.

W: I guess we'd need sleeping bags, too.

M: That's right.

W: Is there anything else?

M: We have to check the weather forecast for heavy rain or snow. Why don't we go this weekend?

W: Sure! Let's do it.

03

M: Hey, are you busy now?

W: Yes, I am. What do you need?

M: _______ _______ _______ the order for table 3?

W: Yes, here you are. The customer wanted her steak medium-rare, right?

M: No. She asked for it well-done.

W: Oh, I'm sorry. I guess _______ _______ _______.

M: That's okay, but please hurry. She's been waiting too long already.

W: I'll put it back on the grill right now. It will _______ _______ _______ _______ _______.

M: Good. How are her French fries coming along?

W: They are ready. You can take them out to her now.

M: All right. I'll be right back for the steak!

W: It'll be ready when you return.

04

M: It's a perfect day for a picnic. Where should we sit?

W: Maybe we can _______ _______ _______ _______ _______ near that pond.

M: There's a tree next to the pond, but I don't want to sit there. There might be too many insects.

W: Oh, good point. Then how about sitting next to the dragon statue on the right side of the path?

M: Well, there aren't any trees. We need some shade from the sun.

W: What about the picnic table with a parasol _______ _______ _______ _______? If we open the parasol, there will be plenty of shade.

M: Do you mean the one next to the bike path?

W: That's not a bike path. Don't you see the "No Bikes" sign? It's _______ _______ _______.

M: I see it now. Anyway, let's sit there.

05

W: I'm thinking of buying a car so I can drive to work.

M: Oh, really? _______ _______ _______ _______ _______ the bus?

W: Yes. It's too crowded, and it doesn't come often.

M: Well, if you plan to buy a car, _______ _______ _______ _______ _______ first.

W: I'm thinking of buying a used car, so I need your advice. You bought a used car, right?

M: Yeah. Be sure to check the car's accident and maintenance history.

W: Okay. Is that all?

M: No. There are many other things. I'll show you an online guide to buying a used car.

W: Thanks, but I'm not sure if I can _______ _______ _______ _______ _______. Can you go with me?

M: Sure. I'll be happy to help you.

06

W: Here, Marvin. Why don't you have a glass of milk with these cookies?

M: No thanks, Bonnie. I don't drink milk.

W: Really? Are you _______ _______ _______ _______ _______ _______?

M: No, but recently I haven't been feeling well after I drink milk.

W: That's strange. Maybe you're allergic to dairy products.

M: I don't think so. I can still eat yogurt and cheese _______ _______ _______. It's only milk that hurts my stomach.

W: I see. Well, that's a shame. These cookies _______ _______ _______ with milk!

M: I bet they do! I am pretty thirsty, though. Do you have anything else to drink?

W: How about some orange juice?

M: That would be great.

07

[Telephone rings.]

W: Continental Hotel. How can I help you?

M: Hello. I'm calling to book a room for next week.

W: All right. We have _______ _______ _______ _______.

M: How much do they cost?

W: Our regular suites are $100 per night, and the deluxe suites are $150. And for just $15 more, _______ _______ _______ _______.

M: Well, I just want the cheapest room, and I don't need breakfast.

W: Okay. Our standard rooms are $80.

M: I'll take one from Monday until Friday.

W: Oh, if you're staying _______ _______ _______ _______, you can get a 25 percent discount on a regular suite.

M: That's great! I'll take a regular suite instead.

W: So four nights in a regular suite without breakfast?

M: That's right.

08

W: Wow, this pizza is great! It was _______ _______ _______.

M: I agree. What is it called?

W: It's called a Margherita pizza. It's topped with tomatoes, basil, and mozzarella cheese.

M: Hmm... I've never heard of it before.

W: It was created in 1889 and _______ _______ _______ Queen Margherita.

M: Really? Why was that?

W: According to an old story, Queen Margherita really liked pizza.

M: I see.

W: When she visited Naples, a pizza maker named Raffaele Esposito created a special pizza _______ _______ _______ _______.

M: Wow! It was made just for her?

W: Yes! Esposito chose ingredients that represent the colors of the Italian flag: green, white, and red.

M: What an interesting story!

09

M: Hello, everyone. You all know what a jellyfish is. It is a sea animal that has a transparent body. Today, I want to talk about Jellyfish Lake. ________ ________ ________ ________ ________ in the country of Palau, it is a saltwater lake that was once connected to the ocean. About 12,000 years ago, however, it was cut off from the sea. ________ ________ ________, many jellyfish were trapped in the lake. Without any enemies to eat them, their population expanded rapidly. They ________ ________ ________ ________ around the lake, following the light of the sun. People can swim in the lake because the stingers of the jellyfish don't cause any pain.

10

W: These music class packages look great. Are you going to take one?

M: I already signed up for one. It's on Wednesdays.

W: Oh, ________ ________ ________ ________ ________ ________, but I have to work on Wednesday and Friday afternoons.

M: I see. There are still four other packages to choose from. Do you like singing?

W: No. I just want to learn ________ ________ ________ ________ ________.

M: What about the drums?

W: That would be great, but I can only afford a package that's less than $100 a month.

M: Oh, this one is very cheap. And you can use the practice room for free.

W: But ________ ________ ________ the other one. I can learn to play two instruments.

M: That one looks like a good choice, too.

11

W: Joe, are you ________ ________ ________ for Italy?

M: Yes. I packed everything, and I have my passport.

W: What time does your flight leave?

M: (It takes off in three hours, so I should leave now.)

12

M: Hi, may I take your order?

W: Yes, I'll have the steak and a glass of red wine.

M: I'm sorry, but we've ________ ________ ________ ________. Could I bring you something else?

W: (Yes, but let me look at the menu first, please.)

13

M: Mom, I'm going to school now.

W: Aren't you going to have breakfast?

M: No. I don't ________ ________ ________ ________ ________.

W: But breakfast is an important meal. Eating it will help you study well at school.

M: Do you mean that it will help me focus in class?

W: Exactly. You won't be distracted by hunger, so you'll probably learn more.

M: Oh, I didn't think of that.

W: In addition, eating a healthy breakfast will ________ ________ ________ ________ at lunch.

M: That makes sense. When I skip breakfast, I eat a huge lunch. Then I feel bad.

W: When you ________ ________ ________, you're less likely to eat too much at one meal.

M: (You're right. I'll have breakfast before I leave.)

14

[Cell phone rings.]

M: Good afternoon. This is Officer Rosenberg.

W: Hello, Mr. Rosenberg. This is Susan Edison, Liam's teacher.

M: Ah, yes. Is everything okay, Ms. Edison?

W: Yes, sir. Liam is doing wonderfully in class. Actually, I'm calling to _______ _______ _______ _______.

M: All right. What is it?

W: Well, your son talked about you in class today. He said that you're a police officer.

M: Yes, that's correct.

W: You see, the students are _______ _______ _______ this month.

M: Yes, Liam showed me his homework.

W: So I'm wondering if you could visit someday in your uniform and talk to them about your job.

M: Of course. Can I check my schedule and _______ _______ _______?

W: (Sure. Just let me know when you are available.)

15

W: Ethan is eating lunch in the school cafeteria when his friend Julie asks him to lend her $10. So he _______ _______ _______ _______ and gives Julie $10. Then the bell rings, and they rush to class. After class, Ethan finds that his wallet is gone! He _______ _______ _______ _______ about where he went that day. He finally remembers having taken his wallet out in the cafeteria. He runs back to the cafeteria and checks the table where he was sitting. Some other students are sitting there. He thinks they _______ _______ _______ his wallet. In this situation, what would Ethan most likely say to them?

Ethan : (Excuse me, did any of you see a brown wallet here?)

16-17

M: Your pet dog probably begs at the dinner table. You can safely give it certain foods, such as eggs, fruit and vegetables. These are not harmful to dogs. But it's different _______ _______ _______ _______ chocolate. If dogs eat chocolate, they can become sick or even die. This is because chocolate contains a substance that is toxic to dogs. If your dog accidentally eats chocolate, it might first _______ _______ _______, such as anxiously walking around the room. Next, it will probably vomit and have an irregular heartbeat. In the worst case, your dog could _______ _______ _______ _______. If you see any of these signs, bring your pet to an animal hospital right away. A vet can help, but the best way to protect your dog is to keep it away from chocolate at all times.

22 Word & Expressions

01
- □ **airline** 항공사
- □ **be satisfied with** …에 만족하다
- □ **unpleasant** 불쾌한
- □ **delay** 미루다; *지연시키다
- □ **fully** 완전히
- □ **furthermore** 뿐만 아니라, 더욱이
- □ **crew** 승무원
- □ **pay attention to** …에 주의를 기울이다
- □ **passenger** 승객
- □ **flight attendant** 승무원
- □ **overall** 전반적으로
- □ **disappointing** 실망스러운
- □ **improve** 개선되다, 나아지다

02
- □ **supply** 공급; *(*pl.*) 보급품, 물자
- □ **waterproof** 방수의
- □ **sleeping bag** 침낭
- □ **weather forecast** 일기 예보

03
- □ **medium-rare** 약간 덜 익힌
- □ **well-done** 완전히 익힌
- □ **confused** 혼란스러워하는

04
- □ **pond** 연못
- □ **insect** 곤충
- □ **statue** 조각상
- □ **path** 길
- □ **shade** 그늘

05
- □ **be tired of** …에 질리다
- □ **crowded** 붐비는, 복잡한
- □ **shop around** 가게를 돌아다니다
- □ **used car** 중고차
- □ **maintenance** 유지, 보수
- □ **on one's own** 혼자, 혼자 힘으로

06
- □ **be on a diet** 다이어트를 하다
- □ **allergic** 알레르기가 있는
- □ **dairy product** 유제품
- □ **shame** 딱한 일

07
- □ **regular** (크기가) 보통의
- □ **suite** (호텔의) 스위트룸
- □ **deluxe** 호화로운
- □ **standard** 보통의

08
- □ **top** 위에 놓다[얹다]
- □ **name for** …의 이름을 따서 붙이다
- □ **in honor of** …에게 경의를 표하여
- □ **represent** 대표하다; *상징하다

09
- □ **jellyfish** 해파리
- □ **transparent** 투명한
- □ **saltwater** 해수의
- □ **cut off** …을 차단하다[가로막다]
- □ **enemy** 적
- □ **population** 개체 수
- □ **expand** 확대하다, 팽창하다
- □ **stinger** (쏘는) 침

10
- □ **sign up for** …을 신청하다
- □ **instrument** 악기
- □ **afford** …할 형편이[여유가] 되다
- □ **feature** 특징, 특성
- □ **fee** 수수료; *요금

11
- □ **passport** 여권

12
- □ **run out of** …이 동나다[떨어지다]

13
- □ **appetite** 식욕
- □ **distract** 산만하게 하다
- □ **overeat** 과식하다
- □ **make sense** 이해가 되다
- □ **on schedule** 정시에 맞춰서

14
- □ **(police) officer** 경찰관
- □ **ask ... a favor** …에게 부탁하다
- □ **career** 직업, 직장 생활
- □ **wonder** 궁금하다, 궁금해하다
- □ **uniform** 제복, 교복

15
- □ **cafeteria** 구내식당
- □ **take out** …을 꺼내다
- □ **wallet** 지갑
- □ **rush** 서두르다
- □ **over and over** 여러 번 되풀이하여

16-17
- □ **beg** 간청하다; *(개가) 두 앞발을 들다
- □ **dinner table** 식탁, 밥상
- □ **harmful** 해로운
- □ **when it comes to** …에 대해서
- □ **substance** 성분
- □ **toxic** 유독성의
- □ **display** 전시하다, 내보이다
- □ **unusual** 특이한, 흔치 않은
- □ **anxiously** 근심[걱정]하여, 걱정스럽게
- □ **vomit** 토하다
- □ **irregular** 불규칙한
- □ **heartbeat** 심장 박동
- □ **coma** 혼수상태
- □ **sign** 징후, 조짐
- □ **keep away from** …에 가까이하지 않다
- □ **downside** 단점
- □ **warn against** …에 대해 주의를 주다[경고하다]

23 영어듣기 모의고사

1번부터 17번까지는 듣고 답하는 문제입니다.
1번부터 15번까지는 한 번만 들려주고, 16번부터 17번까지는 두 번 들려줍니다. 방송을 잘 듣고 답을 하기 바랍니다.

01

다음을 듣고, 여자가 하는 말의 목적으로 가장 적절한 것을 고르시오.

① 실내 환기의 중요성을 알리려고
② 새로 개업한 약국을 홍보하려고
③ 안구 건조 예방 제품을 광고하려고
④ 올바른 에어컨 사용법을 설명하려고
⑤ 여름철 건강 관리의 중요성을 강조하려고

02

대화를 듣고, 여자의 의견으로 가장 적절한 것을 고르시오.

① 밤보다는 아침에 공부하는 것이 좋다.
② 공부를 하기 전에 계획을 세워야 한다.
③ 너무 오래 자는 것은 건강에 좋지 않다.
④ 수면을 취하는 것은 기억력에 도움이 된다.
⑤ 시험 직전에 복습을 하는 것이 효율적이다.

03

대화를 듣고, 두 사람의 관계를 가장 잘 나타낸 것을 고르시오.

① 세입자 — 집주인　② 고객 — 은행 직원
③ 투숙객 — 호텔 직원　④ 집주인 — 열쇠 수리공
⑤ 고객 — 이삿짐 센터 직원

04

대화를 듣고, 그림에서 대화의 내용과 일치하지 않는 것을 고르시오.

05

대화를 듣고, 여자가 남자에게 부탁한 일로 가장 적절한 것을 고르시오. 3점

① to help her hand out flyers to students
② to return her books to the school library
③ to hang some handwritten posters for their club
④ to make book club posters to promote their club
⑤ to make 200 copies of a flyer within 20 minutes

06

대화를 듣고, 남자가 자원봉사를 하려는 이유를 고르시오.

① 친구를 응원하려고
② 증정 티셔츠를 받으려고
③ 내년 마라톤에 참가하려고
④ 다양한 사람들을 만나려고
⑤ 봉사 활동 시간을 채우려고

07

대화를 듣고, 여자가 지불할 금액을 고르시오. 3점

① \$16　② \$19　③ \$21
④ \$22　⑤ \$25

08

대화를 듣고, 수석 주방장 지원 자격 요건으로 언급되지 않은 것을 고르시오.

① 경력　② 요리 대회 입상 여부
③ 자격증　④ 협동 능력
⑤ 프랑스어 구사 능력

09

calamansi에 관한 다음 내용을 듣고, 일치하지 않는 것을 고르시오.

① 포도알 크기 정도의 작은 녹색 과일이다.
② 필리핀 이외의 지역에서도 재배된다.
③ 실내에서만 재배할 수 있다.
④ 껍질을 벗기기가 쉽고 신맛이 난다.
⑤ 비타민 C를 많이 함유하고 있다.

정답 및 해설 p.68-71

10

다음 표를 보면서 대화를 듣고, 여자가 구입할 화장대를 고르시오.

< Dresser Options >

	Model	Number of Drawers	Material	Color	Price
①	A	Two	Metal	Pink	$40
②	B	Three	Wooden	White	$45
③	C	Three	Metal	White	$60
④	D	Four	Wooden	Pink	$70
⑤	E	Four	Wooden	White	$55

11

대화를 듣고, 남자의 마지막 말에 대한 여자의 응답으로 가장 적절한 것을 고르시오.

① I'll get you one in a different color.
② It fits well, but I don't like the color.
③ I'll see if I can find a larger size for you.
④ But we can't give you a refund without a receipt.
⑤ Certainly. The changing room is right over there.

12

대화를 듣고, 여자의 마지막 말에 대한 남자의 응답으로 가장 적절한 것을 고르시오.

① If you run, you won't be late.
② I can go to a drugstore for you.
③ I'm feeling much better than before.
④ Then why don't you go to the doctor?
⑤ I already took two tablets this morning.

13

대화를 듣고, 여자의 마지막 말에 대한 남자의 응답으로 가장 적절한 것을 고르시오.

Man: ______________________________

① I would drop that class if I were you.
② He gave us a perfect speech on that day.
③ If you keep practicing, your skills will improve.
④ Take some notes so you don't forget your speech.
⑤ I guess so. But you really wanted to take that class.

14

대화를 듣고, 남자의 마지막 말에 대한 여자의 응답으로 가장 적절한 것을 고르시오. 3점

Woman: ______________________________

① You should find a brighter place to work.
② It would be wise to tell your boss the problem.
③ You just need to relax and stop worrying about it.
④ You'd better change your appointment with the doctor.
⑤ Make sure you look away from the screen from time to time.

15

다음 상황 설명을 듣고, Brian이 배달원에게 할 말로 가장 적절한 것을 고르시오. 3점

Brian: ______________________________

① As I told you, the pizza hasn't arrived yet.
② I think I should have received a large pizza.
③ If you don't mind, can I pay you tomorrow?
④ I'm sorry, but we didn't order a cheese pizza.
⑤ Unfortunately, I don't know how much it costs.

[16-17] 다음을 듣고, 물음에 답하시오.

16

남자가 하는 말의 목적으로 가장 적절한 것은? 3점

① to suggest a treatment for chronic headaches
② to emphasize the role and importance of the neck
③ to explain the causes of FHP and how to prevent it
④ to describe certain postures that people should avoid
⑤ to note the correlation between FHP and the immune system

17

언급된 증상이 아닌 것은?

① 두통 ② 뻐근한 목
③ 어깨 근육 뭉침 ④ 만성 피로
⑤ 목 디스크

23 DICTATION

녹음을 다시 한 번 듣고, 빈칸에 알맞은 말을 쓰시오.

01

W: As this summer has been extra hot, you may be turning up your air conditioner. This may be comfortable, but it can cause a lot of health problems. People usually use their air conditioners _______ _______ _______ _______. And the poor air circulation makes their eyes dry and tired. That's why many people _______ _______ _______ _______ during the summer months. But there's a way to solve this problem. TearX is a new product that can _______ _______ _______ _______ all summer long. Just put one drop in each eye every three hours. It's available at most drugstores, so go out and get some today.

02

W: Why are you still up, Mike? It's nearly midnight.

M: I know, Mom, but I have an important science exam tomorrow afternoon.

W: That's exactly why you need to go to bed soon.

M: What do you mean? I _______ _______ _______ _______ and studying for a few more hours.

W: That's not a good idea. Have you gone over all the material already?

M: Yes, but I want to review it once more.

W: That could do _______ _______ _______ _______. Your memory needs sleep to function well.

M: Does it? I didn't know that.

W: It's true. If you sleep well, you'll be able to remember everything you studied better.

M: Okay. I'll _______ _______ _______ _______, and then I'll go to bed.

03

W: Excuse me. _______ _______ _______ _______.

M: Certainly. There isn't anything wrong with your room, is there?

W: No, the room is fine. It's very big and has a nice view.

M: I'm glad to hear that. So how can I help you?

W: Well, I think I _______ _______ _______ _______ _______ my room.

M: That's too bad. Wait one moment, and I'll get another one for you. What is your room number?

W: I'm staying in room 201.

M: Unfortunately, you'll have to pay $10 _______ _______ _______. It's our policy.

W: I understand.

M: Wait a moment while I get you another key card.

W: Sure. Thanks again.

04

[Cell phone rings.]

M: Hello?

W: Hi, Jason. I seem to have left my wallet at home. Can you _______ _______ _______ _______ _______?

M: Sure. *[Pause]* Well, it's not on your desk. There are just two books and a ruler there.

W: Can you check on my dresser?

M: It looks like there are only cosmetics there.

W: How about on my bed _______ _______ _______?

M: Only a teddy bear.

W: Did you check the floor next to my bed, too?

M: Yeah, there is only a pair of slippers. Oh, wait! I found it.

W: Really? _______ _______ _______! Where was it?

M: It was on the table next to the lamp.

W: Ah, I remember now. Thank you.

05

M: Amy, how many posters have we made so far?

W: We've already made 20.

M: Now we need to put them up _______ _______ _______ _______.

W: That's right. By the way, did you make copies of our flyer?

M: Yes, I made 200 copies.

W: Good. Then I'll distribute them.

M: Can you _______ _______ _______? Or do you want me to help you?

W: Don't worry. Some other club members will help me. Can you just _______ _______ _______ _______ these posters instead?

M: Okay. Should I put one in the library?

W: No, I'll do that. I have to return some books anyway. You can put some up in the student union building.

M: Okay.

06

W: Do you have any plans this Saturday, James?

M: Yes, I _______ _______ _______ the City Marathon on that day.

W: Oh. I didn't know you were running in the marathon.

M: I'm not, but I _______ _______ _______ _______ free T-shirts to the runners who finish.

W: Sounds fun. Is it part of your volunteer work requirement?

M: No, I already finished that a few months ago.

W: Did you? Then why are you doing this?

M: I think it seems like a good opportunity to meet lots of different people.

W: Yeah, it probably is. People from _______ _______ _______ _______ will be attending.

M: Exactly. Would you like to come?

W: No, thanks. I plan on spending the day at the mall.

07

M: Hi! Welcome to Adventure Land—the best amusement park in the world!

W: Thank you. How much do admission tickets cost?

M: Well, each adult ticket costs $7.

W: _______ _______ _______ _______ for children?

M: Yes. Tickets for children under 13 are $2 cheaper.

W: All right. I'll take two adult tickets and one child's ticket.

M: Would you like tickets for our mini-train too? _______ _______ _______ all around the park. It can be nice on a hot day like today.

W: How much do those tickets cost?

M: Each train ticket costs $1, for both children and adults.

W: Then I'll _______ _______ _______ _______ too.

M: Here you go. Enjoy your day at Adventure Land!

08

W: So, you're interested in our head chef position?

M: Yes, I am.

W: Well, we need someone who has been a head chef for at least ten years.

M: I have fifteen years of experience. And I _______ _______ _______ in the national cooking contest.

W: That's great. Our new head chef must be a cooking contest winner.

M: Terrific. Is there anything else required?

W: Yes, you must have demonstrated the ability to work _______ _______ _______ _______ _______.

M: I have. I worked with 20 other chefs at a French restaurant when I was younger.

W: So can you speak French fluently?

M: Unfortunately, no. Is that important?

W: Yes, it's actually necessary. Most of our kitchen staff only speaks French.

M: That's too bad. I _______ _______ _______ _______ _______.

09

M: I'm sure you're all familiar with many kinds of fruit, but have you heard of the calamansi? Also known as the Philippine lime, it is a small, green fruit _______ _______ _______ _______ a grape. Although it is most commonly used in Filipino cooking, it is grown in many places, including Florida. The small trees are easy to grow and can be kept indoors or outdoors. Their small flowers _______ _______ _______ _______. The fruit itself is easy to peel and has a very sour flavor. _______ _______ _______, it contains a lot of vitamin C, so it's good for you, too.

10

M: Good afternoon. What are you looking for?

W: I want to buy a new dresser for my daughter.

M: We have _______ _______ _______ _______. How many drawers do you need?

W: At least three. My daughter has a lot of clothes.

M: Okay. What do you think of this metal one?

W: I would _______ _______ _______ _______ to match my daughter's wooden bed frame.

M: I see. Well, many girls like pink, so how about this pink one?

W: Hmm... I don't think my daughter would like that color.

M: Okay. Then there are two options left. Which one would you like?

W: The cheaper one, of course. Can I _______ _______ _______ _______?

M: Sure.

11

M: Excuse me. Do you have this shirt in a large?

W: I think a medium will fit you. These shirts are rather large.

M: I see. But I want to _______ _______ _______ first.

W: (Certainly. The changing room is right over there.)

12

W: I have a terrible headache today.

M: I'm sorry to hear that. Is there _______ _______ _______ _______ for you?

W: Well, I need to buy some aspirin but I don't have time now.

M: (I can go to a drugstore for you.)

13

M: Ellen! I heard you're taking a speech class. How is it?

W: Yes. _______ _______ _______ _______ _______, but I'm not enjoying it.

M: Really? What happened?

W: There's nothing wrong, actually. I just feel depressed whenever I finish my speeches.

M: I can't believe it. You're very outgoing, so I thought you'd be doing well.

W: Well, I get very nervous when I _______ _______ _______ _______ _______. Sometimes I forget everything that I'm supposed to say.

M: Maybe that's because you don't have much experience.

W: I'm not sure. Anyway, I don't think I want to attend class anymore.

M: I understand how you feel. But you know what? _______ _______ _______.

W: What does that mean?

M: (If you keep practicing, your skills will improve.)

14

W: Your eyesight is getting worse, Mr. Petrelli.

M: That's just a natural part of getting older, isn't it?

W: _______ _______. I think some bad habits could be damaging your vision.

M: Really? What kinds of habits are you talking about?

W: _______ _______ _______ _______ is one example.

M: Well, I don't do that. I always use my desk lamp when I read.

W: That's good. Another common bad habit is spending too much time staring at a computer screen.

M: Oh. I'm a web designer, so I _______ _______ _______ most of my time in front of a computer.

W: Then you need to give your eyes a rest sometimes.

M: So, what do you suggest I do?

W: (Make sure you look away from the screen from time to time.)

15

W: Brian _______ _______ _______ a pizza for dinner. Before he called his usual pizza place, he found an advertisement flyer from a different restaurant. The flyer said if he ordered a pizza online, he would get a free upgrade to a larger size. So he ordered a medium cheese pizza on the restaurant's website. He _______ _______ _______ a large one for the same price. When the delivery man arrived, however, he found that the man had brought a medium cheese pizza. Now he _______ _______ _______ the situation to the delivery man. In this situation, what would Brian most likely say to the delivery man?

Brian: (I think I should have received a large pizza.)

16-17

M: Many people suffer from problems caused by poor posture. One of the most common types of bad posture is called Forward Head Posture, or FHP. It occurs when a person holds his or her head in a forward position rather than _______ _______ _______ _______. Sitting with one's shoulders and head bent while working on a computer or driving can lead to FHP. So can sleeping in an awkward position. The most common symptoms of people with FHP are headaches, a tense neck, and tight shoulder muscles. Long-term FHP can lead to slipped discs in the neck. _______ _______ _______ to avoid this condition is to be aware of your posture. If you have any bad habits, try to correct them. Exercising the neck muscles is another way to _______ _______ _______ and decrease your chances of developing FHP.

23회

23 Word & Expressions

01
- □ **extra** 특별히
- □ **comfortable** 편안한, 쾌적한
- □ **poor** (질적으로) 좋지 못한
- □ **circulation** 순환
- □ **suffer from** …로 고통받다
- □ **product** 제품
- □ **drop** 방울
- □ **available** 구할 수 있는

02
- □ **up** 깨어 있는
- □ **midnight** 자정
- □ **stay up** 안 자다
- □ **go over** …을 복습하다
- □ **review** 검토하다
- □ **do more harm than good** 득보다는 해가 되다
- □ **function** 작동하다
- □ **section** 부분

03
- □ **replacement** 교체
- □ **policy** 정책, 규정

04
- □ **ruler** 자
- □ **dresser** 화장대
- □ **cosmetics** 화장품
- □ **pillow** 베개
- □ **What a relief!** 정말 다행이다!

05
- □ **put up** …을 게시하다
- □ **flyer** (광고용) 전단
- □ **distribute** 배포하다
- □ **student union** 학생회
- □ **handwritten** 손으로 쓴
- □ **promote** 홍보하다

06
- □ **attend** 참가하다
- □ **volunteer** 자원하다; 자원봉사자
- □ **hand out** …을 나누어 주다
- □ **requirement** 필요조건, 요건
- □ **opportunity** 기회

07
- □ **admission ticket** 입장권
- □ **make a stop** 멈추다

08
- □ **chef** 주방장
- □ **win a prize** 상을 타다
- □ **national** 전국의
- □ **terrific** 아주 좋은
- □ **require** 필요로 하다
- □ **demonstrate** 입증하다
- □ **fluently** 유창하게
- □ **necessary** 필요한, 필수적인

09
- □ **be familiar with** …에 익숙하다
- □ **known as** …로 알려진
- □ **commonly** 흔히, 보통
- □ **indoors** 실내에서
- □ **outdoors** 야외에서
- □ **peel** 껍질을 벗기다
- □ **sour** 신맛이 나는
- □ **flavor** 맛

10
- □ **drawer** 서랍
- □ **metal** 금속의
- □ **frame** 틀
- □ **material** 재료

11
- □ **medium** 중간의
- □ **rather** 꽤, 약간
- □ **refund** 환불
- □ **receipt** 영수증
- □ **changing room** 탈의실

12
- □ **terrible** 심각한
- □ **drugstore** 약국
- □ **tablet** 알약, 정제

13
- □ **depressed** 우울한
- □ **outgoing** 외향적인
- □ **be supposed to-v** …하기로 되어 있다
- □ **drop** 떨어지다; *그만두다

14
- □ **eyesight** 시력
- □ **damage** 손상시키다
- □ **vision** 시력
- □ **stare at** …을 응시하다
- □ **can't help v-ing** …하지 않을 수 없다
- □ **look away** 눈길을 돌리다
- □ **from time to time** 이따금, 때때로

15
- □ **advertisement** 광고
- □ **delivery** 배달

16-17
- □ **posture** 자세
- □ **rather than** …보다는
- □ **awkward** 어색한
- □ **symptom** 증상
- □ **tense** 뻐근한, 긴장된
- □ **slipped disc** (척추) 디스크
- □ **condition** 조건; *질환
- □ **chronic** 만성적인
- □ **emphasize** 강조하다
- □ **correlation** 연관성, 상관관계
- □ **immune system** 면역체계

24 영어듣기 모의고사

정답 및 해설 p.71-74

1번부터 17번까지는 듣고 답하는 문제입니다.
1번부터 15번까지는 한 번만 들려주고, 16번부터 17번까지는 두 번 들려줍니다. 방송을 잘 듣고 답을 하기 바랍니다.

01

다음을 듣고, 여자가 하는 말의 목적으로 가장 적절한 것을 고르시오.

① 알레르기약을 홍보하려고
② 봄에 할 수 있는 활동을 소개하려고
③ 알레르기 증상의 심각성을 경고하려고
④ 알레르기를 일으키는 원인을 설명하려고
⑤ 알레르기를 예방하는 법에 대해 조언하려고

02

대화를 듣고, 두 사람이 하는 말의 주제로 가장 적절한 것을 고르시오.

① 제습기의 다양한 기능
② 공기 오염의 주된 원인
③ 실내 청결 유지의 중요성
④ 벽에 생긴 곰팡이 제거 방법
⑤ 적절한 실내 습도 유지의 필요성

03

대화를 듣고, 두 사람의 관계를 가장 잘 나타낸 것을 고르시오.

① 수리공 — 고객　② 집주인 — 세입자
③ 투숙객 — 호텔 종업원　④ 관리소 직원 — 입주민
⑤ 부동산 중개인 — 고객

04

대화를 듣고, 그림에서 대화의 내용과 일치하지 않는 것을 고르시오.

05

대화를 듣고, 여자가 남자에게 부탁한 일로 가장 적절한 것을 고르시오.

① to clean the house that evening
② to help her finish a project late at night
③ to cook dinner for her before she gets home
④ to pick up their son from the day-care center
⑤ to pick up some laundry from the dry-cleaners

06

대화를 듣고, 여자가 기한을 연장해 주지 않은 이유를 고르시오.

① 공정하지 않아서
② 과제가 어렵지 않아서
③ 이미 충분한 시간을 줘서
④ 아직 기한이 많이 남아서
⑤ 어머니의 증세가 심하지 않아서

07

대화를 듣고, 남자가 지불할 금액을 고르시오. 3점

① $28　② $30　③ $35
④ $37　⑤ $40

08

대화를 듣고, 영화제에 관해 두 사람이 언급하지 않은 것을 고르시오.

① 행사 기간　② 개막작 제목
③ 표 가격　④ 표 구입 장소
⑤ 상영관

09

Anuta Island에 관한 다음 내용을 듣고, 일치하지 않는 것을 고르시오.

① 태평양에 위치한 섬이다.
② 화산으로 생성되었다.
③ 세계에서 인구 밀도가 가장 낮다.
④ 주민들은 고유의 언어를 사용한다.
⑤ 협동과 연민과 같은 가치를 중요시하는 문화가 있다.

24회

10

다음 표를 보면서 대화를 듣고, 여자가 주문할 음료를 고르시오.

< Green Leaf Café Menu >

	Beverage	Caffeine	Hot/Cold	Price	Discount
①	A	O	Hot	$2.50	1+1
②	B	X	Cold	$2.75	20% off
③	C	X	Hot or cold	$4.00	1+1
④	D	X	Hot or cold	$3.00	20% off
⑤	E	X	Hot	$2.50	1+1

11

대화를 듣고, 남자의 마지막 말에 대한 여자의 응답으로 가장 적절한 것을 고르시오.

① Sure. What time should I be there?
② Sounds great. Let's meet at my house.
③ That was the best party I've ever been to.
④ I'd have to cancel my housewarming party.
⑤ I'd love to, but I didn't receive an invitation.

12

대화를 듣고, 여자의 마지막 말에 대한 남자의 응답으로 가장 적절한 것을 고르시오.

① I'm sorry, but I don't like puppies.
② That's too bad. I got bitten by a cat once.
③ No, thanks. I have too many pets already.
④ I'd love to, but my mom doesn't allow pets.
⑤ Cats give birth to four to six kittens at a time.

13

대화를 듣고, 남자의 마지막 말에 대한 여자의 응답으로 가장 적절한 것을 고르시오. 3점

Woman: ______________________________

① If so, we should go there this winter.
② Sorry, but I prefer the south coast to Busan.
③ No. I really don't want to go to Busan again.
④ I don't know. Crowded beaches aren't very fun.
⑤ Great. We can go to the beach some other time.

14

대화를 듣고, 여자의 마지막 말에 대한 남자의 응답으로 가장 적절한 것을 고르시오.

Man: ______________________________

① That dress is just too expensive for you.
② I don't think the shop has beautiful dresses.
③ I guess you will have to put off your wedding.
④ Honestly, I just don't like any of these choices.
⑤ I'll ask her for some information about the shop.

15

다음 상황 설명을 듣고, Kevin이 Lisa에게 할 말로 가장 적절한 것을 고르시오.

Kevin: ______________________________

① I'm sorry for not voting for your friend.
② Why are you running for president, too?
③ You need to make more friends at school.
④ Would you help me during the campaign?
⑤ Whom are you voting for in this election?

[16-17] 다음을 듣고, 물음에 답하시오.

16

남자가 하는 말의 주제로 가장 적절한 것은?

① the main causes of fire on boats
② the importance of giving first aid
③ a variety of ways to fish on a boat
④ the ocean's unpredictable weather
⑤ safety equipment needed on boats

17

언급된 장비가 아닌 것은?

① lights
② a fire extinguisher
③ a whistle
④ a life jacket
⑤ a first aid kit

정답 및 해설 p.74

녹음을 다시 한 번 듣고, 빈칸에 알맞은 말을 쓰시오.

01

W: It's springtime again, which means there are beautiful flowers everywhere. But some people don't like spring because it's also allergy season. If you have springtime allergies, listen up! ________ ________ ________ ________ that can really help you control your symptoms. Remember, most allergies come from pollen in the air. When you're outside, you should always wear a mask to ________ ________ ________ pollen. You should also wash your hands often to avoid rubbing pollen in your eyes. These simple tips could save you from your seasonal allergies. If you ________ ________ ________ them, you can enjoy the spring.

02

W: How's your new apartment, Harry?

M: It's not bad. But I found some mold ________ ________ ________ ________ yesterday.

W: Oh, that's a shame.

M: I was really surprised because I've been keeping the house very clean.

W: It's not caused by uncleanliness. It's ________ ________ ________, especially in summer.

M: Humidity? You mean the amount of water in the air?

W: Yes. Indoor air needs to be carefully monitored. It shouldn't be too wet or too dry.

M: Oh, I didn't think about that.

W: Humidity can affect your health as well. If the air is too dry, for example, you ________ ________ ________ ________.

M: I see. In that case, I should probably buy a dehumidifier.

W: That's a great idea.

03

[Telephone rings.]

M: Hello?

W: Hi. My name is Jodie Bryant. I live in Building B.

M: Hello, Ms. Bryant. What can I help you with?

W: Well, I ________ ________ ________ in the underground parking garage yesterday.

M: I see. Did something happen to it?

W: Yes. I found a big dent in the door this morning. Someone must have hit it last night.

M: I'm sorry to hear that. Would you like me to review the CCTV video from last night?

W: Yes, please. I ________ ________ ________ ________ ________ my car.

M: All right. I need to know your apartment number and your parking space.

W: My apartment is B201, and the parking space is 39C.

M: Okay. I'll ________ ________ ________ and contact you this afternoon.

04

W: How was your family vacation in the Philippines, Jihoon?

M: It was great! We went scuba diving and ________ ________ ________. Look at this!

W: Wow! Are the two people holding hands on the left side your parents?

M: Yes. And the person next to them making a fist is my sister.

W: Look at those fish swimming above her!

M: They were amazing. ________ ________ ________ which person I am?

W: Are you the boy making a heart with his arms next to your sister?

M: Nope. That's my older brother.

W: Then you must be the person with his hand on the turtle's shell.

M: That's right! I ________ ________ ________ ________ ________ playing with the turtle.

05

[Cell phone rings.]

W: Hello?

M: Hi, dear. I just got home. What time will you get home?

W: Oh, sorry, honey. I _______ _______ _______ _______ at the office tonight to finish a big project.

M: Really? I understand. Then I'll cook dinner for myself and clean the house this evening.

W: Thanks. That would be a big help.

M: Should I pick up Jeffrey from the day-care center?

W: _______ _______ _______ _______. I already asked my mother to pick him up.

M: Good. Is there anything else that needs to be done?

W: Actually, there's one thing. I _______ _______ _______ _______ at the dry-cleaners a few days ago. Could you go get them?

M: Sure, I can do that.

W: Great.

06

M: Mrs. Green, can I talk to you?

W: Of course, Peter. What is it?

M: Is it okay if I _______ _______ _______ _______ one day late?

W: What's the reason?

M: My mom has the flu, so I need to take care of her.

W: I'm sorry to hear that. But isn't there anyone else who can take care of her?

M: No, I'm the only one. So I'm worried I won't be able to finish the paper in time.

W: I'm sorry, but I can't let you have more time. _______ _______ _______ to the other students.

M: I understand. I'll try to finish it then. Thank you anyway.

W: I hope your mother _______ _______ _______.

07

[Telephone rings.]

W: Thanks for calling Pizza Express. How can I help you?

M: I'd like to order two potato pizzas, please.

W: Sure. Would you like regular or large pizzas?

M: What's the price difference _______ _______ _______?

W: Large pizzas are $15 each, and regular ones are $10 each.

M: Okay, then I'll take two large ones. And I also need five medium colas.

W: Okay, those are $2 each.

M: All right. And I _______ _______ _______ _______ for 10% off.

W: I see. But that coupon is only for the pizza. The colas are still full price.

M: That's fine. And can you deliver it to 123 Evergreen Terrace in Springfield?

W: Certainly. Your food will be delivered _______ _______ _______ _______.

M: Excellent. Thanks a lot.

08

W: Do you know that the Harrisville Film Festival starts October 1st?

M: No. _______ _______ _______ _______ _______?

W: For one week. Why don't you come see the opening film with me?

M: Sorry. I have an exam that day.

W: Okay. There's a good movie playing on October 4th.

M: Great. What's it called?

W: *Wonder World.* It's a comedy about _______ _______ _______ _______.

M: Sounds good. How much are the tickets?

W: We can get one-day tickets for $15 each. But we have to buy them at the ticket office.

M: Are the films being shown at the City Cinemas again this year?

W: Yes. It's _______ _______ _______ _______ last year.

M: Oh, then we can just take the subway.

09

M: Anuta Island has been featured on many television documentaries lately. As a result, more and more people are _______ _______ _______ this tiny island located in the Solomon Islands in the Pacific Ocean. It was formed by a volcano, and it has an area of only 0.37 square kilometers. _______ _______ _______ _______, about 300 people live there. Therefore, it has one of the highest population densities in the world. People living on this island speak their own language, Anuta. Their culture _______ _______ _______ _______ _______ called aropa. Basically, this means that they believe in cooperation and sympathy.

10

M: Hi. How can I help you?

W: I want to order something to drink. What would you recommend?

M: We have lots of drinks to choose from. Would you like something with caffeine?

W: No. I need to _______ _______ _______ caffeine.

M: I see. Would you like something hot or cold?

W: I'd like something hot.

M: Well, we have three hot options.

W: Actually, I only have three dollars right now. So that limits my choices.

M: We also _______ _______ _______ on all our drinks. Some are "one plus one," and others are 20% off.

W: I'll choose the one that is 20% off.

M: All right. I will _______ _______ _______ _______ in just a minute.

11

M: Linda, do you have any plans for this Saturday?

W: No, not really. _______ _______ _______ _______?

M: I'm having a housewarming party, and I'd like you to come.

W: (Sure. What time should I be there?)

12

W: Brian, have you ever thought about getting a pet?

M: Yes. I don't have one now, but _______ _______ _______ _______.

W: Great! My cat had four kittens last week. You can take one.

M: (I'd love to, but my mom doesn't allow pets.)

13

M: I would really love to go to Busan for our vacation next week.

W: Well, I would too. But there are too many people on the beach _______ _______ _______ _______.

M: I guess you're right. Let's pick a different place.

W: We could go to the south coast. The weather there is nice in summer.

M: Yes, but we went there last summer. I don't want to _______ _______ _______ _______ _______.

W: Then how about going to Pyeongchang?

M: That sounds nice, but it's better to go there in the winter.

W: True. But _______ _______ _______ _______ the cool valleys will be on hot days.

M: You've convinced me. Let's go there!

W: (Great. We can go to the beach some other time.)

14

W: My wedding is in just one month, but I _______ _______ _______ a dress yet.

M: Well, you should try on a variety of dresses and find the one that's right for you.

W: That's a good idea, but the price has to be within my budget.

M: How much money can you spend?

W: I can only spend up to $1,000. So I need to find a shop with dresses _______ _______ _______ _______.

M: Don't worry. I can help you out.

W: How?

M: One of my friends _______ _______ _______. She said she got her dress at a discounted price.

W: Wow, I'd like to know where she bought it.

M: (I'll ask her for some information about the shop.)

15

W: Kevin is a sophomore in high school. He has decided to _______ _______ _______ _______. He is friendly with many of his male classmates. While he is confident that they will vote for him, he _______ _______ _______ the female students. Most of them don't know him well and might decide to vote for someone else. However, his sister Lisa also goes to his school, and she has many female friends. Kevin thinks that he'll _______ _______ _______ _______ _______ winning the election with her assistance. So he wants to ask for her help. In this situation, what would Kevin most likely say to Lisa?

Kevin: (Would you help me during the campaign?)

16-17

M: Fishing is a fun and relaxing hobby. And fishing from a boat can be even more exciting. However, before you _______ _______ _______ _______ _______, you should make sure the boat contains proper safety equipment. First of all, every boat should have lights. Even if you're fishing during the day, lights can help prevent collisions if it becomes rainy or foggy. You should also make sure there's a fire extinguisher. In case of a fire, it's better to _______ _______ _______ than abandon the boat. There should also be a whistle on board. You can use it to attract rescuers in case of an emergency. And, finally, always bring a first aid kit with you. If someone gets hurt, it can _______ _______ _______ _______ to get to a doctor. So being able to treat injuries is important.

24 Word & Expressions

01
- □ allergy 알레르기
- □ symptom 증상
- □ pollen 꽃가루
- □ breathe in …을 들이마시다
- □ rub 문지르다, 비비다
- □ seasonal 계절적인

02
- □ mold 곰팡이
- □ uncleanliness 불결함
- □ humidity 습도
- □ monitor 감시하다, 관리하다
- □ have trouble v-ing …하는 데 어려움을 겪다
- □ dehumidifier 제습기

03
- □ parking garage 주차장
- □ dent 움푹 들어간 곳

04
- □ scuba diving 스쿠버 다이빙
- □ make a fist 주먹 쥐다
- □ turtle 거북이
- □ shell 껍데기, 껍질

05
- □ pick up …을 데리러 가다, …을 데려오다
- □ day-care center 어린이집
- □ drop off …을 맡기다
- □ dry-cleaners 드라이클리닝점
- □ laundry 세탁물

06
- □ hand in …을 제출하다
- □ have the flu 독감에 걸리다
- □ in time 시간 맞춰, 늦지 않게
- □ fair 공평한
- □ get well 나아지다

07
- □ regular 규칙적인; *(크기가) 보통인
- □ medium (크기가) 중간인
- □ full price 적정 가격, 정가
- □ deliver 배달하다

08
- □ film festival 영화제
- □ last 지속하다, 계속되다

09
- □ feature 특징을 그리다; *(방송에서) …을 특집으로 다루다
- □ documentary 다큐멘터리, 기록물
- □ tiny 아주 작은
- □ volcano 화산
- □ area 지역; *면적
- □ square kilometer 제곱킬로미터
- □ despite …에도 불구하고
- □ density 밀도
- □ be based on …에 기초하다
- □ basically 기본적으로
- □ cooperation 협동
- □ sympathy 연민

10
- □ caffeine 카페인
- □ cut down on …을 줄이다
- □ limit 제한하다

11
- □ housewarming party 집들이
- □ cancel 취소하다
- □ invitation 초대, 초대장

12
- □ kitten 새끼 고양이
- □ bite 물다
- □ allow 허락하다
- □ give birth to …을 낳다[출산하다]

13
- □ coast 해안
- □ valley 계곡
- □ convince 설득하다, 수긍하게 하다
- □ crowded 붐비는, 복잡한

14
- □ a variety of 다양한
- □ budget 예산
- □ range 범위
- □ put off …을 연기하다

15
- □ sophomore 2학년생
- □ run for …에 입후보하다
- □ vote for …에 투표하다
- □ chance 가능성
- □ election 선거
- □ assistance 도움, 지원
- □ campaign 선거 운동

16-17
- □ proper 적절한, 제대로 된
- □ equipment 장비
- □ collision 충돌
- □ foggy 안개가 낀
- □ fire extinguisher 소화기
- □ in case of …의 경우
- □ put out (불을) 끄다
- □ abandon 버리고 떠나다
- □ whistle 호루라기
- □ attract 끌어들이다
- □ rescuer 구조자, 구출자
- □ emergency 비상사태
- □ first aid kit 구급상자
- □ injury 부상
- □ first aid 응급 처치
- □ unpredictable 예측할 수 없는
- □ life jacket 구명조끼

25 영어듣기 모의고사

1번부터 17번까지는 듣고 답하는 문제입니다.
1번부터 15번까지는 한 번만 들려주고, 16번부터 17번까지는 두 번 들려줍니다. 방송을 잘 듣고 답을 하기 바랍니다.

01

다음을 듣고, 여자가 하는 말의 목적으로 가장 적절한 것을 고르시오.

① 특별 배달 서비스를 홍보하려고
② 아파트 관리인의 사임을 알리려고
③ 범죄 피해 신고 절차를 안내하려고
④ 도난 사건 예방에 대한 조언을 하려고
⑤ 휴가철 안전사고에 대비할 것을 당부하려고

02

대화를 듣고, 두 사람이 하는 말의 주제로 가장 적절한 것을 고르시오.

① 흰 빵의 기원
② 다양한 밀 정제법
③ 흰 빵의 색이 하얀 이유
④ 빵을 만드는 다양한 재료
⑤ 통밀빵과 흰 빵의 차이점

03

대화를 듣고, 두 사람의 관계를 가장 잘 나타낸 것을 고르시오.

① 학생 — 교사　② 매니저 — 쇼핑객
③ 승무원 — 승객　④ 여행사 직원 — 고객
⑤ 우체국 직원 — 여행자

04

대화를 듣고, 그림에서 대화의 내용과 일치하지 <u>않는</u> 것을 고르시오.

05

대화를 듣고, 여자가 남자에게 부탁한 일로 가장 적절한 것을 고르시오.

① 음식 주문하기
② 닭 요리 재료 사기
③ 식당 위치 검색하기
④ 맛집 블로그 검색하기
⑤ 식당 전화번호 찾아보기

06

대화를 듣고, 여자가 동창회에 참석하지 <u>못하는</u> 이유를 고르시오.

① 출장을 가야 해서
② 운동하다가 다쳐서
③ 가족 여행을 가기로 해서
④ 테니스 수업을 들어야 해서
⑤ 어머니 생신 파티에 참석해야 해서

07

대화를 듣고, 남자가 지불할 금액을 고르시오. 3점

① $46　② $59　③ $65
④ $69　⑤ $75

08

대화를 듣고, 뮤지컬에 관해 두 사람이 언급하지 <u>않은</u> 것을 고르시오.

① 공연 시작일　② 상연 장소　③ 제목
④ 공연 내용　⑤ 공연 횟수

09

바리스타 연수회에 관한 다음 내용을 듣고, 일치하지 <u>않는</u> 것을 고르시오.

① 주말에만 열릴 것이다.
② 각 수업은 2시간 동안 진행된다.
③ 지역 문화 회관에서 열릴 것이다.
④ 참가자는 25명으로 제한할 것이다.
⑤ 참가 비용은 무료이다.

정답 및 해설 p.75-77

10

다음 표를 보면서 대화를 듣고, 남자가 구입할 물건을 고르시오.

< Headphones & Earphones >

	Model	Built-in Microphone	Cable Length	Type	Price
①	A	O	1.25 m	Headphones	$20
②	B	X	1.25 m	Earphones	$12
③	C	O	2.00 m	Headphones	$15
④	D	O	1.25 m	Earphones	$16
⑤	E	X	2.00 m	Headphones	$13

11

대화를 듣고, 남자의 마지막 말에 대한 여자의 응답으로 가장 적절한 것을 고르시오.

① Sure, I heard they are great actors.
② Sorry, but I've already seen that film.
③ Yeah, they both like watching movies.
④ I want to make a sci-fi movie sometime.
⑤ We should ask Julie what she wants to see.

12

대화를 듣고, 여자의 마지막 말에 대한 남자의 응답으로 가장 적절한 것을 고르시오.

① I also need to buy a new bag.
② Well, how about right after class?
③ Sorry, I don't think I'll be able to make it.
④ I'll meet you in front of the shopping mall.
⑤ I've heard that they're having a sale tomorrow.

13

대화를 듣고, 여자의 마지막 말에 대한 남자의 응답으로 가장 적절한 것을 고르시오.

Man: ______________________

① Doctors say it's best to eat each meal slowly.
② That's the secret to maintaining a good figure!
③ Then we'll increase the amount of weight you lift.
④ It seems so, but that can be very bad for your health.
⑤ Drinking water with your meals upsets your stomach.

14

대화를 듣고, 남자의 마지막 말에 대한 여자의 응답으로 가장 적절한 것을 고르시오. 3점

Woman: ______________________

① I'm sorry but it's sold out.
② Actually, iced drinks cost 50 cents more.
③ I'm sorry. I'll bring a new one right away.
④ You can use the coupon for any kind of drink.
⑤ That's fine. I'm okay with drinking hot coffee.

15

다음 상황 설명을 듣고, Hailey가 이웃에게 할 말로 가장 적절한 것을 고르시오.

Hailey: ______________________

① How can we reduce the amount of trash?
② Would you mind not putting waste in the hall?
③ Why don't we complain to the landlord about it?
④ Where should I go if I want to throw my trash out?
⑤ How did you know that I broke the building's rules?

[16-17] 다음을 듣고, 물음에 답하시오.

16

남자가 하는 말의 목적으로 가장 적절한 것은?

① 새로운 호신 제품을 광고하려고
② 공원 산책 시 조심할 것을 경고하려고
③ 안전한 동네를 고르는 법을 설명하려고
④ 사람들에게 도시에 살 것을 권장하려고
⑤ 미행을 당할 때의 행동 수칙을 알려주려고

17

언급된 용품이 아닌 것은?

① whistle
② gas gun
③ stun gun
④ pepper spray
⑤ stick

25 DICTATION

녹음을 다시 한 번 듣고, 빈칸에 알맞은 말을 쓰시오.

01

W: Good morning, residents. As your building manager, I need to _______ _______ _______ _______. As the holiday season is approaching, many people will be away from their apartments. However, the number of thefts in our neighborhood has been increasing. So we need to be careful. If you will be away for a long time, please _______ _______ _______ _______, such as newspapers and milk. The delivered goods outside your door can make your home a target for theft. Please also lock your windows, especially if you're living on lower floors, to prevent someone from breaking into your apartment. Please keep these tips in mind _______ _______ _______. Thank you.

02

M: Mom, what's this? Whole wheat bread? You know _______ _______ _______ _______.

W: I know, but whole wheat bread is better for you.

M: It's the same thing as white bread. They're both made from wheat, but white bread is much softer.

W: White bread _______ _______ _______ _______ whole wheat bread. So although it might be softer, it's not healthier.

M: What does that mean?

W: It means that many important nutrients such as vitamins and minerals are removed.

M: Really? What about whole wheat bread?

W: Since it is made with whole wheat, it contains lots of nutrients.

M: I didn't know that. I guess I can _______ _______ _______ _______ whole wheat bread.

W: I'm glad to hear that.

03

W: Can I help you with something?

M: Yes, please. I'm visiting from another country, and I just bought these postcards.

W: I see. Would you like to send them?

M: Well, I have to write on them first. But I was wondering _______ _______ _______ _______ to send them to Canada.

W: Well, a regular postcard stamp costs $3.

M: If I send them that way, how long will it take?

W: About a week. But if you send them _______ _______ _______, it will take two days.

M: That's better. And how much does that cost?

W: Just $5 per postcard.

M: Excellent. Then I'll _______ _______ _______ _______ to send these. Thanks for your help.

W: It was my pleasure.

04

M: How do you like the new children's library, Mary?

W: Wow! It looks fantastic! Why did you choose a round table instead of a square one?

M: Well, the corners of square tables can be dangerous for children.

W: _______ _______ _______. Oh, you put the bookshelves in the back of the room.

M: Yes. And I put the teddy bear to the left of them.

W: It's so cute! But why did you put that vase on the table? It can be dangerous for children reading books.

M: I didn't think of that. I guess I should _______ _______ _______ _______.

W: And what are you going to put on the bulletin board beside the clock?

M: Well, I'll probably put _______ _______ _______ _______ to read on it.

W: That's a good idea!

05

M: I'll ________ ________ ________ ________ tonight.
W: I don't think there's much food in the refrigerator, though.
M: Oh, then how about going out for dinner instead?
W: Sorry, but I'm too tired to go out. Why don't we just ________ ________ ________?
M: That would be nice, too. Is there anything in particular you want?
W: ________ ________ ________ that new Chinese restaurant, Dragon Palace?
M: Good idea! I've heard that their sesame chicken is delicious.
W: Do you know what their phone number is?
M: I'm not sure. How can we find out?
W: It's probably on their website. Why don't you look it up? And then I'll call and place an order.
M: Sure, I'll do that right now.

06

M: Are you going to our high school reunion this weekend, Melissa?
W: Probably. It ________ ________ ________ ________ ________ ________. How about you?
M: I'm going. I have a tennis lesson on that day, but I switched it to Sunday.
W: Wait a minute. I thought the reunion was on Sunday.
M: No, it's on Saturday.
W: In that case, I can't go. I have plans on Saturday.
M: Really? Can't you cancel them?
W: No. My family is ________ ________ ________ ________ for my mother's birthday.
M: You told me your mom's birthday was next weekend.
W: It is, but my mother will be away ________ ________ ________ ________ next weekend.
M: I see. Well, I'm disappointed you won't be coming.

07

M: Hi. I'd like to rent some skis.
W: How many pairs do you need?
M: I need two pairs of adult skis and a child's pair.
W: Adult skis are $10 per hour, and children's are usually $5. However, we ________ ________ ________ ________ on children's skis right now.
M: Do you? How much are they?
W: Children's skis are $3 an hour today. How long will you be on the slopes?
M: We'll be here for ________ ________ ________ ________.
W: Then would you like to pay for two hours?
M: No, I'll pay for three hours in case we ________ ________ ________ ________.
W: No problem, sir. Do you have a membership card?
M: Oh, yes. I can get a $10 discount with it, right?
W: That's correct.

08

M: Hey, Tammy. I haven't seen you around lately.
W: I've been busy because I ________ ________ ________ ________ in a new musical!
M: A musical? That's great. Is it playing soon?
W: Yes. It starts next Tuesday.
M: That's very soon. Where will it be showing?
W: We'll be performing at the Wren Theater.
M: I ________ ________ ________ ________ ________. What's the name of the show?
W: It's called *The Wonderful West*. It's about a woman ________ ________ ________ ________ to live on a ranch.
M: Sounds interesting. So are you the star of the show?
W: I wish, but Vicky Green, the director, chose someone else.
M: That's too bad. But I'm sure you'll be great in your role.

25회

09

M: Are you interested in _______ _______ _______ in the coffee business? Our eight-day barista workshop will teach you how to make coffee-based drinks. You'll also get information on how to set up and run your own coffee shop. It will be held on Saturdays and Sundays for the four weeks of September. Each session _______ _______ _______ _______. Topics will include selecting the best coffee, choosing the ideal location and operating coffee-making equipment. The workshop will be held in the local community center, and _______ _______ _______ _______ will be limited to 25. If you're interested, sign up and bring the $150 workshop fee.

10

W: Can I help you find something, sir?

M: Well, I need a pair of headphones or earphones.

W: All right. Do you need a pair with a built-in microphone?

M: Yes, I do. I want to use them with my smartphone.

W: Okay. How about _______ _______ _______ _______ _______?

M: I'm not sure. How long are they usually?

W: Most are 1.25 meters long. But some are two meters. Normally, 1.25 meters _______ _______ _______ _______ _______.

M: I will get the normal size.

W: I see. Then we have two different models for you to choose from.

M: It doesn't matter. I'll just take the cheaper pair.

W: Sure. You can _______ _______ _______ at the front counter.

11

M: Julie and I are _______ _______ _______ _______ _______. Would you like to come?

W: I love movies, but it depends. What are you going to see?

M: Julie and I both want to see *Space Explorers*.

W: (Sorry, but I've already seen that film.)

12

W: Hey, Dave. Would you like to go shopping together tomorrow?

M: Sure. I need to buy some new clothes and a pair of shoes.

W: Great. _______ _______ _______ _______?

M: (Well, how about right after class?)

13

M: And that's the shower room over there.

W: I see. Thanks for showing me around the gym.

M: My pleasure. _______ _______ _______ _______, we'll set up a workout routine for you.

W: Okay. As my personal trainer, do you have any advice for me?

M: Well, first I need to know your reason for joining the gym.

W: I just want to _______ _______ _______.

M: My tip is to exercise regularly and drink a lot of water.

W: Okay. How many glasses should I drink a day?

M: About eight. Also, make sure you eat _______ _______ _______ _______ _______.

W: Really? I've found skipping meals is a good way to lose weight quickly.

M: (It seems so, but that can be very bad for your health.)

14

[Knocking on door]

M: Who is it?

W: I have a coffee delivery for Peter Diaz.

M: Oh, come on in. You can put it on that desk.

W: All right. It's three cappuccinos and a latte.

M: Did you bring the receipt? I want to check because you _______ _______ _______ last time.

W: Yes, I'm sorry about that. I was confused. Anyhow, here's your receipt and a coupon.

M: Oh! It's _______ _______ _______ _______!

W: It's an apology from the manager for our mistake last time.

M: That's very nice. Uh-oh, I think there's a mistake with this latte.

W: Is there? Didn't you order one?

M: Yes, but it _______ _______ _______ _______ _______.

W: (I'm sorry. I'll bring a new one right away.)

15

W: Hailey moved to a new apartment, and she _______ _______ _______ _______ it. On the day she moved in, her neighbor came and introduced himself. He was very nice and friendly. One day, however, she finds that her neighbor has put his trash _______ _______ _______ _______ _______. Hailey guesses he did this because he wants to throw out all his trash at one time. As time goes by, it starts to smell bad and looks awful whenever Hailey passes it. She thinks the waste has to be removed _______ _______ _______ _______. In this situation, what would Hailey most likely say to her neighbor?

Hailey: (Would you mind not putting waste in the hall?)

16-17

M: Many people often _______ _______ _______ _______ alone late at night. However, this is very dangerous because you could be a target of crime. If someone starts to follow you at night, don't panic. Instead, use the following tips. First of all, try to _______ _______ _______ _______ where there are other people. If the person tries to grab you before you can find a place, yell loudly for help. Blowing a whistle can also be helpful. But if nothing else works, you may have to fight. A gas gun is an effective weapon. You can also use a stun gun, or if _______ _______ _______ _______ _______, pepper spray is good for self-protection as well. It can be used to stop attackers and temporarily blind them. If you follow these tips, you can be safe when you walk alone at night.

25회

25 Word & Expressions

01
- □ **resident** 거주민
- □ **approach** 다가가다[오다]
- □ **be away from** …로부터 떨어져있다
- □ **theft** 절도, 도난 사건
- □ **regular** 보통의; *정기적인
- □ **target** 목표, 대상
- □ **break into** …에 침입하다
- □ **at all times** 항상, 언제나

02
- □ **whole wheat bread** 통밀빵
- □ **process** 가공[처리]하다
- □ **nutrient** 영양소
- □ **mineral** 무기질, 미네랄
- □ **remove** 없애다, 제거하다
- □ **get used to** …에 익숙해지다

03
- □ **postcard** 그림엽서, 엽서
- □ **stamp** 우표
- □ **express** 속달의

04
- □ **square** 정사각형 모양의
- □ **make sense** 타당하다, 말이 되다
- □ **bookshelf** 책꽂이
- □ **vase** 꽃병
- □ **bulletin board** 게시판

05
- □ **refrigerator** 냉장고
- □ **in particular** 특별히
- □ **sesame** 참깨
- □ **look up** …을 찾아보다
- □ **place an order** 주문하다

06
- □ **reunion** 동창회
- □ **switch** 바꾸다
- □ **cancel** 취소하다
- □ **business trip** 출장
- □ **disappointed** 실망한

07
- □ **rent** 빌리다, 대여하다
- □ **slope** 경사지; *스키장
- □ **in case** …할 경우에 대비해서

08
- □ **role** 역할, 배역
- □ **perform** 공연하다
- □ **ranch** 목장
- □ **star** (연극 등의) 주연, 주역
- □ **director** (연극 등의) 감독

09
- □ **workshop** 워크숍, 연수회
- □ **based** 기반을 둔
- □ **set up** …을 시작하다[설립하다]
- □ **run** (사업체 등을) 운영하다
- □ **session** 기간; *수업 (시간)
- □ **operate** 작동하다
- □ **equipment** 장비, 용품
- □ **community center** 시민 문화 회관
- □ **participant** 참가자
- □ **limit** 제한하다

10
- □ **built-in** 내장된
- □ **microphone** 마이크
- □ **length** 길이
- □ **cable** 전선
- □ **normally** 보통(은)

11
- □ **explorer** 탐험가
- □ **sci-fi** 공상 과학 소설의

12
- □ **make it** 시간 맞춰 가다

13
- □ **show around** …을 구경시켜주다
- □ **gym** 체육관, 헬스장
- □ **workout** 운동
- □ **routine** 정해진 순서
- □ **regularly** 규칙적으로
- □ **balanced** 균형 잡힌, 안정된
- □ **skip** 거르다, 빼먹다
- □ **secret** 비밀;*비결
- □ **maintain** 유지하다
- □ **weight** 무게; (역기의) 웨이트
- □ **upset** 속상하게 하다; *배탈이 나게 하다

14
- □ **receipt** 영수증
- □ **miscalculate** 잘못 계산하다
- □ **confused** 혼란스러워하는
- □ **apology** 사과
- □ **be supposed to-v** …하기로 되어있다, …해야 한다

15
- □ **be satisfied with** …에 만족하다
- □ **neighbor** 이웃
- □ **introduce** 소개하다
- □ **throw out** …을 버리다
- □ **awful** 끔찍한
- □ **remove** 없애다, 제거하다
- □ **complain** 불평[항의]하다
- □ **landlord** 집주인

16-17
- □ **panic** 겁에 질리다
- □ **following** 다음에 나오는
- □ **grab** 잡다
- □ **whistle** 호루라기
- □ **effective** 효과적인
- □ **weapon** 무기
- □ **stun gun** 전기 충격기
- □ **pepper spray** 페퍼 스프레이(호신용 분사액체)
- □ **self-protection** 자기방어
- □ **temporarily** 일시적으로

26 영어듣기 모의고사

정답 및 해설 p.78-80

1번부터 17번까지는 듣고 답하는 문제입니다.
1번부터 15번까지는 한 번만 들려주고, 16번부터 17번까지는 두 번 들려줍니다. 방송을 잘 듣고 답을 하기 바랍니다.

01

다음을 듣고, 여자가 하는 말의 목적으로 가장 적절한 것을 고르시오.

① 신발 제작 과정을 보여주려고
② 발 건강의 중요성을 강조하려고
③ 수제화 제작 업체를 홍보하려고
④ 편한 신발 고르는 방법을 알려주려고
⑤ 고객의 신발 구매 성향을 설명하려고

02

대화를 듣고, 남자의 의견으로 가장 적절한 것을 고르시오.

① 치실 사용을 게을리하면 안 된다.
② 하루에 세 번 양치질을 해야 한다.
③ 식사 후에 바로 양치질을 해야 한다.
④ 주기적으로 스케일링을 받아야 한다.
⑤ 치아 건강을 해치는 습관을 없애야 한다.

03

대화를 듣고, 두 사람의 관계를 가장 잘 나타낸 것을 고르시오.

① 독자 — 소설가
② 고객 — 서점 직원
③ 학생 — 국어 선생님
④ 출판업자 — 도서관 사서
⑤ 도서관 이용객 — 도서관 사서

04

대화를 듣고, 그림에서 대화의 내용과 일치하지 않는 것을 고르시오.

05

대화를 듣고, 남자가 할 일로 가장 적절한 것을 고르시오.

① 여행 계획 세우기
② 호텔 투숙 연장하기
③ 불꽃놀이 시간 알아보기
④ 인터넷으로 호텔 예약하기
⑤ 돌아가는 항공편 변경하기

06

대화를 듣고, 여자가 아르바이트를 하는 이유를 고르시오.

① 컴퓨터를 사려고
② 근무 경력을 쌓으려고
③ 여행 경비를 마련하려고
④ 다음 학기 등록금을 내려고
⑤ 선생님께 선물을 사 드리려고

07

대화를 듣고, 남자가 지불할 금액을 고르시오. 3점

① $32 ② $36 ③ $40
④ $45 ⑤ $50

08

대화를 듣고, 장학금에 관해 두 사람이 언급하지 않은 것을 고르시오.

① 자격 ② 지원 방법
③ 지원 마감일 ④ 면접 날짜
⑤ 금액

09

Dugong에 관한 다음 내용을 듣고, 일치하지 않는 것을 고르시오.

① 두껍고 주름진 피부를 가지고 있다.
② 꼬리를 위아래로 움직여 헤엄친다.
③ 주로 작은 물고기를 잡아먹는다.
④ 호주 연안에 집단으로 서식한다.
⑤ 고기와 기름을 얻기 위해 사냥당했다.

10

다음 표를 보면서 대화를 듣고, 여자가 렌트할 정수기를 고르시오.

< Water Purifier Rental Service >

	Model	Hot Water	Ice Maker	Filter Refill Frequency	Monthly Rental Fee
①	A	Y	N	once / year	$65
②	B	Y	N	once / month	$25
③	C	Y	Y	once / three months	$30
④	D	N	N	once / month	$15
⑤	E	Y	N	once / six months	$55

11

대화를 듣고, 남자의 마지막 말에 대한 여자의 응답으로 가장 적절한 것을 고르시오.

① I think it will be at least 20 minutes.
② You should have made a reservation.
③ We open at eleven o'clock in the morning.
④ Unfortunately, we only have tables for two now.
⑤ I'm sorry, but we are closing the restaurant soon.

12

대화를 듣고, 여자의 마지막 말에 대한 남자의 응답으로 가장 적절한 것을 고르시오.

① Then it would be perfect for you.
② I'd love to make some new friends.
③ Are you a member of the language club?
④ I'm not interested in learning a language.
⑤ Why don't you learn something else instead?

13

대화를 듣고, 여자의 마지막 말에 대한 남자의 응답으로 가장 적절한 것을 고르시오.

Man: ______________________

① If we meet later, we might miss the show.
② The show was amazing. I'll never forget it.
③ Why don't we choose a band we both like?
④ All right. We should meet in front of Stage A.
⑤ They're supposed to play on Stage C later tonight.

14

대화를 듣고, 남자의 마지막 말에 대한 여자의 응답으로 가장 적절한 것을 고르시오. 3점

Woman: ______________________

① Can you show me how to make candles?
② Sorry, but I don't have time to bake cakes.
③ We can just buy some at the bakery instead.
④ Yes, it's really nice to have an enjoyable hobby.
⑤ You should have told me before I made this candle.

15

다음 상황 설명을 듣고, 선생님이 Joyce에게 할 말로 가장 적절한 것을 고르시오.

Teacher: ______________________

① I will take part in the contest as a judge.
② You should've tried harder than last year.
③ Just do what you did before, and you'll be fine.
④ You can try again next year, so don't be disappointed.
⑤ You had better not take part in the competition this year.

[16-17] 다음을 듣고, 물음에 답하시오.

16

남자가 하는 말의 주제로 가장 적절한 것은? 3점

① 성격을 바꾸는 방법
② 좋은 첫인상을 남기는 방법
③ 친구를 사귀기에 좋은 성격
④ 첫 방문에 가져갈 선물 고르는 방법
⑤ 집안의 물건으로 알 수 있는 사람의 성격

17

언급된 단서가 아닌 것은?

① decorations ② pictures
③ nature photos ④ electronics
⑤ books

정답 및 해설 p.80

녹음을 다시 한 번 듣고, 빈칸에 알맞은 말을 쓰시오.

01

W: ________ ________ ________ ________ shoes, you should pay close attention to how well they fit. Choosing shoes that don't fit can lead to pain and even injury. Normal shoes sometimes cause this kind of problem. ________ ________ ________ ________, custom shoes are designed specifically for the wearer, so they can give you the most comfortable fit. At Johnson and Sons, we make some of the best custom shoes in the world. For over 50 years, our family has been making classic, unique shoes ________ ________ ________ ________. Our shoes are made of high quality materials. Come into our store and choose from more than 40 styles!

02

M: Hello, Amy. ________ ________ ________ ________ today?

W: I have a toothache, Dr. Smith.

M: Let me see... *[Pause]* You have a cavity, but it's not that serious.

W: That's good. But I don't understand why I got a cavity.

M: Hmm... Have you been ________ ________ ________ ________?

W: Yes, I brush them for three minutes at least three times a day.

M: Well, brushing isn't always enough. You need to have regular scaling treatments, too.

W: Is that really necessary?

M: Yes. When a lot of plaque builds up on your teeth, you can't always ________ ________ ________ ________ ________.

W: Oh, I see. How often should I come?

M: You should come in every six months.

W: Okay.

03

M: Excuse me. ________ ________ ________ you can help me.

W: Sure. What can I do for you?

M: Well, I'm looking for a book called *The History of the Wild West.*

W: Do you know the author's name?

M: Yes, I do. The author is Benjamin Horne.

W: *[Typing sound]* Hmm... It looks like that book has ________ ________ ________ ________ by someone else.

M: I see. When was it checked out?

W: It was checked out just last week. Would you like us to contact you ________ ________ ________ ________?

M: That would be great. Here is my phone number.

W: We will let you know as soon as it is returned.

04

M: Honey, I'm home!

W: I was waiting for you. I rearranged the kitchen.

M: Really?

W: Yes! Come take a look. I put the spice jars ________ ________ ________ ________ the stove.

M: That's a good idea. It was inconvenient when we had them in the cupboard above the stove.

W: I also put the kitchen tool holder on the wall ________ ________ ________ ________.

M: I see. Oh, what's that in front of the spice jars?

W: It's a toaster. I just bought it this morning.

M: Good. We needed one. And you moved the coffeemaker next to the water purifier.

W: Yes, that should ________ ________ ________ to make coffee.

M: I agree. You did a great job!

05

W: This has been a great trip. I can't believe it's almost over.

M: Yes. _______ _______ _______ _______ _______ one more day.

W: So do I. Why don't we change our plans and leave tomorrow instead of this evening?

M: That sounds good. If we do, we can watch the fireworks show tonight!

W: Great! Oh, wait! We should check if we can _______ _______ _______ first.

M: You're right. I will check to make sure we can change it to tomorrow.

W: Great. Why don't you call the airline right away?

M: Sure. We also need to reserve the room for one more night. _______ _______ _______ _______ that?

W: No problem. I'll take care of it while you call about the flight.

06

M: Hi, Kate. What are you doing here?

W: Hi, Kevin. I'm _______ _______ _______ now.

M: Really? Why did you get a part-time job?

W: I want to make some extra money.

M: I see. I guess it's good work experience to put on your résumé.

W: I guess so, but I want to be a teacher after I graduate.

M: That's a good goal. So, what are you _______ _______ _______?

W: I want to travel around Europe this summer.

M: That sounds fun. But it must be pretty expensive, too.

W: Yes. That's why I got this job.

M: Well, I'm sure _______ _______ _______ _______ _______. Traveling is a great experience.

W: I hope so.

07

W: Welcome to the Mint Museum of Toys. How may I help you?

M: I'd like to buy some tickets. How much are they?

W: _______ _______ _______ _______. Do you need tickets for adults or children?

M: There are four of us: two adults and two children.

W: All right. Tickets are $15 for adults and $10 for children under 12.

M: I see. I have a four-year-old daughter and a son who is 11.

W: Oh, children under 5 _______ _______ _______ _______, sir.

M: Great! In that case, I don't need a ticket for my daughter. And can I _______ _______ _______?

W: Let me check. *[Pause]* Sure. This will give you 10% off the total price.

M: Excellent! Then, three tickets, please.

08

[Telephone rings.]

W: Good afternoon, Mansfield College administrative office.

M: Hi. _______ _______ _______ the scholarships.

W: Okay. Well, to qualify, you must currently be a high school senior living in the city of Mansfield.

M: All right. How can I apply?

W: You can _______ _______ _______ _______ from our website, fill it out, and email it to us.

M: When should I send it?

W: Well, we must receive it by June 1st.

M: I see. How will I know _______ _______ _______ _______?

W: We will email that information to you on June 15th.

M: Great. I have one more question. How much are the scholarships for?

W: There are three scholarships available, and they are worth $3,000 each.

09

M: The dugong is a sea mammal. It is ________ ________ ________ ________ the elephant. Like an elephant, it has thick, wrinkly skin. It also has a whale-like tail that it ________ ________ ________ ________ to swim. It grows up to three meters in length and weighs up to 500 kg. It feeds on its mother's milk when it's young. After about 18 months, however, it begins to eat seaweed. It mainly lives in large herds in coastal waters near Australia where seaweed grows. Unfortunately, the dugong ________ ________ ________ ________ its meat and oil for thousands of years. It is now protected, but its population is continuously shrinking.

10

M: Welcome to Water World. How may I help you?
W: ________ ________ ________ ________ a water purifier.
M: Okay. What kind would you like?
W: Well, do you have any that can make hot water?
M: Of course. Do you want one that has a built-in icemaker as well?
W: No, I don't need that. And I don't want to ________ ________ ________ ________.
M: Well, the more expensive ones require fewer filter changes. Filters can be very expensive.
W: Hmm... I don't like changing the filters. ________ ________ ________ is too often.
M: Then you only have two options. Which one do you prefer?
W: The cheaper one, of course.

11

M: I'd like a table for two, please.
W: I'm sorry, but you'll need to ________ ________ ________ ________ ________.
M: Oh. We're in a bit of a rush. How long is the wait?
W: (I think it will be at least 20 minutes.)

12

W: What do you think of the French club?
M: It's great. My French ________ ________ ________ ________ since I joined.
W: I'd really like to join a club and learn French.
M: (Then it would be perfect for you.)

13

M: Wow! There are so many different bands to see.
W: Yeah. This will be the best rock festival ever!
M: The first show is at five. There are three stages to choose from.
W: Well, I want to see Red Rock play at five. They're on Stage B.
M: But ________ ________ ________ the Quiet Monkeys. They're on Stage C.
W: Hmm... I think we should see ________ ________ ________.
M: So do I. Then we should split up. You want to see Dexter's Shadow at eight on Stage A, right?
W: Of course! They're my favorite!
M: Okay. I want to watch their performance, too.
W: Then ________ ________ ________ now and meet somewhere before eight.
M: (All right. We should meet in front of Stage A.)

26회

14

W: Hi, Ken. Did you have a nice weekend?

M: Yes. I _______ _______ _______ _______ _______. What about you, Brenda?

W: I made some candles. It's something I really enjoy doing.

M: That's interesting. Why do you like making candles?

W: Hmm... It's fun, and it helps me relax.

M: That's good. Our lives _______ _______ _______ _______, so relaxing is important.

W: Yes. Also, I like giving candles to people as gifts.

M: That makes sense. I feel the same way about baking.

W: I didn't know you like to bake. What kinds of things do you bake?

M: I like making cakes. _______ _______ _______ my friends eating something I made, I feel happy.

W: (Yes, it's really nice to have an enjoyable hobby.)

15

W: Joyce won the Middleton High School speech contest yesterday. Now she is going to enter the regional competition and _______ _______ _______ from other schools. She won the school speech contest last year as well. But when she got to the regional finals, she _______ _______ _______ in the top three. Now she's really nervous about trying again. So she goes to ask her favorite teacher for some advice. Her teacher thinks she can win if she _______ _______ _______ like the one from the school contest. In this situation, what would Joyce's teacher most likely say to her?

Teacher: (Just do what you did before, and you'll be fine.)

16-17

M: Imagine you visit the home of someone you've never met before. Do you think you could learn about the person's personality just _______ _______ _______? One social psychologist believes we can learn a lot about people simply by looking at the things in their homes. For example, if people's shelves are full of decorations, they are probably outgoing. And if they have lots of pictures, _______ _______ _______ _______ they are creative. People who hang nature photos on their walls tend to be quiet and shy. Bookshelves can also provide big clues. People with books from many different genres, for example, are usually flexible. These things might not always be true. But you should still _______ _______ _______ what people put on their shelves or hang on their walls. It might give you some clues about their personalities.

26 Word & Expressions

01
- □ **when it comes to** …에 관한 한
- □ **injury** 부상
- □ **custom** 맞춘, 주문한
- □ **specifically** 분명히, 명확하게; *특별히
- □ **classic** 최고 수준의
- □ **unique** 독특한, 특별한
- □ **material** 재료

02
- □ **toothache** 치통
- □ **cavity** 충치
- □ **properly** 제대로, 적절히
- □ **scaling** 스케일링, 치석 제거
- □ **treatment** 치료, 처치
- □ **necessary** 필요한, 필수적인
- □ **plaque** (치아에 끼는) 플라크, 치태
- □ **build up** 늘다, 축적되다
- □ **get off** …을 제거하다

03
- □ **author** 작가, 저자
- □ **check out** (책 등을) 대출하다
- □ **contact** 연락하다

04
- □ **rearrange** 재배치하다
- □ **spice jar** 양념 통
- □ **stove** 가스레인지
- □ **inconvenient** 불편한
- □ **cupboard** 찬장
- □ **kitchen tool** 부엌 도구
- □ **water purifier** 정수기

05
- □ **firework** (*pl.*) 불꽃놀이
- □ **airline** 항공사
- □ **reserve** 예약하다
- □ **take care of** …을 처리하다

06
- □ **extra** 추가의
- □ **résumé** 이력서
- □ **be worth** …의 가치가 있다

07
- □ **vary** 서로[각기] 다르다
- □ **for free** 공짜로, 무료로

08
- □ **administrative office** 행정실
- □ **scholarship** 장학금
- □ **qualify** 자격을 갖추다
- □ **currently** 현재, 지금
- □ **application** 지원(서)
- □ **fill out** …을 작성하다
- □ **select** 선발하다, 선정하다

09
- □ **mammal** 포유류
- □ **relative** 친척
- □ **wrinkly** 주름진
- □ **feed on** …을 먹고살다
- □ **seaweed** 해조, 해초
- □ **mainly** 주로
- □ **herd** (동물의) 무리
- □ **population** 인구; *개체수
- □ **continuously** 계속해서
- □ **shrink** 줄어들다

10
- □ **built-in** 내장된
- □ **icemaker** 제빙기
- □ **filter** 필터, 여과 장치

11
- □ **in a rush** 아주 바쁘게
- □ **make a reservation** 예약하다

12
- □ **improve** 개선되다, 나아지다

13
- □ **split up** 헤어지다, 나뉘다
- □ **be supposed to-v** …하기로 되어 있다

14
- □ **be full of** …로 가득 차 있다
- □ **enjoyable** 즐길 수 있는

15
- □ **regional** 지역의
- □ **competition** 대회, 경쟁
- □ **compete against** …와 경쟁하다
- □ **final** 결승전
- □ **fail** 실패하다
- □ **nervous** 초조한, 불안해하는
- □ **give a speech** 연설하다
- □ **judge** 판사; *심판, 심사위원

16-17
- □ **personality** 성격, 인격
- □ **social psychologist** 사회 심리학자
- □ **decoration** 장식물
- □ **outgoing** 외향적인
- □ **tend** (…하는) 경향이 있다
- □ **clue** 단서
- □ **flexible** 융통성 있는
- □ **electronics** 전자기기

27 영어듣기 모의고사

1번부터 17번까지는 듣고 답하는 문제입니다.
1번부터 15번까지는 한 번만 들려주고, 16번부터 17번까지는 두 번 들려줍니다. 방송을 잘 듣고 답을 하기 바랍니다.

01

다음을 듣고, 여자가 하는 말의 목적으로 가장 적절한 것을 고르시오.

① 십 대 청소년들이 바쁜 이유를 설명하려고
② 음악을 활용한 기억력 향상 방법을 소개하려고
③ 시간을 효율적으로 활용하는 방법을 알려주려고
④ 전자 기기 사용을 줄여야 하는 이유를 알려주려고
⑤ 여러 일을 동시에 하는 것의 비효율성을 설명하려고

02

대화를 듣고, 두 사람이 하는 말의 주제로 가장 적절한 것을 고르시오.

① 콘택트렌즈 착용의 부작용
② 눈 건강을 향상시키는 방법
③ 피로한 눈의 여러 가지 원인
④ 사무실 근무 시 휴식의 중요성
⑤ 눈을 건조하게 만드는 나쁜 습관들

03

대화를 듣고, 두 사람의 관계를 가장 잘 나타낸 것을 고르시오.

① 화가 — 수강생 ② 헤어 디자이너 — 고객
③ 사진작가 — 모델 ④ 패션 디자이너 — 연예인
⑤ 박물관 안내원 — 관람객

04

대화를 듣고, 그림에서 대화의 내용과 일치하지 않는 것을 고르시오.

05

대화를 듣고, 남자가 여자를 위해 할 일로 가장 적절한 것을 고르시오.

① 회의 참석하기
② 디자이너 추천하기
③ 웹사이트 디자인하기
④ 디자이너에게 연락하기
⑤ 자신의 웹사이트 보여 주기

06

대화를 듣고, 여자가 하와이에 다시 가고 싶지 않은 이유를 고르시오.

① 벌레가 많아서
② 등산을 싫어해서
③ 음식이 맞지 않아서
④ 날씨가 좋지 않아서
⑤ 비행기 멀미가 심해서

07

대화를 듣고, 여자가 지불할 금액을 고르시오. 3점

① $60 ② $80 ③ $100
④ $120 ⑤ $160

08

대화를 듣고, 드야 동물 보호 구역에 관해 두 사람이 언급하지 않은 것을 고르시오.

① 위치 ② 크기 ③ 관광객 수
④ 설립 연도 ⑤ 거주민

09

Anderson Cooper에 관한 다음 내용을 듣고, 일치하지 않는 것을 고르시오.

① 미국에서 가장 잘 알려진 기자 중 한 명이다.
② 부유하고 유명한 가정에서 태어났다.
③ 가족의 죽음으로 삶과 죽음의 문제에 관심을 가졌다.
④ 미얀마와 아프리카 지역의 분쟁을 보도했다.
⑤ 뛰어난 보도 기사를 많이 썼지만 상을 받은 적은 없다.

정답 및 해설 p.81-83

10

다음 표를 보면서 대화를 듣고, 여자가 선택할 배송 방법을 고르시오.

< International Shipping Choices >

	Choice	Type of Shipping	Package Type	Tracking
①	A	Express	Box	X
②	B	Standard	Bubble Pack	X
③	C	Standard	Box	O
④	D	Standard	Bubble Pack	O
⑤	E	Express	Bubble Pack	O

11

대화를 듣고, 남자의 마지막 말에 대한 여자의 응답으로 가장 적절한 것을 고르시오.

① You can call the zoo to cancel the trip.
② Make sure that you follow all of the rules.
③ Field trips are a great experience for students.
④ The zoo is the best place to see a variety of animals.
⑤ As long as the weather is good, there'll be no problem.

12

대화를 듣고, 여자의 마지막 말에 대한 남자의 응답으로 가장 적절한 것을 고르시오.

① I'm sure that it is too big.
② Help me put these books on it.
③ I got it at that new furniture store.
④ Let's see if it will fit in your bedroom.
⑤ There's enough space in the living room.

13

대화를 듣고, 남자의 마지막 말에 대한 여자의 응답으로 가장 적절한 것을 고르시오. 3점

Woman: ________________

① I already promised to lend it to her.
② I'll apologize to her tomorrow morning.
③ That would be more helpful than fighting.
④ I'm very disappointed that you don't trust me.
⑤ I'll never get the stain out of my sister's dress!

14

대화를 듣고, 여자의 마지막 말에 대한 남자의 응답으로 가장 적절한 것을 고르시오.

Man: ________________

① I'm sorry I didn't finish it on time.
② I believe you. Tomorrow is just fine.
③ Your foot should heal in a few weeks.
④ You should go to the hospital right away.
⑤ That's okay. My friend will be there soon.

15

다음 상황 설명을 듣고, Megan이 고객에게 할 말로 가장 적절한 것을 고르시오.

Megan: ________________

① May I have your order number?
② I'd like to, but your address is incorrect.
③ It is possible, but I don't know what to send.
④ There will be an additional shipping charge.
⑤ You shouldn't have given the wrong number.

[16-17] 다음을 듣고, 물음에 답하시오.

16

남자가 하는 말의 주제로 가장 적절한 것은? 3점

① the side effects of healthy food
② the various kinds of super food
③ foods that prevent heart disease
④ the benefits of eating blueberries
⑤ how to strengthen the immune system

17

언급된 슈퍼푸드가 아닌 것은?

① 시금치　② 호두
③ 사과　④ 마늘
⑤ 블루베리

녹음을 다시 한 번 듣고, 빈칸에 알맞은 말을 쓰시오.

01

W: It's common to find people _______ _______ _______ _______ _______. For example, people often listen to music while studying or working, or chat on their phones while watching a movie. Why do people want to do two things at the same time? Well, many people think that it is more efficient than doing just one thing at a time. However, that's not true. Doing more than one thing at a time can actually make it _______ _______ _______ _______ them. Also, it can overstimulate your brain and affect your short-term memory negatively. So when you're studying, just _______ _______ _______ _______. The results will surely be better.

02

W: Dr. Green, my eyes _______ _______ _______ by the end of the day.

M: Do you spend a lot of time staring at computer screens and TVs?

W: I do. I work in an office on a computer all day.

M: I see. Unfortunately, staring at a computer screen _______ _______ _______ _______ _______.

W: What should I do?

M: Take a five-minute break every hour to rest your eyes.

W: What if that doesn't work?

M: I suggest using eye drops when your eyes get dry and not wearing contact lenses for too long.

W: Okay. I'll _______ _______ _______ _______.

M: In addition, you shouldn't stay too close to air conditioners or heaters.

W: I won't. Thank you for your advice, doctor.

03

M: Okay, Penelope. How would you like it today?

W: Honestly, Jonathan, I am open-minded. Do you _______ _______ _______?

M: Well, you've had it this way for over a year. How about something short this time?

W: That could be nice. How short?

M: Here, look at the models in these pictures. I could cut it shoulder-length.

W: Hmm... How about _______ _______ _______ _______? I like this style.

M: Wow, you're brave! But don't worry. I'll make it look fabulous.

W: Okay. I also want to dye my hair blonde.

M: But you dyed your hair just two months ago. If you dye it again, it might become damaged.

W: Oh, then I'll just _______ _______ _______ _______ _______.

04

M: This photo album is amazing! Did you make it?

W: Yes, I made it for my brother!

M: Oh, it says "Happy Birthday!" _______ _______ _______ _______ the left page.

W: Yes, it is a birthday present.

M: I like these three circular photos _______ _______ _______ _______. But the square one is the best.

W: I agree. I also like the big rectangular photo of my family on the right page.

M: It looks good! Is that your family's dog in the other picture?

W: Yes, it is. She's my brother's best friend. That's why I cut the picture into _______ _______ _______ _______ _______.

M: I see. Is that a note next to your dog's picture?

W: Yes. I wrote it myself.

05

M: Hey, Mary. What are you doing?

W: I'm just ________ ________ ________ ________ ________. I want to make the main page look better.

M: It sounds difficult.

W: It's not easy, but I'm enjoying it. Now I need to find a web designer, though.

M: I know lots of really good web designers. Would you like me to recommend someone?

W: Actually, I already have ________ ________ ________ ________. I just need to decide on one.

M: That should be easy.

W: Maybe, but I have four meetings today, so I don't have much time. Can you help me choose one?

M: Sure. Just email me the list and I'll ________ ________ ________.

W: Great! I really appreciate it!

06

M: Hey, Amy. How was your vacation?

W: It was okay, but I'm ________ ________ ________ ________.

M: Where did you go?

W: I went to Hawaii with my family.

M: That sounds nice. Was the weather good?

W: Yeah. The weather was mostly great.

M: Good! By the way, you look pretty tanned!

W: Yeah. I spent a lot of time outside. It was a perfect vacation ________ ________ ________ ________.

M: Uh-oh. Did you get sick on the flight?

W: No. Actually, there were many mosquitoes and ants where we were staying. They drove me crazy.

M: Oh! ________ ________ ________ ________ as well.

W: It was a beautiful place, but I don't want to go again.

07

M: How may I help you?

W: I'm looking for some shoes I can ________ ________ ________ ________.

M: We have three kinds of water shoes. They cost $80.

W: That's pretty expensive, but I really like that pair.

M: Do you have a membership card? If so, you can save 25%.

W: Yes. I also ________ ________ ________ ________ 50% off. I want to buy a second pair of the same shoes for my sister.

M: Oh, this coupon would only ________ ________ ________ ________.

W: Then I guess I will use it next time.

M: Well, you could buy one pair with the membership card and the other with the coupon.

W: That sounds great!

08

W: What are you reading, Steve?

M: It's a blog post about the Dja Faunal Reserve.

W: Oh, what's that?

M: It's ________ ________ ________ in Cameroon. The post says it is 5,260 square kilometers.

W: Then there must be a lot of different animals and plants there.

M: Yes. It says more than 1,500 plant species and 107 mammal species live there.

W: Wow, it is a really amazing place. Oh, look. The blogger wrote ________ ________ ________ ________ 1950.

M: And it has been on the UNESCO World Heritage Site list since 1987.

W: What does "Baka" mean? Is it a plant's name?

M: No, it is ________ ________ ________ ________ ________ who live there.

W: Well, it looks like an interesting post.

09

M: Anderson Cooper is one of the best-known journalists in America. _______ _______ _______ _______ a wealthy and famous family. However, when he was very young, his family was struck by tragedy. When he was only ten, his father died during heart surgery. About ten years later, his brother committed suicide. Deeply affected by these events, Cooper _______ _______ _______ questions of life and death. He became a journalist and reported on wars. After reporting on conflicts in Myanmar and parts of Africa, he became an international correspondent. And he _______ _______ _______ for his outstanding reporting.

10

M: How may I help you?

W: I'd like to send a package to my friend in Canada.

M: Okay. You have two options: express shipping or standard shipping.

W: Hmm... It's not urgent, so _______ _______ _______ would be better.

M: Okay. Are you going to use a standard box?

W: What I'm sending is fragile, so it _______ _______ _______ _______ _______.

M: In that case, I'd recommend the bubble pack.

W: Okay. Can I track where the package is?

M: If you want to track your package, you can register it. But that requires _______ _______ _______.

W: That's okay. I definitely want to track it. How much is the total price?

11

M: I can't wait to go on the school field trip next Monday.

W: Oh, where will you go?

M: We're going to the zoo! I really hope _______ _______ _______ _______ _______.

W: (As long as the weather is good, there'll be no problem.)

12

W: Can you help me move this bookshelf into my bedroom?

M: Hmm... I think it's _______ _______ _______ _______ in there.

W: Where do you think we can put it then?

M: (There's enough space in the living room.)

13

M: Karen. You seem to _______ _______ _______ _______ _______.

W: Oh, I had a big fight with my younger sister.

M: That's too bad. What happened?

W: She borrowed one of my dresses without permission.

M: That doesn't seem like a very big deal.

W: Normally I wouldn't care, but she _______ _______ _______ _______ _______ and lied about taking it.

M: How did you know she had taken it?

W: I hadn't worn it in weeks, but I found it in the laundry basket.

M: Are you sure your sister took it?

W: Yes. She's done it before. Plus, my mom saw her wearing it.

M: I see. I think you'd better _______ _______ _______ for lending her your things from now on.

W: (That would be more helpful than fighting.)

14

[Cell phone rings.]

W: Hello?

M: Hello, this is Professor Johnson.

W: Oh, Professor! I'm sorry I missed your class this morning.

M: Yes. I'm curious why you didn't attend class.

W: Actually, I _______ _______ _______ _______ and broke my foot this morning. I was in the hospital for hours.

M: Oh, that's too bad. Are you all right now?

W: I _______ _______ _______. I just wish I hadn't missed class.

M: Don't worry about it. You've never missed a class before.

W: What about my report due today, though? Should I have someone bring it to you tonight?

M: You can just drop it off at my office tomorrow morning.

W: Really? But I don't want you to think I didn't _______ _______ _______ _______.

M: (I believe you. Tomorrow is just fine.)

15

W: Megan is a customer service employee at an online shopping company. One afternoon, she _______ _______ _______ _______ an angry customer. He says he has been waiting for his order to arrive for three weeks. She discovers the shipment was sent out properly, but the shipping address was incorrect. When she explains this, he says that he recently moved to a new place and _______ _______ _______ his address on the website. He asks her to resend the package _______ _______ _______ _______. Since it's the customer's mistake, he has to pay the shipping charge. In this situation, what would Megan most likely say to the customer?

Megan: (There will be an additional shipping charge.)

16-17

M: Hello, everyone. My name is Miriam Jordan, and I'm a nutrition expert. Today many people _______ _______ _______ their health. They eat various kinds of healthy foods, including spinach, apples, and garlic, to keep healthy. These healthy foods are called "super foods" because of their beneficial effects on the body. Here is one more super food that you should know about—blueberries! Blueberries are high in antioxidants, which help strengthen your immune system. They have also been shown to help us _______ _______ _______ and memory as we age. They even help fight heart disease and cancer. Moreover, because blueberries consist of 85% water, they help you to lose weight and _______ _______ _______. With all of these health benefits, blueberries are one of the world's healthiest foods. Why don't you try adding blueberries to your breakfast cereal or yogurt for a healthy start to your day?

27회

27 Word & Expressions

01
- □ **efficient** 효율적인
- □ **complete** 완료하다
- □ **overstimulate** 과도하게 자극하다
- □ **negatively** 부정적으로
- □ **concentrate on** …에 집중하다

02
- □ **stare at** …을 응시하다
- □ **eye drop** 안약
- □ **contact lens** 콘택트렌즈

03
- □ **open-minded** 마음이 열린
- □ **shoulder-length** 어깨까지 오는, 어깨 길이의
- □ **fabulous** 기막히게 멋진
- □ **dye** 염색하다
- □ **blonde** 금발인

04
- □ **circular** 원형의
- □ **square** 정사각형 모양의
- □ **rectangular** 직사각형 모양의

05
- □ **work on** …을 작업하다
- □ **main page** 초기 화면
- □ **make a recommendation** 추천하다
- □ **appreciate** 고맙게 생각하다

06
- □ **tanned** 햇볕에 탄
- □ **sick** 아픈; *메스꺼운, 토할 것 같은
- □ **mosquito** 모기
- □ **drive ... crazy** …을 미치게 하다
- □ **bother** 귀찮게 하다, 성가시게 하다

07
- □ **save** 구하다; *절약하다
- □ **apply to** …에 적용되다

08
- □ **post** 게시글
- □ **faunal** 동물상의
- □ **reserve** 보호 구역
- □ **square kilometer** 제곱킬로미터
- □ **species** (분류상의) 종
- □ **mammal** 포유동물
- □ **native people** 원주민

09
- □ **journalist** 기자
- □ **strike** (갑자기) 발생하다
- □ **tragedy** 비극
- □ **commit suicide** 자살하다
- □ **conflict** 갈등; *분쟁
- □ **correspondent** 특파원
- □ **outstanding** 뛰어난
- □ **reporting** 보도

10
- □ **package** 소포; 포장하다
- □ **express** 신속한, 속달의
- □ **standard** 일반적인; 표준 규격에 맞춘
- □ **urgent** 긴급한
- □ **fragile** 깨지기 쉬운
- □ **track** 추적하다
- □ **register** 등록하다
- □ **require** 필요[요구]하다
- □ **additional** 추가의
- □ **definitely** 분명히

11
- □ **field trip** 현장 학습
- □ **cancel** 취소하다
- □ **make sure** 반드시 …하다

13
- □ **be in a bad mood** 기분이 나쁘다
- □ **permission** 허락
- □ **stain** 얼룩
- □ **laundry** 세탁물

14
- □ **miss** 놓치다
- □ **drop off at** …에 갖다 놓다
- □ **heal** 낫다

15
- □ **shipment** 수송; *수송품
- □ **properly** 제대로, 적절히
- □ **incorrect** 부정확한
- □ **resend** 다시 보내다
- □ **shipping charge** 배송료
- □ **additional** 추가의

16-17
- □ **be concerned with** …에 관심이 있다
- □ **beneficial** 유익한
- □ **antioxidant** 산화 방지제
- □ **strengthen** 강화되다, 강화하다
- □ **immune system** 면역 체계
- □ **consist of** …로 이루어지다[구성되다]
- □ **belly** 배, 복부
- □ **side effect** 부작용

28 영어듣기 모의고사

정답 및 해설 p.84-86

1번부터 17번까지는 듣고 답하는 문제입니다.
1번부터 15번까지는 한 번만 들려주고, 16번부터 17번까지는 두 번 들려줍니다. 방송을 잘 듣고 답을 하기 바랍니다.

01

다음을 듣고, 여자가 하는 말의 목적으로 가장 적절한 것을 고르시오.

① 새 직원을 소개하려고
② 신입 사원 채용을 공지하려고
③ 사내 행사 참여에 감사하려고
④ 신제품 개발 성공을 축하하려고
⑤ 직원들 간의 협력을 당부하려고

02

대화를 듣고, 두 사람이 하는 말의 주제로 가장 적절한 것을 고르시오.

① 환불 정책의 불합리성
② 온라인 쇼핑의 장단점
③ 대형 쇼핑몰 이용의 이점
④ 좋은 옷감을 고르는 요령
⑤ 옷의 얼룩을 제거하는 방법

03

대화를 듣고, 두 사람의 관계를 가장 잘 나타낸 것을 고르시오.

① 고객 — 택배 기사
② 고객 — 컴퓨터 수리공
③ 아파트 주민 — 경비원
④ 고객 — 슈퍼마켓 점원
⑤ 집주인 — 부동산 중개인

04

대화를 듣고, 그림에서 대화의 내용과 일치하지 않는 것을 고르시오.

05

대화를 듣고, 여자가 남자를 위해 할 일로 가장 적절한 것을 고르시오.

① 약 사 오기
② 상자 옮기기
③ 서랍 정리하기
④ 얼음팩 만들어오기
⑤ 병원에 데려다주기

06

대화를 듣고, 여자가 로스쿨 진학을 고려하는 이유를 고르시오.

① 부모님이 권유해서
② 돈을 많이 벌고 싶어서
③ 역할 모델처럼 되고 싶어서
④ 변호사가 되는 것이 꿈이어서
⑤ 법학과 교수님이 추천을 해서

07

대화를 듣고, 남자가 집안일로 소모한 칼로리를 고르시오. 3점

① 300 kcal ② 420 kcal ③ 450 kcal
④ 540 kcal ⑤ 690 kcal

08

대화를 듣고, 공원에 관해 두 사람이 언급하지 않은 것을 고르시오.

① 위치 ② 크기 ③ 개장 시기
④ 부대 시설 ⑤ 이름

09

사이버 게임 토너먼트에 관한 다음 내용을 듣고, 일치하지 않는 것을 고르시오.

① 9월 30일에 출전 등록을 마감한다.
② 센터 회원이 아니어도 참가할 수 있다.
③ 개인 키보드, 마우스, 헤드셋을 가져올 수 있다.
④ 부스에서 음료를 포함한 모든 음식물의 섭취는 금지된다.
⑤ 1위부터 3위까지 메달이 수여된다.

10

다음 표를 보면서 대화를 듣고, 두 사람이 선택할 프로그램을 고르시오.

< Newtown Aquarium Daily Programs >

	Program	Time	Age Limit	Price
①	Penguin Feeding	10:30 a.m.	None	$25
②	Meet the Sharks	3:00 p.m.	7 and up	$50
③	Sea Life Safari	2:30 p.m.	7 and up	$80
④	Diving Class	3:45 p.m.	13 and up	$90
⑤	Fun with Seals	4:30 p.m.	13 and up	$90

11

대화를 듣고, 남자의 마지막 말에 대한 여자의 응답으로 가장 적절한 것을 고르시오.

① That's great. Can I buy two of them?
② You still have lots of time to buy one.
③ Tomorrow is the last day to buy tickets.
④ Sorry, I don't know anything about the party.
⑤ You're right. When will the event take place?

12

대화를 듣고, 여자의 마지막 말에 대한 남자의 응답으로 가장 적절한 것을 고르시오.

① I hope you find your cell phone soon.
② Can you go shopping with me tomorrow?
③ Please call me any time you need my help.
④ I just found my phone in the lost and found.
⑤ I already did, but they said they didn't have it.

13

대화를 듣고, 여자의 마지막 말에 대한 남자의 응답으로 가장 적절한 것을 고르시오.

Man: ____________________

① You can borrow my notes from class.
② In that case, you can't apply this semester.
③ I think you had better go see a doctor today.
④ I'm sorry to hear that. I hope you get better soon.
⑤ When you improve your grades, you can apply again.

14

대화를 듣고, 남자의 마지막 말에 대한 여자의 응답으로 가장 적절한 것을 고르시오. 3점

Woman: ____________________

① Please give it back to me tomorrow.
② I wish I could help, but this is a library book.
③ Okay, I'll try hard to remember where I put it.
④ Sorry, but I still don't remember even borrowing it.
⑤ No problem. I finished reading that book last week.

15

다음 상황 설명을 듣고, Amy가 George에게 할 말로 가장 적절한 것을 고르시오.

Amy: ____________________

① You should have told me you were sick.
② When will your band play? I'd love to go.
③ Can you complete the poster without me?
④ I'm sad to hear the performance was canceled.
⑤ Thank you for taking me to the hospital today.

[16-17] 다음을 듣고, 물음에 답하시오.

16

남자가 하는 말의 목적으로 가장 적절한 것은?

① to suggest backpacking around South America
② to explain why South American cities attract tourists
③ to offer discounts on hotels in South American cities
④ to announce reduced prices on airfares to South America
⑤ to encourage preservation of the environment in South America

17

언급된 도시가 아닌 것은?

① Brasilia
② Lima
③ Bogota
④ Buenos Aires
⑤ Santiago

정답 및 해설 p.86

녹음을 다시 한 번 듣고, 빈칸에 알맞은 말을 쓰시오.

01

W: Good morning, everyone. First of all, I'd like to thank all of you for attending today's staff meeting. I'd like to ________ ________ ________ ________ a special announcement. This is Mr. Scott Brady. He will be our new financial advisor. He ________ ________ ________ ________ accounting and more than ten years of work experience. I believe that Mr. Brady will help our team in many ways. His hard work and knowledge will also help the entire company succeed and grow in the future. Please help Mr. Brady feel comfortable as he adjusts to ________ ________ ________ our corporate family.

02

M: Is that a new dress, Hailey?

W: Yes. I ________ ________ ________, but there's a huge stain on it.

M: Oh, that's awful. That's why I prefer to buy clothes at a store.

W: What do you mean?

M: That way you can ________ ________ ________ and see exactly what you're getting.

W: Online shopping is much cheaper, though. Actually, I got this dress for 20% off the store price.

M: But you have to re-pack it and mail it back to return it.

W: It's easy to return.

M: If you had bought the dress at a store, you could quickly exchange it for a new one.

W: That's true. I'll probably just ________ ________ ________ ________ this time.

03

[Cell phone rings.]

W: Hello.

M: Hello. Is this Ms. Johnson?

W: Yes, this is she. ________ ________ ________?

M: My name is Rob. You called our service center. I'm outside your apartment now.

W: I waited for you all morning, but now I'm at the supermarket.

M: Then is it okay for me to come back tomorrow?

W: I really need to use my computer this afternoon. It's already been three days since ________ ________ ________ ________. Can you wait there for a little bit?

M: How long do you think it will take?

W: I'll be home in ten minutes.

M: Okay, then I'll ________ ________ ________.

W: Thank you very much.

M: No problem.

04

M: How should we arrange the living room in our new apartment?

W: Well, first, let's hang these curtains ________ ________ ________ ________ up.

M: All right. Now, what about our big photograph of the Eiffel Tower?

W: How about hanging it on the wall to the left of the window?

M: That sounds good. And the rectangular table can go under it.

W: No, let's put the sofa under it.

M: Okay, that sounds fine.

W: Then we can put the table ________ ________ ________.

M: All right. I think we should put this small picture frame on it.

W: I don't agree. ________ ________ ________, our houseplant would look better.

M: Hmm... Good suggestion, honey!

28회

05

M: Ahh!

W: What's wrong, honey?

M: I just _______ _______ _______ in my neck while I was carrying this box. It really hurts. I can't turn my head.

W: Oh no! Do you want me to take you to see the doctor?

M: You may need to later. But I'm okay for now.

W: I think you should _______ _______ _______ for the pain. Should I get some at the drugstore?

M: No. There's some in the drawer. I'll take some right now.

W: Then how about some ice? I can _______ _______ _______ _______ for your neck.

M: Oh, that's a great idea.

W: I'll go make one right now.

M: Thanks, honey. You're the best.

06

M: How is the writing assignment about your future goals going?

W: I finished it _______ _______ _______ _______. I wrote about how I'm considering law school.

M: Really? Is that what your parents want you to study?

W: No. My parents just want me to study _______ _______ _______.

M: So does law interest you, or do you want a well-paying career?

W: We need money to live comfortably, but I started considering law because of Jeannie Suk.

M: Who is she? Is she your role model?

W: Yes. She is the first Asian American woman to become a professor at Harvard Law School.

M: So you want to _______ _______ _______ _______?

W: Exactly.

07

M: Do you know doing housework can be _______ _______ _______ _______?

W: Really? How so?

M: Look at this blog. You burn approximately 300 calories per hour scrubbing dishes.

W: Then I guess you burned some off when you did the dishes earlier for half an hour.

M: Yes, I did. Plus, I vacuumed the whole house today, _______ _______ _______ _______.

W: Let's see... It says that an hour of vacuuming burns about 150 calories.

M: I also spent 30 minutes washing the windows.

W: _______ _______ _______ did that burn?

M: According to this blog, it's about 240 an hour.

W: Wow! You really burned a lot of calories in total.

08

W: Hi, Tom. Where are you going?

M: Hey, Anne. I'm going to the new park that was recently _______ _______ _______ _______.

W: Oh, I've heard about it. Where is it exactly?

M: It's located four blocks north of here, next to city hall.

W: I see. How big is it?

M: It's about _______ _______ _______ _______ our school's playground. It takes about 20 minutes to walk across it.

W: I didn't know it was open to the public already. I thought they were still working on it.

M: It just opened last Monday.

W: That's great. It's called Roger's Park, right?

M: Yes. _______ _______ _______ if you would like to go sometime. Maybe we can go together.

W: Okay!

09

M: The city's number-one electronics retailer, Circuit Center, will host the annual Cyber Games Tournament on October 10th. _______ _______ _______ _______ is September 30th, so please hurry. If you have a Circuit Center membership, participation is free! If not, the entry fee is only $3 per player. You _______ _______ _______ _______ your own keyboard, mouse, and headset. However, in order to prevent cheating and hacking, no wireless equipment is allowed. Contestants are allowed to drink beverages during matches, but food is not allowed in the game booths. _______ _______ _______ _______ to first, second, and third place winners. For more information, please visit our website: www.circuitcenter.com.

10

W: Honey, we promised to take Peter to the Newtown Aquarium tomorrow.

M: I remember. Here's the schedule for the daily programs at the aquarium.

W: Okay. _______ _______ _______ _______ Peter.

M: What time do you think we'll get there?

W: The aquarium is far from here, so we'll probably _______ _______ _______ _______.

M: Right. Peter loves seals, so how about this one?

W: The time works, but Peter is only eight.

M: Then we should _______ _______ _______ _______ _______ programs.

W: Yes. Hmm... Do you think this one is worth $80?

M: No, I think that's a little expensive. And the other one sounds exciting.

W: I agree. Let's sign Peter up for that. I think he'll love it.

11

M: Are you going to take part in the fundraising event next Saturday?

W: I'd love to, but I heard that _______ _______ _______ _______ _______.

M: Don't worry. I have some extra tickets.

W: (That's great. Can I buy two of them?)

12

W: You look worried. What's the matter?

M: I lost my cell phone somewhere in the mall. I don't remember _______ _______ _______ _______.

W: Why don't you go and check the lost and found?

M: (I already did, but they said they didn't have it.)

13

M: Hi, can I help you?

W: Yes, please. I'd like to _______ _______ _______ _______ for next semester.

M: All right. Have you applied for one before?

W: No, I haven't. This will be my first time.

M: I see. Well, you need to be a first or second-year student.

W: _______ _______ _______ _______ _______ here.

M: That's good. You also must have Bs or higher in all your classes.

W: Actually, I've gotten straight As every semester.

M: Excellent. The final requirement is a perfect attendance record for this semester.

W: Oh. I _______ _______ _______ earlier this month. I had the flu.

M: (In that case, you can't apply this semester.)

14

M: _______ _______ _______ _______ that book I lent you?

W: Umm... I'm not sure which one you're talking about.

M: I'm talking about my favorite book, *A Tale of Two Cities*. You borrowed it a few months ago.

W: Really? But I don't remember borrowing it at all.

M: What? Are you kidding?

W: Oh, wait. Now I remember it, but _______ _______ _______ _______ where I left it.

M: I can't believe this. You're the most careless person I know!

W: I'm really sorry about this. I can't even recall if I finished reading it.

M: Please find it soon. I want it back _______ _______ _______ _______.

W: (Okay, I'll try hard to remember where I put it.)

15

W: George and Amy are in the school band. Next month, they will perform in the school auditorium. To advertise it, they are going to make a poster together this week. They _______ _______ _______ _______ _______. But suddenly Amy gets a severe stomachache, and she has to go to the hospital. She is told that she has to stay in the hospital _______ _______ _______ _______ _______. At this point, Amy calls George to say that she cannot work on the poster anymore and asks him to _______ _______ _______. In this situation, what would Amy most likely say to George?

Amy: (Can you complete the poster without me?)

16-17

M: For many people, traveling to South America is _______ _______ _______ _______ _______. It is very far away, and it costs a lot of money to get there. But thanks to Trans Atlantic Airlines, this continent of exciting cities is easier to reach than ever before. Starting tomorrow, all round-trip tickets to Brasilia and Lima are just half their normal price. In addition, you can visit Buenos Aires and Santiago at 20% off the regular ticket price. This amazing sale will _______ _______ _______ _______ _______, so please act quickly. Tickets must be booked for the months of March, April, or May of this year. Tickets must be purchased on the Trans Atlantic website and cannot be changed or refunded. For more information, go to our website. We _______ _______ _______ _______ you wherever you want to go.

28 Word & Expressions

01
- □ announcement 발표
- □ financial advisor 재정 고문
- □ degree 도; *학위
- □ accounting 회계(학)
- □ adjust to …에 적응하다
- □ corporate 기업의

02
- □ stain 얼룩
- □ exactly 정확히
- □ exchange 교환하다
- □ refund 환불

03
- □ arrange 배치하다
- □ vertical 수직의, 세로의
- □ rectangular 직사각형의
- □ picture frame 액자
- □ houseplant 실내용 화초

05
- □ pull a muscle 근육을 접질리다
- □ drugstore 약국

06
- □ assignment 과제
- □ consider 고려하다
- □ interest 흥미[관심]을 끌다
- □ well-paying 보수가 좋은
- □ career 직업
- □ role model 역할 모델
- □ footstep 발자취

07
- □ burn calories 칼로리를 소모하다
- □ approximately 대략
- □ scrub 문질러 닦다
- □ vacuum 진공청소기로 청소하다

08
- □ neighborhood 이웃, 동네
- □ located …에 위치한
- □ be open to the public 대중에게 개방되다

09
- □ electronics 전자기기
- □ retailer 소매상
- □ host 주최하다
- □ annual 연례의
- □ deadline 마감일
- □ registration 등록
- □ participation 참가
- □ entry fee 참가비
- □ cheating 부정 행위
- □ hacking 해킹
- □ wireless 무선의
- □ equipment 장비, 용품
- □ contestant 대회 참가자
- □ beverage 음료
- □ award 수여하다

10
- □ aquarium 수족관
- □ seal 바다표범, 물개
- □ worth …의 가치가 있는

11
- □ take part in …에 참석하다
- □ fundraising 모금
- □ sold out 매진된
- □ extra 여분, 추가분

12
- □ lost and found 분실물 취급소

13
- □ apply for …에 지원하다
- □ scholarship 장학금
- □ semester 학기
- □ straight A 모두[전과목] A
- □ requirement 요건
- □ attendance 출석

14
- □ careless 부주의한
- □ recall 기억해 내다, 상기하다

15
- □ auditorium 강당
- □ advertise 광고하다
- □ divide 나누다
- □ severe 극심한
- □ complete 완료하다
- □ cancel 취소하다

16-17
- □ nothing more than …에 지나지 않는
- □ continent 대륙
- □ round-trip ticket 왕복 티켓
- □ look forward to v-ing …하기를 고대[기대]하다
- □ backpacking 배낭
- □ attract 끌어들이다
- □ airfare 항공 요금
- □ preservation 보존

29 영어듣기 모의고사

1번부터 17번까지는 듣고 답하는 문제입니다.
1번부터 15번까지는 한 번만 들려주고, 16번부터 17번까지는 두 번 들려줍니다. 방송을 잘 듣고 답을 하기 바랍니다.

01

다음을 듣고, 여자가 하는 말의 목적으로 가장 적절한 것을 고르시오.

① 출퇴근 시간 변경을 알리려고
② 사무실 책상 교체를 요청하려고
③ 사무실의 청결 상태를 보고하려고
④ 전자 제품 사용 시 유의 사항을 안내하려고
⑤ 사무실 바닥 청소에 따른 유의 사항을 공지하려고

02

대화를 듣고, 여자의 의견으로 가장 적절한 것을 고르시오.

① 십 대들을 위한 공간을 확충할 필요가 있다.
② 십 대들을 위한 센터가 다시 문을 열어야 한다.
③ 아동의 안전을 고려하여 건물을 설계해야 한다.
④ 스트레스를 줄이기 위해 시험 횟수를 줄여야 한다.
⑤ 노후한 건물을 보수하는 데는 신중을 기해야 한다.

03

대화를 듣고, 두 사람의 관계를 가장 잘 나타낸 것을 고르시오.

① 손님 — 약사 ② 환자 — 접수자
③ 요리사 — 영양사 ④ 고객 — 식료품 직원
⑤ 애완견 주인 — 수의사

04

대화를 듣고, 그림에서 대화의 내용과 일치하지 않는 것을 고르시오.

05

대화를 듣고, 남자가 여자를 위해 할 일로 가장 적절한 것을 고르시오.

① 세탁하기
② 사진 출력하기
③ 사진 보내주기
④ 카메라 빌려주기
⑤ 여행 계획 세우기

06

대화를 듣고, 여자가 회의에 늦는 이유를 고르시오. 3점

① 늦게 일어나서
② 도로에 차가 막혀서
③ 병원에 들러야 해서
④ USB 메모리 스틱을 분실해서
⑤ 발표 자료를 집에 두고 나와서

07

대화를 듣고, 남자가 환불 받은 금액을 고르시오. 3점

① \$4 ② \$10 ③ \$14
④ \$16 ⑤ \$20

08

대화를 듣고, 어휘 학습 애플리케이션에 관해 두 사람이 언급하지 않은 것을 고르시오.

① 이름 ② 개발사 ③ 어휘 수
④ 가격 ⑤ 고객 반응

09

기아 체험 행사에 관한 다음 내용을 듣고, 일치하지 않는 것을 고르시오.

① 4월 10일 학교 강당에서 열린다.
② 24시간 동안 물 이외에는 아무것도 먹을 수 없다.
③ 세계 기아에 관한 영화 관람이 포함되어 있다.
④ 참가비는 굶주리고 있는 어린이들에게 기부된다.
⑤ 참가 희망자는 미리 온라인으로 등록을 해야 한다.

정답 및 해설 p.87-89

10

다음 표를 보면서 대화를 듣고, 여자가 방문할 식당을 고르시오.

< Restaurants List >

	Restaurant	Vegetarian Option	Location	Cuisine
①	Sombrero Grill	No	Downtown	Mexican
②	Tokyoya	Yes	Suburbs	Japanese
③	Taste of Paris	Yes	Downtown	French
④	Caesar's	No	Suburbs	Italian
⑤	Jade Garden	Yes	Downtown	Chinese

11

대화를 듣고, 남자의 마지막 말에 대한 여자의 응답으로 가장 적절한 것을 고르시오.

① Then can you tell me where the theater is?
② In that case, I'll call you as soon as I arrive.
③ You don't need to hurry. I'm running late too.
④ Let's meet at 6 p.m. I'll wait for you in the lobby.
⑤ That's okay. We have plenty of time before the movie.

12

대화를 듣고, 여자의 마지막 말에 대한 남자의 응답으로 가장 적절한 것을 고르시오.

① Why don't we stop by the pharmacy?
② We'd better ask someone for directions.
③ I prefer taking the bus to taking the subway.
④ If you take some medicine, you'll feel better.
⑤ Don't worry. I'll get you to the bus stop on time.

13

대화를 듣고, 여자의 마지막 말에 대한 남자의 응답으로 가장 적절한 것을 고르시오. 3점

Man: ____________________

① I agree, but you should ask for a discount.
② Most stores reduce the prices of older models.
③ I think you should always compare prices online.
④ You shouldn't buy a camera without trying it first.
⑤ Yes, and I don't care if other people have touched it.

14

대화를 듣고, 남자의 마지막 말에 대한 여자의 응답으로 가장 적절한 것을 고르시오.

Woman: ____________________

① I'll give you my essay as soon as I finish it.
② Why? I don't think you should deduct any points.
③ You're right. I should have submitted it last week.
④ Don't worry too much. I'm feeling much better now.
⑤ I will go to the hospital and bring it to you tomorrow.

15

다음 상황 설명을 듣고, Vanessa가 택시 기사에게 할 말로 가장 적절한 것을 고르시오.

Vanessa: ____________________

① Can you take me back to my apartment?
② How long does it take to get to the station?
③ Can you check to see if I left a present in your car?
④ Please go to the train station as quickly as you can.
⑤ Could you drop me off at the shopping mall instead?

[16-17] 다음을 듣고, 물음에 답하시오.

16

남자가 하는 말의 주제로 가장 적절한 것은?

① types of direct bodily contact
② tips for raising a healthy baby
③ the proper method of breastfeeding
④ how a baby's environment affects intelligence
⑤ why early childhood education is so important

17

캥거루식 돌보기의 효과로 언급되지 않은 것은? 3점

① 심장 박동 안정　② 수면 시간 증가
③ 체중 증가　④ 면역력 강화
⑤ 체온 유지

녹음을 다시 한 번 듣고, 빈칸에 알맞은 말을 쓰시오.

01

W: Good afternoon. This message is for all the employees at Worldcorp International. _______ _______ _______ _______ on Friday evening, please put your chairs on your desks. Also, unplug all your electronic devices including your computer and place everything on your desk. This will _______ _______ _______ _______ for the cleaning crew to polish the floors. In addition, do not come to the office over the weekend because you will not _______ _______ _______ your desk. When you come to the office on Monday morning, the office floor will be freshly polished. Thank you for your cooperation, and have a nice weekend.

02

M: I'm glad that our exams are over.

W: Me, too. _______ _______ _______ _______ all week. Let's do something fun.

M: Do you want to see a movie?

W: No. I want to do something more social.

M: Then how about visiting the teen center?

W: Well, it's been closed since last month.

M: Really? Then what can we do around here? _______ _______ _______ _______.

W: How frustrating! I feel like everything in this neighborhood is designed for children or adults.

M: I know! We need a place just for teens.

W: Right! I wish there were somewhere for us to _______ _______ _______ _______ _______.

M: I agree.

03

W: Thank you for taking the time to see Carter.

M: You're welcome. What's wrong with him?

W: _______ _______ _______ _______ since yesterday.

M: What did you feed him yesterday?

W: I gave him some food and watermelon.

M: That's the problem. The watermelon gave Carter a stomachache because dogs _______ _______ _______ so much water.

W: Wow, I had no idea. What can I do to help him?

M: Please make sure not to give him any more watermelon.

W: Okay, I won't. What else can I do?

M: Please pick up this prescription at the pharmacy. Carter should take two tablets a day _______ _______ _______ _______ _______.

W: Thank you!

04

W: What are you working on, dear?

M: These are the plans for our country house.

W: I love the big rectangular window. It will _______ _______ _______ _______ _______.

M: What do you think of the stairs that lead up to the house from the front gate?

W: They are nice.

M: Does the square table _______ _______ _______ _______ the stairs look okay?

W: Yes, it looks fine.

M: Good. I thought the tree next to it would protect it from the sun.

W: That was smart. Is that a basketball hoop to the right of the stairs?

M: Yes. You know _______ _______ _______ _______ to play basketball.

W: Yes, I do. It looks like it will be a very nice house to live in!

05

[Cell phone rings.]

M: Hello, Anne. How are you today?

W: I'm fine, Hank. _______ _______ _______. Our hike up Mount Halla yesterday was tiring.

M: I'm tired, too. But wasn't it fun?

W: Definitely. _______ _______ _______ _______ _______ were really worth it.

M: Yeah. We could see almost all of Jeju Island.

W: We should plan another trip sometime soon.

M: I agree. By the way, I took a lot of great photos.

W: Good! Could you send me some of the pictures?

M: Sure. I haven't printed any of them yet, though.

W: Why don't you send them to me by email then?

M: Sure. I'm _______ _______ _______ now, but I'll do that as soon as I finish.

W: Thanks!

06

[Cell phone rings.]

M: Hello?

W: Hi, Carl. I think I'll be a bit late for the meeting.

M: What happened? Are you sick?

W: No, I'm fine.

M: Did you forget to _______ _______ _______ _______?

W: Well, I got up early and left home 30 minutes ago.

M: Then what's the problem?

W: Well, all of my presentation materials were on a USB memory stick and I forgot to bring it.

M: Oh, you certainly need that. Do you _______ _______ _______ _______ now?

W: Yes. As long as I don't get stuck in traffic, I should be at the meeting in about 30 minutes.

M: All right. I'll _______ _______ _______ that we will start the meeting a bit late.

07

W: Hello. Can I help you with something?

M: Yes. I was just here _______ _______ _______.

W: I remember. You purchased four tickets to a musical.

M: That's right. They were $20 each. But I'm afraid _______ _______ _______ _______.

W: Oh, really?

M: I should have gotten some discounts. One ticket is for my father, and he is over 65.

W: In that case, he gets a 20% senior citizen discount on his ticket.

M: That's great. Also, the show is on my sister's birthday.

W: Then birthday tickets _______ _______ _______.

M: That's perfect. Here are their IDs.

W: All right. *[Pause]* And here is your refund.

M: Thanks for your help. I really appreciate it.

08

W: Wow, Greg. Your Chinese vocabulary _______ _______ _______ since last semester.

M: Thanks, Sally. I studied a lot over summer break.

W: How did you study? You must have a secret.

M: Well, I downloaded a really helpful application called WordZone on my smartphone.

W: Oh, I've heard of it. Wasn't it developed by Lingua Limitless?

M: Yeah. All of their applications are great for _______ _______ _______.

W: Maybe I should get it, too. How much is it?

M: It costs $10.

W: Oh, really? That's a bit expensive for an application.

M: _______ _______ _______ _______, though. And all of the reviews have been positive!

W: Wow. Then I should give it a try.

09

M: Hello, students! As you probably know, _______ _______ _______ around the world go with almost no food every day. So to raise awareness about world hunger, the student council is planning a special event. It will be held at the school auditorium on April 10th. For a whole 24 hours, the participants will not eat anything. They will only _______ _______ _______ _______ _______. In addition, we will be showing a film about global hunger. There is a small $5 fee to participate, but this money _______ _______ _______ _______ starving children. Interested students need to sign up outside the auditorium on the day of the event.

10

M: Hi, Alice. I heard your parents are visiting this weekend.

W: Right. Could you recommend a nice restaurant _______ _______ _______ _______ _______?

M: Sure. I know a lot of good places around here.

W: Good. Just remember, I'm a vegetarian.

M: I see. Can you _______ _______ _______ _______?

W: No, I want to stay in the city. After having dinner, we'll go downtown to see the sights.

M: Okay. Is there any kind of cuisine that you _______ _______ _______?

W: Not really. My parents don't like Chinese food, though.

M: I see. Then I have a great recommendation for you.

W: Great! What is it? We'll go there.

11

[Cell phone rings.]

M: Hello, Linda. Have you _______ _______ _______ _______ _______?

W: Yes. I just got here. We're meeting at 6 p.m., right?

M: Well, I'm running about 20 minutes late.

W: (That's okay. We have plenty of time before the movie.)

12

W: We've walked a lot, but I still don't see the subway station.

M: I thought it was going to be just past the pharmacy.

W: _______ _______ _______. What if we are on the wrong street?

M: (We'd better ask someone for directions.)

13

W: That's a nice camera. Where did you get it?

M: Thanks. I bought it at the electronics shop downtown last week.

W: I haven't seen that model before. Is it new?

M: Yes, it's brand-new. And you won't believe _______ _______ _______ _______.

W: Let me guess... $500?

M: Well, the regular price was $550. But I paid only $300.

W: That's great! Was it on sale?

M: No. But this _______ _______ _______ _______.

W: Does the camera work alright?

M: Yes, it works perfectly. People usually don't want to buy display items, so the store reduces their prices.

W: Well, I think _______ _______ _______ _______ _______.

M: (Yes, and I don't care if other people have touched it.)

14

W: Excuse me, Mr. Stewart. Here's my essay.

M: Well, Jenny, this essay was due last week.

W: I'm sorry, but I was really sick last week.

M: Oh, really? What was wrong?

W: I had food poisoning. I had to go to the emergency room and _______ _______ _______ _______ for a few days.

M: Oh my goodness. I didn't know that.

W: That's why I wasn't able to _______ _______ _______ _______ on time.

M: In that case, I will accept your essay.

W: Thank you very much, Mr. Stewart!

M: But you need to _______ _______ _______ _______ _______ _______ to prove that you were sick.

W: (I will go to the hospital and bring it to you tomorrow.)

15

W: Vanessa is going to _______ _______ _______ over the weekend. She hasn't seen her family in a few months, so she is very excited. On her departure day, she gets into a taxi and tells the driver to _______ _______ _______ _______ _______ _______. Suddenly she realizes that her little sister's birthday is this weekend. However, she forgot to buy her a present. But luckily, there is a shopping mall _______ _______ _______ _______ the train station, and she has some extra time. She thinks she can buy her sister a present at the mall. In this situation, what would Vanessa most likely say to the taxi driver?

Vanessa: (Could you drop me off at the shopping mall instead?)

16-17

M: Hello, expecting mothers! I know you all want your babies to _______ _______ _______ _______ _______. Here are some of my best tips. First, I really recommend breastfeeding. It's the best food for babies. It contains various nutrients that boost the baby's immune system. Next, make sure your home is clean. Babies _______ _______ _______ _______ infection, and an unclean environment will likely increase their risk of developing allergies. Lastly, skin-to-skin contact is good for babies. Have you heard of kangaroo care? It's simple. Just hold your baby to your bare chest. This method is especially effective for premature babies. Through kangaroo care, the baby's heartbeat stabilizes, and his or her breathing becomes steady. The baby is able to get more sleep and will even _______ _______ _______. Also, the baby's body temperature will remain warm. I hope this information has been helpful. See you next time!

29 Word & Expressions

01
- □ **unplug** 플러그를 뽑다
- □ **electronic device** 전자기기
- □ **cleaning crew** 청소부
- □ **polish** 광을 내다
- □ **have access to** …에 접근하다
- □ **cooperation** 협동, 협조

02
- □ **stressed out** 스트레스를 받는
- □ **social** 사회적인; *사교적인
- □ **frustrating** 좌절감을 주는
- □ **neighborhood** 인근, 근처
- □ **hang out with** …와 시간을 보내다

03
- □ **watermelon** 수박
- □ **digest** 소화하다
- □ **prescription** 처방전
- □ **tablet** 알약

04
- □ **rectangular** 직사각형의
- □ **let in** …을 들어오게 하다
- □ **square** 정사각형 모양의
- □ **hoop** 테[고리]; *(농구의) 링

05
- □ **tiring** 피곤하게 만드는, 피곤한
- □ **definitely** 당연히, 분명히
- □ **worth** …할 만한 가치가 있는
- □ **do the laundry** 빨래하다

06
- □ **set an alarm clock** 자명종을 맞추다
- □ **material** 재료; *자료
- □ **certainly** 틀림없이, 분명히
- □ **get stuck** 꼼짝 못 하게 되다
- □ **traffic** 교통(량)

07
- □ **overpay** 초과 지급하다
- □ **senior citizen** 노인, 고령자
- □ **ID** 신분증
- □ **refund** 환불(금)
- □ **appreciate** 고맙게 생각하다

08
- □ **secret** 비밀; *비결
- □ **download** (데이터를) 다운로드하다
- □ **application** 지원; *응용 프로그램
- □ **memorize** 암기하다
- □ **totally** 전적으로, 완전히
- □ **give it a try** 시도하다

09
- □ **awareness** 의식
- □ **hunger** 기아
- □ **student council** 학생회
- □ **auditorium** 강당
- □ **participant** 참가자
- □ **donate** 기부하다
- □ **starving** 굶주리는

10
- □ **recommend** 추천하다 (n. recommendation 추천)
- □ **vegetarian** 채식주의자
- □ **suburb** 교외
- □ **downtown** 시내에
- □ **sight** 시력; *(*pl.*) (도시에 있는) 명소, 관광지
- □ **cuisine** 요리

11
- □ **plenty of** 많은, 충분한

12
- □ **stop by** 잠시 들르다
- □ **pharmacy** 약국
- □ **direction** 방향; *(*pl.*) 길

13
- □ **electronics** 전자 제품
- □ **brand-new** 신제품의
- □ **regular price** 정가
- □ **display** 전시
- □ **reduce** 줄이다; *(가격을) 낮추다

14
- □ **food poisoning** 식중독
- □ **emergency room** 응급실
- □ **turn in** …을 제출하다
- □ **accept** 받아주다
- □ **note** (특정한 목적의) 증서
- □ **deduct** 공제하다, 감하다

15
- □ **departure** 출발
- □ **drop off** …을 내려놓다

16-17
- □ **expecting mother** 임신부
- □ **breastfeeding** 모유 수유
- □ **nutrient** 영양소
- □ **boost** 신장시키다, 북돋우다
- □ **immune system** 면역 체계
- □ **resistance** 저항력
- □ **infection** 감염
- □ **develop** 성장하다; *(병·문제가) 생기다
- □ **skin-to-skin contact** 피부를 맞대고 있는 접촉
- □ **bare** 벌거벗은, 맨
- □ **premature** 조산의
- □ **heartbeat** 심장 박동
- □ **stabilize** 안정되다
- □ **steady** 일정한, 규칙적인

30 영어듣기 모의고사

정답 및 해설 p.90-92

1번부터 17번까지는 듣고 답하는 문제입니다.
1번부터 15번까지는 한 번만 들려주고, 16번부터 17번까지는 두 번 들려줍니다. 방송을 잘 듣고 답을 하기 바랍니다.

01

다음을 듣고, 여자가 하는 말의 목적으로 가장 적절한 것을 고르시오.

① 항공편 지연을 공지하려고
② 공항 탑승구 변경을 안내하려고
③ 항공편 결항에 대해 사과하려고
④ 특별 할인 항공권을 광고하려고
⑤ 공항 내 개업한 식당을 홍보하려고

02

대화를 듣고, 두 사람이 하는 말의 주제로 가장 적절한 것을 고르시오.

① 새집 증후군 완화 방안
② 심한 기침에 좋은 민간요법
③ 자신에게 맞는 집 고르는 방법
④ 새집에 사용되는 화학 물질의 종류
⑤ 실내에서 식물을 기를 때 유의할 점

03

대화를 듣고, 두 사람의 관계를 가장 잘 나타낸 것을 고르시오.

① 환자 — 의사 ② 시민 — 경찰
③ 고객 — 옷 가게 점원 ④ 탑승객 — 지하철역 직원
⑤ 아파트 주민 — 경비원

04

대화를 듣고, 그림에서 대화의 내용과 일치하지 않는 것을 고르시오.

05

대화를 듣고, 남자가 여자에게 부탁한 일로 가장 적절한 것을 고르시오.

① 회의 참석하기
② 저녁거리 사 오기
③ 휴대전화 구입하기
④ 휴대전화 수리 맡기기
⑤ Timmy를 데리러 가기

06

대화를 듣고, 여자가 늦는 이유를 고르시오.

① 늦잠을 자서
② 기차가 연착해서
③ 교통 체증이 심해서
④ 기차표를 잃어버려서
⑤ 기차 출발 시간을 착각해서

07

대화를 듣고, 여자가 지불할 금액을 고르시오. 3점

① $160 ② $170 ③ $200
④ $220 ⑤ $230

08

대화를 듣고, 졸업식에 관해 두 사람이 언급하지 않은 것을 고르시오.

① 장소 ② 졸업생 수 ③ 연설자
④ 밴드 공연 ⑤ 복장

09

자연 사진 콘테스트에 관한 다음 내용을 듣고, 일치하지 않는 것을 고르시오.

① 사진 두 장을 제출해야 한다.
② 사진의 주제는 자연이다.
③ 접수는 웹사이트에서 가능하다.
④ 제출할 사진 파일의 형식에 제한이 있다.
⑤ 3명을 뽑아 상금을 준다.

10

다음 표를 보면서 대화를 듣고, 여자가 구입할 구두를 고르시오.

< Shoes Selection >

	Heel Height	Style	Color	Price
①	6 cm	Open toe	Black	$65
②	4 cm	Closed toe	Brown	$55
③	3 cm	Open toe	Red	$50
④	5 cm	Open toe	Brown	$55
⑤	7 cm	Closed toe	Black	$45

11

대화를 듣고, 남자의 마지막 말에 대한 여자의 응답으로 가장 적절한 것을 고르시오.

① I try to do it every single day.
② No, I usually take a bus to get there.
③ I mostly just run or swim at the gym.
④ I'm going on a diet to lose some weight.
⑤ How about exercising together tomorrow?

12

대화를 듣고, 여자의 마지막 말에 대한 남자의 응답으로 가장 적절한 것을 고르시오.

① Yes, that scarf looks really good on you.
② I haven't purchased a present for her, either.
③ You should come to the party early anyway.
④ I'd love that. I don't know how to thank you.
⑤ Good. She said she needed one the other day.

13

대화를 듣고, 여자의 마지막 말에 대한 남자의 응답으로 가장 적절한 것을 고르시오.

Man: ______________________________

① You should get some rest before the test.
② I don't want you to disappoint me anymore.
③ Please promise me to study harder next time.
④ That's not true. You made very few mistakes.
⑤ All you can do is to wait and see what happens.

14

대화를 듣고, 남자의 마지막 말에 대한 여자의 응답으로 가장 적절한 것을 고르시오. 3점

Woman: ______________________________

① Not really. I don't have a lot of money.
② That's okay. I don't need any help now.
③ It sure does. That's why I'm helping her.
④ You should have sent me a letter like her.
⑤ I spend most of my allowance buying books.

15

다음 상황 설명을 듣고, Brian이 웨이터에게 할 말로 가장 적절한 것을 고르시오.

Brian: ______________________________

① Is there any dish that you recommend?
② I suffered from food poisoning last week.
③ I can't eat this since I'm allergic to oysters.
④ Could you give me the recipe for this dish?
⑤ This dish tastes strange. Can I get a new one?

[16-17] 다음을 듣고, 물음에 답하시오.

16

남자가 하는 말의 목적으로 가장 적절한 것은?

① to encourage people to eat orange peels
② to give tips on how to peel oranges easily
③ to suggest eating more oranges for health
④ to introduce ways of keeping oranges fresh
⑤ to inform people about uses of orange peels

17

언급된 효능이 아닌 것은?

① 감기 예방
② 모기 퇴치
③ 피부 청결
④ 치아 미백
⑤ 콜레스테롤 저하

정답 및 해설 p.92

녹음을 다시 한 번 듣고, 빈칸에 알맞은 말을 쓰시오.

01

W: Attention, all passengers. There is a flight change you should be aware of. Due to the typhoon, West Airlines Flight 90 to San Diego will _______ _______ _______ _______. We now expect the plane to depart at approximately 8:30 p.m. This is unavoidable, as high winds and heavy rain are expected to last for some time. The storm should clear up soon, though, and no further delays are expected. To _______ _______ _______ _______ _______, passengers waiting to board Flight 90 will receive a ten-dollar meal coupon. It can be used at any restaurant in the airport. Thank you _______ _______ _______.

02

M: Hi, Judy. How's your new house?
W: It's great. It was built recently, so it's nice and clean. But there is one problem.
M: Really? What is it?
W: It is _______ _______ _______. When I'm home, I get headaches and cough a lot. But I don't know why.
M: It's probably sick building syndrome.
W: Oh, what's that?
M: The chemicals in new buildings can sometimes make you sick.
W: Really? Is there anything I can do?
M: Yes. Just open your windows _______ _______ _______ _______ to let in more fresh air. Growing some house plants will also help clean the air.
W: Wow, you know a lot about this! I'll _______ _______ _______. Thanks!

03

W: Hello, can you please help me?
M: Yes, but first, please _______ _______. Are you hurt?
W: No, no. I'm okay.
M: All right. What is the problem?
W: I was walking to the subway station, but suddenly, a man ran up to me and _______ _______ _______!
M: Okay. Did you see what he looked like?
W: No, he ran away too fast. I just remember that he was wearing a black hat and jeans.
M: I see. Was there anything valuable in your bag?
W: Yes. My money and my cell phone.
M: Okay. Let's go back to _______ _______ _______ _______ _______. We can check to see if there were any security cameras there.
W: Thank you so much.

04

W: We're finally at the amusement park!
M: Here's a map. Let's look and _______ _______ _______ _______.
W: Well, I really want to see the flower garden on the right side of the entrance.
M: Okay. The roller coaster is right behind the garden.
W: Let's go to the garden first and then ride the roller coaster.
M: After that, let's go to the café _______ _______ _______ _______ of the entrance.
W: Yeah, we can get drinks there and take a break.
M: Okay. How about going to the ice rink across from the roller coaster?
W: Great. And then we can stop by the fountain _______ _______ _______ _______ the park and take a picture together.
M: That sounds good. Let's do it!

05

M: My cell phone got wet and isn't working.

W: You should go to the customer service center. You can _______ _______ _______ there.

M: But it's too far away. Honestly, I think it's better to buy a new one.

W: That makes sense. Your phone is quite old. Are you going to buy a new one tomorrow?

M: I want to, but my meeting _______ _______ _______ _______ o'clock.

W: The store closes at seven. Isn't that enough time?

M: Well, someone has to pick up Timmy from basketball practice after work. Could you do that for me?

W: Sure, I'll do that.

M: Really? Thanks. I'll buy us something to eat for dinner _______ _______ _______ _______ then.

W: That sounds perfect.

06

[Cell phone rings.]

W: Hello, Dad.

M: Hi, Amy. Are you on your way?

W: Yes. Actually, I just _______ _______ _______ _______ now. I'm going to be a bit late.

M: What happened? Did you get up late?

W: No, I got up on time.

M: Oh. Was there a lot of traffic on the way to the train station, then?

W: No. I just _______ _______ _______ _______. I thought my train was leaving at 10:30, but it actually left at 10:00.

M: I see.

W: I arrived at 10:10, but the train had already left. So I had to wait for the 11 o'clock train.

M: That's fine. We will _______ _______ _______ at the station when you arrive.

W: Thanks, Dad. I'll see you soon.

07

W: Hello, I'd like to buy a dress for my school dance.

M: Where do you go to school?

W: Hatfield High School.

M: Great! _______ _______ _______, Hatfield students get $10 off any purchase.

W: Really? Do you have something like the red dress in this photo?

M: Yes. How about this one? It's $200.

W: _______ _______ _______ _______. *[Pause]* It's too big. Do you have it in a smaller size?

M: I'm afraid I don't. But we can _______ _______ _______ for an extra $30.

W: Great. I also have this 30% discount coupon.

M: If you use the coupon, you can't get the $10 discount. And you can't use it for the mending fee.

W: Okay. I'll just use the coupon.

08

M: Can you believe we're _______ _______ _______ _______ tomorrow?

W: No! It seems like we were freshmen just yesterday!

M: Time flies. The ceremony _______ _______ _______ _______ the school auditorium, right?

W: Yes. There is a really big stage there.

M: Is anyone going to give a speech?

W: I heard the principal and the two students with the best grades are going to speak.

M: Cool. I heard that the school band _______ _______ _______ _______, too.

W: That's right. And after the performance we will receive our diplomas.

M: Great! Do we have to wear our school uniforms?

W: Yes. Our teacher said we have to.

M: That will be the last time we will ever wear our school uniforms!

09

M: Hello, students. I have an exciting announcement for you! The annual Nature Photo Contest will be held next week. To enter, just send in _______ _______ _______ _______ _______. Since the theme is nature, there should be things like lakes, mountains, trees, or animals in your photos. Go to the Hearst College website and _______ _______ _______ _______. Input your name and student number and upload your photos. The photos can be saved _______ _______ _______ _______ image file. The deadline is May 21st. We will be selecting first, second, and third place winners. They will receive a cash prize. Good luck!

10

M: How may I help you today?

W: I'm looking for some new shoes. I need _______ _______ _______ _______ _______.

M: Okay. How about these? They have 7 cm heels.

W: That's too high for me. I don't want the heels to be any higher than 6 cm.

M: I see. What about these then? _______ _______ _______ _______ _______, open toe or closed toe?

W: Actually, I like open-toed shoes.

M: Okay. We have ones in black, red, and brown.

W: Well, I like the black ones and the brown ones, but I can't _______ _______ _______ $60 for shoes.

M: I think this pair is the best choice, then.

W: I agree. I'll buy these.

11

M: Wow, Sarah. You look so slim. What's your secret?

W: I've just been exercising a lot at the school gym recently.

M: Really? _______ _______ _______ _______ _______ at the gym?

W: (I try to do it every single day.)

12

W: Isn't Mom's birthday next Friday?

M: Yes, it is. I already bought a present for her.

W: Really? I'm _______ _______ _______ _______ a new scarf. What do you think?

M: (Good. She said she needed one the other day.)

13

M: What's wrong? You _______ _______ _______ _______.

W: I'm just worried about the science test I took yesterday. I think I made a lot of mistakes.

M: You studied very hard, so I'm sure you did fine.

W: But it was so hard. There wasn't _______ _______ _______ _______ on the whole test.

M: Well, all of your classmates are in the same situation. So don't worry about it too much.

W: But I'm concerned about my grades. The English test yesterday _______ _______ _______.

M: You probably did well on that, too. Anyway, being overly concerned won't help anything.

W: I don't know what to do when there's so much to worry about!

M: (All you can do is to wait and see what happens.)

30회

14

M: What are you reading, Rachael?

W: It's a letter that was sent to me by a girl I'm sponsoring.

M: Sponsoring? Are you _______ _______ _______ _______ _______?

W: Yes. I give some money to a group that helps children in different countries.

M: That's very _______ _______ _______.

W: I just save a little bit of my allowance and send $20 every month. Look, this is a photo of the girl I help.

M: She looks very cute. Where does she live?

W: She lives in Ethiopia. She sent me these drawings, too.

M: That's nice. It must _______ _______ _______ _______ to help improve someone's life.

W: (It sure does. That's why I've been helping her.)

15

W: Brian is having dinner at a nice restaurant with his sister. They order a few nice dishes to share, _______ _______ _______ _______ oysters. When the food arrives, Brian tries one of the oysters. It tastes a little strange, so he picks up another and smells it. It doesn't smell right. Brian suspects that _______ _______ _______ _______. He is afraid of getting food poisoning, so he decides to call the waiter over. He wants to let the waiter know about the problem and _______ _______ _______ for a new one. In this situation, what would Brian most likely say to the waiter?

Brian: (This dish tastes strange. Can I get a new one?)

16-17

M: Hi, everyone. I'm here to _______ _______ _______ _______ about oranges with you. Oranges are one of the world's most popular fruits, and it's easy to see why. They are delicious and nutritious. But most people don't realize that they often throw away _______ _______ _______ _______ _______—the peel. You can keep mosquitoes away if you dry orange peels and burn them. You can also grind orange peels into powder and add it to bathwater. This will make your skin _______ _______ _______. Or, you can make your teeth whiter by rubbing the inside of the peel on them before brushing. Finally, drinking orange peel tea and eating ground peels on your food helps lower your cholesterol. Doesn't it seem like a waste to throw away orange peels?

30 Word & Expressions

01
- □ depart 출발하다
- □ approximately 대략
- □ unavoidable 불가피한
- □ clear up (날씨가) 개다
- □ make up for …에 대해 보상하다

02
- □ cough 기침하다
- □ sick building syndrome 새집 증후군
- □ chemical 화학 물질
- □ from time to time 이따금
- □ suggestion 제안

03
- □ calm down 진정하다
- □ steal 훔치다
- □ run away 달아나다
- □ valuable 소중한; *값비싼
- □ security camera 보안 카메라

04
- □ flower garden 꽃밭
- □ entrance 입구
- □ take a break 휴식을 취하다
- □ fountain 분수(대)

05
- □ repair 수리하다
- □ honestly 솔직히
- □ make sense 이해가 되다
- □ pick up …을 태우러 가다

06
- □ traffic 교통(량)
- □ misread 잘못 읽다

07
- □ try on …을 입어보다
- □ reduce 줄이다
- □ mending 수선

08
- □ graduate from …을 졸업하다
- □ freshman 신입생
- □ ceremony 의식, 식
- □ auditorium 객석; *강당
- □ give a speech 연설하다
- □ diploma 졸업장
- □ school uniform 교복

09
- □ announcement 발표
- □ annual 연례의
- □ theme 주제
- □ input 입력하다
- □ upload 업로드하다
- □ cash prize 상금

10
- □ heel (신발의) 굽
- □ open-toed 발가락 부분이 트인

11
- □ slim 날씬한
- □ mostly 주로, 일반적으로

12
- □ the other day 지난번에, 일전에

13
- □ be worried[concerned] about …에 대해 걱정하다
- □ tricky 까다로운
- □ overly 지나치게

14
- □ sponsor 후원하다
- □ in need 어려움에 처한
- □ generous 너그러운
- □ allowance 용돈
- □ improve 개선하다, 향상시키다

15
- □ oyster 굴
- □ suspect 의심하다
- □ go bad (음식이) 상하다
- □ call over …을 불러오다
- □ suffer from …로 고생하다
- □ allergic 알레르기가 있는
- □ recipe 조리법

16-17
- □ useful 유용한
- □ nutritious 영양가가 높은
- □ peel (과일의) 껍질
- □ keep away …을 멀리 하다
- □ mosquito 모기
- □ grind 갈다
- □ rub 문지르다, 비비다
- □ lower 낮추다
- □ cholesterol 콜레스테롤
- □ encourage 격려하다; *권장하다
- □ inform 알리다

31 영어듣기 모의고사

1번부터 17번까지는 듣고 답하는 문제입니다.
1번부터 15번까지는 한 번만 들려주고, 16번부터 17번까지는 두 번 들려줍니다. 방송을 잘 듣고 답을 하기 바랍니다.

01

다음을 듣고, 여자가 하는 말의 목적으로 가장 적절한 것을 고르시오.

① 호텔을 홍보하려고
② 등산을 권장하려고
③ 레스토랑의 개업을 알리려고
④ 저렴한 여행사를 추천하려고
⑤ 리조트 예약 방법을 안내하려고

02

대화를 듣고, 두 사람이 하는 말의 주제로 가장 적절한 것을 고르시오.

① 올바른 동물 사육 방법
② 균형 잡힌 식사의 필요성
③ 신체 호르몬 변화의 원인
④ 단기 체중 감량의 부작용
⑤ 육류에 첨가된 호르몬의 위험성

03

대화를 듣고, 두 사람의 관계를 가장 잘 나타낸 것을 고르시오.

① 비서 — 사장 ② 건축가 — 고객
③ 수리공 — 고객 ④ 화가 — 관람객
⑤ 건설사 직원 — 건물 관리인

04

대화를 듣고, 그림에서 대화의 내용과 일치하지 않는 것을 고르시오.

05

대화를 듣고, 남자가 여자를 위해 할 일로 가장 적절한 것을 고르시오.

① 대신 소포 부쳐주기
② 내일 소포 배송하기
③ 미용실에 소포 맡기기
④ 여자의 이웃집 방문하기
⑤ 경비실에서 소포 찾아가기

06

대화를 듣고, 여자가 함께 저녁을 먹으러 가지 않는 이유를 고르시오.

① 배탈이 나서
② 배달 음식을 주문해서
③ 집에서 도시락을 싸 와서
④ 남편과 저녁 약속이 있어서
⑤ 급히 마쳐야 할 업무가 있어서

07

대화를 듣고, 남자가 지불할 금액을 고르시오. 3점

① $13 ② $15 ③ $18
④ $20 ⑤ $28

08

대화를 듣고, 동영상 콘테스트에 관해 두 사람이 언급하지 않은 것을 고르시오.

① 목적 ② 참가 자격
③ 마감 기한 ④ 우승 상금
⑤ 동영상 길이

09

자전거 전용 도로 건설에 관한 다음 내용을 듣고, 일치하지 않는 것을 고르시오. 3점

① 공사는 다음 달에 시작된다.
② 총 4개의 도로를 건설할 예정이다.
③ 두 곳에 자전거 보관대가 생길 것이다.
④ 세금을 인상하여 공사 비용을 충당할 것이다.
⑤ 올여름 초까지 완공될 것이다.

정답 및 해설 p.93-95

10

다음 표를 보면서 대화를 듣고, 남자가 신청할 온라인 중국어 강좌를 고르시오.

< Online Chinese Classes >

	Class	Level	Price	Books	Number of Lectures
①	A	Basic	$70	Provided	25
②	B	Basic	$75	X	30
③	C	Basic	$85	X	35
④	D	Intermediate	$75	X	40
⑤	E	Intermediate	$85	Provided	45

11

대화를 듣고, 여자의 마지막 말에 대한 남자의 응답으로 가장 적절한 것을 고르시오.

① Sure. I know a good store we can go to.
② I think you had better postpone your trip.
③ Okay. I want you to help me pack for my trip.
④ No, I don't need them. It is raining in New York.
⑤ Yes, you can borrow mine. Drop by my house any time.

12

대화를 듣고, 남자의 마지막 말에 대한 여자의 응답으로 가장 적절한 것을 고르시오.

① No wonder it's so crowded here.
② Be careful. The pizza is very hot.
③ Well, it doesn't seem very popular.
④ That was the best pizza I've ever tasted.
⑤ I've been standing in line for 30 minutes.

13

대화를 듣고, 남자의 마지막 말에 대한 여자의 응답으로 가장 적절한 것을 고르시오.

Woman: ______________________

① I think you just need to plan ahead.
② I really can't wait to see a movie with you.
③ Please give me a bigger allowance next week.
④ I'm impressed that you've saved so much money.
⑤ Yes, I was surprised at how expensive it was, too.

14

대화를 듣고, 여자의 마지막 말에 대한 남자의 응답으로 가장 적절한 것을 고르시오.

Man: ______________________

① It sounds like you are really depressed.
② The doctor said you will feel better in no time.
③ I missed some English classes because I was sick.
④ Everyone has a hard time adjusting to a new place.
⑤ You'll learn English much more quickly living here.

15

다음 상황 설명을 듣고, Mike가 Ellen에게 할 말로 가장 적절한 것을 고르시오.

Mike: ______________________

① Why don't you find a job that you enjoy?
② As a new employee, you should work harder.
③ This project is important, so concentrate on it.
④ I think you need to focus more on your health.
⑤ Improve your weak points, and you'll succeed.

[16-17] 다음을 듣고, 물음에 답하시오.

16

남자가 하는 말의 주제로 가장 적절한 것은? 3점

① how to raise babies to be independent
② the importance of touch between mother and child
③ problems caused by providing babies with less food
④ the difference between human and animal emotions
⑤ how memories of early childhood affect personality

17

실험에 이용된 것으로 언급되지 않은 것은?

① a baby monkey
② a wire mother
③ a cloth mother
④ a bottle of milk
⑤ a bottle of water

31 DICTATION

녹음을 다시 한 번 듣고, 빈칸에 알맞은 말을 쓰시오.

01

W: Do you like spending time in the mountains? Are you looking for a place where you can _______ _______ _______? Then you should make a reservation at the Cloudview Hotel. Located in the Green Mountains, our hotel has several hiking trails just outside our front door. Our rooms all have comfortable beds and wonderful views. We _______ _______ _______ _______ and 24-hour room service. You can also enjoy fine dining at our restaurant, which serves fresh local food prepared by premier chefs. Check our website to see if any of our special packages meets your needs. We hope our hotel can be your _______ _______ _______ _______.

02

M: Anna, why don't we have dinner at that new steakhouse?

W: No, thanks. To be honest, I'm trying to avoid meat these days.

M: Really? _______ _______ _______ _______ animal cruelty?

W: No, it's not that. I heard there are a lot of hormones in meat.

M: Hormones? What do you mean?

W: Some farmers use hormones to make their animals _______ _______.

M: Oh, I see. If we eat that meat, then those hormones can enter our bodies, right?

W: Yes. And they can be harmful over time.

M: But they're not dangerous in small amounts, are they?

W: Nobody is sure. But I don't want to _______ _______ _______.

M: I understand what you mean.

03

[Cell phone rings.]

M: Hello?

W: Hi, this is Alicia Smith. I received your email this morning.

M: Oh, yes. Do you have any questions?

W: Actually, I would like to _______ _______ _______. The restroom seems to be too small.

M: Okay. I'll make some changes to that.

W: Thank you. Considering the number of employees, it definitely _______ _______ _______ _______.

M: No problem. Is there anything else you would like me to change?

W: That's all. Do you think you can finish the renovation work by December 20th?

M: Well, I'm not sure. First, I will need to _______ _______ _______ _______.

W: I see. Can you show me the new plans by Monday?

M: Sure, I can do that.

04

M: Honey, I've _______ _______ _______ the backyard.

W: Already? Let's see. *[Pause]* Wow! It looks great.

M: I bought a rectangular table with a big umbrella _______ _______ _______. Do you like it?

W: Yes. It will be perfect for sitting and relaxing.

M: I think so, too. And don't you think the kids will love the slide behind the table?

W: Definitely. They will enjoy that bench swing next to the slide, too.

M: Also, I dug a round pond _______ _______ _______ _______ the table and put some fish in it.

W: Great idea. The tree to the right of the pond looks nice. Are those flowers around it new?

M: Yes, I planted them this afternoon.

W: They look beautiful.

05

[Cell phone rings.]

W: Hello?

M: Hi. This is Steve Black from Express Delivery Services. Is this Judy Kim?

W: Yes. Has my package from New York arrived already?

M: Yes, it has. I'm at your house now, but no one is ______ ______ ______.

W: Oh! I'm at work right now. Can you ask my next-door neighbors to take it?

M: I already tried, but ______ ______ ______ ______.

W: I see.

M: The only other option would be to deliver it tomorrow.

W: Oh, but I really need that package tonight.

M: There's a hair salon around the corner. I can leave it there.

W: Okay, I guess ______ ______ ______ ______. I know the owner.

06

M: Patricia, let's ______ ______ ______ ______. It's almost 7:00.

W: Already? I didn't realize how late it was.

M: Is it because you're doing the monthly sales report?

W: Yes, but I've just finished it.

M: That's great. By the way, would you like to have dinner with Julie and me today?

W: I'd love to, but ______ ______ ______ have dinner with my husband.

M: I see. Didn't you say that he's been sick with stomach problems?

W: Yes, but he's fully recovered now. So I will ______ ______ ______ ______ ______ downtown today.

M: That's nice. Have a good time with him.

W: Thanks. Have a nice dinner with Julie!

07

[Cell phone rings.]

W: Hi, honey.

M: Hi. I ______ ______ ______ ______ on the way home. Don't we need some fruit to serve for dessert at the housewarming party?

W: Yes! I almost forgot! Would you please buy some while you're there?

M: Sure. What would you like me to get?

W: How about some oranges and apples?

M: That's a good idea. They are $2 each, but right now oranges are 50% off.

W: Great! ______ ______ ______ ______.

M: We invited eight people to the party, so five oranges and five apples should be enough.

W: I think so, but please buy 5 extra oranges. The kids love them, too.

M: Good idea. It's better to buy them while ______ ______ ______.

08

M: Olivia, have you heard about the contest Smithtown Park is having?

W: No, I haven't. What's it for?

M: They want people to make videos about the park. The winning videos ______ ______ ______ ______ commercials for the park.

W: Cool! Can anyone participate?

M: No, only people living in Smithtown can apply.

W: Good thing we both live in Smithtown.

M: Yes. But ______ ______ ______ Earth Day, which is April 22nd. That's in five days!

W: We can finish it by then. What's the prize?

M: The top three videos will air on local TV. The grand prize winner will receive $2,000.

W: We could both get $1,000! Let's ______ ______ ______ ______ now!

09

M: Ladies and gentlemen, I'd like to announce the town council's plan for new bicycle lanes. We are building these new lanes to _______ _______ _______ _______ for cyclists. Construction will start next month. There will be four new routes, so people _______ _______ _______ _______ will be able to use these lanes. There will also be bicycle racks placed outside Town Hall and Memorial Park. Therefore, parking will be convenient for anyone coming into town. The money to construct these lanes will come from the city's budget, so we won't have to raise taxes to build them. Construction will be completed _______ _______ _______ _______ this summer.

10

M: I want to learn Chinese, so I decided to _______ _______ _______ _______.

W: That's great. Which class will you take?

M: Well, I've never studied Chinese before, so an intermediate class would be too hard.

W: I see. What's your budget?

M: I can't pay over $80.

W: There are a couple of classes in your price range. This one provides a book.

M: _______ _______ _______ to me.

W: In that case, I recommend this one. It offers more lectures.

M: Yes. I think I'll take that one.

W: But it's a little more expensive than the other one.

M: That's okay. I _______ _______ _______ _______. Thanks for your help!

11

W: I think I need sunglasses for my trip to New York.

M: Right. It's really sunny in New York _______ _______ _______ _______.

W: Yes. I'm going to buy a pair. Will you help me choose some?

M: (Sure. I know a good store we can go to.)

12

M: Why don't we buy some pizza here?

W: Sure. But there are so many people _______ _______ _______! Is the pizza here that good?

M: They're offering mushroom pizza at half price.

W: (No wonder it's so crowded here.)

13

W: How about going to the movies tonight, Jason?

M: I'd love to, but I'm _______ _______.

W: Already? But you just got your allowance last week.

M: Right. But I spent it all in just a couple of days.

W: Why did you do that?

M: I didn't intend to. I guess _______ _______ _______ _______. I just bought a few things that I liked right away.

W: That can be a real problem. You need to be smarter with your money.

M: I totally agree with you. But I don't know how.

W: It's _______ _______ _______ to be responsible.

M: Well, what should I do?

W: (I think you just need to plan ahead.)

14

M: I'm going to meet some friends at a coffee shop. Do you want to come?

W: No, thanks. I think I'll just stay home tonight.

M: _______ _______ _______. Are you feeling sick?

W: No, I'm fine. I just feel like being alone for a while.

M: Hmm... I think you _______ _______ _______ _______.

W: You're right. I'm starting to really miss my family and friends back home.

M: That's too bad.

W: And I'm not familiar with this new culture yet.

M: Don't worry. You've been here for just a month. It's perfectly normal. _______ _______ _______ _______ when I came here for the first time.

W: What do you mean?

M: (Everyone has a hard time adjusting to a new place.)

15

W: Mike's friend Ellen recently _______ _______ _______ _______. The company is good, and her coworkers are friendly. However, she's been working late nearly every night, including weekends. When Mike asks her if she was okay with it, she says she doesn't mind. She feels like she needs to work hard on her project because she is _______ _______ _______. Mike understands, but he has noticed that she seems tired all the time. She also has severe headaches. He thinks she needs to consider her health and _______ _______ _______. In this situation, what would Mike most likely say to Ellen?

Mike: (I think you need to focus more on your health.)

16-17

M: Harry Harlow, a scientist, was interested in the bond between mothers and infants. Some scientists said that newborn babies only see their mothers _______ _______ _______ _______ _______. But others disagreed. In the 1950s, Harlow _______ _______ _______ with baby monkeys. He took them away from their mothers soon after they were born. Then he gave them two fake "mothers" to choose from. The first was made from cold, hard wire, and the second was covered in soft, warm cloth. The wire mother held a bottle full of milk, but the cloth mother offered nothing. Interestingly, most of the baby monkeys chose the cloth mother. They only crawled over to the wire mother to feed, and then returned to the cloth mother. This proved that newborn babies _______ _______ _______ _______ for comfort, not just for food.

31 Word & Expressions

01
- □ **comfort** 안락, 편안
- □ **reservation** 예약
- □ **hiking trail** 하이킹 코스
- □ **wireless** 무선의
- □ **dining** 식사, 정찬
- □ **premier** 최고의, 일류의
- □ **home away from home** 제2의 고향

02
- □ **cruelty** 학대
- □ **hormone** 호르몬
- □ **harmful** 해로운
- □ **amount** 양
- □ **take a risk** 위험을 감수하다

03
- □ **request** 요구하다
- □ **consider** 고려하다
- □ **employee** 직원
- □ **renovation** 수리, 보수
- □ **draw up** …을 작성하다
- □ **plan** (*pl.*) 도면, 설계도

04
- □ **set up** …을 세우다
- □ **backyard** 뒤뜰
- □ **slide** 미끄럼틀
- □ **dig** 파다

05
- □ **package** 소포
- □ **answer the door** (손님을 맞이하러) 현관으로 나가다
- □ **neighbor** 이웃
- □ **owner** 주인

06
- □ **call it a day** 그만 끝내다
- □ **be supposed to-v** …하기로 되어 있다
- □ **stomach problem** 위장병
- □ **fully** 완전히, 충분히

07
- □ **serve** (음식을) 제공하다, 대접하다
- □ **housewarming** 집들이
- □ **extra** 추가의

08
- □ **commercial** 광고 (방송)
- □ **participate** 참가하다
- □ **air** 방송하다
- □ **grand prize** 대상

09
- □ **town council** 시 의회
- □ **bicycle lane** 자전거 전용 도로
- □ **cyclist** 자전거 타는 사람
- □ **construction** 건설, 공사(v. construct 건설하다)
- □ **bicycle rack** 자전거 보관대
- □ **memorial** 기념하기 위한, 추모의
- □ **convenient** 편리한
- □ **budget** 예산

10
- □ **intermediate** 중급의
- □ **price range** 가격
- □ **lecture** 강의
- □ **afford** …할 여유가 있다

11
- □ **postpone** 연기하다
- □ **drop by** 잠깐 들르다

12
- □ **stand in line** 줄을 서다
- □ **no wonder** …하는 것도 당연하다
- □ **crowded** 붐비는, 복잡한

13
- □ **broke** 빈털터리의
- □ **allowance** 용돈
- □ **intend** 의도하다, (…하려고) 생각하다
- □ **pay attention** 주의를 기울이다
- □ **totally** 완전히, 전적으로
- □ **responsible** 책임감 있는
- □ **ahead** 앞으로; *미리
- □ **impressed** 감명을 받은

14
- □ **feel homesick** 향수병에 걸리다
- □ **depressed** 우울한
- □ **in no time** 곧, 즉시
- □ **adjust to** …에 적응하다

15
- □ **coworker** 동료
- □ **concentrate on** …에 집중하다
- □ **weak point** 약점

16-17
- □ **bond** 유대감
- □ **infant** 신생아
- □ **source** 원천, 근원
- □ **experiment** 실험
- □ **fake** 가짜의
- □ **wire** 철사
- □ **crawl** 기다
- □ **newborn** 갓 난
- □ **depend on** …에 의존하다
- □ **independent** 독립적인
- □ **emotion** 감정
- □ **personality** 성격

32 영어듣기 모의고사

정답 및 해설 p.96-98

1번부터 17번까지는 듣고 답하는 문제입니다.
1번부터 15번까지는 한 번만 들려주고, 16번부터 17번까지는 두 번 들려줍니다. 방송을 잘 듣고 답을 하기 바랍니다.

01

다음을 듣고, 여자가 하는 말의 목적으로 가장 적절한 것을 고르시오.

① 선물의 다양한 의미를 설명하려고
② 선물을 거절하는 방법을 알려주려고
③ 물질보다는 마음이 중요함을 강조하려고
④ 외국인들이 좋아할 만한 선물을 소개하려고
⑤ 외국인에게 선물할 때 주의할 점을 조언하려고

02

대화를 듣고, 여자의 의견으로 가장 적절한 것을 고르시오.

① 식당은 서비스의 질이 가장 중요하다.
② 실내 디자인이 식당 사업의 성공을 좌우한다.
③ 식당이 성공하기 위해서는 음식 맛이 중요하다.
④ 손님을 끌기 위해 음식의 가격을 낮추어야 한다.
⑤ 음식 맛을 위해 우수한 요리사를 채용해야 한다.

03

대화를 듣고, 두 사람의 관계를 가장 잘 나타낸 것을 고르시오.

① 사진 작가 — 모델　② 서점 주인 — 작가
③ 삽화가 — 도서 편집자　④ 웹 디자이너 — 의뢰인
⑤ 장난감 가게 주인 — 손님

04

대화를 듣고, 그림에서 대화의 내용과 일치하지 않는 것을 고르시오.

05

대화를 듣고, 여자가 남자에게 부탁한 일로 가장 적절한 것을 고르시오.

① 함께 캠핑 여행 가기
② 대신 텐트 구입해주기
③ 최근에 산 텐트를 빌려주기
④ 캠핑용품 가게 위치 알려주기
⑤ 캠핑용 텐트 고르는 것 도와주기

06

대화를 듣고, 남자가 화가 난 이유로 가장 적절한 것을 고르시오.

① 수학 시험에 낙제해서
② 학교에서 친구와 다퉈서
③ 여동생이 방을 어질러놔서
④ 여동생이 게임기를 망가뜨려서
⑤ 어머니가 여동생을 혼내지 않아서

07

대화를 듣고, 여자가 지불할 금액을 고르시오. 3점

① $50　② $56　③ $58
④ $63　⑤ $70

08

대화를 듣고, 불꽃놀이에 관해 두 사람이 언급하지 않은 것을 고르시오.

① 날짜　② 장소　③ 표 가격
④ 시작 시각　⑤ 종료 시각

09

Radio Seoul K-pop 콘서트에 관한 다음 내용을 듣고, 일치하지 않는 것을 고르시오. 3점

① 13명의 한국 가요 가수들이 출연할 것이다.
② 토요일 저녁 8시에 시작한다.
③ 학생 표 가격은 성인 것보다 5달러가 저렴하다.
④ 표는 웹사이트에서만 구입할 수 있다.
⑤ 비가 오면 공연이 취소될 것이다.

10

다음 표를 보면서 대화를 듣고, 여자가 선택할 아파트를 고르시오.

< Apartments >

	Apartment	Bedrooms	Balcony	Bathrooms	Rent
①	A	Two	No	One	$700
②	B	Three	Yes	One	$900
③	C	Three	Yes	Two	$1,100
④	D	Two	Yes	One	$800
⑤	E	Three	No	Two	$950

11

대화를 듣고, 여자의 마지막 말에 대한 남자의 응답으로 가장 적절한 것을 고르시오.

① You can buy a round-trip ticket.
② That's true. Maybe I will purchase it then.
③ Why didn't you tell me that before my trip?
④ I enjoyed my trip, but I spent too much money.
⑤ Okay, but we'll have to wake up early tomorrow.

12

대화를 듣고, 남자의 마지막 말에 대한 여자의 응답으로 가장 적절한 것을 고르시오.

① Go another block and turn left again.
② Yes, I definitely recommend that store.
③ There is a shortcut to get there quickly.
④ There is a big bookstore across from it.
⑤ It'll be easy if you found some landmarks.

13

대화를 듣고, 남자의 마지막 말에 대한 여자의 응답으로 가장 적절한 것을 고르시오. 3점

Woman: ______________________________

① Please fax the document to this number.
② Please try to check your email frequently.
③ Lend me your tablet computer for a few days.
④ Can you pick me up at the airport in three hours?
⑤ Call the airline and tell them that I missed my flight.

14

대화를 듣고, 여자의 마지막 말에 대한 남자의 응답으로 가장 적절한 것을 고르시오.

Man: ______________________________

① Sure, just leave your phone number.
② You're a lucky customer. It's our last one.
③ Let me know where you saw it last week.
④ I'm sorry, but we don't have anything cheaper.
⑤ Why don't you see how it looks with your outfit?

15

다음 상황 설명을 듣고, Edward가 팀원들에게 할 말로 가장 적절한 것을 고르시오.

Edward: ______________________________

① You should have asked for help.
② Would you please help out more?
③ It will be better if I just finish this alone.
④ Why did you do everything by yourself?
⑤ I'd like to thank all of you for your hard work.

[16-17] 다음을 듣고 물음에 답하시오.

16

남자가 하는 말의 주제로 가장 적절한 것은?

① 여성 탈모가 증가하는 원인
② 탈모를 예방하기 위한 방법
③ 스트레스와 탈모의 상관관계
④ 헤어스타일이 첫인상에 미치는 영향
⑤ 두피를 건강하게 해 주는 머리 손질 요령

17

언급된 탈모 원인이 아닌 것은?

① 스트레스 ② 오염
③ 화학 물질 ④ 호르몬 교란
⑤ 유전적 요인

정답 및 해설 p.98

녹음을 다시 한 번 듣고, 빈칸에 알맞은 말을 쓰시오.

01

W: Giving gifts is a great way to show people that you're thinking about them. Usually, it doesn't really matter what the gift is. ________ ________ ________ ________, "It's the thought that counts." But when giving gifts to people from other countries, you need to be careful. Certain gifts can send the wrong message. In China, for example, clocks are associated with death. Therefore, they ________ ________ ________. And in Japan, giving someone scissors or a knife means you want to cut off your friendship. So, always ________ ________ ________ before giving gifts to foreigners. By being culturally aware, you won't send the wrong message.

02

W: The opening of our restaurant is just a month away!

M: I can't wait! Is the interior decorating completed?

W: It was finished yesterday.

M: Great! I'm sure it looks wonderful. Did you contact the chef we ________ ________ ________ ________?

W: No, I forgot. I'll call him right now.

M: I think he'll bring in the customers. Chefs are the most important factor for the restaurant's success.

W: Actually, I think service is ________ ________ ________ ________. We should make sure to hire friendly waiters.

M: Well, no one remembers a nice waiter if the food is terrible.

W: But the customers will not ________ ________ ________ ________ if they are not treated well.

M: That's true. I guess both things are important.

03

M: I've finished designing the page you requested. Take a look.

W: I love the two little kids ________ ________ ________ in the middle of the page.

M: Great. And I put the name "Toy Land" at the top of the page.

W: Yes, it looks good.

M: And if the customers click on the "Best Sellers" button, they can see the company's best-selling toys.

W: I see. Is there a place ________ ________ ________ ________ ________?

M: Of course. Do you see the login button shaped like a bear's face?

W: Oh. It's very cute!

M: Also, customers ________ ________ ________ on the website from the menu bar.

W: Everything looks great. Thank you so much for all your hard work.

04

M: I'm working on the stage design for our school musical. Will you take a look?

W: Sure. *[Pause]* Wow, it looks wonderful!

M: Thanks. The story takes place on Christmas Eve. That's why there's a big Christmas tree there.

W: And I can see ________ ________ ________ ________ ________. They look beautifully wrapped.

M: Thank you. I also made that fireplace in the background.

W: It looks great. By the way, where are the Christmas stockings?

M: I ________ ________ ________ on the Christmas tree.

W: Now I see them. I think they'd look better hung on the fireplace.

M: I'll think about that. What do you think about the armchair right next to the tree?

W: It ________ ________ ________ the setting.

32회

05

W: Hi, Gary. You recently bought a small tent, didn't you?

M: Yes, I bought a two-person tent last month. The price was quite reasonable.

W: That's exactly _______ _______ _______. I'm going on a camping trip next week.

M: Would you like to borrow mine?

W: Thanks, but I want to _______ _______ _______. Where did you get it?

M: At Outdoor Equipment. It's right next to my office.

W: Great. I think I'll go there and buy one tomorrow.

M: I'm a member of that store, so I can get a 30% discount.

W: Really? Then could you buy it for me?

M: Sure, no problem. _______ _______ _______ _______ tomorrow evening and pick it up.

W: Thanks!

06

M: Mom, can I talk to you for a minute?

W: Sure, Andy. You look upset. Did something bad happen at school?

M: No. Actually, I had a good day. I _______ _______ _______ _______ my math test.

W: I'm glad to hear that.

M: But when I got home, I saw that the screen on my portable game player was cracked.

W: Oh, really? Who did that?

M: Tara did. She took it from my room _______ _______ _______ and broke it.

W: Did she? Well, I'll go have a talk with your sister right now.

M: Thanks, Mom. She's always using my stuff. She acts like it's hers.

W: This won't happen again. I'll _______ _______ _______ _______ _______.

07

W: Excuse me. How much does this red swimsuit cost?

M: That one is $50. It's very popular this summer.

W: Yes, it's quite nice. Oh, how much is the blue one?

M: That one is $40. But they're both 20% off this week.

W: That's great. _______ _______ _______ _______ _______. And what about this beach hat?

M: It's $20. Would you like that as well?

W: I'm not sure. _______ _______ _______ _______ _______ this week?

M: No. Only the swimsuits are on sale.

W: Hmm... I need a hat, though. And I have this coupon for 10% off.

M: I'm sorry, but that coupon _______ _______ _______ on sale items.

W: Oh, okay. I'll just use it for the hat. Here's my card.

08

W: Hey, Sam! What are you doing next Saturday?

M: August 30th? I don't have any plans. Is there _______ _______ _______ _______?

W: Yes, there's going to be a fireworks display at Harris Stadium.

M: Really? I love watching fireworks. Is it a free show?

W: No, but the tickets are only $2 each.

M: Then _______ _______ _______ _______. But wait... Don't you work on Saturdays?

W: Yes, I do. But only for a couple of hours.

M: Oh, I see. In that case, when will you be finished?

W: I finish at 7 o'clock, and the show _______ _______ _______ 8.

M: That's great. Then I'll pick you up at work.

W: Sounds perfect! See you then!

09

M: Radio Seoul ________ ________ ________ announce an exciting concert next weekend. It will be hosted by Radio Seoul DJs, and it will feature 13 K-pop singers. The concert starts at 8 p.m. on Saturday evening and lasts until eleven. It will take place on the outdoor stage in Riverside Park, and tickets are just $15 for adults and $10 for students. Remember that tickets ________ ________ ________ ________ on the Radio Seoul website. Book yours quickly because the seats are limited and they won't last long. This concert will take place ________ ________ ________ ________, and there are no refunds. If you'd like more information, check out our website.

10

W: Hi, I'm looking for a new apartment.

M: Okay. ________ ________ ________ ________ some available places. What are you looking for?

W: I need an apartment with two bedrooms.

M: All right. We have a few places with two bedrooms.

W: Oh, I almost forgot. I also need an extra bedroom to use ________ ________ ________ ________.

M: I see. What else do you need?

W: I would love to have a balcony.

M: Well, there are a few with balconies. What about the number of bathrooms?

W: ________ ________ ________.

M: How much are you willing to spend?

W: My limit is $1,000 a month. I can't afford more.

M: Then this one is the best place for you.

11

W: Did you buy the special sightseeing pass for your trip?

M: No, it's too expensive.

W: Well, if you visit many tourist attractions with it, you'll ________ ________.

M: (That's true. Maybe I will purchase it then.)

12

M: Excuse me. Do you know where the Quick Way Supermarket is?

W: Yes, I do. Go straight three blocks and then turn right.

M: Great. Are there any landmarks ________ ________ ________ ________?

W: (There is a big bookstore across from it.)

13

[Cell phone rings.]

M: Hello.

W: Hi, Paul. This is Jennifer.

M: Oh, hi. I heard ________ ________ ________ New York today. Are you at the airport?

W: Yes, I'm in the airport lounge. But there is something I forgot to bring with me.

M: You didn't leave your tablet computer in the meeting room, did you?

W: No, I've got that with me right here.

M: Then what is it?

W: I just realized that I left a document on the table in your office.

M: Oh! You ________ ________ ________ ________ with something like that!

W: I know. Are you by any chance in your office right now?

M: Yes, I just arrived. Can I ________ ________ ________ somehow?

W: (Please fax the document to this number.)

14

M: Hello. Can I help you find something?

W: Yes. I saw a very nice purse here last week. But I don't see it today.

M: I see. Do you remember the brand name?

W: Sorry, I don't. But it was the white one _______ _______ in that corner there.

M: I think I know which one you mean. The strap is a gold chain, right?

W: Yes, exactly!

M: That is a very popular item. But unfortunately it's temporarily _______ _______ _______.

W: Oh, that's too bad.

M: Is there anything else you're interested in?

W: Well, I came here specifically to buy that purse. Could you contact me _______ _______ _______ _______ later?

M: (Sure, just leave your phone number.)

15

W: Edward is taking a literature class and _______ _______ _______ _______ _______ with some classmates. Edward and his team members decide to divide the work. However, over the course of the week, the other members say they are _______ _______ _______ _______ their parts. So, Edward begins to do their work for them. Soon, he realizes he has done _______ _______ _______ _______ _______ by himself. Furthermore, because of this, he couldn't focus on his other schoolwork. He thinks his team members should do their fair share of the work. In this situation, what would Edward most likely say to his team members?

Edward: (Would you please help out more?)

16-17

M: These days, many people change the style or color of their hair _______ _______ _______ _______ themselves better. Unfortunately, more and more people are experiencing hair loss for _______ _______ _______ reasons. These include stress, pollution, chemical substances contained in hair products, and genetic factors. To prevent this from happening, here are some tips for you to follow. You should not damage your hair by dyeing or perming it too often. Also, you need to wash your hair regularly and let it dry naturally. And be sure to always _______ _______ _______ and find time to relax. Finally, make sure you eat plenty of vegetables. Tomatoes and carrots contain a rich amount of nutrients that help prevent hair loss. If you keep these tips in mind, you'll have one less thing to worry about.

32 Word & Expressions

01
- □ **proverb** 속담
- □ **count** (수를) 세다; *중요하다
- □ **be associated with** …와 관련되다
- □ **scissors** (*pl.*) 가위
- □ **culturally** 문화적으로

02
- □ **interior decorating** 실내 장식
- □ **complete** 완료하다, 끝마치다
- □ **contact** 연락하다
- □ **chef** 요리사
- □ **success** 성공
- □ **treat** 대하다, 대우하다

03
- □ **request** 요청하다
- □ **take a look** 한번 보다
- □ **best-selling** 베스트셀러의, 가장 많이 팔리는

04
- □ **take place** 일어나다
- □ **wrap** 싸다, 포장하다
- □ **fireplace** 벽난로
- □ **background** 배경
- □ **stocking** 긴 양말, 스타킹
- □ **match** 어울리다, 맞다
- □ **setting** 배경, 무대

05
- □ **reasonable** 타당한; *(가격이) 적당한
- □ **outdoor** 야외의
- □ **equipment** 장비, 용품
- □ **come by** 잠깐 들르다

06
- □ **upset** 속상한, 마음이 상한
- □ **portable** 휴대용의
- □ **crack** 금이 가다, 갈라지다
- □ **stuff** 것, 물건
- □ **apologize** 사과하다

08
- □ **fireworks display** 불꽃놀이
- □ **definitely** 분명히, 틀림없이

09
- □ **announce** 발표하다, 알리다
- □ **host** 주최하다; *진행하다
- □ **feature** 특별히 나오다
- □ **check out** …을 살펴보다

10
- □ **available** 구할 수 있는
- □ **extra** 추가의, 여분의
- □ **balcony** 발코니
- □ **be willing to-v** 기꺼이 …하다
- □ **afford** (…할) 여유가 되다

11
- □ **sightseeing** 관광
- □ **pass** 합격; *출입증, 통행증
- □ **tourist attraction** 관광 명소
- □ **round-trip ticket** 왕복표

12
- □ **landmark** 랜드마크, 주요 지형지물
- □ **shortcut** 지름길

13
- □ **lounge** 라운지, 대합실
- □ **document** 서류
- □ **careless** 부주의한
- □ **by any chance** 혹시라도
- □ **somehow** 어떻게든
- □ **fax** 팩스로 보내다

14
- □ **purse** (여성용) 지갑
- □ **on display** 전시된, 진열된
- □ **strap** 끈, 줄
- □ **temporarily** 일시적으로
- □ **out of stock** 재고가 없는
- □ **specifically** 특별히
- □ **outfit** 옷, 복장

15
- □ **literature** 문학
- □ **divide** 나누다
- □ **over the course of** … 동안
- □ **fair** 공정한
- □ **share** 몫

16-17
- □ **a variety of** 다양한
- □ **pollution** 오염
- □ **chemical substance** 화학 물질
- □ **genetic factor** 유전적 요인
- □ **dye** 염색하다
- □ **plenty of** 많은
- □ **nutrient** 영양소, 영양분

33 영어듣기 모의고사

1번부터 17번까지는 듣고 답하는 문제입니다.
1번부터 15번까지는 한 번만 들려주고, 16번부터 17번까지는 두 번 들려줍니다. 방송을 잘 듣고 답을 하기 바랍니다.

01

다음을 듣고, 여자가 하는 말의 목적으로 가장 적절한 것을 고르시오.

① 휴식의 필요성을 설명하려고
② 수면과 건강의 연관성을 알려주려고
③ 사내 휴가 정책의 변경을 공지하려고
④ 업무 스트레스 해소 방법을 제안하려고
⑤ 휴가 후유증을 극복하는 법을 소개하려고

02

대화를 듣고, 두 사람이 하는 말의 주제로 가장 적절한 것을 고르시오.

① how to reduce stress eating
② what to do when feeling sick
③ the best ways to relieve stress
④ healthy foods to eat when stressed
⑤ problems that come from overeating

03

대화를 듣고, 두 사람의 관계를 가장 잘 나타낸 것을 고르시오.

① 고객 — 판매원
② 교장 — 교사
③ 조종사 — 승무원
④ 사장 — 비서
⑤ 여행객 — 여행사 직원

04

대화를 듣고, 그림에서 대화의 내용과 일치하지 않는 것을 고르시오.

05

대화를 듣고, 여자가 남자에게 부탁한 일로 가장 적절한 것을 고르시오.

① to take care of her pet
② to go on a business trip
③ to help her pack her bags
④ to take her cat to the hospital
⑤ to show her around Los Angeles

06

대화를 듣고, 여자가 이사하려는 이유를 고르시오.

① 직장을 옮겨서
② 정원이 필요해서
③ 주택을 세놓으려고
④ 침실이 더 많이 필요해서
⑤ 자녀의 통학 거리가 멀어서

07

대화를 듣고, 남자가 지불할 금액을 고르시오. 3점

① $35
② $39
③ $43
④ $48
⑤ $50

08

대화를 듣고, 여자의 아르바이트에 관해 두 사람이 언급하지 않은 것을 고르시오.

① 업무 종류
② 근무 횟수
③ 근무지
④ 근무 시간
⑤ 보수

09

fittonia에 관한 다음 내용을 듣고, 일치하지 않는 것을 고르시오. 3점

① 남아메리카의 열대 우림이 원산지이다.
② 극한 기후에서는 생존할 수 없다.
③ 잎에 혈관 모양의 줄무늬가 있는 종이 있다.
④ 잎은 거의 항상 녹색이다.
⑤ 꽃을 피우지는 않는다.

정답 및 해설 p.99-101

10

다음 표를 보면서 대화를 듣고, 여자가 구입할 중고차를 고르시오.

< SUVs >

	Model	Year	Kilometers	Accident Record	Price
①	A	2010	80,000 km	2	$7,500
②	B	2013	70,000 km	0	$7,500
③	C	2014	50,000 km	0	$11,500
④	D	2015	40,000 km	1	$11,500
⑤	E	2016	55,000 km	0	$14,500

11

대화를 듣고, 여자의 마지막 말에 대한 남자의 응답으로 가장 적절한 것을 고르시오.

① I apologize for the late delivery.
② Oh, I'm sorry. I'll get you one more.
③ There are more cupcakes than I expected.
④ Then would you like a dozen boxes to go?
⑤ Sure, those were baked fresh this morning.

12

대화를 듣고, 남자의 마지막 말에 대한 여자의 응답으로 가장 적절한 것을 고르시오.

① There's nothing else we can do.
② We should just turn the heater off.
③ I'd better bring a blanket next week.
④ We enjoy skiing and snowboarding in winter.
⑤ I've never used so much electricity in summer.

13

대화를 듣고, 여자의 마지막 말에 대한 남자의 응답으로 가장 적절한 것을 고르시오.

Man: ______________________________

① Try to protect your skin when you swim.
② It sounds like the spray type will work best.
③ Don't spend too much on buying skin protectors.
④ You should find another way to protect your skin.
⑤ Just remember to apply it every two to three hours.

14

대화를 듣고, 남자의 마지막 말에 대한 여자의 응답으로 가장 적절한 것을 고르시오.

Woman: ______________________________

① They cleaned up before we arrived.
② I think there's another trash can near here.
③ You need to separate the trash to be recycled.
④ People should be responsible when they're here.
⑤ Don't you care about protecting the environment?

15

다음 상황 설명을 듣고, Gina가 Eric에게 할 말로 가장 적절한 것을 고르시오.

Gina: ______________________________

① I don't agree with you about the ticket price.
② I really can't wait to meet our friends tonight.
③ Our magic show will definitely be a big success.
④ I hope that a lot of people come and enjoy the show.
⑤ The safety of the audience is the first thing to consider.

[16-17] 다음을 듣고, 물음에 답하시오.

16

남자가 하는 말의 주제로 가장 적절한 것은?

① how to communicate well with others
② ways of making a good first impression
③ characteristics of careless and lazy people
④ the best way to change your current image
⑤ the relationship between word choice and personality

17

영향을 주는 것으로 언급되지 않은 것은?

① 의상 ② 말 ③ 머리 모양
④ 자세 ⑤ 표정

33 DICTATION

녹음을 다시 한 번 듣고, 빈칸에 알맞은 말을 쓰시오.

01

W: Nothing is more relaxing than a nice vacation. But when you get back to work, you may find that your work has been piling up. And you _______ _______ _______ concentrating again. This is known as post-vacation syndrome. The best way to deal with it is to set your biorhythm. First, try to regulate the times you go to sleep and wake up. Also, _______ _______ _______ _______ will help you feel rested. Finally, you can deal with your piles of work in order of priority. Then it will be _______ _______ _______ _______ _______ into the swing of things after returning from vacation.

02

W: Are you alright, Michael? You _______ _______ _______ _______.

M: I'm not sick, just really full.

W: Did you eat too much for dinner?

M: Yes. I was stressed out, so I wanted some good food. But I overate.

W: Hmm... I think you were stress eating.

M: Stress eating? What's that?

W: It's when you eat a lot to relieve stress. But it only _______ _______ _______ _______.

M: I see. But how can I stop?

W: You have to think before you eat. Ask yourself if you are really hungry.

M: That's a good idea. But if I don't eat, what can I do?

W: Try another activity to _______ _______ _______. Take a walk or sing a song.

03

M: Good morning.

W: Hi, sir. How are you today?

M: I'm great.

W: Glad to hear that. _______ _______ _______ _______ _______ for the seminar in New York tomorrow.

M: Thanks. Hmm... Is there an earlier one?

W: If you want, I can try to find one. Is something wrong?

M: This one arrives at 10:00 a.m., but the seminar starts at 11:00 a.m. The schedule _______ _______ _______ _______.

W: I'm sorry. I'll change your ticket for an earlier flight. Also, the sales meeting is today at three o'clock.

M: Right. Thank you _______ _______ _______. Who's presenting today?

W: It's Nick from the Sales Department.

M: Okay. Please bring me the materials before the meeting.

04

M: Is the office ready for the New Year's party?

W: Yes. I set up a big rectangular table in the middle of the room.

M: Oh, good. And the cake?

W: Of course. I put it in the middle of the table.

M: Excellent. I hope the atmosphere will be _______ _______ _______.

W: Me, too. And there is a big banner on the wall.

M: Does it say "Happy New Year"?

W: Yes. And I put heart-shaped balloons _______ _______ _______ _______ the banner.

M: That sounds great. Also, you didn't forget to put some champagne on the table, did you?

W: No. I also put two beverage machines _______ _______ _______ _______ the table.

M: Excellent!

05

W: Do you have any plans for the next several days?
M: Nothing special. What's going on?
W: Well, I just found out I have to go to LA _______ _______ _______ _______.
M: Wow! LA is a great city. When do you leave?
W: My flight is tomorrow morning, and I come back next Thursday. So I'm worried about Sandy.
M: Who is Sandy?
W: My new cat. If you don't mind, could you _______ _______ _______ _______?
M: Sure. I'd be glad to. You know I also have a cat, right?
W: Actually, that's why I asked you. Thanks, John! I'll bring her and her stuff to your house.
M: Yes, _______ _______ _______ _______. I'll be happy to see her.
W: Thanks a lot.

06

W: Hi, Patrick. How have you been?
M: I'm doing fine, Rebecca. I heard that your daughter _______ _______ _______.
W: Yes. She's very excited. By the way, I'm looking for a new house.
M: Oh, are you moving somewhere near your daughter's school?
W: No, she's going to take the school bus.
M: Then why are you moving? You like your house, especially your garden.
W: We need _______ _______ _______ _______ _______.
M: Why do you need more?
W: My twin boys are sharing a room now, but I think they should each have their own space.
M: I see. Actually, _______ _______ _______ _______ is a real estate agent. If you want, I'll ask him.
W: That would be great. Thank you.

07

W: Welcome to Water Planet. Would you like to _______ _______ _______?
M: Yes. I'm here with my two sons. How much do tickets cost?
W: Adult tickets are $15 each, and children's tickets are $10 each.
M: All right. Do those tickets include access to all of the water slides?
W: You'll _______ _______ _______ all of the rides, except for the Aqua Plunge.
M: How much does the Aqua Plunge cost?
W: The tickets are $3 for adults and children.
M: Okay. Then I'll _______ _______ _______ _______ as well.
W: All right. If you have a membership card, you can get a $5 discount.
M: Great. Here is my membership card and my credit card.

08

M: Molly! Are you free to go to the movies this evening?
W: I'm not sure. I'm _______ _______ _______. I just started a new part-time job last Tuesday.
M: Really? What are you doing?
W: I'm working as a waitress three evenings a week.
M: I see. How long do you work each evening?
W: Five hours. I'm enjoying it so far, but it's hard work.
M: I'm sure it is, but that's fine if you _______ _______ _______.
W: Right. I'm earning $200 more a week now.
M: That's great. Then do you have any plans tonight after you finish?
W: No. I finish at ten. Could we see the movie at ten-thirty?
M: Sure. Just call me _______ _______ _______.

09

M: Have you ever heard of fittonia? It is a plant that _______ _______ _______ South American rainforests and is mainly found in Peru. It doesn't like extreme temperatures, so it can't live in very cold places, deserts, or places with lots of direct sunlight. There are 15 species of fittonia, but _______ _______ _______ has vein-like markings on its leaves. These lines stretch outward from the center of the leaf to the tip. All of the species _______ _______ _______. The leaves are almost always green, but the lines can be white or even pink. They all have hairs on their stems and produce small white flowers.

10

M: Hello, may I help you?

W: Yes. _______ _______ _______ a used car. It would be best if it was an SUV made after 2013.

M: We have _______ _______ _______ _______ SUVs here.

W: Great. I want one that has been driven less than 60,000 kilometers.

M: Okay. Then you should take a look at these three.

W: Have any of them _______ _______ _______ _______?

M: Yes, one of them has, but the other two have not.

W: Oh, that's important. I'd like one that hasn't been in any accidents.

M: I see. How much can you spend?

W: My budget is $13,000.

M: Then we have the perfect SUV for you.

11

W: Excuse me. I think _______ _______ _______ with my order.

M: Oh, really? What's the problem?

W: I asked for a dozen cupcakes, but there are only eleven in this box.

M: (Oh, I'm sorry. I'll get you one more.)

12

M: Lisa, don't you think it's too cold?

W: Yes. I've heard the heater in the office _______ _______ _______ until Friday.

M: You mean we have to suffer through this freezing cold all week?

W: (There's nothing else we can do.)

13

M: I heard you're going to the beach this weekend.

W: That's right. I _______ _______ _______ _______.

M: That sounds great! But don't forget to wear sunscreen.

W: Yeah. I'll buy some. But I'm not sure which type I should buy.

M: The sunlight will be strong, so I'd recommend using one with SPF 50.

W: Oh, right. But what if the water _______ _______ _______?

M: Just make sure you get sunscreen that is waterproof.

W: Okay. I just wish it didn't take so long to apply it over my whole body.

M: Why don't you try the spray type?

W: You know a lot about sunscreen! What else should I _______ _______ _______?

M: (Just remember to apply it every two to three hours.)

14

W: That was a great camping trip. But now it's time to go.

M: Let's make sure we pack everything.

W: Okay. What about this table?

M: That table _______ _______ _______ _______.

W: Okay. But let's wipe it off first and put it back.

M: Did you bring trash bags? We'll need some to throw away our trash.

W: Of course, but... Look at that pile of trash.

M: That's awful. Bottles, cans, food wrappers... Why didn't those people _______ _______ _______ _______?

W: The public trash can is just around the corner. How could they be so lazy?

M: Even without trash bags, they could have cleaned up. That's _______ _______ _______.

W: (People should be responsible when they're here.)

15

W: Eric and Gina have been preparing an outdoor magic show. Most of the tickets have been sold, and a lot of people _______ _______ _______ _______. However, the weather forecast suddenly changes, and heavy rain and high winds are expected on the day of the show. Still, Eric insists that the magic show should _______ _______ _______ _______ for the audience. Gina doesn't agree with him, though. She thinks that the event should be canceled. So, she decides to persuade Eric that there might be _______ _______ _______. In this situation, what would Gina most likely say to Eric?

Gina: (The safety of the audience is the first thing to consider.)

16-17

M: Today, I'm going to talk about first impressions. Throughout your life, you will _______ _______ _______ _______. Most of them will make a decision about you as soon as they meet you for the first time. That's why you need to make sure that their first opinion is a good one. You can control this by presenting yourself _______ _______ _______ _______ _______. For example, wearing dirty clothes might make people think you're careless and lazy. So always dress neatly. Also, when you speak, choose your words carefully. Using the proper words will make others think that you're intelligent and thoughtful. The way that you stand or sit and the look on your face are important as well. You should _______ _______ _______ _______ all of these things. I'm sure that people will have a positive reaction when they meet you.

33 Word & Expressions

01
- □ **relaxing** 편안한, 느긋한
- □ **pile up** 쌓이다
- □ **post-vacation syndrome** 휴가 후유증
- □ **deal with** …을 처리하다
- □ **biorhythm** 바이오리듬
- □ **regulate** 조절하다
- □ **priority** 우선 사항
- □ **get into the swing of** …에 익숙해지다

02
- □ **stressed out** 스트레스를 받는
- □ **overeat** 과식하다
- □ **relieve** 완화하다, 줄이다

03
- □ **tight** 단단한; *빡빡한, 빠듯한
- □ **remind** 상기시키다
- □ **present** 발표하다
- □ **department** 부서
- □ **material** 재료; *자료

04
- □ **set up** …을 세우다[놓다]
- □ **rectangular** 직사각형의
- □ **atmosphere** 분위기
- □ **festive** 축제의
- □ **beverage** 음료
- □ **machine** 기계

05
- □ **business trip** 출장
- □ **stuff** 물건
- □ **take care of** …을 돌보다
- □ **pack** (짐을) 싸다
- □ **show around** …을 구경시켜 주다

06
- □ **especially** 특히
- □ **garden** 뜰, 정원
- □ **share** 함께 쓰다, 공유하다
- □ **real estate agent** 부동산 중개인

07
- □ **access** 접근, 입장 허가
- □ **slide** 미끄럼틀
- □ **have access to** …에 접근할 수 있다
- □ **ride** 놀이 기구
- □ **except for** …을 제외하고는
- □ **plunge** 낙하

08
- □ **so far** 지금까지는
- □ **earn** (돈을) 벌다

09
- □ **native** 원산의, 토종의
- □ **rainforest** (열대) 우림
- □ **mainly** 주로
- □ **extreme** 극도의, 극한적인
- □ **temperature** 온도, 기온
- □ **direct sunlight** 직사광선
- □ **species** (생물의) 종
- □ **common** 흔한
- □ **vein-like** 정맥 같은
- □ **marking** 표시, 무늬
- □ **stretch** 늘이다; *뻗다
- □ **outward** 바깥쪽으로
- □ **stem** 줄기

10
- □ **used car** 중고차
- □ **a wide variety of** 매우 다양한 …
- □ **accident** 사고

11
- □ **order** 주문
- □ **dozen** 12의, 1다스의
- □ **delivery** 배달

12
- □ **properly** 제대로, 적절히
- □ **suffer** 고통받다; *겪다
- □ **freezing** 얼어붙을 것 같은

13
- □ **sunscreen** 자외선 차단제
- □ **wash away** …을 씻어 없애다
- □ **waterproof** 방수의
- □ **apply** 바르다

14
- □ **campground** 캠프장
- □ **wipe off** …을 닦아 내다
- □ **wrapper** 포장지
- □ **clean up** …을 치우다
- □ **lazy** 게으른
- □ **shame** 창피, 부끄러움
- □ **separate** 분리하다

15
- □ **weather forecast** 일기예보
- □ **suddenly** 갑자기
- □ **insist** 주장하다
- □ **audience** 관객, 관중
- □ **persuade** 설득하다
- □ **safety** 안전
- □ **issue** 문제
- □ **consider** 고려하다

16-17
- □ **throughout** … 동안 죽, 내내
- □ **make a decision** 결정[판단]을 내리다
- □ **opinion** 의견
- □ **present** 나타내다, 보이다
- □ **careless** 부주의한
- □ **neatly** 단정하게
- □ **intelligent** 지적인
- □ **thoughtful** 사려 깊은
- □ **pay attention to** …에 주의를 기울이다
- □ **positive** 긍정적인
- □ **characteristic** 특징
- □ **current** 현재의
- □ **relationship** 관계
- □ **personality** 성격

34 영어듣기 모의고사

정답 및 해설 p.102-104

1번부터 17번까지는 듣고 답하는 문제입니다.
1번부터 15번까지는 한 번만 들려주고, 16번부터 17번까지는 두 번 들려줍니다. 방송을 잘 듣고 답을 하기 바랍니다.

01

다음을 듣고, 여자가 하는 말의 목적으로 가장 적절한 것을 고르시오.

① 오디션 참여를 독려하려고
② 음악 축제 행사를 안내하려고
③ 학교 축제 일정 변경을 공지하려고
④ 시험공부 하는 학생들을 격려하려고
⑤ 축제 기간 중 주의 사항을 당부하려고

02

대화를 듣고, 남자의 의견으로 가장 적절한 것을 고르시오.

① 다양한 기능이 있는 가전제품이 더 좋다.
② 가전제품의 디자인은 집에 어울려야 한다.
③ 에너지 효율이 높은 가전제품을 구입해야 한다.
④ 가구는 온라인으로 구입하는 것이 더 저렴하다.
⑤ 비싼 가전제품이 모두 성능이 우수한 것은 아니다.

03

대화를 듣고, 두 사람의 관계를 가장 잘 나타낸 것을 고르시오.

① 만화책 작가 — 팬
② 서점 직원 — 고객
③ 도서관 사서 — 이용객
④ 인형 가게 직원 — 고객
⑤ 골동품 가게 주인 — 기자

04

대화를 듣고, 그림에서 대화의 내용과 일치하지 않는 것을 고르시오.

05

대화를 듣고, 남자가 할 일로 가장 적절한 것을 고르시오.

① 대신 주차해 주기
② 주차 요금 지불하기
③ 사무실에 짐 옮기기
④ 주차장 위치 알려주기
⑤ 관리사무소에 차량 등록하기

06

대화를 듣고, 여자가 집에 늦게 오는 이유를 고르시오.

① 운동을 하고 가야 해서
② 음식을 사서 가야 해서
③ 회의가 늦게 시작되어서
④ 저녁 식사 약속이 있어서
⑤ 학교에서 딸을 데려와야 해서

07

대화를 듣고, 남자가 지불할 금액을 고르시오. 3점

① $330
② $445
③ $450
④ $455
⑤ $675

08

대화를 듣고, 자동차에 관해 두 사람이 언급하지 않은 것을 고르시오.

① 제조사
② 색상
③ 차종
④ 가격
⑤ 연비

09

Salar de Uyuni에 관한 다음 내용을 듣고, 일치하지 않는 것을 고르시오. 3점

① 세계에서 가장 큰 소금 평지이다.
② 안데스 산맥의 높은 고도에 위치해 있다.
③ 과거에 큰 호수의 일부였다.
④ 많은 양의 리튬을 함유하고 있다.
⑤ 동식물이 전혀 살지 않는다.

10

다음 표를 보면서 대화를 듣고, 남자가 구입할 태블릿 컴퓨터를 고르시오.

< Tablet Computers >

	Model	Storage	Screen Size	Price	Battery Life
①	A	16 GB	10 inches	$380	12 hrs.
②	B	32 GB	12 inches	$400	15 hrs.
③	C	32 GB	14 inches	$420	10 hrs.
④	D	32 GB	14 inches	$440	15 hrs.
⑤	E	64 GB	14 inches	$500	18 hrs.

11

대화를 듣고, 여자의 마지막 말에 대한 남자의 응답으로 가장 적절한 것을 고르시오.

① Then we should get chocolate.
② It's too expensive for me to buy.
③ In that case, it's worth waiting for.
④ You should not cut in line, though.
⑤ I thought they were open until ten.

12

대화를 듣고, 남자의 마지막 말에 대한 여자의 응답으로 가장 적절한 것을 고르시오.

① I just bought a new computer.
② Let's check if the computer is working.
③ Why don't you go to the hospital then?
④ Sorry, but I need it for a project tomorrow.
⑤ Then try deleting the programs you don't use.

13

대화를 듣고, 남자의 마지막 말에 대한 여자의 응답으로 가장 적절한 것을 고르시오.

Woman: ______________________

① I guess I need to get some sleep.
② Then I should stop drinking coffee.
③ In that case, I should take a vacation.
④ I'd better not drink so many energy drinks.
⑤ I should feel better after a good night's sleep.

14

대화를 듣고, 여자의 마지막 말에 대한 남자의 응답으로 가장 적절한 것을 고르시오.

Man: ______________________

① He said that everything was delicious.
② Okay. I'll try growing vegetables, too.
③ Send me the recipe and I'll try it tonight.
④ Sorry. We don't have time to cook dinner.
⑤ Vegetables are essential for a healthy diet.

15

다음 상황 설명을 듣고, 선생님이 Jennifer의 부모님에게 할 말로 가장 적절한 것을 고르시오.

Teacher: ______________________

① Jennifer doesn't know what she wants to study.
② Please give Jennifer a chance to follow her dream.
③ Jennifer has the potential to become a great doctor.
④ I believe Jennifer will win first prize in the contest.
⑤ I advised her to study harder to enter a good university.

[16-17] 다음을 듣고, 물음에 답하시오.

16

남자가 하는 말의 주제로 가장 적절한 것은? 3점

① why cats make sounds
② what makes cats good pets
③ why cats sometimes scratch
④ how to choose a healthy cat
⑤ how to understand cats' moods

17

언급된 고양이의 신체 부위가 아닌 것은?

① backs ② tails ③ eyes
④ ears ⑤ legs

정답 및 해설 p.104

녹음을 다시 한 번 듣고, 빈칸에 알맞은 말을 쓰시오.

01

W: Good morning, everyone. I'd like to make an announcement about the upcoming school festival. ________ ________ ________ ________, the festival will be held two weeks from today. However, auditions for the singing contest will take place next Tuesday. ________ ________ ________ to take part in the contest is welcome to audition. You can try out as an individual or as a group. Ten people or teams will be selected from the auditions for the contest. Please submit your name and the title of the song you will sing to the music teacher, Ms. Swann, ________ ________ ________ this Friday. The place and time of the auditions will be announced soon. Thank you.

02

W: Jim, have you finished buying the appliances for your new house?

M: Yes. The refrigerator and the TV will be delivered soon.

W: Do you think they'll match your new apartment?

M: Well, I didn't ________ ________ ________ ________ the way they looked.

W: Really? Design is very important to me. So are any special functions.

M: Special functions don't matter that much to me, either.

W: Then what do you consider when buying appliances?

M: I ________ ________ ________ ________, since I don't want my electric bill to go up.

W: Aren't energy-efficient appliances usually expensive?

M: Sometimes. But ________ ________ ________ ________ money in the future, I'm willing to buy them.

W: That makes sense.

03

M: Excuse me.

W: Hello, sir. How can I help you?

M: I'm looking for my favorite comic book, *The Dream of Carter*. Do you have it?

W: I ________ ________ ________ ________. Do you know who wrote it?

M: Yes. It was written and illustrated by Tom Riley. I'd like to give it to my grandson for his birthday.

W: Okay. I'll ________ ________ ________ ________.

M: Take your time.

W: I found it! It's ________ ________ ________ ________.

M: That's wonderful! How much is it?

W: The hardcover copy is $30 and the paperback copy is $20. Which one do you prefer?

M: The hardcover copy, please.

04

M: Hey, Susan, I heard you ________ ________ ________ a publishing company.

W: Yeah. Now, I have my own private office. There is a big desk in the middle of the room.

M: Great. How about a bookshelf?

W: I put a big bookshelf behind my desk.

M: Good. I guess you need a printer, too.

W: Sure. It's ________ ________ ________ my desk.

M: That's really convenient. Oh, I recommend getting a plant to ________ ________ ________ ________.

W: I already have one! It's next to my printer.

M: It sounds like everything is set up perfectly. Does the office get a lot of sunlight?

W: Not enough. So I put a big standing lamp next to the desk.

33회

05

M: Oh, I've _______ _______ _______ _______ _______ from our building's maintenance office.

W: What? That's ridiculous. Did you park in the correct parking spot?

M: Yes. We can park in spaces 12 through 20, right?

W: Right. They must have made a mistake.

M: Weren't our parking privileges _______ _______ _______ yesterday?

W: That's right.

M: And did you submit a copy of the vehicle registration documents to the maintenance office?

W: Oh, actually, I forgot to do that. I've been so busy moving things into this new office.

M: Well, then that's the problem. I will turn them in right away.

W: Okay. In that case, they should _______ _______ _______ _______.

M: I certainly hope so.

06

[Cell phone rings.]

M: Hello?

W: Hi, honey. Where are you?

M: I'm _______ _______ _______ _______ _______ now. We finished early today.

W: That's great. Unfortunately, I'm on my way to a meeting now.

M: Oh, really? So you'll be home late?

W: Yes. It was supposed to be at four o'clock, but it _______ _______ _______ _______ _______.

M: That's too bad. I guess you won't be able to join me at the gym.

W: Right, I won't be able to. Could you pick up Jenny from school?

M: Sure. Do you think you'll be home for dinner?

W: Yes. Let's _______ _______ _______ tonight.

M: Good idea. See you at home!

07

W: How can I help you today?

M: I'm looking for an anniversary gift for my wife.

W: Then I recommend this gold necklace. It was $700, but it's available now _______ _______ _______ _______ of $550.

M: Hmm... It's a bit expensive. How about a bracelet?

W: Sure. This gold bracelet _______ _______ _______ _______. It was $550, but now it's $325.

M: That looks perfect. I'll take it.

W: And if you spend more than $300, you can get 20% off _______ _______ _______ _______. The original price of this pair is $150.

M: Those are nice. I'll take them, too. Can you gift-wrap everything?

W: Sure. Standard gift-wrapping is $5, and special gift-wrapping is $10.

M: Standard, please.

08

W: Wow! Is that your new car? _______ _______ _______ this model before.

M: Yeah. I just bought it yesterday. It's the latest model from Modern Motors.

W: I love the color.

M: Thanks. I was going to get a red one, but I eventually decided to _______ _______ _______ _______.

W: That was a good choice. I bet it was expensive, though.

M: It was about $23,000, but I think it was worth it.

W: Does it get good gas mileage?

M: It gets about 30 miles per gallon.

W: That's _______ _______ _______ _______.

M: Me too. I'm really happy with the purchase. Do you want to go for a ride?

W: Why not!

09

M: Hello, everyone. Today I will talk about an amazing salt flat. The world's largest salt flat, called Salar de Uyuni, is in southwestern Bolivia. ________ ________ the Andes Mountains, it sits at a very high altitude. Thousands of years ago, it was actually part of a giant lake. Over time, the lake dried up and the salt flat was formed. Interestingly, it contains ________ ________ ________ lithium, which is used to make batteries. Because of its desert climate, there are few plants and animals there. Since it is such an interesting place, Salar de Uyuni has become one of Bolivia's ________ ________ ________ ________.

10

W: Good morning, sir. What are you looking for?

M: Hi, I'm here to buy a tablet computer.

W: Okay. ________ ________ ________ do you need?

M: Well, I download a lot of movies, so I need one with at least 32 GB of storage.

W: How about this one? The 14-inch screen would be great for watching movies.

M: I think so, too.

W: May I ask what price range you were thinking of?

M: Well, I'd like to spend ________ ________ ________ $450.

W: Okay. Do you have any other particular features in mind?

M: I'd like one that has a long battery life.

W: ________ ________ ________, this model would be the best for you.

M: Great.

11

W: Look at that long line outside the ice cream shop!

M: What's happening there?

W: That sign says if you buy one ice cream you can ________ ________ ________ ________.

M: (In that case, it's worth waiting for.)

12

M: My computer is driving me crazy. It's too slow!

W: Does it have anti-virus software?

M: Yes, but it doesn't ________ ________ ________.

W: (Then try deleting the programs you don't use.)

13

M: Gee, Anna. You look awfully tired.

W: Yeah. I haven't been sleeping well at all lately.

M: Maybe ________ ________ ________.

W: Well, I don't feel very stressed. In fact, I just finished a big project and I'm not very busy.

M: In my case, I ________ ________ ________ after I have a lot of caffeine. Do you drink a lot of coffee?

W: Not coffee. I like to drink energy drinks, though.

M: I bet that's your problem.

W: Why? ________ ________ ________ ________ energy drinks.

M: Well, they contain large amounts of caffeine. Some of them have even more than coffee.

W: (I'd better not drink so many energy drinks.)

14

M: Did you do anything interesting last weekend, Kathy?

W: Yes. I went to my vegetable garden in the countryside with my daughter. We pulled some carrots.

M: I didn't know that you had a garden.

W: Well, it's just a small one. My family and I _______ _______ _______ _______ together.

M: That's great. Does your daughter enjoy working in the garden?

W: Of course. She loves eating vegetables, too.

M: Wow! _______ _______ _______ _______ get my son to eat vegetables.

W: Before we had a garden, my daughter also refused to eat them.

M: So, do you think growing vegetables changed her mind?

W: Definitely! You should _______ _______ _______ _______ _______.

M: (Okay. I'll try growing vegetables, too.)

15

W: Jennifer is a high school student who loves studying sociology. She _______ _______ _______ _______ _______ sociology at a university. Her parents, on the other hand, want her to become a doctor. They believe her grades are good enough _______ _______ _______ _______ a good medical school. Not knowing what to do, they visit her homeroom teacher to get some advice. But her homeroom teacher knows Jennifer's passion for sociology. He wants to persuade Jennifer's parents to let her _______ _______ _______ _______. In this situation, what would the teacher most likely say to Jennifer's parents?

Teacher: (Please give Jennifer a chance to follow her dream.)

16-17

M: Many people think that cats are easy to take care of because they're so independent. So, _______ _______ _______ _______ have them as pets. However, despite their independence, they still need love and attention. Cats express their emotions in their own way, so people might not know what they're saying. To understand their cats, people need to take a close look at their behavior. For example, when cats are angry, their backs curve and their tails _______ _______ _______ _______ quickly. But if they're happy, it moves slowly. Closing their eyes halfway sends the same message. But if they point their ears back and make sounds, they're ready to attack. Finally, when cats start rubbing back and forth against your legs, it means they _______ _______ _______. A pet cat may be hard to understand at first, but once you do, you can be their lifelong friend.

34 Word & Expressions

01
- □ announcement 발표(v. announce 발표하다)
- □ upcoming 다가오는
- □ take place 개최되다, 일어나다
- □ take part in …에 참가하다
- □ try out (선발에) 지원하다
- □ individual 개인
- □ submit 제출하다
- □ no later than 늦어도 …까지는

02
- □ appliance (가정용) 기기
- □ function 기능
- □ consider 고려하다
- □ energy efficiency 에너지 효율
- □ electric bill 전기 요금 고지서
- □ energy-efficient 에너지 효율이 좋은
- □ be willing to-v 기꺼이 …하다

03
- □ comic book 만화책
- □ illustrate 삽화를 넣다
- □ hardcover 양장본, 표지가 딱딱한 책
- □ paperback 페이퍼백, 종이 표지를 한 책

04
- □ publishing company 출판사
- □ private 개인을 위한, 개인적인
- □ convenient 편리한

05
- □ parking fee 주차 요금
- □ maintenance 관리, 유지
- □ ridiculous 말도 안 되는
- □ privilege 혜택
- □ be supposed to-v …하기로 되어 있다
- □ vehicle 차량, 탈것
- □ registration 등록
- □ document 서류, 문서
- □ turn in …을 제출하다

06
- □ delay 지연시키다
- □ pick up …을 태우러 가다

07
- □ anniversary 기념일
- □ available 이용할[구할] 수 있는
- □ bracelet 팔찌
- □ original 원래의, 본래의
- □ gift-wrap 선물용으로 포장하다

08
- □ gas mileage 연비
- □ gallon 갤런(용량의 단위)
- □ purchase 구매
- □ go for a ride 드라이브하러 가다

09
- □ flat 평평한; *평지
- □ altitude 고도
- □ lithium 리튬
- □ climate 기후
- □ tourist destination 관광지

10
- □ storage 저장; *저장량
- □ price range 가격대
- □ particular 특정한
- □ feature 특징
- □ battery life 배터리 수명

11
- □ cut in line 새치기하다

12
- □ anti-virus software 바이러스 방어 프로그램
- □ detect 감지하다
- □ delete 삭제하다

13
- □ awfully 정말, 몹시
- □ stressed out 스트레스를 받는
- □ fall asleep 잠들다
- □ caffeine 카페인

14
- □ countryside 시골 지역
- □ pull 당기다; *뽑다
- □ take care of …을 돌보다
- □ refuse 거부하다
- □ definitely 분명히
- □ recipe 조리법
- □ essential 필수적인

15
- □ sociology 사회학
- □ major in …을 전공하다
- □ medical school 의과 대학
- □ homeroom teacher 담임 교사
- □ passion 열정
- □ persuade 설득하다
- □ pursue 추구하다; *계속하다
- □ potential 잠재력

16-17
- □ independent 독립적인(n. independence 독립)
- □ household 가정
- □ attention 주목; *관심, 흥미
- □ emotion 감정
- □ take a close look at …을 주의 깊게 보다
- □ behavior 행동
- □ halfway 반쯤
- □ rub 문지르다, 비비다
- □ lifelong 평생의
- □ scratch 긁다, 할퀴다

35 영어듣기 모의고사

1번부터 17번까지는 듣고 답하는 문제입니다.
1번부터 15번까지는 한 번만 들려주고, 16번부터 17번까지는 두 번 들려줍니다. 방송을 잘 듣고 답을 하기 바랍니다.

01

다음을 듣고, 여자가 하는 말의 목적으로 가장 적절한 것을 고르시오.

① 기숙사생을 모집하려고
② 기숙사 규칙을 안내하려고
③ 기숙사 내 취사를 금지하려고
④ 기숙사 절도 사건을 보고하려고
⑤ 새로 온 기숙사 사감을 소개하려고

02

대화를 듣고, 남자의 의견으로 가장 적절한 것을 고르시오.

① 지하철 요금을 인상해야 한다.
② 지하철의 승차감을 개선해야 한다.
③ 공공장소에서 타인을 배려해야 한다.
④ 지하철에 버려지는 쓰레기의 양을 줄여야 한다.
⑤ 휴대전화 영상 통화 기능 사용을 자제해야 한다.

03

대화를 듣고, 두 사람의 관계를 가장 잘 나타낸 것을 고르시오.

① 고객 — 은행원 ② 영업자 — 거래처 사장
③ 고용주 — 인사 담당자 ④ 기자 — 웹사이트 관리자
⑤ 아르바이트 지원자 — 마트 주인

04

대화를 듣고, 그림에서 대화의 내용과 일치하지 않는 것을 고르시오.

05

대화를 듣고, 남자가 여자에게 부탁한 일로 가장 적절한 것을 고르시오.

① to repair a broken laptop computer
② to place pop-up ads on his homepage
③ to show him how to send text messages
④ to install antivirus software on his computer
⑤ to tell him the name of an ad-blocking program

06

대화를 듣고, 남자가 달리기 경주에 참가하지 못하는 이유를 고르시오.

① 달리기 연습을 해야 해서
② 자선 행사에 참석해야 해서
③ 생일 파티를 준비해야 해서
④ 친구를 응원하러 가야 해서
⑤ 그룹 프로젝트 모임이 있어서

07

대화를 듣고, 남자가 지불할 금액을 고르시오. 3점

① $25 ② $30 ③ $34
④ $36 ⑤ $40

08

대화를 듣고, 여자가 건강을 위해 하는 일로 언급되지 않은 것을 고르시오.

① 요가하기 ② 수영하기
③ 조깅하기 ④ 균형 잡힌 식사하기
⑤ 비타민제 복용하기

09

Best Chef Korea에 관한 다음 내용을 듣고, 일치하지 않는 것을 고르시오. 3점

① 12주 동안 진행될 것이다.
② 매주 두 명의 탈락자가 발생할 것이다.
③ 탈락자는 3명의 심사위원만이 선택할 것이다.
④ 최후의 3명에게 취업 기회가 주어질 것이다.
⑤ 우승자는 3억원의 상금을 받을 것이다.

정답 및 해설 p.105-107

10

다음 표를 보면서 대화를 듣고, 두 사람이 남자를 만날 게이트를 고르시오.

< Arrival Gates >

	Gates	Flight No.	From	Arrival Time
①	1	632	Tokyo	3:00 p.m.
②	2	430	Beijing	3:10 p.m.
③	3	425	Tokyo	3:30 p.m.
④	4	575	Beijing	3:45 p.m
⑤	5	410	Tokyo	4:15 p.m

11

대화를 듣고, 여자의 마지막 말에 대한 남자의 응답으로 가장 적절한 것을 고르시오.

① It looks like a great place to travel.
② May I have a small paper bag, please?
③ Thanks, but my brother bought me one.
④ It looks nice, but I need something practical.
⑤ I know where I can find it at a reasonable price.

12

대화를 듣고, 남자의 마지막 말에 대한 여자의 응답으로 가장 적절한 것을 고르시오.

① You don't have to do that.
② Sure, I'll sign it right now.
③ That's too bad. It sounds fun.
④ I'll bring it to class tomorrow.
⑤ They're not interested in coming.

13

대화를 듣고, 남자의 마지막 말에 대한 여자의 응답으로 가장 적절한 것을 고르시오.

Woman: ______________________

① You're right. I should have taken a taxi.
② Yes, I'll just call my mom to pick me up.
③ Great. Thanks for lending me the phone.
④ Are you sure you have the time? It's far away.
⑤ You're kind, but you don't need to drive me home.

14

대화를 듣고, 여자의 마지막 말에 대한 남자의 응답으로 가장 적절한 것을 고르시오.

Man: ______________________

① I'll let you know how much they cost.
② You should write about climate change.
③ No problem. I'm happy to help a friend.
④ I'm sorry. I have to return the books today.
⑤ You should have finished the report on time.

15

다음 상황 설명을 듣고, Julie가 Eric에게 할 말로 가장 적절한 것을 고르시오.

Julie: ______________________

① Why don't you buy tickets at the cafeteria?
② Do you know the bands that are performing?
③ I'm sorry, but I can't go to the festival with you.
④ You can have my ticket to the festival if you want.
⑤ Can you work for me at the restaurant on that day?

[16-17] 다음을 듣고, 물음에 답하시오.

16

남자가 하는 말의 목적으로 가장 적절한 것은?

① to introduce a tour provided in a park
② to talk about the dangers of hot weather
③ to describe the history of the Grand Canyon
④ to explain how to register for a camping trip
⑤ to advertise a newly opened park near the city

17

프로그램에 대해 언급되지 않은 것은?

① 체험 내용　　② 준비물
③ 참가 비용　　④ 참가 인원
⑤ 운영 기간

녹음을 다시 한 번 듣고, 빈칸에 알맞은 말을 쓰시오.

01

W: Good morning. Welcome to your new college dormitory. As the dormitory manager, I supervise the building and the building's residents. If there are any problems, _______ _______ _______ _______ me. Now, I'd like to tell you about some rules. First, you are not allowed to cook in the dormitory. The reason for this is that _______ _______ _______ _______ _______. Second, you should never give the front-door password to anyone who doesn't live here. Doing so could result in problems such as theft. Finally, you will have to pay for any damage you may cause. If something breaks, please _______ _______ _______ right away.

02

M: Liz, you look upset. What's wrong?

W: A person on the subway was eating some food and throwing his trash on the floor.

M: Really? That's pretty annoying.

W: I agree. In addition, a woman made a video call _______ _______ _______!

M: Oh, no! Was she loud?

W: Yes. I couldn't concentrate on my book.

M: I guess some people don't care what others think about their behavior.

W: You're right. People _______ _______ _______ _______ on the subway these days.

M: It's a public place. They should think of others.

W: Exactly. Everyone should understand that their actions affect others.

M: If people remembered that, riding the subway would be _______ _______ _______ _______ for everyone.

03

[Telephone rings.]

M: Hello?

W: Hello. Is this Brian Mraz?

M: Speaking. Who's this?

W: This is Katie Wilson, and _______ _______ _______ your application on the Happy Mart website.

M: Oh, yes. I applied for it last month. Is it still available?

W: Yes, but there is one blank about your work experiences on the form.

M: Oh, I forgot it. I've _______ _______ _______ _______ at a big supermarket for one year.

W: Great. And working hours are Monday through Saturday from 7 a.m. to 3 p.m.

M: That sounds good.

W: A lot of products will need to be organized at the store tomorrow morning. Why don't you come then and _______ _______ _______?

M: Sure! I'd love to.

04

M: Hi, Christine. I heard you're _______ _______ _______ _______.

W: Oh, hi, David. That's right. Actually, I'm working on the election poster right now.

M: Oh, I wonder what it looks like. Can I see it?

W: Sure. I put my picture on the poster. And my name is written _______ _______ _______.

M: It looks good. You used a picture of our school for the background.

W: Yes. And I put my slogan below my picture.

M: I like your slogan. It's "We Can Make a Difference!"

W: Thanks. I made a campaign song, too.

M: Is this QR code _______ _______ _______ _______ _______ of the poster for your song?

W: Yes, you can scan it and listen to the song.

05

M: I'm so tired of seeing ads when I use the Internet.

W: _______ _______ _______ _______ are you talking about, James?

M: Pop-up ads. They're all over the Internet. They're so annoying.

W: I know how you feel. They can be pretty irritating.

M: _______ _______ _______ _______ _______. I want to get rid of them.

W: Well, there is an ad blocker that stops pop-ups. After I installed it, I don't have that problem anymore.

M: What's the name of the program?

W: It's on the tip of my tongue. I can't think of the name right now. I need to _______ _______ _______ at home.

M: Can you send me a message when you do?

W: Sure.

06

M: Hi, Susie! Can you come to Jason's birthday party this afternoon?

W: I don't think I can. I'm going jogging after school.

M: Jogging? Are you training to _______ _______ _______ _______?

W: Sort of. I'm running in a 10-kilometer race tomorrow. It's for charity.

M: Wow. That sounds fun. Good luck!

W: Thanks. Hey, how about running with me tomorrow? You can _______ _______ _______ _______ _______.

M: Hmm... When does it start?

W: It starts at 9:30 a.m.

M: I don't think I can. I have to meet some classmates for a group project at 8:30 a.m.

W: Why don't you come after you finish, then? You can _______ _______ _______ instead.

M: That sounds good. See you tomorrow.

07

W: Welcome to Book World.

M: Hi. I want to buy a few books as gifts.

W: Then you're lucky. We're _______ _______ _______ _______ this week.

M: That's great. How much can I save?

W: _______ _______ _______ which kinds of books you buy.

M: Okay, I'll go look around. *[Pause]* How much are these novels?

W: They're four dollars each.

M: I see. How about these children's books? The price tags on all the children's books say six dollars.

W: Actually, this week they're 50% off _______ _______ _______.

M: Okay. I'll take all of these. How much is the total?

W: You have four novels and three children's books. Let me add everything.

08

M: Megan, you look really healthy these days. Is there a special reason?

W: Actually, I wasn't feeling well a few weeks ago, so I went to see a doctor. He gave me tips on _______ _______ _______ _______ _______.

M: What did he tell you?

W: He told me to exercise more and to be careful about what I eat.

M: So did you take his advice?

W: Yes. I'm _______ _______ _______ _______.

M: Wow. That will improve your flexibility!

W: I also swim twice a week to increase my endurance.

M: That's great. What else are you doing to stay healthy?

W: I always try to _______ _______ _______. I also take vitamins every day.

M: Good for you!

09

M: Do you know who the best chef in Korea is? Best Chef Korea is going to find out! This show will _______ _______ _______ _______ on the Food Channel starting next week. Each week, chefs will compete in a variety of challenges. The show will start with 25 chefs, but two will leave every week. The final three will then _______ _______ _______ _______ _______. Each week, a panel of three food experts and an audience of 50 people will choose the week's losers. And all three finalists will _______ _______ _______ _______ _______ at world-famous restaurants. The winner will also get 300 million won.

10

M: I'm so happy to finally see Greg again.

W: Well, it's three o'clock now. Do you know which gate he will arrive at?

M: Actually, I'm not sure. I forgot to _______ _______ _______ _______ he arrives.

W: Let's take a look at this flight schedule.

M: Good idea. I bet if we work together we can _______ _______ _______ to meet him.

W: Okay. I remember that his flight number was in the four hundreds.

M: Good. And we obviously don't have to consider Beijing.

W: Then that narrows the range of choices.

M: Right. Plus, he said he would arrive _______ _______ _______ 4 p.m.

W: Well, I think we've figured it out!

M: Let's go find him!

11

W: Hello, sir. How can I help you?

M: _______ _______ _______ a strong, medium-sized backpack.

W: Well, how about this one? It's very stylish and popular these days.

M: (It looks nice, but I need something practical.)

12

M: Wendy, will you attend the class field trip on Monday?

W: Yes, Mr. Kang. I'm really excited.

M: That's good, but you haven't _______ _______ _______ _______ _______ signed by a parent yet.

W: (I'll bring it to class tomorrow.)

13

M: Hey, you need to wake up.

W: Oh, no! Where am I?

M: This is the last stop. You need to _______ _______ _______ _______.

W: I can't believe I fell asleep on the bus! Would you tell me how to get to City Hall?

M: You need to _______ _______ _______ and use that bus stop over there. Bus number 272 will take you there.

W: Thank you.

M: Oh, wait. I'm afraid you just missed the last bus.

W: Oh, no. What should I do?

M: I think you'll have to take a taxi.

W: But I _______ _______ _______ _______ for a taxi.

M: Hmm... You'd better ask your parents for help.

W: (Yes, I'll just call my mom to pick me up.)

14

M: Final exams are finally over! We're free!

W: You may be, but I'm not. I still have work to do.

M: What do you mean? Do you still have exams?

W: No, I finished all of my exams, too. But I _______ _______ _______ _______ _______.

M: Really? That's too bad. What's the report about?

W: It's about climate change.

M: You didn't submit that report yet? It was _______ _______ _______!

W: Yeah. Luckily, my teacher gave me an extension.

M: I have the reference books I used to write that report. If you want, I can _______ _______ _______ _______.

W: Really? Oh, thank you. That would help a lot.

M: (No problem. I'm happy to help a friend.)

15

W: Eric and Julie are talking about a music festival. It is going to be held on Saturday in the school auditorium. _______ _______ _______ _______ will attend. Julie says that one of her friends gave her a ticket to the festival, but she can't go. She works part-time at Burger Chef and _______ _______ _______ to work on Saturday. Eric says that he really loves music and wishes that he could go. But he wasn't able to buy a ticket because they _______ _______ _______ _______. So, Julie decides to give him her ticket. In this situation, what would Julie most likely say to Eric?

Julie: (You can have my ticket to the festival if you want.)

16-17

M: Welcome to Grand Canyon National Park. Today, I'd like to introduce the Adventure Time trip. On this two-day camping trip, you can enjoy the beautiful scenery of the canyon while learning _______ _______ _______ _______. We'll ride horses from the top of the canyon to the bottom and stop at some special locations _______ _______ _______. The sun is strong, so remember to bring lots of water and sunscreen. I'd also recommend that you wear a hat. When we reach the bottom, we'll camp for the night, look up at the stars, and relax. Then we'll come back up to the top of the canyon. Everything is _______ _______ _______, so don't worry about the cost. But this program is only offered from mid-July through mid-August. If you're interested, please hurry and sign up now.

35 Word & Expressions

01
- □ dormitory 기숙사
- □ supervise 감독하다
- □ resident 거주자
- □ feel free to-v 마음 놓고 …하다
- □ result in …을 야기하다
- □ theft 절도

02
- □ upset 화난, 기분이 상한
- □ annoying 짜증이 나는
- □ concentrate on …에 집중하다
- □ please 기쁘게 하다; *…하고 싶다
- □ enjoyable 즐거운

03
- □ application 지원(서)
- □ cashier 출납원
- □ product 생산물, 제품
- □ organize 조직하다; *정리하다

04
- □ run for …에 입후보하다[출마하다]
- □ student president 학생회장
- □ election 선거
- □ slogan 구호 문구, 슬로건

05
- □ pop-up ad 팝업 광고
- □ irritating 짜증이 나는
- □ get rid of …을 없애다
- □ install 설치하다
- □ on the tip of one's tongue 생각이 날 듯 말 듯한
- □ look up …을 찾아보다

06
- □ charity 자선
- □ on the spot 현장에서
- □ cheer on …을 응원하다

07
- □ price tag 가격표
- □ regular price 정가

08
- □ flexibility 유연성
- □ endurance 인내; *지구력
- □ balanced 균형 잡힌

09
- □ run (얼마의 기간 동안) 계속되다
- □ a variety of 다양한
- □ episode 에피소드, 1회 방영분
- □ panel 판; *위원단, 패널
- □ finalist 결승전 진출자

10
- □ figure out …을 이해하다[알아내다]
- □ obviously 분명히
- □ narrow 좁아지다
- □ range 범위
- □ no later than 늦어도 …까지는

11
- □ backpack 배낭
- □ practical 실용적인
- □ reasonable (가격이) 적정한, 비싸지 않은

12
- □ permission 허락, 허가

13
- □ get off (버스에서) 내리다
- □ fall asleep 잠들다

14
- □ climate change 기후 변화
- □ submit 제출하다
- □ extension (기간의) 연장
- □ reference 참고

15
- □ auditorium 강당
- □ work part time 파트타임으로 근무하다, 아르바이트하다
- □ sold out 매진된

16-17
- □ canyon 협곡
- □ location 장소
- □ sunscreen 자외선 차단제
- □ camp 야영하다
- □ free of charge 무료의
- □ cost 비용
- □ register 등록하다

수능만만
기 본

기출 영어듣기 모의고사

—

01회 -05회

01 기출 영어듣기 모의고사

정답 및 해설 p.108-110

1번부터 17번까지는 듣고 답하는 문제입니다.
1번부터 15번까지는 한 번만 들려주고, 16번부터 17번까지는 두 번 들려줍니다. 방송을 잘 듣고 답을 하기 바랍니다.

01

다음을 듣고, 여자가 하는 말의 목적으로 가장 적절한 것을 고르시오.

① 수영장 안전 수칙을 안내하려고
② 실내 수영장 개장을 홍보하려고
③ 야외 수영장 임시 폐쇄를 알리려고
④ 음식물의 수영장 반입 금지를 알리려고
⑤ 호텔 외부 유리창 청소 일정을 안내하려고

02

대화를 듣고, 두 사람이 하는 말의 주제로 가장 적절한 것을 고르시오.

① 전자기기 구입 시 유의점
② 전자 폐기물로 인한 문제점
③ 친환경적인 쓰레기 처리 방법
④ 무분별한 자원 개발의 위험성
⑤ 빈곤국에 대한 국제 원조의 필요성

03

대화를 듣고, 두 사람의 관계를 가장 잘 나타낸 것을 고르시오.

① 구조대원 — 등산객
② 의사 — 환자
③ 여행 가이드 — 관광객
④ 코치 — 운동선수
⑤ 의료기 판매원 — 고객

04

대화를 듣고, 그림에서 대화의 내용과 일치하지 않는 것을 고르시오.

05

대화를 듣고, 여자가 남자를 위해 할 일로 가장 적절한 것을 고르시오.

① 여권 복사하기
② 여행 가방 싸기
③ 휴대전화 해지하기
④ 국제학생증 수령하기
⑤ 여행자 보험 가입하기

06

대화를 듣고, 남자가 English Composition을 수강할 수 없는 이유를 고르시오.

① 강좌가 폐강되어서
② 신청 인원이 초과되어서
③ 수강 신청 기간이 지나서
④ 수강 가능 학년이 아니어서
⑤ 다른 강좌와 시간이 중복되어서

07

대화를 듣고, 여자가 지불할 금액을 고르시오. 3점

① $28　② $30　③ $35
④ $37　⑤ $40

08

대화를 듣고, book signing event에 관해 두 사람이 언급하지 않은 것을 고르시오.

① 저자명　② 요일　③ 책 제목
④ 장소　⑤ 시작 시간

09

Roseville Fitness Club에 관한 다음 내용을 듣고, 일치하지 않는 것을 고르시오.

① 신규 회원은 첫 달에 50% 할인을 받는다.
② 신규 회원은 사물함 이용이 무료이다.
③ 요가 프로그램을 제공한다.
④ 밤 11시까지 이용할 수 있다.
⑤ 음료를 마실 수 있는 카페가 있다.

10

다음 표를 보면서 대화를 듣고, 남자와 여자가 구매하기로 선택한 티켓을 고르시오.

	Ticket Type	Duration	Audio Guide	Sydney Harbor Cruise	Total Price
①	A	24 hours	X	X	$50
②	B	24 hours	O	O	$90
③	C	48 hours	X	X	$95
④	D	48 hours	O	X	$100
⑤	E	48 hours	O	O	$130

11

대화를 듣고, 남자의 마지막 말에 대한 여자의 응답으로 가장 적절한 것을 고르시오.

① You'll get better at it soon.
② Try harder to be more flexible.
③ I was a yoga instructor myself.
④ The class is too difficult to follow.
⑤ Not many places offer yoga classes.

12

대화를 듣고, 여자의 마지막 말에 대한 남자의 응답으로 가장 적절한 것을 고르시오.

① No, the game starts at 7 p.m.
② Actually, I'm a big fan of baseball.
③ Well, I usually get sleepy at this hour.
④ You should take part in the next game.
⑤ Lack of sleep is a serious problem nowadays.

13

대화를 듣고, 여자의 마지막 말에 대한 남자의 응답으로 가장 적절한 것을 고르시오. 3점

Man: ______________________________

① Not at all. I look forward to seeing you.
② Not really. I think I'm getting used to it.
③ Don't bother. I'll change my phone number.
④ Never mind. I'll keep my eye on your phone.
⑤ Don't worry. I'm comfortable working with you.

14

대화를 듣고, 남자의 마지막 말에 대한 여자의 응답으로 가장 적절한 것을 고르시오. 3점

Woman: ______________________________

① My tennis training session starts in two days.
② Your behavior is crossing the line as a student.
③ Try to memorize new words with their images.
④ Keep imagining hitting the ball inside the court lines.
⑤ I'm going to exchange my tennis racket for a new one.

15

다음 상황 설명을 듣고, Julia가 Paul에게 할 말로 가장 적절한 것을 고르시오.

Julia: ______________________________

① Why don't we catch a movie tonight?
② Please don't tell me any more about it.
③ If you miss this movie, you'll regret it.
④ The main actor is not my favorite anyway.
⑤ The ending is different from what I expected.

[16-17] 다음을 듣고, 물음에 답하시오.

16

남자가 하는 말의 주제로 가장 적절한 것은? 3점

① dangers of a one-food diet among teenagers
② misunderstandings about the nutrients in food
③ ways of growing fruits and vegetables at home
④ reasons coloring books are great for mental health
⑤ benefits of eating fruits and vegetables of various colors

17

언급된 음식이 아닌 것은?

① blueberries ② watermelons ③ carrots
④ lemons ⑤ broccoli

정답 및 해설 p.110

녹음을 다시 한 번 듣고, 빈칸에 알맞은 말을 쓰시오.

01

W: Attention, please. This is an announcement for Moonlight Hotel guests. We _______ _______ _______ _______ you that pieces of broken glass have been found in the outdoor pool. The pool will be closed since it _______ _______ _______ _______ swimming. If you want to enjoy swimming, you can use the indoor pool on the seventh floor. We will let you know as soon as _______ _______ _______ _______ _______. Sorry for the inconvenience and thank you for your cooperation.

02

W: Daniel, what are you doing?
M: I'm watching a documentary about e-waste.
W: E-waste? You mean electronic waste?
M: Yes. The documentary says thrown away electronic devices like cell phones _______ _______ _______.
W: Oh, I learned about that in class. Harmful metals from e-waste pollute drinking water and soil, right?
M: Exactly. Besides, e-waste from developed countries is illegally exported and dumped in poor nations.
W: It must _______ _______ _______ _______ _______ the environment in those countries.
M: Right. I think _______ _______ _______ _______ to solve this problem.
W: I agree with you.

03

M: Are you okay?
W: Not really. I'm cold and my ankle really hurts.
M: Here, take this blanket to warm up. *[Pause]* Can you walk?
W: Not at all. I think my ankle is broken.
M: What happened?
W: I was walking down this mountain and I suddenly slipped. I _______ _______ _______ my leg.
M: Don't worry, ma'am. We'll take you to a nearby hospital.
W: I'm so relieved. I thought I might have _______ _______ _______ _______ by myself.
M: It's a good thing you explained where you were to our emergency operator so well.
W: I was lucky that my cell phone was still working this deep in the mountains.
M: Yes, you were. I'll bandage your leg _______ _______ _______ _______.
W: Thank you. Please go ahead.

04

W: Mr. Morris, I finished designing the set for our musical. Here's my sketch.
M: Let me see. *[Pause]* I like the entrance door in the middle.
W: Thanks. On the left side, I put a fireplace _______ _______ _______.
M: Great. And hanging that portrait above the fireplace is a very good idea. The portrait is very important for many scenes.
W: I agree. How about the sofa?
M: It looks good in front of the fireplace.
W: And check out the round table _______ _______ _______. Do you like it?
M: Perfect. I like the vase, too.
W: One more question. Is having a rocking chair _______ _______ _______ okay?
M: It's great. You did a really good job!

05

W: Steve, are you ready to leave tomorrow?

M: Yes, Mom. I can't believe I'm going to the U.S. as an exchange student.

W: I'm so proud of you. Did you buy medical and travel insurance?

M: Yeah. And I ______ ______ ______ ______.

W: Good. Have you canceled your cell phone yet?

M: Not yet. I can do that at the airport tomorrow.

W: Okay. And don't forget to photocopy your passport ______ ______ ______.

M: Right, thanks for reminding me. But I have to pick up my international student ID first.

W: Then I'll photocopy it for you while you get your ID.

M: Thanks, Mom. I'm meeting some friends ______ ______ ______ ______.

W: Okay. Don't be late.

07

M: Hello. What can I do for you?

W: I'd like to buy some body lotion.

M: Sure. How about this product? It is organic and ______ ______.

W: How much is it?

M: It's ten dollars per bottle. But you can get a ten percent discount if you have a membership.

W: Good. Then, I'll buy three. ______ ______ ______ ______.

M: Okay. Anything else?

W: Oh, I also need some hand cream.

M: This brand new one is selling well these days. It's five dollars per tube. But there is no discount on this item.

W: Okay. Then I'll ______ ______ ______ ______.

M: So, three body lotions and two hand creams, right?

W: Yes, here is my credit card.

06

W: Hello, what can I do for you?

M: Hi, I want to change my course to another one.

W: What course did you ______ ______?

M: English Grammar. But I want to change it to English Composition. Is it too late to change?

W: No, it's possible until this Friday. Can I have your ID card?

M: Here you are.

W: *[Pause]* Oh, I'm sorry. You're ______ ______ ______ ______ this course.

M: What's the matter? Is it full?

W: No, it's not. But English Composition is ______ ______ ______ third year students.

M: Oh, I thought first year students could take it.

W: I'm afraid you can't. You have to find another course.

08

[Telephone rings.]

M: Greenlight Bookstore. How can I help you?

W: Hello. I'd like to register for the upcoming book signing event. I heard the author is Cindy Wallace.

M: You mean this Saturday's event?

W: Yes.

M: I'm sorry. ______ ______ ______ an hour ago.

W: Oh, no! Is there any other way for me to attend?

M: The event will take place in our main lobby. You can ______ ______ ______ there.

W: Oh, really? That's good! When will the event start?

M: It'll be from 3 p.m. to 5 p.m.

W: I see. Do I need to buy her new book ______ ______ ______ ______?

M: No, you don't need to. You can bring any of her books.

W: Okay. Thank you very much.

M: My pleasure.

09

M: Hello, this is Roseville Fitness Club. Come and enjoy our latest promotion. Our fitness club offers a 50% discount for your first month. Plus, you can _______ _______ _______ _______. Our various programs include swimming, yoga, Latin dance classes, as well as weight training. Our personal trainers and up-to-date equipment will _______ _______ _______ _______ _______. Our club is open everyday from 6 a.m. until 10 p.m. We also have a café with _______ _______ _______ sports drinks and fruit juices for your refreshment needs. Please visit us and sign up for your club membership today! Thank you.

10

M: Wow! We're finally in Sydney. Where should we go?

W: I just picked up this city tour leaflet. Take a look.

M: How about this 24-hour ticket? It _______ _______ _______ _______ for 24 hours.

W: But we're staying here for three days. Isn't it better to buy a 48-hour ticket instead?

M: That makes sense. Do we need an audio guide?

W: Of course. It'll definitely _______ _______ _______ to know more about Sydney's attractions.

M: Okay. How about the Sydney Harbor Cruise?

W: Let me see... Don't you think spending $130 is too much for a city tour?

M: Yeah. If we _______ _______ _______ _______ _______, we can visit a museum later.

W: Then let's take the one without the cruise.

M: Good. Let's go.

11

M: Did you go to the yoga class at the community center yesterday?

W: Yes, I did. But I don't think that class _______ _______ _______ _______.

M: Why do you think that?

W: (The class is too difficult to follow.)

12

W: Kevin, you look tired. Are you okay?

M: I didn't get _______ _______ _______ _______. I watched baseball on TV until 2 a.m.

W: Oh, I didn't know you liked baseball that much.

M: (Actually, I'm a big fan of baseball.)

13

M: How's your preparation for the final exam going?

W: I was stuck at my desk all day long, but I couldn't focus because of my smart phone.

M: I know it's _______ _______ _______ using a smart phone while studying.

W: Right. It's very difficult.

M: Actually I _______ _______ _______ the same problem just like you, but I found a way to handle it.

W: Really? How did you deal with it?

M: I made my room into a "no smart phone" zone.

W: What do you mean by that?

M: It means when I study in my room, I don't bring my phone with me.

W: Then where do you keep your phone?

M: Usually I leave it in the living room while I study.

W: Aren't you uncomfortable _______ _______ _______ _______ _______?

M: (Not really. I think I'm getting used to it.)

14

M: Wow, your tennis skills _______ _______ _______ _______ every day! What's your secret?

W: I use a technique called "image training."

M: Image training? What's that?

W: It's _______ _______ _______ that you want to improve in your head repeatedly.

M: Hmm, can you explain it in more detail?

W: Sure. Watch the games of great tennis players and imagine you're moving just like them.

M: Developing skills while imagining! Sounds awesome!

W: If you keep doing that, your body will follow eventually.

M: Then, do you think it'll _______ _______ _______ _______ _______, too?

W: Of course! Tell me about it, and I'll help you with this technique.

M: Whenever I hit my tennis ball, it goes too far. It goes past the court lines.

W: (Keep imagining hitting the ball inside the court lines.)

15

W: Julia is a high school student _______ _______ _______. One day, Julia finds that her favorite actor plays the main character in a newly released movie. She wants to watch the movie with her friend, Paul. When she asks him if he wants to watch the movie with her, Paul says he _______ _______ _______ and really liked the ending. Julia notices that he's going to tell her all about the movie. She doesn't want Paul to _______ _______ _______ _______ of the movie. In this situation, what would Julia most likely say to Paul?

Julia: (Please don't tell me any more about it.)

16-17

M: Hello, I'm Jason from *Five Minutes for Health*. Do you have the blues these days? I'm not talking about your mood _______ _______ _______ _______! Did you know that you can get what your body needs by eating colorful fruits and vegetables? Different nutrients actually give different colors to the foods they're in. For example, the nutrient that makes blueberries blue can help _______ _______ _______ _______. The nutrient that makes watermelons and tomatoes red can help protect against certain cancers. Also, the nutrient that makes carrots orange-colored can help keep your bones strong and your eyes healthy. Last, the nutrient in green vegetables like broccoli can help _______ _______ _______. So if you want to get healthy, make sure you have the bright colors of the rainbow on your plate.

Word & Expressions

01
- □ announcement 발표, 소식
- □ inform 알리다
- □ as soon as …하자마자
- □ inconvenience 불편
- □ cooperation 협조

02
- □ documentary 다큐멘터리
- □ electronic 전자의
- □ device 장치, 기기
- □ cause 유발하다, 초래하다
- □ pollute 오염시키다
- □ developed country 선진국
- □ illegally 불법적으로
- □ export 수출하다
- □ dump 버리다
- □ threat 협박, 위협
- □ action 행동, 조치

03
- □ blanket 담요
- □ slip 미끄러지다
- □ get stuck 꼼짝 못 하게 되다
- □ by oneself 혼자서
- □ emergency 응급, 비상
- □ operator 전화 교환원
- □ bandage 붕대를 감다

04
- □ entrance door 출입문
- □ fireplace 벽난로
- □ request 요청하다
- □ portrait 초상화
- □ scene (영화·연극·책에 나오는) 장면
- □ rocking chair 흔들의자

05
- □ medical 의학의, 의료의
- □ insurance 보험
- □ photocopy (복사기로) 복사하다
- □ passport 여권
- □ remind 상기시키다, 알려주다
- □ pick up …을 찾아오다

06
- □ course 강의, 강좌
- □ register for …에 등록하다
- □ composition 작문, 짧은 에세이
- □ be allowed to-v …하는 것이 허용되다
- □ available 이용할 수 있는

07
- □ product 상품, 제품
- □ organic 유기농의
- □ brand new 아주 새로운, 신제품인

08
- □ upcoming 다가오는, 곧 있을
- □ book signing 책 사인회
- □ author 작가, 저자
- □ registration 등록 (v. register 등록하다)
- □ attend 참석하다
- □ take place 개최되다
- □ wait in line 줄을 서서 기다리다
- □ signature 서명

09
- □ latest 최근의, 최신의
- □ promotion 승진; *홍보 (활동)
- □ for free 공짜로, 무료로
- □ equipment 비품, 설비
- □ refreshment 다과, 간식
- □ need 필요(성)
- □ sign up for …을 신청하다

10
- □ leaflet 전단
- □ unlimited 무제한의
- □ make sense 타당하다, 말이 되다
- □ attraction 명소, 명물
- □ harbor 항구

11
- □ community center 지역 문화 센터

12
- □ take part in …에 참가하다

13
- □ preparation 준비, 대비
- □ be stuck 꼼짝도 못 하다
- □ resist 참다, 견디다
- □ deal with …을 처리하다
- □ uncomfortable 불편한
- □ get used to …에 익숙해지다
- □ keep one's eye on …에서 눈을 떼지 않다

14
- □ technique 기법, 기술
- □ picture 상상하다, 마음속에 그리다
- □ movement 움직임
- □ in detail 상세하게
- □ keep v-ing 계속해서 …하다

15
- □ main character 주인공
- □ release 풀어주다; *개봉하다
- □ notice 알아차리다
- □ give away …을 폭로하다

16-17
- □ nutrient 영양소, 영양분
- □ blood pressure 혈압
- □ plate 접시
- □ misunderstanding 오해
- □ mental 정신의, 마음의

기출 영어듣기 모의고사

1번부터 17번까지는 듣고 답하는 문제입니다.
1번부터 15번까지는 한 번만 들려주고, 16번부터 17번까지는 두 번 들려줍니다. 방송을 잘 듣고 답을 하기 바랍니다.

01

다음을 듣고, 여자가 하는 말의 목적으로 가장 적절한 것을 고르시오.

① 장학금 신청 관련 정보를 안내하려고
② 졸업을 위한 자격 요건을 알려주려고
③ 지도자 양성 프로그램을 홍보하려고
④ 교내 경시대회 수상 기준을 공지하려고
⑤ 장학 기금 모금 행사 참여를 권장하려고

02

대화를 듣고, 남자의 의견으로 가장 적절한 것을 고르시오.

① 대중교통을 많이 이용해야 한다.
② 운전면허 시험 제도를 개선해야 한다.
③ 과속 운전에 대한 단속을 강화해야 한다.
④ 장거리 운전 시 충분한 휴식을 취해야 한다.
⑤ 운전 시 앞차와의 안전거리를 유지해야 한다.

03

대화를 듣고, 두 사람의 관계를 가장 잘 나타낸 것을 고르시오.

① 은행원 — 고객　　② 공항 세관원 — 여행객
③ 지하철 역무원 — 승객　　④ 문화 해설사 — 관람객
⑤ 관광 안내소 직원 — 관광객

04

대화를 듣고, 그림에서 대화의 내용과 일치하지 <u>않는</u> 것을 고르시오.

05

대화를 듣고, 여자가 남자에게 부탁한 일로 가장 적절한 것을 고르시오.

① 호텔 예약하기　　② 손님 마중 나가기
③ 선물 구입하기　　④ 이름표 만들기
⑤ 통역사 구하기

06

대화를 듣고, 여자가 New York에 가려는 이유를 고르시오.

① 미술 작품을 구입해야 해서
② 친구의 포트폴리오를 제출해야 해서
③ 자신의 작품 전시회에 참석해야 해서
④ 미술관 개관식 축사를 해야 해서
⑤ 미술관을 관람해야 해서

07

대화를 듣고, 여자가 지불할 금액을 고르시오. 3점

① $90　　② $100　　③ $160
④ $180　　⑤ $200

08

대화를 듣고, skin problem에 관해 두 사람이 언급하지 <u>않은</u> 것을 고르시오.

① 증상　　② 발병 시기　　③ 발병 원인
④ 치료 방법　　⑤ 치료 기간

09

Gainesville Community Center에 관한 다음 내용을 듣고, 일치하지 <u>않는</u> 것을 고르시오.

① 5월 17일에 개장했다.
② 모든 연령대가 사용할 수 있다.
③ 컴퓨터실과 도서실을 갖추고 있다.
④ 등록하려면 신분증이 필요하다.
⑤ 평일에는 오후 5시에 문을 닫는다.

10

다음 표를 보면서 대화를 듣고, 두 사람이 구입할 자전거를 고르시오.

< Top 5 Bicycles for Kids >

	Model	Rider height	Bicycle weight	Folding	Price
①	A	110-130 cm	7 kg	O	$260
②	B	130-150 cm	8 kg	X	$210
③	C	130-150 cm	9 kg	O	$290
④	D	140-160 cm	9 kg	O	$320
⑤	E	140-160 cm	12 kg	X	$260

11

대화를 듣고, 남자의 마지막 말에 대한 여자의 응답으로 가장 적절한 것을 고르시오.

① Yes, I like watching movies.
② Sure, I will borrow it from you.
③ No, I don't like the characters in it.
④ That's why people call you a walking dictionary.
⑤ Sorry, but I have to return it to the library today.

12

대화를 듣고, 여자의 마지막 말에 대한 남자의 응답으로 가장 적절한 것을 고르시오.

① No way. It's not the same at all.
② Right. The restaurant was very good.
③ No worries. It was my pleasure helping you.
④ Thank you. I'm happy you came to my house.
⑤ Sorry. I don't have time to help you with that.

13

대화를 듣고, 남자의 마지막 말에 대한 여자의 응답으로 가장 적절한 것을 고르시오. 3점

Woman: ______________________

① At least you should have said sorry.
② How about forgiving her for being late?
③ I can't understand why you feel that way.
④ Sometimes it's good to express your anger.
⑤ Why don't you write an apology letter to her?

14

대화를 듣고, 여자의 마지막 말에 대한 남자의 응답으로 가장 적절한 것을 고르시오.

Man: ______________________

① Right. It saved us from a lot of waiting in line.
② Sorry. I don't know how to buy tickets online.
③ Not really. Booking is not necessary.
④ Good. Let's choose a movie first.
⑤ No problem. It's not your fault.

15

다음 상황 설명을 듣고, Daniel이 Sarah에게 할 말로 가장 적절한 것을 고르시오. 3점

Daniel: ______________________

① This is yours. It was delivered to my mailbox.
② The housewarming party was great. Thank you.
③ Sure. Hiring a moving company would be better.
④ Right. I'd like to get a refund on these hairpins.
⑤ This apartment has a nice view. I'd like to move in.

[16-17] 다음을 듣고, 물음에 답하시오.

16

남자가 하는 말의 주제로 가장 적절한 것은? 3점

① home remedies for mosquito bites
② cultural influences on medical practice
③ health risks of mosquito-related diseases
④ the increasing popularity of natural cures
⑤ misconceptions about insect bite remedies

17

언급된 재료가 아닌 것은?

① baking soda ② onions ③ salt
④ lemons ⑤ honey

녹음을 다시 한 번 듣고, 빈칸에 알맞은 말을 쓰시오.

01

W: Good morning, students. May I have your attention, please? This announcement is for our seniors. The County Bank Foundation is awarding three $5,000 scholarships to seniors based not just on academics or athletics, but also on citizenship. If you ______ ______ ______ to be a future leader and have a B average or better, you could receive this scholarship. Does this ______ ______ ______? Then go to www.countybank.com or ask your guidance counselor for the application for the Richard Citizenship Award. The deadline to apply is November 30, 2016. I hope many of you will ______ ______ ______ this opportunity. Thank you for listening.

02

M: I saw a car accident on Alington Avenue today.

W: Really? What happened?

M: A truck suddenly stopped and a taxi ______ ______ ______ ______.

W: How terrible! Is anybody hurt?

M: The taxi driver was injured. I think he ______ ______ ______ ______ ______.

W: What do you mean?

M: He was driving too close to the truck.

W: You mean there was ______ ______ ______ between the truck and the taxi, right?

M: Yes. Keeping a safe distance from the car ahead is important, but he didn't do so.

W: I see.

03

M: Welcome. How may I help you?

W: Hello. Where can I exchange money?

M: There is a bank ______ ______ ______.

W: Thanks. And can I get a subway map for tourists?

M: Sure. We have maps written in English, Japanese, and Chinese.

W: Good. I will take an English one, please.

M: Sure. Anything else ______ ______ ______ ______ ______?

W: Oh, I need some information about hotels as well. The hotel I stayed at last night was terrible.

M: Sorry to hear that. ______ ______ ______ ______ nearby hotels and contact numbers.

W: Thank you so much for helping me.

M: You're welcome. Helping tourists is my job.

04

W: Jason, look at this.

M: What is it?

W: A blogger posted a picture after she ______ ______ ______.

M: Oh, it looks great. I like the round rug on the floor.

W: I think it goes well with the striped curtains.

M: You're right. And the floor lamp next to the bed is just the type that I want to buy.

W: We can ask the blogger ______ ______ ______ ______. Look at the heart-shaped cushion on the chair.

M: It looks really comfortable.

W: Yes. The blanket ______ ______ ______ looks nice, too.

M: Right. I think this blog will be helpful when we decorate our room.

05

M: Hi, Jenny. You look busy. What's going on?

W: Hi, Nick. Chinese buyers are _______ _______ _______ today. I am preparing for their visit.

M: Oh, I see. How is it going?

W: Almost done now. I _______ _______ for hotel rooms and bought some gifts for them.

M: They may not understand Korean. Did you get an interpreter?

W: Yes. She will come soon. Now I'm making some nametags for them.

M: Is there anything I can help you with?

W: Actually, I need _______ _______ _______ _______ the buyers at the airport. Could you do that for me?

M: Sure, no problem. What time do you want me to be there?

W: By 5 o'clock. Thank you so much, Nick.

06

M: Amy, what's with all the clothes and bags?

W: Oh, I need to pack some things to go to New York.

M: New York? How come?

W: Well... The Modern Art Gallery in New York is going to _______ _______ _______ next month!

M: Really? Congratulations! This is the opportunity you've been waiting for.

W: Thanks. I'm so excited. A lot of visitors will come and see my paintings.

M: Good for you. How did you _______ _______ _______?

W: Last month, I sent my portfolio to that gallery.

M: And?

W: I got an invitation letter from them this morning! They sent me a plane ticket, too.

M: Your efforts are finally _______ _______.

W: I'm looking forward to being there for the opening.

07

M: Welcome to New York City Sightseeing. How may I help you?

W: Hi. I'm here to purchase city tour package tickets for today.

M: Okay. There are one-day and half-day package tours. Which would you like?

W: _______ _______ _______?

M: The one-day tour includes three routes and five attractions, and the half-day tour includes only one route and two attractions.

W: Umm. The one-day tour _______ _______ _______ my family. How much is it?

M: It's $60 for adults and $40 for children.

W: I see. I want tickets for two adults and two kids. Can I get a discount with a Metropolitan Membership Card?

M: Yes. You'll get a 10% discount _______ _______ _______.

W: Good. Here's my credit card.

08

W: Good morning. What can I do for you?

M: I _______ _______ _______ _______ on my back.

W: Can you describe it for me?

M: My back was itchy all night. I scratched it and now I have small red dots _______ _______ _______.

W: When did it start?

M: Yesterday evening. I _______ _______ _______ _______ last night.

W: Did you eat or do anything different recently? These problems often happen when people change something in their routine.

M: I guess it could be an allergic reaction to a new soap.

W: Then, I recommend this anti-itching cream.

M: Okay. But what if it doesn't work?

W: In that case, you should see a doctor. It's probably nothing serious, but better safe than sorry.

M: Right! Thank you.

09

M: Finally, the Gainesville Community Center opened on May 17th. It is for _______ _______ _______ _______ and different interests. It offers a computer lab, a dance studio, a library, and a playground. Registration is required before you can use the center's facilities. _______ _______ _______ _______, you need to visit the community center with your ID card. The center _______ _______ _______ 9 a.m. to 9 p.m. on weekdays and from 9 a.m. to 5 p.m. on weekends. For further information, you can visit our website or call our information center. Thank you.

10

W: Honey, have you _______ _______ a bicycle for Jimmy?

M: Not yet. Take a look at these five models. Which one do you think is good?

W: Well, he's 145 cm tall, so this one would be too small for him.

M: That's right. And I'd like it to be _______ _______ _______ _______.

W: I agree. A heavy bicycle would be harder for Jimmy to ride.

M: Yeah. And I think a folding bicycle would be better so that we could carry it in our car.

W: You're right. We'd better choose one from these two. But I don't want to _______ _______ _______ $300.

M: Then I think this is the best option for us.

W: Okay. Let's buy that one.

11

M: Jane, are you done with the novel?

W: Yes, I read the whole book in just two days. It was really interesting.

M: I want to read that book, too. Can I _______ _______ _______ _______?

W: (Sorry, but I have to return it to the library today.)

12

W: Thank you so much for the help with my computer yesterday.

M: Oh, it was nothing. It only took me 10 minutes.

W: No, it meant a lot to me. I'd like to _______ _______ _______ _______ or something.

M: (No worries. It was my pleasure helping you.)

13

W: Tom, how was your day at school?

M: It was a tough day, Mom.

W: What happened?

M: Jessie _______ _______ _______ me.

W: Why? You two are best friends.

M: Every Thursday we _______ _______ _______. But I'm always late.

W: Are you? Being late is not a good habit.

M: I know. So last week I _______ _______ _______ _______ _______. But today I was 30 minutes late again.

W: No wonder Jessie got angry. Did you say sorry to her?

M: Yes. But she was so upset that she went home without accepting my apology. What should I do?

W: (Why don't you write an apology letter to her?)

14

W: Let's _______ _______. The movie will begin soon.

M: Sure. I'm really excited to finally watch this movie.

W: Me, too. I hope it will be fun.

M: I'm sure it will. The main actor has _______ _______ _______.

W: Right. I think he is really talented.

M: I agree. *[Pause]* Wow, there are a lot of people here today.

W: Yes. This movie theater is always crowded on weekends.

M: Look over there. So many people are standing in line to buy movie tickets.

W: I'm glad _______ _______ _______ on the Internet in advance.

M: (Right. It saved us from a lot of waiting in line.)

15

W: Daniel moves to an apartment _______ _______ _______ _______. His friend, Sarah, lives next door. One day, when he comes home, he finds a small package in his mailbox. He takes it to his apartment and opens it. He finds _______ _______ _______ hairpins inside the package. He feels confused and reads the address carefully. Daniel finds that they are for Sarah. The package was mistakenly put into his mailbox. He goes to Sarah's apartment. Daniel _______ _______ _______ _______ Sarah and tries to explain why he has it. In this situation, what would Daniel most likely say to Sarah?

Daniel: (This is yours. It was delivered to my mailbox.)

16-17

M: Hello, everyone. I'm Benjamin Brown from Healthy Talk. These days people are discovering not only the convenience of home remedies, but also their health benefits for such things as mosquito bites. It's the season for mosquito bites, so today, I'll tell you about some of my favorite home remedies _______ _______ _______.
First, found in virtually every kitchen, baking soda is a good remedy. Rub a paste of baking soda and water onto the affected area, and it'll provide relief. How about onions? They can also help _______ _______ _______ _______ _______ a bite. Simply place a fresh slice of onion onto a mosquito bite for several minutes, then the itching will be gone. Lemons are your friends, too. By _______ _______ _______ _______ the bitten area, you can help reduce the chance of developing an infection. Lastly, honey is helpful since it has many antibacterial properties. I hope you find these cures effective this summer.

기출 2회

기출 **02** Word & Expressions

01
- ☐ **foundation** 토대; *재단
- ☐ **scholarship** 장학금
- ☐ **senior** 상급자; *졸업반 학생
- ☐ **based on** …에 근거하여
- ☐ **academic** 학업의; *학과
- ☐ **athletics** 체육(실기, 이론)
- ☐ **citizenship** 시민권
- ☐ **potential** 가능성
- ☐ **average** 평균
- ☐ **guidance** 지도
- ☐ **counselor** 상담역; *지도 교사
- ☐ **application** 신청(v. apply 신청하다)
- ☐ **take advantage of** …을 이용하다

02
- ☐ **avenue** (도시의) 거리, -가
- ☐ **terrible** 끔찍한
- ☐ **injure** 부상을 입다
- ☐ **safe distance** 안전거리
- ☐ **ahead** 앞으로, 앞에

03
- ☐ **exchange money** 환전하다
- ☐ **tourist** 관광객
- ☐ **nearby** 인근의
- ☐ **contact number** 연락 전화번호

04
- ☐ **post** (웹사이트에) 올리다, 게시하다
- ☐ **rug** 깔개, 양탄자
- ☐ **striped** 줄무늬가 있는
- ☐ **heart-shaped** 하트 모양의
- ☐ **comfortable** 편안한

05
- ☐ **buyer** 바이어, 구매자
- ☐ **interpreter** 통역사
- ☐ **nametag** 명찰
- ☐ **pick up** …을 태우러 가다

06
- ☐ **exhibit** 전시하다
- ☐ **opportunity** 기회
- ☐ **portfolio** 작품집, 포트폴리오
- ☐ **invitation** 초대, 초청
- ☐ **effort** 노력
- ☐ **pay off** 성공하다, 성과를 올리다
- ☐ **opening** 개막식

07
- ☐ **sightseeing** 관광
- ☐ **purchase** 구입하다
- ☐ **route** 길, 경로
- ☐ **attraction** 명소
- ☐ **metropolitan** 대도시의, 수도의

08
- ☐ **describe** 말하다, 서술하다
- ☐ **itchy** 가려운
- ☐ **scratch** 긁다
- ☐ **routine** 일상
- ☐ **allergic** 알레르기성의
- ☐ **reaction** 반응, 반작용
- ☐ **anti-itching** 가려움 방지
- ☐ **better safe than sorry** 나중에 후회하는 것보다 미리 조심하는 편이 낫다

09
- ☐ **offer** 제의하다; *제공하다
- ☐ **registration** 등록 (v. register 등록하다)
- ☐ **require** 요구하다
- ☐ **facility** 설비, 시설

10
- ☐ **folding** 접을 수 있는
- ☐ **carry** 나르다; *가지고 다니다

11
- ☐ **done with** …가 끝난

12
- ☐ **treat** 다루다; *대접하다

13
- ☐ **upset** 화난, 마음이 상한
- ☐ **accept** 받아들이다
- ☐ **apology** 사과

14
- ☐ **disappoint** 실망시키다
- ☐ **talented** 재능이 있는
- ☐ **crowded** 붐비는, 복잡한
- ☐ **in advance** 미리, 사전에
- ☐ **wait in line** 줄 서서 기다리다
- ☐ **necessary** 필요한, 필수적인

15
- ☐ **view** 경관, 전망
- ☐ **package** 소포
- ☐ **a couple of** 둘의
- ☐ **confused** 혼란스러워하는
- ☐ **mistakenly** 잘못하여, 실수로
- ☐ **hand** 건네주다

16-17
- ☐ **remedy** 치료, 요법; 치료 약
- ☐ **benefit** 혜택, 이득
- ☐ **virtually** 사실상, 거의
- ☐ **paste** 반죽
- ☐ **affected** (병에) 걸린, 침범된
- ☐ **relief** 안심; *경감, 완화
- ☐ **sting** 따가움, 쓰라림
- ☐ **itching** 가려움
- ☐ **apply** 신청하다; *(페인트·크림 등을) 바르다
- ☐ **develop** 발달하다; *(병·문제가) 생기다
- ☐ **infection** 감염
- ☐ **antibacterial** 항균성의
- ☐ **property** 성질, 특성
- ☐ **cure** 치유법
- ☐ **misconception** 오해

03 기출 영어듣기 모의고사

정답 및 해설 p.114-116

1번부터 17번까지는 듣고 답하는 문제입니다.
1번부터 15번까지는 한 번만 들려주고, 16번부터 17번까지는 두 번 들려줍니다. 방송을 잘 듣고 답을 하기 바랍니다.

01

다음을 듣고, 여자가 하는 말의 목적으로 가장 적절한 것을 고르시오.

① 라디오 청취자의 사연을 공모하려고
② 야간 숲 걷기 프로그램을 안내하려고
③ 시 당국에 산책로 조성을 건의하려고
④ 변경된 야외 생방송 일정을 공지하려고
⑤ 등산 시 안전 수칙을 지킬 것을 당부하려고

02

대화를 듣고, 두 사람이 하는 말의 주제로 가장 적절한 것을 고르시오.

① 응급 구조 요청 시 유의사항
② 정기적인 응급 처치 훈련의 필요성
③ 비전문가에 의한 응급 처치의 위험성
④ 교내 안전사고를 유발하는 다양한 요인
⑤ 심장마비 예방을 위한 준비운동의 중요성

03

대화를 듣고, 두 사람의 관계를 가장 잘 나타낸 것을 고르시오.

① 소설가 — 독자　② 인쇄업자 — 고객
③ 사진작가 — 모델　④ 사서 — 도서관 이용객
⑤ 서점 주인 — 출판사 직원

04

대화를 듣고, 그림에서 대화의 내용과 일치하지 않는 것을 고르시오.

05

대화를 듣고, 남자가 여자를 위해 할 일로 가장 적절한 것을 고르시오.

① 셔츠 수선 맡기기
② 저녁 식사 준비하기
③ 아이스크림 사 오기
④ 세탁소에서 옷 찾아 오기
⑤ 사무실로 서류 가져 오기

06

대화를 듣고, 여자의 포스터가 철거된 이유를 고르시오.

① 승인 도장이 없어서
② 공연 날짜가 지나서
③ 담당 직원이 실수해서
④ 게시 기간이 초과되어서
⑤ 게시판 이외의 장소에 부착되어서

07

대화를 듣고, 남자가 지불할 금액을 고르시오. 3점

① $200　② $270　③ $300
④ $330　⑤ $400

08

대화를 듣고, 여자의 USB 램프에 관해 두 사람이 언급하지 않은 것을 고르시오.

① 구입처　② 무게　③ 가격
④ 전구　⑤ 디자인

09

Kennedy Clothing Drive에 관한 다음 내용을 듣고, 일치하지 않는 것을 고르시오.

① 매년 열리는 행사이다.
② 9월 5일부터 9월 9일까지 열린다.
③ 학교 주차장으로 기부 물품을 가져와야 한다.
④ 커튼과 담요를 기부할 수 있다.
⑤ 물품은 비닐봉지에 담아 와야 한다.

10

다음 표를 보면서 대화를 듣고, 여자가 신청할 수영 강좌를 고르시오.

< Dolphin Swimming Center >

	Lesson	Time	Days	Level
①	A	7-8 a.m.	Mon, Wed, Fri	Beginner
②	B	7-8 a.m.	Tues, Thurs	Intermediate
③	C	8-9 a.m.	Mon, Wed, Fri	Beginner
④	D	8-9 a.m.	Tues, Thurs	Intermediate
⑤	E	8-9 a.m.	Mon, Wed, Fri	Intermediate

11

대화를 듣고, 남자의 마지막 말에 대한 여자의 응답으로 가장 적절한 것을 고르시오.

① I took this picture in Paris.
② I'm sure you'll also like her.
③ She has always been good at math.
④ You'll meet her at my birthday party.
⑤ We went to the same school together.

12

대화를 듣고, 여자의 마지막 말에 대한 남자의 응답으로 가장 적절한 것을 고르시오.

① It was so impressive to me.
② I already finished it yesterday.
③ I've read many books this year.
④ The literature class was on Friday.
⑤ You should do the assignment first.

13

대화를 듣고, 여자의 마지막 말에 대한 남자의 응답으로 가장 적절한 것을 고르시오.

Man: ______________________

① Let's start off by using fans, instead.
② Don't you think the air is too humid?
③ We have to contact the travel agency.
④ See if the air conditioner is working well.
⑤ Imagine what our summer holiday will be like.

14

대화를 듣고, 남자의 마지막 말에 대한 여자의 응답으로 가장 적절한 것을 고르시오. 3점

Woman: ______________________

① I wish she were your mother.
② I'm late. Let's get off in a hurry.
③ Okay. Could you bring the lady here?
④ My parents taught me to keep the traffic rules.
⑤ Transfer to the Yellow Line at the next station.

15

다음 상황 설명을 듣고, Ally가 점원에게 할 말로 가장 적절한 것을 고르시오. 3점

Ally: ______________________

① Can I get a refund on this book?
② Will you exchange it for another?
③ Forget about it. I'll keep the book.
④ I'd like you to recommend a good book.
⑤ How long will it take to get a new copy?

[16-17] 다음을 듣고, 물음에 답하시오.

16

여자가 하는 말의 주제로 가장 적절한 것은?

① vitamins' effects on the body
② ways to check eye conditions
③ importance of a healthy diet plan
④ advice for dealing with tired eyes
⑤ necessity of relaxing a stressed mind

17

언급된 식품이 아닌 것은?

① almonds ② avocados ③ broccoli
④ lemons ⑤ potatoes

정답 및 해설 p.116

녹음을 다시 한 번 듣고, 빈칸에 알맞은 말을 쓰시오.

01

W: Good evening, everybody. Welcome to Jennifer's Green Life! Tonight, ______ ______ ______ ______ you some questions. Are you a nature lover? Have you ever wondered what happens in the forest after dark? If your answer is "Yes," there's a perfect program for you. The city is offering a night walk in the forest every Saturday night during April, May, and June. You can ______ ______ ______ ______ ______ with an experienced guide, and enjoy all the wonders of the forest at night. It's ______ ______ ______, but online preregistration is required. Bring your family and friends! Now, it's time for a break. Stay tuned!

02

M: Did you read the newspaper article about the high school heroes?

W: High school heroes? What do you mean?

M: Some high school students saved one of their classmates when he had a heart attack in school.

W: How did they do that?

M: They ______ ______ ______ mouth to mouth and heart massage until the ambulance arrived.

W: Unbelievable! How did they know what to do?

M: The newspaper says the students took regular first aid training classes.

W: Then, ______ ______ ______ ______ ______ practicing first aid regularly?

M: I think so. That's how they could stay calm and save their friend even in that emergency situation.

W: Now I see why practicing first aid regularly is necessary.

M: ______ ______ ______ ______ ______.

03

W: Hello, Mr. Brown.

M: Hello, Ms. Duncan. I just stopped by to check how my order is going.

W: I was ______ ______ ______ ______ to ask about some details.

M: All right. What are they?

W: Please look at this sample. I need your opinion about this overall concept for your brochure.

M: Umm, I like it, but I want you to ______ ______ ______ ______ and the picture smaller.

W: I see. How about the background color and font?

M: I like the font, but I want to make the color a little brighter.

W: Okay. I'll ______ ______ ______ ______ that. You ordered 1,000 copies to be printed, right?

M: Exactly. Please, don't miss the deadline.

W: Of course, I won't.

04

W: How was the magic show last night?

M: Fantastic! Let me show you a picture.

W: The man wearing the hat must be the magician.

M: Right. Look at the bird sitting on the branch. At the start of the show, the bird ______ ______ ______ the magician's hat.

W: Wonderful! And who is the lady with glasses on next to the magician?

M: She was a member of the audience.

W: What did she do?

M: She ______ ______ ______ the box was empty and put it on the table.

W: That box on the table?

M: Yes, unbelievably, the magician pulled flowers out of the box. That's why the flowers are on the floor.

W: Wow, it must have been awesome!

M: Absolutely! I ______ ______ ______ ______ ______ of the stage.

05

[Cell phone rings.]

M: Hello.

W: Honey, it's me. Are you on your way home?

M: No. I'm still in the office, but I can ______ ______ ______ ______.

W: That's great. Then I'm going to start cooking now.

M: What're we having for dinner?

W: I'm thinking about seafood pasta.

M: Sounds delicious. Do you ______ ______ ______ ______ ice cream for dessert?

W: No, I already bought it while I was grocery shopping. *[Pause]* Oh, no!

M: What's wrong?

W: I ______ ______ ______ ______ my blue shirt from the laundry.

M: Don't worry. I'll pick it up for you on my way home.

W: Thanks, honey. See you soon.

06

M: Hello. Can I help you?

W: Yes, please. I recently ______ ______ ______ ______ about my music club's concert on the campus bulletin boards.

M: Is there a problem with them?

W: Yes, this morning, I found all the posters are gone.

M: One of our staff probably ______ ______ ______. Did your posters have stamps of approval?

W: Yes. I got all of them stamped, and I put them up on the boards for clubs only!

M: Then you put them in the right place. Do you remember when you posted them?

W: Um.... I posted them ten days ago.

M: ______ ______ they're all gone. We take down the posters after they've been up for one week.

W: Oh, my! I didn't know that.

07

W: Can I help you?

M: I need T-shirts and caps for my school's sports day.

W: We have ______ ______ ______ shirts and caps. Please take your time and look around.

M: Hmm... Do you have T-shirts under 15 dollars?

W: Sure. How about this blue one? It's only 10 dollars.

M: Sounds good. How much is that red cap ______ ______ ______?

W: It's 5 dollars. How many shirts and caps do you need?

M: Twenty T-shirts and twenty caps.

W: If you're buying that many, I can give you a 10% discount off the total price.

M: That's great. Do you offer lettering on T-shirts like "Way to Go!"?

W: Yes, we offer lettering to students for free.

M: Awesome! Here's my student ID card. I'll ______ ______ ______.

W: Okay.

08

M: Katie, your lamp looks cute. Is it connected to the laptop?

W: You mean this USB lamp? Yes. It's for working at night.

M: I'd like to get one like that. Where did you get it?

W: From ABC Online Store. ______ ______ ______ ______.

M: How much was it?

W: The list price was $20, but I paid only $12.

M: Great. It's quite bright. What kind of bulb does it use?

W: It has an LED bulb. It's energy efficient and ______ ______ ______ ______ ______.

M: I like the design, too. It's modern and simple.

W: Also, you can easily adjust the direction of the light.

M: I think that's exactly ______ ______ ______ ______.

09

W: Hello, students of Kennedy High School. I'm here to tell you about our Kennedy Clothing Drive. We ______ ______ ______ every year to help our neighbors in need. You can clean out your closets and help your community. The event will be held for five days from September 5th to September 9th. Bring your donations to the school parking lot. Remember, we'll ______ ______ ______ there between 8 a.m. and 3 p.m. We're collecting wearable and usable clothing for men, women, and children. Shoes and belts ______ ______ ______ as well. We will not collect curtains or blankets. Please bring your items in plastic bags. We're looking forward to your participation.

10

M: What are you doing on the computer?

W: ______ ______ ______ swimming lessons during summer vacation.

M: What time are the lessons?

W: I think 7 a.m. is ______ ______ ______ ______. I want the lesson that starts at 8 a.m.

M: How often do you want to have a lesson?

W: Three times a week would be better for me.

M: I see. You probably want an intermediate level because you can swim, right?

W: I can swim, but I want to ______ ______ ______.

M: So you want to start from the beginner level?

W: Yes. I'll sign up for this lesson.

11

M: Who is the girl next to you in this picture?

W: She is Sophie, one of my friends.

M: You two ______ ______ ______. How did you first meet each other?

W: (We went to the same school together.)

12

W: Jack, have you read the book *The Great Gatsby*?

M: Sure. I read it in my literature class last year.

W: How did you ______ ______ ______?

M: (It was so impressive to me.)

13

W: Honey, I'm home. Whoa! Why is it so hot in here?

M: I didn't turn on the air conditioner.

W: Why not? You know I ______ ______ ______ ______.

M: Yeah, but look at this. It's our electricity bill for last month.

W: Why is it so high?

M: Obviously, it's because we ______ ______ ______ ______ ______ all month long.

W: Well, but it's really hot and humid. I don't want to sweat all summer just to save a little money.

M: I understand. But honey, it's ______ ______ ______ ______ for this month.

W: I hate the heat, though.

M: Think about it. We have to save some money for our winter holiday.

W: Well then, what should we do?

M: (Let's start off by using fans, instead.)

기출 3회

14

M: The subway is crowded. Oh! There is an empty seat. Lilly, sit down.

W: Thank you. Actually, I'm so tired today.

M: Oh, there is _______ _______ _______ _______ over there. Why don't you give her the seat?

W: But I'm exhausted. Someone else may _______ _______ _______ _______.

M: Look, no one's voluntarily standing up for her.

W: I don't know her. And I was on the subway first.

M: Lilly, imagine she is your grandmother.

W: Hmm... I would make room for my grandmother because she is an angel to me.

M: Well, the lady over there could be precious to someone else.

W: You are _______ _______ _______ _______.

M: Come on. Just do it! We're getting off in three stations, anyway.

W: (Okay. Could you bring the lady here?)

15

M: At a bookstore, Ally buys a novel that she is looking forward to reading. However, when she gets back home and _______ _______ _______ _______ briefly, she finds a few pages printed upside down. She goes back to the bookstore and asks them to _______ _______ _______ for a new copy. But the clerk says the book is sold out at the moment and it will take a few days for new copies to arrive. Ally wants to _______ _______ _______ _______ and go to another store to buy the novel. In this situation, what would Ally most likely say to the clerk?

Ally: (Can I get a refund on this book?)

16-17

W: Hello, students. Here is some health advice for you. Reading or using a computer too long _______ _______ _______ tired eyes. However, eye tiredness can be effectively prevented or reduced by following these simple tips. First, blink every three to four seconds. Blinking helps _______ _______ _______ _______ _______ _______. Second, give your eyes a break. Look away from the book or the computer screen if your eyes feel tired. Third, eat foods that are good for your eyes. Foods high in Vitamin B, like almonds and avocados, are good choices. Broccoli and berries are also recommended since they contain a lot of Vitamin C. Eating foods high in Vitamin E, such as bananas and potatoes, is helpful, too. Please keep these simple tips in mind in order to _______ _______ _______.

기출 03 # Word & Expressions

01
- □ wonder 궁금해하다; 경이(로운 것)
- □ trail 자국; *루트, 코스
- □ experienced 경험이 있는, 능숙한
- □ free of charge 공짜의, 무료의
- □ preregistration 사전 등록
- □ require 요구하다
- □ break 휴식(시간); *(방송 중간의) 광고
- □ tune (방송 채널을) 맞추다

02
- □ article 글, 기사
- □ heart attack 심장마비
- □ take turns …을 교대로 하다
- □ mouth to mouth 구강 대 구강 인공호흡
- □ unbelievable 믿기 어려울 정도인
- □ first aid 응급 처치
- □ thanks to … 덕분에
- □ practice 연습하다, 실습하다
- □ calm 침착한, 차분한
- □ emergency 비상(사태)
- □ necessary 필요한

03
- □ stop by 잠시 들르다
- □ detail 세부 사항
- □ opinion 의견
- □ overall 전반적인, 전체의
- □ concept 개념; *구상, 콘셉트
- □ brochure (안내·광고용) 책자
- □ font 폰트
- □ copy (책·신문 등의) 한 부
- □ deadline 기한

04
- □ magician 마술사
- □ branch 나뭇가지
- □ audience 청중, 관중
- □ empty 비어 있는, 빈
- □ unbelievably 믿을 수 없을 정도로
- □ awesome 경탄할 만한, 엄청난
- □ absolutely 그럼, 물론이지
- □ take one's eyes off …에서 눈을 떼다

05
- □ grocery 식료품 및 잡화
- □ pick up …을 찾아오다
- □ laundry 세탁물; *세탁소

06
- □ put up …을 내붙이다, 게시하다
- □ bulletin board 게시판
- □ take down …을 내리다, 치우다
- □ approval 승인
- □ post 게시하다, 공고하다

07
- □ sports day 운동회
- □ take one's time 천천히 하다
- □ offer 제공하다
- □ lettering 글자 쓰기, 레터링
- □ for free 무료로
- □ pay in cash 현금으로 지불하다

08
- □ connect 잇다, 연결하다
- □ list price 정가
- □ energy efficient 에너지 효율이 높은
- □ adjust 조절하다
- □ direction 방향

09
- □ drive (조직적인) 운동
- □ in need 어려움에 처한
- □ community 주민, 지역 사회
- □ donation 기증(품)
- □ wearable 착용하기에 적합한
- □ usable 사용 가능한
- □ accept 받아주다, 수락하다
- □ participation 참가, 참여

10
- □ consider 고려하다
- □ intermediate 중급의
- □ beginner 초보자
- □ sign up for …을 신청하다

12
- □ literature 문학
- □ impressive 인상적인, 감명 깊은

13
- □ stand 참다, 견디다
- □ bill 고지서, 청구서
- □ obviously 확실히, 분명히
- □ humid 습한
- □ sweat 땀을 흘리다
- □ budget 예산
- □ start off (…하는 것으로) 시작하다

14
- □ crowded 붐비는, 복잡한
- □ exhausted 기진맥진한
- □ voluntarily 자발적으로
- □ make room for …을 위해 자리를 양보하다
- □ precious 소중한
- □ guilty 죄책감이 드는
- □ get off 내리다, 하차하다

15
- □ look through …을 훑어보다
- □ briefly 잠시, 간단히
- □ upside down 거꾸로, 뒤집혀
- □ at the moment 지금

16-17
- □ lead to …을 유발하다
- □ tiredness 피로
- □ effectively 효과적으로
- □ blink 눈을 깜빡이다
- □ look away from …로부터 눈길을 돌리다
- □ maintain 유지하다
- □ necessity 필요(성)

04 기출 영어듣기 모의고사

1번부터 17번까지는 듣고 답하는 문제입니다.
1번부터 15번까지는 한 번만 들려주고, 16번부터 17번까지는 두 번 들려줍니다. 방송을 잘 듣고 답을 하기 바랍니다.

01

다음을 듣고, 남자가 하는 말의 목적으로 가장 적절한 것을 고르시오.

① 홈스테이 제공 가정을 모집하려고
② 학부모 대상 중국어 강좌를 안내하려고
③ 새로 부임한 중국어 교사를 소개하려고
④ 해외 교환 학생 프로그램을 홍보하려고
⑤ 자매결연 학교 방문 학생을 선발하려고

02

대화를 듣고, 여자의 의견으로 가장 적절한 것을 고르시오.

① 학생들에게 숙제를 내주는 것이 필요하다.
② 자신만의 스트레스 해소법을 찾아야 한다.
③ 방과 후 프로그램을 다양화해야 한다.
④ 복습은 수업 직후에 하는 것이 좋다.
⑤ 게임을 활용한 학습은 효과적이다.

03

대화를 듣고, 두 사람의 관계를 가장 잘 나타낸 것을 고르시오.

① 앱 개발자 — 의뢰인　② 내과 의사 — 환자
③ 택배 기사 — 주문자　④ 휴대폰 수리 기사 — 고객
⑤ 컴퓨터 강사 — 수강생

04

대화를 듣고, 그림에서 대화의 내용과 일치하지 않는 것을 고르시오.

05

대화를 듣고, 남자가 여자에게 부탁한 일로 가장 적절한 것을 고르시오. 3점

① to run hot water in the sink
② to call the maintenance office
③ to repair the pipe in the kitchen
④ to empty the cabinet under the sink
⑤ to send her address to the repairman

06

대화를 듣고, 여자가 지난 주말에 자전거를 타지 못한 이유를 고르시오.

① 독감에 걸려서
② 조카를 돌봐야 해서
③ 날씨가 좋지 않아서
④ 시험공부를 해야 해서
⑤ 자원봉사 일정이 변경되어서

07

대화를 듣고, 여자가 지불할 금액을 고르시오. 3점

① $35　② $38　③ $42
④ $44　⑤ $48

08

대화를 듣고, 호텔 예약에 관해 두 사람이 언급하지 않은 것을 고르시오.

① 특별 혜택　② 투숙 기간　③ 객실 전망
④ 숙박 요금　⑤ 퇴실 시간

09

Annapurna Adventure Bike Ride에 관한 다음 내용을 듣고, 일치하지 않는 것을 고르시오.

① 1년에 16번 출발한다.
② 히말라야 산맥의 계곡을 따라 이동한다.
③ 전 구간을 자전거를 타고 간다.
④ 산악자전거와 헬멧을 제공한다.
⑤ 자전거 수리공과 여행 가이드가 동행한다.

정답 및 해설 p.117-119

10

다음 표를 보면서 대화를 듣고, 두 사람이 선택할 상품을 고르시오.

< Vitamin Product >

	Product	Ingredient	Type	Quantity	Price
①	A	Vitamin C	Jelly	60	$12
②	B	Vitamin C	Pill	60	$14
③	C	Vitamin C	Jelly	120	$24
④	D	Vitamin D	Pill	60	$10
⑤	E	Vitamin D	Jelly	120	$20

11

대화를 듣고, 여자의 마지막 말에 대한 남자의 응답으로 가장 적절한 것을 고르시오.

① Can I get a bigger one?
② Let's go and ask the clerk.
③ I don't have enough money.
④ Thank you for visiting our shop.
⑤ No problem. I like it very much, too.

12

대화를 듣고, 남자의 마지막 말에 대한 여자의 응답으로 가장 적절한 것을 고르시오.

① That's true. I've grown them for years.
② I learned how to grow plants from my parents.
③ Good. You must have a talent for growing plants.
④ Having plants in your room will help you feel good.
⑤ Maybe that's why. Too much water can harm the roots.

13

대화를 듣고, 여자의 마지막 말에 대한 남자의 응답으로 가장 적절한 것을 고르시오. 3점

Man: ______________________________

① Don't worry. It was just a dream.
② That's right. I like monster movies.
③ Try hard, and you'll achieve your dream.
④ Okay. I'll wake you up tomorrow morning.
⑤ That's strange. Nothing happened to me today.

14

대화를 듣고, 남자의 마지막 말에 대한 여자의 응답으로 가장 적절한 것을 고르시오.

Woman: ______________________________

① I know how to start the engine.
② You can't use my car this Sunday.
③ I'll ask him if he can come help us.
④ There is a car repair shop near my home.
⑤ My brother doesn't know anything about cars.

15

다음 상황 설명을 듣고, Bill이 Rachel에게 할 말로 가장 적절한 것을 고르시오.

Bill: ______________________________

① I think we should not be late for the exams.
② Why don't we join the student drama contest?
③ Let's put off practicing until the exams are done.
④ Please tell me when the performance will be held.
⑤ We'd better practice more often than you've planned.

[16-17] 다음을 듣고, 물음에 답하시오.

16

여자가 하는 말의 주제로 가장 적절한 것은?

① safety guidelines for exercise
② ways to exercise in everyday life
③ advantages of working out at a gym
④ roles of exercise in dealing with stress
⑤ effects of listening to music while exercising

17

언급된 장소가 아닌 곳은?

① 사무실 ② 공원 ③ 지하철역
④ 쇼핑몰 ⑤ 거실

녹음을 다시 한 번 듣고, 빈칸에 알맞은 말을 쓰시오.

01

M: Thank you all for coming today. Before we end this parents' meeting, we have something to tell you. As you know, our school has _______ _______ _______ _______ Beijing Secondary School since last year. Five Chinese teachers from that school will come next semester to teach our students. So, we're looking for families _______ _______ _______ _______. They'll be joining us in January and staying until the end of the semester. Having them stay in your home would be a great opportunity for your family _______ _______ _______ a new culture. If you're interested, please contact Mr. Gilmore in the school office.

02

M: Honey, here is an interesting article.
W: What's it about?
M: It's about school homework. It says that homework _______ _______ _______.
W: I don't understand. Why does the writer think so?
M: He says students study all day at school, so giving them homework can make them stressed out.
W: But doing homework is a good way to review _______ _______ _______ at school.
M: According to the article, students need time to relax and play with their friends after school.
W: _______ _______ _______. But I'm worried that students will play computer games all day long if they have no homework to do.
M: I'm worried about that, too.
W: I think giving them homework is necessary.
M: I agree. That might be helpful for students.

03

M: Good morning. How can I help you?
W: Hi. I bought this recently, but it _______ _______ _______ _______.
M: Can I see it?
W: Yes, here it is.
M: *[Pause]* It's infected with a virus, and that's causing your phone to shut down.
W: I see. Can it be fixed?
M: Yes, but if the virus _______ _______ _______, your cell phone will need to be reset.
W: What will happen to all the applications and files on my phone if it is reset?
M: Don't worry. I will back up all your apps and files before I _______ _______ _______.
W: I appreciate that. When can I pick it up?
M: It'll be done by 4 p.m. You can come back to the service center after that.

04

M: Amy, are you buying something from that furniture catalog?
W: I'm planning to. I need to buy some furniture _______ _______ _______.
M: Hmm.... The bookcase on the wall looks great.
W: I've wanted something like that. This bookcase would look perfect on my wall.
M: How about this notice board under the bookcase? You can _______ _______ _______ _______ it.
W: I like it! And the lamp on the desk would be nice for reading books.
M: And the drawers under the desk look useful.
W: Yeah, I think so. I can keep a lot of things in them.
M: I like the chair with four wheels.
W: So do I. It looks comfortable and _______ _______ _______ _______ in.
M: You seem to like everything in this page.
W: Actually, I do.

05

[Telephone rings.]

M: Lanson Apartment maintenance office. May I help you?

W: Yes, I live in unit 14. I have a problem with my kitchen sink.

M: Would you be more specific, please?

W: I just ran some water in my kitchen sink, and the water isn't ______ ______ ______ ______.

M: Okay. We'll send a repairman to your apartment this afternoon.

W: ______ ______ ______ ______ I'll be home at that time. Could you tell him to call me before coming? My phone number is 520-234-8500.

M: Okay. Do you have anything in the cabinet under the sink?

W: Yes, I put some cooking tools and other things there.

M: Then, please ______ ______ so the repairman can check the pipe under the kitchen sink.

W: Okay, I will. Thank you.

06

M: Hi, Olivia. How was your bike ride last weekend?

W: Well, ______ ______ ______ ______ ride it.

M: Why? The weather was perfect for bike riding.

W: I know. But just when I was about to leave, my sister called me.

M: Was it something important?

W: She had the flu, so ______ ______ ______ ______ I could take care of her baby.

M: So, you had to babysit your nephew instead of riding your bike?

W: Yes. I still had a lot of fun with him, though.

M: Great. But ______ ______ ______ ______ for the test last week, so the bike ride would have refreshed you.

W: There's always a next time. I guess I'll have to wait until I finish my volunteer work next week.

07

W: Hi, can you help me? I need to buy mini-cupcake pans.

M: Okay. We have metal and silicone pans. Metal pans are 20 dollars each and silicone pans are 15 dollars each.

W: Well, since metal is ______ ______ ______ silicone, I'll take two metal pans.

M: We're running a special promotion. If you buy two cupcake pans, you can get a 10 percent discount.

W: That sounds great! Maybe I'll get some gift boxes for the cupcakes, too.

M: The boxes are over there.

W: Wow, this red box looks cute. I'll ______ ______ ______ ______.

M: They're two dollars each. Anything else?

W: That's all for now. Are the boxes ______ ______ ______ ______?

M: I'm afraid not.

W: That's okay. Here's my credit card.

08

[Telephone rings.]

M: Good morning, Healing Spa Hotel. How may I help you?

W: I'd like to make a reservation. I got an e-mail saying your hotel ______ ______ ______ ______.

M: Yes, ma'am. This month, if you stay for 2 nights, we'll give you a third night for free.

W: Good. I'd like to ______ ______ ______ ______ from the 20th to the 23rd.

M: That would be for three nights, right?

W: Yes. Do you have a room with an ocean view?

M: Let me check. *[Pause]* Yes. But, we only have one left ______ ______ ______. It's $100 per night including tax.

W: It sounds reasonable. I'll reserve the room. When can I check in?

M: You can check in after 3 p.m.

W: Great! See you then.

09

M: Are you _______ _______ from your busy city life? Annapurna Adventure Bike Ride offers a week of great adventures in the heart of the Himalayas. We have 16 departures per year. You can ride along the beautiful Himalayan valleys. Are you worried if it might be too dangerous? Don't worry. The steep and dangerous parts of the course are _______ _______ _______. We supply new quality mountain bikes and helmets for your safe and smooth ride. Also, a qualified bike mechanic and a travel guide _______ _______ _______ each team. For more information, visit our homepage at www.annapurnaadventure.com.

10

W: Honey, look at this website! I'm thinking about buying some vitamins for Mike.

M: That's good. I heard vitamins are very _______ _______ _______.

W: I've also heard that. That's why I want to buy some for him.

M: Which product do you _______ _______ _______?

W: I think it's a good idea to start with vitamin C, because it's the most common.

M: You're right. That'll certainly be good for Mike. Oh, there are two types of vitamin C, jelly and pill.

W: Of course Mike would love to have the jelly type.

M: I agree. Now we _______ _______ _______ _______.

W: Why don't we get the smaller amount first? Just in case Mike doesn't like it.

M: Okay. Plus, it costs less than 20 dollars. Let's buy it now.

11

W: Wow, look at that pink blouse _______ _______!

M: It's gorgeous. I think it'll suit you very well.

W: Yeah, I like it. I hope they have my size.

M: (Let's go and ask the clerk.)

12

M: Wow, your plants look great! I don't know why mine look so unhealthy.

W: _______ _______ _______ _______ _______ your plants?

M: I make sure to water them several times every day.

W: (Maybe that's why. Too much water can harm the roots.)

13

M: Jessica, you don't look well.

W: I feel a little tired today.

M: Is something the matter?

W: I _______ _______ _______ _______ last night.

M: A bad dream? Can you tell me about it?

W: A monster was chasing me and I had to run away.

M: That's horrible. What happened next?

W: Just before the monster grabbed me, I _______ _______ _______ _______ _______.

M: That sounds really scary.

W: Yeah. I'm afraid _______ _______ _______ _______ to me today.

M: (Don't worry. It was just a dream.)

14

M: Oh, no! Sue, we've got a problem.

W: What's the matter, Kevin? _______ _______ _______ _______ with your car?

M: I guess so. It won't start.

W: Really? Try again.

M: I'm trying, but it doesn't work. Actually, the same thing happened a few days ago.

W: I think you need to call a car repair shop and _______ _______ _______ immediately.

M: I want to, but today is Sunday. I don't think there is a shop that is open today.

W: You're right. Oh, wait! My brother knows a lot about cars. He might be able to find out what the problem is.

M: Really? _______ _______ _______ right now?

W: (I'll ask him if he can come help us.)

15

W: Bill is a member of his school's drama club. One day, the club members _______ _______ _______ the local student drama contest that'll be held next month. So, Rachel, the leader of the club, tells the club members that they'll have a practice session _______ _______ _______ starting tomorrow. However, their exams are in a week, and Bill is worried about the schedule. He thinks that not many members will like the practice sessions because of the coming exams. Now, he wants to suggest to Rachel that they start practicing after the exams so that they can have _______ _______ _______ _______. In this situation, what would Bill most likely say to Rachel?

Bill: (Let's put off practicing until the exams are done.)

16-17

W: Good morning, everyone. Spring's here and more people are interested in _______ _______ _______. But it's not easy to find time to go to the gym. There are some good ways to exercise in your daily life. At the office, set your alarm so that you can stand up every hour. Do simple exercises before sitting back down. When you commute, walk, walk, and walk. Get off the bus _______ _______ _______ _______ and walk. At the subway station, walk around the platform while waiting for a train. In the shopping mall, _______ _______ _______ _______ to go around the whole mall at least twice before you make a decision. Two hours of shopping burns as much as 300 calories. At home, dance or do some stretching exercises while you're watching TV in your living room. Remember: The more you move your body, the healthier and happier you get!

기출 4회

Word & Expressions

01
- □ **partnership** 협력, 제휴
- □ **semester** 학기
- □ **host** (손님을) 재워주다
- □ **opportunity** 기회
- □ **contact** 연락하다

02
- □ **article** 글, 기사
- □ **ban** 금지하다
- □ **stressed out** 스트레스를 받는
- □ **review** 복습하다
- □ **according to** …에 의하면
- □ **necessary** 필요한

03
- □ **recently** 최근에
- □ **be infected with** …에 감염되다
- □ **shut down** (기계가) 멈추다, 정지하다
- □ **application** 지원; *응용 프로그램(= app)
- □ **appreciate** 고마워하다

04
- □ **study** 학업; *서재
- □ **bookcase** 책장, 책꽂이
- □ **notice board** 게시판
- □ **drawer** 서랍
- □ **useful** 유용한, 도움이 되는
- □ **wheel** 바퀴
- □ **move around** 돌아다니다

05
- □ **maintenance** 보수, 관리
- □ **specific** 구체적인, 명확한
- □ **repairman** 수리공
- □ **cabinet** 캐비닛, 보관함

06
- □ **flu** 독감
- □ **take care of** …을 돌보다
- □ **nephew** (남자) 조카
- □ **refresh** 생기를 되찾게 하다
- □ **volunteer work** 자원봉사

07
- □ **metal** 금속
- □ **durable** 내구성이 있는, 오래가는
- □ **promotion** 홍보, 판촉 활동

08
- □ **special offer** 특가 판매
- □ **view** 경관, 전망
- □ **period** 기간, 시기
- □ **including** …을 포함하여
- □ **reasonable** 합리적인; *(가격이) 적정한
- □ **reserve** 예약하다

09
- □ **adventure** 모험
- □ **departure** 출발
- □ **valley** 계곡, 골짜기
- □ **steep** 가파른, 비탈진
- □ **cover** (언급된 거리를) 가다, 이동하다
- □ **quality** 질; *고급의
- □ **smooth** 부드러운
- □ **qualified** 자격이 있는
- □ **mechanic** 정비공

10
- □ **have in mind** …을 염두에 두다
- □ **common** 흔한
- □ **certainly** 틀림없이
- □ **pill** 알약
- □ **amount** 양
- □ **in case** …할 경우에 대비해서

11
- □ **gorgeous** 아주 멋진
- □ **suit** 어울리다
- □ **clerk** 점원

12
- □ **unhealthy** 건강하지 못한, 병든 것 같은
- □ **make sure to-v** 반드시 …하도록 하다
- □ **several** 몇몇의

13
- □ **chase** 뒤쫓다
- □ **run away** 달아나다
- □ **horrible** 지긋지긋한, 끔찍한
- □ **grab** 붙잡다
- □ **sweat** 땀, 식은땀
- □ **scary** 무서운, 겁나는

14
- □ **repair shop** 수리점, 정비소
- □ **immediately** 즉시
- □ **available** (사람들을 만날) 시간이 있는
- □ **start the engine** 엔진의 시동을 걸다

15
- □ **local** 지역의, 현지의
- □ **practice** 연습; 연습하다
- □ **session** (특정한 활동을 위한) 시간
- □ **suggest** 제안하다
- □ **put off** …을 미루다, 연기하다

16-17
- □ **get into shape** 건강을 유지하다, 몸매를 맵시 있게 가꾸다
- □ **gym** 체육관
- □ **daily life** 일상생활
- □ **commute** 통근하다
- □ **ahead** 미리, 앞서서
- □ **platform** 플랫폼, 승강장
- □ **make it a rule to-v** …하는 것을 원칙으로 하다

05 기출 영어듣기 모의고사

정답 및 해설 p.120-123

1번부터 17번까지는 듣고 답하는 문제입니다.
1번부터 15번까지는 한 번만 들려주고, 16번부터 17번까지는 두 번 들려줍니다. 방송을 잘 듣고 답을 하기 바랍니다.

01

다음을 듣고, 남자가 하는 말의 목적으로 가장 적절한 것을 고르시오.

① 치과 개원을 홍보하려고
② 머리 빗는 요령을 설명하려고
③ 칫솔의 생산 과정을 안내하려고
④ 올바른 칫솔질에 대해 알려주려고
⑤ 길에 껌을 뱉는 행동을 비판하려고

02

대화를 듣고, 두 사람이 하는 말의 주제로 가장 적절한 것을 고르시오.

① 좋은 책을 고르는 요령
② 색이 감정에 미치는 영향
③ 발표 불안의 원인과 치료법
④ 그림 그리기의 심리 치료 효과
⑤ 제품 색상과 판매량의 상관관계

03

대화를 듣고, 두 사람의 관계를 가장 잘 나타낸 것을 고르시오.

① 의사 — 환자　② 영화감독 — 배우
③ 방송 작가 — 성우　④ 신문 기자 — 시나리오 작가
⑤ 영화 제작자 — 촬영 감독

04

대화를 듣고, 그림에서 대화의 내용과 일치하지 않는 것을 고르시오.

05

대화를 듣고, 남자가 여자를 위해 할 일로 가장 적절한 것을 고르시오.

① 휴대 전화 언어 변경해 주기
② 공항까지 차로 데려다주기
③ 한국 음식점 소개해 주기
④ 관광지 안내해 주기
⑤ 휴대 전화 빌려주기

06

대화를 듣고, 남자가 봉사활동에 갈 수 없는 이유를 고르시오.

① 중간고사 준비를 해야 해서
② 동물원 구경을 가야 해서
③ 미루어 둔 일이 많아서
④ 동물 털 알레르기 때문에
⑤ 도서관에 가야 하기 때문에

07

대화를 듣고, 남자가 지불할 금액을 고르시오. 3점

① $20　② $32　③ $40
④ $48　⑤ $60

08

대화를 듣고, 여자가 실시할 설문 조사에 관해 두 사람이 언급하지 않은 것을 고르시오.

① 주제　② 대상　③ 방법
④ 기간　⑤ 증정품

09

Ontario Universities' Fair에 관한 다음 내용을 듣고, 일치하지 않는 것을 고르시오.

① 21개 대학이 참여할 것이다.
② 9월 25일부터 3일간 개최된다.
③ 방문하려면 사전 등록을 해야 한다.
④ 대학생과 교수가 직접 상담을 해준다.
⑤ 캐나다에서 가장 큰 교육 박람회이다.

10

다음 표를 보면서 대화를 듣고, 두 사람이 선택할 투어를 고르시오.

< Sherlock Holmes Walking Tours >

	Tour	Day	Length (hours)	Character Dress-up	Price (per person)
①	A	Wednesday	2	×	$20
②	B	Wednesday	2	○	$25
③	C	Friday	2	○	$30
④	D	Friday	3	×	$35
⑤	E	Saturday	3	○	$45

11

대화를 듣고, 여자의 마지막 말에 대한 남자의 응답으로 가장 적절한 것을 고르시오.

① I usually take the bus to work.
② We still have forty minutes left.
③ Sure, the concert will be exciting.
④ Please watch out at the next corner.
⑤ No, I don't want to go to the concert.

12

대화를 듣고, 남자의 마지막 말에 대한 여자의 응답으로 가장 적절한 것을 고르시오.

① No problem. When can I visit you?
② Okay, I'll call the customer service center.
③ Sure, the repairman just fixed the computer.
④ Well, I don't think we need a new computer.
⑤ Hey, why don't we play computer games together?

13

대화를 듣고, 여자의 마지막 말에 대한 남자의 응답으로 가장 적절한 것을 고르시오. 3점

Man: ______________________

① No. There are no seats available in his class.
② Okay. I'll try to take a language class this time.
③ Never mind. You can be a good language teacher.
④ All right. I'll recommend the class to my classmates.
⑤ Sure. He receives good reviews from most beginners.

14

대화를 듣고, 남자의 마지막 말에 대한 여자의 응답으로 가장 적절한 것을 고르시오. 3점

Woman: ______________________

① Then, I'll buy you something to eat.
② Your donation was used for poor children.
③ It's sweet of you to treat me to lunch today.
④ It's impressive that you've donated for a long time.
⑤ You can share my lunch and donate your lunch money.

15

다음 상황 설명을 듣고, Carrie가 Bill에게 할 말로 가장 적절한 것을 고르시오.

Carrie: ______________________

① Don't get out of the car to take pictures.
② Watch out for the animals while driving.
③ I love to take pictures of wild animals.
④ I have an extra camera in the back seat.
⑤ Never walk through the park alone at night.

[16-17] 다음을 듣고, 물음에 답하시오.

16

남자가 하는 말의 주제로 가장 적절한 것은?

① why we should use oils for body care
② how scented candles affect feelings
③ how smells affect flavors of food
④ why people prefer sweet scents
⑤ how to make scented candles

17

언급된 향이 아닌 것은?

① lavender ② vanilla ③ rosemary
④ peppermint ⑤ jasmine

정답 및 해설 p.123

녹음을 다시 한 번 듣고, 빈칸에 알맞은 말을 쓰시오.

01

M: Hi, everyone. I'm very happy to have this precious time with you. I've _______ _______ _______ a dentist for over twenty years. And whenever I meet my patients with serious dental problems, I've wanted to let them know how to _______ _______ _______ _______. Most cavities and gum diseases are caused by bad habits while brushing your teeth. When brushing, you should divide your mouth into four sections and spend 30 seconds on each. Brush the outer and inner tooth surfaces thoroughly _______ _______ _______ _______. Brushing more than three times a day is not ideal, because you can damage your gums. I'll show you the proper process with a cartoon.

02

W: Jake, your big presentation is tomorrow! Are you _______ _______?

M: Yeah, I think I'm ready for it. Wish me luck!

W: I will. *[Pause]* Oh! If it's possible, look at a picture of the sky or the ocean before the presentation.

M: A picture of what? I'm not following you.

W: I'm talking about the color. The color blue _______ _______ _______ _______ helping people feel relaxed and comfortable.

M: Really? I didn't know colors could influence our emotions.

W: Yes, they do, according to the book I read.

M: Interesting! Can you tell me more?

W: Sure. Red can make people energetic and excited.

M: Ah, that's why red _______ _______ _______ _______ cheering at sporting events.

W: Yes. Colors can have an impact on our emotions.

M: Amazing! Thanks for the information.

03

M: Congratulations on _______ _______ _______, Liz.

W: Thanks, John. Your latest movie was also impressive.

M: I appreciate that.

W: I believe the movie is going to be a big hit.

M: I hope so. Recently, I found the perfect scenario for my next film. I'm thinking of you in the starring role.

W: What _______ _______ _______ _______?

M: She is an Alzheimer's patient who is losing her memory at a young age.

W: Oh, no way. The last time I played a cancer patient, I had to lose 10 kilograms.

M: But you _______ _______ _______ this time. I bet once you read the scenario, you'll love it.

W: Okay, I'll read it.

M: Great! I'll have the scenario delivered to your manager's office tomorrow.

W: Good.

M: If you accept the role, we'll start shooting as soon as possible.

04

M: Wow! I didn't know there was a cafe like this near my house.

W: Yeah. I sometimes come here to take a break.

M: This place looks very comfortable. Oh, look at that menu board. It's _______ _______ _______.

W: And the flower pot on the counter makes this place feel cozy.

M: You're right. Why don't we order some coffee?

W: Okay. Go and take a seat while I order.

M: Thanks. Do you want to sit at the long table _______ _______ _______?

W: How about sitting at the round table in the center?

M: That sounds good. Oh, there are some books on the shelves.

W: Yes, we can read them while drinking our coffee.

M: I think it's the perfect _______ _______ _______.

05

M: Hey, Sumin. Over here! Welcome to Hungary.

W: Hi, Dominik. Thanks for coming to the airport ______ ______ ______ ______.

M: It's nothing. You did a lot for me when I was in Korea.

W: I enjoyed ______ ______ ______ in Korea, too.

M: I remember the Korean palaces we saw and the street food we ate together.

W: Yeah. You had a hard time eating spicy food.

M: Oh, by the way, do you need a phone to use here in Budapest?

W: I've already rented a cellphone, but I need to change the language setting into Korean.

M: Do you need help?

W: Yes. The phone is quite different from ______ ______ ______ in Korea.

M: Okay. Just hand it to me.

06

W: Thank goodness! Midterm exams are over.

M: Yes. I feel like ______ ______ ______ ______. Do you have any plans this Saturday, Lisa?

W: I'm going to do some volunteer work at an animal shelter.

M: What are you ______ ______ ______ there?

W: I'm going to help feed the cats and dogs. It'll be fun. Do you want to join me?

M: It sounds really interesting, but I can't go.

W: Why not? Do you have something to do this Saturday?

M: No, I'll be free, but I'm ______ ______ ______ ______.

W: I'm sorry to hear that. Next time, let's go somewhere else like a library, instead.

M: Sounds good.

07

W: How do you like your new hairstyle, sir?

M: This is my first time ______ ______ ______. But, I like it.

W: You look more stylish with your hair permed.

M: Thank you. How much is it?

W: You ______ ______ ______ ______ and permed, didn't you?

M: That's right.

W: Well, the price for the haircut is $20, and the perm is $40.

M: Is there any discount?

W: Yes. We offer a 20% discount for customers ______ ______ ______ before noon.

M: That's great. Then can I get the discount off the total price?

W: Yes, you can. How would you like to pay?

M: I'd like to pay in cash.

08

M: Clare, how's the survey for your report going?

W: It's almost ready. I'm checking ______ ______ ______ ______ before I start.

M: What's your survey about?

W: It's about how smartphones affect our daily lives.

M: Sounds interesting. Who will you survey?

W: I'm thinking of surveying ______ ______ ______ ______ ______.

M: How will you survey them?

W: I'm planning to interview at least 100 students in person.

M: That's a good idea. How about offering some kind of gift to those students?

W: I've already thought about that. I'm going to give them smartphone accessories.

M: Great. You seem to ______ ______ ______. Good luck with your survey.

09

W: Hello, students! Today, I'd like to inform you of the Ontario Universities' Fair, or the OUF. If you're thinking about _______ _______ _______ in Ontario, don't miss this chance. All 21 Ontario universities will _______ _______ _______ _______! The OUF is held for three days from September 25 to 27, at the Metro Toronto Convention Center. All visitors are welcome to the OUF. No admission charge or preregistration is required. At the OUF, you can talk personally with university students and professors to get information about programs, admission requirements, student life and much more. _______ _______ _______ _______ the largest educational fair in Canada! For more information, please visit our website. Thank you.

10

M: Honey, what are we going to do here in London?

W: How about a Sherlock Holmes Walking Tour? I got a brochure from the hotel lobby.

M: Good idea. Let me see.... _______ _______ _______ _______ London?

W: This Saturday morning. So we should go either Wednesday or Friday.

M: Right. We need to choose the tour length, too. There are 2 or 3 hour options.

W: I think 3 hours will be _______ _______ _______ for us in this hot weather.

M: I agree. 2 hours sounds better.

W: Good. Do you _______ _______ _______ _______ characters' costumes? That'll be fun and exciting.

M: Yeah! I can dress up like Sherlock Holmes! Let's choose the character dress-up option.

W: Awesome! Well, two options left. I think the cheaper one is better.

M: I agree. Let's choose this one.

11

W: Oh no. Another traffic jam! We might be late for the concert.

M: Don't worry. Once we get around this corner, it'll be okay.

W: I hope so. How much time do we have _______ _______ _______ _______?

M: (We still have forty minutes left.)

12

M: Why did your computer suddenly shut down?

W: I tried to _______ _______ _______, but I couldn't find what was wrong.

M: Then, I think you need to call the repairman.

W: (Okay, I'll call the customer service center.)

13

M: Good evening, ma'am.

W: Hi, Mr. Taylor. Can I see my French test results?

M: Sure. *[Typing]* Here. _______ _______ _______ in most sections except pronunciation.

W: Hmm.... What class do you think would be good for me _______ _______ _______ my pronunciation?

M: Well, a beginner speaking class would be good for you.

W: Then I'll take a speaking class next month. Are there any classes in the morning?

M: We have one at 7 a.m. on Tuesdays and at 9 a.m. on Thursdays.

W: I think I'll take the Tuesday class.

M: Okay. The instructor is Mr. Martin.

W: Oh, I heard his class is a bit difficult. Do you think _______ _______ _______ _______?

M: (Sure. He receives good reviews from most beginners.)

14

M: Ally, I'm going to a snack bar to buy something for lunch. Do you want to go with me?

W: I'm okay. I brought some sandwiches.

M: Then, do you need _______ _______ _______?

W: No. Actually, I'm not going to buy anything today.

M: Oh, why is that?

W: Today is International Buy Nothing Day.

M: Buy Nothing Day? What's that?

W: You don't buy anything for the day and instead, you donate _______ _______ _______ _______ to charity.

M: That's very meaningful.

W: I started to celebrate the day two years ago, and it _______ _______ _______ _______.

M: I want to participate, but I didn't bring anything for lunch.

W: (You can share my lunch and donate your lunch money.)

15

M: Bill and Carrie both like traveling and taking pictures. Today, they're joining a safari car tour in Tanzania, Africa. Tanzania is _______ _______ _______ _______, especially for the herds of thousands of buffalo which make for beautiful pictures. Bill is excited to take close-up pictures of those buffalo. So when he sees a herd of buffalo, he tries to get out of the car to take pictures of them _______ _______. However, Carrie is worried about the danger of being outside of the car. So, she wants to tell him to _______ _______ _______ _______ when taking pictures. In this situation, what would Carrie most likely say to Bill?

Carrie: (Don't get out of the car to take pictures.)

16-17

M: Hello, everyone! Have you heard about scented candles? They are candles _______ _______ _______. Today, I'm going to tell you about one of the benefits of lighting scented candles. In addition to lighting up a room, they can make an ordinary room special with their smell. Research suggests that the smell of candles does more than just improves the atmosphere; it can also affect _______ _______ _______. Some smells can actually lower stress levels. For example, lavender _______ _______ _______ _______ relieve stress and anxiety. Vanilla is also known to reduce stress with its comforting effect. Some smells tend to promote positive emotions. For example, rosemary provides a feeling of satisfaction. Jasmine can help to overcome sadness and depression. Why don't you use scented candles to revive yourselves?

Word & Expressions

01
□ precious 귀한, 소중한
□ dental 치아의
□ cavity 구멍; *충치
□ gum 고무; *잇몸
□ section 부분, 구획
□ surface 표면
□ thoroughly 철저히
□ proper 적절한, 제대로 된
□ process 절차, 방법
□ cartoon 만화

02
□ presentation 발표
□ prepared 준비가 된
□ possible 가능한
□ follow 이해하다, (내용을) 따라잡다
□ relaxed 느긋한, 여유 있는
□ influence 영향을 주다
□ emotion 감정
□ energetic 힘이 넘치는, 활기찬
□ widely 널리
□ sporting event 스포츠 경기
□ impact 영향을 주다

03
□ impressive 인상적인
□ hit 치기; *대 인기, 히트
□ scenario 시나리오
□ starring role 주역
□ deliver 배달하다
□ accept 받아들이다
□ shoot (영화·사진을) 촬영하다

04
□ decorate 장식하다, 꾸미다
□ flower pot 화분
□ cozy 아늑한, 편안한
□ shelf 책꽂이, 선반
□ rest 쉬다, 휴식하다

05
□ pick up …을 태우러 가다
□ show around …을 구경시켜 주다
□ palace 궁전, 왕실

06
□ volunteer work 자원봉사
□ animal shelter 동물 보호소
□ be supposed to-v …하기로 되어 있다
□ feed 먹이를 주다
□ be allergic to …에 알레르기가 있다

07
□ perm 파마; 파마를 해주다

08
□ survey 설문 조사; 설문 조사하다
□ a couple of 두서너 개의, 몇 개의
□ affect 영향을 미치다
□ in person 직접

09
□ inform 알리다
□ fair 박람회
□ attend 다니다
□ participate in …에 참가하다
□ admission charge 입장료
□ preregistration 사전 등록
□ require 필요하다(n. requirement 필요, 요건)
□ personally 직접, 개인적으로
□ educational 교육의

10
□ length 길이
□ character 성격; *등장인물
□ costume 의상
□ dress up 변장을 하다

11
□ traffic jam 교통 체증

12
□ shut down (기계가) 멈추다, 정지하다
□ figure out …을 이해하다[알아내다]
□ repairman 수리공

13
□ result 결과
□ score 점수를 받다
□ section 부분
□ pronunciation 발음
□ work on …에 애쓰다, 공들이다
□ keep up (진도 등을) 따라가다
□ review 평가, 비평

14
□ snack bar 간이 식당
□ donate 기부하다(n. donation 기부, 기증)
□ charity 자선 단체
□ meaningful 의미 있는
□ celebrate 기념하다, 축하하다
□ participate 참여하다

15
□ wildlife 야생동물
□ especially 특히
□ herd 떼, 무리
□ close-up 근접 촬영(한 사진)

16-17
□ scented 향기로운(n. scent 향기)
□ light 불을 붙이다; 밝게 하다
□ ordinary 보통의, 평범한
□ atmosphere 대기; *분위기
□ relieve 없애주다, 덜어주다
□ anxiety 불안(감)
□ reduce 줄이다
□ comforting 기운을 북돋우는
□ promote 조성하다, 촉진하다
□ positive 긍정적인
□ satisfaction 만족
□ overcome 극복하다
□ depression 우울
□ revive 활기를 되찾다

지은이

NE능률 영어교육연구소

NE능률 영어교육연구소는 혁신적이며 효율적인 영어 교재를 개발하고
영어 학습의 질을 한 단계 높이고자 노력하는 NE능률의 연구조직입니다.

수능만만 〈기본 영어듣기 35+5회〉

펴 낸 이 주민홍
펴 낸 곳 서울특별시 마포구 월드컵북로 396(상암동) 누리꿈스퀘어 비즈니스타워 10층
㈜NE능률 (우편번호 03925)
펴 낸 날 2022년 1월 5일 개정판 제1쇄 발행
2024년 1월 15일 제7쇄
전 화 02 2014 7114
팩 스 02 3142 0356
홈페이지 www.neungyule.com
등록번호 제1-68호
I S B N 979-11-253-3738-6 53740
정 가 18,000원

NE 능률

고객센터

교재 내용 문의 : contact.nebooks.co.kr (별도의 가입 절차 없이 작성 가능)
제품 구매, 교환, 불량, 반품 문의 : 02-2014-7114
☎ 전화문의는 본사 업무시간 중에만 가능합니다.

NE능률 교재 MAP

아래 교재 MAP을 참고하여 본인의 현재 혹은 목표 수준에 따라 교재를 선택하세요.
NE능률 교재들과 함께 영어실력을 쑥쑥~ 올려보세요!
MP3 등 교재 부가 학습 서비스 및 자세한 교재 정보는 www.nebooks.co.kr 에서 확인하세요.

초1-2 | 초3 | 초3-4 | 초4-5 | 초5-6

초6-예비중 | 중1 | 중1-2 | 중2-3 | 중3

중2-3
- 첫 번째 수능 영어 기초편

중3
- 첫 번째 수능 영어 유형편
- 첫 번째 수능 영어 실전편

예비고-고1
- 기강잡고 독해 잡는 필수 문법
- 기강잡고 기초 잡는 유형 독해
- The 상승 직독직해편
- 올클 수능 어법 start
- 얇고 빠른 미니 모의고사 10+2회 입문

고1
- 빠바 기초세우기
- 능률기본영어
- The 상승 문법독해편
- 수능만만 기본 영어듣기 20회
- 수능만만 기본 영어듣기 35+5회
- 수능만만 기본 문법·어법·어휘 150제
- 수능만만 기본 영어독해 10+1회
- 맞수 수능듣기 기본편
- 맞수 수능문법어법 기본편
- 맞수 구문독해 기본편
- 맞수 수능유형 기본편
- 수능유형 PICK 독해 기본
- 수능유형 PICK 듣기 기본
- 수능 구문 빅데이터 기본편
- 얇고 빠른 미니 모의고사 10+2회 기본

고1-2
- 빠바 구문독해
- The 상승 어법어휘+유형편
- The 상승 구문편
- 맞수 수능듣기 실전편
- 맞수 수능문법어법 실전편
- 맞수 구문독해 실전편
- 맞수 수능유형 실전편
- 맞수 빈칸추론
- 특급 독해 유형별 모의고사
- 수능유형 PICK 독해 실력
- 수능 구문 빅데이터 수능빈출편
- 얇고 빠른 미니 모의고사 10+2회 실전

고2-3, 수능 실전
- 빠바 유형독해
- 빠바 종합실전편
- The 상승 수능유형편
- 수능만만 어법어휘 228제
- 수능만만 영어듣기 20회
- 수능만만 영어듣기 35회
- 수능만만 영어독해 20회
- 특급 듣기 실전 모의고사
- 특급 빈칸추론
- 특급 어법
- 특급 수능·EBS 기출 VOCA
- 올클 수능 어법 완성
- 능률 EBS 수능특강 변형 문제 영어(상), (하)
- 능률 EBS 수능특강 변형 문제 영어독해연습(상), (하)

수능, 학평 기출
- 다빈출코드 영어영역 고1독해
- 다빈출코드 영어영역 고2독해
- 다빈출코드 영어영역 듣기
- 다빈출코드 영어영역 어법·어휘

수능 이상/ 토플 80-89· 텝스 600-699점 | 수능 이상/ 토플 90-99· 텝스 700-799점 | 수능 이상/ 토플 100· 텝스 800점 이상

만만한
수능영어

NE 능률

수능 만만

기본

영어듣기
35+5회

정답 및 해설

만만한
수능영어

영어듣기
35+5회

정답 및 해설

01 영어듣기 모의고사

본문 ▶ p.6

01 ③	02 ②	03 ⑤	04 ⑤	05 ⑤	06 ②
07 ③	08 ③	09 ⑤	10 ①	11 ⑤	12 ④
13 ③	14 ②	15 ④	16 ⑤	17 ③	

01 ③

여: 우리 시에서 사는 것에는 많은 이점들이 있습니다. 안타깝게도, 많은 문제점들 또한 있습니다. 최악의 문제점들 중 두 가지는 대기 오염과 교통입니다. 만약 더 많은 사람들이 자전거를 타면 이 두 문제는 줄어들 수 있습니다. 하지만, 우리 시에는 자전거 전용 도로가 아예 없어서, 자전거를 타는 것은 위험할 수 있습니다. 만약 우리가 자전거 전용 도로를 건설하면, 자전거를 타는 것은 훨씬 더 안전하고 더 즐거워질 것입니다. 그리고 더 많은 사람들이 자전거를 타기 시작하면, 도시 전체가 혜택을 볼 것입니다. 교통량이 더 감소하고, 공기는 더 깨끗해지고, 사람들은 더 건강해질 것입니다. 대단하지 않습니까?

02 ②

여: Eric, 너 그 콜라 버릴 거니?
남: 응. 그거 김이 빠져버렸고, 냉장고 공간 좀 만들려고 해.
여: 버리지 마. 그걸 다른 용도로 사용할 수 있어.
남: 정말? 예를 들면?
여: 어떤 사람들은 변기와 욕실 세면대를 청소하기 위해 사용한다고 들은 적이 있어. 그것은 심지어 금속의 녹을 벗겨낼 수 있어.
남: 와, 그건 몰랐어.
여: 청소뿐만 아니라, 사람들은 생선을 요리하기 전에 콜라로 생선을 문지르기도 해.
남: 그거 흥미롭긴 한데, 맛이 이상하지 않을까?
여: 실은 콜라가 비린내를 없애주고 생선이 단맛이 나도록 해줘.
남: 아, 멋지다. 그렇다면 여기 냉장고 안에 놔둬야겠다.

03 ⑤

[전화벨이 울린다.]
여: 여보세요, Hertz Company입니다. 무엇을 도와드릴까요?
남: 안녕하세요. 제 예약을 확인하려고 전화했습니다.
여: 알겠습니다. 고객님의 성함을 알려주시겠어요?
남: Andrew Stevenson입니다. 지난주에 예약했어요.
여: 잠시만요. *[잠시 후]* 네. 7일부터 3일간 고객님을 위해 마련된 미니밴이 있습니다. 맞으신가요?
남: 맞아요. 하루에 120달러인 것도 확인하고 싶은데요, 맞나요?
여: 네. 하지만 저희가 이번 달에 특별 할인 요금을 제공하고 있습니다. 고객님께서는 하루에 100달러만 내시면 됩니다.
남: 좋네요. 언제 지불하면 되나요?
여: 차를 받을 때 지불하시면 됩니다. 고객님의 차는 내일 오전 8시 전에 준비될 것입니다.
남: 알겠습니다. 내일 오전 8시경에 가겠습니다.

04 ⑤

남: 여기가 Tom의 새로운 놀이방이에요? 근사해 보여요!
여: 고마워요. 어젯밤에 만들었어요. 엄청난 일이었어요.
남: 멋지게 해낸걸요. 창문 옆에 있는 해변 그림이 마음에 들어요.
여: 그건 Tom 그린 거예요. 그리고 오른쪽 벽에 농구 골대를 걸었어요.
남: 그거 멋지군요. Tom이 농구를 정말 좋아하잖아요. 구석에 있는 저건 뭔가요?
여: 그건 놀이용 텐트예요. 귀엽지 않아요?
남: 그러네요. Tom을 위해 장난감 자동차도 샀군요!
여: 네. 그 애는 그걸 타면서 즐거워할 거예요. 이 포도 모양의 매트는 어때요?
남: 멋지네요. 어디서 구한 거예요?
여: 제 여동생이 우리에게 선물로 준 거예요.
남: 그렇군요. Tom은 이 방을 아주 좋아할 거예요.

05 ⑤

남: 안녕, Kara. 결혼 때문에 긴장되니?
여: 응, 조금.
남: 결혼 준비는 어떻게 되어가고 있어?
여: 음, 지난주에 드레스를 골랐고 가구도 좀 샀어.
남: 잘했네. 결혼식 축가를 불러 줄 사람은 구했어?
여: 내 사촌에게 부탁할 거야. 하지만 신혼여행이 더 걱정이야. 나 신혼여행 계획을 아직 못 세웠어.
남: 내가 너에게 괜찮은 여행사 전화번호를 줄 수 있어. 거기서 내 신혼여행을 계획해줬었거든.
여: 그거 괜찮네. 고마워. 그런데, 괜찮은 결혼식 사진작가 아니?
남: 아니. 안타깝게도, 내 결혼식 사진작가는 별로 잘 못 찍는 것 같아.
여: 그거 안됐구나. 아무튼, 도와줘서 고마워.

06 ②

[휴대전화가 울린다.]
여: 안녕, Tom.
남: 안녕, Kelly. 오늘 밤 야구 경기를 보러 갈 준비는 됐니?
여: 실은, 갈 수 없다고 말하려고 너에게 전화하려던 참이야. 정말 미안해.
남: 괜찮아. 왜 올 수 없어?
여: 일정이 바뀌었어.
남: 아, 네 여동생이 계획했던 것보다 더 일찍 널 보러 오기로 결정했대?
여: 아니야. 다음 주 목요일에 있을 발표가 내일로 바뀌었어.
남: 아, 그렇구나. 그러면 그걸 준비해야겠구나.
여: 맞아. 아무튼, 다음번에는 우리 경기 보러 갈 수 있을 거야.
남: 물론이지. 다음 경기를 보러 가도록 하자.

07 ③

남: 오늘은 머리를 어떻게 하고 싶으세요?
여: 뭔가 새로운 걸 하고 싶어서, 파마를 하고 싶어요.
남: 좋습니다. 어깨까지 오는 길이로 웨이브 파마를 하시는 것이 고객님께 잘 어울릴 것 같아요.
여: 네, 그게 바로 제가 원하는 거예요. 얼마인가요?

남: 파마는 70달러예요. 하지만 머리도 자르셔야 할 것 같네요. 그건 추가로 10달러입니다.
여: 알겠습니다. 저는 갈색으로 염색도 하고 싶어요.
남: 그건 40달러인데, 그러면 커트는 무료예요.
여: 좋아요. 그리고 이 쿠폰도 가지고 있어요.
남: 알겠습니다. 이 쿠폰으로 10달러 할인을 해드릴게요.
여: 그거 좋네요.
남: 저쪽에 있는 저 의자에 앉으세요.

문제풀이

파마 비용이 70달러이고 염색 비용이 40달러인데, 10달러 할인 쿠폰이 있으므로 여자가 지불할 금액은 총 100달러(= $70+$40-$10)이다. 염색을 하면 커트 비용은 무료라는 것에 유의한다.

08 ③

남: 이번 여름 우리의 배낭여행 계획에 대해 얘기해보자.
여: 좋아. 나는 이탈리아, 스페인, 그리고 프랑스 이렇게 세 나라에 가고 싶어.
남: 음, 프랑스 대신 스위스에 가는 건 어때? 나는 전에 프랑스에 가본 적이 있거든.
여: 좋아. 스위스도 가면 좋을 거야.
남: 7월 1일에 출발하는 비행기를 타도 괜찮을까?
여: 실은, 나는 그날 일해야 해. 7월 2일에 출발하면 안되니?
남: 아냐, 괜찮아. 그리고 우리는 돈을 아끼기 위해 유스호스텔에서 숙박해야 해.
여: 맞아. 그렇게 하면, 우리는 음식과 관광에 더 많은 돈을 쓸 수 있을 거야.
남: 응, 우리는 항공권을 포함해서 각자 3천 달러 넘게 쓸 수는 없어.
여: 나도 알아.

09 ⑤

남: 안녕하세요, 여러분! 첫 번째 연례 Berryville 책 교환 행사가 Hansontown 도서관에서 다음 주 일요일에 개최될 것입니다. 아직 상태가 괜찮은 중고책들을 좀 가져오세요. 여러분은 12권까지 책을 가져오셔서 다른 책들과 교환하실 수 있습니다. 행사는 오후 12시 30분에 시작하며 4시까지 계속될 것입니다. 책 교환은 무료이지만, 2달러의 입장료가 있습니다. 모금된 돈은 도서관의 새 책들을 구입하는 데 사용될 것입니다. 참석하시는 모든 분을 위해 간식과 음료도 무료로 제공될 것입니다. 더 많은 정보를 원하시면, 사서들 중 한 명과 이야기하세요. 여러분 모두 다음 주에 뵙길 바랍니다!

10 ①

남: Express Café에 오신 걸 환영합니다. 오늘은 무엇을 드릴까요?
여: 점심 세트 메뉴 중 하나를 주문하고 싶은데 어떤 것을 골라야 할지 모르겠어요.
남: 구운 돼지고기는 어떠세요? 그건 가장 인기 있는 세트 메뉴예요.
여: 실은, 저는 고기를 먹지 않아요. 채식주의자거든요.
남: 알겠습니다. 저희는 채식주의자를 위한 세트 메뉴도 가능합니다. 어떤 사이드 요리를 좋아하시나요?
여: 옥수수만 빼고 다 좋아요. 옥수수에는 알레르기가 있거든요.
남: 알겠습니다. 그러면 이 두 세트 메뉴 중 어느 것이 좋으세요?
여: 어디 한번 보죠. 음, 저는 커피를 안 마시니까, 저걸로 할게요.
남: 좋습니다. 앉아계시면, 주문하신 음식이 준비됐을 때 알려드릴게요.

11 ⑤

남: 안녕, Lisa. 뭘 들고 가는 거야?
여: 안녕, Mark. 내가 어제 온라인에서 산 책들이 들어 있는 상자야.
남: 무거워 보이네. 도움이 필요하니?
여: 고맙지만, 내가 들 수 있어.

문제풀이

① 물론이야, 내가 너를 도와줄 수 있어.
② 미안하지만, 난 지금 바빠.
③ 난 그것들을 저렴한 가격에 샀어.
④ 난 시험을 위해 이 책들이 필요해.

12 ④

여: 네가 다음 주에 새 일을 시작한다고 들었어. 신나니?
남: 응, 너무 기다려져! 하지만 사무실이 꽤 멀어.
여: 아, 그래? 거기까지 가는 데 얼마나 걸려?
남: 버스로 약 한 시간 걸려.

문제풀이

① 나는 다음 주 월요일에 시작할 거야.
② 그래, 하지만 그건 좋은 일자리야.
③ 좋아, 우리는 함께 갈 수 있어.
⑤ 나는 일주일 동안 일하고 있어.

13 ③

여: 안녕, Oliver. 오늘 기분은 어때?
남: 좋지 않아. 지하철에 내 가방을 두고 내렸거든. 난 보통 그런 것을 잊지 않는데 말이야.
여: 정말? 가방을 거기에 두고 온 게 확실해?
남: 응, 앉기 전에 그걸 머리 위 선반에 올려뒀던 걸 기억해.
여: 그러면 분실물 취급소에 전화해야지. 거기에 있을지도 몰라.
남: 그건 이미 해봤어. 오늘 가방을 가져온 사람은 아무도 없대.
여: 그거 안됐구나. 지하철에 언제 있었는데?
남: 바로 30분 전에.
여: 그런 경우엔, 아마 누군가가 그걸 발견했는데 아직 분실물 취급소에 가져가지 않았나 봐.
남: 한두 시간 후에 다시 전화해봐야겠다.

문제풀이

① 미안하지만, 네 가방은 여기에 없어.
② 네가 그걸 어디에 뒀는지 기억하려고 노력해봐.
④ 버스를 타는 것이 아마 더 나을 거야.
⑤ 지하철로 거기에 어떻게 가는지 잘 모르겠어.

14 ②

남: Jennifer, 너 괜찮니? 안 좋아 보이는구나.

여: 몸이 별로 좋지 않아요, 아빠.
남: 무슨 일이니?
여: 콧물이 흐르고, 재채기도 계속 해요.
남: 넌 감기에 걸린 것 같구나.
여: 저도 그런 것 같아요. 요즘 날씨가 추워서 그런가 봐요.
남: 내 생각엔 요즘 네가 입고 다니는 옷이 너무 얇은 것 같구나.
여: 하지만 그 옷들은 지금 정말 유행하는 거예요. 저는 멋있어 보이고 싶어요.
남: 네가 어떻게 보이는지는 중요하지 않단다. 네 건강이 가장 중요한 거야.
여: 아빠 말씀이 맞는 것 같아요. 아프고 싶진 않거든요.
남: 넌 지금부터 더 따뜻한 옷을 입고 목도리를 해야 해.
여: 알겠어요. 명심할게요.

문제풀이

① 날씨가 점점 추워지고 있어요.
③ 고마워요. 이제 훨씬 나아졌어요.
④ 아빠 말씀이 맞아요. 병원에 가야겠어요.
⑤ 어서 아빠와 함께 쇼핑을 가고 싶어요.

15 ④

여: Frances는 대학생이다. 어느 날, 그녀와 그녀의 두 친구들은 커피를 마시려고 만나기로 한다. 그들이 커피숍에 도착할 때, 그곳은 매우 붐빈다. 음료를 산 후, 그들은 빈 테이블 하나를 발견하지만, 의자는 두 개밖에 없다. 그들은 가게를 둘러보고 한 남자가 테이블에 혼자 앉아 있는 것을 본다. 그의 옆에 빈 의자가 하나 있지만, 그는 누군가를 기다리고 있는 것처럼 보이지 않는다. Frances는 그 의자를 자신의 테이블로 가져오고 싶어 한다. 이런 상황에서, Frances가 그 남자에게 할 말로 가장 적절한 것은 무엇인가?
Frances : 실례지만, 저희가 이 의자를 사용해도 될까요?

문제풀이

① 저희와 합석하시겠어요?
② 그런 일을 하시다니 매우 무례하셨네요.
③ 고맙지만, 저는 친구들과 같이 있어서요.
⑤ 근처에 커피숍이 있는지 아세요?

16 ⑤ 17 ③

남: 여러분이 한 곡을 성공적으로 연주하고 싶다면 무엇이 필요하다고 생각하시나요? 바로, 음악에 대한 기초 지식이 필수적입니다. 그 이유에 대한 좋은 예가 여기 있습니다. 여러분이 학교 음악 동아리의 일원이라고 상상해보세요. 여러분의 동아리는 학교 축제에서 「도레미」 곡을 연주할 것입니다. 그것은 연주하기 쉬운 곡처럼 보이지만, 실제로는 그렇지 않습니다. 여러분은 이 곡을 다른 네 명의 학생들과 함께 연주할 것입니다. 그들 중 두 명은 실로폰을 연주할 것이고, 또 다른 학생은 피아노를 연주할 것입니다. 다른 한 학생은 바이올린을 연주할 것이고, 여러분은 기타를 연주할 것입니다. 만약 여러분이 그 곡을 훌륭하게 소리 나도록 하고 싶다면, 여러분의 기타는 각각 다른 악기들과 조화를 이루어야 합니다. 따라서 여러분은 각 악기가 어떻게 소리 나는지를 이해해야 합니다. 기초적인 음악적 지식이 없으면, 그것은 매우 어려운 일이 될 수 있습니다!

DICTATION Answers

01 advantages of living in our city / built some bike lanes / be less traffic
02 Don't throw it away / rub cola on fish / makes the fish sweet
03 confirm my reservation / offering a special rate / pick up the car
04 set it up / on the right wall / have fun riding in it
05 picked out the dress / made honeymoon plans / did a good job
06 can't make it / earlier than planned / go to a game
07 get a perm / have your hair cut / have a seat in that chair
08 instead of France / Do you mind leaving / including airline tickets
09 take place next Sunday / bring up to twelve books / buy new books
10 which one to choose / would you prefer / take that one
11 need a hand with that
12 take to get there
13 left my bag / might have it / hasn't brought it
14 don't feel very well / caught a cold / How you look doesn't matter
15 is very crowded / sitting alone / take that chair to her table
16-17 a good example of why / seems like an easy song / needs to harmonize with

02 영어듣기 모의고사

본문 p.13

01 ⑤	02 ①	03 ③	04 ④	05 ①	06 ⑤
07 ③	08 ④	09 ⑤	10 ②	11 ④	12 ①
13 ①	14 ④	15 ⑤	16 ①	17 ④	

01 ⑤

여: 여러분 중 몇몇은 많은 사람들 앞에서 발표나 공연을 하는 것에 대해 긴장감을 느낄지도 모릅니다. 이러한 불안감은 '무대 공포증'이라고 불리는데, 이는 아주 자연스러운 것입니다. 다행히도, 여러분이 이것을 방지하기 위해 할 수 있는 것이 몇 가지 있습니다. 우선, 몇 번 심호흡하세요. 다음으로, 근육이 이완될 수 있도록 편하게 앉거나 서 있으세요. 그런 다음 압박감을 좀 덜기 위해 청중들을 웃게 만들도록 노력하세요. 마지막으로, 여러분이 해야 하는 것에만 집중하세요. 다른 사람들이 어떻게 생각할지에 대해서는 걱정하지 마세요. 이 간단한 것들은 여러분이 무대 공포증을 줄이고 가능한 한 최선의 결과를 얻도록 도울 수 있습니다.

02 ①

남: 안녕, Kate! 여기서 뭘 하고 있니?
여: 안녕, Jack. 연극 동아리 포스터를 붙이고 있어. 우리는 새 멤버를 찾고 있거든.
남: 그렇구나. 학교에서 허가는 받았어?
여: 응, 받았어.
남: 그렇구나. 하지만 여기에 포스터를 붙일 수 없을 것 같은데.
여: 왜 안 되는데? 이곳은 완벽한 장소야. 모든 학생들이 구내식당으로 가는 길에 이 포스터를 볼 거야.
남: 하지만 여기에 포스터를 거는 것은 허용되지 않아. 그것은 게시판에 붙여야 해.
여: 이미 게시판을 확인해 봤어. 다 차 있더라고.
남: 안타깝지만, 그곳이 포스터를 붙일 수 있는 유일한 곳이야.
여: 학교는 게시판을 하나 더 만들어야 해. 그래야 학생들이 더 많은 정보를 공유할 수 있어.
남: 동의해.

03 ③

여: 안녕하세요, 손님. 무엇을 도와드릴까요?
남: 공항 셔틀버스가 내일 몇 시에 출발하는지 좀 궁금해서요.
여: 오전 6시부터 오후 8시까지 매시간 출발합니다.
남: 좋네요. 고맙습니다.
여: 그밖에 더 물어보고 싶은 것이 있으세요?
남: 네, 한 가지 더요. 내일 몇 시에 체크아웃해야 되나요?
여: 체크아웃 시간은 오전 11시입니다.
남: 좀 이르네요. 제가 3시간 후에 체크아웃할 수 있는 방법이 있을까요?
여: 죄송합니다, 손님. 예외는 없어서요. 하지만 저희가 고객님의 짐을 안내 데스크에 맡아 두고, 고객님께서 나중에 찾아가실 수는 있습니다.
남: 아, 그게 좋겠네요.

04 ④

남: 텐트가 다 설치됐어요. 안으로 들어와요.
여: 와, 멋져 보여요. 텐트 가운데에 테이블을 놓았군요.
남: 네. 테이블에 의자도 두 개 놓았어요. 우리는 거기서 저녁을 먹을 수 있어요.
여: 멋져요! 이건 히터예요?
남: 네, 테이블 오른쪽에 작은 히터를 두었어요. 추워지면 그걸 켜면 돼요.
여: 잘했어요. 그리고 테이블 위에는 랜턴이 걸려 있네요. 우리는 밤에 책을 읽거나 게임을 할 수 있겠어요.
남: 맞아요. 오늘 크리스마스이브를 기념하기 위해 작은 크리스마스트리도 두었어요.
여: 네. 테이블 왼쪽에 그게 보이네요.
남: 이번은 근사한 휴가 여행이 될 거예요.

05 ①

남: 안녕, Mary. 네가 봄 휴가 때 플로리다에 갈 거라고 들었어.
여: 응. 내일 떠나서 다음 주까지 거기에 머무를 거야.
남: 너 신나겠다. 플로리다 방문하기 가장 좋은 시기잖아.
여: 나도 그렇게 생각해. 근데 내가 가 있는 동안 부탁 하나 해도 될까?
남: 물론. 내가 뭘 해주면 좋겠니?
여: 우편으로 반품할 게 있거든. 셔츠를 하나 샀는데 맞지 않아.
남: 그것 참 안됐다. 배송 직원이 그걸 가지러 사무실로 오는 거야?
여: 응, 내일 아침에 사무실을 방문할 거야.
남: 알겠어. 걱정하지 마. 내가 그걸 건네줄게.
여: 정말 고마워.

06 ⑤

남: BT 살롱에 오신 걸 환영합니다!
여: 안녕하세요. 제가 2시로 예약을 했어요. 제 이름은 Susan Burns입니다.
남: Susan Burns 씨요? 문제가 있는 것 같네요.
여: 제가 잠시 기다려야 하는 거라면 괜찮아요.
남: 실은, 고객님의 이름이 안 보여서요. 2시에 다른 분이 예약되어 있네요.
여: 하지만 어제 확인하려고 전화도 했는걸요.
남: 죄송합니다, 고객님. 다른 날로 예약을 변경해드릴까요?
여: 아니요, 이번 주에는 지금 말고는 시간이 없어요.
남: 죄송합니다만, 오늘 저녁까지 가능한 시간이 없습니다.
여: 어쩌다 이런 일이 일어난 것인지 이해할 수가 없군요.
남: 다시 한번 정말 죄송합니다만, 제가 해드릴 수 있는 일이 없네요.

07 ③

여: 안녕하세요. 구내식당의 식권을 좀 구입하고 싶은데요.
남: 알겠습니다. 한 장에 2달러입니다.
여: 한꺼번에 10장을 구입하면 할인이 있나요?

남: 네. 10장은 18달러이고, 20장은 35달러입니다.
여: 그러면 20장 살게요.
남: 알겠습니다. 카페 쿠폰도 사시겠어요? 한 장에 1달러인데 도서관 카페에서 커피 한 잔을 드실 수 있습니다.
여: 거기서 그냥 현금을 사용할 수는 없나요?
남: 있습니다만, 카페 쿠폰을 10장 구입하시면, 저희가 한 장을 무료로 드리거든요.
여: 아, 그거 저렴한 거 같네요. 지금 카페 쿠폰도 10장 살게요.

문제풀이

식권은 20장에 35달러이고, 카페 쿠폰은 장당 1달러인데 10장을 사기로 했으므로, 여자가 지불할 금액은 총 45달러(= $35+$10)이다.

08 ④

여: 안녕, Eric. 뭘 읽고 있니?
남: 안녕, Samantha. 나 어니스트 헤밍웨이의 「무기여 잘 있거라」를 읽고 있어.
여: 아, 나 아직 그 책 읽어보지 못했어. 무슨 내용인데?
남: 1차 세계대전 때 이탈리아에서 있었던 사랑 이야기야.
여: 아, 흥미롭게 들린다. 그건 언제 쓰인 거야?
남: 1929년에 처음 출간되었고, 그 이후로 계속 인기가 있었어.
여: 몰랐네. 근데 헤밍웨이는 미국 작가인 걸로 알고 있어. 주인공들도 역시 미국인이니?
남: 아니, 남자 주인공은 미국 군인이야. 여자 주인공은 영국 간호사야.
여: 그렇구나. 아마 난 나중에 도서관에서 빌려야겠어.

09 ⑤

남: 7월에 서울에서 한 달간의 흥미로운 행사가 있을 것입니다. 저희는 시청 앞에 특별한 시장을 세울 것입니다. 판매원들은 전통 의상을 입고, 많은 흥미로운 물건들을 판매할 것입니다. 관광객들은 전통 시장의 독특한 분위기를 경험하면서 기념품들을 구입할 수 있습니다. 그들은 또한 다양한 전통 음식들을 시식하는 것을 즐길 수 있습니다. 시장은 매일 오전 10시부터 오후 7시까지 열릴 것입니다. 주말에는 전통 음악과 춤 공연도 있을 것입니다! 많은 분들이 이 행사에 참여하시길 바랍니다.

10 ②

여: 안녕하세요. 도와드릴까요?
남: 네, 태블릿 컴퓨터를 사고 싶어요.
여: 좋습니다. 저희는 고르실 수 있는 것들이 많습니다. 주로 업무용으로 쓰실 건가요, 아니면 오락용으로 쓰실 건가요?
남: 주로 영화와 TV 프로를 보기 위해 사용할 거예요.
여: 그런 경우라면, 화면이 최소 8인치인 것을 사는 걸 추천해드립니다.
남: 좋아요, 하지만 500달러 넘게 지불하고 싶지 않아요.
여: 문제없습니다. 이것들을 한번 보세요. 8기가바이트면 고객님께 충분한 용량이 될까요?
남: 아니요, 더 많은 용량이 필요해요.
여: 그러면 두 개의 선택권이 남았네요.
남: 저는 더 큰 화면을 가진 것을 고를게요.
여: 좋습니다, 훌륭한 선택이시네요.

11 ④

여: Matthew, 주말 잘 보냈니?
남: 아니. 아버지께서 편찮으셔서, 내가 아버지를 돌봐 드려야 했거든.
여: 아, 그 얘기를 들으니 유감이야. 아버지께서는 회복하셨어?
남: 응, 지금은 훨씬 좋아지셨어.

문제풀이

① 걱정하지 마. 내가 널 도울 수 있어.
② 네가 곧 회복되길 바랄게.
③ 미안하지만, 나는 너와 함께할 수 없어.
⑤ 가족들과 함께한 좋은 시간이었어.

12 ①

남: Jenny, 너는 한가한 시간에 보통 뭘 하니?
여: 나는 영화 보러 가는 걸 정말 좋아해.
남: 아, 정말? 얼마나 자주 극장에 가는데?
여: 한 달에 적어도 두 번은 가.

문제풀이

② 나는 거기에 주로 지하철로 가.
③ 나는 로맨틱 코미디 영화를 가장 좋아해.
④ 나는 한가한 시간에 주로 책을 읽어.
⑤ 이번 주말에 영화 보는 게 어때?

13 ①

[전화벨이 울린다.]
여: 안녕하세요, Globe 여행사입니다. 무엇을 도와드릴까요?
남: 안녕하세요. 이번 여름 휴가 패키지여행에 관한 정보를 좀 얻고 싶습니다.
여: 좋습니다. 모험적인 것을 좋아하시나요, 아니면 휴식을 취하는 것을 좋아하시나요?
남: 그저 휴식을 취하는 것으로 부탁합니다.
여: 그렇다면, 어느 것이 좋으세요? 해변 온천이나 유람선 패키지 중에서요?
남: 저한테는 유람선 패키지가 더 좋을 것 같네요.
여: 좋습니다. 저희는 지중해와 카리브 해 두 곳에 호화로운 유람선 여행 상품이 있습니다.
남: 그거 좋네요. 조금 더 정보를 보내주실 수 있으세요?
여: 물론이죠. 오늘 홍보 책자를 우편으로 보내드릴 수 있어요. 주소 좀 알려주시겠어요?
남: 실은 제가 지금 출장 중이어서 우편물을 받을 수가 없어요.
여: 그러시면 고객님께 이메일로 디지털 브로셔를 보내드리겠습니다.

문제풀이

② 지중해 유람선 여행이 더 나을 것 같네요.
③ 그러면 그 정보는 우편으로 발송될 것입니다.
④ 출장은 언제 가시나요?
⑤ 더 모험적인 여행을 하시는 게 어떠세요?

14 ④

여: 역사 보고서 끝냈니, Brian?
남: 응, 그런데 오늘 그것을 제출하지 못했어.
여: 뭐라고? 그러면 그 보고서에 대해 F를 받을지도 몰라!
남: 응, 나도 알아. 정말 스트레스를 받고 있어.
여: 안됐구나. 왜 제시간에 제출하지 못했어?
남: 오늘 아침에 보고서를 끝내느라 서둘렀거든. 그러고 나서 그걸 학교에 가져오는 것을 잊었어.
여: 아마 네가 너무 서둘렀기 때문일 거야. 왜 미리 하지 않았니?
남: 나는 그냥 그 일을 미뤘어. 어쨌든 나는 보통 마감 직전에 일을 시작하거든.
여: 그거 나쁜 습관인 것 같네. 더 일찍 일을 시작하지 않으면 이런 일이 계속 생길 거야.
남: 맞아. 이번에 교훈을 얻었어.

문제풀이

① 다음엔 더 좋은 주제를 고를 거야.
② 아니, 나는 제시간에 보고서를 제출했어.
③ 걱정하지 마. 내가 널 도울 수 있어.
⑤ 나는 그렇게 생각하지 않아. 나는 보통 미리 하거든.

15 ⑤

여: Gloria는 오후에 학교에서 집으로 가고 있다. 집 근처의 공원을 가로질러 걸어가다가, 그녀는 고양이 한 마리가 바위 사이에 끼어 있는 것을 발견한다. 고양이는 진흙으로 덮여 있고, 떨고 있다. 고양이는 매우 겁먹어 보인다. Gloria는 그 고양이가 아마도 오랫동안 그곳에 끼어 있었다고 생각한다. 하지만, 그녀는 바위를 옮길 수 없기 때문에 그 고양이를 어떻게 도와야 할지 모른다. 그러므로, 그녀는 도움을 요청하기 위해 소방서에 전화를 건다. 이런 상황에서 Gloria가 소방관에게 할 말로 가장 적절한 것은 무엇인가?
Gloria : 이 고양이를 구조하러 공원으로 와주실 수 있으세요?

문제풀이

① 제 다리가 바위 사이에 끼었어요.
② 제 잃어버린 고양이를 찾는 것을 도와주셔서 감사합니다.
③ 저희 집 근처 공원에서 불이 났어요.
④ 공원에서 쓰러진 사람을 발견했어요.

16 ① 17 ④

남: 주목해주시겠습니까? 저는 여러분에게 올해의 Go-Green 음악 축제에 대해 알려드리고자 합니다. 여러분도 아시다시피, 작년의 축제는 매우 재미있었습니다. 그래서 저는 올해에도 음악과 재미있는 활동들을 즐기기 위해 여러분 모두가 다시 오시길 바랍니다. 올해는 더 많은 가수들과 밴드들이 축제에 참여할 것입니다. 또한, 여러분은 다음 사항대로 하시면 표를 특별 할인받으실 수 있습니다. 기부할 헌 옷과 재활용할 폐건전지를 가져오시거나, 녹색 옷을 입고 오시거나, 그냥 저희 소식지를 신청하십시오. 현재 주차가 자주 문제가 되기 때문에, 대중교통을 이용해주십시오. 그것은 여러분이 이곳에 오시는 것을 더 쉽게 해 줄 것이고, 환경에 더 좋을 것입니다. 마지막으로, 여러분의 개인 쓰레기를 담을 쓰레기봉투를 가져오십시오. 저는 4월 20일에 Green Park에서 여러분을 만나 뵐 것을 기대하겠습니다.

DICTATION Answers

01 it is completely natural / just focus on / reduce your stage fright
02 get permission from the school / on their way to / share more information
03 leaves every hour / need to check out / hold your luggage
04 in the center of / turn it on / a great holiday trip
05 until next week / do me a favor / Don't worry about
06 have an appointment / reschedule for a different day / how this happened
07 ten tickets at once / Each one costs / give you another coupon free
08 takes place in / was first published / check it out
09 in traditional clothing / the unique atmosphere / participate in this event
10 have many options available / pay more than / two options left
11 take care of him
12 do in your free time
13 get some information / is better for me / on a business trip
14 hand it in / forgot to bring / before the deadline
15 on her way home / is covered in mud / does not know how to help
16-17 come back again / sign up for our newsletter / for your personal trash

03 영어듣기 모의고사

본문 ▲ p.20

01 ① 02 ② 03 ④ 04 ④ 05 ⑤ 06 ⑤
07 ③ 08 ⑤ 09 ④ 10 ② 11 ① 12 ②
13 ③ 14 ③ 15 ⑤ 16 ⑤ 17 ④

01 ①

여: 안녕하세요, 쇼핑객 여러분. 저희는 여러분 모두가 저희의 연례 배낭 세일을 즐기고 계시길 바랍니다. 저희는 고객님들로부터 세일에 대해 굉장한 호응을 얻고 있습니다. 그 결과, 배낭 모델들 중 하나가 이미 품절이 되었습니다. 저희의 포스터 광고에 나와 있었던 Hello Puppy 배낭은 더 이상 구매하실 수 없습니다. 유감스럽게도, 저희는 그 제품을 더 주문할 수가 없습니다. 불편을 끼쳐 드린 점 사과드립니다. 하지만, 여전히 30~60퍼센트 할인 중인 많은 다른 배낭들이 있습니다. 저희가 여러분에게 딱 맞는 다른 배낭을 보유하고 있을 거라고 확신합니다. Super Mart를 택해주셔서 감사드리며, 남은 쇼핑 즐겁게 하시기 바랍니다.

02 ②

여: 이번 달 전기요금 고지서 봤어요?
남: 네. 정말 많이 나왔어요, 그렇죠?
여: 네, 그래요. 우리는 전기를 더 적게 사용해야 해요.
남: 하지만 우리는 이미 열심히 노력했어요. 우리가 할 수 있는 일이 더 있나요?
여: 나는 있다고 확신해요.
남: 어떻게요? 우리는 외출하기 전에 항상 가전제품 전원을 끄잖아요.
여: 그것도 좋지만, 그것들이 플러그에 꽂혀있을 때에도 여전히 전기를 사용해요.
남: 알았어요. 그것들을 사용하지 않을 때에는 플러그를 뽑아 놓을 것을 기억하기로 해요.
여: 그리고 에어컨 사용을 멈춰야겠어요.
남: 그러나 여전히 낮에는 더워요.
여: 우리는 에어컨보다 선풍기를 사용할 수 있어요.
남: 알겠어요, 시도해 볼게요. 그렇게 하는 걸 시작해보죠.

03 ④

[전화벨이 울린다.]
남: 여보세요?
여: 안녕하세요, Jeff 씨. 저는 Wendy이고 저희 책의 삽화 때문에 전화드렸어요.
남: 안녕하세요, Wendy 씨. 저는 그 일을 막 끝냈어요.
여: 좋아요. 그게 맞는지 확인하고 싶어서요. 삽화에서, 앞에 탄 남자가 뒤를 돌아보고 있는 게 맞지요?
남: 맞아요. 그리고 그는 발가락 부분이 뾰족한 부츠를 신고 있어요.
여: 알겠어요. 그가 머리에 모자를 쓰고 있나요?
남: 아, 미안합니다. 그걸 잊었네요. 이미 색칠하는 걸 끝내서 새로 스케치해야겠네요.
여: 알겠습니다. 스케치하고 채색하는 데 오래 걸릴까요?
남: 아니요, 3시간이면 될 것 같아요.
여: 알겠어요, 그럼 언제 제게 작업하신 걸 모두 보내주실 수 있나요?
남: 오늘 밤까지 이메일로 보내드릴게요.

04 ④

남: 정말 멋진 사진이구나! 동네 수영장에 수영하러 갔었니?
여: 응, 지난주에 가족들과 함께 거기에 갔었어.
남: 팔을 들고 미끄럼틀을 타고 내려오는 남자애는 즐거워 보여.
여: 그건 내 남동생이고, 튜브를 타고 떠 있는 건 나야.
남: 공을 던지고 있는 남자애들은 누구야?
여: 내 사촌들이야. 선글라스를 끼고 의자에 누워 있는 여자분이 우리 이모야.
남: 그렇구나. 수영장 반대편에 있는 남자분은 이모부야?
여: 허리에 손을 올리고 서 있는 사람? 아니. 그 사람은 안전요원이야.
남: 아, 그래? 어쨌든, 네가 재미있게 보낸 것 같아.
여: 응, 그랬어.

05 ⑤

여: Mike, 네가 다음 달에 스페인에 갈 거라고 들었어.
남: 응. 빨리 가고 싶어!
여: 네 여권은 언제 기한이 만료되는지 확인했어?
남: 응, 했어. 아직 몇 년 남았어.
여: 비행기 표는? 이미 비행기 표도 구입했니?
남: 응, 지난달에 샀어. 난 호텔도 예약했고 일정 계획도 짰어.
여: 와! 넌 갈 준비가 다 된 것 같구나.
남: 응, 하지만 내 스페인어가 걱정이야. 전혀 말할 줄 모르거든.
여: 걱정하지 마. 내가 그걸 도와줄 수 있어. 너도 알다시피, 나는 스페인어를 전공했잖아.
남: 그거 잘됐다! 나에게 기초 표현을 좀 가르쳐줄 수 있어?
여: 물론이지. 내일 오후에 여기서 만나자.

06 ⑤

여: 안녕. Eric. 너 오늘 학교 끝나고 무슨 계획 있어?
남: 안녕, Jessica. 나는 전자제품 매장에 새 노트북 컴퓨터를 사러 갈 거야.
여: 너 이미 노트북 컴퓨터 가지고 있지 않아? 네 것이 고장 난 거야?
남: 아니, 그렇지 않아. 그런데 너무 오래됐어. 7년 전에 샀거든.
여: 아, 오랫동안 그걸 사용했구나. 하지만 그게 잘 작동하면, 왜 새것을 사야 하는 거야?
남: 음, 너무 느려서 짜증이 나거든.
여: 전에 서비스 센터에 가져가 본 적은 있어?
남: 물론이지, 그런데 그걸 고치기 위해 해줄 수 있는 게 아무것도 없대.
여: 그렇구나. 그러면 좋은 걸 찾길 바라.
남: 고마워.

07 ③

남: Elaine, 오늘 저녁엔 어떤 영화를 보고 싶니?
여: 오후 6시에 하는 「Summer Love」는 어때?
남: 좋아. 카운터에서 표를 사올게.
여: 아, 잠깐만. 나한테 이 30퍼센트 할인 쿠폰이 있어.
남: 좋아. 표가 장당 10달러니까, 우리는 몇 달러를 절약할 수 있을 거야.
여: 그리고 이 극장은 우리가 Global Rewards 카드를 사용해서 결제하면 총액에서 5달러를 할인해줘.
남: 그거 좋네. 나 그 카드 있어.
여: 기다려 봐. 이 쿠폰은 3D 영화에서는 사용될 수 없다는 걸 지금 알았어. 우리가 볼 영화는 3D야.
남: 아, 그렇구나. 우리는 적어도 신용카드 할인은 받잖아.

문제풀이
남자는 한 장에 10달러인 영화 표를 두 장 구입할 것이고, 극장 할인 카드로 결제하면 5달러를 할인받을 수 있다고 했으므로, 남자가 지불할 금액은 총 15달러(= ($10×2)-$5)이다.

08 ⑤

여: 세계에서 가장 높은 장난감 블록 탑에 대해 들어본 적 있어?
남: 아니, 없어. 그것에 대해 말해줘.
여: 델라웨어 주(州)의 몇몇 학교의 미국 학생들이 만든 거야.
남: 얼마나 높았는데?
여: 그건 112피트였어. 그건 약 11층 건물의 높이야.
남: 와! 그들은 수천 개의 장난감 블록 조각들을 사용한 게 틀림없어.
여: 그건 사실 약 50만 개의 장난감 블록들로 만들어졌어.
남: 그걸 볼 수 있었으면 좋을 텐데.
여: 나도 그래. 그게 만들어지고 며칠 후에 해체된 건 너무 안타까워.
남: 학생들은 세계 신기록을 세우려고 그걸 만들었나 봐.
여: 맞아.

09 ④

남: 만약 여러분이 미국의 중부를 가로질러 여행해본 적이 있다면, 아마도 프레리도그를 보았을지도 모릅니다. 그 이름에도 불구하고, 그것은 개와는 관련이 없습니다. 그것은 사실 다람쥐의 일종입니다. 그것의 길이는 약 40센티미터이며, 풀과 작은 곤충들을 먹습니다. 프레리도그는 북미 토종이고, 지하에서 삽니다. 그들은 수 마일까지 뻗어 있고 수천 마리의 개체들을 포함할 수 있는 큰 공동체를 형성합니다. 이 공동체는 프레리도그를 코요테나 독수리 같은 포식 동물들로부터 보호하도록 돕습니다. 한 마리의 프레리도그가 위험한 동물이 접근하는 것을 보면, 그것은 모든 다른 개체들에게 안전을 위해 지하로 들어가라고 알리는 큰 소리를 냅니다.

10 ②

여: 이리 와서 이것 좀 봐줄래요, 여보?
남: 아, 이건 Olivia의 학교에서 제공하는 여름 캠프 프로그램들인가요?
여: 맞아요. 그 애가 어떤 과목을 좋아할 것 같아요?
남: 음, 그 애는 지난달에 과학 캠프를 했으니, 아마도 다른 과목을 해보고 싶어할 것 같아요.
여: 알겠어요. 그러면 고를 수 있는 것이 네 개 남아요.
남: 그 애가 얼마나 많은 현장 학습에 가고 싶어 할 것 같아요?
여: 음, 그 애는 현장 학습을 좋아하니까 적어도 세 개는 하고 싶어 할 거예요.
남: 내 생각도 그래요. 그러면 선택할 게 두 개가 남네요.
여: 하지만 나는 50달러 이상은 지불하고 싶지 않아요.
남: 저도 그래요. 그러면 선택할 수 있는 게 하나 남는군요.
여: 맞아요. 지금 등록해요.

11 ①

여: 제 뮤지컬 표 여기 있어요. 지금 입장할 수 있나요?
남: 죄송하지만, 간식과 음료를 가지고 입장하실 수 없어요.
여: 정말요? 하지만 이건 단지 팝콘과 청량음료일 뿐이에요.
남: 죄송하지만, 그게 저희 규칙이에요.

문제풀이
② 그것 중 어떤 것도 건강에 별로 좋지 않아요.
③ 모든 손님께서는 표를 보여주셔야 합니다.
④ 표는 카운터에서 구입하실 수 있습니다.
⑤ 그게 저희가 여기서 판매하는 유일한 간식입니다.

12 ②

남: Mary, 새 아파트 마음에 드니?
여: 별로 그렇지 않아. 요즘 밤에 잠을 잘 수가 없어.
남: 왜? 뭐 잘못된 거라도 있어?
여: 이웃들이 너무 시끄러워.

문제풀이
① 나는 지금 너무 졸려.
③ 너는 일찍 잠자리에 들어야 해.
④ 충분한 수면을 취하는 것이 중요해.
⑤ 나는 아파트에 사는 것에 익숙해.

13 ③

여: 안녕하세요, 손님. 뭘 찾으시나요?
남: 제 손이 너무 건조해요. 좋은 핸드크림을 추천해주시겠어요?
여: 음, 몇 가지 선택사항이 있지만, 가격들이 달라요.
남: 아, 전 가격은 신경 안 써요. 전 단지 그게 효과가 있는지 없는지만 신경 써요.
여: 알겠습니다. 이게 제일 잘 나가는 제품들 중 두 가지예요. 둘 다 비싸긴 하지만 수분 함량은 매우 높습니다.
남: 음… 이 두 제품의 차이점이 뭐죠?
여: 음, 이 제품은 비타민이 더 들어있지만, 저 제품은 노화 방지 기능이 있어요.
남: 제 손은 예민한 편이거든요. 둘 다 향은 없나요?
여: 네, 그렇습니다.
남: 둘 다 좋아 보이네요. 어떤 것이 더 좋을지 잘 모르겠어요.
여: 그럼 샘플을 좀 써보시는 건 어떠세요?

문제풀이
① 네, 더 많은 비타민을 먹을게요.
② 오늘 필요한 다른 것은 없나요?

④ 둘의 차이점이 없어요.
⑤ 손님께서는 잘 결정하신 것 같아요.

14 ③

남: 실례합니다. 책을 찾는 게 어려워서요. 저를 도와주실 수 있으세요?
여: 물론이죠. 무슨 책이죠?
남: 「Fantasy World」 책 시리즈를 찾고 있어요.
여: 알겠습니다, 확인해볼게요. *[잠시 후]* 여기 있네요. 이 서가의 세 번째 칸에 있습니다.
남: 아, 고맙습니다. 이 시리즈의 첫 편은 얼마인가요?
여: 시리즈의 각 권은 9달러입니다. 첫 편을 사길 원하시나요?
남: 전 시리즈 전체를 사고 싶어요. 전부 몇 권이 있죠?
여: 시리즈에 다섯 권이 있습니다.
남: 한 번에 모든 책을 구입하면 할인받을 수 있나요?
여: 네. 20퍼센트 할인을 받으실 수 있어요.
남: 그러면 전체 시리즈를 구입할게요.

문제풀이
① 저는 첫 편을 좋아하지 않았어요.
② 저는 그냥 그 DVD를 구입하고 싶어요.
④ 저는 그 책 시리즈를 정말 즐겼어요.
⑤ 그게 할인 판매를 하면 알려주세요.

15 ⑤

여: Amanda는 온라인 쇼핑을 하고 있고, 매우 예쁜 흰 블라우스를 발견한다. 그녀는 그것을 주문하고 그것이 배송되는 것을 며칠 동안 기다린다. 마침내 Amanda의 집으로 상품이 도착한다. 그녀는 그것을 열고 블라우스를 꺼낸다. 처음에 그것은 완벽해 보인다. 하지만 그녀가 그것을 입어보니, 너무 작다. 그녀가 상품 꼬리표를 확인해보고 그 상점이 잘못된 사이즈를 보낸 것을 알게 된다. 그녀는 온라인 상점에 전화를 걸어 그들이 실수를 했다고 말하기로 결정한다. 이런 상황에서, Amanda가 상점 직원에게 할 말로 가장 적절한 것은 무엇인가?
Amanda : 제게 잘못된 사이즈의 블라우스를 보냈어요.

문제풀이
① 그 상품은 너무 늦게 배송됐어요.
② 내가 주문했던 블라우스는 흰색이었어요.
③ 제게 보내준 블라우스가 더럽혀져서 왔어요.
④ 저는 이 블라우스가 할인 판매 중이라고 생각했어요.

16 ⑤ 17 ④

남: 여러분은 아마도 "하루에 사과 한 개면 의사를 멀리한다."라는 표현을 들어본 적이 있을 것입니다. 사과가 인간의 신체에 많은 이익을 주는 것은 사실입니다. 사과를 먹는 것은 콜레스테롤을 낮추고 여러분을 심장병으로부터 안전하게 지키도록 도울 수 있습니다. 사과는 심지어 특정 유형의 암과 노화의 징후를 예방할 수 있습니다. 하지만 단지 매일 평범한 사과를 하나씩 먹는 것은 조금 지루할지도 모릅니다. 그래서 몇 가지 맛있는 요리에 사과를 사용할 방법에 대해 몇 가지 제안을 드립니다. 우선, 저는 매우 간단한 간식을 추천하고 싶습니다. 사과를 얇게 잘라서 그것들을 아무 샐러드에 넣기만 하세요. 두 번째로, 여러분은 사과잼을 직접 만드실 수 있는데, 그것은 토스트에 발라먹으면 맛있습니다. 그리고 누가 사과 파이를 잊을 수 있을까요? 이 디저트는 사과로 가득 차 있답니다! 단지 이 단 음식을 구울 때 버터와 설탕을 더 적게 쓰는 것을 잊지 마세요!

DICTATION Answers

01 already sold out / apologize for any inconvenience / the rest of
02 use less electricity / before we go out / rather than the air conditioner
03 want to make sure / finished coloring it / email it over
04 going down the slide / lying on the chair / with his hands on his waist
05 I can't wait / booked my hotel / Can you teach me
06 have any plans after school / which annoys me / fix it
07 save us a few dollars / That's good to know / At least
08 was built by / made up of / set a world record
09 In spite of / are native to / makes a loud noise
10 Which subject / four left to choose from / sign her up
11 you can't enter with
12 can't sleep at night
13 the prices vary / high in water content / They both look great
14 having trouble finding / let me check / get a discount
15 is shopping online / tries it on / made a mistake
16-17 keeps the doctor away / some suggestions for / is full of apples

04 영어듣기 모의고사

본문 p.27

01 ②	02 ①	03 ②	04 ④	05 ②	06 ⑤
07 ③	08 ④	09 ④	10 ①	11 ④	12 ④
13 ③	14 ⑤	15 ⑤	16 ②	17 ⑤	

01 ②

여: 안녕하세요, 여러분! 저는 학교 신문의 편집장인 Lauren Cooper입니다. 최근 우리 학교의 올해 네 번째 신문이 출간되었습니다. 저는 여러분 모두가 그것을 즐겁게 읽으셨기를 바랍니다. 저희는 현재 신문기사를 쓸 기자들을 찾고 있습니다. 만약 여러분이 기자가 되기 위해 지원하고 싶다면, 두 편의 기사를 제출해주십시오. 각 기사는 학교생활에 관한 것이어야 합니다. 아울러, 각 기사는 약 500자가 되어야 합니다. 마감일은 6월 15일입니다. 선배 기자들이 여러분의 기사를 읽고 평가할 것입니다. 결과는 6월 22일에 학교 게시판에 게재될 것입니다. 시간을 주셔서 감사합니다!

02 ①

남: 이봐, Cindy. 너 최근에 녹차를 많이 마시는구나.
여: 안녕, Logan. 맞아. 녹차에는 건강상 이점이 많아서 나는 요즘 물도 안 마시고 있어.
남: 있잖아, 좋은 것도 너무 지나치면 해가 될 수 있어.
여: 무슨 말이야? 난 기분이 정말 좋아. 난 피곤함도 거의 느끼지 않고 있어.
남: 나도 알아. 그건 녹차에 카페인이 들어 있기 때문이야. 카페인을 너무 많이 섭취하는 것은 좋지 않아.
여: 정말? 난 몰랐어.
남: 그건 또한 너의 칼슘 수치를 낮추고 너의 뼈를 약하게 할 수 있어.
여: 와, 놀랍다.
남: 그러니 너는 녹차를 마시는 것에 주의해야 해.
여: 알았어, 지금부터 덜 마시도록 해볼게.

03 ②

여: 실례합니다. 제가 차를 어디에 주차하면 될까요?
남: 방문 목적이 무엇인가요?
여: 그냥 몇 시간 정도 제 친구를 만나러 여기에 왔어요.
남: 그러면 저한테 주차권을 받으셔야 해요.
여: 정말 그게 필요한가요? 전 여기 잠시만 있을 건데요.
남: 네, 안전상의 이유 때문이에요. 저희는 건물에 들어오시는 모든 방문자들의 기록을 가지고 있어야 해요.
여: 알겠습니다.
남: 방문하신 분 성함과 친구분의 아파트 호수를 적어주세요. 양식의 나머지는 제가 작성할게요.
여: 알겠습니다. *[잠시 후]* 여기 있어요.
남: 좋아요. 이제 이 주차권을 차에 두시고, 지하에 있는 방문자 주차장에 주차하세요.
여: 알겠습니다. 감사합니다.

04 ④

남: 너는 어제 친구와 함께 도시 정원에 갔었니?
여: 응, 갔었어. 그곳은 아름다웠어.
남: 정원 중앙에 큰 풍차가 있다고 들었어.
여: 맞아. 그리고 풍차 뒤에는 둥근 연못이 있어.
남: 튤립도 있었어? 그건 내가 가장 좋아하는 꽃이야.
여: 응, 풍차 앞에 튤립들이 있었어.
남: 정말 멋질 것 같아. 거기서 점심도 먹었니?
여: 응. 풍차 왼편에 있는 하트 모양의 조각상 앞에서 점심을 먹었어.
남: 근사한 것 같아.
여: 나는 또 그네도 탔어. 풍차 오른편에 있는 나무에 매달려 있었거든.
남: 재미있었겠다!

05 ②

여: Patrick, 너 지쳐 보인다. 무슨 일 있어?
남: 안녕, Amy. 나 어젯밤에 잠을 한숨도 못 잤어.
여: 왜? 아팠어?
남: 아니. 내일까지 내야 하는 미술 과제물이 있거든. 밤새 그걸 작업했어.
여: 그래서 그걸 끝냈어?
남: 아니, 못 끝냈어. 나는 아직 온라인으로 정보를 더 찾아야 해.
여: 너는 과제물을 끝내자마자 휴식을 좀 취해야겠다.
남: 그러고 싶어. 하지만 나는 모레 역사 수업 발표도 있어.
여: 너 정말 바쁘구나. 내가 너를 도와줄 수 있는 게 있어?
남: 실은, 있어. 나 대신 책 몇 권을 도서관에 반납해줄 수 있어?
여: 물론이지, 문제없어.

06 ⑤

남: 이봐, Angela! 면접은 어땠어?
여: 실은, 괜찮았는데, 나는 더 잘할 수도 있었어.
남: 음, 너는 몇 주 동안 면접 준비를 정말 많이 했잖아. 네 노력이 결실을 맺을 거라고 확신해.
여: 고마워. 네 말이 맞으면 좋겠어.
남: 표정이 좋아 보이지 않네. 불안하니?
여: 음, 나는 그 일을 정말 원하는데, 아직 회사로부터 아무 소식도 못 들었거든.
남: 언제 결과를 발표할 거래?
여: 이번 주 말까지 알려준다고 했어. 난 떨어진 것 같아.
남: 진정해. 이제 겨우 목요일이야. 네가 그 일자리를 얻을 거라 확신해.
여: 고마워, Robert.

07 ③

남: 안녕하세요. 도와드릴까요?
여: 네. 제 항공편 예약을 취소하고 싶어요.
남: 알겠습니다, 하지만 취소 수수료가 있습니다, 고객님.
여: 얼마죠?
남: 출발 72시간 이전에 취소하시면 티켓 가격의 5퍼센트이고, 그 이후에

취소하시면 10퍼센트입니다.
여: 알겠어요. 그래도 취소하고 싶어요.
남: 알겠습니다. 예약 번호를 알고 계세요?
여: 네, KA50501이에요.
남: 잠시만 기다려주세요. *[잠시 후]* 네, Jolson 씨. 시카고행 티켓을 두 장 예약하셨네요, 맞죠?
여: 네. 그 비행기는 내일 밤 9시에 출발하고요.
남: 맞아요. 각 티켓은 200달러였네요.
여: 네. 예약 취소해주세요.

문제풀이
내일 출발하는 항공권 두 장을 취소하였으므로 취소 수수료는 10퍼센트가 발생하고, 각 항공권의 가격이 200달러였으므로 여자가 환불받을 금액은 총 360달러(= $200×2×0.9)이다.

08 ④

남: 오늘 밤에 새로 생긴 이탈리아 식당에서 외식하는 게 어때요?
여: 우체국 근처에 있는 Jessie's Kitchen 말하는 거예요?
남: 맞아요. 봐요! 방금 블로그에서 그 식당 후기를 발견했어요.
여: 뭐라고 적혀 있어요?
남: 방문한 대부분의 사람들이 훌륭한 서비스와 맛있는 음식에 만족했네요.
여: 좋아요. 그들의 특선 요리가 뭔가요?
남: 그들의 특선 요리는 갈릭 크림 파스타예요.
여: 좋아요. 가격은 어떤가요?
남: 가장 비싼 음식이 10달러 이하예요.
여: 값이 아주 적당하네요. 집에서 얼마나 걸리죠?
남: 우리 집에서 거기까지 걸어서 5분밖에 걸리지 않아요.
여: 완벽해요! 가요!

09 ④

남: 안녕하세요! 흥미진진한 행사에 대해 여러분께 말씀드리려고 합니다. 8월 15일에 Newport 항구에서 야외 (수영) 경기가 있을 예정입니다. 1킬로미터 경기와 5킬로미터 경기가 있을 것입니다. 18세 이상의 모든 수영 선수들이 참가하시는 것을 환영합니다. 각 경기의 우승자들은 Newport 헬스클럽의 1년 회원권을 받으실 것입니다. 프로 수영 선수들은 참가할 수는 있으나 상을 받을 자격은 없습니다. 15달러의 입장료가 있으며, 온라인으로 사전에 등록하실 수 있습니다. 더 많은 정보가 필요하시면, 저희 웹사이트를 방문해주세요!

10 ①

[전화벨이 울린다.]
여: Starlight 극장입니다. 무엇을 도와드릴까요?
남: 안녕하세요. 단체 학생 영화 표를 예약하려고 전화했는데요.
여: 알겠습니다. 어떤 영화를 보고 싶으시죠?
남: 학생들이 코미디를 좋아할 것 같아요. 현재 상영하는 코미디 영화가 있나요?
여: 네, 선택하실 수 있는 몇 가지 영화가 있습니다. 학생들이 몇 살이죠?
남: 14살입니다.
여: 알겠습니다. 고르실 수 있는 영화가 아직 두 편 있네요. 3D 영화를 보시겠어요, 아니면 2D 영화를 보시겠어요?
남: 학생들은 3D로 보는 것을 좋아할 것 같아요.
여: 그렇다면 이 영화가 최고의 선택일 것 같네요.
남: 좋습니다, 그걸로 할게요.

11 ④

여: 지난 주말에 뭘 했니, Kevin?
남: John Wiltshire 작가의 연설을 들었어.
여: 그의 발표는 어땠어?
남: 훌륭했어. 나는 정말 감동받았어.

문제풀이
① 그것은 도서관에서 열렸어.
② 응, 나는 그의 책을 전에 읽어본 적이 있어.
③ 나는 연설을 잘했고 긴장하지 않았어.
⑤ 나는 연설을 잘하는 방법을 배우고 싶어.

12 ④

남: 안녕, Julia. 널 오랫동안 못 봤어! 그동안 어떻게 지냈어?
여: 안녕, Alfred! 나쁘지 않았어. 너 이 거리에 살지, 그렇지?
남: 응, 맞아. 너는 여기 무슨 일이야?
여: 할머니를 뵈러 왔어.

문제풀이
① 나는 지하철을 탔어.
② 아니, 나는 여기서 먼 곳에 살아.
③ 나는 아직 아무것도 안 샀어.
⑤ 나는 어제 길에서 너를 봤어.

13 ③

여: 뭘 하고 있니, Brad?
남: 새 직원이 한 명 필요해서 구인 광고를 쓰고 있어.
여: 네 식당에? 다른 요리사를 뽑는 거야?
남: 아니. 아르바이트 웨이터 중 한 명이 그만두고 싶다고 말했어. 그를 대체해야 해.
여: 정말? 너도 알다시피 내 사촌이 아르바이트를 찾고 있어.
남: Jake 말하는 거야? 그 애는 학생이잖아, 그렇지 않아? 나는 낮에 일할 수 있는 사람이 필요하거든.
여: 그거 잘됐다. 그 애는 이번 학기에 야간 수업만 들어.
남: 식당에서 일해 본 경험은 있어? 나는 경험이 있는 웨이터를 원하는데.
여: 내가 알기로는, 그 애는 해산물 요리 식당에서 2년 동안 일했어.
남: 그러면 그에게 날 보러 오라고 해줘.

문제풀이
① 네 요리사는 요리를 잘하는 것 같아.
② 그거 안됐구나. 그는 곧 직업을 구할 거야.
④ 문제없어. 어제 괜찮은 웨이터를 고용했거든.
⑤ 미안하지만, 오늘 밤엔 해산물을 먹고 싶지 않아.

14 ⑤

여: 나는 우리 여행이 너무 기대돼! 너는 어때?
남: 나도 그래. 난 우리가 다음 주에 아프리카에 있을 거라는 게 믿어지지 않아.
여: 우리가 완벽히 준비되었는지 확인해보자.
남: 우리는 옷을 싸는 걸 끝냈고, 나는 가방에 구급약을 좀 넣었어.
여: 좋아. 우리가 거기서 아프면 그게 필요할지도 몰라.
남: 맞아. 그리고 너 국제 운전 면허증은 발급받은 거지?
여: 응. 지난주에 했어.
남: 잘했어. 돈도 조금 환전했어, 맞지?
여: 응, 했어. 내 지갑에 남아프리카 돈이 있어.
남: 좋아. 그리고 우리는 호텔을 예약했어, 맞지?
여: 응, 내가 어제 예약을 확인했어.

문제풀이

① 그건 여행사 직원의 실수야.
② 걱정하지 마. 네가 짐을 싸는 걸 도와줄게.
③ 고마워. 내일 진료를 받을 거야.
④ 너는 어느 나라를 방문할지 정했어?

15 ⑤

여: Hal은 아파서 역사 수업에 빠졌다. 나중에 그의 반 친구인 Julie는 그가 걱정이 되어 그에게 전화를 한다. 그녀는 수업 시간에 어떤 장을 다루었는지 말해주고, 프로젝트를 위해 반을 그룹으로 나눈 것을 그에게 설명한다. 그들은 같은 그룹에 속해 있다. 그가 없이 그룹의 나머지 구성원들은 이미 프로젝트를 위한 계획을 세웠다. Hal은 그녀가 그 계획에 대해 이메일로 정보를 더 보내주기를 원한다. 이런 상황에서, Hal이 Julie에게 할 말로 가장 적절한 것은 무엇인가?
Hal : 나에게 프로젝트 계획을 이메일로 보내줄 수 있어?

문제풀이

① 친절하게 조언해줘서 고마워.
② 나는 다음 주에는 나아질 것 같아.
③ 내가 너희 팀에 들어가도 괜찮겠어?
④ 수업 시간에 어떤 장을 다루었니?

16 ② 17 ⑤

남: 안녕하세요, 여러분! 저희는 여러분들께 North Lake 호텔에 생길 몇 가지 신나는 변화에 대해 알려드리고자 합니다. 1980년 이후로, North Lake 호텔은 도시의 가장 인기 있는 리조트 중 하나가 되었습니다. 올해, 저희는 객실을 포함한 일부 시설을 개선할 계획입니다. 이러한 개선 덕분에 여러분은 더 편안하고 신나는 시간을 보내실 수 있을 것입니다. 공사는 3월 1일에 시작될 것입니다. 저희의 성대한 재개장은 10월 1일이 될 것입니다. 저희의 객실은 더 크고 더 현대식일 것이며, 저희 건물은 새로운 옥상 수영장을 갖추게 될 것입니다. 저희는 또한 두 개의 식당을 보수하고 리조트 로비에 24시간 커피숍을 만들 것입니다. 보수 공사 기간 동안 저희 리조트를 이용하실 수 없는 점은 정말 유감입니다. 하지만 이번 가을에, 여러분은 틀림없이 이 모든 변화에 감동하실 것입니다. 항상 그랬듯이, 여러분들의 관심에 감사드리고, 10월에 뵙겠습니다!

DICTATION Answers

01 looking for reporters / In addition / be posted on
02 can be harmful / weaken your bones / from now on
03 the purpose of your visit / for a short time / fill in
04 in the center of / in front of / hung from a tree
05 due tomorrow / get some rest / return some books
06 it went well / announce the results / get the job
07 cancel my flight reservation / before departure / departs tomorrow night
08 near the post office / were very satisfied with / How far is it
09 eighteen years or older / qualify for prizes / register beforehand
10 reserve some movie tickets / enjoy a comedy / two options available
11 listened to a speech
12 What brought you here
13 replace him / during the day / a waiter with experience
14 Let's make sure / exchanged some money / booked the hotel
15 missed history class / divided into groups / by email
16-17 improve some facilities / renovate our two restaurants / surely be impressed by

05 영어듣기 모의고사

본문 ☁ p.34

01 ⑤	02 ③	03 ④	04 ⑤	05 ④	06 ②
07 ②	08 ⑤	09 ④	10 ③	11 ②	12 ⑤
13 ①	14 ①	15 ⑤	16 ①	17 ⑤	

01 ⑤

여: 안녕하세요, 학생 여러분. 저는 교감인 Hernandez입니다. 오늘 제가 여러분께 드릴 말씀이 있습니다. 많은 학생들이 학교의 오래된 구내식당에 대해 불평해 왔습니다. 다행히, 우리는 학교 구내식당을 보수하기로 결정했습니다. 학생들은 다음 주 월요일부터 한 달 동안 식당을 이용할 수 없습니다. 식당은 훨씬 더 넓어질 것이고, 새 테이블들과 의자들이 추가될 것입니다. 유리창이 주방 앞에 설치될 것이므로 여러분은 식당 내부를 볼 수 있습니다. 구내식당의 외관뿐 아니라 메뉴도 변경될 것입니다. 곧 새롭고 개선된 구내식당을 즐길 준비를 하세요. 감사합니다.

02 ③

남: 왜 재활용 쓰레기를 다시 가져왔어요, 여보?
여: 건물 관리인이 그걸 지금 버릴 수 없다고 했어요.
남: 왜요? 오늘은 월요일이고 재활용 쓰레기 배출일인 걸요.
여: 관리인이 월요일 오후 6시부터 9시까지만이라고 하네요. 나는 한 시간 늦었고요.
남: 겨우 세 시간이라고요? 그건 너무 짧아요! 우리가 그 시간까지 귀가하지 못하면 어떻게 하죠?
여: 모르겠어요. 그것이 이 아파트 건물의 규칙 중 하나예요.
남: 이해할 수가 없군요. 이 모든 쓰레기가 쌓여서 온 집안을 악취가 나게 만들 거예요.
여: 나도 알지만 그들은 쓰레기장을 가능한 한 깔끔하게 유지하고 싶어 해요.
남: 음, 그래도 시간은 연장돼야 한다고 생각해요.

03 ④

여: 안녕. 무슨 일이니?
남: 무릎에서 피가 나요.
여: 아, 좀 보자. 어쩌다 이렇게 됐니?
남: 축구 경기에서 공을 차는 도중에 넘어졌어요.
여: 학교 운동장에서 그런 거니?
남: 네, 맞아요. 골을 놓쳤어요.
여: 그거 안됐구나. 많이 아프니?
남: 아뇨, 단지 약간 쓰려요.
여: 다행히도, 그렇게 심각해 보이지는 않구나. 상처를 소독해줄게. 그 위에 반창고도 붙여줄게. *[잠시 후]* 좀 낫니?
남: 그런 것 같아요. 고맙습니다. 이제 교실로 돌아갈게요.
여: 더러운 손으로 상처를 만지지 않을 것을 기억하렴.
남: 그럴게요. 고맙습니다.

04 ⑤

여: Paul, 나 오늘 Luigi's 식당에 다녀왔어. 거기 개조되었더라고.
남: 아, 정말? 어떻게 변했어?
여: 음, 줄무늬 벽지를 꽃무늬 벽지로 바꿨어.
남: 그거 멋지다. 낡은 직사각형 테이블들도 바꿨어?
여: 바꿨어. 지금은 직사각형 테이블들 대신 새 둥근 테이블들이 있어.
남: 각 테이블 위에는 여전히 꽃병이 한 개씩 있고?
여: 아니, 대신에 각 테이블에는 작은 양초가 하나씩 있어.
남: 멋지다! 낡은 의자들은 어때? 전에는 등받이가 없었잖아.
여: 이제 등받이가 있는 일반 의자들이 있어.
남: 훨씬 더 좋아졌겠네.
여: 유일하게 바꾸지 않은 건 천장에 있는 공 모양의 전등이었어.

05 ④

남: 너 기분이 안 좋아 보여. 무슨 일이야?
여: 오늘 오후에 Western 쇼핑센터로 영화를 보러 갔었어.
남: 거기서 무슨 일이 있었니?
여: 응. 주차장에 주차를 했는데, 요금으로 40달러를 청구했어.
남: 40달러를 냈다고? 너무 많잖아. 영화 표를 보여주면 할인을 해주잖아, 그렇지 않아?
여: 내가 영화 표를 보여주었는데, 그 서비스를 중단했다고 그랬어.
남: 그래서 전액을 내야 했어?
여: 응. 그들은 고객들에게 정책의 변화에 대해 알렸어야 했어.
남: 거기에 전화를 하거나 그곳 웹사이트에 가보는 게 어때? 네가 어떻게 느끼는지 말해.
여: 온라인으로 내 의견을 말할 거야. 그러면 아마 적어도 안내판은 붙이겠지.

06 ②

여: 소풍 가 있는 동안 내 문자에 왜 대답하지 않았니, Dan?
남: 죄송해요, 엄마. 할 수가 없었어요.
여: 왜? 전화 배터리가 다 됐었니?
남: 아뇨. 실은, 휴대전화를 잃어버렸어요.
여: 또? 너는 몇 달 전에도 휴대전화를 잃어버렸잖아. 이번에는 그걸 어디서 잃어버렸니?
남: 아마 공원 가는 길에 지하철에서인 것 같아요. 지하철에서 휴대전화를 사용했던 것이 기억나요. 그런데 내린 후에 찾을 수가 없었어요.
여: 지하철역에 연락해봤니?
남: 네, 하지만 거기서는 그걸 찾지 못했대요.
여: 아, 이런! 네가 또 휴대전화를 잃어버리다니 믿을 수가 없구나.

07 ②

여: Ice World에 오신 걸 환영합니다. 무엇을 도와드릴까요, 손님?
남: 안녕하세요. 티켓 세 장이 필요합니다. 성인 한 명과 어린이 두 명 입니다.
여: 네, 성인은 6달러이고, 어린이는 4달러입니다. 스케이트는 가져오셨나요?
남: 아뇨. 스케이트도 세 켤레 빌려야 해요.

여: 스케이트 대여료는 모두 2달러니까 6달러입니다.
남: 괜찮네요. 여기 제 신용카드요.
여: 아! 이 신용카드로 결제하시면 티켓에서 50퍼센트 할인을 받으실 수 있어요.
남: 아주 좋네요.
여: 분명히 하자면, 전체 금액에 대한 할인은 아니고요. 티켓에 한해서만 적용된다는 말이에요.
남: 알겠습니다.

문제풀이

티켓 요금은 14달러(= $6+($4×2))이고, 스케이트 대여료는 6달러(= $2×3)인데, 이 중 티켓 요금만 50퍼센트 할인이 되므로 남자가 지불할 금액은 총 13달러 (= ($14×0.5)+$6)이다.

08 ⑤

남: Jane, 다음 주에 미술 전시회에 갈래?
여: 아, 그래. 나 미술 좋아해. 그건 어떤 전시회야?
남: 포스트 모더니즘 작가들에 의해 그려진 100점이 넘는 미술품들을 전시할 거래.
여: 어떤 종류의 미술품이 전시되는데?
남: 회화랑 조각품들이야.
여: 그거 멋지다. 전시회가 언제야?
남: 7월 10일에서 7월 20일까지 열릴 거야. 다음 주 금요일 오후에 같이 가는 게 어때?
여: 그거 좋아.
남: 시내에 있는 Western 미술관에서 열려.
여: 나 거기 알아. 거긴 정말 크잖아.
남: 맞아. 시내에서 점심을 먹고 전시회에 가자.

09 ④

남: 안녕하세요, 여러분. 오늘 우리는 소시지 나무에 관해 배울 것입니다. 그것은 아프리카의 열대 지역에서 자랍니다. 연중 비가 내리는 곳에서, 소시지 나무는 녹색을 유지합니다. 그것은 꽃과 독특한 열매 때문에 종종 장식용으로 재배됩니다. 나무의 빨간색 꽃은 해가 질 때 핍니다. 그리고 꽃이 바닥에 떨어지면, 그 자리에서 열매가 자랍니다. 열매는 매우 큰데, 길이는 거의 30센티미터에서 100센티미터이며 폭이 18센티미터 정도이고, 소시지처럼 생겼습니다. 그러나 그것은 먹을 수는 없습니다. 지역민들은 이것을 피부병을 치료하기 위해 사용합니다. 이 나무는 놀라움으로 가득 차 있습니다, 그렇지 않습니까?

10 ③

남: Marathon 컴퓨터 학원에 오신 걸 환영합니다. 무엇을 도와드릴까요?
여: 안녕하세요. 전 컴퓨터 강의를 신청하고 싶어요.
남: 저희는 많은 강좌들이 있습니다. 어떤 수업을 찾고 계신가요?
여: 저는 제 업무를 위해 몇몇 프로그램을 배우고 싶어요. 근데 엑셀을 더 배워야 해요.
남: 저희의 많은 강좌들이 엑셀 프로그램에 대한 교육을 포함합니다.
여: 그거 좋네요. 또 저는 평일에만 여기 올 수 있어요.
남: 그러시다면 이 강좌들 중에서 고르실 수 있습니다.
여: 알겠습니다. 음, 저는 오후 6시까지 근무를 해야 해서 그 시간 전에 있는 건 불가능해요.
남: 그렇다면 이 수업이 가장 적합하겠네요.
여: 아, 그거 좋겠네요. 다음 달부터 시작할게요.

11 ②

여: 안녕하세요. 저는 새 모자가 필요해요. 인기 있는 것들을 보여주실 수 있나요?
남: 이걸 써 보시는 게 어때요? 이게 요즘 가장 인기가 많아요.
여: 음, 디자인은 좋은데 저는 빨간색을 좋아하지 않아요.
남: 그렇다면 이 파란색 모자는 어떠세요?

문제풀이

① 자 어서 한번 써 보세요.
③ 그 디자인은 저에게 어울리지 않는 것 같아요.
④ 저희 매장에서 쇼핑해주셔서 감사합니다.
⑤ 죄송합니다만, 빨간색은 품절이에요.

12 ⑤

남: 너 스트레스 받는 거 같은데. 괜찮은 거야?
여: 아니, 내 컴퓨터가 계속 다운돼.
남: 누가 곧 그 문제를 해결하러 오기로 했어?
여: 응, 오늘 점심 이후에 누군가 올 거야.

문제풀이

① 응, 나 보통 스트레스를 받아.
② 그거 말이 되네. 그건 매우 힘들어.
③ 일이 정말 편해.
④ 내 컴퓨터가 다운되는 게 멈춘 것 같아.

13 ①

남: 아, 이런! 비가 오네요!
여: 오늘 아침에 일기 예보를 확인했는데, 비에 대해선 아무 말도 하지 않았어요.
남: 맞아요. 나는 출근할 때 우산을 가져오지 않았어요.
여: 비가 곧 멈출 것 같지가 않네요.
남: 그럴 것 같아요. 우산 있으세요?
여: 실은, 난 사무실에 항상 우산 하나를 놔둬요.
남: 당신은 준비가 잘돼 있네요. 나는 우산을 사러 가게에 잠깐 들러야겠어요.
여: 집에 다른 우산들이 있지 않아요?
남: 있어요, 하지만 무슨 다른 방법이 있겠어요? 지금 하나를 사지 않으면, 나는 집에 가는 길에 완전히 젖을 거예요.
여: 잠깐만요! 서랍에 여분의 우산이 하나 있는 게 막 기억났어요.
남: 그러면 내게 그걸 빌려줄 수 있어요?

문제풀이

② 비가 곧 그칠 것 같아요.
③ 나는 일기 예보를 더 이상 믿을 수 없어요.
④ 나와 함께 가게에 가는 게 어때요?
⑤ 당신은 지금 당장 우산을 사야 해요.

14 ①

남: Kelly, 너는 한가한 시간에 주로 뭘 하니?
여: 음, 나는 기타를 쳐. 그건 내가 가장 좋아하는 취미 중 하나야.
남: 아, 정말? 난 네가 기타를 칠 수 있는지 몰랐어. 얼마나 오래 쳤어?
여: 내가 아주 어렸을 때부터 쳐왔어. 아빠가 나에게 연주하는 법을 가르쳐주셨어.
남: 와! 너는 기타를 아주 잘 치겠구나!
여: 그렇지는 않아. 여전히 배울 게 많아.
남: 사실, 나는 기타 치는 걸 배우는 데 항상 흥미가 있었어.
여: 그건 재미있어, 그런데 많이 힘들 수도 있어.
남: 괜찮아. 네가 언젠가 나에게 가르쳐줄 수 있을까?
여: 물론이지. 이번 주 일요일에 시간 되니?

문제풀이

② 너는 계속해서 더 연습을 해야 해.
③ 아니, 나는 기타를 쳐 본 적이 없어.
④ 그래, 나는 훌륭한 선생님들을 많이 알아.
⑤ 나는 네가 좋은 기타를 고르는 걸 도와줄 수 있어.

15 ⑤

여: Justin은 옷 가게에서 쇼핑을 하고 있다. 그는 멋진 셔츠를 발견한다. 가격표에는 그것이 50달러라고 쓰여 있다. 그런 다음 그는 가격표에서 그것이 50퍼센트 할인된다고 쓰여 있는 스티커를 발견한다. Justin은 그 셔츠에 대한 비용으로 25달러면 괜찮은 가격이라고 생각해서, 그는 그것을 사기로 결정한다. 그는 그 셔츠를 계산대로 가져가고, 계산대 점원은 그것을 스캔한다. 그녀는 그에게 가격이 50달러라고 말한다. Justin은 혼란스럽고 오류가 있음이 틀림없다고 생각한다. 이런 상황에서, Justin이 계산대 점원에게 할 말로 가장 적절한 것은 무엇인가?
Justin : 가격이 잘못된 것 같아요.

문제풀이

① 신용카드로 지불해도 될까요?
② 저는 50퍼센트 할인 쿠폰이 있어요.
③ 이 셔츠가 제게 어울린다고 생각하세요?
④ 이 셔츠는 다른 색으로도 나오나요?

16 ① 17 ⑤

남: 주목해 주세요, 모든 학생 여러분! 외국어 실력을 향상시키고 싶나요? 외국어를 학습하는 가장 좋은 방법 중 하나는 다른 나라에서 시간을 보내는 것입니다. 이것은 어렵고 비용이 많이 들 수 있습니다. 하지만, 쉬운 해결책인 저희의 해외 교환 학생 프로그램이 있습니다. 여러분은 다른 나라에서 공부하고 그 문화에 몰두할 수 있습니다. 게다가, 비용도 적절합니다. 학생들은 캐나다, 프랑스, 중국, 일본의 4개국 학교들 중에서 고를 수 있습니다. 지원하시려면, 학생 센터에 오셔서 신청서를 작성하세요. 여러분은 국가를 선택하도록 요청받을 것이고, 여러분이 기숙사나 민박 가정에서 머무는 것을 선호하는지에 대한 질문을 받을 것입니다. 프로그램의 일원이 되기 위해서 학생들은 학점이 3.0 이상이어야 하고 면접 과정을 성공적으로 통과해야 합니다. 지원 마감일은 5월 15일입니다. 더 많은 정보를 얻으시려면, 학교 홈페이지에 있는 공고문을 읽어 주세요.

DICTATION Answers

01 have complained about / be much wider / get ready to enjoy
02 throw it away / can't get home / should be extended
03 I fell over / put bandages on them / Remember not to touch
04 has been renovated / instead of / chairs with backs
05 Did something happen / pay full price / give my opinion online
06 lost my cell phone / on my way to / contact the subway station
07 rent three pairs of skates / pay with this credit card / on the total price
08 go to an art exhibition / will be held / Let's have lunch
09 throughout the year / when the sun sets / looks like
10 sign up for / come here on weekdays / be best for you
11 try this on
12 fix the problem
13 left for work / stop by a store / have an extra umbrella
14 in your free time / taught me how / a lot of hard work
15 The tag says / pay for the shirt / must be an error
16-17 learn a foreign language / fill out an application / pass the interview process

06 영어듣기 모의고사

본문 ▸ p.41

01 ④	02 ⑤	03 ②	04 ④	05 ①	06 ②
07 ④	08 ③	09 ④	10 ②	11 ②	12 ①
13 ⑤	14 ④	15 ③	16 ③	17 ②	

01 ④

여: 안녕하세요, 여러분. 오늘 오후 협조해주셔서 감사합니다. 소방서에서 전체 건물을 확인했는데, 다행히도 화재는 없었다고 말했습니다. 화재경보기가 울렸지만, 그것은 오작동했던 것이었습니다. 그들은 5층 주방에서 발생한 연기가 아마도 경보기를 울렸을 것이라 추정하고 있습니다. 하지만 아직 확실하지는 않습니다. 저희는 문제가 무엇이었는지 알아보기 위해 경보 시스템을 계속 시험할 것입니다. 갑작스러운 혼란으로 인해 아마도 놀라셨겠지만, 걱정하실 필요가 없습니다. 여러분의 도움과 이해에 다시 한번 감사드립니다.

02 ⑤

남: 안녕, Amy. 너 왜 그렇게 걷고 있어?
여: 실은, 오늘 아침부터 허리가 아팠어.
남: 아마 네 매트리스가 문제인 것 같구나.
여: 네 말이 맞아. 그건 너무 오래됐거든. 새것을 사야겠어. 괜찮은 브랜드를 추천해줄 수 있니?
남: 브랜드가 가장 중요한 것이라고 생각하지 않아.
여: 어떤 매트리스가 나에게 적합한지 어떻게 알 수 있어?
남: 그건 쉬워. 매장에 가면, 네가 평소 잠을 자는 자세로 그 위에 누워보면 돼.
여: 아하.
남: 각 매트리스 위에서 대략 5분에서 10분 정도 누워 있어 봐. 그러면 그것이 편한지 아닌지 알 수 있어.
여: 알겠어. 고마워, Jack.

03 ②

여: 안녕하세요, Anderson 선생님. 부탁 좀 드려도 될까요?
남: 물론이야, Cindy. 뭔데?
여: 과제물 기한을 연장해줄 수 있으세요?
남: 하지만 그건 오늘까지야. 마감일을 혼동했니?
여: 그건 알고 있었지만, 그저 그걸 끝낼 시간이 없었어요.
남: 그건 좋은 변명이 아니야. 시간이 더 필요했다면, 나에게 더 일찍 알렸어야 했어.
여: 사실, 제 컴퓨터가 고장이 나서 그걸 타자로 칠 수가 없었어요.
남: 그랬어?
여: 네. 그다음에 저는 과제물을 전부 손으로 쓰려고 했는데, 그건 대략 10페이지예요. 그래서 그걸 제시간에 끝낼 수 없었어요.
남: 그렇다면 내일 제출해도 돼.
여: 감사합니다! 그때까지 제출할 것을 약속드리겠습니다.

04 ④

[휴대전화가 울린다.]
남: 안녕, 여보. 출장은 어때요?
여: 아, 안녕. 좋아요. 새로운 집으로 짐을 옮기는 걸 도와주지 못해서 미안해요.
남: 괜찮아요. 모든 것이 근사해 보여요. 나는 창문 앞에 탁자와 의자 두 개를 놓았어요.
여: 좋아요. 텔레비전도 설치했어요?
남: 네. 창문의 왼쪽 벽에 있어요.
여: 그렇군요. 시계는요?
남: 그건 텔레비전 위에 있어요.
여: 그거 마음에 드네요.
남: 하지만 새로 산 정사각형 모양의 깔개는 바닥에 깔지 못했어요. 그건 너무 커서 지난 집에 있던 둥근 걸 깔았어요.
여: 괜찮아요. 자전거 기구는 어디에 두었어요?
남: 깔개 옆에요. 우리는 TV를 보면서 운동할 수 있어요.
여: 좋은 생각이에요.

05 ①

[휴대전화가 울린다.]
여: 여보세요?
남: 안녕, 여보. 당신이 내게 전화했던 걸 방금 알았어요.
여: 당신 지금 어디예요?
남: 회사에서 집으로 가는 중이에요. 신선한 과일을 좀 사려고 슈퍼마켓에 들렀어요.
여: 좋아요. 어쨌든, 당신이 집에 오는 길에 나를 위해 약을 좀 사다 줄 수 있는지 물으려고 전화했었어요.
남: 물론이죠. 당신 아파요?
여: 네. 온종일 몸이 좋지 않았는데, 이제는 열이 나요.
남: 당신을 병원에 데리고 가면 어떨까요?
여: 음, 체온이 그렇게 높지 않아서 약만 먹어도 충분할 것 같아요.
남: 알겠어요. 곧 집에 갈게요.

06 ②

남: 너 지쳐 보여, Sarah.
여: 응, 피곤해. 요즘 전혀 잠을 잘 자지 못하고 있어.
남: 다음 주 시험 때문에 스트레스받는 거야?
여: 그건 아냐. 나는 많이 공부했고 시험은 상당히 잘 준비했어.
남: 그러면 네 이웃들 때문이야? 아직도 밤에 매우 시끄럽게 하니?
여: 그들은 더 이상 시끄럽지 않아. 그냥 날씨 탓인 것 같아.
남: 정말? 우리 집은 밤에 상쾌하고 시원한데.
여: 그건 네가 산 근처에 살기 때문이지. 우리 집에서는 선풍기를 켜도 여전히 너무 더워.
남: 아, 그거 안됐다. 곧 나아지길 바랄게.

07 ④

남: 안녕하세요. 저희 부모님을 위해 같은 운동화 두 켤레를 사고 싶은데요.

여: 알겠습니다. 여기 있는 이 회색 운동화는 어떠세요? 이건 매우 인기 있어요.

남: 좋아 보이네요. 얼마죠?

여: 한 켤레당 70달러입니다.

남: 240 사이즈와 280 사이즈 있나요?

여: 실은, 이 스타일로 280 사이즈는 없어요.

남: 그러면 저 다른 회색 운동화는요?

여: 이건 최신 모델이라서 한 켤레당 10달러 더 비쌉니다. 하지만 그건 두 가지 사이즈 다 있어요.

남: 그러면 그걸 살게요. 그런데, 제 회원 카드로 5퍼센트 할인받을 수 있는 거죠, 맞죠?

여: 맞습니다.

문제풀이

남자는 한 켤레당 80달러인 최신 모델의 운동화를 두 켤레 사기로 했고 회원 카드로 5%를 할인받을 수 있으므로, 남자가 지불할 금액은 총 152달러(= $80×2×0.95)이다.

08 ③

여: 이봐, Greg. 우리 학교의 학생회장 선거가 3월 25일이야.

남: 맞아! 두 후보 중에서 누구에게 투표할지 정했어?

여: 아직 모르겠어, 하지만 Kate에게 투표할까 생각 중이야. 그녀는 학교에 새로운 정원을 만들겠다고 공약했거든.

남: 그거 멋지겠다. 하지만 나는 다른 후보인 Richard가 좋아.

여: 그는 점심시간을 늘리겠다고 공약했지, 그렇지 않아?

남: 맞아. 나는 정말 점심시간이 더 길면 좋겠어.

여: 그것도 좋아, 하지만 그 공약은 이행되기가 어려울 것 같아.

남: 아마도. 어쨌든 나는 아직 정하지 못했어.

여: 그러면 그것에 대해 조금 더 생각해 봐. 그리고 금요일에 구내식당에서 투표하는 것 잊지 마.

남: 물론이지.

09 ④

남: 안녕하세요, 여러분. 저는 스프링필드 스포츠 클럽이 11월 10일에 마라톤을 개최하는 것을 알리고자 합니다. 이 행사의 목적은 희귀병 환자들을 위한 기금을 마련하는 것입니다. 마라톤은 시내의 시청에서 시작하여 동부 스프링필드의 언덕을 지나갈 것입니다. 그것은 시내에 있는 스프링필드 도서관 앞에서 끝날 것입니다. 모든 참가자들은 무료 티셔츠를 받을 것이고, 우승자는 500달러를 받을 것입니다! 15세 이상이라면 누구나 10달러의 참가비를 내고 참가하실 수 있습니다. 경기에 참가하고 싶다면, 11월 1일까지 저희 웹사이트에서 등록하십시오.

10 ②

[전화벨이 울린다.]

여: 안녕하세요. Phuket Seaside 여행사입니다.

남: 안녕하세요. 다음 주말에 해변에 있는 별장을 예약하고 싶습니다.

여: 좋아요. 여전히 많은 해변 별장들이 이용 가능해요. 침실은 몇 개가 필요하세요?

남: 저를 포함해서 네 명이니까, 적어도 두 개의 침실이 필요해요.

여: 좋습니다. 선택 사항으로 수영장을 더 좋아하시나요, 아니면 바비큐를 더 좋아하시나요?

남: 음, 전 아이들을 데려갈 거라 수영장이 좋겠어요. 그들은 수영장을 좋아할 거예요.

여: 알겠습니다. 그리고 예산이 얼마인가요?

남: 음… 1박에 300달러 이상은 쓰고 싶지 않아요.

여: 그렇다면 이 별장이 고객님께 제격일 것입니다.

남: 좋습니다. 그걸 지금 당장 예약할게요.

11 ②

여: 이 식당의 음식은 맛이 좋아, 그렇지 않니?

남: 응, 그래. 우리가 지난번에 왔을 때보다 훨씬 좋아.

여: 음식이 많이 나아졌어. 뭐가 변한 것인지 궁금해.

남: 내 생각에는 새로운 요리사를 구한 것 같아.

문제풀이

① 지난번이 훨씬 더 나았어.
③ 고맙지만, 나는 이미 배가 불러.
④ 그것은 전부 내 새로운 조리법 덕분이지.
⑤ 나는 더 이상 이 식당을 오지 않을 거야.

12 ①

남: 실례합니다. 게시하셨던 일자리가 아직 있나요?

여: 네. 그 자리는 아직 비어 있어요.

남: 잘됐네요. 지원서를 어떻게 제출하죠?

여: 이메일로 보내시면 됩니다.

문제풀이

② 아니요, 저희는 아무것도 게시하지 않았어요.
③ 저희는 비어 있는 일자리가 많습니다.
④ 저희는 이미 적절한 사람을 찾았습니다.
⑤ 내일까지 그것을 제출하셔야 해요.

13 ⑤

남: 안녕, Vanessa. 너 오늘 기분이 안 좋아 보여. 무슨 일 있어?

여: 안녕, Eric. 음, 나는 학교 뮤지컬의 배역을 위해 오디션을 봤어.

남: 그거 재미있겠다! 문제가 뭔데?

여: 나는 오디션에서 최선을 다했는데 배역을 얻지 못했어.

남: 아, 그거 정말 안됐구나.

여: 많이 연습했는데, 나는 노래를 잘 못 하나 봐.

남: 그건 사실이 아니야. 전에 네가 노래하는 걸 들어봤는데, 너는 정말 좋은 목소리를 가졌어!

여: 그렇게 말해줘서 고마워. 하지만 나는 자신감을 모두 잃었어.

남: 힘내! 다른 기회들이 있을 거야.

문제풀이

① 나는 아직 네가 노래하는 것을 들어본 적이 없어.
② 나에게 노래를 잘 부르는 법을 가르쳐 줘.
③ 그게 네가 항상 연습이 필요한 이유야.
④ 네가 긍정적인 태도를 가져서 기뻐.

14 ④

[전화벨이 울린다.]

남: 안녕하세요. Capital Electric입니다. 무엇을 도와드릴까요?

여: 안녕하세요. 저희 집 전기요금 고지서에 문제가 있는 것 같아요.

남: 문제가 무엇인지 말씀해주실 수 있으세요?

여: 지난달 요금이 너무 많이 부과됐어요. 저는 혼자 살아서 고지서에 적힌 만큼 많은 전기를 사용한다고 생각하지 않아요.

남: 알겠습니다. 고객님의 성함과 주소를 알 수 있을까요?

여: Jodie Smith입니다. 그리고 샌프란시스코 가(街) 52번지에 살아요.

남: 잠시만 기다려주세요. *[잠시 후]* 아, 지지난달 요금을 납부하지 않으셨네요.

여: 아, 이 고지서가 두 달 치라는 말씀이세요?

남: 네. 4월이랑 5월이요.

여: 죄송합니다. 4월 요금을 납부하지 않은 것이 이제 기억나네요.

문제풀이

① 맞아요. 저는 전기를 더 적게 써야 해요.
② 그러면 오늘 환불받을 수 있나요?
③ 그 문제에 대해 전화 주셔서 감사합니다.
⑤ 다음에는 같은 실수를 하지 마세요.

15 ③

여: Sam은 겨울 방학을 맞아 그의 가족을 방문하러 시카고에 있는 집으로 가고 있다. 그가 기차역에 도착하자, 그는 처음이라 승차권 발매기를 사용하는 데 어려움을 좀 겪는다. 마침내 그는 표를 구입할 수 있게 된다. 그는 기차에 타서 좌석을 찾기 시작한다. 곧 그는 좌석을 찾지만, 놀랍게도 거기에는 이미 한 여자가 앉아 있다. 그는 자신의 표를 다시 확인하는데, 그곳이 맞는 좌석이다. 이런 상황에서, Sam이 여자에게 할 말로 가장 적절한 것은 무엇인가?

Sam : 실례지만, 제 자리에 앉아계신 것 같아요.

문제풀이

① 이 기차는 시카고행인가요?
② 승차권 발매기가 어디 있나요?
④ 제가 옆에 앉아도 괜찮으세요?
⑤ 차장을 불러 주실래요?

16 ③ 17 ②

남: 안녕하세요, 청취자 여러분! 여러분 모두가 가장 좋아하는 노래를 위한 (주파수) 89.1에 맞춰주셔서 감사합니다! 그런데 먼저, 이 중요한 안전 수칙에 대해 공유해드리고자 합니다. 사고와 부상은 어디서나 일어날 수 있습니다. 심지어 여러분이 집에 있을 때에도 항상 조심해야 합니다. 그러면 여러분 자신과 가족을 어떻게 안전하게 지킬 수 있을까요? 우선, 화재가 가정 내 부상의 주요 원인들 중 하나입니다. 여러분은 소화기, 작동하는 연기 경보기, 그리고 가족 대피 계획을 확실하게 갖추고 있도록 하십시오. 특히 어린 아이들에게 가정 내 또 다른 위험은, 중독입니다. 의약품, 세정액, 그리고 화장품은 모두 독이 될 수 있습니다. 이 모든 것들이 아이들의 손에 닿지 않도록 하십시오. 심지어 정원도 위험한 장소가 될 수 있습니다. 정원에 있는 버섯과 다양한 다른 식물들은 사실 독성이 있을지도 모릅니다. 이러한 것들을 명심하시면, 여러분은 가정을 더 안전하게 만들 수 있습니다.

DICTATION Answers

01 checked out the whole building / was working improperly / don't have to be anxious
02 has been in pain / right for me / find out
03 give me an extension / should have let me know / hand it in
04 couldn't help move / above the television / beside the rug
05 on my way home / pick up some medicine / have a fever
06 Are you stressed out / making a lot of noise / turn on the fan
07 purchase two pairs / in a size / I'll take those
08 promised to make / difficult to carry out / don't forget to
09 hold a marathon / in front of / enter the race
10 reserve a beach house / Would you prefer / spend more than
11 much better than
12 submit my application
13 look down today / did my best / lost all confidence
14 seems to be a problem / was charged too much / for two months
15 has some trouble using / gets on the train / to his surprise
16-17 tuning in to / the major causes of injury / can all be poisonous

07 영어듣기 모의고사

본문 ▲ p.48

01 ⑤	02 ③	03 ⑤	04 ⑤	05 ②	06 ④
07 ①	08 ④	09 ④	10 ③	11 ②	12 ④
13 ⑤	14 ④	15 ③	16 ②	17 ②	

01 ⑤

여: 요즘 아이들은 공부를 하거나 컴퓨터를 하느라 책상 앞에 앉아서 너무 많은 시간을 보냅니다. 이 때문에, 그들은 충분한 운동을 하지 않습니다. 최근 한 연구에 따르면, 많은 어린아이들이 하루에 겨우 15분 동안만 운동을 한다고 합니다. 이는 건강에 좋지 않고 그들이 비만이 되게 합니다. 의사들은 5세에서 12세 사이의 아이들이 매일 적어도 한 시간 동안은 운동을 해야 한다고 말합니다. 그러므로 우리는 아이들이 시간을 보내는 방식을 바꿀 필요가 있습니다. 그들은 컴퓨터 게임을 하는 데 시간을 덜 쓰고 활동하는 데 더 많은 시간을 써야 합니다.

02 ③

여: 안녕, Mark. 유럽 여행은 어땠어?
남: 재미있었어. 하지만 나는 나쁜 경험을 하나 했어.
여: 아, 무슨 일이었어?
남: 여행이 거의 끝나갈 무렵에, 누군가 내 배낭을 훔쳐갔어. 나는 카메라와 노트북 컴퓨터를 잃어버렸어.
여: 정말 안됐다. 그래서 현지 경찰에게 그걸 신고하고 조서를 받았니?
남: 아니, 그러지 않았어. 조서가 왜 필요해?
여: 만약에 네가 그것을 보험 회사에 제출하면 약간의 돈을 돌려받을 수 있어.
남: 사실, 난 보험이 없었어. 그게 필요할 거라고 생각하지 않았거든.
여: 정말 안타깝다! 해외여행을 할 때는 언제나 여행자 보험에 들어야 해.
남: 음, 다음에 해외에 가면, 그것을 명심할게.

03 ⑤

여: 마침내 당신을 직접 만나서 너무 좋아요!
남: 저를 보러 와 주셔서 감사합니다.
여: 오늘 당신의 공연은 환상적이었어요. 저는 당신이 노래 부른 것이 너무 좋았어요!
남: 정말 감사합니다. 오늘이 이 작품에서 제 마지막 공연이었던 걸 알고 계셨나요?
여: 아, 정말요? 음, 당신이 무대에 다시 서는 것을 보고 싶네요. 다음엔 무엇을 하실 건가요?
남: 실은, 내년에 「Mamma Mia」에 출연할 거예요. 다음 달부터 연습을 시작할 거예요.
여: 정말 흥미로워요! 그건 제가 가장 좋아하는 뮤지컬 중 하나예요.
남: 아, 그래요? 그러면 꼭 오셔서 보세요.
여: 물론이죠. 그런데 사인 좀 받을 수 있을까요?
남: 그럼요.

04 ⑤

[휴대전화가 울린다.]
남: 여보세요?
여: 안녕하세요, Steven 씨. Carol Jones예요. 수리가 어떻게 되어가고 있는지 물어보려고 전화했어요.
남: 아, 안녕하세요, Carol 씨. 실은, 지금 막 끝냈어요. 저희는 막 새 세면대를 왼쪽 벽에 설치했어요.
여: 좋아요. 그 위에 거울이 있나요?
남: 네, 그리고 당신이 요청했던 것처럼 욕조는 뒤편 오른쪽 구석에 있어요.
여: 완벽해요. 수건걸이는요?
남: 그건 욕조 옆 벽에 있어요.
여: 좋아요, 그리고 샤워 커튼도 설치했나요?
남: 네. 커튼이 욕조 앞에 있어요.
여: 음, 모든 것이 멋진 것 같아요. 어서 새 욕실을 보고 싶네요!
남: 직접 오셔서 보셔야 해요!

05 ②

남: 이봐, Jessica! 뭘 하고 있어?
여: 안녕, Nathan. 온라인에서 괜찮은 자전거를 찾고 있어.
남: 아, 하나 사려고?
여: 응, 왜냐하면 매일 아침 학교에 자전거를 타고 가기로 결심했거든.
남: 그거 좋네. 그건 네 건강을 증진시키고 돈을 절약해줄 거야.
여: 하지만 나는 가격이 적당한 자전거를 온라인에서 찾을 수가 없어. 저렴한 자전거를 파는 웹사이트 알아?
남: 아니, 하지만 자기 자전거를 팔고 싶어 하는 친구가 있어.
여: 정말? 얼마나 오래된 건데? 너무 오래된 건 원하지 않거든.
남: 그 애가 그걸 올해 사서 그건 괜찮아 보여.
여: 잘됐다! 그 애한테 전화해서 아직 그걸 팔고 싶어 하는지 물어봐 줄 수 있어?
남: 물론이지.

06 ④

남: 너 이번 주말에 Kelly의 생일 파티에 갈 거야?
여: 정말 가고 싶은데 못 가.
남: 왜? 도서관에서 아르바이트를 해야 해?
여: 아니, 나는 학교 끝나고 주 중에만 일해.
남: 내가 맞혀볼게. 너 시험 있구나, 그렇지?
여: 아니, 연극 동아리에서 곧 공연이 있어. 이번 주말에 연극 리허설을 해.
남: 아, 그래. 맞아. 어떻게 되어가고 있어?
여: 재미있어! 어쨌든, 나는 리허설에 있어야 해서 갈 수 없어.
남: 끝나고 잠깐 들를 수 있어?
여: 그럴 수 있을지 잘 모르겠어. 리허설이 길어질지도 모르거든.
남: 그 말을 들으니 안타깝다. 어쨌든, 난 네 공연에 꼭 갈게!

07 ①

여: 맛있었어. 갈 준비 됐니?

남: 응. 계산서를 보자. 우리는 샐러드를 먹었고, 그건 5달러야.
여: 우리는 또 파스타와 피자를 먹었는데, 그것들은 15달러와 18달러야.
남: 그리고 음료 각각 2달러씩이야.
여: 아, 나에게 '한 잔을 사면 한 잔은 무료'인 음료 쿠폰이 있어.
남: 잘됐다. 그러면 우리는 한 잔 값만 내면 돼.
여: 나는 회원 카드도 있어. 우리가 쿠폰을 사용하고 회원 할인을 함께 받을 수 있을까?
남: 어디 보자. *[잠시 후]* 쿠폰에 회원 카드와 함께 사용될 수 있다고 써 있어.
여: 그거 잘됐네. 그러면 우리는 10퍼센트 할인도 받을 수 있어.
남: 좋아!

문제풀이

샐러드와 파스타, 피자의 가격을 합하면 38달러(= $5+$15+$18)이고 음료는 쿠폰을 사용하면 2달러만 내면 되므로 지불할 음식값은 총 40달러이다. 그런데, 회원 카드로 10퍼센트 할인을 받을 수 있으므로, 두 사람이 지불할 금액은 36달러이다.

08 ④

여: 안녕하세요, 대출 창구가 어딘지 알려주실 수 있나요?
남: 여기입니다. 이 도서관에 오신 게 처음이신가요?
여: 네, 저는 신입생이에요.
남: 아, 그러면 학생증은 가지고 있나요? 책을 빌리려면 그게 필요해요.
여: 다행히 어제 받았어요. 여기 있습니다.
남: 잘됐네요. 그러면 책을 빌릴 수 있습니다.
여: 알겠습니다. 책을 얼마나 오래 대출할 수 있나요?
남: 2주까지요. 만약 연체되면, 한 권당 하루 25센트입니다.
여: 알겠습니다. 또, 도서관은 얼마 동안 여나요?
남: 일요일을 제외하고 매일 오전 8시부터 오후 10시까지 열어요. 하지만 오후 9시 이전에만 책을 대출할 수 있습니다.
여: 알겠습니다. 도와주셔서 감사합니다!

09 ④

남: 여러분은 오카피에 대해 들어본 적이 있나요? 오카피는 중앙아프리카 우림에서 볼 수 있는 동물입니다. 다리에 있는 검정색과 흰색의 줄무늬 때문에, 여러분은 아마도 그것이 얼룩말과 밀접한 관련이 있다고 생각할지도 모릅니다. 하지만, 이것은 사실 기린과 더 밀접하게 관련이 있습니다. 기린처럼 이것은 길고 유연한 혀를 가지고 있습니다. 오카피는 심지어 혀를 이용해 눈꺼풀을 청소하기도 합니다! 그들은 또한 큰 귀를 가지고 있는데, 그것은 작은 소리도 들을 수 있고 오카피가 포식 동물들을 감지하는 것을 도와줍니다. 오카피는 콩고 민주 공화국의 국가적 상징물로 여겨지며 그 나라의 화폐에 실려있습니다.

10 ③

여: 여보, 여기 괌에 있는 호텔 목록이 있어요.
남: 아, 고마워요. 어느 호텔을 고를까요?
여: 먼저 위치를 결정해야 할 것 같아요. 당신은 해변에 있는 호텔이 좋아요 아니면 시내에 있는 호텔이 좋아요?
남: 나는 바다가 내려다보이는 호텔에서 머물고 싶어요. 경치를 즐기고 싶거든요.
여: 저도 그래요. 그리고 아침 식사는 필요하지 않을 것 같아요.
남: 사실은, 나는 더 편리하기 때문에 아침 식사를 제공하는 호텔을 원해요.
여: 음… 당신 말이 맞아요. 조식을 제공하는 호텔을 고르는 게 더 낫겠어요.
남: 네. 그러면 우리에게는 두 가지 선택권이 있네요.
여: 그런 경우라면, 더 저렴한 것이 더 낫죠. 다른 것들을 즐기기 위해 돈을 절약할 수 있으니까요.
남: 나도 그렇게 생각해요. 지금 당장 방을 예약하죠!

11 ②

여: Paul, 네가 내년에 외국에서 공부할 계획이라 들었어.
남: 응, 나는 그게 정말 신이 나.
여: 어느 나라로 갈지 정했어?
남: 나는 캐나다에서 공부할 거야.

문제풀이

① 나는 여기 머물기로 결정했어.
③ 그 계획은 취소됐어.
④ 나는 단지 쉬고 싶어.
⑤ 나는 내년 3월에 갈 거야.

12 ④

남: 너 뭘 하고 있니, Hailey?
여: 학교 웹사이트에서 오늘 점심 메뉴를 찾고 있어.
남: 웹사이트에서? 그게 거기에 게시되는지 몰랐어.
여: 응, 매주 그걸 새로 올려줘.

문제풀이

① 너는 요리를 잘하는구나.
② 제가 주문을 받아도 될까요?
③ 미안하지만 난 벌써 점심을 먹었어.
⑤ 그는 웹사이트에 자기 사진을 올렸어.

13 ⑤

[휴대전화가 울린다.]
여: 안녕, Nick. 어떻게 지내?
남: 나쁘진 않은데, 오늘 저녁 식사에 제시간에 갈 수 없을 것 같아.
여: 하지만 그건 Matthew의 생일 파티야. 넌 우리가 그를 위해 만든 동영상을 놓칠 거야.
남: 알아. 일을 마치고 바로 가고 싶었는데, 일이 생겼어.
여: 무슨 일인데?
남: 오늘이 딸아이의 학교에서 열리는 '아버지 방문의 날'인 걸 완전히 잊었지 뭐야.
여: 아, 이해해. 그걸 놓쳐서는 안 되지. 너와 네 딸에게 중요한 날이잖아.
남: 맞아. 하지만 행사가 끝나자마자 Matthew의 생일 파티에 갈게.
여: 네가 너무 늦지 않길 바라.
남: 알겠어. 가능한 한 빨리 거기에 도착하도록 할게.

문제풀이

① 미안하지만, 나는 거기에 갈 수 없어.
② 나는 회의에 제시간에 갈게.
③ 그를 위한 동영상을 함께 만들자.
④ 내 딸이 매우 행복해할 거라고 생각해.

14 ④

남: Sally, 너 스트레스를 받는 것 같아. 무슨 일이야?
여: Sheridan 선생님께서 내주신 조별 과제 때문이야.
남: 왜? 너무 어려워?
여: 아니, 그런데 우리 조원 몇몇이 전혀 일을 안 하고 있어.
남: 무슨 말인지 알겠어. 항상 그런 사람들이 있지.
여: 그러고는 그들은 열심히 일하는 사람들과 같은 성적을 받아. 그건 공평하지 않아.
남: 나도 작년에 조별 프로젝트에서 비슷한 문제를 겪었어.
여: 너는 그걸 어떻게 해결했어?
남: 우리는 각 조원에게 그룹 과제를 위한 다른 역할을 주었어. 그래서 과제를 끝내려면 모두가 참여해야만 했어.
여: 다음에 우리 조와 만날 때 그렇게 해봐야겠어.

문제풀이
① 응, 요리사가 너무 많으면 수프를 망치지.
② 나는 모두에게 같은 성적을 주지 않을 거야.
③ 나는 프로젝트를 위해 더 열심히 일할 것을 약속할게.
⑤ 네가 왜 그 문제를 해결할 수 없었는지 이제 알겠어.

15 ③

여: Jane의 어머니는 저녁 식사를 요리 중이다. 그녀는 Jane에게 가게에 가서 몇 가지 재료를 사 오라고 부탁한다. 슈퍼마켓에서 Jane은 세 가지 물건을 고른다. 그녀가 그것들을 계산하러 갈 때, 그녀는 5개 물품 이하를 가진 사람들을 위한 특별한 줄에서 기다린다. 하지만 그녀는 그녀 앞에 있는 남자가 5개보다 많은 물품들을 가지고 있는 것을 알아챈다. 사실, 그는 대략 15가지의 물품들을 가지고 있다. Jane은 아주 바쁘고 더 오래 기다리고 싶지 않다. 이런 상황에서, Jane이 남자에게 할 말로 가장 적절한 것은 무엇인가?
Jane : 실례지만, 당신은 잘못된 줄에 서 계세요.

문제풀이
① 이 물품들을 계산하려면 어디로 가면 되나요?
② 저 대신 슈퍼마켓에 다녀올 수 있으세요?
④ 다른 사람들 앞에 끼어드는 것은 옳지 않아요.
⑤ 죄송하지만, 저는 당신이 거기에 서 있는 것을 보지 못했어요.

16 ② 17 ②

남: 환영합니다, 학생 여러분. 제 이름은 Andy Wilson이고, 이번 학기에 서양 철학 입문을 가르칠 것입니다. 이 수업의 목표는 여러분에게 서양 철학에 대한 기초적인 개관을 알려주는 것입니다. 우리는 이 강의실에서 매주 화요일과 금요일 오후 3시부터 4시 30분까지 만날 것입니다. 교재로는 「서양 철학의 역사」를 사용할 것입니다. 저는 또한 온라인에 부가적인 읽기 자료들을 게시할 것입니다. 여러분의 성적은 여러분이 이번 학기 동안 쓸 세 편의 에세이를 바탕으로 정해질 것입니다. 물론 여러분의 기말고사도 성적에 영향을 줄 것입니다. 저는 또한 여러분의 출석과 수업 참여를 볼 것입니다. 저는 이번 학기에 여러분에게 강의를 하는 것이 아주 기대됩니다. 질문이 있으면, 이메일을 통해 언제든지 제게 연락해도 됩니다.

DICTATION Answers

01 get enough exercise / at least one hour / being active
02 had one bad experience / get some money back / keep that in mind
03 meet you in person / begin practicing / get your autograph
04 coming along / like you requested / in front of
05 searching online for / any affordable bicycles / call and ask him
06 but I can't / rehearsing for a play / take a while
07 look at the check / get one free / can be used with
08 to borrow a book / Up to two weeks / every day except Sunday
09 in the rainforest / catch small sounds / a national symbol of
10 overlooking the sea / more convenient / the cheaper one
11 which country to go to
12 it was posted
13 can't make it / something came up / an important day for
14 look stressed out / It's not fair / be involved to finish
15 pick up / in the special line / in a rush
16-17 a basic overview / based on three essays / look forward to teaching

08 영어듣기 모의고사

본문 ▸ p.55

01 ②	02 ⑤	03 ③	04 ④	05 ②	06 ①
07 ③	08 ⑤	09 ⑤	10 ②	11 ⑤	12 ③
13 ②	14 ⑤	15 ②	16 ⑤	17 ⑤	

01 ②

여: 여러분은 물리학이 어려운 과목이라고 생각하시나요? 물리학 수업 시간에 지루하고 졸린가요? 자, 여러분이 저희의 새로운 박물관에 오시면, 물리학이 얼마나 흥미로운지 아실 수 있습니다. 이번 주 금요일, 저희 박물관은 마침내 대중들에게 개관할 것입니다. 저희는 여러분에게 물리학이 재미있고 매력적이고 흥미진진하다는 것을 보여드리고 싶습니다. 다른 박물관에서와는 달리, 여러분은 모든 것을 만지고 교감하는 것이 허용됩니다. 여러분은 저희의 재미있는 활동들을 즐기실 수 있습니다. 저희는 오전 10시부터 오후 6시까지 개관하지만, 매주 화요일에는 휴관합니다. 만약 더 많은 정보를 원하시면, 저희의 웹사이트인 www.funphysics.com을 방문해주십시오.

02 ⑤

여: 안녕, Robert. 뭘 읽고 있어?
남: 내 여동생의 프랑스어 수업 과제물을 읽고 있어. 그녀가 나한테 오류를 확인해달라고 부탁했거든.
여: 네 역사 과제는 다 했어?
남: 아니, 아직. 나는 또 친구가 수학 시험공부를 하는 것도 도와주기로 했어.
여: 내 생각에는 너 자신의 과제를 먼저 끝내야 할 것 같아.
남: 나는 도움이 필요한 사람들에게 '안돼'라고 말하는 게 너무 어려워. 나는 누군가를 실망시키고 싶지 않아.
여: 나도 알아. 하지만 넌 때로는 다른 사람들의 부탁을 거절해야 해. 그들도 이해할 거야.
남: 네 말이 맞아. 나는 지금부터 내 일을 먼저 끝내도록 노력할 거야.
여: 그거 좋은 생각일 것 같아.

03 ③

남: 무엇을 도와드릴까요?
여: 저는 디자인 경연 대회에 제 디자인 작품집을 제출하려고 왔습니다.
남: 아, 죄송합니다만, 마감일 이후로는 어떤 것도 받을 수가 없습니다.
여: 뭐라고요? 오늘이 디자인을 제출하는 마지막 날인 걸로 생각했는데요.
남: 사실, 어제까지 마감이었습니다.
여: 하지만 저는 몇 달 동안이나 제 디자인 작업을 했어요.
남: 제출 마감 시간에 대해서는 우리가 따르고 있는 매우 엄격한 규정이 있습니다.
여: 그건 명백한 착오였어요. 제 디자인은 모두 어제 끝났어요.
남: 정말 안됐지만, 제가 할 수 있는 것이 없군요.
여: 이번 한 번만 예외를 둘 수는 없는 건가요?
남: 죄송합니다만, 우리는 모든 참가자를 공정하게 대해야 합니다.

04 ④

여: 여기로 와서 이것 좀 봐줄 수 있어요, 여보?
남: 물론이죠. 뭔데요?
여: 나는 막 주방 찬장을 정리하는 걸 끝냈어요.
남: 차와 커피를 가운데 칸에 두었어요?
여: 네, 그리고 과일 주스는 맨 아래 왼 칸에 두었어요.
남: 그렇군요, 그리고 면류는 맨 위 오른 칸에 모여 있군요. 그런데 꿀 병은 왜 맨 위 칸에 있어요? 위험할 수도 있을 것 같아요.
여: 우리는 그걸 자주 사용하지 않아서 괜찮을 것 같아요.
남: 아, 그렇군요.
여: 그리고 우리가 거의 사용하지 않는 커피머신은 찬장 꼭대기에 올려놨요.
남: 그거 좋네요. 당신이 정리한 방식이 다 마음에 들어요.

05 ②

여: 오늘 오후에 뭘 할 거니, Tommy?
남: 2시에 영어 수업에 가야 해요.
여: 음, 나는 막 식료품을 사러 가려던 참이야. 나 대신 뭐 좀 해줄 수 있니?
남: 그럼요. 제가 뭘 하길 원하세요, 엄마?
여: 수업에 가기 전에 새에게 모이를 주고 꽃에 물을 줄 수 있니?
남: Sarah가 이미 오늘 아침에 그걸 했어요.
여: 그렇구나. 음, 나는 또 누군가가 설거지를 하고 너희 아빠의 드라이 클리닝한 세탁물을 찾아왔으면 해. 그것들 중 하나를 해줄 수 있니?
남: 제가 수업 끝나고 집에 오는 길에 드라이 클리닝한 세탁물을 찾아올게요.
여: 좋아. 그러면 Sarah에게 설거지를 하라고 부탁해야겠어.
남: 네.

06 ①

[휴대전화가 울린다.]
여: 안녕, Mike. 무슨 일이야?
남: 안녕, Ann. 너 지금 어디 있어?
여: 쇼핑몰에 있는데. 왜 묻는 건데?
남: 너 잊어버렸어? 우리는 과학 프로젝트 작업을 하려고 도서관에서 만나기로 했었잖아!
여: 아, 정말 미안해! 그걸 완전히 잊고 있었어.
남: 네가 이런 걸 잊어 버린 게 이번이 처음이 아니야. 지난주에 너는 야구 경기에도 나타나지 않았어.
여: 미안해. 다음에는 잊어버리지 않겠다고 약속할게.
남: 어떻게 기억할 건데?
여: 잘 모르겠어. 나는 항상 무언가 잊어버려.
남: 내 생각에 너는 해야 할 것을 일정 계획표에 모두 적어둬야 할 것 같아.
여: 알겠어, 그렇게 해볼게.

07 ③

남: 국립 미술관에 오신 걸 환영합니다. 도와드릴까요?
여: 네. 티켓 구매를 하려고요. 얼마죠?
남: 성인은 12달러이고 13세 미만의 어린이들은 6달러입니다.
여: 그러면 성인 티켓 두 장과 어린이 티켓 두 장을 살게요.
남: 알겠습니다. 저희는 또한 오디오 가이드 서비스를 제공하고 있습니다. 그걸 사용하길 원하시나요?
여: 아, 그것에 대해 들어본 적이 없는데요. 그게 뭐죠?
남: 헤드폰을 통해서 미술 작품에 대한 정보를 들려드리는 서비스입니다.
여: 그거 좋을 것 같아요. 미술 작품을 더 잘 이해하는 데 도움이 되겠네요.
남: 물론이죠.
여: 그건 얼마인가요?
남: 한 사람당 겨우 2달러입니다.
여: 좋아요. 넷 다 할게요. 여기 제 신용카드요.

문제풀이

12달러인 성인 티켓 두 장과 6달러인 어린이 티켓 두 장을 샀고, 인당 2달러인 오디오 가이드 서비스를 네 명 신청했으므로, 여자가 지불할 금액은 총 44달러(= ($12×2)+($6×2)+($2×4))이다.

08 ⑤

여: Roger, 학교 축제가 다음 주말이야!
남: 그래! 너는 행사에 참여할 거야?
여: 응, 나는 Hamilton 동물 보호소를 위해 쿠키를 팔 거야.
남: 멋지다! 너는 「Dan and Kate」를 볼 거야? 그건 학교의 연극 동아리가 공연하는 연극이야.
여: 응, 볼 거야. 연극이 끝나면, 내 가장 친한 친구가 드럼을 연주할 거라서 밴드 콘서트에 갈 거야.
남: 아, 나는 거기엔 갈 수 없어. 내가 그 시간에 미술 전시회를 하거든.
여: 정말? 그건 몰랐어. 네 전시회에 가지 못해 매우 유감이야.
남: 괜찮아. 그런데 작년에 캐리커처를 그렸던 미술가가 올해에는 다시 오지 않을 거라고 들었어.
여: 아, 이런. 나는 그걸 기대하고 있었는데.

09 ⑤

남: 안녕하세요, 여러분. 오늘 저는 남미에 있는 로라이마 산에 대해 말씀드리겠습니다. 그 산의 정상은 테이블처럼 평평합니다. 그것은 사방에 400미터 높이의 절벽이 있습니다. 산의 정상에는 거의 매일 비가 옵니다. 그것은 매우 높은 몇몇 폭포들이 있다는 것을 의미합니다. 산 표면의 대부분은 단지 헐벗은 사암일 뿐입니다. 하지만 산에는 일부 식물들이 잘 자라는 축축하고 진흙이 있는 몇몇 지역이 있습니다. 무엇보다도, 로라이마 산은 도보 여행을 하기에 매우 좋습니다. 하지만 도보 여행자들은 오후 2시 이후에는 도보 여행을 시작하는 것이 허용되지 않습니다.

10 ②

[전화벨이 울린다.]
여: Newtown 버스 터미널입니다. 무엇을 도와드릴까요?
남: 안녕하세요. 저는 내일 여기서 스프링필드로 가는 버스 티켓이 필요해요.
여: 몇 시에 출발하고 싶으세요? 선택하실 수 있는 것이 몇 가지 있습니다.
남: 오전에 출발해야 해요. 정오 이전이면 아무 때나 괜찮습니다.
여: 그러면 세 가지 선택권이 남아요. 직행으로 가실 수 있지만, 그건 더 비싸요.
남: 아, 정차하는 것은 상관없어요. 저는 더 저렴한 티켓이 더 좋아요.
여: 알겠습니다. 내일 오전에 출발하는 두 대의 버스가 있네요, 정차를 하고요.
남: 그것들 중에 더 큰 의자가 있는 게 있나요?
여: 네, 하지만 편안한 좌석은 더 비쌉니다.
남: 그러면 저는 그냥 일반 좌석을 골라야겠네요.
여: 알겠습니다. 그건 25달러입니다.

11 ⑤

남: 무엇을 도와드릴까요?
여: 이 재킷을 사고 싶은데요. 이걸로 6사이즈가 있나요?
남: 아, 저희는 지금 그 사이즈가 떨어졌지만, 제가 고객님을 위해 주문해 드릴 수는 있습니다.
여: <u>그거 괜찮네요. 기다리는 건 상관없어요.</u>

문제풀이

① 탈의실이 어디죠?
② 고맙습니다만, 전 그걸 온라인으로 주문했어요.
③ 아니요. 저는 더 작은 사이즈의 것은 필요 없어요.
④ 그건 비싸네요. 그렇게 (돈을) 많이 쓸 수는 없어요.

12 ③

여: 지난 주말에 뭐 특별한 걸 했니?
남: 응, 여동생이랑 같이 N서울 타워에 걸어 올라갔어.
여: 그거 힘들 것 같다. 왜 케이블카를 타지 않았어?
남: <u>우리는 운동 삼아 걷고 싶었거든.</u>

문제풀이

① 나는 케이블카 타는 걸 좋아해.
② 나는 언덕을 걸어 올라가는 걸 좋아하지 않아.
④ 안타깝게도, 나는 차가 없어.
⑤ 사실, 지하철이 끊겼었어.

13 ②

남: 무엇을 도와드릴까요, 손님?
여: 제가 요즘 아주 피곤함을 느껴요. 비타민 보충제 좀 섭취해야 할 것 같아요.
남: 그러시군요. 특별히 마음에 두신 것이 있으세요?
여: 아니요. 저에게 비타민 좀 추천해 주실 수 있으세요?
남: 이 비타민 B 보충제는 어떠세요? 피로를 회복하는 데 좋습니다.
여: 그거 좋은 것 같네요. 매일 복용해야 하나요?
남: 네, 아침 식사 후에 두 알씩 드셔야 합니다.
여: 알겠습니다. 그밖에 추천해주실 게 있나요?

남: 이 철분 보충제도 드셔보세요. 손님의 면역 체계가 강하게 유지되도록 도와줍니다.
여: 알겠습니다. 그건 얼마나 자주 복용해야 하나요?
남: 하루에 두 번 한 알씩 드셔야 합니다.

문제풀이

① 다 합쳐서 30달러입니다.
③ 손님께서는 드시는 것에 주의하셔야 합니다.
④ 비타민 B 알약을 드시는 걸 잊지 마세요.
⑤ 손님께서는 철분제를 드시면 안 됩니다.

14 ⑤

[전화벨이 울린다.]
여: 안녕하세요. City International의 Darcy Wilson입니다. 무엇을 도와드릴까요?
남: 안녕하세요, Darcy 씨. 저는 Tom Green이에요.
여: 아, 안녕하세요, Tom 씨. 어떻게 지내세요?
남: 다 잘 되고 있어요, 근데 뭔가 확인하고 싶은 게 있어서요.
여: 그게 뭔가요?
남: 당신 조수가 어제 제게 새 계약서를 팩스로 보내주기로 했었는데, 전 그걸 받지 못했어요.
여: 사실 이번 주 내내 저희 팩스 기계에 문제가 있었어요.
남: 그렇군요. 그런데 저희는 그 계약서가 가급적 빨리 필요합니다.
여: 그러면 제가 오늘 저녁 일을 마친 후에 그걸 당신께 직접 가져다 드릴게요.
남: 잘됐네요. 근데 저녁 8시까지 확실히 그렇게 해줄 수 있나요?
여: 네, 당신 사무실에 저녁 7시경에 갈게요.

문제풀이

① 제가 오늘 그 계약서를 팩스로 보낼 수 있어요.
② 원하시면 언제든지 저를 방문하셔도 돼요.
③ 제 조수에게 그렇게 하라고 부탁하는 걸 잊었어요.
④ 아뇨, 수리공은 내일 올 거예요.

15 ②

여: Ryan은 최근에 밤에 잠을 자는 데 어려움을 겪고 있다. 그는 항상 피곤함을 느끼고 때로는 수업 중에 잠이 들기도 해서 이것은 큰 문제이다. 게다가 그의 성적은 떨어지고 있다. 그의 선생님은 그가 걱정되어서, 그를 학교 상담 선생님과 상담을 하도록 보낸다. 상담 선생님은 Ryan의 이야기를 듣고 그가 하루에 서너 잔의 커피를 마신다는 것을 알게 된다. 그녀는 커피의 카페인이 그가 밤에 잠들지 못하게 하고 있다고 생각한다. 이런 상황에서, 상담 선생님이 Ryan에게 할 말로 가장 적절한 것은 무엇인가?
상담 선생님 : 너는 매일 커피를 더 적게 마셔야 해.

문제풀이

① 너는 너희 선생님과 이야기해보는 것이 어떠니?
③ 너는 수업 중에 깨어 있도록 해야 해.
④ 내가 너라면, 그렇게 많은 게임을 하지는 않을 거야.
⑤ 잠을 자려고 할 때 음악을 틀지 마라.

16 ⑤ 17 ⑤

남: 안녕하세요, 입주민 여러분. 최근 밤에 일어나는 소음에 대한 불편사항들이 접수되고 있어서, 여러분에게 몇 가지 조언을 공유해드리고자 합니다. 만약 여러분의 이웃들이 불평하는 것을 원하지 않으면, 소음을 줄이는 데 도움이 되는 이 조언들을 시도해보시길 바랍니다. 첫째로, 두꺼운 카펫을 까십시오. 이것은 여러분의 가족이 낼 수도 있는 소리의 대부분을 흡수할 것입니다. 덧붙여서, 여러분은 여러분의 가족 구성원들이 걸어 다닐 때 너무 많은 소음을 발생시키지 않도록 슬리퍼를 마련할 수도 있습니다. 여러분은 또한 이웃들의 수면을 방해하지 않도록 밤에는 TV의 음량을 줄여야 합니다. 끝으로, 밤에 너무 늦게 샤워하는 것을 피하십시오. 사람들이 자려고 할 때 여러분이 샤워를 하면, 물소리가 매우 성가실 수 있습니다. 이것들을 명심하시고 더 조심하려고 노력하십시오. 시간 내주셔서 감사합니다.

DICTATION Answers

01 get bored and sleepy / are allowed to / be closed
02 check for mistakes / hard to say no / refuse others' requests
03 after the due date / working on my designs / make an exception
04 finished organizing / on the top shelf / we rarely use
05 I'm about to go / do the dishes / pick up
06 were supposed to meet / show up / write down everything
07 for adults / lets you hear / take four of them
08 participate in any events / is putting on / won't be back
09 flat like a table / some very high waterfalls / are not permitted to
10 Anytime before noon / prefer the cheaper ticket / just choose economy seating
11 order one for you
12 Why didn't you take
13 anything particular in mind / good for overcoming / How often should I
14 Things are going well / was supposed to fax / as soon as possible
15 has trouble sleeping / sends him to talk with / preventing him from
16-17 had some complaints / help reduce noise / turn down your TV

09 영어듣기 모의고사

본문 ▲ p.62

01 ②	02 ②	03 ②	04 ④	05 ④	06 ②
07 ③	08 ③	09 ⑤	10 ②	11 ④	12 ①
13 ②	14 ③	15 ④	16 ①	17 ③	

01 ②

여: 여러분은 셰익스피어를 좋아하시나요? 만약 그렇다면, 주의 깊게 들으십시오. 영어과에서는 셰익스피어의 희곡에 관한 일일 세미나를 열 것입니다. 세미나는 10월 18일에 Lincoln Hall에서 개최될 것입니다. 세미나 동안, 참석자들은 「로미오와 줄리엣」과 「햄릿」과 같은 그 작가의 가장 유명한 희곡들 중 일부를 논의할 것입니다. 이 주제에 관심이 있는 분이라면 누구나 환영합니다. 참가비는 20달러이며, 당일 세미나가 시작되기 전에 홀 앞 데스크에서 등록하실 수 있습니다. 세미나에 대해 더 알고 싶으시면, 저희 웹사이트를 방문해 주십시오.

02 ②

남: 이봐 Gina, 뭘 하고 있어?
여: 온라인으로 드레스를 쇼핑하고 있어.
남: 왜 새 드레스가 필요한 거야?
여: 다음 달에 댄스파티가 있거든. 파티를 위해 예쁜 드레스를 사고 싶어서.
남: 그렇구나. 드레스는 고른 거야?
여: 거의. 그런데 내가 원하는 드레스는 몇몇 웹사이트에서 판매되고 있어.
남: 그렇다면, 너는 최저 가격을 찾기 위해서 모든 웹사이트를 확인해야겠다.
여: 응, 나는 지금 가격을 비교하고 있어. 다른 온라인 상점들이 같은 제품을 다른 가격에 판매해.
남: 배송비도 잊지 마!
여: 물론이지. 난 어느 상점에서 무료배송을 해주는지 확인하고 있어. 나는 또 환불이나 교환을 할 수 있는지도 확인 중이야.
남: 네 말이 맞아. 그것 또한 중요하지.

03 ②

남: 잘했어, Beth! 좋은 경기였어.
여: 고맙습니다.
남: 너는 2등으로 들어왔어! 너는 은메달을 받게 될 거야!
여: 네, 괜찮은 것 같네요.
남: 괜찮다고? 무슨 말을 하고 있는 거야? 그건 굉장한 거야!
여: 제가 속도를 계속 유지했더라면 1등을 할 수 있었을 거예요. 제가 마지막에 왜 뒤처지기 시작했는지 모르겠어요.
남: 네가 경기 중간에 팔 젓기를 짧게 하기 시작했는데, 그것이 너의 속도를 늦추게 했단다. 매번 손을 내 저을 때마다 팔을 완전히 뻗는 것을 잊지 마라.
여: 네, 선생님. 다음번 경기에서 더 잘할 수 있도록 계속 연습해야겠어요.
남: 좋아. 너무 자학하지 마라.

04 ④

여: 자선 바자회가 내일이야! 매장에 물건들을 어떻게 배열해야 하지?
남: 음, 우리에게는 테이블 두 개, 선반 하나와 옷걸이가 있어. 우선, 직사각형 모양의 테이블을 중앙에 놓고 그 위에 인형들을 놓자.
여: 좋은 생각이야. 이 모자들은 어떻게 하지?
남: 그건 인형 옆에 놓자.
여: 알겠어. 그리고 우리는 둥근 테이블을 직사각형 모양의 테이블 앞에 놓을 수 있어. 나는 그 위에 넥타이들을 두고 싶어.
남: 좋아. 스카프들은 어떻게 할 거야? 벽에 있는 선반 위에 두어야 할까?
여: 그래. 그러면 사람들이 그걸 쉽게 찾을 수 있어.
남: 알겠어. 그리고 마지막으로, 이 옷들을 옷걸이에 걸어서 오른쪽에 놓자.
여: 완벽해!

05 ④

여: 아, 이런! 새로 산 내 노트북 컴퓨터가 작동을 멈췄어.
남: 아마 배터리 때문일 거야. 그건 별로 오래 지속되지 않거든.
여: 하지만 나는 이걸 오늘 아침에 충전했어. 그때 이후로 나는 이걸 별로 사용하지 않았는데.
남: 넌 노트북이 고장 났다고 생각하니?
여: 잘 모르겠어. 내 생각엔 이걸 서비스 센터에 가지고 가야 할 것 같아.
남: 좋은 생각이야. 시내에 하나 있어, 기차역 맞은편에.
여: 맞아, 그런데 나는 오늘 오후 회의에 노트북 컴퓨터가 필요해. 네 것을 써도 될까?
남: 그럼. 나는 오늘 하이킹하러 갈 거라서 필요 없어.
여: 잘됐다. 내가 회의 끝나고 바로 돌려줄 수 있어.
남: 괜찮아. 그냥 오늘 밤에 나에게 돌려줘.
여: 정말 고마워.

06 ②

여: 안녕, Tom. 손에 든 그 책은 뭐야?
남: 인터넷으로 주문한 소설이야.
여: 아, 제목이 뭐야?
남: 「Twelve Days」야. 빨리 이걸 읽기 시작하고 싶어.
여: 너 요즘 바쁘지 않니? 그걸 읽을 시간이 있어?
남: 음, 매일 밤 자기 전에 30분 동안 읽을 수 있을 거야.
여: 그거 베스트셀러야?
남: 아니, 하지만 모든 서평들이 훌륭해서, 난 망설이지 않고 그것을 골랐어.
여: 누가 그 책을 썼니?
남: Douglas Kennedy야. 나는 그 이름에 익숙하지 않지만, 이 소설은 읽어 볼 만한 가치가 있을 것 같아.
여: 그렇구나. 네가 그 책을 재미있게 읽었으면 좋겠어.

07 ③

여: 제주 렌터카에 오신 걸 환영합니다. 무엇을 도와드릴까요?
남: 3일 동안 차를 빌리려고요.
여: 좋아요. 저희는 5인승 자동차와 7인승 자동차가 있어요.
남: 하루에 얼마인가요?
여: 5인승 자동차는 하루에 30달러이고 7인승 자동차는 50달러입니다.
남: 저희 가족은 여섯 명이에요. 7인승 차 한 대를 원해요.
여: 좋습니다. 구형 모델도 괜찮으세요? 최신 모델을 원하시면 하루에 10 달러의 추가 비용이 있습니다.
남: 음, 신형은 필요 없습니다.
여: 알겠습니다, 그리고 보험을 원하세요?
남: 그건 얼마죠?
여: 하루에 추가로 5달러입니다.
남: 네, 해주세요.

문제풀이

남자는 하루에 대여료가 50달러인 7인승 자동차를 3일 동안 대여하기로 했고, 하루에 추가 비용이 5달러 발생하는 보험에 가입하기로 했으므로, 남자가 지불할 금액은 총 165달러(= ($50+$5)×3)이다.

08 ③

여: 강당이 2월 20일에 재개관하는 거 들었어?
남: 정말? 폭설로 인한 피해가 정말 심각했는데. 모든 것이 수리된 거야?
여: 응, 모든 것이 마침내 수리되었어.
남: 그거 정말 좋은 소식이다!
여: 맞아. 그리고 개관하는 날, 뮤지컬 「The Lions」 공연이 있을 거야.
남: 아, 멋지다. 누가 공연해?
여: 학교 연극 동아리가 공연할 거야.
남: 티켓은 얼마야?
여: 실은, 공짜야.
남: 그거 좋다. 어디에서 티켓을 구할 수 있어?
여: 내일 학생 센터에서 수령할 수 있을 거야.
남: 알겠어. 빨리 그 공연을 보고 싶어!

09 ⑤

남: 안녕하세요, 여러분. 저는 여러분에게 오늘 오후에 있을 특별 행사를 상기시켜드리고 싶습니다. 여러분께서 이미 공지받은 대로, 저희는 오후 3시에 '우정의 날' 행사를 가질 예정입니다. 그것은 학교 도서관에서 개최될 것입니다. 그곳에는 카드와 색연필, 그리고 도서 목록이 있는 책상이 있을 것입니다. 여러분은 친구를 한 명 골라 그들에게 카드를 쓰면 됩니다. 그 후에, 여러분은 도서 목록에서 친구와 공유하고 싶은 책 한 권을 고르실 수 있습니다. 저희는 이번 주 금요일에 그 책을 카드와 함께 여러분의 친구에게 전달할 것입니다. 여러분의 우정을 보여 줄 이번 기회를 잡으시길 바랍니다!

10 ②

남: 안녕, Julie. 여기 무슨 일이니?
여: 안녕하세요, Olson 선생님. 저는 웨이트리스로 일하는 아르바이트를 찾고 있어요. 저를 도와주실 수 있으세요?
남: 물론이지, 그게 내 일인걸. 어디 보자… *[타자치는 소리]* 웨이트리스를 찾는 식당들이 많이 있구나. 몇 시간 일하는 걸 원하니?
여: 하루에 5시간 넘게 일하고 싶지는 않아요.
남: 그렇구나. 너는 식당에서 일한 경험이 있니?
여: 네, 저는 작년에 5개월 동안 웨이트리스로 일했어요.
남: 그러면 너에게 고를 수 있는 두 가지 선택권이 있구나.
여: 음, 저는 보수를 더 주는 식당에 지원할게요.
남: 알겠어. 내가 너에게 그 식당의 연락처를 주마.
여: 감사합니다!

11 ④

[휴대전화가 울린다.]
남: 여보세요, 여보. 당신 집에 오는 길이에요?
여: 아니요, 이미 집이에요. 밖에 비가 오고 있어요. 우산 가져갔어요?
남: 안타깝게도, 안 가져 왔어요. 사무실로 저를 태우러 올 수 있어요?
여: 그럼요, 30분 안에 거기로 갈게요.

문제풀이

① 네, 당신은 지금 저를 태우러 와도 돼요.
② 저를 사무실까지 태워줄 수 있으세요?
③ 당신의 우산은 내일 돌려줄게요.
⑤ 우리는 약속을 취소해야 해요.

12 ①

여: Charlie, 너 우울해 보여. 무슨 일 있어?
남: 실은, 오늘 아침 운전면허 시험에서 떨어졌어.
여: 필기시험에는 합격했다고 했잖아, 그렇지 않아?
남: 맞아, 그런데 도로주행 시험에서 떨어졌어.

문제풀이

② 네가 두 시험에 모두 통과하지 못했다니 안됐구나.
③ 음, 내 생각에 넌 운전을 잘하는 거 같아.
④ 나는 직업을 위한 필기시험을 곧 볼 거야.
⑤ 나는 몇 년 전에 운전면허증을 땄어.

13 ②

남: 갈 준비됐어요?
여: 잠깐만요. 내 지갑을 찾을 수가 없어요.
남: 또요? 지난번에 당신이 그걸 잃어버렸을 때, 우리는 집안 전체를 살펴봤는데, 결국 당신은 그걸 당신의 외투 주머니에서 발견했죠.
여: 나도 그걸 기억해요, 그래서 내 주머니를 다 확인해봤어요.
남: 당신은 물건들을 잃어버리지 않게 항상 그것들을 같은 자리에 둬야 해요.
여: 당신 말이 맞아요. 그걸 명심하도록 노력할게요.
남: 어쨌든, 당신이 오늘 아침에 했던 모든 일을 생각해보고, 당신이 지갑을 마지막으로 가지고 있던 때를 기억하려고 해봐요.
여: 생각 좀 해볼게요… *[잠시 후]* 아! 생각났어요!
남: 기억나요?
여: 그걸 어제 차에 둔 것 같아요.

문제풀이

① 아니요. 내 주머니를 확인하지 않았어요.

③ 걱정 말아요. 내가 당신에게 돈을 좀 빌려줄게요.
④ 여동생이 내 생일 선물로 그걸 줬어요.
⑤ 정리정돈을 더 잘하도록 노력하세요.

14 ③

남: Sarah, 너 이번 겨울 방학에 무슨 계획 있니?
여: 응! 나는 뉴질랜드로 2주 동안 여행을 갈 거야.
남: 와! 그거 멋지다. 난 네가 거기서 멋진 시간을 보낼 거라고 확신해.
여: 아, 너는 전에 거기 가본 적 있다고 하지 않았어? 단순히 거기 여행 간 거였어?
남: 실은, 나는 영어를 공부하느라 웰링턴에 몇 달 있었어.
여: 아, 나도 거기 가는데. 그 도시 날씨는 어때?
남: 기후는 온화해. 그런데 바람이 매우 많이 불어.
여: 너는 그 나라에서 뭘 가장 좋아했어?
남: 아마 풍경이었을 거야. 내가 갔던 어디나 정말 아름다웠어.
여: 멋지다! 가볼 만한 곳 좀 추천해줄 수 있어?
남: 물론이지. 장소 몇 군데를 이메일로 보내줄게.

문제풀이
① 미안하지만 그럴 수 없어. 나는 거기 가본 적이 없거든.
② 걱정하지 마. 내가 같이 가서 너를 안내해줄게.
④ 너는 거기 가면 조심해야 해.
⑤ 멋진 장소들이 많이 있다는 것에 동의해.

15 ④

여: Kimberly는 영화에서 연기를 하고 싶어서, 많은 오디션을 보러 다닌다. 하지만 그녀는 한 번도 합격하지 못한다. 그녀는 자신의 연기가 충분히 좋지 않아서라고 생각한다. 그러나 그녀는 정확한 문제가 무엇인지 모른다. 그녀는 자신의 친구인 Ben이 좋은 배우이기 때문에 그에게 조언을 구하기로 결심한다. Ben은 그녀에게 독백을 해보라고 말한다. 그녀가 연기하는 것을 보고, 그는 그녀의 문제를 알아챈다. 그녀의 목소리가 매우 조용하고 발음이 불명확해서, 그는 그녀가 말하는 것을 이해할 수가 없다. 이런 상황에서, Ben이 Kimberly에게 할 말로 가장 적절한 것은 무엇인가?
Ben : 너는 더 크고 더 명확하게 말을 해야 해.

문제풀이
① 시선을 더 잘 마주치려고 노력해봐.
② 너는 다음에는 오디션에 합격할 거야.
③ 잠깐 쉬는 게 어때?
⑤ 네가 또 떨어졌다니 유감이야.

16 ① 17 ③

남: 오늘 우리는 독도가 왜 역사적으로 그리고 국제적으로 중요한지를 배웠습니다. 오늘의 수업을 마치기 전에, 저는 이야기할 것이 한 가지 더 있습니다. 제가 이번 학기 초에 언급했던 것처럼, 저는 여러분의 마지막 과제로 독도에 관한 에세이를 쓰는 것을 원합니다. 여러분은 독도와 관련되어 있는 한 어떤 것이든 선택해서 쓸 수 있습니다. 하지만 그 섬의 위치, 기후, 인구, 그리고 역사를 포함해야 합니다. 에세이를 300단어 이내로 써야 한다는 것을 기억하세요. 타자를 치고 A4지에 출력하세요. 여러분이 쓴 것을 다음 수업에 가져오세요. 여러분 중 일부는 과제를 학급 학생들과 공유하도록 요청받게 될지도 모릅니다. 충실한 발표를 하는 사람은 추가 점수를 받을 것입니다. 여러분이 제출하는 것을 볼 것이 기대됩니다.

DICTATION Answers

01 will be held / Anyone who / before the seminar begins
02 for a dress online / get the best price / get a refund
03 came in second place / gotten first place / in the next competition
04 arrange the items / next to the dolls / put them on the right
05 last very long / across from the train station / give it back
06 ordered on the Internet / have time for reading / be worth reading
07 rent a car / There are six members / will that be
08 has finally been repaired / be performed by / pick one up
09 remind you of / be held in / share with
10 What brings you here / more than five hours / apply to the restaurant
11 pick me up
12 passed the written test
13 I can't find my wallet / keep that in mind / I got it
14 going on a trip / spent a few months / recommend some places
15 she never passes / for advice / what she says
16-17 to talk about / print it out / Anyone who gives

10 영어듣기 모의고사

본문 ▲ p.69

01 ② 02 ② 03 ② 04 ⑤ 05 ② 06 ②
07 ④ 08 ④ 09 ④ 10 ③ 11 ④ 12 ①
13 ③ 14 ⑤ 15 ⑤ 16 ④ 17 ③

01 ②

여: 주목해주십시오. 저희의 댄스 공연에 와주셔서 감사합니다. 저희는 여러분 모두가 공연을 즐기시길 바랍니다. 공연이 시작되기 전에, 저희는 여러분께 한 가지 부탁을 드리고 싶습니다. 저희가 여러분께 드린 종이를 읽으시고, 그 질문들에 답해 주십시오. 저희는 저희 댄스 극장을 곧 보수할 계획입니다. 그래서 저희가 어떻게 보수해야 하는지에 대한 여러분의 의견을 듣고 싶습니다. 여러분의 의견은 저희의 보수 계획에 반영될 것입니다. 이 설문조사는 작성하는 데 겨우 몇 분밖에 걸리지 않을 겁니다. 나가실 때 종이를 작은 상자에 넣어주시는 걸 기억해주세요. 감사드리며 즐거운 관람 되십시오!

02 ②

남: 밖이 추워지고 있어. 겨울이 코앞이야.
여: 아, 이런! 내 피부는 겨울엔 항상 건조해져.
남: 맞아, 히터를 켜고 실내에 있는 것은 우리의 피부를 극도로 건조하게 만들어.
여: 그렇지만 너의 피부는 정말 좋아 보여. 비법이 뭐야?
남: 음, 난 종일 약 2리터 정도의 물을 마시려 노력해.
여: 그거 좋은 생각이다.
남: 난 또한 가끔 사용된 녹차 티백이나 오이 조각을 피부 위에 올려놔.
여: 아, 난 비타민 C가 우리의 피부에 아주 좋다고 들었어.
남: 맞아, 많은 과일과 채소를 먹는 것이 많은 비타민 C를 섭취하는 데 도움을 줄 거야.
여: 조언 고마워. 내 피부를 건강하게 유지하기 위해 그 조언들을 이용해 봐야겠어!

03 ②

여: 안녕하세요. 저는 Kate Smith입니다.
남: 만나서 반가워요, Kate 씨.
여: 저도 만나서 반갑습니다. 제가 몇 가지 질문을 드려도 괜찮으시겠어요?
남: 그럼요. 무엇을 알고 싶으신가요?
여: 성공적으로 투어 콘서트를 끝내셨잖아요. 그에 대해 소감이 어떠세요?
남: 매우 만족스럽습니다. 그리고 저는 제 팬들과 저를 도와주신 모든 분들께 감사합니다.
여: 그분들도 틀림없이 매우 행복했을 겁니다. 새 앨범에 대한 계획이 있으신가요?
남: 네, 새 앨범은 크리스마스이브에 발매될 것입니다.
여: 앨범에 대해 더 상세히 알려주실 수 있으신가요?
남: 그럼요. 곡 대부분은 사랑에 관한 발라드입니다.
여: 분명 당신의 팬들이 그것을 빨리 듣고 싶어 할 거예요. 시간 내주셔서 감사합니다.

04 ⑤

[전화벨이 울린다.]
여: 여보세요. Ace 디자인입니다.
남: 안녕하세요, Murphy 씨. 저 Max입니다. 키즈 카페를 리모델링하는 걸 마치셨나요?
여: 그럼요, 오늘 오후에 끝냈어요.
남: 미끄럼틀은 방의 모퉁이에 두었죠?
여: 네, 전 그것을 왼쪽 뒤 모퉁이에 두었어요. 그리고 저는 또한 큰 볼 풀을 카페 왼쪽에 두었어요.
남: 그거 좋네요. 장난감 자동차는요?
여: 고객님께서 요청하신 대로 그것들을 중앙에 두었습니다.
남: 좋아요. 그러면 차들을 운전할 수 있는 충분한 공간이 있겠네요. 장난감 기차 선로는 어디에 설치하셨나요?
여: 그것을 오른쪽 뒤 모퉁이에 설치했어요.
남: 좋아요. 아이들이 앉아서 먹을 곳은 있나요?
여: 장난감 기차 선로 앞에 두 개의 원형 테이블이 있어요.

05 ②

[전화벨이 울린다.]
여: 여보세요. IT 부서입니다. 저는 Cassie입니다.
남: Cassie 씨, 저 John이에요. 저 좀 도와줄 수 있어요?
여: 물론이죠. 하와이에서 휴가 중이신 거 아니에요?
남: 맞아요, 그런데 도움이 필요해요. 본사에서 보낸 팩스가 도착했나요?
여: 확인해볼게요. *[잠시 후]* 아, 네. 여기 당신에게 온 팩스가 하나 있네요. 제가 무엇을 해드리길 원하세요?
남: 그걸 Jones 씨에게 나 대신 팩스로 보내줄 수 있어요? 그의 팩스 번호는 제 책상 위에 있어요.
여: 같은 팩스를 그에게 보내는 걸 원하시는 거죠?
남: 네. 오늘 퇴근하기 전에 언제든지 괜찮아요.
여: 그건 해드릴 수 있어요. 보답으로, 제 기념품을 사오실 거죠? *[웃음]*
남: 물론이죠. 도와줘서 고마워요!

06 ②

여: 서울에 있는 Star 호텔에 대한 광고 봤어요? 새로운 지배인을 찾고 있더라고요.
남: 아니요, 못 봤어요. 그 일에 대해 조금 더 말해줄 수 있어요?
여: 그럼요. 당신은 다음 달부터 시작해야 해요.
남: 그럴 수 있어요. 다른 건요?
여: 그들은 호텔 경영을 전공한 사람을 찾고 있어요.
남: 아, 그건 제 전공이었어요.
여: 그리고 당신은 지배인으로서 최소 5년의 경력이 필요해요.
남: 저는 두 개의 다른 호텔에서 총 8년 동안 일했어요.
여: 마지막 요구 조건은 당신이 중국어에 유창해야 한다는 거예요.
남: 정말요? 저는 중국어를 전혀 하지 못해요.
여: 아, 그렇다면 이건 당신에게 적합한 자리가 아닌 것 같네요.

07 ④

여: 안녕하세요. 놀이공원 표를 좀 사고 싶어요.

남: 알겠습니다. 성인 표는 장당 15달러이고, 12세 이하 어린이들은 장당 5달러입니다. 몇 장을 원하세요?

여: 성인 표 한 장과 어린이 표 두 장이 필요해요.

남: 알겠습니다. 잠시 기다리세요.

여: 그런데 모든 놀이기구가 그 표에 포함되어 있나요?

남: 대부분이요, 하지만 Devil's Spine을 타시려면 한 사람당 5달러를 더 내셔야 해요.

여: 아, 그건 좀 비싸군요.

남: 하지만 그것은 저희 카페 중 하나에서의 무료 점심 쿠폰을 포함합니다.

여: 무료 점심이요? 그거 훌륭하네요! 그러면 저희 전부 Devil's Spine을 포함하는 표를 살게요.

문제풀이

여자는 장당 15달러인 성인 표 1장과 5달러인 어린이 표 2장을 사려고 하다가 각각 5달러를 추가하여 특별 놀이기구와 무료 점심을 이용할 수 있는 표를 사기로 했으므로, 총 40달러(= $20+($10×2))를 지불할 것이다.

08 ④

여: 이봐, Jerry! 너를 여기서 만날 줄 몰랐네.

남: 아. 안녕, Betty! 여기 무슨 일이니?

여: 나는 가족들을 위한 선물을 사러 여기 왔어.

남: 정말 착하구나. 무엇을 샀니?

여: 어머니를 위해서 찻잔 세트를 샀어.

남: 아버지는?

여: 아버지를 위해서는 한국산 녹차를 좀 샀어.

남: 너희 부모님은 네 선물을 분명 좋아하실 거야. 네 여동생은?

여: 그녀는 한국 대중가요의 열렬한 팬이라서 그녀에게 줄 CD를 좀 샀어.

남: 아, 그녀가 그걸 엄청 좋아할 게 분명해. 네 남동생에게 줄 것도 샀어?

여: 물론이지. 그 애는 한국 문화에 호기심이 많아서 한국의 전통 탈을 샀어.

09 ④

남: 안녕하세요, North Star 헬스클럽의 소중한 회원님. 저희 수영장의 리모델링이 마침내 끝났습니다. 다음 주부터 여러분은 새로운 수영장을 이용하실 수 있습니다. 저희는 세 개의 레인을 추가해서 이제 열 개의 레인이 있습니다. 또한, 저희는 샤워장과 탈의실을 확장했습니다. 그리고 저희는 모든 사물함을 더 큰 것으로 교체했습니다. 저희는 다음 달에 수영장을 무료로 이용하실 수 있도록 기존 회원님들을 초대합니다. 회원 카드만 보여 주시면 입장하실 수 있습니다. 새로운 수영장은 오전 6시부터 저녁 9시까지 개장합니다. 오셔서 이 모든 훌륭한 새로운 특징들을 즐기시길 바랍니다!

10 ③

남: Jennifer, 내가 방금 온라인에서 연극 일정을 찾았어. 내일 볼 연극을 하나 고르자.

여: 좋아. 너는 어떤 것을 보고 싶어?

남: 오후 1시 이후에 시작하면 그것들 중 어떤 것이든 괜찮아. 난 내일 아침에 체육관에 가야 하거든.

여: 좋아. 「Ms. Jessica」를 보는 게 어때? 우리 언니가 그것이 정말 재미있었다고 했어.

남: 실은, 나는 그걸 지난주에 봤어.

여: 그러면, 우리에게는 두 개의 다른 선택권이 남았어.

남: 그래. 네가 좋아하지 않는 장르가 있니? 나는 모든 장르를 좋아하거든.

여: 음, 나는 로맨스 연극은 보고 싶지 않아.

남: 정말? 그러면 남은 선택권은 딱 하나네.

여: 좋아. 그 표를 사자.

11 ④

남: 안녕하세요. 새로운 소파를 사는 데 관심이 있어서요.

여: 좋아요. 마음에 두고 있는 특정한 제품이 있으세요?

남: 그렇지는 않아요. 할인 판매 중인 것이 있나요?

여: 가죽 소파들은 현재 10% 할인 중입니다.

문제풀이

① 저희는 매주 월요일에 문을 닫습니다.
② 이건 이미 품절되었습니다.
③ 죄송하지만 그것들은 판매하는 것이 아닙니다.
⑤ 저희는 다른 가구들도 있어요.

12 ①

여: 안녕, Andy! 오랜만이야. 너 휴가였니?

남: 아니, 나 3일 동안 입원해 있었어.

여: 그거 안됐구나. 무슨 일 있었어?

남: 심한 복통이 있었어.

문제풀이

② 병원에 가보는 게 어때?
③ 길을 건널 때 조심해.
④ 나는 아직 아무런 휴가 계획을 세우지 않았어.
⑤ 그는 수술을 위해 입원 중이야.

13 ③

남: 난 스마트폰이 없는 세상을 상상할 수 없어.

여: 나도 동의해. 나는 요즘 내 스마트폰을 항상 사용하거든.

남: 정말? 그걸로 보통 뭘 하니?

여: 나는 이메일을 확인하고, 인터넷을 검색하고, 게임을 하고, 그 외 더 많은 것들을 하는 데 그걸 사용해.

남: 너는 하루에 그걸 몇 시간 사용한다고 생각해?

여: 하루 종일 사용해.

남: 그건 너무 많아. 너는 스마트폰에 중독된 것처럼 들려!

여: 그럴지도 몰라. 스마트폰을 가지고 있지 않으면 심지어 불안함을 느끼기 시작하거든.

남: 너는 그것을 너무 자주 사용하는 것을 멈춰야 할 것 같아.

문제풀이

① 너는 네 스마트폰으로 공부를 할 수 있어.
② 응, 스마트폰은 많은 이점들이 있어.
④ 너는 전화를 너무 자주 바꾸는 것 같아.
⑤ 많은 십 대들이 스마트폰에 중독되어 있어.

14 ⑤

여: 인터넷으로 뭘 하고 있니, Gary?
남: 난 신청서를 작성하고 있어. 달리기 경주를 신청하고 있거든.
여: 마라톤을 하려고? 정말 멋지다!
남: 아니, 나는 단지 10킬로미터 경주를 뛸 거야.
여: 그것도 그래도 대단해. 그게 언제야?
남: 6월 8일이야. 너도 함께 하는 게 어때?
여: 아쉽지만 나는 못 할 것 같아. 나는 그날 제주도에 있을 거야.
남: 와. 너는 거기로 휴가 가는 거야?
여: 아니, 휴가는 아니야. 난 세미나에 참석해야 해.
남: 그렇구나. 네가 그 행사에 함께 할 수 없어서 유감이야.
여: 괜찮아. 나중에 함께 경주에 참가하자.

문제풀이
① 아, 너는 그것에 대해 어떻게 알아냈어?
② 나는 너와 함께 제주도로 여행 가고 싶어.
③ 고마워. 나는 지금 그 경주를 신청할게.
④ 내가 그 행사에 대해 더 많은 정보를 얻을 수 있을까?

15 ⑤

여: Alice는 늦게 일어나 학교 버스를 놓쳐서 대신 공공 버스를 타기로 결정한다. 그녀는 버스 정류장으로 달려가서 버스가 도착하기 직전에 그곳에 도착한다. 하지만 그녀는 책상 위에 지갑을 두고 온 것을 알게 된다. 그녀는 집으로 돌아가 그녀의 지갑을 가져올 시간이 없기 때문에 좌절감을 느낀다. 바로 그때, 그녀의 반 친구인 John이 그녀를 향해 다가와서, "안녕"이라고 말한다. 그녀는 그에게서 버스 요금을 낼 돈을 조금 빌리고 싶다. 이런 상황에서, Alice가 John에게 할 말로 가장 적절한 것은 무엇인가?
Alice : 내게 버스를 탈 돈 좀 빌려줄 수 있니?

문제풀이
① 어떤 버스가 우리 학교로 가니?
② 학교 버스는 어디서 정차하니?
③ 우리 학교 버스는 언제 여기에 도착할까?
④ 학교에 도착하는 데 얼마나 걸리니?

16 ④ 17 ③

남: 올해 당신의 크리스마스트리는 어떻게 생겼나요? 그것은 작년과 같은 전등과 장식물을 달고 있나요? 크리스마스가 다가오고 있고, 많은 집들이 크리스마스트리를 장식하기 시작했습니다. 매년 사람들은 같은 물건들로 크리스마스트리를 장식합니다. 하지만 올해에 특별하고 기억할 만한 크리스마스를 보내고 싶으시다면, 다른 것들을 시도해보세요. 음식들로 크리스마스트리를 장식해 보는 것이 어떻습니까? 그 음식들은 쉽게 상하지 않을 것들이어야 합니다. 그것들은 쿠키, 사탕, 견과, 그리고 말린 과일과 같은 어떤 것도 될 수 있습니다. 그것들을 색깔이 있는 작은 상자에 넣고 나무에 매달아보세요. 크리스마스 파티가 끝난 후에는, 당신은 그 음식을 여러분의 가족이나 친구들과 함께 나눠 먹을 수 있습니다. 그들은 분명 그것을 좋아할 것입니다. 어른들뿐만 아니라 아이들도 그 경험을 즐길 것입니다. 그러니 이 새롭고 맛있는 크리스마스 전통을 여러분의 집에서 시작해보는 것이 어떤가요?

DICTATION Answers

01 ask you a favor / will be reflected / remember to put
02 makes our skin extremely dry / throughout the day / keep my skin healthy
03 Do you mind if / will be released / can't wait to hear
04 put the slide / as you requested / two round tables
05 on vacation / fax it to / In return
06 looking for a new manager / who majored in / be fluent in Chinese
07 twelve years old or younger / all of the rides included / get the tickets
08 pick up presents / a big fan of / He's curious about
09 As of next week / replaced all the lockers / for free
10 Let's choose one / have two other options / only one option left
11 anything on sale
12 was in the hospital
13 all the time / searching the Internet / you're addicted to
14 filling out / Why don't you join me / take part in
15 take the public bus / left her wallet / borrow some money
16-17 have begun decorating / won't go bad easily / Children as well as adults

11 영어듣기 모의고사

본문 ☁ p.76

01 ④	02 ④	03 ②	04 ④	05 ③	06 ④
07 ③	08 ③	09 ⑤	10 ④	11 ①	12 ③
13 ②	14 ②	15 ①	16 ③	17 ③	

01 ④

여: 안녕하세요. 여러분이 뉴스에서 들으셨을지도 모르지만, 주말에 이곳 로스앤젤레스에 매우 큰 폭풍이 닥쳤습니다. 우리 사무실 근처의 많은 지역들이 일시적으로 정전이 되었습니다. 또한, 일부 도로들은 정돈되어야 합니다. 결과적으로, 저희의 전화 영어 프로그램의 교사들 중 일부가 오늘 사무실에 오지 못합니다. 그래서 몇몇 수업들이 취소되었습니다. 수업이 취소된 학생들은 사전에 문자 메시지를 받을 것입니다. 보충 수업은 가능한 한 빨리 일정이 잡힐 것입니다. 불편을 끼쳐드려 사과드립니다. 감사합니다.

02 ④

여: 너 걱정이 있는 것 같구나. 무슨 문제라도 있어?
남: 나 최근에 몸무게가 늘었어. 아마 내가 밤늦게 먹기 때문인가 봐.
여: 아, 그거 안됐구나. 체중을 줄이려고 노력해봤어?
남: 응. 간식을 먹지 않으려고 노력 중이야, 특히 밤에.
여: 그거 좋은 시작인 것 같아. 운동도 하니?
남: 그렇지는 않아. 운동을 할 충분한 시간이 없어. 그저 때때로 근력 운동을 해.
여: 왜 시간이 없어? 규칙적인 운동은 체중을 줄이는 가장 좋은 방법 중 하나야.
남: 나는 보통 밤늦게까지 사무실에서 일해.
여: 그래도, 너는 규칙적으로 운동할 시간을 좀 찾아야 해. 네 식단을 조절하는 것은 한계가 있어.
남: 그건 사실이야. 시간을 내보도록 할게.

03 ②

남: 실례합니다.
여: 네, 손님. 무엇을 도와드릴까요?
남: 음, 저는 불만이 있습니다.
여: 그러시다니 정말 유감입니다. 무엇이 문제인가요?
남: 제 방에 만족을 못 하겠어요. 침대 시트에 얼룩이 있어요.
여: 아, 사과드립니다. 청소부가 시트를 교체하는 걸 잊은 게 분명해요.
남: 또한 누군가 거기서 담배를 피운 것 같은 냄새가 납니다.
여: 지금 당장 방을 청소하라고 사람을 보내겠습니다.
남: 음, 전 정말 방이 청소될 때까지 기다리고 싶지 않아요. 그냥 다른 방으로 옮겨 주시겠어요?
여: 물론 그렇게 할 수 있어요. 불편을 드려서 다시 한번 정말로 죄송합니다.
남: 괜찮습니다. 도와주셔서 감사해요.

04 ④

여: 안녕하세요. 무엇을 도와드릴까요?
남: 제 아내를 위해 생일 케이크를 주문하고 싶습니다.
여: 좋습니다. 마음에 두고 계신 특별한 케이크가 있나요?
남: 음, 아랫단에 하트들이 있는 3단 케이크를 원해요.
여: 알겠습니다, 그리고 가운데 단은요?
남: 주위에 줄무늬만 좀 넣어주세요.
여: 알겠습니다.
남: 하지만 가장 윗단을 어떻게 장식해야 할지 모르겠어요.
여: 음, 작은 점들은 어떤가요?
남: 아, 그거 괜찮을 것 같네요. 또, 케이크 꼭대기에 별 모양의 장식품을 놓아주실 수 있으세요?
여: 그럼요. 근사할 것 같네요. 그리고 아랫단 주위에 약간의 꽃들을 더 하는 건 어떠세요?
남: 네, 멋지겠네요!

05 ③

남: 안녕, Wendy. 너 새로운 일자리를 찾고 있지, 맞아?
여: 맞아, Bob. 실은, 내일 면접이 있어.
남: 와! 네가 일자리를 구하길 바랄게.
여: 음, 잘 모르겠어. 나는 면접이 정말 긴장돼.
남: 그냥 긴장을 풀어봐. 네가 그 회사에 대한 정보를 찾는 걸 내가 도와줄게. 그 정보로 면접관에게 깊은 인상을 줄 수 있어.
여: 고마워, 하지만 난 이미 많은 조사를 했어.
남: 그러면 내가 네 면접 연습을 도와주는 건 어때?
여: 좋은 생각이야! 네가 면접관들이 물어볼 만한 면접 질문들을 좀 해줄 수 있어?
남: 그럼. 지금 바로 시작하자.
여: 고마워. 그러면 나는 훨씬 덜 긴장될 거야.

06 ④

[전화벨이 울린다.]
여: 안녕하세요. EZ 전자제품 고객 서비스입니다.
남: 안녕하세요. 저는 Kevin Taylor라고 합니다. 제가 지난주에 귀사의 웹사이트에서 스마트폰을 주문했거든요.
여: 네, Taylor 씨. 아직 배송을 받지 못하셨나요?
남: 아니요, 어제 받았어요. 그런데 문제가 있어요.
여: 아, 무엇이 문제죠?
남: 개봉했을 때 그것이 파손되어 있었어요.
여: 그러시다니 정말 유감입니다. 그것이 어떻게 파손되어 있었나요?
남: 스마트폰의 액정이 깨져 있었어요.
여: 그렇군요. 그걸 새것으로 교환하시고 싶으신가요?
남: 아니요, 환불을 원해요.
여: 알겠습니다. 그러시면 제품을 다시 저희에게 보내주세요. 물건이 도착하면, 저희가 고객님의 계좌로 돈을 환불해드리겠습니다. 다시 한번, 정말 죄송합니다.

07 ③

여: 안녕하세요. 무엇을 도와드릴까요?
남: 저희 회사의 신년 파티를 위해 홀을 하나 대관하고 싶습니다.
여: 알겠습니다. 파티가 언제죠?
남: 12월 31일입니다. 45명이 갈 거예요.
여: 그러시면 Rose 홀이 그날 오후 3시부터 8시까지 이용 가능해요.
남: 저는 그 홀을 오후 3시부터 7시까지 대관하고 싶어요.
여: 아주 잘됐네요. 대관료는 한 시간에 150달러입니다. 하지만 음향 시스템을 사용하시면 한 시간에 50달러의 추가 요금이 있습니다.
남: 저희는 음향 시스템도 필요해요.
여: 알겠습니다. 준비해드릴게요. 40명이 넘으시기 때문에 단체 할인을 받으실 수 있습니다. 전체 금액에서 10퍼센트 할인됩니다.
남: 그거 좋군요.

문제풀이

시간당 대관료가 150달러인 강당을 4시간 동안 빌리기로 했고, 시간당 50달러의 추가 요금이 발생하는 음향 시스템도 사용하기로 했으므로, 800달러(= ($150+$50)×4)의 비용이 발생한다. 그런데 단체 할인으로 10퍼센트를 할인받을 수 있으므로 남자가 지불할 금액은 총 720달러(= $800×0.9)이다.

08 ③

[전화벨이 울린다.]
여: 안녕하세요. Happy Times 유치원입니다.
남: 안녕하세요. 제 딸을 이 유치원에 등록시킬까 하는데요, 몇 가지 질문이 있어요.
여: 좋습니다. 무엇을 알고 싶으신가요?
남: 그곳 선생님들은 교사 경력이 있으신가요?
여: 네. 그들은 모두 최소 3년의 교사 경력이 있어요.
남: 그거 좋네요. 한 반에는 몇 명의 학생들이 있습니까?
여: 각 반에는 15명에서 18명의 학생들이 있습니다.
남: 그렇군요. 그리고 특별 수업도 있나요?
여: 네. 발레와 태권도 수업이 있습니다.
남: 알겠습니다, 그리고 마지막 질문이 있어요. 유치원까지 셔틀버스가 있나요?
여: 네, 물론이죠. 이 근처에 살고 계시면 그 버스를 이용하실 수 있어요.
남: 좋네요. 정보를 주셔서 감사합니다.

09 ⑤

남: 안녕하세요, 쇼핑객 여러분. Hearst 백화점에서 쇼핑해주셔서 감사합니다. 오늘, 여러분께 저희의 특별 프로그램에 대해 알려드리려고 합니다. 지금부터 이번 달 말까지, 저희는 나무 심기 캠페인을 할 것입니다. 이 기간 동안 모든 판매 금액의 1%는 나무를 심는 일에 보탬이 될 것입니다. 저희는 이 돈을 중국의 사막에 나무를 심는 데 쓸 것입니다. 저희는 5,000그루가 넘는 나무를 심을 계획입니다. 1층 정문에 모금함도 있습니다. 고객님들 누구나 돈을 기부하실 수 있습니다. 여러분이 원하는 만큼 기부하실 수 있습니다. 이곳에서 쇼핑해주셔서 감사드립니다. 즐거운 하루 되십시오.

10 ④

남: 안녕하세요. 무엇을 도와드릴까요?
여: 태블릿 컴퓨터를 찾고 있어요.
남: 알겠습니다, 이쪽으로 오세요. *[잠시 후]* 이것들이 저희가 가진 태블릿 컴퓨터들입니다.
여: 그렇군요. 64기가바이트나 그 이상인 것이 있나요? 저는 대용량 메모리가 있는 모델이 필요하거든요.
남: 그럼요. 이 세 제품 중에서 고르실 수 있습니다. 화면 크기는요?
여: 저는 태블릿 컴퓨터로 비디오를 보고 싶어요. 큰 화면이 있는 걸 원해요.
남: 그러시면, 11인치 화면을 가진 것이 좋을 겁니다. 생각하고 계신 특정한 가격이 있나요?
여: 네, 850달러보다는 싼 태블릿 컴퓨터를 원해요.
남: 그러시면 이것이 손님에게 적당한 거네요.
여: 그러네요. 그걸로 할게요.

11 ①

여: 안녕, Gary. 너 Tony가 지난주에 수술받은 거 들었어?
남: 응. 나는 지금 그 애를 보려고 병원에 가는 중이야.
여: 그러면 곧 회복하길 바란다고 전해줘.
남: 네가 그렇게 말했다고 그 애에게 알려줄게.

문제풀이

② 그는 왼쪽 무릎에 수술이 필요했어.
③ 그는 내일 병원에 갈 거야.
④ 고마워. 나는 매우 빨리 회복했어.
⑤ 그러면 거기서 3시에 만나자.

12 ③

남: Driving World에 오신 걸 환영합니다. 도와드릴까요?
여: 네. 앞으로 이틀 동안 차를 한 대 빌리고 싶은데요.
남: 그렇군요. 어떤 종류의 차를 원하시나요?
여: 승합차를 찾고 있어요.

문제풀이

① 저는 그걸 3일 동안 빌릴 거예요.
② 저는 최신 모델을 구입했어요.
④ 당신의 운전 면허증을 볼 수 있을까요?
⑤ 당신은 화요일까지 차를 돌려주셔야 합니다.

13 ②

[전화벨이 울린다.]
남: 안녕하세요! Life Saver 보험사의 Bob입니다. 무엇을 도와드릴까요?
여: 안녕하세요, 언제 제 자동차 보험 증권 사본을 받을 수 있는지 알고 싶어서요.
남: 물론이죠. 성함을 말씀해주시겠어요?
여: 제 이름은 Jennifer Smith입니다. 어제 다른 사람에게 그것을 이메일로 보내 달라고 요청했는데요.
남: 확인해볼게요. *[잠시 후]* 네, 어제 고객님께 그걸 이메일로 보내 드린 걸로 나오는데요. 이메일을 다시 확인해보시겠어요?
여: 제가 방금 확인했는데, 아무것도 없었어요.

남: 전에 저희로부터 이메일을 받은 적 있으세요?
여: 아니요, 없어요.
남: 가끔은 저희 이메일이 스팸 메일 폴더로 가기도 합니다.
여: 아, 그 폴더를 지금 당장 확인해볼게요.

문제풀이
① 네, 그것은 계속 받은편지함에 있었어요.
③ 제가 폴더를 만들면 알려드릴게요.
④ 죄송합니다. 저는 그냥 자동차 보험이 필요하지 않아요.
⑤ 걱정하지 마세요. 제가 이메일로 사본을 보내 드릴게요.

14 ②

여: Harrison 선생님, 잠깐 시간 좀 있으세요?
남: 물론이지. 무슨 일로 왔니?
여: 제 보고서가 왜 D를 받았는지 여쭤보고 싶었어요.
남: 음, 네가 인터넷에서 일부 정보를 베낀 것을 발견했단다. 너는 단어 하나조차 바꾸지 않았더구나.
여: 하지만 그것은 단지 몇 문장일 뿐이었는걸요, Harrison 선생님.
남: 너는 모든 걸 너의 말로 적어야 했단다, Rachel. 내가 그걸 수업 중에 설명했단다.
여: 만일 제가 다시 쓴다면요?
남: 모든 사람들이 이 과제를 끝내는 데 같은 양의 시간이 주어졌어, Rachel.
여: 다시 한번 기회를 얻을 수는 없을까요? 당장 다시 할게요.
남: 미안하지만 그건 공정하지 않아.

문제풀이
① 아니다, 다음에는 그냥 인터넷을 이용하거라.
③ 나에게 제발 다시 한번 기회를 주렴.
④ 유감이지만 너는 사본을 한 부 더 만들 수 없단다.
⑤ 너는 웹사이트에서 정보를 찾았어야 했어.

15 ①

여: Hailey는 쇼핑몰에서 쇼핑을 한 뒤 그녀의 차로 걸어가고 있다. 그녀가 차에 도달했을 때, 그녀는 그녀가 산 것을 차 트렁크에 넣기 시작한다. 그때, 한 남자가 그녀 옆을 지나가고, 그의 지갑이 주머니에서 나와 땅에 떨어진다. 그는 알아차리지 못한 것처럼 보이고 계속 걸어간다. Hailey는 다른 누군가가 그것을 주워서 가져갈까 봐 걱정한다. 그녀는 그 남자에게 그것에 대해 알려주고 싶다. 이런 상황에서, Hailey가 그 남자에게 할 말로 가장 적절한 것은 무엇인가?
Hailey : 당신이 지갑을 떨어뜨리신 것 같아요!

문제풀이
② 실례지만, 어디를 가고 계시죠?
③ 어딘가에서 제 지갑을 보셨나요?
④ 쇼핑몰이 어디인지 아세요?
⑤ 제가 이 가방들을 트렁크에 넣는 걸 도와주세요.

16 ③ 17 ③

남: 여러분이 팀의 일원으로 일을 해본 적이 있다면, 다른 사람들과 함께 일을 하는 것이 이점이 있다는 것을 알 것입니다. 그것이 제가 학교 연극 동아리에 가입했을 때 배운 것입니다. 함께 일을 하는 것의 가장 좋은 점은 우리가 더 창의적인 대본을 만들 수 있었다는 것이었습니다. 동아리에는 20명의 사람들이 있었기 때문에, 우리는 선택할 수 있는 많은 아이디어들이 있었습니다. 또한, 일이 우리 모두에게 배분되어서 스트레스를 많이 주지 않았습니다. 저는 주로 연기를 했음에도 불구하고, 가끔은 분장이나 의상 제작에 대한 의견을 제시하였습니다. 게다가 우리는 연극을 리허설을 할 때 서로에게 조언을 해주었습니다. 그 결과, 우리는 지역 연극 대회에서 1등을 차지했고 전국 연극 대회에 출전할 기회를 얻었습니다. 저는 우리의 팀워크 덕분에 우리가 이러한 훌륭한 결과를 얻게 되었다고 생각합니다.

DICTATION Answers

01 a very big storm / have been canceled / as soon as possible
02 gained weight recently / don't have enough time / Controlling your diet
03 have a complaint / must have forgotten to change / move to a different room
04 put some stripes / how to decorate / add some flowers
05 you get the job / impress the interviewers / give me some interview questions
06 get your shipment / It was damaged / I want a refund
07 is available / The rental fee / get a group discount
08 enrolling my daughter / How many students / a shuttle bus
09 let you know / in some deserts / as much as you wish
10 looking for / choose among these three items / to be less than
11 he recovers soon
12 rent a car
13 a copy of / email it to me / there was nothing
14 copied some information / in your own words / have a second chance
15 shopping at the mall / slips out of his pocket / let the man know
16-17 working with others / was divided among / got a chance to participate

12 영어듣기 모의고사

본문 ☁ p.83

01 ②	02 ②	03 ④	04 ④	05 ②	06 ⑤
07 ③	08 ④	09 ⑤	10 ②	11 ⑤	12 ②
13 ⑤	14 ④	15 ③	16 ④	17 ④	

01 ②

여: 안녕하세요! 저는 교장 Johns입니다. 일기 예보에 따르면, 오늘 밤에 강력한 태풍이 온다고 합니다. 따라서 저는 여러분들이 교실을 보호하기 위해 무엇을 해야 하는지를 말씀드리고 싶습니다. 우선, 오늘 교실을 나가기 전에 모든 창문을 반드시 닫아주세요. 그것은 태풍이 여러분의 컴퓨터와 TV를 파손하지 않도록 해줄 것입니다. 두 번째로, 커튼을 닫는 것도 중요합니다. 만약 태풍이 창문을 깨뜨리면, 커튼은 유리 파편들이 교실 곳곳에 흩어지는 것을 막아줄 수 있습니다. 학교를 나가기 전에 이러한 것들이 되어 있는지 확인해주세요. 감사합니다.

02 ②

여: 너 피곤해 보여, Mark. 괜찮아?
남: 그냥 최근에 잠을 잘 못 자고 있는데, 왜 그런지 잘 모르겠어.
여: 음, 충분한 잠을 자는 건 네 건강에 정말 중요해. 너는 운동을 많이 하니?
남: 그냥 조금. 왜? 운동이 수면에 좋아?
여: 물론이지. 적절한 운동은 네가 더 잘 그리고 더 깊게 자도록 도와줄 거야.
남: 그렇구나.
여: 취침 시간 전에 따뜻한 물로 샤워하는 것도 중요해. 그건 네 몸의 긴장을 풀어줘.
남: 알겠어. 책을 읽는 건 어때? 나는 그게 잠이 드는 걸 더 쉽게 해준다고 들었는데.
여: 그건 사실이 아니야. 독서는 사실 네가 잠들려고 애쓸 때 너의 뇌를 깨어있게 해.
남: 아, 그건 몰랐어.

03 ④

[전화벨이 울린다.]
여: 여보세요, Food Network입니다. 무엇을 도와드릴까요?
남: 여보세요, 저는 유명한 요리사인 Nigel Sparks와 함께하는 요리 수업에 참석할 기회를 주는 행사에 응모했는데요. 이제 결과가 나왔는지 알고 싶어서요.
여: 그럼요. 성함을 말씀해주시겠어요?
남: 네. 제 이름은 Edward James입니다.
여: 확인 좀 해볼게요. *[잠시 후]* 축하드립니다! 당신은 이 요리 수업에 참여할 8명 중의 한 명입니다.
남: 놀라워요! 수천 명의 사람들이 이 행사에 지원했다고 들었어요.
여: 네, 이 행사가 한 해에 한 번만 제공되기 때문에 항상 응모자들이 많습니다.
남: 대단히 감사합니다. 이 기회를 얻게 되어 정말 고맙네요.
여: 다시 한번 축하드립니다, James 씨.

04 ④

남: 나는 내 생일 파티 초대장을 만들고 있어. 나를 도와줄 수 있어?
여: 물론이지. 그 위에 네 사진을 붙이는 건 어때? 네 생일이잖아!
남: 좋아. 그걸 왼쪽에 붙일게. 그런데 초대장 맨 위에 무엇을 적어야 할지 모르겠어.
여: "당신은 초대되었습니다!"가 좋은 것 같아.
남: 좋아. 이제 어디에 날짜, 시간 그리고 장소를 적어야 할까?
여: 그거 전부를 오른편에 적는 건 어때?
남: 좋아, 하지만 하단에는 무엇을 넣어야 할까?
여: 뭔가를 그리는 건 어때?
남: 밝은 별들이 좋을 것 같아.
여: 그거 멋지겠다. 네 전화번호를 넣는 것을 잊지 마.
남: 그건 별들 바로 아래에 넣을게.

05 ②

남: 안녕, Vanessa. 내일 세미나 장소가 바뀌었다는 거 들었어?
여: 아니, 못 들었어. 왜 바뀌었는데?
남: 좌석이 모든 사람이 앉기에 충분하지 않았던 거 같아.
여: 그랬구나. 그밖에 변경된 것이 있니?
남: 아니, 그게 전부야. 그런데 새로운 장소는 더 멀어. 그래서 우리는 계획한 것보다 더 일찍 출발해야 해.
여: 아, 그 새로운 장소가 어디인지 알아?
남: 응. 모두에게 지도를 이메일로 보냈어.
여: 정말? 나에게 한 부 출력해줄 수 있어?
남: 물론이지. 내 사무실로 올라가자, 그러면 내가 그걸 출력해줄게.
여: 좋아. 네가 나에게 새로운 소식을 알려줘서 다행이야. 나는 잘못된 장소로 갈 뻔했어!

06 ⑤

남: Amy, 내가 어제 널 시내에서 본 것 같아.
여: 아, 정말? 나는 그 지역에서 아파트를 보고 있었어. 다른 곳으로 이사갈 생각을 하고 있거든.
남: 하지만 너는 지금 사는 곳으로 최근에 이사하지 않았어?
여: 맞아, 그리고 나도 우리 아파트가 정말 좋아. 넓기도 하고 멋진 조망이 있거든.
남: 그런데 왜 이사하려는 거야? 너무 비싸?
여: 아니, 집세는 괜찮아. 난 그저 교통이 얼마나 불편한지 생각하지 못했어. 사무실에 가는 데 거의 두 시간이 걸리거든.
남: 그렇구나. 그래서 괜찮은 곳을 찾았어?
여: 아니. 그것들은 전부 1층이었어. 나는 더 높은 곳을 원하거든.
남: 곧 찾을 거라고 확신해.

07 ③

남: 안녕하세요, Coffee King에 오신 걸 환영합니다. 무엇을 드릴까요?

여: 안녕하세요, 아메리카노는 얼마예요?
남: 보통 크기 아메리카노는 2달러이고, 큰 것은 3달러입니다.
여: 큰 아메리카노 한 잔 주세요.
남: 뜨거운 걸로 드릴까요, 아니면 아이스로 드릴까요? 아이스 음료는 50센트가 추가됩니다.
여: 아이스로 주세요. 그리고 저 바나나 머핀 중 하나를 살게요. 맛있어 보여요.
남: 알겠습니다. 그건 1달러 50센트지만, 단 2달러에 두 개를 구입하실 수 있으세요.
여: 저는 하나만 살게요. 그리고 여기 제 할인카드요.
남: 알겠습니다. 그러면 총액에서 10퍼센트 할인됩니다.
여: 고맙습니다.

문제풀이

여자는 3달러 50센트인 큰 사이즈의 아이스 아메리카노와 1달러 50센트인 바나나 머핀 한 개를 샀고, 10퍼센트의 카드 할인을 받았으므로 총 4달러 50센트(= ($3.50+$1.50)×0.9)를 지불해야 한다.

08 ④

여: 안녕하세요. 이곳이 아이들 장난감들을 빌려주는 가게인가요?
남: 네. 저희는 3세에서 7세 사이의 아이들을 위한 많은 장난감들이 있습니다.
여: 그거 좋네요. 저는 세 살짜리 아들을 위한 장난감이 필요해요.
남: 그러면 이것들을 좀 보세요. 어린아이들이 이 장난감을 갖고 노는 것을 좋아합니다.
여: 얼마 동안 빌릴 수 있나요?
남: 장난감은 2주 동안 대여됩니다.
여: 그렇군요. 대여료는 얼마인가요?
남: 모든 장난감들은 각 3달러입니다.
여: 제가 2주 이내에 반납하지 못하면 어떻게 되나요?
남: 그러면 하루에 1달러의 연체료를 부과합니다.
여: 알겠어요. 영업시간은 어떻게 되죠?
남: 일요일을 제외하고 매일 오전 9시부터 오후 8시까지 영업합니다.
여: 좋네요.

09 ⑤

남: 안녕하세요, 학생 여러분. 새로운 학기가 막 시작되었고, 방과 후 수업을 등록할 시간이 다가오고 있습니다. 학생들은 세 개의 수업까지 참여할 수 있고, 모든 학생들은 적어도 하나의 수업에는 참석해야 합니다. 각 수업은 5달러입니다. 학교 웹사이트에 수업들이 사진과 함께 소개되어 있습니다. 등록 마감은 다음 주 수요일 오후 6시입니다. 등록을 하기 위해서는 부모님의 서명이 있는 동의서가 필요합니다. 동의서는 각 교실의 뒤편에 있습니다. 등록 기간은 내일 아침에 시작됩니다. 질문이 있다면, 선생님들에게 물어보십시오. 감사합니다!

10 ②

여: 여기 기차 시간표가 있어. 우리가 탈 기차를 정해보자.
남: 좋아. 우리는 내일 파리로 가는 아침 기차를 타야 해.
여: 고속 열차를 타자. 그건 30분밖에 안 걸려.
남: 좋아. 우리는 몇 시에 거기에 가야 하지?
여: 회의가 10시에 시작하니까 9시 30분 전에 도착하면 괜찮아.
남: 맞아, 그런데 우리가 더 이른 기차를 타면, 우리는 회의 전에 아침을 먹을 시간이 있을 거야.
여: 아, 동의해. 하지만 그러려면 우리는 식당 칸을 타면 돼.
남: 음, 나는 기차에서 먹고 싶지는 않아. 또한, 식당 칸이 있는 기차는 더 비싸잖아.
여: 알겠어. 파리에서 아침을 먹자.
남: 좋아. 그러면 이걸 타자.

11 ⑤

여: 너는 공항에 곧 가야 하지, 그렇지 않아?
남: 그래. 비행기가 오후 6시에 출발해서 난 지금 가는 게 좋겠어.
여: 네가 원한다면 내가 널 태워줄 수 있어.
남: 괜찮아. 공항 셔틀버스를 타면 돼.

문제풀이

① 나는 방금 공항에 도착했어.
② 어머니께서 어제 나를 태워주셨어.
③ 좋아. 기꺼이 너를 태워줄게.
④ 공항에서 오후 5시에 만나자.

12 ②

남: 엄마, 우리는 얼마나 많은 오렌지를 사야 하죠?
여: 한 상자에 오렌지 30개가 있어. 한 상자를 전부 사자.
남: 하지만 너무 많은 것 같은데요. 우린 그걸 전부 먹을 수 없어요.
여: 그렇다면, 반 상자만 살게.

문제풀이

① 그래, 우린 돈을 더 아껴야 해.
③ 나도 알아. 오렌지를 재배하는 것은 쉽지 않아.
④ 정확해. 넌 껍질 또한 이용할 수 있어.
⑤ 맞아, 우리는 과일을 더 자주 먹어야 해.

13 ⑤

남: 나는 내일 역사 수업 시간에 발표를 해야 해.
여: 아, 정말? 주제가 뭐야?
남: 한국의 조선 왕조에 대해 이야기할 거야.
여: 그거 멋지다. 너는 아시아 역사에 대해 많이 알잖아, 그렇지 않니?
남: 응, 그래. 그리고 난 많이 조사했어.
여: 좋아. 너 정말 잘할 거야!
남: 나는 그것에 대해서는 걱정이 안 돼. 그런데 나는 학급 전체 앞에서 말하는 건 싫어.
여: 왜? 긴장되니?
남: 많이. 나는 말할 것을 잊을까 봐 걱정돼.
여: 발표할 내용을 오늘 밤에 스스로 계속 반복해봐.
남: 그게 도움이 될 것 같아?
여: 물론이지. 연습은 네가 실수를 덜 하도록 도와줄 거야.

문제풀이

① 아니. 나는 역사 과목을 잘 못했어.

② 아마도. 너는 더 쉬운 주제가 필요해.
③ 응. 그것을 피할 방법이 없어.
④ 미안해. 너를 도와줄 충분한 시간이 없어.

14 ④

여: Colin, 여름 휴가 계획 있어?
남: 특별히 없어. 하지만 이번 여름에는 뭔가 특별한 것을 해보고 싶어.
여: 그럼 우리 하이킹을 가는 게 어때?
남: 좋은 생각이야. 어디를 갈까?
여: 설악산에 가자. 내가 괜찮은 등반 코스를 알아.
남: 멋진 것 같아! 나는 그 산 정상에 정말 올라가보고 싶어. 얼마나 머무를 거야?
여: 이틀 정도가 좋을 거야. 우리는 산장에서 밤을 보낼 수 있어.
남: 정말 신난다! 어서 가고 싶어.
여: 한 가지 더. 우리는 온라인으로 산장을 예약해야 해. 그걸 해줄 수 있어?
남: 웹사이트를 알려주면, 지금 당장 예약할게.

문제풀이
① 난 너와 함께 갈 수 없을 것 같아.
② 아, 산장을 예약해줘서 고마워.
③ 음, 우리는 장소를 바꾸는 게 낫겠어.
⑤ 만일에 대비하여 우리는 따뜻한 옷가지와 먹을 걸 싸야 해.

15 ③

여: Todd는 어머니가 원하셔서 요즘 여섯 개의 학원에 다닌다. 그는 수학, 영어, 한국어, 역사, 과학, 그리고 중국어를 공부한다. 그는 그것들을 공부하는 것을 좋아하지만, 그는 스트레스를 받기 시작한다. 그는 모든 숙제를 할 충분한 시간이 없다. 그는 몇 개의 학원을 가는 것을 그만둬야 한다고 생각한다. 게다가, 한국어와 역사, 과학에 관해서는, 그는 혼자 공부할 수 있다고 생각한다. 그는 어머니에게 자신이 어떻게 느끼는지를 말하고 싶어 한다. 이런 상황에서, Todd가 어머니에게 할 말로 가장 적절한 것은 무엇인가?
Todd : 엄마, 저는 수업 중 몇 개를 그만두어야 할 것 같아요.

문제풀이
① 저는 괜찮은 무료 온라인 강의를 찾았어요.
② 학교 끝나고 수업을 하나 더 들어도 될까요?
④ 저는 반 친구들과 과학 수업을 들을 거예요.
⑤ 저를 학원까지 태워주시면 안 돼요?

16 ④ 17 ④

남: 인간의 몸에는 수백 개의 뼈가 있습니다. 밖에서는 보이지 않지만, 그것들은 매우 중요합니다. 그리고 만약 뼈가 아동기에 잘 발달하지 못한다면, 아이들은 제대로 자라지 못합니다. 놀랍게도, 어떤 연구는 요즘 아동의 뼈는 매우 약하다는 것을 보여줍니다. 그래서 튼튼한 뼈를 가지고 자라게 하기 위해 아이들은 건강한 습관을 기르는 것이 필요합니다. 우선, 아이들이 콩과 우유와 같이 칼슘이 많이 들어 있는 음식을 먹어야 합니다. 두 번째로, 비타민 D 또한 건강한 뼈 성장에 필수적입니다. 붉은 고기, 계란, 그리고 기름진 생선은 비타민 D의 좋은 원천이므로, 그 음식들을 자주 섭취하는 것이 중요합니다. 게다가, 매일 10분에서 15분 동안 야외에서 햇빛을 받으며 보내는 것은 또한 비타민 D를 체내에 공급합니다. 마지막으로, 규칙적으로 운동하는 것은 언제나 좋습니다. 심지어 가벼운 운동을 하는 것도 뼈가 튼튼해지도록 도와줍니다.

DICTATION Answers

01 According to the weather forecast / be sure to close / these things are done
02 getting enough sleep / relaxes your body / trying to fall asleep
03 the results are out / one of the eight people / once a year
04 put your picture / on the right side / Don't forget to add
05 farther away / Do you mind printing / would have gone to
06 looking at apartments / has a nice view / get to the office
07 can I get you / fifty cents extra / off of your total
08 between three to seven / are rented out / charge a late fee
09 up to three classes / The deadline for / begins tomorrow morning
10 take an express train / time to eat breakfast / more expensive
11 give you a ride
12 that's too much
13 give a presentation / did a lot of research / over and over again
14 why don't we go hiking / go up to the peak / reserve the cabin
15 feel stressed out / when it comes to / how he feels
16-17 hundreds of bones / grow up with strong bones / good to exercise regularly

13 영어듣기 모의고사

본문 ▲ p.90

01 ⑤	02 ②	03 ⑤	04 ③	05 ③	06 ②
07 ⑤	08 ④	09 ③	10 ①	11 ⑤	12 ①
13 ①	14 ④	15 ⑤	16 ⑤	17 ②	

01 ⑤

여: 주목해주시겠습니까? 여러분 모두가 아시다시피, 이 기숙사 건물의 몇 구역은 보수가 필요합니다. 즉시 수리되어야 하는 몇 개의 누수 파이프들이 있습니다. 또한, 낡은 카펫들은 교체되어야 합니다. 이 작업이 이번 주말에 시행될 것이며, 그 기간 동안, 모든 거주자들은 다른 곳에 머물러야 합니다. 여러분은 일요일 오후 5시 이후에 기숙사에 들어오실 수 있습니다. 만약 머무실 곳이 없으면, 기숙사 대표에게 말씀해주세요, 그러면 그가 다른 기숙사에 방을 준비해줄 것입니다. 불편을 끼쳐드려 죄송합니다.

02 ②

남: 이봐, Janet! Janet, 너 내 말 들려?
여: 아. 안녕, Ralph. 미안해, 나 이어폰을 끼고 있었어.
남: 나도 알아. 너의 음악을 들을 수 있었거든.
여: 아, 음악 소리가 조금 컸나 보다.
남: 응, 넌 볼륨을 낮추는 걸 고려해봐야 해. 큰 소리는 너의 청력을 손상시킬 수 있어.
여: 나도 알아, 하지만 볼륨을 높이지 않으면 나는 아무것도 듣지 못해.
남: 그래도, 넌 너의 귀를 보호해야 해. 또한 네가 길을 걷는 동안에는 이어폰을 끼면 안 돼.
여: 왜 그래야 해?
남: 자동차나 자전거가 네 쪽으로 오는 것을 네가 알아차리지 못할 수도 있기 때문이야. 너는 다칠 수도 있어.
여: 맞아. 더 조심하도록 노력할게.

03 ⑤

여: 안녕하세요! 무엇을 도와드릴까요?
남: 제 피부가 최근에 매우 건조해지고 있어요. 특히 얼굴이 그래요.
여: 그건 겨울에 흔한 문제에요. 차갑고 건조한 공기가 우리 피부에 나쁠 수 있어요.
남: 도움이 될 만한 걸 추천해주실 수 있나요?
여: 물론이죠! 여기 이 크림은 매우 강한 보습제예요. 저희의 가장 잘 팔리는 제품들 중 하나죠.
남: 음… 근데 이건 향이 굉장히 강하네요. 향이 별로 강하지 않은 다른 제품이 있나요?
여: 네. 이건 어떠세요? 이건 어떤 향도 없지만, 분명 고객님의 피부를 부드럽고 매끈하게 유지시켜줄 거예요.
남: 그거 좋아 보이는군요. 이거 한 병을 살게요.
여: 좋아요. 여기 있어요.

04 ③

여: 크리스마스가 다가오고 있어! 아름다운 장식품들을 모두 빨리 보고 싶어.
남: 아, 나는 어제 쇼핑몰에서 아름다운 크리스마스트리를 봤어.
여: 그랬어? 그건 어떻게 생겼어?
남: 음, 그건 매우 높았고, 꼭대기에 큰 별이 있었어.
여: 와! 다른 장식품들도 달려 있었어?
남: 응. 별 아래에 큰 리본이 하나 있었어. 그리고 그것 아래에 긴 크리스마스 양말을 하나 걸어놨어.
여: 예쁘겠네. 또 다른 건?
남: 트리 하단에 작은 종들이 몇 개 매달려 있었어.
여: 트리 아래에 선물들도 있었어?
남: 응, 다섯 개의 선물 상자들이 있었어!
여: 멋진 것 같다. 나도 그걸 보고 싶어!

05 ③

[문 두드리는 소리]
남: 들어오세요!
여: 안녕, David. 짐 풀고 있어?
남: 응, 거의 끝났어. 이제 몇 개만 남았어.
여: 내가 도와줄 수 있는 일이 있어?
남: 괜찮아. 네가 날 위해 이 집을 찾아줬으니, 너는 이미 나를 충분히 도와줬어.
여: 그건 아무것도 아니야. 나는 그저 신문에서 광고를 보고 알려줬을 뿐이야.
남: 음, 다시 한번 고마워. 어쨌든, 나는 곧 저녁 식사를 만들 식료품을 사러 가야 해.
여: 너는 하루 종일 짐을 풀어서 분명 피곤할 거야. 중국 음식을 주문 하는 게 어때?
남: 아, 하지만 나는 이 지역에 대해 아직 아무것도 몰라. 괜찮은 식당 아는 곳 있어?
여: 응, 내가 전화번호를 알아. 내가 전화할게.

06 ②

남: 안녕, Sally. 너 여전히 다음 달에 우리와 함께 스페인에 가는 것에 관심이 있니?
여: 아쉽지만, 난 당분간 어떤 여행도 갈 수 없어.
남: 정말? 왜? 몸이 별로 안 좋아?
여: 나는 괜찮아. 단지 일정이 매우 빡빡할 뿐이야.
남: 아, 맞아. 네가 다음 달에 새 아파트로 이사 간다는 걸 잊었네.
여: 사실, 그건 문제가 아니야. 내 출장이 너희의 스페인 여행과 같은 시기라는 걸 방금 들었어.
남: 아, 그거 안됐구나. 스페인에 가기에 완벽한 때인데!
여: 나도 알아. 나는 정말 가고 싶었는데.
남: 걱정 마. 너는 거기에 다음에 갈 수 있을 거야.
여: 맞아. 어쨌든 재미있게 보내!

07 ⑤

[휴대전화가 울린다.]
남: Jane, 너 어디니? 너 지금 시카고니?
여: 나 아직 집으로 가는 공항에 있어.
남: 왜? 난 네가 지금쯤 이미 여기 있을 거라고 생각했는데.
여: 비행기가 정오에 출발하기로 되어 있었는데, 눈보라 때문에 지연되고 있어.
남: 아, 그거 안됐다. 그러면 비행기는 언제 출발해?
여: 오후 3시에. 나는 워싱턴 DC에서 다른 비행기로 갈아타야 해.
남: 워싱턴 DC에 도착하는 데는 얼마나 걸려?
여: 두 시간. 거기다, 갈아타기 전에 거기서 또 두 시간을 기다려야 해.
남: 그렇구나. 그 후에 너는 거기에서 시카고로 한 시간 비행을 해야 하지, 맞아?
여: 맞아.
남: 알겠어. 우리 일정을 좀 바꿔야겠어.

문제풀이

여자는 오후 3시에 출발하여 워싱턴 DC까지 두 시간 동안 가는 비행기를 타고, 워싱턴 DC에서 두 시간을 대기한 후에 시카고까지 한 시간 동안 비행기를 타게 되므로, 시카고에는 오후 8시에 도착할 것이다.

08 ④

여: 이 상점을 둘러보자. 나는 새 코트를 사야 해.
남: 그래. 여기 이건 어때? 디자인이 마음에 들어.
여: 나도 그래. 그리고 노란색이 정말 눈에 띄어. 그 색은 디자인과 완벽하게 어울려.
남: 나도 그렇게 생각해. 그리고 꼬리표에는 그것이 고품질의 모직으로 만들어져 있다고 쓰여 있어.
여: 응. 그건 정말 중요해. 나를 따뜻하게 해줄 거야
남: 그리고 가벼운 것 같아.
여: 맞아. 여기에 200그램보다 적게 나간다고 쓰여 있어.
남: 하지만 약간 비싸네. 코트 하나에 320달러는 비싸.
여: 그건 괜찮아. 나는 인터넷에서 검색해본 다음에 그 정도는 지불할 것으로 이미 예상했어.
남: 그렇다면, 너는 이걸 사야겠네.

09 ③

남: 만약 여러분이 홍콩으로 여행을 계획 중이라면, 여러분은 Central-Mid-Levels 에스컬레이터에 가보셔야 합니다. 그것은 그 도시의 가장 독특한 관광 명소 중 한 곳입니다. 그것은 지붕이 있는 세계에서 가장 긴 야외 에스컬레이터 시스템입니다. 그것은 원래 사람들이 그들의 집과 홍콩의 중심가에 있는 사무실 사이를 오가는 것을 돕기 위해 1993년에 지어졌습니다. 지금은, 6만 명이 넘는 사람들이 매일 그 에스컬레이터를 이용합니다. 오전 6시부터 오전 10시까지, 그 에스컬레이터는 내리막 방향으로 움직입니다. 그러고 나서 오전 10시 30분부터 자정까지, 그것이 오르막 방향으로 움직입니다. 그것은 타는 것은 무료이고, 편도는 약25분이 걸립니다. 그것은 당신이 쉽게 잊을 수 없는 재미있는 경험이 될 것입니다!

10 ①

남: 실례합니다, 저 좀 도와주실 수 있으신가요?
여: 그럼요, 손님. 무엇을 도와드릴까요?
남: 두통이 있는데, 어떤 약을 사야 할지 모르겠어요.
여: 알겠습니다. 이것들이 저희가 갖고 있는 모든 두통약들입니다. 이 중에서 하나 고르시면 됩니다.
남: 어느 것을 추천하시겠어요?
여: 어디 한번 봅시다. 통증이 얼마나 심한가요?
남: 아주 심한 건 아니라서, 강한 약이 필요한 것 같지는 않아요.
여: 알겠습니다. 그러면 물약을 드셔도 괜찮으세요?
남: 저는 물약 맛을 좋아하지 않기 때문에 알약이 더 좋아요.
여: 알겠습니다. 여기 두 종류가 있습니다. 가격에 차이가 약간 있어요.
남: 더 저렴한 걸로 주세요.

11 ⑤

여: Kevin, 너 지난달에 전화를 많이 썼니?
남: 아니요, 안 그랬어요. 무슨 문제가 있어요?
여: 이번 달 전화 요금이 평소보다 더 많이 나왔단다.
남: 아, 전화로 게임을 하나 산 걸 잊고 있었어요.

문제풀이

① 제게 문자 메시지를 보내실 수 있어요.
② 저는 다음 달에 새 스마트폰을 살 거예요.
③ 제가 스마트폰을 어디에 뒀는지 기억이 안 나요.
④ 제가 이미 인터넷뱅킹으로 요금을 납부했어요.

12 ①

남: 내가 너에게 이메일로 보낸 보고서 읽었니?
여: 아니, 파일을 열 수가 없었어.
남: 다른 사람들도 똑같이 말했어. 무엇이 문제인지 모르겠네.
여: 네 파일에 바이러스가 있을 수도 있어.

문제풀이

② 내가 네 보고서를 검토했어. 그건 완벽해.
③ 괜찮아. 나는 그 파일을 열 수 있었어.
④ 너는 보고서를 화요일까지 제출해야 해.
⑤ 내가 내 노트북 컴퓨터로 이메일을 다시 보내줄게.

13 ①

여: 너는 어린이날 무슨 계획이라도 있니?
남: 응, 나는 10킬로미터 경주에 참가할 거야.
여: 와! 네가 달리기 선수인지 몰랐네.
남: 진짜 선수는 아냐. 하지만 이 경주는 좋은 목적을 위해 열리는 거라 난 참가하기로 결정했어.
여: 아, 무엇을 위해서?
남: 자선 단체를 위한 기금을 모금하기 위한 거야. 그 기금은 지역 병원에 있는 암에 걸린 아이들을 위한 거야.
여: 그거 훌륭하네! 이 경주를 위해서 어떻게 준비해왔어?
남: 난 매일 저녁마다 한 시간 동안 뛰어왔어. 너도 함께할래?
여: 나도 정말 하고 싶지만, 난 그렇게 먼 거리를 뛰어 본 적이 없어.
남: 초보자들을 위한 5킬로미터 경주도 있어.

여: 그거 좋은 거 같다. 어떻게 신청할 수 있어?

문제풀이

② 나는 네가 나보다 더 빨리 달릴 수 있다고 생각하지 않아.
③ 달리기 경주는 네 건강에 매우 좋아.
④ 내일 아침에 병원에서 만나자.
⑤ 자선 단체를 위한 것이 아니면 나는 마라톤을 뛰지 않을 거야.

14 ④

[전화벨이 울린다.]

여: 안녕하세요. White Teeth 병원입니다.

남: 안녕하세요. 제 이름은 Harvey Bloom이고, 어제 치아 하나를 뽑았어요.

여: 네, 기억나요. 문제가 있으세요?

남: 음, 전 수술 이후에 엄청난 통증에 시달렸어요.

여: 그건 일반적인 겁니다. 아마 약 2~3일 정도 지속될 거예요. 지금도 아프세요?

남: 약간요. 하지만, 전 언제 또 나빠질지 몰라 걱정돼요.

여: 의사 선생님께서 처방해주신 진통제를 복용하셨나요? 그게 도움이 될 거예요.

남: 알겠습니다. 또, 의사 선생님께서 어떤 음식들을 먹는 것을 피하라고 말씀해주셨는데, 기억을 못 하겠어요.

여: 저희는 환자들을 위한 서면 안내서가 있습니다. 그걸 이메일로 보내드릴까요?

남: 좋습니다. 제 이메일 주소를 알려드릴게요.

문제풀이

① 통증을 줄이시려면 약을 복용하세요.
② 알겠습니다, 오늘 오후에 제가 가지러 갈게요.
③ 통증은 몇 시간 후면 사라질 겁니다.
⑤ 네, 내일 예약할게요.

15 ⑤

여: Amy는 오늘 저녁에 가장 친한 친구의 집들이에 갈 것이다. 그녀의 친구 집은 10마일 떨어져 있고, Amy는 그곳에 운전을 해서 갈 예정이다. Amy의 아버지인 Smith 씨는 라디오로 지역 일기 예보를 듣는다. 일기 예보에서는 폭우가 내릴 것이라고 하고, 그는 딸이 그렇게 나쁜 날씨에 운전을 하지 않는 편이 낫다고 생각한다. Amy의 친구 집 근처에는 지하철역이 있어서 Smith 씨는 Amy가 지하철을 타고 그곳에 가기를 원한다. 이런 상황에서, Smith 씨가 Amy에게 할 말로 가장 적절한 것은 무엇인가?

Mr. Smith : 운전하는 대신 지하철을 타는 게 어떠니?

문제풀이

① 네 친구의 집이 어디라고 말했니?
② 나는 네가 오늘 저녁에 집에 있어야 할 것 같구나.
③ 내가 네 친구의 집까지 태워다 주마.
④ 내일 일기 예보를 확인해 봐라.

16 ⑤ 17 ②

남: 모든 사람들이 녹차가 훌륭한 건강상의 이점이 있다는 것을 알고 있습니다. 그것은 암과 심장병을 예방할 수 있습니다. 또한, 그것은 노화의 징후를 예방해주고 체중 감량을 촉진합니다. 따라서, 많은 사람들이 녹차를 마시는 것을 즐깁니다. 하지만 사람들은 그것을 마신 후 무엇을 해야 할까요? 보통, 사람들은 티백을 그저 버립니다. 하지만 티백 그 자체는 많은 쓸모가 있습니다. 예를 들어, 여러분은 몇 개의 사용한 티백을 넣어 목욕을 하면 피부를 부드럽게 할 수 있습니다. 또는 여러분에게 화분이 몇 개 있다면 화분 바닥에 있는 구멍에 티백 몇 개를 두세요. 화분은 더 천천히 수분을 잃어갈 것이고, 티백으로부터 영양분이 흙으로 들어갈 것입니다. 여러분은 티백을 사용하여 어두운 가죽 신발을 닦을 수도 있습니다. 그러니 이제부터, 녹차를 마신 후에 반드시 티백을 보관하도록 하세요.

DICTATION Answers

01 in need of repair / take place over the weekend / arrange a room
02 a little too loud / turn up the volume / coming your way
03 getting very dry / has a strong scent / take a bottle of
04 a big star / a long stocking / five gift boxes
05 almost done / go buy some groceries / I'll call them
06 can't take any trips / the same time as / have fun
07 was supposed to depart / transfer to another flight / make some changes to
08 stands out / keep me warm / pay that much
09 planning a trip to / was originally built / free to ride
10 which medicine to buy / are you okay with / difference in price
11 higher than usual
12 couldn't open the file
13 I'm going to run / raise money for charity / for beginners
14 had a tooth pulled / Are you in pain / email it to you
15 is ten miles away / had better not drive / take the subway
16-17 has great health benefits / you can soften your skin / keep your tea bags

14 영어듣기 모의고사

본문 p.97

01 ⑤	02 ④	03 ⑤	04 ④	05 ③	06 ⑤
07 ③	08 ⑤	09 ⑤	10 ②	11 ①	12 ⑤
13 ⑤	14 ④	15 ④	16 ⑤	17 ⑤	

01 ⑤

여: 안녕하세요, 여러분. 오늘 회의에 와주셔서 감사합니다. 여러분들이 아시다시피, 우리 시는 요즘 점점 더 다문화화 되어가고 있습니다. 그 결과, 여러분은 언제 어디서나 다른 나라에서 온 많은 사람들을 만날 수 있습니다. 그래서 우리 시의 새로운 구성원들을 환영하는 것뿐만 아니라 그들의 문화를 이해하는 것이 중요합니다. 그것이 바로 다문화 교육 센터를 건립해야 하는 이유입니다. 저는 이미 그런 센터를 건립하는 것을 요청하는 서한을 작성했습니다. 이것을 시 정부에 보내기 전에, 저는 여러분의 지지가 필요합니다. 동의하신다면, 앞으로 나오셔서 이 서한에 서명해주십시오. 감사합니다.

02 ④

여: Peter, 너 화나 보여.
남: 응. 나는 내 룸메이트랑 문제가 있어.
여: 무슨 일인데?
남: 그는 주방을 사용한 후에 결코 치우지를 않아.
여: 아, 그렇구나.
남: 나는 이제 심지어 전자레인지도 사용할 수가 없어. 그 안에 온통 음식 찌꺼기가 있거든.
여: 그는 네가 어떻게 느끼는지 모를지도 몰라. 그 애한테 그걸 청소하라고 말을 하는 게 어때?
남: 그 애한테 뭐라고 말해야 할지 모르겠어. 나는 그의 감정을 상하게 하고 싶지 않아.
여: 너희 둘은 마음을 터놓고 대화를 할 필요가 있어. 그 애한테 네가 어떻게 느끼는지 말을 해야 해.
남: 네 말이 아마 맞는 것 같아.
여: 그러면 그는 바라건대 변할 거야.

03 ⑤

남: 어서 오세요! 여기 앉으세요.
여: 고맙습니다.
남: 자, 무엇을 도와드릴까요?
여: 음, 저는 막 이직을 해서요, 새로운 아파트를 찾고 있어요.
남: 알겠습니다. 마음에 두고 계신 특정 지역이 있으신가요?
여: 시청 근처에 있는 걸 찾을 수 있으면 좋겠어요.
남: 한 달에 얼마를 지불하실 수 있으세요?
여: 500달러 넘게 지불하고 싶지는 않아요.
남: 흠… 그 가격으로 시청 근처 아파트는 찾기 어려울 겁니다.
여: 그러면 기념 공원은 어떤가요?
남: 거기는 괜찮을 것 같아요. 그 지역에 있는 아파트를 몇 개 보는 게 어떠세요?
여: 그거 좋네요.

04 ④

여: 나는 방금 토론실을 준비하는 것을 끝냈어.
남: 와. 정말 근사해 보여.
여: 정말 고마워. 내가 벽에 건 '토론 대회' 현수막이 마음에 드니?
남: 응. 그건 눈에 잘 띄어.
여: 직사각형의 테이블은 어때? 그게 둥근 것보다 더 나을 거라고 생각했어.
남: 네 말이 맞아. 그리고 저 물병 네 개를 준비한 것은 좋은 생각이야.
여: 고마워. 나는 토론자들이 목이 마를 수도 있을 거라고 생각했어.
남: 테이블 위에 있는 고양이처럼 생긴 저건 뭐야?
여: 그건 시계야. 그리고 앞쪽에 있는 '찬성'과 '반대'라고 적힌 둥근 팻말은 어때?
남: 완벽해 보여. 정말 수고했어.

05 ③

여: 멋진 집들이였어. 그렇지 않아?
남: 응, 모든 사람들이 즐거운 시간을 보낸 거 같아.
여: 그런데 치울 것들이 많네. 꽤 시간이 걸릴 거 같아.
남: 지금 당장 시작하자. 내가 남은 음식을 냉장고에 넣을게.
여: 그러면 내가 설거지할게. 접시들을 모아서 싱크대로 가져와 줄래?
남: 그건 괜찮아. 내가 음식을 치운 후에 설거지할게.
여: 그러면 나는 바닥을 쓸기 시작할게.
남: 대신 쓰레기를 분리수거 하는 건 어때? 플라스틱과 유리를 문 옆에 놔줘.
여: 좋아. 그런데 장식품들은 누가 치울까?
남: 그건 급하지 않아. 그건 내가 내일 할게.
여: 좋아.

06 ⑤

[전화벨이 울린다.]
여: LTG 은행입니다. 무엇을 도와드릴까요?
남: 제가 인터넷뱅킹으로 송금하는 데 문제가 있어요. 시스템에 문제라도 있나요?
여: 전 그렇게 생각하지 않습니다. 고객님의 성함과 계좌번호를 제게 말씀해주시겠어요?
남: 제 이름은 Brian Smith입니다. 제 계좌 번호는 46890입니다.
여: 감사합니다. 잠시만 기다려 주세요. *[타자치는 소리]* 이제 문제를 알겠네요.
남: 무슨 일인가요?
여: 고객님께서는 지난 방문 때 저희가 드린 보안 카드를 등록하지 않으셨어요.
남: 아, 전 그것이 필요한지 몰랐어요. 제가 지금 그걸 전화로 할 수 있나요?
여: 아니요, 고객님. 고객님께서 온라인으로 그 카드를 등록하셔야 합니다.
남: 아, 알겠습니다. 도와주셔서 감사합니다.

07 ③

[전화벨이 울린다.]
남: 여보세요. Red Wings 여행입니다. 무엇을 도와드릴까요?
여: 안녕하세요, 제가 예약했던 항공편의 날짜를 바꾸고 싶습니다.
남: 알겠습니다. 예약 번호가 무엇이죠?
여: TS003507입니다.
남: 잠깐만 기다리세요. *[타자치는 소리]* 특별 행사가로 구입하셨네요. 항공편으로 300달러를 지불하셨고요.
여: 네. 그게 문제가 되나요?
남: 이와 같은 티켓에는, 저희가 고객님께서 지불하신 금액의 20퍼센트를 청구합니다.
여: 괜찮습니다. 저는 8월 5일로 날짜를 바꾸고 싶어요. 그날 가장 저렴한 항공편은 얼마인가요?
남: 500달러입니다. 그래서 고객님께서는 재예약 비용뿐만 아니라 그 차액도 지불하셔야 합니다. 괜찮으시겠어요?
여: 음, 선택의 여지가 없네요.

문제풀이
여자는 원래 항공권 요금의 20퍼센트에 해당하는 재예약 비용 60달러(= $300×0.2)와 새 항공권 요금과의 차액인 200달러(= $500-$300)를 더 내야 하므로, 총 260달러를 추가로 지불해야 한다.

08 ⑤

남: 안녕, Jennifer! 터키 여행 어땠어?
여: 굉장했어. 나는 많은 흥미로운 기념품들을 가져왔어.
남: 아, 뭘 샀는데?
여: 아름다운 무늬가 있는 카펫을 샀어.
남: 그거 멋진 거 같다. 다른 건 뭘 샀어?
여: 전통 시장에서 선물로 스카프 몇 장과 손거울 몇 개를 샀어.
남: 너는 사려 깊구나. 애플티는? 너는 그걸 맛보고 싶다고 했잖아.
여: 아, 맞아. 그게 정말 맛있어서 나를 위해 좀 샀어.
남: 잘했네. 그런데, 나는 터키의 접시들이 아름답다고 들었어. 그것도 샀어?
여: 아니, 그건 들고 오기가 너무 어려웠을 거야.

09 ⑤

남: 국제 에세이 대회에 오신 걸 환영합니다. 시작하기 전에, 먼저 이 대회의 규칙에 대해 설명드리겠습니다. 여러분은 국제 사안들에 관한 두 가지 에세이 주제를 받게 될 것입니다. 하나를 고르셔서 그것에 관한 에세이를 쓰십시오. 저희는 여러분께 에세이를 600에서 700단어로 제한하실 것을 부탁합니다. 답안지에 어떤 메모도 적지 마십시오. 만약 (메모하기를) 원하시면, 주제가 나열된 종이의 여백을 이용하십시오. 또한, 답안지에 여러분의 이름과 에세이의 제목을 적는 것을 잊지 마십시오. 에세이를 완성하는 데 두 시간이 주어집니다. 질문 있으신가요?

10 ②

남: 안녕하세요. 선풍기를 사러 여기 왔는데요. 가지고 계신 모든 선풍기를 보여주실 수 있을까요?
여: 당연하죠. 저를 따라오세요. *[잠시 후]* 여기 모델들이 있습니다. 리모컨이 있는 선풍기가 필요하신가요?
남: 그렇진 않아요. 선풍기를 제 책상 위에 둘 거거든요.
여: 책상 위에요? 그러면 소형이나 중간 크기의 선풍기가 좋을 거예요.
남: 네, 그런데 저는 소형 선풍기가 더 좋습니다.
여: 알겠습니다. 여기 이것이 가장 잘 팔리는 상품이에요. 3단 변속이에요.
남: 좋아요, 그런데 40달러는 너무 비싸요. 가능한 한 가장 저렴한 걸로 사고 싶어요.
여: 그럼 이건 어떠세요? 이것은 더 저렴하고, 2단 변속이에요.
남: 괜찮은 것 같네요. 그것을 살게요.
여: 잘 선택하셨습니다.

11 ①

여: 너는 무엇을 찾고 있니?
남: 내 자동차 열쇠. 모든 곳을 다 살펴봤는데, 그걸 찾을 수가 없어.
여: 주방 테이블 위는 봤어? 너는 자주 그걸 거기에 두잖아.
남: 봤어, 그런데 그건 거기에 없었어.

문제풀이
② 주방 테이블을 치워줄 수 있니?
③ 그건 사실이야. 나는 그걸 차에 두고 왔어.
④ 나는 테이블을 움직일 수 없을 것 같아.
⑤ 너를 도와주고 싶지만, 나는 가야 해.

12 ⑤

남: 이 재킷은 너한테 잘 어울려.
여: 응, 나는 이게 정말 좋아. 그런데 약간 비싸네.
남: 그러면 그걸 인터넷으로 사보는 게 어때? 그게 보통 더 저렴하거든.
여: 네 말이 맞아. 그걸 온라인에서 사야겠어.

문제풀이
① 지금 먼저 이걸 입어봐.
② 나는 새 재킷이 필요 없어.
③ 나는 이걸 인터넷에서 샀어.
④ 미안하지만, 이건 내 스타일이 아니야.

13 ⑤

여: 오늘 기분 어때, Jimmy?
남: 다음 주에 있을 합창 대회 때문에 매우 긴장돼.
여: 걱정하지 마. 난 네가 잘할 거라고 확신해. 연습은 어떻게 되어가고 있어?
남: 실은, 큰 문제가 있어. 어제 피아니스트가 자동차사고를 당했어. 그래서 그녀는 몇 주 동안 병원에 입원할 거야.
여: 그거 안됐구나. 그러면 그녀는 그날 피아노를 칠 수 없겠네.
남: 맞아. 어떻게 해야 할지 모르겠어.
여: 다른 피아니스트를 찾아야지!
남: 하지만 나는 피아노를 칠 수 있는 다른 사람을 몰라.
여: 음… 있잖아, Tom이 피아노를 잘 쳐. 그에게 부탁하는 건 어때?
남: 아, 고마워. 그에게 지금 당장 전화해볼게.

문제풀이

① 나는 그에게 몇 가지 질문을 했어.
② 그 피아니스트는 지금 나아지고 있어.
③ 우리는 그 대회에 준비가 되어 있어.
④ 나는 피아노를 잘 치지 못해.

14 ④

여: 안녕, Patrick, 너는 과학 과제를 위한 발표를 끝냈니?
남: 아직. 여전히 작업 중이야.
여: 언제가 마감이야?
남: 이번 주 목요일이야. 그런데 10분 시간제한이 있어서 걱정이야.
여: 왜? 넌 네가 그렇게 오래 얘기하지 못할 거라고 생각해?
남: 아니, 내가 발표를 그 시간 안에 끝낼 수 있을 거 같지 않아.
여: 내가 그 자료를 한번 봐도 될까?
남: 당연하지. *[잠시 후]* 어떻게 생각해?
여: 음, 정보가 너무 많아. 조금 복잡해 보여. 더 간단하게 만들어야 할 것 같아.
남: 아, 내가 어떻게 하면 더 이해하기 쉽게 만들 수 있을 것 같아?
여: 너는 도표들을 좀 사용해야 할 것 같아.

문제풀이

① 발표 시간이 너무 짧아.
② 음, 너는 그것을 제시간에 제출해야 해.
③ 심호흡을 해 보는 게 어때?
⑤ 나는 네 작업에 매우 감명받았어.

15 ④

여: Mike는 디지털카메라를 위한 새 메모리 카드가 필요해서 인터넷으로 그것을 검색한다. 그는 적절한 것을 찾고 인터넷뱅킹 계좌를 이용하여 그것을 구매한다. 그러나 돈을 보낸 후에, 그는 자신이 실수를 한 것을 깨닫는다. 그것은 가격이 23달러인데 그는 33달러를 보냈다. 그는 10달러를 다시 자신의 계좌로 이체해달라고 상점에 말하고 싶다. 그는 상점의 고객 서비스 센터에 전화를 걸어 그 문제를 설명한다. 그러자 고객 서비스 직원은 Mike에게 그가 어떻게 돈을 돌려받고 싶은지 묻는다. 이런 상황에서, Mike가 고객 서비스 직원에게 할 말로 가장 적절한 것은 무엇인가?
Mike : 돈을 제 계좌로 보내 주실 수 있나요?

문제풀이

① 저는 환불을 받고 싶어요.
② 제 주문을 취소해주세요.
③ 저는 신용카드로 지불할게요.
⑤ 당신네 웹사이트에 오류가 있었어요.

16 ⑤ 17 ⑤

남: 안녕하세요, 청취자 여러분! 오늘 전 음식에 관해서 말씀드리려 합니다. 사람들은 보통 음식은 단지 먹기 위한 것이라고만 생각합니다. 하지만 그들은 음식이 다른 목적으로도 사용될 수 있다는 것을 모릅니다. 예를 들어, 베이킹소다는 제과점에서 보는 구운 음식을 만드는 데 사용됩니다. 그러나 그것은 옷에 있는 악취를 제거할 수도 있습니다. 또한 여러분은 냄새를 제거하기 위해 우유 한 그릇을 냉장고에 넣어 둘 수 있습니다. 만약 여러분이 오렌지를 먹는 것을 좋아한다면, 껍질을 보관하여 그것을 피부에 문지르세요. 이것은 모기를 쫓도록 도와줄 것입니다. 심지어 콜라도 예상 밖의 용도가 있습니다. 그저 콜라로 녹슨 자전거를 문지르면, 여러분은 녹이 사라지는 것을 볼 수 있습니다! 이러한 간단한 정보들을 기억하면, 여러분은 음식들을 다른 방식들로 활용할 수 있습니다. 다음번에는, 다른 유용한 정보들을 가지고 돌아오겠습니다.

DICTATION Answers

01 more and more multicultural / but also to understand / need your support
02 having trouble with / clean it up / how you feel
03 a certain location / pay per month / at that price
04 organizing the room / It stands out / looks like a cat
05 a lot to clean up / separate the trash / It's not urgent
06 transferring money through / account number / register the security card
07 change the date of / a special deal / in addition to
08 I brought back / at a traditional market / too difficult to carry
09 two essay topics / on your answer sheets / complete your essay
10 with a remote control / prefer a compact one / what about this one
11 I've looked everywhere
12 buy it on the Internet
13 be in the hospital / find another pianist / is good at playing
14 finished making the presentation / take a look at / a bit complicated
15 searches for one / made a mistake / get his money back
16-17 for other purposes / get rid of / make use of

15 영어듣기 모의고사

본문 ▲ p.104

01 ①	02 ④	03 ②	04 ④	05 ②	06 ①
07 ④	08 ④	09 ⑤	10 ③	11 ④	12 ②
13 ⑤	14 ⑤	15 ②	16 ④	17 ④	

01 ①

여: 여러분은 빵을 먹는 것을 더 좋아하나요 아니면 밥을 먹는 것을 더 좋아하나요? 요즘 많은 사람들은 편리하기 때문에 빵을 먹는 것을 좋아합니다. 그리고 작년에 우리는 그전 어느 때보다 더 적게 쌀을 소비했습니다. 이 때문에, 우리나라의 농부들은 경제적인 어려움에 직면하고 있습니다. 그러나 우리는 몇 가지 작은 일을 함으로써 농부들을 도울 수 있습니다. 아침 식사로 빵 대신에 밥을 먹는 것은 큰 도움이 됩니다. 여러분은 또한 휴일과 기념일을 축하하는 선물로 떡을 줄 수도 있습니다. 또한 쌀을 이용하면서 농부들을 돕는 많은 다른 방법들이 있습니다. 우리가 할 수 있는 한 자주 쌀을 꼭 먹도록 합시다!

02 ④

여: 안녕, Justin. 동네 게시판에 있는 포스터 봤니?
남: 나무 심기 행사에 관한 포스터 말하는 거야?
여: 응. 다음 주에 우리 학교 근처에서 열릴 거야.
남: 실은, 나는 벌써 신청했어. 너는 이미 신청 했어?
여: 나는 곧 할 거야! 나는 나무가 더 많아지는 것이 우리 마을을 아름답게 해주고, 우리에게 더 깨끗한 공기를 제공할 것이라고 생각해.
남: 맞아. 그러면 그것은 우리 동네를 더 살기 좋게 만들 거야!
여: 그리고 그것은 생태계에도 도움을 줄 거야. 나무는 새들과 다른 작은 동물들에게 집을 제공해줄 거야.
남: 와! 네 말이 맞아. 우리가 참여하게 되어서 정말 기뻐.
여: 나도 그래. 더 많은 학생들이 그 행사에 참여하면 좋겠어.

03 ②

남: 나를 위해서 새 책상을 정리해 줘서 고마워요, Newton 씨.
여: 천만에요, 사장님. 프린터를 컴퓨터 옆에 놓은 것이 괜찮나요?
남: 네. 사용하기 더 편리하겠어요.
여: 마음에 드신다니 기쁩니다.
남: 다시 한번 고마워요. 내 오후 스케줄 좀 보여주겠어요?
여: 그럼요, 사장님. 음… 오후 2시에 Jones 씨와 회의가 있습니다.
남: 알겠어요. 오늘 오후에 내가 다른 약속이 있나요?
여: 아니요. 그런데 Smith 씨와 저녁 7시에 저녁을 드시기로 되어 있습니다.
남: 아, 거의 잊어버릴 뻔했어요.
여: 그밖에 다른 알고 싶으신 것이 있으세요, 사장님?
남: 그게 다예요. 내가 필요할 때 부를게요.

04 ④

[휴대전화벨이 울린다.]
여: 여보세요?
남: 안녕, 여보. 우리 딸의 생일 파티를 준비하는 것을 끝냈어요?
여: 네. 체크무늬의 테이블보가 깔린 긴 직사각형의 테이블을 세웠어요.
남: 현수막은요? 당신이 그걸 샀다고 말했잖아요.
여: 그건 테이블 앞에 있어요. 'Happy Birthday'라고 쓰여 있어요.
남: 그거 좋군요. 그리고 케이크도 구웠어요?
여: 네, 2단 케이크이고, 그걸 테이블 가운데에 두었어요.
남: 선물은요?
여: 우리가 마련한 세 개의 선물을 포장했고 테이블의 오른편에 놓았어요.
남: 그거 멋지네요!
여: 또, 왼편에는 우리 딸의 사진들도 있어요.
남: 어서 그것들을 보고 싶네요. 곧 거기로 갈게요.

05 ②

여: 네 보고서는 어떻게 되어 가고 있니, Sam?
남: 나는 아직도 많은 조사를 해야 해.
여: 정말? 나는 조사를 끝내고 쓰기 시작했어.
남: 나도 쓰기 시작해야 해. 나는 이미 뒤처지고 있어.
여: 네가 설문조사를 하는 데 도움이 필요하니?
남: 응, 나는 설문조사를 받을 30명의 사람들이 필요해. 나를 도와줄 수 있어?
여: 물론이지. 내가 반 친구들에게 물어볼 수 있어. 내가 설문지 질문을 그들에게 읽어줘야 할까?
남: 아니, 그냥 그 애들에게 설문지를 나눠 주면 돼. 작성하는 데 3분에서 5분 정도 걸릴 거야.
여: 그리고 그다음에 내가 설문지를 수거해서 너에게 돌려줘야 하네, 그렇지?
남: 정확해.

06 ①

[전화벨이 울린다.]
여: Forest 초등학교입니다. 저는 Jane Smith입니다.
남: 안녕하세요. 당신의 학교에서 체육 교사를 구하고 있다고 들었어요. 그 일에 지원하고 싶습니다.
여: 네, 그렇습니다. 저희에게 이번 주 금요일까지 이력서를 보내주세요.
남: 그렇게 하겠습니다. 체육 교사가 가르쳐야 하는 특별한 프로그램이 있나요?
여: 네. 체육 교사는 방과 후 축구 프로그램을 지도할 것입니다.
남: 잘됐네요! 저는 축구를 지도한 경력이 있습니다.
여: 완벽하네요. 몇 년이나 가르치셨어요?
남: 졸업 이후에 3년 동안 가르쳤습니다.
여: 아, 안됐네요. 저희는 최소 5년의 경력을 가진 사람을 찾고 있습니다.
남: 그렇군요. 알려주셔서 감사합니다. 그리고 시간 내주셔서 감사합니다.
여: 천만에요, 선생님. 좋은 하루 보내세요.

07 ④

여: 무엇을 도와드릴까요, 손님?

남: 가족들을 위해서 스키 장비를 대여하려고요.
여: 알겠습니다. 가족이 몇 명인가요?
남: 어른 두 명과 아이 두 명입니다.
여: 알겠습니다. 어떤 물품들을 대여하고 싶으세요?
남: 음, 저희는 모든 것을 대여해야 해요. 1일 이용권도 필요해요.
여: 그렇다면, 저희의 기본 패키지가 고객님께 최적이겠네요. 그것은 스키, 폴, 부츠, 그리고 1일 이용권을 포함합니다.
남: 좋네요. 그건 얼마죠?
여: 어른은 장당 50달러이고 아이들은 장당 30달러입니다.
남: 스키복도 있나요?
여: 네. 옷 대여료는 한 사람당 10달러입니다.
남: 그러면 우리 모두를 위한 스키복도 대여할게요.

문제풀이

남자는 어른은 50달러, 아이는 30달러인 기본 패키지를 어른 2명과 아이 2명을 위해 구입하기로 했고, 대여료가 한 명당 10달러인 스키복을 4명 모두를 위해 대여하기로 했으므로, 남자가 지불할 금액은 총 200달러(=($50×2)+($30×2)+($10×4))이다.

08 ④

여: Shawn, 과학 수업 숙제 다 했니?
남: 거의 다 했어. 투명 개구리에 대해서 쓰고 있어.
여: 투명 개구리라고? 나는 그것에 대해 들어본 적이 없어.
남: 그것들은 보통 대부분의 개구리들처럼 초록색이야. 하지만 그것들의 배에 있는 투명한 피부를 통해서 그것들의 내부를 볼 수 있어.
여: 우와, 그래서 그게 그것들이 투명 개구리라고 이름이 지어진 이유구나. 그것들은 어디 살아?
남: 그것들은 강을 따라서 사는데, 그곳에서는 사람들이 그것들을 찾기가 어려워.
여: 그것들은 언제 처음 발견됐어?
남: 그것들은 1872년에 처음 발견되었어.
여: 얼마나 커?
남: 길이가 약 1인치에서 3인치 정도야.
여: 꽤 작구나. 그것들은 흥미로운 동물인 것처럼 들린다.

09 ⑤

남: 안녕하세요, 학생 여러분. 우리 학교 축제가 다음 주에 시작됩니다. 축제 동안에, 저희는 음료와 샌드위치를 판매하는 카페를 설치할 것입니다. 모인 금액 전부는 학교 도서관을 위해 더 많은 책을 구입하는 데 사용될 것입니다. 카페는 학교 정문 앞에 위치할 것입니다. 현재, 저희는 학생 자원봉사자들을 찾고 있습니다. 관심이 있으시면, Garcia 선생님께 얘기해주세요. 도와줄 수 없으시다면, 축제 동안에 카페에 잠시 들러주세요. 많은 학생들이 들러주길 바랍니다. 카페는 오전 11시부터 오후 4시까지 운영할 것입니다. 여러분을 그때 뵙길 바랍니다.

10 ③

여: 실례합니다. 제 아들을 위한 자전거를 찾고 있어요.
남: 어떤 종류의 자전거를 찾고 계시죠? 선택하실 수 있는 것이 많고 다양하거든요.
여: 음, 그 아이는 큰 것이 필요한 것 같아요.
남: 아드님이 몇 살이죠?
여: 9살이에요.
남: 그러면 17인치가 넘는 바퀴가 아드님에게 좋을 겁니다.
여: 알겠습니다. 또, 그 아이가 자전거를 들 수 있어야 해서 자전거가 가볍기도 하면 좋겠어요.
남: 틀림없이 7킬로그램 이하의 자전거가 좋을 것입니다. 그러면 선택하실 수 있는 게 이 두 가지가 남네요.
여: 그것들은 아주 멋져 보이네요. 어떤 것이 더 저렴하죠?
남: 이것이요. 이것은 저희의 가장 잘 팔리는 제품들 중 하나이기도 합니다.
여: 훌륭하네요. 그걸 살게요.

11 ④

남: Kate, 오늘 밤에 영화 보러 가는 게 어때?
여: 재미있겠다. 뭘 보고 싶은데?
남: 오늘 새로운 공포 영화가 개봉했어.
여: 미안하지만, 난 무서운 영화는 좋아하지 않아.

문제풀이

① 나는 항상 앞줄에 앉아.
② 나는 오늘 외출하고 싶지 않아.
③ 나는 지난달에 영화 두 편을 봤어.
⑤ 나는 요즘 공포 소설을 읽고 있어.

12 ②

여: Tim, 왜 집들이에 안 왔어?
남: 미안하지만, 그날 바빴어. 집들이는 어땠어?
여: 많은 사람들이 와서 파티를 즐겼어.
남: 나도 거기에 갔어야 했는데.

문제풀이

① 음식은 훌륭했어.
③ 나는 제시간에 파티에 갈게.
④ 네가 그걸 놓치다니 유감이야.
⑤ 네 파티는 정말 즐거웠어.

13 ⑤

남: Becky, 너 우울해 보여. 괜찮아?
여: 그냥 지리학 수업 때문에 약간 스트레스를 받는 것뿐이야.
남: 아, 너 Baker 선생님의 수업 들어?
여: 응. 오늘이 학기 첫 수업이었는데, 너무 어려운 것 같아.
남: 걱정하지 마. 분명 재미있을 거야.
여: 하지만 나는 지리학을 정말 못하는 데다 공부할 게 너무 많아.
남: 만약 도움이 필요하면, 나에게 부탁해. 나는 그 선생님 수업을 지난 학기에 들었거든.
여: 잘됐다! 그런데 나는 너에게 많은 질문들을 할지도 몰라.
남: 괜찮아. 친구 좋다는 게 뭐겠니?
여: 고마워. 그런데 나는 지금 그 교과서를 사러 서점에 가는 길이야.

남: 내 책을 사용하는 건 어때? 난 아직 그걸 가지고 있거든.

문제풀이
① 정말 고마워. 나중에 보자.
② 나는 전에 그 수업을 들은 적이 없어.
③ 너는 그 교과서를 어디서 샀니?
④ 네 역사 수업에서 행운을 빌어.

14 ⑤

여: 너 곧 여행 간다고 했어, 그렇지? 여행 준비는 됐니?
남: 음, 나는 여행을 위해 모든 짐을 다 쌌어.
여: 확실해? 다시 한번 확인해보는 게 어때?
남: 걱정하지 마. 이미 했어.
여: 여행 일정은 어때? 일정은 정했어?
남: 아니, 나는 비행기 티켓이랑 호텔 방만 예약했어.
여: 그러면 매일 뭘 할 거야?
남: 아직 모르겠어. 매일 아침에 계획을 세울 거야.
여: 그거 나쁘진 않겠네. 그런데 가기 전에 계획을 세우는 것이 훨씬 나아.
남: 나도 알지만, 지금은 정보를 검색할 충분한 시간이 없어.
여: 그렇다면 넌 좋은 여행 책자를 한 권 가져가야 해.

문제풀이
① 외국으로 여행하는 것은 항상 신나.
② 나도 그래. 그게 그것을 할 가장 좋은 방법이야.
③ 네가 미리 계획을 세운 것은 잘한 일이야.
④ 알겠어. 내가 널 위해 호텔 방을 예약할게.

15 ②

여: Tom과 Betsy는 결혼한 부부이다. 그들은 둘 다 매일 아침 일을 하러 가고 오후 6시경에 집으로 돌아온다. 그들이 직장에서 집으로 오면, Betsy는 집안일을 하기 시작하고 아이들을 돌본다. 하지만 Tom은 그저 소파에 앉아 TV를 본다. Betsy는 이것이 불공평하다고 생각한다. 그는 좀처럼 집안일을 하거나 아이들을 돌보지 않는다. 그는 항상 피곤하다고 말한다. Betsy는 Tom이 그녀처럼 집안일을 하면 더 좋을 것 같다고 생각한다. 이런 상황에서, Betsy가 Tom에게 할 말로 가장 적절한 것은 무엇인가?
Betsy : 집안일을 공정하게 나눠요.

문제풀이
① 내가 일을 그만둘 것 같아요.
③ 피곤하면 쉬어요.
④ 우리는 로봇 청소기를 사야 해요.
⑤ 나는 집안일을 해줄 사람을 고용했어요.

16 ④ 17 ④

남: 대부분의 사람들은 파티를 위해 많은 음식을 준비해야 할 때 부담감을 느낍니다. 많은 사람들은 파티룸을 예약하는 것이 그 상황을 처리하는 가장 좋은 방법이라고 생각할지도 모릅니다. 하지만 이제 여러분은 여러분의 집에서 파티를 여는 것을 두려워하지 않으셔도 됩니다. Order to Your Door는 여러분이 어떤 파티에서도 이용하실 수 있는 저렴하고 편리한 식사 서비스입니다. Order to Your Door와 함께라면, 여러분은 온라인으로 음식을 구입하고 그것을 여러분의 집으로 배달시킬 수 있습니다. 여러분이 원하는 음식과 접대할 사람들의 수를 그냥 고르기만 하세요. 여러분은 스테이크, 파스타, 치킨 샐러드, 볶음밥, 그리고 훨씬 더 많은 음식들을 즐기실 수 있습니다. 그러면 저희가 여러분의 주문 음식을 여러분의 집으로 제시간에 바로 배달해드릴 것입니다. 적어도 이틀 전에만 미리 주문해주세요. Order to Your Door는 여러분의 파티를 더 쉽게 해줄 최고의 방법입니다.

DICTATION Answers

01 ate less rice than / instead of bread / as often as we can
02 It's going to take place / make our town beautiful / join the event
03 It was my pleasure / have a meeting / Is there anything else
04 with a checkered tablecloth / bake a cake / on the left side
05 do a lot of research / already running behind / hand the survey out
06 apply for the job / have experience coaching soccer / at least five years
07 rent ski equipment / our standard package / The clothing rental fee
08 never heard of / they were named / were first discovered
09 be used to buy / If you're interested / stop by the café
10 needs something big / to be light / one of our best sellers
11 That sounds like fun
12 enjoyed the party
13 a little stressed out / I'm terrible at / on my way to
14 have everything packed / Did you arrange it / much better to plan
15 get home from work / this is unfair / do the housework
16-17 deal with the situation / have it delivered / place an order

16 영어듣기 모의고사

본문 ▲ p.111

01 ②	02 ②	03 ⑤	04 ⑤	05 ①	06 ⑤
07 ③	08 ④	09 ④	10 ⑤	11 ④	12 ⑤
13 ⑤	14 ⑤	15 ⑤	16 ⑤	17 ④	

01 ②

여: 겨울이 더 추워지면서, 사람들은 난방기에 더 의존합니다. 이러한 난방기는 집을 따뜻하게 유지해주지만, 공기를 건조하게 하기도 합니다. 그러므로 사람들은 가습기를 이용하기 시작합니다. 하지만 여러분이 조심하지 않으면 이것 또한 문제들을 유발할 수 있습니다. 문제들을 예방하기 위해서, 여러분은 우선 가습기를 청결하게 유지해야 합니다. 세균이 번식하는 것을 막기 위해 가습기의 안팎 모두를 청소하세요. 그리고 반드시 물을 매일 교체하세요. 먼저 끓인 후에 식힌 물을 사용하는 것이 가장 좋습니다. 마지막으로, 여러분의 집안 공기가 너무 습해지지 않게 하세요. 이것은 곰팡이가 번식하게 할 수 있습니다.

02 ②

남: 이봐, Gwen. 너 약 먹는 거니?
여: 안녕, Shawn. 실은, 이건 종합 비타민이랑 칼슘 보충제야. 너도 좀 먹어볼래?
남: 난 괜찮아, 고마워. 그런데 그 둘을 같이 먹니?
여: 응. 문제가 있어?
남: 실은, 그것들을 동시에 먹어서는 안 돼.
여: 그건 왜 그러는데?
남: 칼슘은 몸이 종합비타민에 있는 철분을 흡수하는 것을 힘들게 해. 그것들을 같은 날 다른 시간대에 섭취하는 것이 더 좋아.
여: 정말? 난 그걸 몰랐어.
남: 그래. 그리고 또 종합비타민은 음식과 함께 먹어야 해.
여: 아, 그렇구나. 말해줘서 고마워!

03 ⑤

여: 실례합니다. 저를 도와주실 수 있으세요?
남: 물론이죠. 무엇을 도와드릴까요?
여: 「Happy Holidays」를 보고 싶은데, 목록에서 보이지 않네요.
남: 그건 다음 주에 상영할 거예요.
여: 제가 일정을 잘못 읽었나 보네요. 다른 영화를 추천해주실래요? 저는 로맨틱 코미디를 좋아해요.
남: 오후 6시에 상영하는 다른 로맨틱 코미디가 있어요.
여: 아, 정말요? 그건 제목이 뭐죠?
남: 「We Are in Love」요. 요즘 가장 인기 있는 영화들 중 하나예요.
여: 음… 그러면 그 영화를 볼게요. 극장 중앙에 있는 자리로 티켓 한 장 구매할 수 있을까요?
남: 정말 운이 좋으시네요. 고급 좌석 구역에 자리가 하나 남아 있어요.
여: 잘됐네요.

04 ⑤

남: Janet, 겨울 축제 포스터 끝냈어?
여: 응, 끝냈어. 포스터에 대해 어떻게 생각해?
남: 와, 가운데에 스노보드를 타고 있는 사람이 정말 멋져 보여.
여: 고마워. 나는 그가 포스터를 더 흥미진진하게 보이게 해서 그를 추가했어.
남: 배경에는 눈으로 덮인 산들도 넣었구나.
여: 맞아, 그것들은 포스터에 겨울 느낌이 더 나도록 해줘. 나는 또 눈사람 옆에 1월 1일부터 1월 15일까지라고 날짜도 적었어.
남: 응. 그게 거기 있으니까 더 눈에 잘 띈다!
여: 정말 그래.
남: 무엇보다도 나는 '겨울 축제'가 스노보드를 타고 있는 사람 위에 적혀 있는 방식이 마음에 들어.
여: 그리고 나는 오른쪽 상단 구석에 불꽃놀이를 넣는 걸 잊지 않았어.
남: 응, 그거 멋져 보여.

05 ①

남: 너 토요일 오후에 바쁘니, Anne?
여: 아니, 특별히 계획한 건 없어. 왜 물어봐?
남: 음, 너 내가 학교 댄스 동아리에 가입한 거 기억해?
여: 응, 네가 내게 말했었어. 토요일에 행사가 있니?
남: 응, 우리는 학교 체육관에서 공연을 해. 모든 동아리 멤버가 그 행사에 참여할 거야.
여: 그거 멋지다. 너 정말 신나겠다.
남: 그래. 하지만 나는 누군가가 내 사진을 찍어주면 좋겠어. 네가 그걸 해줄 수 있어?
여: 물론이지. 내가 지난달에 새 카메라를 구입한 것 너도 알잖아. 그건 몇 시에 시작해?
남: 오후 3시에. 그런데 좋은 자리를 맡기 위해 네가 그보다는 더 일찍 와줬으면 해.
여: 알겠어. 문제없어.

06 ⑤

여: 음, Taylor 씨, 지금 막 당신의 검사 결과를 받았습니다.
남: 그럼 제 발목은 어떤가요? 지난주보다는 훨씬 더 나은 것 같아요.
여: 네, 부러진 뼈는 거의 치유됐네요.
남: 거의요? 완전히 회복하려면 얼마나 걸릴까요?
여: 약 2주 더 걸릴 겁니다. 그때쯤 되면 괜찮아질 겁니다.
남: 정말요? 그 말씀을 들으니 기쁘네요.
여: 어떤 계획이라도 있나요?
남: 실은 한 달 후에 중요한 테니스 대회가 있거든요. 그 대회에 출전하고 싶어요.
여: 그렇군요. 음, 그 대회에 참가하실 수 있을 거라고 생각합니다.
남: 그거 좋은 소식이군요. 제가 우승할 가능성이 크다고 생각하거든요!
여: 잘됐네요. 2주 후에는 가벼운 운동을 시작하실 수 있습니다.

07 ③

남: 도와드릴까요?

여: 네, 저는 제 스마트폰을 수리해야 해요. 화면이 깨졌어요.
남: 알겠습니다. 제가 한번 볼게요. *[잠시 후]* 음… 바깥쪽과 안쪽 화면 둘 다 깨졌네요. 음, 제 생각엔 둘 다 교체하셔야 할 것 같아요.
여: 그렇게 심각한가요? 그건 얼마나 들죠?
남: 각각의 화면을 교체하는 데 100달러씩 들어요.
여: 아, 제가 그걸 둘 다 지불하면 비싸겠네요.
남: 이 전화기를 언제 구입하셨어요? 1년 미만이면 저희가 30퍼센트 할인해드릴게요.
여: 아, 그거 잘됐네요. 저는 이걸 6개월 전에 샀어요.
남: 그러면 할인을 받으실 수 있어요.

문제풀이

바깥쪽과 안쪽 화면을 모두 교체하는 비용은 원래 200달러인데, 구입한 지 1년 미만이어서 30퍼센트의 할인을 받을 수 있으므로, 여자가 지불할 금액은 총 140달러(= $200×0.7)이다.

08 ④

여: 이 놀라운 하와이 사진 좀 봐!
남: 아름답지 않니? 사실, 나는 영어를 공부하려고 1년 동안 하와이에 살았었어.
여: 정말? 나는 언젠가 그곳에 여행 가고 싶어.
남: 꼭 가야 해. 거긴 일 년 내내 따뜻해서 여행하기 아주 좋은 곳이야.
여: 멋진 것 같아. 그건 어디에 있어?
남: 미국 본토의 남서쪽에 있어.
여: 그렇구나. 그건 그냥 하나의 섬이야?
남: 사실, 그건 8개의 큰 섬과 100개가 넘는 작은 섬들로 구성되어 있어.
여: 섬들이 매우 많구나. 거기엔 얼마나 많은 사람들이 살아?
남: 약 140만 명이 거기에 산다고 들었어.
여: 아, 인구가 적구나.
남: 맞아. 그래서 사람들이 붐비지 않고, 휴식을 취하기에 좋은 곳이야.

09 ④

남: International Electronics는 특별 여름 세일을 할 것입니다. 저희의 모든 노트북 컴퓨터와 태블릿 컴퓨터가 다음 주부터 할인될 것입니다. 이 모든 제품들은 원래 가격에서 25퍼센트 할인된 가격으로 판매될 것입니다. 이번 세일은 7월 7일부터 9일까지 3일 동안만 진행될 것입니다. 하지만 여러분이 특별 세일가를 받기 위해서는 저희 매장의 회원 카드를 가지고 계셔야 합니다. 또한, 이번 세일은 저희의 시내에 있는 매장에서만 시행될 것입니다. 저희의 다른 매장들은 이 행사를 하지 않습니다. 저희는 평소처럼 문을 열지만, 문을 닫는 것은 평소보다 한 시간 더 늦게 닫을 것입니다. 이 좋은 기회를 놓치지 마세요!

10 ⑤

여: 안녕하세요. 무엇을 도와드릴까요?
남: 안녕하세요. 저는 아파트 하나를 임차하고 싶은데요. 적절한 것을 찾는 것을 도와주시겠어요?
여: 알겠습니다. 어떤 크기의 아파트를 찾고 계신가요?
남: 저는 혼자 살아서 한두 개의 침실이면 충분할 거예요.
여: 그렇군요. 그리고 월 예산이 얼마인지 여쭤봐도 될까요?
남: 저는 한 달에 800달러 이상 쓸 수는 없습니다.
여: 알겠습니다. 저희에게 손님의 요구에 꼭 맞는 아파트가 세 개 있네요.
남: 그거 잘됐네요. 그리고 제 임대차 계약이 곧 만료가 되어서, 가능한 한 빨리 이사해야 합니다.
여: 아, 언제까지 이사를 들어가셔야 하나요?
남: 5월 21일이요.
여: 그러면 이것이 손님께서 임차하셔야 할 아파트네요.

11 ④

남: 네 음악이 너무 시끄러워. 내 방에서도 계속 들려.
여: 미안해. 소리를 줄일게.
남: 아직도 너무 시끄러워. 내가 공부에 집중을 할 수가 없어.
여: <u>그러면 내가 헤드폰을 쓸게.</u>

문제풀이

① 너는 더 크게 말해야 해.
② 우리 함께 공부하는 게 어때?
③ 괜찮아. 나는 네 말을 똑똑히 들을 수 있어.
⑤ 내가 그에게 음량을 낮춰달라고 부탁할게.

12 ⑤

여: 이번 주 토요일의 중요한 야구 경기를 빨리 보고 싶어!
남: 정말 부러워. 나는 야구를 정말 좋아하는데!
여: 그렇다면 우리와 함께 경기장에 가는 게 어때?
남: <u>그러고 싶지만, 할머니를 뵈러 가야 해.</u>

문제풀이

① 응, 그건 정말 흥미로운 경기였어.
② 직진하다가 모퉁이에서 왼쪽으로 돌아.
③ 아니, 나는 야구 경기에 흥미가 없어.
④ 나는 경기장에서 너를 오랫동안 기다렸어.

13 ⑤

남: 나랑 같이 Smoothie World에 갈래?
여: 나도 가고 싶지만, 지금 당장 돈이 없어.
남: 또? 용돈을 벌써 다 쓴 거야?
여: 응. 그냥 사라져 버리는 것 같아. 내가 어디에 돈을 썼는지조차 기억을 못하겠어.
남: 그건 심하다. 너는 네가 사는 모든 것을 적기 시작해야 할 것 같아.
여: 실은, 그렇게 하려고 애써봤지만, 기억하기가 힘들어.
남: 네 스마트폰에 애플리케이션을 다운로드하는 게 어때? 네가 지출을 기록하는 게 더 쉬워질 거야.
여: 아, 그건 생각해본 적이 없어. 좋은 생각이야!
남: 응, 너는 항상 전화를 가지고 다니니까 그게 더 쉬울 거야.
여: <u>맞아. 나는 당장 그걸 다운로드할게.</u>

문제풀이

① 나는 더 많은 용돈을 요구해야 해.
② 내 생각에, 그건 돈 낭비야.
③ 좋아, 하지만 나는 이미 스마트폰을 가지고 있어.
④ 아니, 그 애플리케이션을 사용하는 건 어려웠어.

14 ⑤

[휴대전화벨이 울린다.]

여: 안녕, Patrick. 우리 오늘 어디에서 만날까?

남: 무슨 말이야? 오늘 우리 약속 있어?

여: 잊었어? 우리 함께 영화를 보기로 했잖아.

남: 아, 정말 미안해. 그걸 완전히 잊고 있었어. 나는 지금 내 사촌들을 보러 가는 길이야.

여: 정말? 언제 돌아오는데?

남: 주말 내내 거기에 있을 거야. 하지만 일요일 밤에 돌아올 거야.

여: 음, 그거 실망스럽네. 하지만 네가 재미있게 보내길 바랄게. 네가 시간이 있을 때 보자.

남: 정말 미안해. 다음 주 토요일에 약속을 잡을 수 있을까?

여: 그래. 이번에는 잊지 마!

남: 잊지 않을게. 달력에 그걸 적어 둘게.

문제풀이

① 응, 그건 정말 흥미진진했어.
② 실은, 난 그날 너무 바빴어.
③ 잘됐다! 오늘 오후에 보자!
④ 나는 갈 수 없어. 일요일은 어때?

15 ⑤

여: Michelle은 역사 프로젝트를 위한 보고서를 작성해야 해서, 그녀는 도서관에 가서 다섯 권의 책을 빌린다. 그녀가 집으로 오는 길에, 갑자기 비가 내리기 시작했지만, 그녀는 우산을 가지고 있지 않다. 그녀는 가능한 한 빨리 비를 뚫고 집으로 달려가기로 결심한다. 집에 도착할 때, 그녀는 책 중 한 권이 너무 젖어서 표지가 심각하게 파손된 것을 알게 된다. 다음 날, 그녀는 자신이 어떻게 할 수 있는지 묻기 위해 도서관으로 다시 간다. 이런 상황에서, Michelle이 사서에게 할 말로 가장 적절한 것은 무엇인가?

Michelle : 이 책이 파손되었어요. 제가 어떻게 해야 하죠?

문제풀이

① 오늘 새로 들어온 책이 있나요?
② 제가 몇 권의 책을 대출할 수 있나요?
③ 제가 어디에서 그 책을 잃어버렸는지 모르겠어요.
④ 제가 빌릴 수 있는 여분의 우산이 하나 있나요?

16 ⑤ 17 ④

남: 많은 사람들은 두통으로 고통받고 있습니다. 스트레스와 수면 부족과 같은 다양한 두통의 원인들이 있습니다. 두통은 또한 굶주림이나 수면 과다에 의해서 생길 수 있습니다. 보통 사람들은 통증을 덜기 위해서 약을 복용하는데, 왜냐하면 그것이 그 문제를 해결하는 쉽고 빠른 방법이기 때문입니다. 하지만 약을 복용하는 것이 항상 좋은 것은 아닌데, 그 이유는 그것이 몇몇 부작용을 가지고 있을 수 있기 때문입니다. 따라서 만약 두통이 심하지 않으면, 여러분은 두통과 맞설 다른 방법들을 먼저 시도해볼 수 있습니다. 머리에 차가운 얼음 팩을 놓는 것은 통증을 약간 줄일 수 있습니다. 뜨거운 물로 목욕을 하는 것 또한 여러분을 편안하게 하는 데 도움이 될 수 있습니다. 심지어 두통이 발생하기도 전에 여러분이 할 수 있는 일들도 있습니다. 항상 하루 종일 충분한 물을 마시고, 규칙적으로 운동을 하려고 노력해보세요. 이러한 조언들은 여러분이 두통을 완화하는 것을 도와줄 수 있습니다.

DICTATION Answers

01 depend more on / To prevent any problems / cause mold to grow
02 taking them together / at the same time / It's better to
03 will be showing / the most popular movies / There is one seat left
04 look more exciting / more noticeable there / in the upper right corner
05 anything special planned / have a performance / take pictures of
06 has almost healed / coming up in one month / a really good chance of
07 have my smartphone repaired / replace both of them / get the discount
08 a great place to travel / it consists of / it's not crowded
09 be on sale / only take place at / closing one hour later
10 What size apartment / can't spend more than / my lease expires
11 focus on my studies
12 why don't you come
13 seems to disappear / downloading an application / be easier
14 watch a movie together / are you coming back / when you have time
15 On her way home / as fast as she can / goes back to
16-17 relieve the pain / Taking a hot bath / try to exercise regularly

17 영어듣기 모의고사

본문 ▲ p.118

01 ①	02 ⑤	03 ②	04 ⑤	05 ②	06 ③
07 ④	08 ④	09 ⑤	10 ④	11 ④	12 ③
13 ④	14 ③	15 ⑤	16 ①	17 ⑤	

01 ①

여: 안녕하세요, 여러분. 여러분도 아시다시피, 내일 아침부터 전국에 눈이 내릴 것입니다. 눈이 많이 내릴 것으로 예상되니, 이런 날씨에 운전하실 때는 특히 조심하셔야 합니다. 빙판길에서 차를 멈추는 것은 평소보다 훨씬 더 오래 걸립니다. 천천히 운전하세요. 그뿐만 아니라, 앞에 있는 차와 간격을 유지하세요. 그리고 너무 갑자기 브레이크를 밟지도 마세요. 그것은 여러분의 차를 미끄러지게 할지도 모릅니다. 또한, 낮이라 해도 전조등을 반드시 켜도록 하세요. 이것은 다른 운전자들이 눈 사이로 여러분을 볼 수 있도록 도와줍니다.

02 ⑤

남: 아, 봐봐! 그 건물이 바로 저기 있어.
여: 잘됐다. 하지만 우리는 서두르는 게 좋겠어. 회의가 몇 분 후에 시작해.
남: 네 말이 맞아. 하지만 우선 우리는 차를 지하 주차장에 주차해야 해.
여: 음, 그냥 건물 앞에 주차하는 건 어때? 회의는 길지 않을 거야.
남: 안돼, 우리는 거기에 주차할 수 없어.
여: 왜? 우리가 거기에 주차하면 늦지 않을 거야.
남: '장애인 주차' 표지판이 있어. 보여?
여: 아, 그걸 지금 봤네. 하지만 그들이 우리 차를 확인하지 않을 거 같은데.
남: 그렇다 하더라도, 우리는 거기에 주차하면 안 돼. 만약 우리가 거기 주차하고 누군가가 그곳을 정말 필요로 한다면, 그들은 그곳을 사용하지 못할 거야.
여: 알겠어, 네 말이 맞아.

03 ②

남: 어서 오세요!
여: 안녕하세요. 여기에서 정말 좋은 냄새가 나네요.
남: 감사합니다. 오늘 찾으시는 특별한 것이 있으세요?
여: 아직 결정을 못 했어요. 우선 둘러볼게요.
남: 알겠습니다. 질문이 있으면 알려주세요.
여: 여기 모든 것은 신선한가요?
남: 네, 모두 매일 아침에 갓 만들어집니다.
여: 좋네요. 유기농 재료를 사용하세요?
남: 네. 밀가루와 다른 재료 모두가 100퍼센트 유기농입니다.
여: 좋네요. 어떤 것이 가장 잘 팔리는 건가요?
남: 여기 이 밀로 만든 것이 가장 인기 있는 종류입니다. 그리고 한 덩어리를 사시면, 한 덩어리를 무료로 드립니다.
여: 좋아요! 그걸 살게요.

04 ⑤

남: 나는 교실 뒤쪽 벽을 장식하는 걸 끝냈어.
여: 정말? 그것에 대해 내게 말해줘.
남: 음, 나는 맨 위에 둥근 시계를 걸었어.
여: 너는 급훈도 걸었니?
남: 응, "항상 웃어라!"라는 급훈은 시계 바로 아래에 있어.
여: 내가 만들었던 시간표는?
남: 그건 게시판의 왼쪽에 붙였어. 바로 그 옆에는 우리 반 친구들의 사진들이 있어.
여: 그거 멋지다! 그런데, 너는 교실 규칙 목록도 붙였어? 우리 선생님이 그걸 추가하길 원하셨잖아.
남: 응, 나는 그걸 사진들 바로 옆에 붙였어.
여: 잘했어. 나는 선생님이 그것을 마음에 들어 하시면 좋겠어.

05 ②

남: 이봐, Amy, 이번 주말에 영화 보는 게 어때?
여: 그거 좋다! 어떤 것을 보고 싶어?
남: 「Now You See My Eyes」는 어때? 그건 로맨스 영화야.
여: 그거 사랑에 빠지는 화가들에 관한 거 아니야?
남: 맞아. 들어본 적 있어?
여: 응, 내 친구가 감동적이라고 했어. 나는 정말 그걸 보고 싶어.
남: 좋아. 내 전화기로 이번 주말에 가능한 표가 있는지 확인해보자. *[잠시 후]* 아, 못 확인하겠다.
여: 뭐가 잘못됐어?
남: 내 전화기가 꺼졌어. 어젯밤에 충전하는 걸 잊었어. 네 걸로 티켓을 확인해줄 수 있어?
여: 그럼. 잠깐만 기다려.
남: 고마워.

06 ③

남: 안녕, Melissa. 너 여기서 뭘 하고 있니? 회사에 있어야 하는 거 아냐?
여: 아, 안녕, Peter. 아니야, 나 지난달에 그만뒀어.
남: 왜? 할 일이 너무 많았어?
여: 아니, 그렇게 바쁘진 않았어. 일은 감당할 만했어.
남: 그러면 네 동료들을 좋아하지 않았기 때문이야?
여: 아니, 나는 그들을 좋아했어. 나와 함께 일했던 사람들은 정말 좋았어. 나는 단지 내 미래에 대해 생각할 시간을 좀 더 원했어.
남: 아, 알겠다. 너는 네 일에서 스트레스를 받았던 게 틀림없어.
여: 그게 문제가 아니야. 나는 단지 내 꿈을 위해 일하고 싶어.
남: 아. 네 꿈이 뭔데?
여: 나는 소설가가 되고 싶어.
남: 와! 그거 멋지다. 행운을 빌어!

07 ④

여: 도와드릴까요, 손님?
남: 네. 닭이 얼마죠?
여: 한 마리에 10달러입니다. 그걸 잘게 자르고 싶으시면, 2달러가 추가됩

니다.
남: 그러면 닭 한 마리를 잘게 잘라 주세요. 저는 또 당근이랑 양파도 좀 필요해요.
여: 당근은 개당 2달러이고, 양파는 개당 1달러입니다. 얼마나 필요하세요?
남: 당근 한 개랑 양파 두 개요.
여: 알겠습니다. 다른 것도 필요하세요?
남: 네. 감자 하나가 필요해요.
여: 알겠습니다. 감자는 개당 2달러입니다. 이게 전부인가요?
남: 네. 이제 닭고기 수프를 만들기 위한 모든 게 있네요. 감사합니다.
여: 별말씀을요.

문제풀이

자른 닭 한 마리가 12달러, 당근 한 개가 2달러, 양파 두 개가 2달러, 감자 한 개가 2달러이므로, 남자가 지불 할 금액은 총 18달러(= $12+$2+$2+$2)이다.

08 ④

남: 저희 여행의 다음 행선지는 도쿄 타워입니다.
여: 그건 사무실용 건물인가요?
남: 아니요. 그건 사실 에펠탑과 더 비슷합니다. 그건 주로 통신탑으로서 기능하죠.
여: 그렇군요. 높이가 어느 정도 되나요? 그건 에펠탑만큼 크겠네요, 맞죠?
남: 네. 하지만 약 10미터 더 높습니다. 그건 또 무게가 약 4천 톤 정도 됩니다.
여: 와! 그건 무거운 구조물이네요.
남: 네, 맞습니다. 사실 그것은 강철로 만들어졌어요.
여: 이해가 되네요. 관광객들이 많나요?
남: 그렇습니다. 그것이 1958년에 개장한 이래로 1억 5천만 명이 넘는 사람들이 그곳을 방문했습니다.
여: 음, 그걸 볼 것이 기대되네요!

09 ⑤

남: 안녕하세요, 신사 숙녀 여러분. 연례 주 도서 전시회가 시립 컨벤션 센터에서 8월 9일부터 11일까지 열릴 것입니다. 그곳에는 다양한 기업의 많은 출판업자가 올 것입니다. 여러분은 소규모 출판사들의 새 책들을 일부 읽어보실 수 있습니다. 또한, 여러분은 몇몇 흥미로운 발표를 보고 독서 토론회에 참가하실 수 있을 것입니다. 전시회의 입장료는 15달러이지만, 12세 이하의 어린이는 무료입니다. 더욱이, 전시회 수익금은 어린이 교육을 지원하는 자선 단체에 기부될 것입니다. 시간 내 주셔서 감사합니다.

10 ④

남: 무엇을 도와드릴까요?
여: 전 배드민턴 라켓이 필요해요.
남: 음, 이것들이 저희의 가장 좋은 알루미늄 라켓들입니다. 정말 좋아요.
여: 좋아 보이지만, 저는 무거운 라켓을 원하지 않아요.
남: 가벼운 것을 원하시면, 80그램보다 적게 나가는 것이 좋을 겁니다. 손잡이 사이즈도 신경 쓰시나요?
여: 네. 저는 손이 작아서 큰 손잡이 사이즈는 제게 맞지 않을 거예요.
남: 손을 잠깐만 볼게요. *[잠시 후]* 3.5인치보다 작은 손잡이가 손님께 맞을 거예요. 이 둘 중의 하나를 고르시면 됩니다. 어떤 것이 더 마음에 드세요?
여: 더 저렴한 걸 사고 싶어요.
남: 그러면 이것이 손님께서 원하시는 겁니다.
여: 좋네요!

11 ④

여: 나 몸이 안 좋은 거 같아. 두통과 열이 있어.
남: 아, 정말? 진찰을 받는 게 어때?
여: 그런데 오늘은 일요일이야. 병원이 문을 닫아.
남: 내가 일요일에 문을 여는 병원을 알아.

문제풀이

① 나는 이미 이 약을 먹었어.
② 다행히 나는 열은 없어.
③ 네가 이제 나아졌다니 기뻐.
⑤ 네가 병원에 간 건 잘한 일이야.

12 ③

남: 무엇을 도와드릴까요?
여: 어제 이 재킷을 샀는데, 반품하고 싶어요.
남: 알겠습니다. 문제가 무엇인지 여쭤봐도 될까요?
여: 네. 뒤쪽에 작은 구멍을 발견했어요.

문제풀이

① 저는 그 색을 아주 많이 좋아해요.
② 실은, 그 재킷은 품절되었어요.
④ 아니에요, 모든 것이 완벽히 좋아요.
⑤ 그것에 만족하지 못하셨다니 유감입니다.

13 ④

여: 그 식당 어땠어?
남: 끔찍했어!
여: 응, 근데 그렇게 나쁠 거라고는 전혀 생각도 못 했어. 나의 기대가 너무 높았었나 봐.
남: 나도 너무 큰 기대를 했던 것 같아. 하지만 음식이 전혀 맛이 없었어.
여: 우리는 그런 맛 없는 음식에 너무 많은 돈을 낭비했어.
남: 맞아. 우리는 다른 식당에 가야 했어.
여: 그리고 서비스도 형편없었어.
남: 나는 다시는 절대 거기에 가고 싶지 않아. 네가 아주 인기 있는 곳이라고 말하지 않았어?
여: 응, 그리고 블로그 호평들이 많았거든.
남: 그것들은 그 식당에서 쓴 일종의 광고임이 틀림없어.
여: 우리는 온라인에 있는 모든 걸 믿어서는 안 되겠어.

문제풀이

① 나는 내 블로그에 후기를 쓰지 않았어.
② 하지만 나는 그들의 서비스에는 만족해.
③ 그 음식을 만드는 법을 내게 알려줘.

⑤ 물론이야. 그 식당에 또 가자.

14 ③

남: 무슨 일이야, Jane? 너 속상해 보여.
여: 우리 언니 May가 나한테 화났어. 난 무엇을 해야 할지 모르겠어.
남: 정말? 무슨 일인데?
여: 내가 언니 가방을 빌렸는데, 그 위에 커피를 쏟았거든. 그걸 빨았는데, 여전히 얼룩이 남았어.
남: 무슨 종류의 가방이었는데? 새것이었어?
여: 새것은 아니었어, 하지만 그건 언니가 가장 좋아하는 가방이거든.
남: 음, 왜 너의 언니가 화났는지 이해할 수 있을 거 같아.
여: 나도 알아. 나도 그것이 너무 유감이야.
남: 우리는 모두 실수를 해. 너는 그냥 언니에게 네가 얼마나 미안해하는지 말해야 해.
여: 내가 어떻게 해야 할까? 언니는 나랑 말하는 걸 거부해.
남: 편지로 사과하는 건 어때?

문제풀이

① 화가 날 이유는 없어.
② 너는 거짓말하는 걸 그만둬야 해. 그건 나빠.
④ 걱정하지 마. 너는 내 가방을 빌려도 돼.
⑤ 내 생각에 그녀는 나에게 직접 말하기를 원하는 것 같아.

15 ⑤

여: Susan은 휴가를 보내려고 캐나다에서 호주로 비행기를 타고 간다. 그녀가 착륙하자, 그녀는 세관원에 의해 제지를 당한다. 그 세관원은 그녀의 여행 가방에 과일, 채소, 또는 육류가 있는지를 묻는다. 그녀는 그에게 "아니요"라고 말하지만, 그가 그녀의 여행 가방을 열자 거기엔 사과 한 봉지가 있다. 그녀는 그것에 대해 완전히 잊고 있었기 때문에 깜짝 놀라고 당황스러워한다. 세관원은 그녀가 벌금을 내야 한다고 말하고, 벌금은 340달러이다! Susan은 사과를 하고 그것이 실수였다고 말하고 싶다. 이런 상황에서, Susan이 세관원에게 할 말로 가장 적절한 것은 무엇인가?
Susan : 죄송하지만, 저는 그걸 완전히 잊고 있었어요!

문제풀이

① 그건 제 것이 아니에요!
② 제가 얼마를 내야 하나요?
③ 왜 제가 그 물건들을 가져갈 수 없나요?
④ 저는 비행기에서 그것 중 몇 개를 먹었어요.

16 ① 17 ⑤

남: 안녕하세요, Better Health Channel 청취자 여러분! 오늘의 쇼에 다시 오신 걸 환영합니다. 오늘 저는 에너지 음료에 대해 말하고자 합니다. 요즘, 많은 사람들이 일을 하거나 공부를 하는 동안 깨어 있기 위해 에너지 음료에 의존합니다. 그들은 또한 그것의 달콤하고 상쾌한 맛을 좋아할지도 모릅니다. 하지만, 에너지 음료는 많은 카페인과 설탕을 함유하고 있는데, 이것은 둘 다 심각한 부작용을 초래할 수 있습니다. 카페인은 불면증을 일으킬 수 있는데, 이것은 여러분의 기억력과 건강에 나쁜 영향을 미칩니다. 이것은 또한 불규칙한 심장 박동을 유발할 수 있습니다. 더욱이, 에너지 음료 안의 높은 당 함량은 충치를 유발할 수 있습니다. 설탕은 또한 체중 증가의 원인이 될 수도 있습니다. 이러한 이유로, 에너지 음료를 피하는 것은 좋은 생각입니다. 여러분은 깨어 있을 더 건강에 좋은 방법을 찾아야 합니다. 좋습니다. 더 많은 정보를 위해 채널을 고정해 주세요.

DICTATION Answers

01 is expected to / drive slowly / be sure to turn on
02 we'd better hurry / won't be late / shouldn't park there
03 anything in particular / is freshly made / you get one free
04 hung a round clock / right below the clock / be pleased with
05 fall in love / there are tickets available / forgot to charge
06 handle the job / felt stressed out / want to be a novelist
07 cut it up / How many do you need / need one potato
08 as big as / it's made of steel / looking forward to seeing
09 will be held / take part in / be donated to
10 a heavy racket / won't fit me / get the cheaper one
11 go to see a doctor
12 I'd like to return it
13 It was awful / don't want to go / some kind of advertisement
14 spilt some coffee on it / feel terrible about / refuses to speak
15 is stopped by / a bag of apples / it was a mistake
16-17 rely on / cause serious side effects / avoid energy drinks

18 영어듣기 모의고사

본문 ☁ p.125

01 ①	02 ②	03 ⑤	04 ⑤	05 ②	06 ④
07 ④	08 ③	09 ⑤	10 ①	11 ①	12 ②
13 ②	14 ③	15 ④	16 ②	17 ⑤	

01 ①

여: 안녕하세요, 여러분. 캘리포니아 미술관에 방문해주셔서 감사합니다. 오늘 여러분께 말씀드릴 것이 있습니다. 저희는 다음 주 월요일부터 보수 공사에 들어갈 것입니다. 보수 공사는 한 달 동안 지속될 것입니다. 미술관의 에어컨이 현재 몇몇 전시실에서 고장이 나 있습니다. 그것은 교체될 것입니다. 1층과 2층에는 저희 예술품에 대한 비디오 설명이 나오는 터치스크린 디스플레이도 생길 것입니다. 이 기간 동안 안타깝게도 보수 공사 중인 모든 층이 폐쇄될 것입니다. 하지만 여러분은 다른 층에서는 여전히 전시품들을 관람하실 수 있습니다. 미술관은 보수 공사 동안 오전 10시부터 오후 5시까지의 정상 운영 시간을 유지할 것입니다. 감사합니다.

02 ②

남: 안녕, Sarah. 난 네가 건설 회사에 취업했다고 들었어. 축하해!
여: 고마워, Doug. 나는 지난달에 거기서 일하기 시작했어.
남: 나도 빨리 직업을 구할 수 있으면 좋겠어.
여: 최근에 어떤 자리에 지원해본 적 있어?
남: 응, 해봤어. 하지만 아직 어떤 면접 요청도 받은 적은 없어.
여: 걱정하지 마. 계속 시도해보면 반드시 기회를 얻을 수 있을 거야.
남: 내가 면접을 할 가능성을 높이기 위해서 내가 뭘 해야 할지 아니?
여: 음, 네 이력서를 가능한 한 인상적이게 만들어 봐. 너무 장황하게 만들지 말고.
남: 무슨 말이야?
여: 네 근무 경력에 초점을 맞추고, 네가 그 일에 준비되어 있다는 것을 보여줘.
남: 알겠어. 조언해줘서 고마워!

03 ⑤

여: 안녕하세요. 도와드릴까요?
남: 네. 전 당신과 방에 대해 얘기하고 싶어요.
여: 좋아요. 우리는 이용 가능한 방들이 많이 있습니다. 정확히 어떤 것을 찾고 있나요?
남: 음, 실은, 제 아파트에 세를 줄 방이 하나 있어요.
여: 아, 그렇군요. 방을 임대하길 원하시는군요. 그것도 도와드릴 수 있습니다.
남: 좋습니다. 제가 무엇을 해야 할까요?
여: 먼저, 이 양식을 작성해 주세요. 이것은 당신의 방과 방세로 당신이 얼마를 청구할지를 설명하는 거예요.
남: 알겠습니다. 그밖에는 뭘 해야 하죠?
여: 실은, 그게 전부입니다. 그 방에 관심이 있는 누군가를 찾으면 연락 드리겠습니다.
남: 알겠습니다. 전화 기다리겠습니다.

04 ⑤

남: 와, 창문 밖을 봐. 정말 멋진 광경이다!
여: 응! 바다 위를 나는 저 두 마리 새들을 봐!
남: 아름다워! 해변 근처의 저 작은 배도 멋져 보여.
여: 정말 그래. 이 경치는 거의 그림처럼 보여.
남: 맞아. 저 모래성을 봐. 아마 저건 몇 아이들에 의해 만들어졌을 거야.
여: 응, 내가 어렸을 때 그것들을 만들곤 했었어.
남: 나도 그래. 아침 식사 후에 해변에 가자.
여: 좋은 생각이야. 우리는 저 큰 야자수 아래에 있는 두 개의 해변 의자 위에 앉을 수 있어.
남: 응, 그러고 나서 언덕 위의 깃발이 있는 카페에 갈까?
여: 그래.

05 ②

남: 뭘 하고 있니, Amanda?
여: 내 친구인 Amy의 신부 파티를 위한 장식품을 찾고 있어.
남: 신부 파티가 뭔데?
여: 그건 결혼식 전 신부를 위한 파티야. 친구들은 그녀에게 선물이나 재미있는 물건 같은 것을 줘.
남: 그렇구나. 그걸 어디에서 할 건데?
여: 아직 모르겠어. 좋은 장소를 찾아야 해.
남: 호텔 방은 어때?
여: 호텔 방? 그건 비싸지 않을까?
남: 음, 우리 아버지께서 호텔에서 일하셔서 나는 가족 할인을 받을 수 있어. 네가 원한다면, 내가 너를 위해 방을 예약해줄게.
여: 정말? 그러면 나를 위해 예약해줄 수 있니? 거기에서 신부 파티를 하고 싶어.
남: 물론이지.

문제풀이

① 예식장 예약하기
② 호텔 방 예약하기
③ 파티 장식품 사기
④ 친구들을 파티에 초대하기
⑤ 웨딩드레스 고르기

06 ④

여: Dan, 뭐 하나 물어봐도 돼?
남: 당연하지, 뭔데?
여: 너는 어떤 종류의 신용카드를 사용하니?
남: 나는 Trust 은행 신용카드를 사용해. 왜 물어보는 거야?
여: 음, 나는 신용카드를 바꿀까 생각 중이거든.
남: 아, 연회비가 너무 비싸?
여: 그런 건 아냐. 하지만 나는 휘발유에 많은 돈을 쓰는데, 내 카드는 어떤 할인도 제공하지 않거든.
남: Trust 은행에 가보는 게 어때? 거기에는 주유소에서 5퍼센트 할인을

해주는 카드가 있어.
여: 그거 괜찮네.
남: 그들은 또한 고객 서비스가 훌륭해. 네가 어떤 문제가 생기면 거기에 언제든지 전화할 수 있어.
여: 좋아. 오늘 그 은행에 가봐야겠어.

07 ④

여: Marley Stadium에 오신 것을 환영합니다! 무엇을 도와드릴까요?
남: 오늘 야구 경기 표를 사고 싶어요.
여: 알겠습니다. 하지만 블루석과 레드석 표만 남았어요.
남: 그건 얼마죠?
여: 블루석 표는 15달러이고, 레드석 표는 10달러예요.
남: 왜 블루석이 더 비싼가요?
여: 거기 좌석들이 경기장과 훨씬 더 가까워요.
남: 그렇다면, 블루석 표 두 장 주세요. 그리고 받을 수 있는 할인이 있나요?
여: 회원 카드가 있으면 10 퍼센트 할인을 받을 수 있으세요.
남: 잘됐네요. 여기 제 회원 카드랑 현금이요.
여: 여기 표 두 장이요.

문제풀이

남자는 한 장에 15달러인 블루석 표 두 장을 구입하기로 했으므로 30달러인데, 회원 카드로 10 퍼센트의 할인을 받았으므로 지불한 금액은 총 27달러(= $15×2×0.9)이다.

08 ③

남: 호주 여행은 어땠니, Ashley?
여: 굉장했어! 나는 마침내 시드니 하버 브리지를 봤어.
남: 멋지다. 그건 어땠어?
여: 너도 아마 알다시피, 그건 세계에서 가장 큰 철강 다리 중 하나이고, 전체 길이가 3,770피트야. 그건 장관이었어.
남: 틀림없이 그랬을 것 같아.
여: 그것의 별명이 '옷걸이'라는 거 알고 있었어?
남: 아니, 하지만 왜 그런지 알 것 같아. 그건 아치형 모양 때문이지?
여: 응. 그건 건설하기 어려웠을 게 틀림없어. 건설하는 데 거의 10년이 걸렸다는 것을 읽었었어.
남: 와! 그건 긴 시간이야.
여: 나는 다리 꼭대기에도 올라갔었어. 그게 이번 여행에서 나의 가장 좋았던 기억이야.
남: 너는 좋은 시간을 보낸 것 같구나.

09 ⑤

남: Boyana 교회로 넘어가 봅시다. 이것은 불가리아의 수도인 소피아 근처에 위치해 있습니다. 이것은 세 개의 건물로 구성되어 있습니다. 첫 번째 건물은 10세기에 건축되었습니다. 13세기 초반에는 2층짜리 두 번째 건물이 추가되었습니다. 이 두 번째 건물은 벽에 많은 그림들이 있습니다. 그것들은 동유럽 중세 미술의 가장 좋은 본보기들 중 일부입니다. 그 그림들 때문에, Boyana 교회는 유네스코 세계 문화유산으로도 지정되었습니다. 그 교회의 세 번째 건물은 19세기 초에 건설되었습니다. 그 그림들을 보호하기 위해서, 우리는 15분 동안만 그것들을 관람할 수 있습니다. 즐거운 관람 되시기 바랍니다.

10 ①

남: 안녕하세요. 뭐 찾으시는 거 있으세요?
여: 네, 저는 새 매트리스를 사고 싶어요.
남: 알겠습니다, 고객님께서는 딱 맞는 곳에 오셨네요. 저희는 좋은 매트리스들이 많이 있습니다. 어떤 사이즈를 원하세요?
여: 저는 그냥 싱글 사이즈를 찾고 있어요.
남: 이건 어떠세요? 이건 폭신하고 정말 편안해요.
여: 좋아 보이네요. 근데 저는 요즘 허리 통증이 있어서 단단한 매트리스를 원해요.
남: 아, 그렇다면 이것들 중 두 개가 손님의 요구에 맞을 겁니다.
여: 그렇군요. 그것들 사이에 가격 차이가 있나요?
남: 네, 그것들 중 하나가 100달러 더 저렴합니다.
여: 그렇다면 더 저렴한 걸로 살게요.

11 ①

여: 안녕하세요. Applewood 공공 도서관으로 가주세요.
남: 들어본 적이 전혀 없는데요. 거기가 어디죠?
여: 저도 몰라요. 저는 여기가 처음이거든요.
남: 그러면 제가 GPS를 확인해볼게요.

문제풀이

② 당신의 주소를 여기에 남기세요.
③ 문제없습니다. 저는 그곳이 어디인지 알아요.
④ 도서관은 이 시간에는 문을 닫아요.
⑤ 모든 도서관 책들은 오늘 반납되어야 합니다.

12 ②

남: 잘 지내니, Rebecca? 너 신나 보여.
여: 안녕, John. 실은, 오늘 저녁에 연극을 볼 거야.
남: 와. 그 연극 제목이 뭐야?
여: 「The Lost World」야.

문제풀이

① 연극은 6시 30분에 시작해.
③ 그건 Grace 홀에서 공연될 거야.
④ 그건 역대 최고의 연극 중 하나였어.
⑤ 어머니와 함께 연극을 볼 거야.

13 ②

남: 안녕하세요. 제 이름은 Harry Rose입니다.
여: 안녕하세요, Rose 씨. 오늘 Kaine 선생님과 예약이 돼 있으신가요?
남: 네, 했습니다. 어제 전화 드렸었어요.
여: 아, 네. 이제 기억나네요. 무슨 문제인지 말씀해주실 수 있나요?
남: 전 두통이 심해요. 어제 어지러운 걸 느끼기 시작했는데, 그것이 아직도 저를 괴롭히고 있어요.
여: 전에도 비슷한 증상을 경험하신 적이 있나요?

남: 아니요. 이번이 처음이에요. 저는 평소에 상당히 건강합니다.
여: 그렇군요. 이 양식을 작성해주시고 대기실에 앉아 계세요.
남: 알겠습니다. 진찰을 받으려면 얼마나 기다려야 할까요?
여: 길어봐야 몇 분이면 됩니다.

문제풀이

① 식사 후에 이 알약을 드세요.
③ 제 두통이 훨씬 더 심해졌어요.
④ 저는 오랫동안 기다리고 있었습니다.
⑤ 그는 어제 다른 예약이 있었어요.

14 ③

남: 안녕하세요! 오늘은 무엇을 도와드릴까요?
여: 안녕하세요. 이 안경을 여기서 약 두 달 전에 샀어요.
남: 아, 네. 그건 저희의 가장 인기 있는 테 중 일부네요. 무슨 문제가 있나요?
여: 음, 제가 최근에 이걸 몇 번 떨어뜨렸는데, 이제는 잘 보이지가 않아요. 제 생각에 렌즈가 긁힌 것 같아요.
남: 제가 살펴볼게요. *[잠시 후]* 렌즈 표면에 긁힌 자국들이 많이 있네요. 렌즈를 교체하고 싶으세요?
여: 네. 그건 비용이 얼마나 들죠?
남: 50달러입니다.
여: 적당한 것 같네요. 언제 찾을 수 있나요?
남: 네 시까지는 준비될 겁니다.

문제풀이

① 고맙습니다! 이제 잘 볼 수 있어요.
② 저는 테도 바꾸고 싶어요.
④ 손님은 렌즈를 바꿀 필요가 없으세요.
⑤ 손님은 몇 주 전에 그걸 찾아가셨어요.

15 ④

여: Diana는 고등학교 2학년 학생이다. 그녀는 수학 수업에 힘겨워했었고 성적에 대해 스트레스를 받곤 했다. 하지만 그녀는 지금 훨씬 더 잘하고 있다. 그녀는 6개월 동안 온라인 수학 수업을 들었기 때문에 실력이 향상되었다. 오늘, 그녀와 그녀의 반 친구들은 중간고사 성적을 받았고, Diana는 A를 받았다. 그러나, 그녀의 가장 친한 친구인 Nick은 매우 실망한 것처럼 보인다. 그는 매우 낮은 점수를 받았다. 그는 Diana에게 자신의 수학 실력을 향상시키는 것을 도와달라고 부탁한다. Diana는 그에게 자신이 했던 것을 해보라고 조언하고 싶다. 이런 상황에서, Diana가 Nick에게 할 말로 가장 적절한 것은 무엇인가?
Diana: 온라인 강좌를 들어보는 게 어때?

문제풀이

① 나도 수학을 잘하지 못해.
② 성적을 올리는 법을 말해줘.
③ 너는 다음 기말고사에서 더 잘할 거야.
⑤ 너는 수학 수업에 집중해야 해.

16 ② 17 ⑤

남: 여기 여러분을 위한 좋은 소식이 있습니다. 요즘 많은 사람들은 저렴하고 편리하기 때문에 온라인에서 쇼핑하는 것을 좋아합니다. 하지만 좋은 쇼핑몰에서 쇼핑을 하는 것이 훨씬 더 즐거울 수 있습니다. 그것이 바로 여러분께서 새롭게 개장한 Western 쇼핑몰을 방문하셔야 하는 이유입니다. 이 쇼핑몰은 저렴한 가격으로 고품질의 상품들을 제공합니다. 이곳은 고객들이 50개의 모든 매장들을 쉽게 돌아다닐 수 있도록 설계되었습니다. 쇼핑몰의 대형 주차장에는 주차 공간이 많습니다. 게다가, 이곳에는 여러분이 쉴 수 있는 옥상 정원이 있습니다. 17번 버스가 쇼핑몰 바로 맞은 편에 정차합니다. 쇼핑몰은 이번 주 일요일 오전 9시에 처음으로 개장할 것입니다. 그날, 여러분은 쇼핑몰을 방문하시기만 해도 특별한 선물들을 받으실 수 있습니다. 그러므로 시내로 나오셔서 친구들과 함께 쇼핑하는 데 몇 시간을 보내세요.

DICTATION Answers

01 undergo renovations / out of order / maintain its regular hours
02 you got a job / applied for any positions / Focus on
03 plenty of rooms available / fill out this form / who is interested in it
04 flying over the sea / used to make them / with the flag
05 looking for decorations / find a nice place / make a reservation
06 thinking of changing / doesn't offer any discounts / have excellent customer service
07 for today's baseball game / more expensive / any discounts available
08 its total length / difficult to build / my favorite memory
09 consists of three buildings / some of the best examples / To protect the paintings
10 a single size / having back pain / difference in price
11 never heard of it
12 the name of the play
13 have an appointment / feeling dizzy / fill out this form
14 most popular frames / got scratched / pick them up
15 in her second year / took an online math class / advise him to do
16-17 be much more enjoyable / has been designed so that / spend a few hours shopping

19 영어듣기 모의고사

본문 ▲ p.132

01 ①	02 ⑤	03 ④	04 ⑤	05 ②	06 ④
07 ①	08 ⑤	09 ④	10 ③	11 ①	12 ⑤
13 ③	14 ⑤	15 ⑤	16 ④	17 ④	

01 ①

여: 자연에서 쉬는 것은 주말을 보내는 훌륭한 방법이며, Rock Creek 캠프장은 그렇게 하기에 좋은 장소입니다. 캠프장은 도시 외곽으로 불과 한 시간 거리에 위치하고 있고, 50개가 넘는 텐트를 위한 충분한 공간이 있습니다. 저희 시설에는 욕실, 수영장과 여러분이 바비큐를 할 수 있는 피크닉장이 있습니다. 여러분은 또한 강으로 래프팅을 하러 가거나 근처 호수를 탐험하기 위해 카누를 빌릴 수도 있습니다. 하지만 최소한 일주일 전에 미리 예약을 하셔야 합니다. 오늘 저희에게 전화하셔서 신선한 공기와 재미가 있는 주말 계획을 세우기 시작하세요.

02 ⑤

여: 그 셔츠가 흥미로워, Troy. 그걸 어디서 샀니?
남: 실은, 내가 업사이클링해서 만들었어.
여: 업사이클링? 그게 뭐야?
남: 업사이클링이란 낡은 것을 가져다가 그걸 새것으로 바꾸는 거야. 재활용이랑 비슷하지.
여: 그래서 넌 몇몇의 낡은 것들로 이 새 셔츠를 만들었구나, 그렇지? 와. 멋지다.
남: 그래, 그리고 그것은 지구를 돕는 훌륭한 방법이야. 난 항상 환경을 보호할 새로운 방법들을 찾고 있어.
여: 나도 그래. 나는 전자 기기를 사용하지 않을 때는 전원을 꺼. 그리고 종이컵 대신 머그잔에 음료를 마시는 것으로 쓰레기를 줄여.
남: 그것들도 도움이 되는 좋은 방법들이야.
여: 고마워. 나도 동의해. 우리가 가진 것을 낭비하지 않음으로써 우리는 지구를 보호할 수 있어.
남: 맞아.

03 ④

남: 손님, 실례합니다만, 아직 탑승구를 통과하실 수 없습니다.
여: 왜 안 되죠? 저는 표와 여권을 갖고 있어요.
남: 이건 단지 보안 검사입니다. 손님 가방 안을 봐야 합니다.
여: 아, 알겠습니다. 여기 있어요.
남: 100밀리리터가 넘는 액체가 담긴 병이 있습니까?
여: 아니요, 저는 모든 액체를 위탁 수하물에 담았어요.
남: 주머니칼과 같은 날카로운 물건은요? 그와 같은 것을 가지고서는 비행할 수 없습니다.
여: 아니요, 그런 건 없어요. 저는 가방 안에 지갑, 디지털카메라, 그리고 휴대전화를 갖고 있어요.
남: 알겠습니다. *[잠시 후]* 네, 좋습니다. 이제 손님은 탐지기를 통과하시면 됩니다.
여: 알겠습니다.
남: 협조해주셔서 감사합니다. 좋은 여행 되세요!

04 ⑤

여: Jeremy, 이것은 건강한 생활 방식 콘테스트를 위한 네 포스터니?
남: 응, 맞아. 나는 상단에 "걸어서 그리고 자전거를 타고 통학해라!"라고 제목을 썼어.
여: 그렇구나. 그것은 구름에 약간 덮인 태양 근처에 있네.
남: 맞아. 나는 그것이 실제처럼 보이기를 원했어.
여: 정말로 그래. 그리고 좌측에 있는 나무도 멋져 보여. 거기에 달려 있는 사과 몇 개가 보이네.
남: 고마워. 학교의 큰 시계는 그리기 가장 어려운 부분이었어.
여: 멋져 보이는데! 그것은 실제 시계와 정말로 똑같아.
남: 두 학생에 대해서는 어떻게 생각해? 한 명은 걷고 있고 다른 한 명은 자전거를 타고 있어.
여: 완벽해. 나는 네가 상을 받을 거라고 확신해.
남: 나도 그러길 바라!

05 ②

남: Tom의 생일 파티 준비는 어떻게 되어가고 있어, Kate?
여: 잘되고 있어. 모두에게 식당에 일찍 오라고 이야기했지, 그렇지?
남: 응. 내가 뭐 도와줄까? 장식을 달거나 풍선을 불어줄 수 있어.
여: 아니야, 우리가 그런 것들은 이미 다 했어.
남: 그럼 나는 나중에 식당에 들르기만 하면 되겠네.
여: 실은, 다른 일을 해줄 수 있어?
남: 물론이지, 뭔데?
여: 나는 네가 여섯 시에 Tom을 식당으로 데리고 와 주었으면 해. 그런데 그를 속여야 해.
남: 알았어. 내가 방과 후에 그와 배드민턴을 칠게. 그러고 나서 우리가 여섯 시에 저녁을 먹으러 식당에 들를게.
여: 좋은 계획인 것처럼 들리는걸!

문제풀이

① 사람들에게 일찍 오라고 전화하기
② 그의 친구를 파티에 데려오기
③ 그의 친구와 배드민턴 치기
④ 식당에 테이블 예약하기
⑤ 풍선과 장식을 달기

06 ④

남: Jessica, 네 전공이 컴퓨터 공학이 맞지?
여: 맞아. 그것은 완벽한 선택이었어.
남: 나도 내 전공에 대해 똑같이 말할 수 있으면 좋을 텐데.
여: 아, 안됐다. 네 전공은 철학이 맞지? 그걸 좋아하지 않니?
남: 실은, 부모님이 그걸 추천해 주셨고, 나도 좋아해. 그렇지만 난 전공을 바꾸려고 생각 중이야.
여: 뭐가 문제야? 너무 어렵니?
남: 음, 힘들긴 하지만 너무 어렵진 않아. 그런데 나는 내 미래가 걱정이 돼.
여: 아, 알겠다. 그것이 직장 생활을 시작하기에 좋은 전공은 아니라서 그

런 것 같은데.
남: 맞아. 나는 더 실용적인 것을 전공해야 할 것 같아.
여: 음, 컴퓨터 공학은 어때?
남: 아니, 괜찮아! 나는 컴퓨터에 관련된 것은 아무것도 좋아하지 않아.

07 ①

남: 도와드릴까요?
여: 네. 저는 이 커피 머그잔을 교환하고 싶어요.
남: 문제가 있나요?
여: 그렇진 않아요. 그것을 선물로 받았는데, 저는 스테인리스강으로 된 것을 원해요. 이것은 플라스틱이에요.
남: 알겠습니다. 여기 스테인리스강으로 된 것들이 있어요. 두 가지 다른 크기가 있어요.
여: 더 작은 크기가 좋을 것 같아요. 아, 이건 좋은 거네요. 얼마인가요?
남: 음, 그건 손님이 갖고 오신 것보다 더 비쌉니다. 35달러예요.
여: 괜찮아요. 이걸로 할게요.
남: 알겠습니다. 플라스틱 머그잔은 20달러였습니다.
여: 제게 이 10달러 상품권이 있어요. 그걸 사용하고 나머지는 현금으로 지불해도 되나요?
남: 물론 그러셔도 됩니다.

문제풀이
여자는 선물로 받은 20달러짜리 머그잔을 35달러짜리 머그잔으로 교환하고 10달러짜리 상품권을 냈으므로, 나머지인 5달러(= $35-$20-$10)만 현금으로 지불하면 된다.

08 ⑤

남: 이곳이 초콜릿이 만들어지는 장소입니다.
여: 와. 그러니까 카카오 콩이 주요 원료란 말이군요, 그렇죠?
남: 네, 그런데, 설탕, 우유, 그리고 인공 향미료가 첨가됩니다.
여: 그렇군요. 그런데 초콜릿은 원래 어디에서 생산되나요?
남: 중앙아메리카에서 생산됩니다. 스페인 사람들이 아즈텍 부족으로부터 초콜릿을 만드는 방법을 배웠습니다.
여: 흥미롭군요. 그런데 초콜릿은 일반적으로 건강에 해롭지 않나요, 그렇죠?
남: 실은, 그렇습니다. 그러나, 다크초콜릿은 몇 가지 건강상의 이점을 가지고 있습니다. 그것은 혈압과 스트레스를 낮춰줍니다.
여: 그건 몰랐군요.
남: 사실입니다. 다음에는 기념품점을 방문하겠습니다. 그곳에서 초콜릿을 구매하실 수 있습니다.
여: 좋네요.

09 ④

남: Portsmouth 시립 오케스트라에서 새로운 바이올린 연주자를 찾고 있습니다. 지원자는 오케스트라에서 연주한 경력이 적어도 3년은 있어야 합니다. 음악 연주 학위가 선호됩니다. 저희에게 이력서, 자기소개서와 최근 연주 영상을 보내주십시오. 지원서를 검토한 후에, 상위권 지원자에게 연락할 것입니다. 오디션은 9월 초로 예정되어 있습니다. 만약 필요하다면, 그 직후에 2차 오디션도 보게 될 것 입니다. 저희는 9월 15일까지 최종 결정을 내릴 것으로 예상하고 있습니다. 8월 22일까지 지원서를 보내주시기 바랍니다. 만약 질문이 있다면, hiring@pco.org로 이메일을 보내시기 바랍니다.

10 ③

남: 안녕하세요, 무엇을 도와드릴까요?
여: 카메라를 찾고 있는데요. DSLR 카메라에 관심이 있어요.
남: 그렇군요. 염두에 두고 있는 특정 모델이 있습니까?
여: 딱히 있지는 않지만, 가벼운 것을 원합니다. 어디든 그것을 가지고 다니고 싶어요.
남: 제가 생각하기에 500그램 미만의 카메라가 가지고 다니기에 편리할 것 같습니다.
여: 네, 좋은 것 같아요. 아, 지금 흰색 DSLR이 있다고 들었어요.
남: 맞습니다. 흰색 카메라는 바로 1년 전에 출시되었어요.
여: 전 충전지가 있는 흰색 카메라를 원해요.
남: 알겠습니다. 이 카메라가 손님에게 완벽하겠는데, 가격이 500달러가 넘어요.
여: 괜찮아요. 그걸로 할게요.

11 ①

여: Rob, 너 Eric 생일 선물 샀니?
남: 아직 안 샀어. 뭘 사야 할지 생각이 안 나.
여: 나도 그래. 그에게 필요한 게 뭔지 물어보는 게 어때?
남: 좋은 생각이야. 내가 지금 당장 그에게 전화할게.

문제풀이
② 나는 이미 그를 위해 무엇을 사줘야 할지 알겠어.
③ 나는 네가 그에게 사준 것을 그가 좋아할 것이라고 확신해.
④ 나는 내일 새 바지 한 벌을 사야 해.
⑤ 나는 작년 그의 생일에 그에게 선물을 주지 않았어.

12 ⑤

남: 실례합니다. 찰스 디킨스의 「위대한 유산」이 있나요?
여: 죄송합니다. 모든 책이 지금 대출 중이네요.
남: 그렇군요. 언제 제가 한 부 가져갈 수 있을까요?
여: 내일 그중 한 권이 반납될 거예요.

문제풀이
① 제가 그것을 다 읽으면, 당신에게 전화할게요.
② 그 소설은 제가 가장 좋아하는 책들 중 하나예요.
③ 당신은 2주 후에 그 책을 반납해야 해요.
④ 죄송합니다만, 할인해드릴 수 없어요.

13 ③

남: 안녕, Julia. 왜 그렇게 시무룩해 있니?
여: 내 여동생이 내가 어젯밤에 또 잠꼬대를 했다고 말해줬는데, 난 아무것도 기억나지 않아.
남: 흥미롭네. 자주 그러니?
여: 유감스럽게도 그래. 그 애가 말하길 일주일에 서너 번은 그렇게 한대.
남: 꽤 자주 그러는구나. 어젯밤에는 뭐라고 말했어?

여: 그 애가 말하길 내가 야구 경기에 대해서 이야기를 하고 있었대. 나는 다음번에 무슨 말을 하게 될지 약간 겁이 나.
남: 음, 그게 위험하다고 생각되지는 않는데.
여: 나도 그렇게 생각하지 않아. 하지만 결국 그게 문제를 일으킬지도 몰라. 난 그것을 멈추는 법을 알고 싶어.
남: 그러면 전문가와 이야기해 보는 것이 좋겠어.
여: 빨리 의사와 약속을 잡아야겠다.

문제풀이
① 이상한 수면 습관은 아주 무서울 수 있어.
② 네가 몽유병에 관해서 전문가여서 다행이야.
④ 너는 그때 야구에 대한 꿈을 꿨음이 틀림없어.
⑤ 나는 다른 사람들도 잠꼬대한다는 것을 알게 돼서 기뻐.

14 ⑤

여: 아, 이런! 비밀번호를 또 잊어버렸어.
남: 요새 이런 일이 자주 일어나니?
여: 응, 그리고 나 전화번호도 기억이 안 나.
남: 난 그 문제를 알 것 같아. 너는 디지털 치매에 걸렸음이 틀림없어.
여: 그 병은 나이 든 사람들이 무언가를 잊어버리게 만드는 병 아니니?
남: 그건 좀 다른 거야. 그건 우리가 전자 기기에 비밀번호 같은 것들을 저장하기 때문에 그것들을 잊어버리게 된다는 걸 의미해.
여: 알겠다. 그러면 어떤 걸 외우는 것 대신에 전화기나 컴퓨터에 의존하는 것이 우리에게 나쁜 거지?
남: 그래. 우리가 계속해서 그렇게 한다면, 우리의 컴퓨터, 전화기, 그리고 태블릿 컴퓨터가 우리의 기억력이 될 거야.
여: 끔찍하다. 어떻게 해야 하지?
남: 전자 기기에 덜 의지하려고 노력해야 해.

문제풀이
① 너의 모든 정보를 스마트폰에 저장해.
② 길에서 인터넷 검색을 너무 많이 하지 마.
③ 더 큰 메모리가 있는 전자 기기를 구매해.
④ 한 가지 주제보다는 다양한 주제를 공부해.

15 ⑤

여: Angela는 호주 여행을 마치고 고국인 캐나다로 돌아온다. 그녀는 공항에 도착했을 때, 짐이 많아서 택시를 타기로 결정한다. 그녀는 서둘러서 짐 가방을 찾아 택시를 타고 집으로 간다. 그러나, 그녀는 집에 도착하자, 자신의 전화기가 사라진 것을 알게 된다. 그녀는 그것에 대해 생각해 보고 택시에 탔을 때 전화기를 갖고 있었다고 확신한다. 그녀는 집 전화기로 택시 회사 고객 서비스 번호로 전화를 건다. 이런 상황에서, Angela가 고객 서비스 상담원에게 할 말로 가장 적절한 것은 무엇인가?
Angela : 택시들 중 하나에서 분실된 전화기를 찾았나요?

문제풀이
① 새 전화기를 고르는 것을 도와주시겠어요?
② 공항에 전화를 걸기 위해 당신의 전화기를 사용해도 될까요?
③ 제 전화기를 찾아 주셔서 정말 감사합니다.
④ 여행 가방을 어디서 살 수 있는지 알고 계세요?

16 ④ 17 ④

남: Earth News Today에 오신 것을 환영합니다. 여러분은 아마 과일이 건강에 좋다는 것을 이미 알고 계실 겁니다. 그러나 과일이 좋은 건 그게 전부가 아닙니다. 과일 한 조각을 다 드신 후에, 그 껍질로 할 수 있는 것이 많습니다. 예를 들면, 오렌지 껍질은 소금과 섞어서 더러운 냄비나 프라이팬을 닦는 데 사용할 수 있습니다. 그리고 신발 얼룩의 대부분은 바나나 껍질로 쉽게 닦아낼 수 있습니다. 또한, 포도 껍질은 접시와 그릇에서 마늘 냄새를 없애는 데 아주 좋습니다. 마지막으로, 파인애플을 잊지 마세요. 파인애플의 거친 껍질은 가스레인지나 전자레인지의 먼지와 얼룩을 제거하는 데 사용될 수 있습니다. 그러니 다음에 과일을 즐기고 있을 때, 껍질을 쓰레기통에 버리기 전에 다시 생각해 보세요. 아마 껍질을 가지고 할 수 있는 다른 무언가가 있을 겁니다.

문제풀이
16 ① 가장 맛이 좋은 과일 껍질
② 과일을 쉽게 깎는 도구
③ 과일 껍질의 건강상 이점
④ 과일 껍질을 활용하는 방법
⑤ 부엌에서 냄새를 제거하는 방법

DICTATION Answers

01 spend a weekend / go river rafting / making your plans
02 similar to recycling / turn off electronics / protect the earth
03 look inside your bag / nothing like that / for your cooperation
04 partly covered by / the same as / win the prize
05 hang up decorations / need you to bring / stop at the restaurant
06 say the same about / worried about my future / related to computers
07 as a gift / more expensive than / pay the rest in cash
08 the main ingredient / It comes from / has some health benefits
09 at least three years / reviewing the applications / make a final decision
10 I'm interested in / carry it everywhere / with a rechargeable battery
11 Why don't we ask
12 get a copy
13 talked in my sleep / I'm a little scared / talk to an expert
14 forgot my password / makes older people forget / What should I do
15 comes back home / her phone is missing / dials the number
16-17 is good for your health / can be easily wiped away / think twice before

20 영어듣기 모의고사

본문 ☁ p.139

01 ①	02 ①	03 ②	04 ④	05 ③	06 ③
07 ②	08 ③	09 ③	10 ②	11 ⑤	12 ④
13 ⑤	14 ⑤	15 ②	16 ③	17 ④	

01 ①

여: Tower Manor 거주자 여러분, 주목해주십시오. 여러분 중 몇 분들은 이미 알고 계시듯이, 1층의 거주자가 도둑맞았습니다. CCTV 녹화물을 분석한 후에, 저희는 용의자를 확인할 수 있었습니다. 여러분의 안전을 보장하기 위해, 저희는 몇 가지 즉각적인 변화를 주기로 결정했습니다. 저희는 외부인의 접근에 대해 더 엄격한 통제를 두고 있습니다. 정문에 더 강화된 보안 장치가 설치되었습니다. 그것은 관리사무소에서 알려주는 새 비밀번호로 보호됩니다. 새 비밀번호를 받기 위해서 사무소에 방문하시고, 그것을 비공개로 해 주십시오. 질문이 있으면, 자유롭게 관리 사무소에 연락해주시기 바랍니다. 감사합니다.

02 ①

남: Jessie, 우리의 하와이 여행 계획을 세웠니?
여: 아직 못했어. 너는 무엇을 하고 싶어?
남: 나는 그곳에서 하이킹, 수영, 파도타기, 스쿠버 다이빙 같은 많은 야외 활동을 하고 싶어.
여: 정말 그 모든 것을 다 해보고 싶어?
남: 음… 너는 내 생각이 마음에 들지 않는 것 같은데.
여: 우리가 그렇게 많은 활동들을 할 수 있을 것 같지 않아. 우리는 거기에 3일만 있을 거야.
남: 그러면 너는 무엇을 하고 싶어?
여: 나는 차라리 해변에서 휴식을 취하고 햇볕을 즐기며 시간을 보내고 싶어.
남: 그건 나에게 좀 지루하게 들리는데.
여: 음, 나는 지금보다 더 피곤해져서 휴가에서 돌아오고 싶지 않아.
남: 알았어. 우리는 아마도 그냥 하나 혹은 두 개의 활동을 할 수 있겠구나.

03 ②

[휴대전화벨이 울린다.]
여: 여보세요?
남: 안녕하세요, Johnson 씨. Harry Goldman입니다. 오늘 아침에 당신의 메시지를 받았어요. 무엇을 도와드릴까요?
여: 아, 전화에 답해 주셔서 감사해요. 집에 문제가 있어요.
남: 무엇이죠?
여: 창고 천장에 누수가 있는 거 같아요.
남: 바로 지난여름에 제가 천장을 수리받았는데요. 확실한가요?
여: 네. 비가 왔을 때, 물이 들어왔어요. 내가 거기에 놓은 모든 것이 젖었어요.
남: 그 말을 들으니 유감이네요. 제가 오늘 오후에 들러서 살펴보면 어떨까요?
여: 그게 좋겠어요.
남: 제가 새는 곳을 때우지 못하면, 수리공이 와서 그것을 하도록 전화할게요.
여: 감사해요.

04 ④

여: Joe, 기숙사로 이사하는 것을 다 마쳤니?
남: 응. 방이 정말 마음에 들어.
여: 멋지다! 1인실이라고 했니?
남: 맞아. 약간 작지만, 자연광이 많이 들어오게 하는 큰 창이 있어.
여: 아, 그거 멋지다.
남: 두꺼운 커튼도 있어서 하루 중 아무 때나 잘 수 있어.
여: 잘됐네. 방 안에 또 다른 건 뭐가 있어?
남: 창문 옆에 큰 옷장이 있어.
여: 좋네. 책장은?
남: 내 책상 바로 옆에 세 개의 선반이 있는 책장이 있어.
여: 좋구나. 거기서 잠을 잘 잘 것 같아?
남: 그럼. 방 오른쪽 구석에 멋지고 편안한 침대가 있어.

05 ③

남: Amanda, 오늘 저녁 식사로 제안할 게 있니?
여: 실은, 내가 정말 가보고 싶은 새 식당이 있어.
남: 아. 이름이 뭐야?
여: Pasta Heaven이야.
남: 나도 들어 봤어. 음식이 정말 맛있을 것 같다. 그런데 거기에서 자리를 잡기가 힘들 것 같아.
여: 맞아, 그리고 그 식당은 예약도 받지 않아.
남: 그럼 지금 당장 출발하는 게 어떨까?
여: 좋아. 그런데 나 정확한 위치를 모르고, 내 전화 배터리가 다 됐어.
남: 그건 큰 문제가 아냐. 내 전화에서 찾아볼 수 있어.
여: 잘됐다. 거기를 찾을 수 있는지 봐.
남: 알았어. 지금 해볼게.

06 ③

남: 여보, 당신 화가 나 보여요. 무슨 일이에요?
여: 음, 내 차에 어떤 일이 생겨서 정비공에게 가져갔어요.
남: 정말요? 차에 무슨 일이 있었어요?
여: 주차장에 주차되어 있는 동안에 누가 차를 들이받고 그냥 가버렸어요.
남: 그거 심하네요. 아마도 보안 카메라가 차량 번호판을 촬영했을 거예요.
여: 유감스럽게도, 우리가 주차하는 곳에는 카메라가 없어요.
남: 말도 안 돼요! 우리는 수요일에 입주자 회의에서 이것에 대해 항의해야 해요.
여: 음, 난 갈 수가 없어요. 나는 수요일에 고객과 약속이 있어요.
남: 괜찮아요. 내가 혼자 가서 더 많은 보안 카메라를 설치해야 한다고 주장할게요.
여: 고마워요, 여보. 그게 좋겠네요.

07 ②

여: Fitness Zone에 오신 것을 환영합니다. 무엇을 도와드릴까요?
남: 회원권을 구매할까 해요.
여: 좋습니다. 몇 개월 동안 등록하고 싶으세요?
남: 결정하지 못했어요. 한 달에 얼마인가요?
여: 한 달은 100달러입니다.
남: 여러 달을 등록하면 할인을 받을 수 있나요?
여: 네. 3개월에서 5개월간 등록할 경우, 10퍼센트의 할인을 받습니다. 6개월 이상은, 30퍼센트 할인입니다.
남: 그러면 6개월을 등록할게요. 또한, 저에게 10 퍼센트 할인 쿠폰이 있어요.
여: 죄송합니다만, 이 쿠폰은 만료되었네요. 그러나 여전히 신규회원으로 10달러 할인을 받을 수 있습니다.
남: 좋네요. 도와주셔서 감사합니다.

문제풀이

남자는 한 달에 100달러인 회원권을 6달 동안 등록하기로 했으므로 30퍼센트 할인을 받을 수 있고, 신규회원으로 10달러를 추가 할인받을 수 있기 때문에 총 410달러(= ($100×6×0.7)-$10)를 지불할 것이다.

08 ③

남: Tina, 지역 게시판에 있는 공고문 읽었어?
여: 아니. 뭐라고 쓰여 있어?
남: 다음 주말에 벼룩시장이 있을 거래.
여: 정말 신난다! 어떤 종류의 물품을 팔 거래?
남: 많은 미술품과 공예품, 그러니까 그림, 가구, 도자기, 그리고 온갖 것들이 있을 거라고 들었어.
여: 흥미로울 것 같네. 벼룩시장을 하는 특별한 이유가 있어?
남: 우리 마을에 있는 지역 예술가들의 작품을 홍보하기로 되어 있어.
여: 정말 좋은 생각이네! 나도 가서 지역 예술가들이 만드는 것을 보고 싶다.
남: 우리 같이 가는 게 어때? City Square에서 개최될 예정이야.
여: 완벽한데. 빨리 가고 싶어.

09 ③

남: 우리의 다음 목적지는 칠레에 있는 Atacama 사막입니다. 그곳은 지구상 가장 건조한 곳 중 하나입니다. 이곳의 평균 강우량은 연간 약 15밀리미터에 불과합니다. 그곳에는 심지어 비가 전혀 내리지 않는 곳도 있습니다. 이는 놀라운데, 왜냐하면 그 사막이 태평양 근처의 칠레 해변과 바로 나란히 있기 때문입니다. 그리고 높은 고도 때문에, 밤에는 매우 추워집니다. 그러나 낮 동안에는 온도가 섭씨 30도보다 높이 올라갑니다. 그런 극단적인 환경 때문에, Atacama 사막은 화성과 비교되어 왔습니다. 그곳은 심지어 화성에 관한 영화를 위한 촬영 장소로도 사용되었습니다.

10 ②

[전화벨이 울린다.]
남: Five-Star 여행사입니다. 무엇을 도와드릴까요?
여: 저는 다음 달에 Shoreville에 가는데, 호텔 객실을 2박 동안 예약하고 싶어요.
남: 좋습니다. 마음에 두고 있는 특별한 곳이 있습니까?
여: 꼭 그렇지는 않지만, 제 예산으로는 1박에 150달러 넘게는 쓸 수 없어요.
남: 알겠습니다. 해변, 산 근처, 그리고 도시에 호텔이 있어요. 어디를 선호하세요?
여: 산 근처만 아니면 아무 곳이나 상관없습니다.
남: 알겠습니다. 아침 식사가 포함되길 원하세요, 아니면 포함되지 않길 원하세요?
여: 저는 보통 아침을 먹지 않으니까, 필요하지 않습니다.
남: 그럼 고객님의 요구에 맞는 호텔을 찾은 것 같네요.

11 ⑤

남: 실례합니다만, 여기가 런던행 기차를 타는 플랫폼이 맞습니까?
여: 네, 그런데 기차가 연착되었어요.
남: 얼마나 연착되는지 아십니까?
여: 기차는 30분 늦게 출발합니다.

문제풀이

① 기차는 연착되지 않을 것입니다.
② 당신은 잘못된 플랫폼에 있습니다.
③ 저는 너무 오래 기다렸습니다.
④ 런던에 도착하려면 두 시간이 걸립니다.

12 ④

여: 오늘 발표를 준비하면서 밤을 새웠어.
남: 그랬어? 발표는 했어?
여: 응. 수업은 방금 끝났어. 나는 정말 진이 다 빠졌어.
남: 그러면 집에 가서 잠을 자야겠네.

문제풀이

① 네가 발표를 잘하길 바랄게.
② 20분 전에 약을 먹었어.
③ 너는 언제 끝날 것 같니?
⑤ 나도 그녀가 발표하는 동안에 정말 피곤했어.

13 ⑤

여: 안녕하세요. Greenstone 국립 공원에 오신 것을 환영합니다.
남: 감사합니다. 저는 이곳에 개와 함께 산책하려고 왔습니다.
여: 아, 죄송합니다, 손님. 공원에 애완동물을 데리고 올 수 없습니다.
남: 정말이요? 왜 안 되나요?
여: 그건 공원의 규칙입니다. 손님의 애완동물이 공원에 있는 작은 동물을 다치게 하거나 죽일 수 있어요.
남: 아, 그건 생각을 못 했어요.
여: 저희는 또한 애완동물이 (공원을) 훼손할 수 있기 때문에 애완동물을 허용하지 않습니다.
남: 무슨 뜻인가요?
여: 음, 애완동물이 잔디나 꽃을 파헤칠 수 있거든요.
남: 아, 이제 이해가 되네요. 그렇다면 개를 집으로 데리고 가고 나중에 혼자서 다시 오겠습니다.

여: 불편을 끼쳐 드려 대단히 죄송합니다.
남: 천만에요. 당신은 당신의 일을 하고 있을 뿐인데요.

문제풀이

① 전 최선을 다했습니다. 화내지 마세요.
② 당신의 행동에는 변명할 여지가 없습니다.
③ 당신의 개가 괜찮길 바랄 뿐입니다.
④ 내일 다른 곳에서 만납시다.

14 ⑤

남: 엄마, 저 집에 왔어요.
여: 아, 안녕, Ted. 말하기 대회는 어땠니?
남: 그것에 대해서 말을 꺼내지 마세요, 엄마. 끔찍했어요.
여: 이런. 뭐가 잘못되었니?
남: 네. 몹시 긴장해서 내 연설을 까맣게 잊어버렸어요.
여: 그렇게 많은 사람들 앞에서 연설해 본 건 처음이었잖아. 네가 긴장한 것은 당연하지.
남: 잘 모르겠어요… 지금은 쓸모없는 일에 시간을 낭비한 것 같은 기분이 들어요.
여: 그것이 쓸모없다고 생각하니?
남: 네. 대신 곧 있을 시험 공부를 했어야 했어요.
여: 난 그렇게 생각하지 않아.
남: 왜요? 이제 저는 시험에서도 나쁜 점수를 받을지도 몰라요.
여: 이번 경험은 장차 너를 발전시키는 데 도움이 될 거야.

문제풀이

① 네가 좋은 점수를 받았다니 기쁘구나.
② 똑같은 일이 다음에도 일어날 거야.
③ 너는 선천적으로 연설을 하는 데 소질이 있어.
④ 네가 우승을 하면 대회는 절대 시간 낭비가 아니야.

15 ②

여: James는 여자 친구인 Amy와 오늘 오후에 데이트하러 가는 것을 기대하고 있다. 그들은 정말 재미있어 보이는 새로 개장한 놀이공원에 방문할 계획을 세웠다. 집을 나서기 전에, James는 배가 고파서 샌드위치를 먹는다. 그런데 집을 나서려는 바로 그 순간, 배가 아파오기 시작한다. 그는 약을 먹었으나, 상태는 점점 심해진다. 그는 정말 아파서 걱정하기 시작한다. 그는 Amy에게 나중에 다시 만나기를 원한다고 알리려고 전화를 한다. 이런 상황에서, James가 Amy에게 할 말로 가장 적절한 것은 무엇인가?
James : 미안한데, 우리 계획을 연기할 수 있을까?

문제풀이

① 내가 점심으로 샌드위치를 좀 가져갈게.
③ 너는 가능한 한 빨리 병원에 가야 해.
④ 내가 약간 늦을 것 같으니, 기다려 줄 수 있어?
⑤ 놀이공원 대신에 다른 곳으로 가자.

16 ③ 17 ④

남: 이번 여름 방학에 특별한 계획이 있습니까? 다른 사람들을 도우면서 여행을 하게 해주는 멋진 프로그램에 참여하는 게 어떻습니까? 올해 Jameson 고등학교의 자원봉사 동아리는 미얀마로 여행을 갑니다. 우리는 어려움에 처한 사람들에게 약품과 음식을 제공하면서 2주 동안 그곳에 머물 겁니다. 여러분은 또한 학교에 새로운 교실을 만드는 것을 돕고, 아이들에게 영어를 가르쳐줄 겁니다. 이 프로그램에 관심이 있는 학생은 누구나 지원할 수 있습니다. 왜 가고 싶은지와 어떤 기술을 가지고 있는지에 대한 1페이지 분량의 짧은 글을 제출해 주십시오. 지원서는 4월 30일에 마감이고, 학교 활동 사무실에 제출하면 됩니다. 질문이 있다면, 언제든지 사무실로 와서 질문하십시오. 시간을 내주셔서 감사합니다.

문제풀이

16 ① 수학여행 변경 사항을 알리기 위해
② 교내 자원봉사 행사를 검토하기 위해
③ 자원봉사 프로그램에 학생들을 모집하기 위해
④ 다른 사람들을 도와주는 것이 중요한 이유를 설명하기 위해
⑤ 방학 동안 할 수 있는 다양한 활동을 소개하기 위해

DICTATION Answers

01 guarantee your safety / was installed on / keep it private
02 What would you like / It sounds like / I'd rather spend
03 There seems to be / water came through / patch the leak
04 It's a bit small / any time of the day / one with three shelves
05 What is it called / hard to get a table / my phone battery is dead
06 something happened to my car / in the area where / I can't make it
07 How many months / sign up for several months / as a new member
08 read the notice / What kinds of items / is supposed to promote
09 one of the driest places / reach higher than / been used as
10 book a hotel room / Which do you prefer / fits your needs
11 has been delayed
12 stayed up all night
13 take a walk with / What do you mean / come back later by myself
14 Don't bring it up / It was the first time / should have been studying
15 looking forward to / Before leaving home / gets worse
16-17 take part in / for people in need / feel free to

21 영어듣기 모의고사

본문 ▲ p.146

01 ④	02 ①	03 ④	04 ⑤	05 ②	06 ②
07 ②	08 ④	09 ⑤	10 ④	11 ④	12 ①
13 ①	14 ①	15 ①	16 ①	17 ④	

01 ④

여: 우리 대학교는 수년간 국제 교환 학생을 위한 최고의 목적지가 되어 왔습니다. 오늘, 우리는 우리의 교환 학생 프로그램에 관심이 있는 학생들을 위한 중요한 발표가 있습니다. 우리의 평소 학업 프로그램의 대부분이 올해에도 제공될 것입니다. 그러나 지난해에 다섯 명 미만의 학생들이 특별 과학 교환 프로그램에 신청했습니다. 그러므로 그것은 더 이상 제공되지 않을 것입니다. 또한, 우리 프로그램의 지원 마감일은 10월 30일에서 10월 15일로 변경될 것입니다. 그러나 몇 가지 좋은 소식도 있습니다 — 프로그램 비용이 10퍼센트 감소할 것입니다. 만약 질문이 있으시면, 여러분 학교의 국제 교환 학생 고문과 상담하시기 바랍니다.

02 ①

여: 안녕, John. 너에 대한 안 좋은 소식을 들었어. 괜찮은 거야?
남: 안 좋은 소식? 무슨 말을 하는 거야?
여: 네가 수학 시험에서 낙제했다고 들었어.
남: 아. 그건 내가 아니었어, Mary.
여: 정말? 하지만 나는 그것을 보조 교사로부터 들었는데.
남: 사실, 우리 반에 'John'이라는 이름의 다른 애가 있어. 선생님이 잘못해서 우리 수학 시험 성적을 바꾸셨어!
여: 그렇게 된 거였구나. 나도 비슷한 문제가 있었던 적이 있어. 내 제일 친한 친구 이름도 'Mary'거든.
남: 그거 정말 혼동되겠다.
여: 응, 누군가 "안녕, Mary"라고 말할 때마다, 우리는 언제나 "어떤 Mary?"라고 말해야 하지.
남: 우리 같은 이름으로 생기는 문제인 거 같네.
여: 내가 좀 더 독특한 이름을 갖고 있으면 좋을 텐데!

03 ④

[전화벨이 울린다.]
남: 안녕하세요, 도와드릴까요?
여: 네, 저는 보험금을 청구하려고 해요.
남: 알겠습니다. 성함을 알려주시겠어요?
여: 네, 제 이름은 Jessica Morgan입니다.
남: 잠시 기다리세요. *[타자 치는 소리]* 됐습니다. 고객님께서는 몇 년 동안 저희 보험을 보유하고 계셨네요.
여: 맞아요.
남: 그래서 무슨 일이 있었는지 여쭤봐도 될까요?
여: 네. 지난주에 저는 차에 치여서 3일간 입원했어요.
남: 그거 안됐군요. 수술이 필요했나요?
여: 아니요, 그러지 않았어요. 하지만 그들은 제 왼쪽 다리에 깁스를 해줬어요.
남: 음, 좋은 소식이 있습니다. 고객님께서는 완전히 보장받으십니다. 저희에게 병원비 영수증을 보내 주시면 지급해 드리겠습니다.
여: 그거 좋네요! 감사합니다.

04 ⑤

여: Chen, International Day를 위한 중국 부스 설치를 끝냈니?
남: 응. 난 방금 둥근 등 두 개를 부스의 양 끝에 달았어.
여: 그거 예쁘다. 아, 가운데 있는 저건 용 등이야?
남: 응. 용은 중국에서 매우 특별해.
여: 그렇구나. 너는 많은 중국 전통 의상들도 준비했네.
남: 응. 방문객들은 옷걸이에서 아무거나 입어 볼 수 있어.
여: 재밌겠다. 둥근 탁자 위에 있는 건 중국 보드게임이야?
남: 응. 그리고 다른 탁자 위에는 중국 찻주전자와 컵이 있어.
여: 아, 뒤에는 판다 그림이 있네. 정말 귀엽다!
남: 맞아. 눈길을 끌지 않니? 중국 사람들은 판다를 좋아해.
여: 모든 것들이 좋아 보인다!

05 ②

여: Kevin, 너는 어떻게 인턴직을 찾았니?
남: 난 그저 구직 웹사이트를 보고 흥미로워 보이는 것에 지원했어.
여: 나도 해야 하는데. 그런데 너무 긴장돼.
남: 무엇이 긴장되니?
여: 난 면접을 좋아하지 않아. 난 무슨 말을 해야 할지 모르겠어.
남: 그냥 상냥하게 굴고 자신감을 가지고, 모든 질문에 솔직하게 대답해.
여: 조언 고마워. 그나저나, 인턴직에서 너의 이력서도 요구했니?
남: 응. 이력서를 잘 쓰는 것이 매우 중요해.
여: 나는 아직 이력서가 하나도 없어. 네 이력서를 한번 봐도 될까?
남: 물론이지, 오늘 밤에 네게 그것 한 부를 이메일로 보내 줄게.
여: 고마워. 바라건대, 나도 곧 인턴직을 구할 수 있으면 좋겠다.

문제풀이
① 구직 웹사이트 찾기
② 그녀에게 그의 이력서를 보여 주기
③ 그녀에게 솔직한 답 해주기
④ 면접에 관한 조언을 더 공유해주기
⑤ 인턴직 추천하기

06 ②

남: 안녕, Jenny. 네 커피숍에서 무료 커피 수업을 하고 있다고 들었어.
여: 응, 하고 있어.
남: 내가 다음 주 금요일 수업을 들을 수 있을까?
여: 유감스럽게도 다음 주 수업은 취소됐어. 월요일부터 일주일 동안 가게 문을 닫을 거야.
남: 왜? 가게 인테리어를 바꿀 거니? 아니면 어디 여행이라도 가니?
여: 아니. 실은, 내 딸이 다음 주 월요일에 수술을 받을 거야.
남: 아, 이런! 심각한 거니?
여: 그렇지는 않아. 간단한 수술이지만, 그 애가 회복하는 동안 내가 함께 있어 줘야 해.

남: 음, 그 애가 빠르게 회복되길 바랄게.
여: 고마워, Frank. 곧 다시 가게 문을 열 거야.

07 ②

여: 안녕하세요, 고객님. 도움이 필요하세요?
남: 네. 전 이 USB 플래시 드라이브에 있는 사진 몇 장을 인화해야 해요.
여: 문제없습니다. 어떤 크기의 사진을 원하시나요? 고객님께서는 기본 사이즈와 큰 사이즈 중에 선택할 수 있습니다.
남: 가격이 어떻게 다른가요?
여: 기본 사이즈 사진은 한 장당 1달러이고, 큰 사이즈 사진은 한 장당 3달러입니다.
남: 그러면 15장은 기본 사이즈로 하고 5장은 큰 사이즈로 할게요.
여: 알겠습니다. 그런데, 고객님께서 Springfield 대학교 학생이라면, 전체 금액에서 20퍼센트 할인을 받을 수 있습니다.
남: 그런가요? 저는 Springfield 대학에 다녀요.
여: 저에게 고객님의 학생증을 보여주시겠어요?
남: 그럼요. 여기 있습니다.
여: 감사합니다. 고객님의 사진은 15분 후에 준비될 것입니다.

문제풀이
남자는 1달러인 기본 사이즈 15장, 3달러인 큰 사이즈 5장을 인화하기로 했으므로 총 30달러를 지불해야 하지만, 20퍼센트 할인을 받게 되어 총 24달러(= ($\$1\times15+\$3\times5)\times0.8$)를 지불할 것이다.

08 ④

남: 그게 뭐야, 미리야? 그것은 작은 기타처럼 보여.
여: 이건 우쿨렐레야.
남: 아! 그건 하와이 악기야, 그렇지 않아?
여: 응, 그런데 사실 포르투갈 이민자들이 19세기에 그것을 하와이로 가지고 왔어.
남: 그렇구나. 난 전에 파인애플처럼 생긴 것을 본 적이 있어.
여: 맞아, 다양한 모양이 있어. 어떤 것들은 기타처럼 생겼는데, 다른 것들은 타원형이거나 정사각형 모양이야.
남: 흥미롭네. 그것들은 네 것처럼 모두 4개의 현이 있니?
여: 대부분 그래, 하지만 6현이나 8현도 있어.
남: 그렇구나. 난 그것을 연주하는 법을 배우고 싶어. 그것들은 가격이 어느 정도 돼?
여: 20달러로 저렴한 것도 있지만, 4천 달러에 팔리고 있던 것도 본 적이 있어.
남: 와, 가격대가 다양하구나!

09 ⑤

남: 전 특별한 개봉 행사를 발표하게 되어 기쁩니다. 12월 10일 Circle 극장에서 액션 영화인 「Disaster Train」의 첫 상영이 있겠습니다. 영화 대부분이 바로 우리 마을에서 촬영되었기 때문에, 감독은 이곳에서 그 행사를 개최하기로 했습니다. 이 영화에 출연한 많은 남자 배우와 여자 배우가 참석할 예정입니다. 영화를 관람한 후, 감독과 스타들과 함께하는 사인회가 열릴 것입니다. 여러분이 일생에 한 번 있을 이 행사에 참석하고자 한다면, 12월 1일까지 마을 회관에 들러 신청하세요. 저희는 추첨을 하여 무료 참석 티켓을 받을 50명을 무작위로 선발하겠습니다. 이 기회를 놓치지 마세요.

10 ④

남: Sunny 여행사에 오신 것을 환영합니다. 도와드릴까요?
여: 네. 다음 주말에 Yellow Lake 근처 리조트의 방을 예약하고 싶어요.
남: 알겠습니다. 그 지역에는 몇 개의 멋진 리조트가 있습니다. 고객님의 예산을 여쭤봐도 될까요?
여: 전 하룻밤에 150달러 넘게 내고 싶진 않아요.
남: 손님이 원하시는 가격대의 리조트가 몇 군데 있어요. 하지만 가장 저렴한 방은 수영장이 없어요.
여: 안돼요, 그건 좋지 않네요. 저는 반드시 수영장이 있는 장소가 필요해요.
남: 알겠습니다. 음, 주방은 어떤가요? 꼭 필요한가요?
여: 네. 저는 직접 요리를 할 거라서, 아침 식사 서비스도 필요하지 않아요.
남: 그러면 이곳이 고객님의 모든 요구에 딱 들어맞을 것 같네요.

11 ④

남: 벌써 방과 후 동아리에 가입했니?
여: 아직 안 했어. 난 어떤 것에 가입해야 할지 모르겠어.
남: 난 테니스 동아리에 가입할 거야. 너도 가입할 수 있어!
여: 괜찮아. 사실 난 운동하는 걸 좋아하지 않아.

문제풀이
① 잘됐다. 나도 정말 기뻐!
② 미안해. 오늘 오후에는 시간이 없어.
③ 그거 좋다. 나는 과학을 배우는 것을 좋아해.
⑤ 그런데 축구 동아리는 이미 다 찼다고 하던데.

12 ①

여: 내 친구들이 다음 주에 캠핑을 간다는데, 나는 안 가려고.
남: 왜? 캠핑 가는 거 안 좋아하니?
여: 솔직히 말해서, 전에 가 본 적이 없어. 캠핑에 대해서 전혀 몰라.
남: 내 생각엔 네가 시도해봐야 할 것 같아.

문제풀이
② 내게 사실을 말해줘서 고마워.
③ 그게 나도 그것을 좋아하는 이유야.
④ 그들은 너를 캠핑에 초대했어야 했어.
⑤ 아마도 너를 위해서 우리가 일정을 바꿀 수 있을 거야.

13 ①

여: 안녕, Dan. 피곤해 보이네.
남: 응. 난 요즘 처리해야 할 일이 많아.
여: 응, 네 동료 두 명이 일을 그만두었다고 들었어.
남: 맞아. Helen과 Laura가 학교에 복학하기 위해서 회사를 그만두었어.
여: 그렇구나. 적어도 그들에겐 잘된 일이네.
남: 나도 그렇게 생각하지만, 나는 이전보다 일을 더 많이 해야 해. 솔직히 말하면, 난 약간 스트레스를 받고 있어.

여: 너무 기분 나빠하지 마. 네게 좋은 소식이 있어.
남: 그게 뭔데?
여: 회사가 너희 팀에 새 직원을 몇 명 채용할 계획이라고 들었어.
남: 아, 정말? 그게 바로 내가 듣기를 기다려 온 거야.
여: 응. 새 직원들은 다음 달 초에 일을 시작할 거야.
남: 그게 압박감을 좀 덜어 주면 좋겠다.

문제풀이

② 그들이 다시 돌아온다는 소식을 들으니 기뻐.
③ 너는 왜 그 일자리에 지원하고 싶어?
④ 네가 맞아. 나는 곧 다른 도시로 이사 가.
⑤ 나 좀 도와줘. 혼자서 이 일을 처리하지 못하겠어.

14 ①

남: 이봐, Abby, 너 여름 방학 계획이 있니?
여: 응. 나는 브라질로 여행을 갈 계획이야.
남: 아, 친구들과 함께 가니?
여: 아니, 혼자서 여행할 거야. 나는 자유롭게 나만의 일정을 짜고 싶어.
남: 좋은 생각이야. 그럼, 네가 어떤 곳이 마음에 들면, 네가 원하는 만큼 오래 그곳에 머물 수 있어.
여: 맞아. 또한, 혼자서 여행을 할 때 새로운 사람을 만나고 친구를 사귈 수 있어.
남: 그건 사실이야. 그런 것들은 네가 단체로 여행할 때는 하기 힘들어.
여: 맞아. 그밖에도, 내가 좋아하는 음식은 무엇이든지 먹을 수 있어. 나는 현지 음식을 먹어보는 걸 정말 좋아해.
남: 그거 좋다. 다만 혼자 있을 때 위험한 장소는 반드시 피하도록 해.
여: 알았어, 그걸 명심할게.

문제풀이

② 거기에 혼자 있는 것은 무서웠어.
③ 내 여행은 7월 중순으로 예정되어 있어.
④ 나는 현지 음식을 좀 먹어 보고 싶어.
⑤ 나는 친구들과 브라질에 가고 싶어.

15 ①

여: Greg은 종종 그의 누나인 Jenny와 함께 있을 때 짜증이 난다. 왜냐하면 그녀는 늘 그에게 무엇을 해야 하는지를 말하기 때문이다. 어느 날 그들은 점심을 같이 먹지만, Greg은 식사 후에도 여전히 배가 고프다. 그래서 그는 치즈버거를 하나 더 주문하고 싶어 한다. 그러나 그의 누나는 그에게 살을 빼야 한다고 말하고, 대신에 그가 샐러드를 주문하게 한다. 이제 그들은 옷을 사고 있다. Greg은 멋진 청바지 한 벌을 발견하지만, 그녀의 누나가 그 바지가 유행이 아니라서, 그것을 사지 말아야 한다고 말한다. 그는 매우 화가 난다. 그는 누나가 그에게 무엇을 해야 하는지 말하는 것을 좋아하지 않는다. 이런 상황에서, Greg이 Jenny에게 할 말로 가장 적절한 것은 무엇인가?
Greg : 누나는 내가 스스로 결정을 내리도록 해야 해.

문제풀이

② 내 친구가 내게 이 청바지가 유행이라고 했어.
③ 나는 과체중이 아니고, 내가 원하는 것은 무엇이든지 먹을 거야.
④ 건강에 좋지 않은 음식을 먹지 말아야 하는 건 바로 누나야.
⑤ 누나의 판단을 믿기 때문에, 난 그것을 사지 않을 것 같아.

16 ① 17 ④

남: 우리의 도시는 매일 점점 더 국제화되어 가고 있습니다. 더 많은 사람이 세계 각지에서 이곳으로 오면서, 다른 문화가 함께 섞이고 있습니다. 우리 중 많은 사람들은 이것에 익숙하지 않을 수도 있습니다. 그래서, 주민들이 우리의 새로운 다문화 사회에 대해 더 배우도록 돕기 위해, 우리는 이번 달에 우리의 연례 '세계 화합의 날'을 개최할 것입니다. 해마다, 500명 넘는 사람들이 다른 문화에 대해 배우기 위해 Riverview Park에 모입니다. 20개가 넘는 다른 나라에서 온 무료 음악과 음식이 있을 것이며, 불꽃놀이와 다른 재미있는 행사도 함께 할 겁니다. 티켓 한 장당 5달러밖에 안 하는데, 이것은 최고로 할인된 가격 중 하나입니다. 이 행사는 올해 7월 27일 일요일에 개최되며, 정오에 시작하여 밤까지 계속될 것입니다. 질문이 있으면, 시청에 518-9211로 전화하시면 됩니다. 여러분을 곧 만나기를 기대합니다!

문제풀이

16 ① 다문화 행사를 홍보하려고
② 학교 기념행사를 알리려고
③ 전 세계의 축제를 설명하려고
④ 다문화주의의 개념을 소개하려고
⑤ 다른 문화가 섞이는 이유를 설명하려고

DICTATION Answers

01 a top destination / signed up for / There is some good news
02 failed the math exam / switched our grades / must be confusing
03 make a claim / had a policy with / was in the hospital
04 finish setting up / try on anything / on the other table
05 applied for / Thanks for the advice / take a look at yours
06 attend a class / have an operation / makes a quick recovery
07 Which size prints / show me your student ID / be ready in 15 minutes
08 brought it to / have four strings / how to play it
09 The first showing / be in attendance / be given free tickets
10 book a room / within your price range / fits all of your needs
11 join the tennis club
12 To be honest
13 work to deal with / more than ever before / hire some new employees
14 set my own schedule / when traveling by myself / On top of that
15 tells him what to do / needs to lose weight / getting very upset
16-17 be accustomed to this / learn about other cultures / one of the best bargains

22 영어듣기 모의고사

본문 ☁ p.153

01 ⑤	02 ②	03 ②	04 ⑤	05 ③	06 ⑤
07 ②	08 ④	09 ⑤	10 ②	11 ⑤	12 ⑤
13 ⑤	14 ④	15 ④	16 ④	17 ③	

01 ⑤

여: 제 이름은 Tanya Parker입니다. 저는 수년 동안 귀 항공사로 여행했고, 귀사의 서비스에 늘 만족했습니다. 그러나 최근에 저는 불쾌한 경험을 했습니다. 7월 19일 시카고에서 발리로 가는 제가 탈 항공편이 악천후로 인해 지연되었습니다. 저는 그 상황을 충분히 이해했습니다만, 냉방도 안 되는 비행기 안에서 몇 시간을 기다려야만 했습니다. 그뿐만 아니라, 승무원은 승객들에게 주의를 많이 기울이지 않았습니다. 제가 물을 요청했을 때, 승무원은 기다리라고 말하고 아무것도 하지 않았습니다. 전반적으로 서비스가 매우 실망스러웠습니다. 앞으로는 귀사의 서비스가 개선되기를 바랍니다.

02 ②

여: 나는 겨울이 싫어. 야외에서 무언가를 할 수 있으면 좋겠어.
남: 나랑 캠핑 가는 게 어때?
여: 요즘은 너무 추워서 캠핑을 갈 수가 없어.
남: 음, 여름이 캠핑하기에 가장 좋은 계절이지. 하지만 네가 알맞은 물품을 가져가면, 겨울에 캠핑하는 것도 즐거울 수 있어.
여: 그래? 음… 우리는 무엇이 필요할까?
남: 따뜻하면서 방수가 되는 옷을 입어야 해. 그리고 잠을 잘 텐트도 필요해.
여: 침낭도 필요할 것 같네.
남: 맞아.
여: 또 다른 건 없어?
남: 우리는 폭우나 폭설에 대비해서 일기 예보를 확인해야 해. 이번 주말에 가는 게 어때?
여: 좋아! 그렇게 하자.

03 ②

남: 저기요, 지금 바쁘세요?
여: 네, 그래요. 무엇이 필요하세요?
남: 3번 테이블의 주문은 끝내셨나요?
여: 네, 여기 있습니다. 여자분이 약간 덜 익힌 스테이크를 원했어요, 그렇죠?
남: 아니요. 그분은 완전히 익혀 달라고 요청했어요.
여: 아, 미안해요. 제가 혼동했나 봐요.
남: 괜찮습니다, 하지만 서둘러 주세요. 그 여자분이 이미 너무 오랫동안 기다렸어요.
여: 당장 그것을 그릴 위에 다시 올릴게요. 2분 후에 끝날 거예요.
남: 좋아요. 같이 나오는 프렌치프라이는 어떤가요?
여: 그건 준비가 되었어요. 그 여자분에게 지금 가져갈 수 있어요.
남: 알겠습니다. 스테이크를 가지러 곧 다시 올게요!
여: 당신이 돌아올 때는 준비가 되어 있을 거예요.

04 ⑤

남: 소풍 가기에 완벽한 날이에요. 우리 어디 앉을까요?
여: 아마 연못 근처에서 앉을 장소를 찾을 수 있을 거예요.
남: 연못 옆에 나무 한 그루가 있는데, 난 거기 앉고 싶지 않아요. 거기엔 많은 벌레가 있을 거예요.
여: 아, 좋은 지적이에요. 그러면 길의 오른쪽에 있는 용 조각상 옆에 앉는 게 어때요?
남: 음, 거기에는 나무가 한 그루도 없어요. 우리는 햇빛을 가려 줄 그늘이 필요해요.
여: 조각상 옆에 파라솔이 있는 소풍용 테이블은 어때요? 우리가 파라솔을 펴면, 충분한 그늘이 생길 거예요.
남: 자전거 도로 옆에 있는 걸 말하는 거예요?
여: 그건 자전거 도로가 아니에요. 저기 '자전거 금지' 표시가 안 보여요? 그건 산책로예요.
남: 이제 보이네요. 어쨌든, 거기에 앉도록 하죠.

05 ③

여: 나는 회사에 운전해서 가려고 차를 살까 생각 중이야.
남: 아, 정말? 버스 타는 데 질린 거야?
여: 응. 너무 붐비고 자주 오지도 않아.
남: 음, 만약 차를 살 계획이면, 우선 가게를 둘러보도록 해.
여: 난 중고차를 살까 생각 중이어서 네 조언이 필요해. 너는 중고차를 샀잖아, 그렇지?
남: 응. 그 차의 사고와 유지 관리 기록을 꼭 확인해야 해.
여: 알았어. 그게 다야?
남: 아니. 다른 것들도 많아. 중고차 구매에 관한 온라인 지침서를 보여줄게.
여: 고맙지만, 나는 혼자 차를 고를 수 있을지 잘 모르겠어. 나랑 같이 가줄래?
남: 물론이지. 너를 도와줄 수 있어서 기뻐.

06 ⑤

여: 자, Marvin. 이 쿠키와 함께 우유 한 잔을 마시는 게 어떠니?
남: 괜찮아, Bonnie. 나는 우유를 마시지 않아.
여: 정말? 너 어떤 특별한 종류의 다이어트를 하고 있니?
남: 아니, 그런데 최근에 우유를 마시고 난 후에 몸이 안 좋아.
여: 그거 이상하다. 아마 네가 유제품에 알레르기가 있나 봐.
남: 그런 것 같지 않아. 나는 여전히 요구르트나 치즈는 아무 문제 없이 먹을 수 있어. 우유를 먹을 때만 배가 아파.
여: 알겠어. 음, 안됐다. 이 쿠키는 우유랑 함께 먹으면 훨씬 더 맛이 좋은데!
남: 정말 그럴 거 같아! 그런데 나 아주 목이 말라. 다른 마실 건 없니?
여: 오렌지 주스는 어때?
남: 그거 좋겠다.

07 ②

[전화벨이 울린다.]

여: Continental 호텔입니다. 무엇을 도와드릴까요?

남: 여보세요. 다음 주에 쓸 방을 예약하려고 전화했어요.

여: 알겠습니다. 몇 가지 이용 가능한 옵션이 있습니다.

남: 그것들은 얼마인가요?

여: 보통 스위트룸은 1박에 100달러이고, 고급 스위트룸은 150달러입니다. 그리고 15달러만 추가하시면, 아침 식사를 하실 수 있습니다.

남: 음, 저는 그냥 가장 저렴한 방을 원하고, 아침 식사는 필요하지 않아요.

여: 알겠습니다. 보통 객실은 80달러예요.

남: 저는 월요일부터 금요일까지 그 방을 쓸게요.

여: 아, 만약에 고객님께서 3일 넘게 머무르시면, 보통 스위트룸을 25퍼센트 할인받으실 수 있어요.

남: 그거 좋네요! 대신 보통 스위트룸으로 하겠습니다.

여: 그럼 아침 식사 없이 보통 스위트룸 4박이신 거죠?

남: 맞아요.

문제풀이

남자는 1박에 100달러인 스위트룸에서 4박을 하기로 했으므로 400달러를 지불해야 하나, 3박 이상을 머물러서 25퍼센트 할인을 받을 수 있으므로 총 300달러(= $400×0.75)를 지불할 것이다.

08 ④

여: 와, 이 피자 정말 맛있다! 훌륭한 선택이었어.

남: 나도 동의해. 이거 이름이 뭐야?

여: 이건 Margherita 피자야. 토마토, 바질, 모차렐라 치즈가 위에 얹어져 있어.

남: 음… 난 전에 그것에 대해 들어 본 적이 없어.

여: 그것은 1889년에 만들어졌고 Margherita 여왕의 이름을 따서 지어졌어.

남: 정말? 왜 그랬던 거야?

여: 옛이야기에 따르면, Margherita 여왕이 피자를 정말 좋아했대.

남: 그렇구나.

여: 여왕이 나폴리를 방문했을 때, Raffaele Esposito라는 이름의 피자 만드는 사람이 그녀에게 경의를 표하여 특별한 피자를 만들었어.

남: 와! 그건 그녀만을 위해 만들어진 거야?

여: 응! Esposito는 이탈리아 국기의 색인 초록색, 흰색, 빨간색을 상징하는 재료를 선택했어.

남: 정말 흥미로운 이야기네!

09 ⑤

남: 안녕하세요, 여러분. 아마 여러분은 모두 해파리가 무엇인지 알고 있을 겁니다. 그것은 투명한 몸체를 가진 바다 동물입니다. 오늘 저는 해파리 호수에 대해서 이야기하려고 합니다. Palau라는 나라의 작은 섬에 위치해 있는 이곳은 한때 바다와 연결되어 있던 해수 호수입니다. 그러나 약 12,000년 전에, 이곳은 바다와 단절되었습니다. 그 결과 많은 해파리가 그 호수에 갇히게 되었습니다. 그것들을 먹을 천적이 없어서, 그들의 개체 수는 급격히 증가했습니다. 그들은 태양 빛을 따라서 호수 주위를 헤엄치며 낮 시간을 보냅니다. 사람들은 호수에서 수영할 수 있는데, 해파리의 침이 어떠한 통증도 일으키지 않기 때문입니다.

10 ②

여: 이 음악 수업 패키지는 좋아 보인다. 너는 하나 수강할 거야?

남: 난 이미 하나 등록했어. 수업은 수요일이야.

여: 아, 너랑 함께하면 좋을 텐데, 나는 수요일과 금요일 오후에 일을 해야 해.

남: 그렇구나. 그래도 여전히 선택할 수 있는 다른 네 개의 패키지가 있어. 넌 노래하는 거 좋아해?

여: 아니. 나는 그냥 악기를 연주하는 법을 배우고 싶어.

남: 드럼은 어때?

여: 그것도 좋을 거 같은데, 난 한 달에 100달러 미만의 수업 패키지만 들을 형편이 돼.

남: 아, 이건 정말 저렴하다. 그리고 무료로 연습실을 사용할 수 있어.

여: 그렇지만 나는 차라리 다른 것을 선택할래. 난 두 개의 악기를 연주하는 법을 배울 수 있어.

남: 그것도 좋은 선택인 것 같다.

11 ⑤

여: Joe, 이탈리아로 떠날 준비 됐니?

남: 응. 모든 짐을 다 쌌고, 여권도 가지고 있어.

여: 비행기는 언제 출발하니?

남: <u>세 시간 후에 이륙할 거니까, 지금 가야 해.</u>

문제풀이

① 난 비행기에서 읽을거리가 많아.
② 공항은 바로 30분 거리에 있어.
③ 그의 비행기가 오늘 오전 7시에 떠났어.
④ 이탈리아에 도착하는 데 약 10시간이 걸려.

12 ⑤

남: 안녕하세요, 주문하시겠어요?

여: 네, 스테이크 하나와 적포도주 한 잔을 주문할게요.

남: 죄송합니다만, 스테이크가 다 떨어졌습니다. 다른 것을 드려도 될까요?

여: <u>네, 하지만 먼저 메뉴판을 볼게요.</u>

문제풀이

① 아뇨, 괜찮습니다. 저는 고기를 먹지 않아요.
② 그러면 그냥 스테이크 2개를 주문할게요.
③ 제 친구 중 한 명이 그 와인을 추천했어요.
④ 이 와인이 스테이크와 잘 어울릴까요?

13 ⑤

남: 엄마, 저 지금 학교에 가요.

여: 아침은 안 먹을 거니?

남: 네. 안 먹으려고요. 식욕이 별로 없어요.

여: 하지만 아침은 중요한 식사야. 아침을 먹는 것은 네가 학교에서 공부

를 잘하게 도와줄 거야.
남: 그것이 제가 수업에 집중하도록 도와준다는 거예요?
여: 맞아. 너는 배고픔에 주의가 산만해지지 않아서 아마 더 많이 배우게 될 거야.
남: 아, 그건 생각하지 못했어요.
여: 게다가, 건강한 아침 식사를 하는 것은 네가 점심에 과식하지 않도록 해준단다.
남: 말이 되네요. 아침을 거르면, 점심을 많이 먹어요. 그러면 기분이 안 좋아져요.
여: 정시에 맞춰서 식사하면, 한 끼에 너무 많이 먹을 가능성이 적어져.
남: 엄마 말씀이 맞아요. 출발하기 전에 아침 식사를 할게요.

문제풀이

① 거한 점심은 항상 저를 졸리게 해요.
② 전 점심으로 참치 샌드위치를 먹고 싶어요.
③ 전 아침으로 보통 우유와 시리얼을 먹어요.
④ 전 식욕을 돋우는 방법을 찾아야겠어요.

14 ④

[휴대전화벨이 울린다.]
남: 안녕하세요. Rosenberg 경찰관입니다.
여: 안녕하세요, Rosenberg 씨. 저는 Liam의 교사인 Susan Edison입니다.
남: 아, 그렇군요. 별 문제 없나요, Edison 선생님?
여: 네, 아버님. Liam은 수업 시간에 아주 잘하고 있어요. 사실, 부탁드릴 것이 있어서 전화 드렸습니다.
남: 알겠습니다. 무엇인가요?
여: 음, 아드님이 오늘 수업 시간에 아버님에 관해서 이야기했어요. 그는 아버님이 경찰관이라고 말했습니다.
남: 네, 맞습니다.
여: 아시다시피, 학생들이 이번 달에 직업에 대해서 배우는 중입니다.
남: 네, Liam이 제게 숙제를 보여줬어요.
여: 그래서 전 아버님께서 언젠가 제복을 입고 방문하셔서 학생들에게 아버님의 직업에 대해 이야기해주실 수 있는지 궁금합니다.
남: 물론이죠. 제가 스케줄을 확인하고 다시 전화드려도 될까요?
여: 그럼요. 언제 시간이 되시는지 알려 주세요.

문제풀이

① Liam이 숙제를 끝낼 수 있도록 도와주세요.
② 수업 시간에 오실 필요가 없을 것 같아요.
③ 네, 다음 달에 약간 한가한 시간이 있을 거예요.
⑤ 세탁소에서 당신의 제복을 가지고 올게요.

15 ④

여: Ethan이 학교 구내식당에서 점심을 먹고 있을 때 그의 친구인 Julie가 그에게 10달러를 빌려 달라고 부탁한다. 그래서 그는 지갑을 꺼내 Julie에게 10달러를 준다. 그때 수업 종이 울리고, 그들은 급히 수업에 간다. 수업이 끝난 후, Ethan은 그의 지갑이 없어진 것을 발견한다! 그는 그날 어딜 갔었는지 계속 생각한다. 마침내 그는 구내 식당에서 지갑을 꺼냈던 것을 기억한다. 그는 구내 식당으로 뛰어 돌아가서 그가 앉아 있었던 테이블을 확인한다. 몇몇 다른 학생들이 그곳에 앉아 있다. 그는 그들이 그의 지갑을 틀림없이 보았을 것이라고 생각한다. 이런 상황에서, Ethan이 학생들에게 할 말로 가장 적절한 것은 무엇인가?
Ethan : 미안한데, 여기서 갈색 지갑을 본 사람 있어?

문제풀이

① 테이블에서 주스 좀 마시자.
② 나에게 돈을 좀 빌려줄 수 있어?
③ 미안한데, 지금은 돈이 없어.
⑤ 내가 운동장에서 네 지갑을 찾는 것을 도와줄게.

16 ④ 17 ③

남: 여러분의 애완견은 아마도 밥상에 두 발을 들고 있을 것입니다. 여러분은 안전하게 그 개에게 계란, 과일이나 채소와 같은 특정한 음식을 줄 수 있습니다. 이런 것들은 개에게 해롭지 않습니다. 하지만 초콜릿에 관한 경우는 다릅니다. 만약에 개가 초콜릿을 먹으면, 그들은 병이 들고 심지어 죽을 수도 있습니다. 이는 초콜릿이 개에게 독이 되는 물질을 함유하고 있기 때문입니다. 만약에 여러분의 개가 잘못하여 초콜릿을 먹었다면, 그 개는 불안하게 방 주위를 걷는 것과 같은 특이한 행동을 보일 것입니다. 그다음에, 아마 그 개는 토하고 불규칙한 심장박동을 보일 겁니다. 최악의 경우에는, 여러분의 개는 혼수상태로 빠져들 수 있습니다. 만약 여러분이 이런 징후를 목격하면, 당장 애완동물을 동물 병원으로 데려가십시오. 수의사가 도움을 줄 수 있지만, 여러분의 개를 보호하는 최선의 방법은 항상 개와 초콜릿을 멀리 떨어뜨려 놓는 것입니다.

문제풀이

16 ① 개에게 먹이를 주는 방법을 설명하려고
② 새로운 개 초콜릿을 광고하려고
③ 개를 기르는 것의 단점을 보여주려고
④ 개에게 초콜릿을 먹이지 않도록 경고하려고
⑤ 왜 과일이 개의 건강에 좋은지 보여주려고

DICTATION Answers

01 been satisfied with / pay much attention to / improve your service
02 do something outside / the best season for camping / a tent to sleep in
03 Have you finished / I got confused / be done in two minutes
04 find a place to sit / next to the statue / only for walking
05 Are you tired of taking / be sure to shop around / choose one on my own
06 on some kind of special diet / without any problem / taste much better
07 a few options available / you can have breakfast / more than three days
08 an excellent choice / was named for / in honor of her
09 Located on a small island / As a result / spend their days swimming
10 I wish I could join you / how to play an instrument / I'd rather choose
11 ready to leave
12 run out of steak
13 have much of an appetite / keep you from overeating / eat on schedule
14 ask you a favor / learning about careers / call you back
15 takes out his wallet / thinks over and over / must have seen
16-17 when it comes to / display unusual behavior / go into a coma

23 영어듣기 모의고사

본문 ▲ p.160

01 ③ 02 ④ 03 ③ 04 ⑤ 05 ③ 06 ④
07 ④ 08 ③ 09 ③ 10 ② 11 ⑤ 12 ②
13 ③ 14 ⑤ 15 ② 16 ③ 17 ④

01 ③

여: 이번 여름이 유난히 더워서, 여러분은 아마 에어컨을 세게 틀고 있을지도 모릅니다. 이는 쾌적할 것 같지만, 많은 건강 문제를 일으킬 수 있습니다. 사람들은 보통 창문을 닫은 채로 에어컨을 사용합니다. 그리고 좋지 못한 공기 순환이 사람들의 눈을 건조하고 피로하게 만듭니다. 이것이 많은 사람들이 여름철 동안 건조한 눈으로 고생하는 이유입니다. 하지만 이 문제를 해결할 수 있는 방법이 있습니다. TearX는 여러분의 눈을 여름 내내 건강하게 지켜줄 수 있는 새로운 제품입니다. 그저 3시간마다 양쪽 눈에 한 방울씩 넣어주세요. 이 제품은 대부분의 약국에서 구입하실 수 있으니, 오늘 나가서 좀 구입하세요.

02 ④

여: 왜 아직도 안 자고 있니, Mike? 거의 자정이야.
남: 알아요, 엄마, 하지만 내일 오후에 중요한 과학 시험이 있어요.
여: 그게 바로 네가 곧 잠자리에 들어야 하는 이유야.
남: 무슨 말씀이세요? 저는 안 자고 몇 시간 더 공부할 계획이에요.
여: 그건 좋은 생각이 아니야. 이미 모든 자료는 다 보았니?
남: 네, 하지만 한 번 더 복습하고 싶어요.
여: 그건 네게 득보다는 해가 될 수 있어. 네 기억력이 잘 작동하기 위해서는 잠이 필요해.
남: 그래요? 그건 몰랐어요.
여: 사실이란다. 네가 잠을 잘 잔다면, 공부한 모든 것을 더 잘 기억할 수 있을 거야.
남: 알았어요. 이 부분만 끝내고 나서 자러 갈게요.

03 ③

여: 실례합니다. 도움이 좀 필요해요.
남: 그럼요. 방에 문제가 있는 건 아니죠, 그렇죠?
여: 아니요, 방은 괜찮아요. 매우 크고 경치도 좋아요.
남: 그 말을 들으니 기쁘네요. 그럼 무엇을 도와드릴까요?
여: 음, 제 방의 카드 키를 분실한 것 같아요.
남: 유감이네요. 잠시만 기다려 주시면 다른 것을 가져다 드리겠습니다. 방 호수가 어떻게 되시죠?
여: 저는 201호에 머물고 있어요.
남: 유감스럽게도 교체를 하려면 10달러를 지불하셔야 합니다. 그게 저희 규정입니다.
여: 이해합니다.
남: 제가 다른 카드 키를 가져다 드릴 동안 잠시 기다려 주세요.
여: 물론입니다. 다시 한번 감사합니다.

04 ⑤

[휴대전화벨이 울린다.]

남: 여보세요?

여: 안녕, Jason. 나 지갑을 집에 두고 온 것 같아. 그곳에 있는지 확인해 줄래?

남: 물론이야. *[잠시 후]* 음, 네 책상 위에는 없어. 거기에는 책 두 권이랑 자만 있네.

여: 내 화장대 위를 확인해 줄래?

남: 거기에는 화장품밖에 없는 것 같아.

여: 침대 위 베개 옆은?

남: 곰 인형 하나만 있어.

여: 침대 옆의 바닥도 확인했어?

남: 응, 슬리퍼 한 켤레밖에 없네. 아, 잠깐! 찾았다.

여: 정말? 정말 다행이야! 어디에 있었어?

남: 네 테이블 위 전등 옆에 있었어.

여: 아, 이제 기억난다. 고마워.

05 ③

남: Amy, 우리가 지금까지 포스터를 몇 개나 만들었니?

여: 우리는 벌써 20개나 만들었어.

남: 이제 그것들을 학교 전체에 게시해야 해.

여: 맞아. 그나저나 광고용 전단을 복사했니?

남: 응, 200부 복사했어.

여: 잘했어. 그럼 내가 전단을 배포할게.

남: 그걸 혼자 할 수 있겠어? 아니면 내가 널 도와줄까?

여: 걱정하지 마. 다른 클럽 회원들이 날 도와줄 거야. 대신에 내가 이 포스터를 게시하는 걸 도와줄래?

남: 그래. 내가 도서관에 하나 게시할까?

여: 아니, 내가 할게. 어쨌든 난 책을 몇 권 반납해야 하거든. 너는 학생회관 건물에 몇 장 게시해 줘.

남: 알았어.

문제풀이

① 그녀가 학생들에게 전단 배포하는 것을 돕기
② 그녀의 책을 학교 도서관에 반납하기
③ 그들의 클럽을 위해 손으로 쓴 포스터 몇 장 게시하기
④ 그들의 클럽을 홍보하기 위해 북클럽 포스터 만들기
⑤ 20분 내에 전단을 200부 복사하기

06 ④

여: 이번 주 토요일에 계획 있니, James?

남: 응, 그날 City Marathon에 참가해야 해.

여: 아. 네가 마라톤에서 뛰는 것을 몰랐어.

남: 내가 뛰는 건 아니지만, 나는 완주한 주자들에게 무료 티셔츠를 나눠주는 일에 자원했어.

여: 재미있겠네. 네 자원봉사 요건의 일부인 거야?

남: 아니야, 난 이미 그걸 몇 달 전에 끝냈어.

여: 그랬어? 그럼 왜 이걸 하는 거야?

남: 나는 그것이 많은 다양한 사람들을 만날 좋은 기회라고 생각해.

여: 그래, 아마 그럴 거야. 전국에서 온 사람들이 참여할 테니까.

남: 맞아. 너도 올래?

여: 아냐, 괜찮아. 나는 그날 쇼핑몰에서 시간을 보낼 계획이야.

07 ④

남: 안녕하세요! 세계 최고의 놀이공원인 Adventure Land에 오신 걸 환영합니다!

여: 감사합니다. 입장권은 얼마인가요?

남: 음, 성인 표는 한 장당 7달러입니다.

여: 어린이 할인이 있나요?

남: 네. 13세 미만 어린이 표는 2달러 더 저렴합니다.

여: 알겠습니다. 그럼 성인 표 2장과 어린이 표 1장을 사겠습니다.

남: 미니 기차표도 구매하시겠어요? 공원 전체에 기차가 정차합니다. 오늘 같이 더운 날에 좋을 거예요.

여: 그 표는 얼마에요?

남: 어린이와 성인 모두 기차표는 각각 1달러입니다.

여: 그럼 기차표도 3장 살게요.

남: 여기 있습니다. Adventure Land에서 좋은 하루 보내세요!

문제풀이

여자는 장당 7달러인 성인 입장권 2장과 성인 입장권보다 2달러 저렴한 어린이 입장권 1장, 그리고 장당 1달러인 기차표 3장을 구입했으므로, 총 22달러(= ($7×2)+$5+($1×3))를 지불할 것이다.

08 ③

여: 자, 저희 수석 주방장 자리에 관심이 있으시다고요?

남: 네, 그렇습니다.

여: 음, 저희는 적어도 10년간 수석 주방장으로 근무했던 사람이 필요합니다.

남: 저는 15년의 경력이 있습니다. 그리고 전국 요리 대회에서 1등 상을 탔어요.

여: 잘됐네요. 저희 수석 주방장은 요리 대회 우승자이어야 합니다.

남: 아주 좋습니다. 그밖에 또 필요한 것이 있습니까?

여: 네, 당신은 팀의 일원으로 일할 수 있는 능력을 입증했어야 합니다.

남: 그렇게 했습니다. 저는 더 젊었을 때 20명의 다른 주방장과 프랑스 식당에서 일했습니다.

여: 그러면 당신은 프랑스어를 유창하게 할 수 있나요?

남: 유감스럽게도 그렇지 않아요. 그게 중요합니까?

여: 네, 실은 필수입니다. 저희 주방 직원 대부분이 프랑스어만 하거든요.

남: 유감이네요. 저는 프랑스어를 전혀 할 줄 모릅니다.

09 ③

남: 여러분 모두가 많은 종류의 과일에 친숙할 거라고 확신하지만, 칼라만시에 대해 들어보셨습니까? 필리핀 라임이라고도 알려진 이것은 포도알 크기 정도 되는 작은 초록색 과일입니다. 그것은 필리핀 요리에 가장 흔히 사용되지만, 플로리다를 포함해서 많은 지역에서 재배됩니다. 그 작은 나무는 기르기 쉽고 실내 또는 야외에서 기를 수 있습니다. 칼라만시의 작은 꽃들은 훌륭한 향기를 갖고 있습니다. 과일 자체는 껍질을 벗기기 쉽고 매우 신 맛을 냅니다. 가장 좋은 것은, 칼라만시는 많은 비타민 C를 함유하고 있어서 여러분에게도 좋다는 겁니다.

10 ②

남: 안녕하세요. 무엇을 찾고 계세요?
여: 제 딸을 위해서 새 화장대를 사고 싶어요.
남: 몇 가지 가능한 선택 사항이 있습니다. 서랍이 몇 개 필요한가요?
여: 적어도 세 개요. 딸이 옷을 많이 가지고 있거든요.
남: 알겠습니다. 이 금속 화장대는 어떠세요?
여: 딸의 나무 침대 틀과 어울리려면 나무 화장대가 더 좋겠어요.
남: 알겠습니다. 음, 많은 여자아이들이 분홍색을 좋아하니 이 분홍색 화장대는 어떠세요?
여: 음… 제 딸은 그 색을 좋아할 것 같지 않네요.
남: 알겠습니다. 그러면 두 가지 선택 사항이 남았네요. 어떤 것이 맘에 드세요?
여: 물론 가격이 더 저렴한 거죠. 신용카드로 지불해도 되나요?
남: 물론입니다.

11 ⑤

남: 실례합니다. 이 셔츠 큰 사이즈로 있나요?
여: 중간 사이즈가 손님께 맞을 것 같습니다. 이 셔츠는 다소 큽니다.
남: 알겠습니다. 하지만 먼저 입어 보고 싶어요.
여: 물론이죠. 탈의실은 바로 저기에 있습니다.

문제풀이

① 다른 색으로 가져다 드리겠습니다.
② 잘 맞습니다만, 색이 마음에 들지 않아요.
③ 고객님을 위해 더 큰 사이즈를 찾을 수 있는지 알아보겠습니다.
④ 하지만 영수증이 없으면 환불해 드릴 수 없습니다.

12 ②

여: 나 오늘 두통이 심해.
남: 그거 안됐다. 내가 너를 위해 해줄 수 있는 게 있니?
여: 음, 나 아스피린 좀 사야 하는데 지금은 시간이 없어.
남: 내가 널 위해 약국에 갔다 올 수 있어.

문제풀이

① 네가 뛰면, 늦지 않을 거야.
③ 이전보다 훨씬 나아졌어.
④ 오늘 아침에 벌써 알약 두 개를 먹었어.
⑤ 그럼 진료를 받는 게 어때?

13 ③

남: Ellen! 너 연설 강의를 수강한다고 들었어. 어때?
여: 응. 2주밖에 안 됐지만, 난 그것을 좋아하지 않아.
남: 정말? 무슨 일 있었어?
여: 사실 잘못된 건 없어. 내가 연설을 끝낼 때마다 그냥 기분이 우울해져.
남: 믿을 수가 없네. 너는 매우 외향적이어서 잘하고 있을 거라 생각했는데.
여: 음, 난 사람들 앞에 서 있을 때 매우 긴장이 돼. 때때로 내가 말하려고 했던 모든 것을 다 잊어버려.
남: 그건 아마도 네가 경험이 별로 없어서 그럴 거야.
여: 잘 모르겠어. 어쨌든, 나는 더는 수업에 들어가고 싶지 않아.
남: 네 기분 이해해. 그런데 그거 알아? 연습이 완벽을 만든대.
여: 그게 무슨 뜻이야?
남: 네가 계속 연습을 하면, 너의 기술이 향상될 거야.

문제풀이

① 내가 너라면 그 수업을 그만둘 거야.
② 그는 그날 우리에게 완벽한 연설을 해주었어.
④ 너의 연설을 잊어버리지 않게 필기를 해.
⑤ 그런 거 같아. 하지만 너는 정말 그 수업을 수강하기를 원했잖아.

14 ⑤

여: 시력이 점점 나빠지시는군요, Petrelli 씨.
남: 그건 노화의 자연스러운 부분일 뿐이잖아요, 그렇지 않나요?
여: 반드시 그런 건 아닙니다. 어떤 나쁜 습관이 시력에 손상을 주고 있는 것 같습니다.
남: 정말요? 어떤 종류의 습관에 대해서 말씀하시는 건가요?
여: 어두운 방에서 독서하는 것이 하나의 예죠.
남: 음, 저는 그렇게 하지 않아요. 독서할 때 항상 탁상용 스탠드를 사용해요.
여: 좋네요. 또 다른 흔한 나쁜 습관은 컴퓨터 화면을 보며 너무 많은 시간을 보내는 것입니다.
남: 아. 저는 웹디자이너라 컴퓨터 앞에서 제 대부분의 시간을 보내지 않을 수 없어요.
여: 그러면 때때로 눈에 휴식을 줄 필요가 있어요.
남: 그럼 제가 무엇을 해야 좋을까요?
여: 때때로 꼭 화면에서 눈길을 돌리도록 하세요.

문제풀이

① 당신은 더 밝은 작업 공간을 찾아야 합니다.
② 당신의 상사에게 문제를 말하는 것이 현명할 것입니다.
③ 당신은 그저 휴식을 취하고 그것에 대해서 그만 걱정해야 합니다.
④ 의사와의 예약을 변경하는 것이 낫겠습니다.

15 ②

여: Brian은 저녁으로 피자를 주문하기로 했다. 평소 주문하는 피자 가게에 전화를 걸기 전에, Brian은 다른 식당의 광고 전단을 발견했다. 그 전단에는 인터넷으로 피자를 주문하면 더 큰 크기로 무료 업그레이드를 받을 수 있다고 적혀 있었다. 그래서 그는 그 식당의 웹사이트에서 중간 크기의 치즈 피자를 주문했다. 그는 같은 가격으로 큰 크기의 피자를 받을 것이라고 기대했다. 그러나 배달원이 왔을 때, 그는 그 배달원이 중간 크기의 치즈 피자를 가지고 온 것을 알게 되었다. 지금 그는 배달원에게 상황을 설명해야 한다. 이런 상황에서, Brian이 배달원에게 할 말로 가장 적절한 것은 무엇인가?
Brian: 제가 큰 크기의 피자를 받았어야 하는 것 같은데요.

문제풀이

① 제가 당신에게 말했듯이, 피자는 아직 도착하지 않았어요.
③ 괜찮으시다면, 내일 돈을 내도 될까요?
④ 죄송하지만, 저희는 치즈 피자를 주문하지 않았어요.
⑤ 유감스럽게도, 저는 그게 얼마인지 몰라요.

16 ③ 17 ④

남: 많은 사람들이 나쁜 자세로 인해 생기는 문제로 고통받습니다. 가장 흔한 종류의 나쁜 자세 중 하나는 거북목 증후군 또는 FHP라고 불립니다. 이는 사람이 자신의 머리를 어깨 위로 곧게 두기보다는 앞으로 기울어진 위치에 둘 때 발생합니다. 컴퓨터로 일하거나 운전을 하는 동안 어깨와 머리를 구부리고 앉는 것이 FHP를 일으킬 수 있습니다. 어색한 자세로 잠을 자는 것도 마찬가지입니다. FHP가 있는 사람들의 가장 흔한 증상들은 두통, 뻐근한 목, 그리고 조이는 듯한 어깨 근육입니다. 장기간 지속되는 FHP는 목에 디스크를 일으킬 수도 있습니다. 이 질환을 피하는 가장 쉬운 방법은 여러분의 자세를 인지하는 것입니다. 여러분이 어떤 나쁜 습관을 갖고 있다면, 그것을 교정하도록 노력하세요. 목 근육 운동은 여러분의 자세를 개선시키거나 FHP에 걸릴 확률을 감소시키는 또 다른 방법입니다.

문제풀이

16 ① 만성 두통 치료법을 제시하려고
② 목의 역할과 중요성을 강조하려고
③ FHP의 원인과 예방법을 설명하려고
④ 사람들이 피해야 할 어떤 자세들을 이야기하려고
⑤ FHP와 면역 체계 간의 연관성을 언급하려고

DICTATION Answers

01 with their windows closed / suffer from dry eyes / keep your eyes healthy
02 plan on staying up / more harm than good / just finish this section
03 I need some help / lost the key card to / for the replacement
04 check if it is there / beside the pillow / What a relief
05 all around the school / do it alone / help me put up
06 have to attend / volunteered to hand out / all over the country
07 Is there a discount / It makes stops / take three train tickets
08 won first prize / as part of a team / can't speak French at all
09 about the size of / have a wonderful smell / Best of all
10 a few options available / prefer a wooden one / pay by credit card
11 try it on
12 anything I can do
13 It's only been two weeks / stand in front of people / Practice makes perfect
14 Not necessarily / Reading in dark rooms / can't help spending
15 decided to order / expected to receive / needs to explain
16-17 straight above the shoulders / The easiest way / improve your posture

24 영어듣기 모의고사

본문 ▶ p.167

01 ⑤	02 ⑤	03 ④	04 ④	05 ⑤	06 ①
07 ④	08 ②	09 ③	10 ④	11 ①	12 ④
13 ⑤	14 ⑤	15 ④	16 ⑤	17 ④	

01 ⑤

여: 봄이 다시 왔는데요, 그것은 어디에나 아름다운 꽃이 있다는 것을 의미합니다. 하지만 봄은 또한 알레르기 철이기 때문에 어떤 사람들은 봄을 좋아하지 않습니다. 만약 여러분에게 봄철 알레르기가 있다면, 잘 들으세요! 여기 여러분이 증상을 통제하도록 정말로 도움을 줄 수 있는 몇 가지 조언이 있습니다. 대부분의 알레르기는 공기 중에 있는 꽃가루에서 온다는 것을 기억하세요. 여러분은 밖에 있을 때, 꽃가루를 들이마시지 않도록 하기 위해 항상 마스크를 써야 합니다. 여러분은 또한 꽃가루를 눈에 비비지 않도록 하기 위해 손을 자주 씻어야 합니다. 이러한 간단한 조언들이 여러분을 계절성 알레르기로부터 보호할 수 있습니다. 만약 여러분이 그것들을 따를 것을 기억한다면, 봄을 즐길 수 있습니다.

02 ⑤

여: 네 새 아파트는 어때, Harry?
남: 나쁘지 않아. 하지만 어제 벽에서 곰팡이가 자라고 있는 것을 발견했어.
여: 아, 유감이야.
남: 나는 집을 매우 청결하게 유지해 왔기 때문에 정말 놀랐어.
여: 그건 불결함으로 생기는 게 아니야. 그건 모두 습도에 관한 문제야, 특히 여름철에.
남: 습도? 공기 중에 있는 물의 양을 말하는 거니?
여: 응. 실내 공기는 주의 깊게 관리되어야 해. 너무 축축해도 안 되고 너무 건조해도 안 돼.
남: 아, 그것에 대해서는 생각 못 했어.
여: 습도는 네 건강에도 영향을 미칠 수 있어. 예를 들어서, 공기가 너무 건조하면 숨을 쉬는 데 곤란을 겪을 수도 있어.
남: 알았어. 그렇다면 나는 제습기를 사야 할 거 같아.
여: 그거 좋은 생각이야.

03 ④

[전화벨이 울린다.]
남: 여보세요?
여: 안녕하세요. 제 이름은 Jodie Bryant입니다. 저는 B동에 살아요.
남: 안녕하세요, Bryant 씨. 무엇을 도와드릴까요?
여: 음, 저는 어제 지하 주차장에 주차를 했는데요.
남: 그러시군요. 차량에 무슨 문제가 발생했나요?
여: 네. 오늘 아침에 문에 크게 움푹 들어간 자국을 발견했어요. 누군가가 어젯밤에 차를 박은 게 틀림없어요.
남: 유감이에요. 제가 어젯밤 CCTV 영상을 확인해 보기를 바라세요?

여: 네, 그렇게 해 주세요. 누가 제 차에 손상을 입혔는지 알고 싶어요.
남: 알겠습니다. 아파트 호수와 주차 자리를 알아야 합니다.
여: 제 아파트는 B201호이고, 주차 자리는 39C입니다.
남: 알겠습니다. 영상을 확인하고 오늘 오후에 연락 드리겠습니다.

04 ④

여: 필리핀 가족 여행은 어땠어, 지훈아?
남: 정말 좋았어! 우리는 스쿠버 다이빙을 하러 가서 사진을 좀 찍었어. 이것 봐!
여: 와! 왼편에 손을 잡고 있는 두 분이 네 부모님이시니?
남: 응. 그리고 그들 옆에 주먹을 쥐고 있는 사람이 내 여동생이야.
여: 그 애 위에서 헤엄치고 있는 물고기를 봐!
남: 그것들은 멋졌어. 어떤 사람이 나인지 맞출 수 있겠어?
여: 여동생 옆에서 팔로 하트 모양을 하고 있는 소년이 너니?
남: 아니. 그건 내 형이야.
여: 그러면 너는 거북이 등껍질 위에 손을 올리고 있는 사람임에 틀림없어.
남: 맞아! 거북이랑 놀면서 정말 즐거운 시간을 보냈어.

05 ⑤

[휴대전화벨이 울린다.]
여: 여보세요?
남: 안녕, 여보. 나 방금 집에 왔어요. 몇 시에 집에 올 것 같아요?
여: 아, 미안해요, 여보. 큰 프로젝트를 끝내야 해서 오늘 밤늦게까지 사무실에 있어야 해요.
남: 정말요? 이해해요. 그럼 오늘 저녁에 혼자 저녁 식사를 요리하고 집을 청소할게요.
여: 고마워요. 그러면 큰 도움이 될 거예요.
남: 내가 어린이집에서 Jeffrey를 데려와야 하나요?
여: 그럴 필요 없어요. 내가 이미 어머니한테 그 애를 데려와 달라고 부탁했어요.
남: 잘했어요. 그밖에 해야 할 다른 일이 있나요?
여: 실은, 한 가지가 있어요. 내가 며칠 전에 옷 몇 벌을 드라이클리닝점에 맡겼어요. 가서 가져올 수 있어요?
남: 물론, 그렇게 할 수 있죠.
여: 좋아요.

문제풀이
① 그날 저녁에 집 청소하기
② 여자가 밤늦게 프로젝트 끝내는 걸 도와주기
③ 여자가 집에 도착하기 전에 그녀를 위해 저녁 식사 요리하기
④ 어린이집에서 아들 데려오기
⑤ 세탁소에서 세탁물 찾아오기

06 ①

남: Green 교수님, 이야기 좀 할 수 있을까요?
여: 물론이지, Peter. 무슨 일이니?
남: 제가 과제를 하루 늦게 제출해도 괜찮을까요?
여: 이유가 뭐니?
남: 엄마가 독감에 걸리셔서 제가 엄마를 간호해야 해요.
여: 유감이구나. 그런데 어머니를 간호해 줄 다른 사람이 없니?
남: 없어요, 저 혼자에요. 그래서 시간 맞춰 보고서를 끝내지 못할 것 같아서 걱정이 되네요.
여: 미안하지만, 너에게 시간을 더 줄 수 없어. 다른 학생들에게 공평하지 않아.
남: 이해합니다. 그러면 그것을 끝내도록 노력할게요. 어쨌든 감사합니다.
여: 어머니께서 빨리 나아지시기를 바란다.

07 ④

[전화벨이 울린다.]
여: Pizza Express에 전화 주셔서 감사합니다. 무엇을 도와드릴까요?
남: 포테이토 피자 두 판을 주문하고 싶은데요.
여: 네. 보통 크기의 피자를 원하세요, 아니면 큰 크기의 피자를 원하세요?
남: 그 두 개의 가격 차이가 어떻게 되나요?
여: 큰 크기의 피자는 한 판에 15달러이고, 보통 크기의 피자는 한 판에 10달러예요.
남: 네, 그러면 큰 크기의 피자 두 판으로 할게요. 그리고 중간 크기 콜라 5개도 필요해요.
여: 알겠습니다, 콜라는 개당 2달러예요.
남: 좋습니다. 그리고 저한테 10퍼센트 할인 쿠폰이 있어요.
여: 그렇군요. 하지만 그 쿠폰은 피자에만 해당돼요. 콜라는 여전히 정가예요.
남: 괜찮아요. 그리고 스프링필드의 Evergreen Terrace 123번지로 배달해 주시겠어요?
여: 물론이죠. 주문하신 음식은 약 30분 후에 도착할 거예요.
남: 좋네요. 정말 감사합니다.

문제풀이
남자는 한 판에 15달러인 큰 크기의 피자 두 판과 2달러짜리 콜라 5개를 주문했는데 피자에만 적용되는 10퍼센트 할인 쿠폰을 갖고 있으므로, 총 37달러(= ($15×2×0.9)+($2×5))를 지불할 것이다.

08 ②

여: 너 Harrisville 영화제가 10월 1일에 시작하는 거 아니?
남: 아니. 얼마 동안 열리는데?
여: 일주일 동안. 나랑 가서 개막작을 보는 게 어때?
남: 미안해. 난 그날 시험이 있어.
여: 알았어. 10월 4일에 상영하는 좋은 영화가 있어.
남: 잘됐다. 제목이 뭐야?
여: 「Wonder World」야. 여행자 무리에 관한 코미디야.
남: 좋아. 티켓은 얼마야?
여: 우리는 1일 티켓을 한 장당 15달러에 구매할 수 있어. 그런데 그것을 매표소에서 사야 해.
남: 올해에도 또 City 극장에서 영화가 상영되니?
여: 응. 지난해와 같은 장소야.
남: 아, 그러면 우리는 지하철만 타면 되겠네.

09 ③

남: 최근에 Anuta 섬이 많은 텔레비전 다큐멘터리들에 나오고 있습니다. 그 결과, 점점 더 많은 사람들이 태평양의 솔로몬 제도에 위치한 이 작은 섬에 관심을 가지게 되었습니다. 이 섬은 화산에 의해서 형성되었으며, 면적이 0.37제곱킬로미터에 불과합니다. 작은 크기에도 불구하고, 약 300명의 사람들이 그곳에 삽니다. 그러므로 이 섬은 세계에서 가장 높은 인구 밀도를 지닌 곳 중 하나입니다. 이 섬에 사는 사람들은 Anuta라는 그들만의 언어를 사용합니다. 그들의 문화는 aropa라고 불리는 가치에 기초를 두고 있습니다. 기본적으로 이는 그들이 협동과 연민을 믿는다는 것을 의미합니다.

10 ④

남: 안녕하세요. 무엇을 도와드릴까요?
여: 마실 것을 주문하고 싶어요. 무엇을 추천해 주시겠어요?
남: 저희에게는 선택할 수 있는 음료가 많습니다. 카페인이 있는 것을 원하세요?
여: 아니요. 저는 카페인을 줄여야 해요.
남: 알겠습니다. 뜨거운 것이 좋으세요 아니면 차가운 것이 좋으세요?
여: 뜨거운 걸 마시고 싶어요.
남: 음, 뜨거운 걸로 선택하실 수 있는 게 세 가지 있어요.
여: 실은 제가 지금 당장은 3달러밖에 없는데요. 그래서 제 선택이 제한적이에요.
남: 저희는 또한 모든 음료를 특가로 제공합니다. 어떤 것들은 '1+1'이고 다른 것들은 20퍼센트 할인을 해 드립니다.
여: 저는 20퍼센트 할인되는 것을 선택할게요.
남: 좋습니다. 딱 1분 후에 음료를 준비해 드리겠습니다.

11 ①

남: Linda, 이번 토요일에 무슨 계획이 있니?
여: 아니, 별거 없어. 무슨 일 있어?
남: 내가 집들이 파티를 할 건데, 네가 와줬으면 좋겠어.
여: 물론이야. 몇 시에 거기로 가면 되니?

문제풀이

② 좋은 생각이야. 우리 집에서 만나자.
③ 내가 이제까지 가 봤던 파티 중 최고의 파티였어.
④ 내 집들이를 취소해야 할 것 같아.
⑤ 그러고 싶은데, 난 초대장을 받지 못했어.

12 ④

여: Brian, 애완동물 키우는 거 생각해 본 적 있어?
남: 응. 지금은 없지만, 난 늘 원했어.
여: 잘됐다! 내 고양이가 지난주에 새끼 고양이 4마리를 낳았어. 한 마리 데려가도 돼.
남: 나도 그러고 싶지만, 우리 엄마가 애완동물을 허락하지 않으셔.

문제풀이

① 미안하지만, 나는 강아지를 좋아하지 않아.
② 안됐다. 나는 고양이에게 한 번 물렸어.
③ 아니, 괜찮아. 나는 이미 애완동물이 너무 많이 있어.
⑤ 고양이는 한 번에 4마리에서 6마리의 새끼를 낳아.

13 ⑤

남: 다음 주 우리의 휴가로 부산에 정말 가고 싶어.
여: 음, 나도 그래. 하지만 연중 이맘때에는 해변에는 사람이 너무 많아.
남: 네 말이 맞는 것 같아. 그럼 우리 다른 곳을 고르자.
여: 우리는 남해안으로 갈 수 있어. 여름에 그곳은 날씨가 좋아.
남: 그래, 그렇지만 거긴 작년 여름에 갔잖아. 난 같은 곳에 가고 싶지 않아.
여: 그러면 평창에 가는 건 어떨까?
남: 좋은 생각인 거 같은데, 거기에는 겨울에 가는 것이 더 나아.
여: 맞아. 하지만 더운 날에 시원한 계곡이 얼마나 좋을지 생각해봐.
남: 나를 수긍하게 했어. 거기로 가자!
여: 좋아. 우리는 언젠가 다시 해변에 갈 수 있어.

문제풀이

① 그렇다면, 이번 겨울에 거기에 가야겠다.
② 미안하지만, 나는 부산보다 남해안이 더 좋아.
③ 아니. 나는 정말로 다시는 부산에 가고 싶지 않아.
④ 모르겠어. 붐비는 해안은 별로 즐겁지 않아.

14 ⑤

여: 내 결혼식이 한 달밖에 안 남았는데, 아직 드레스를 결정하지 않았어.
남: 음, 넌 다양한 드레스를 입어 보고 네게 맞는 것을 찾아야 해.
여: 좋은 생각이지만, 가격이 내 예산 안이어야 해.
남: 돈을 얼마나 쓸 수 있니?
여: 나는 1,000달러까지만 쓸 수 있어. 그래서 내 가격 범위 안에 있는 드레스가 있는 매장을 찾아야 해.
남: 걱정하지 마. 내가 도와줄 수 있어.
여: 어떻게?
남: 내 친구 중 한 명이 최근에 결혼했어. 그녀가 할인 가격으로 드레스를 구했다고 했어.
여: 와, 그녀가 어디서 드레스를 샀는지 알고 싶어.
남: 내가 그녀한테 매장에 대한 정보를 물어볼게.

문제풀이

① 그 드레스는 너에게 너무 비싸.
② 그 매장은 아름다운 드레스가 있는 것 같지 않아.
③ 나는 네가 결혼을 미뤄야 할 것 같아.
④ 솔직히 말하면, 선택된 이것들 중 어떤 것도 마음에 들지 않아.

15 ④

여: Kevin은 고등학교 2학년 학생이다. 그는 학교 회장 선거에 출마하기로 결심했다. 그는 많은 남학생들과 친하다. 그는 남학생들이 자신에게 투표할 것이라는 확신이 있는 반면에, 여학생들에 대해서는 그다지 확신이 없다. 여학생들 대부분은 그를 잘 알지 못해서 다른 사람에게 투표하기로 결정할지도 모른다. 하지만 그의 여동생 Lisa 역시 그의 학교에 다니고 있고, 그녀는 많은 여자 친구들이 있다. Kevin은 그녀의 도움을 받으면 선거에서 이길 가능성이 높아질 것이라고 생각한다. 그래서 그는 그녀에게 도와달라고 부탁하고 싶다. 이런 상황에서, Kevin이 Lisa에게 할 말로 가장 적절한 것은 무엇인가?
Kevin: 선거 운동을 할 동안 나를 도와줄래?

문제풀이

① 네 친구에게 투표를 하지 않아서 미안해.
② 왜 너도 회장 선거에 출마하려고 하니?
③ 너는 학교에서 더 많은 친구를 사귈 필요가 있어.
⑤ 이번 선거에서 누구에게 투표를 할 거니?

16 ⑤ 17 ④

남: 낚시는 재미있고 느긋한 취미입니다. 그리고 배 위에서 하는 낚시는 훨씬 더 즐거울 수 있습니다. 그러나 낚시 여행을 가기 전에, 여러분은 배가 제대로 된 안전 장비를 갖추고 있는지를 확인해야 합니다. 우선, 모든 배는 조명을 갖추고 있어야 합니다. 낮에 낚시를 하더라도, 조명은 비가 오거나 안개가 낀다면 충돌을 막도록 도와줍니다. 또한 여러분은 소화기가 있는지 확인해야 합니다. 화재가 날 경우, 배를 버리는 것보다 불을 끄는 것이 더 낫습니다. 또한 선상에 호루라기가 있어야 합니다. 여러분은 비상사태가 발생할 경우에 구조자를 이끄는 데 호루라기를 사용할 수 있습니다. 그리고 마지막으로, 항상 구급상자를 가지고 다니십시오. 만약 누군가 다치게 되면, 의사에게 가기까지 시간이 오래 걸릴 수 있습니다. 그래서 상처를 치료할 수 있는 것이 중요합니다.

문제풀이

16 ① 선상 화재의 주요 원인
② 응급 처치의 중요성
③ 배낚시의 다양한 방법들
④ 바다의 예측할 수 없는 날씨
⑤ 선상에서 필요한 안전 장비

DICTATION Answers

01 Here are some tips / avoid breathing in / remember to follow
02 growing on the walls / all about humidity / could have trouble breathing
03 parked my car / want to know who damaged / check the video
04 took some pictures / Can you guess / had a lot of fun
05 need to stay late / You don't have to / dropped off some clothes
06 hand in my paper / It's not fair / gets well soon
07 between the two / have a discount coupon / in about 30 minutes
08 How long does it last / a group of travelers / the same place as
09 becoming interested in / Despite its small size / is based on a value
10 cut down on / have special offers / have your drink ready
11 Is something going on
12 I've always wanted one
13 this time of year / go to the same place / think about how nice
14 haven't decided on / in my price range / recently got married
15 run for school president / isn't sure about / have a better chance of
16-17 go on a fishing trip / put it out / take a long time

25 영어듣기 모의고사

본문 ▲ p.174

01 ④	02 ⑤	03 ⑤	04 ④	05 ⑤	06 ⑤
07 ②	08 ⑤	09 ⑤	10 ④	11 ②	12 ②
13 ④	14 ③	15 ②	16 ⑤	17 ⑤	

01 ④

여: 안녕하세요, 주민 여러분. 건물 관리자로서, 저는 몇 가지 중요한 정보를 공유하려고 합니다. 휴가철이 다가오면서, 많은 사람이 아파트를 떠나 있게 될 것입니다. 그러나 우리 인근에서 도난 사건 수가 증가하고 있습니다. 그러므로 우리는 주의해야 합니다. 만약 여러분이 오랫동안 나가 있게 된다면, 신문과 우유 같은 모든 정기적인 배달을 중단하십시오. 문밖의 배달된 상품이 여러분의 집을 절도의 대상으로 만들 수 있습니다. 특히 아래층에 살고 있다면, 누군가가 아파트에 침입하는 것을 막기 위해서 창문을 잠그십시오. 이 조언들을 항상 염두에 두십시오. 감사합니다.

02 ⑤

남: 엄마, 이게 뭐예요? 통밀빵이에요? 제가 흰 빵을 더 좋아하는 것을 아시잖아요.
여: 알지만, 통밀빵이 너에게 더 좋단다.
남: 그건 흰 빵하고 똑같은 거예요. 그것들은 모두 밀로 만들어지지만, 흰 빵이 훨씬 더 부드러워요.
여: 흰 빵은 통밀빵보다 더 많이 가공돼. 그래서 흰 빵이 더 부드러울진 몰라도, 건강에 더 좋지는 않아.
남: 그게 무슨 말씀이세요?
여: 비타민과 무기질 같은 많은 중요한 영양소들이 제거된다는 말이야.
남: 정말요? 통밀빵은 어떤데요?
여: 그건 통밀로 만들어지기 때문에, 많은 영양소를 함유해.
남: 그런 줄 몰랐어요. 저는 통밀빵을 먹는 것에 익숙해질 수 있을 것 같아요.
여: 그 말을 들으니 기쁘구나.

03 ⑤

여: 뭘 좀 도와드릴까요?
남: 네, 부탁합니다. 저는 다른 나라에서 왔고, 방금 이 엽서들을 샀어요.
여: 알겠습니다. 엽서를 보내고 싶으세요?
남: 음, 먼저 엽서를 써야 해요. 하지만 캐나다에 엽서를 보내는 데 비용이 얼마나 드는지 궁금했어요.
여: 음, 보통 엽서 우표는 3달러입니다.
남: 제가 엽서를 그렇게 보내면, 시간이 얼마나 걸릴까요?
여: 대략 일주일이요. 하지만 속달 우편으로 보내면, 이틀이 걸릴 거예요.
남: 그게 더 낫네요. 그건 비용이 얼마나 드나요?
여: 엽서당 5달러밖에 안 해요.
남: 아주 좋네요. 그러면 엽서들을 보내러 오늘 오후에 다시 올게요. 도와주셔서 감사합니다.
여: 천만에요.

04 ④

남: 새 어린이 도서관 어때, Mary?
여: 와! 멋져 보여! 그런데 왜 정사각형 테이블 대신 둥근 테이블을 골랐니?
남: 음, 정사각형 테이블의 모서리는 아이들에게 위험할 수 있어.
여: 그럴 수도 있겠다. 아, 방 뒤쪽에 책꽂이를 놓았구나.
남: 응. 그리고 난 그것들 왼쪽에 곰 인형을 놓았어.
여: 정말 귀엽다! 그런데 테이블 위에 저 꽃병은 왜 놓았니? 그건 책을 읽는 아이들에게 위험할 수 있어.
남: 그건 생각 못 했어. 그걸 어딘가 다른 곳에 둬야겠다.
여: 그리고 시계 옆에 있는 게시판에는 무엇을 붙일 거니?
남: 음, 거기에는 읽어야 할 도서의 목록을 붙일 거야.
여: 좋은 생각이야!

05 ⑤

남: 난 오늘 밤 저녁 식사로 뭔가 요리를 할 거야.
여: 그런데 냉장고에 음식이 많이 있지 않은 것 같아.
남: 아, 그럼 대신 저녁을 먹으러 나가는 게 어때?
여: 미안하지만, 너무 피곤해서 외출할 수가 없어. 그냥 뭘 좀 배달시키면 어떨까?
남: 그것도 좋겠다. 특별히 원하는 것이 있니?
여: 새 중국 음식점인 Dragon Palace에서 시켜보는 게 어떨까?
남: 좋은 생각이야! 그곳의 참깨 닭 요리가 맛있다고 들었어.
여: 그 식당의 전화번호가 뭔지 아니?
남: 잘 모르겠어. 어떻게 찾지?
여: 아마 그곳의 웹사이트에 있을 거야. 네가 찾아보는 게 어때? 그러면 내가 전화해서 주문할게.
남: 좋아, 지금 바로 할게.

06 ⑤

남: 이번 주말에 고등학교 동창회에 갈 거니, Melissa?
여: 아마도. 매우 즐거울 것 같아. 너는 어때?
남: 나도 갈 거야. 그날 테니스 강습이 있는데, 난 그것을 일요일로 바꿨어.
여: 잠깐만. 동창회는 일요일이라고 생각했는데.
남: 아니야, 토요일이야.
여: 그렇다면 나는 갈 수 없어. 난 토요일에 계획이 있어.
남: 정말? 그걸 취소할 수 없니?
여: 안 돼. 우리 가족은 어머니 생신 파티를 거하게 할 거야.
남: 너는 나에게 어머니 생신이 다음 주 주말이라고 말했잖아.
여: 맞아, 하지만 어머니가 다음 주말에 출장 중이실 거거든.
남: 알았어. 음, 네가 못 온다니 실망이야.

07 ②

남: 안녕하세요. 저는 스키를 좀 대여하고 싶습니다.
여: 몇 쌍이 필요하세요?

남: 전 성인용 스키 두 쌍과 아동용 한 쌍이 필요해요.
여: 성인용 스키는 시간당 10달러이고, 아동용은 보통 5달러입니다. 그런데, 지금 아동용 스키는 특별 할인 중이에요.
남: 그런가요? 그것은 얼마인가요?
여: 오늘 어린이용 스키는 한 시간에 3달러입니다. 스키장에 얼마나 계실 건가요?
남: 여기에 적어도 두 시간은 있을 거예요.
여: 그러면 두 시간 비용을 지불하시겠어요?
남: 아니요, 더 오래 있고 싶을 경우를 대비해서 세 시간 비용을 지불할게요.
여: 그렇게 하세요, 손님. 회원 카드를 갖고 계십니까?
남: 아, 네. 전 이걸로 10달러를 할인받을 수 있죠, 맞지요?
여: 맞습니다.

문제풀이

남자는 대여료가 시간당 10달러인 성인용 스키 두 쌍과 대여료가 시간당 3달러인 아동용 스키를 한 쌍 대여하기로 했고, 세 시간 동안 대여하겠다고 했으므로 69달러(= ($10×2+$3)×3)를 지불해야 하나, 10달러 할인을 받아 총 59달러를 지불할 것이다.

08 ⑤

남: 안녕, Tammy. 난 너를 최근에 보지 못했었네.
여: 난 새 뮤지컬에서 작은 배역을 맡아서 바빴어!
남: 뮤지컬? 잘됐다. 곧 공연하니?
여: 응. 다음 주 화요일부터 시작해.
남: 얼마 안 남았네. 어디서 공연하니?
여: 우리는 Wren 극장에서 공연할 거야.
남: 나도 보고 싶다. 공연 제목이 뭐니?
여: 「The Wonderful West」라고 해. 목장에서 살려고 도시를 떠나는 여자에 관한 이야기야.
남: 흥미롭네. 그래서 네가 그 공연의 주인공이니?
여: 그러고 싶지, 하지만 감독인 Vicky Green이 다른 사람을 선택했어.
남: 안됐다. 하지만 나는 네가 네 배역을 잘할 거라 확신해.

09 ⑤

남: 커피 사업을 시작하는 데 관심이 있으십니까? 저희의 8일간의 바리스타 연수회는 여러분에게 커피를 기본으로 하는 음료를 만드는 방법을 가르쳐드릴 것입니다. 또한, 여러분은 커피숍을 개업하고 운영하는 방법에 관한 정보도 얻게 될 것입니다. 이 연수는 9월에 4주간 토요일과 일요일에 개최될 예정입니다. 각 수업은 두 시간 동안 진행됩니다. 주제에는 최고의 커피를 선택하는 것, 이상적인 위치를 선택하는 것과 커피 만드는 장비를 작동하는 것이 포함될 것입니다. 이 연수는 지역 문화 회관에서 열릴 것이며, 참가자 수는 25명으로 제한될 것입니다. 만약 관심이 있으시면, 신청하시고 150달러의 연수 비용을 지참하세요.

10 ④

여: 무엇을 찾는 걸 도와드릴까요, 손님?
남: 음, 저는 헤드폰이나 이어폰이 필요해요.
여: 알겠습니다. 마이크가 내장된 것이 필요하신가요?
남: 네, 그래요. 저는 스마트폰과 함께 그것을 사용하고 싶어요.
여: 알겠습니다. 전선 길이는 어떠세요?
남: 잘 모르겠어요. 보통 길이가 어떻게 되나요?
여: 대부분 길이가 1.25미터입니다. 하지만 어떤 것들은 2미터죠. 보통은, 1.25미터가 일상적으로 사용하기에 충분합니다.
남: 보통 길이를 살게요.
여: 알겠습니다. 그렇다면 손님이 선택하실 수 있는 두 가지 다른 종류가 있어요.
남: 상관없어요. 그냥 더 저렴한 것으로 할게요.
여: 알겠습니다. 저 앞쪽 계산대에서 그것 값을 지불하시면 됩니다.

11 ②

남: Julie와 나는 영화를 보러 갈 거야. 너도 올래?
여: 난 영화를 좋아하지만, 영화에 따라 달라. 무엇을 볼 거야?
남: Julie와 나는 둘 다 「Space Explorers」를 보고 싶어.
여: 미안하지만, 나는 이미 그 영화를 봤어.

문제풀이

① 물론이야, 그들이 훌륭한 배우라고 들었어.
③ 그래, 그들은 둘 다 영화 보는 것을 좋아해.
④ 나는 언젠가 공상 과학 영화를 만들고 싶어.
⑤ 우리는 Julie에게 무슨 영화를 보고 싶은지 물어봐야 해.

12 ②

여: 이봐, Dave. 내일 쇼핑하러 같이 가고 싶니?
남: 물론이지. 나는 새 옷과 신발 한 켤레를 사야 해.
여: 잘됐다. 우리 언제 만날까?
남: 음, 수업 끝나고 바로 어때?

문제풀이

① 나도 새 가방을 사야 해.
③ 미안하지만, 나는 시간 맞춰 가지 못할 것 같아.
④ 나는 쇼핑몰 앞에서 너를 만날 거야.
⑤ 나는 그들이 내일 세일을 할 거라고 들었어.

13 ④

남: 그리고 저기가 샤워장입니다.
여: 알겠습니다. 헬스장을 구경시켜 주셔서 감사합니다.
남: 천만에요. 다음에 오실 때, 고객님을 위한 운동 순서를 세워 놓겠습니다.
여: 알겠습니다. 제 개인 트레이너로서, 저에게 조언해 주실 게 있나요?
남: 음, 우선 저는 고객님이 헬스장에 등록하는 이유를 알아야 해요.
여: 그냥 살을 좀 빼고 싶어요.
남: 제 조언은 규칙적으로 운동하고 물을 많이 마시라는 겁니다.
여: 알겠습니다. 하루에 몇 잔을 마셔야 하나요?
남: 대략 여덟 잔입니다. 또한, 매일 꼭 균형 잡힌 세 끼 식사를 하도록 하세요.
여: 정말이요? 식사를 거르는 것이 빨리 살을 빼는 좋은 방법이라고 생각했는데요.

남: 그래 보이지만, 그것은 고객님의 건강에 매우 나쁠 수 있습니다.

문제풀이
① 의사들은 매끼를 천천히 먹는 것이 제일 좋다고 말합니다.
② 그것이 좋은 몸매를 유지하는 비결이군요!
③ 그러면 고객님이 들어 올리는 무게 중량을 늘려 드리겠습니다.
⑤ 식사를 하면서 물을 마시는 것은 배탈이 나게 합니다.

14 ③

[문 두드리는 소리]
남: 누구세요?
여: Peter Diaz 씨에게 커피 배달 왔습니다.
남: 아, 들어오세요. 저 책상에 놔 주세요.
여: 알겠습니다. 카푸치노 세 잔과 라떼 한 잔입니다.
남: 영수증 갖고 오셨나요? 지난번에 가격을 잘못 계산하셨기 때문에 확인해 보고 싶습니다.
여: 네, 그것에 대해서는 죄송합니다. 제가 혼동했습니다. 어쨌든, 여기 영수증과 쿠폰이 있습니다.
남: 아! 무료 음료 쿠폰이군요!
여: 지난번 실수 때문에 매니저가 사과의 의미로 드리는 거예요.
남: 정말 친절하시군요. 이런, 이 라떼가 잘못된 것 같아요.
여: 그렇습니까? 한 잔을 주문하지 않으셨어요?
남: 그렇긴 한데, 얼음을 넣은 것이어야 했어요.
여: 죄송합니다. 당장 새로운 걸 가져다 드리겠습니다.

문제풀이
① 죄송하지만 그것은 다 팔렸습니다.
② 사실, 얼음을 넣은 음료는 비용이 50센트 더 듭니다.
④ 어떤 종류의 음료에도 쿠폰을 사용하실 수 있습니다.
⑤ 괜찮습니다. 저는 뜨거운 커피를 마셔도 괜찮습니다.

15 ②

여: Hailey는 새 아파트로 이사를 왔고, 집에 매우 만족한다. 그녀가 이사를 들어온 날, 그녀의 이웃이 와서 자기를 소개했다. 그는 매우 친절하고 호의적이었다. 그러나 어느 날, 그녀는 그녀의 이웃이 그의 쓰레기를 그의 (집) 문 앞에 놓은 것을 발견한다. Hailey는 그가 한 번에 그의 쓰레기를 모두 버리기를 원하기 때문에 이렇게 했다고 추측한다. 시간이 갈수록, 나쁜 냄새가 나기 시작하고 Hailey가 그 앞을 지나다닐 때마다 그것은 끔찍해 보인다. 그녀는 가능한 한 빨리 쓰레기가 치워져야 한다고 생각한다. 이런 상황에서, Hailey가 그녀의 이웃에게 할 말로 가장 적절한 것은 무엇인가?
Hailey: 복도에 쓰레기를 놓지 말아 주실래요?

문제풀이
① 쓰레기양을 어떻게 줄일 수 있을까요?
③ 이것에 대해서 집주인에게 항의하는 게 어떨까요?
④ 만약 제가 쓰레기를 내다 버리려면 어디로 가야 하나요?
⑤ 제가 건물 규칙을 어겼다는 것을 어떻게 알았나요?

16 ⑤ 17 ⑤

남: 많은 사람들은 종종 자신이 밤늦게 혼자 집에 걸어가고 있는 것을 발견합니다. 그러나, 여러분은 범죄의 대상이 될 수 있으므로 이것은 매우 위험합니다. 밤에 누군가 여러분을 따라오기 시작한다면, 겁먹지 마십시오. 대신에, 다음의 조언을 활용하세요. 우선, 다른 사람들이 있는 장소에 가도록 하세요. 만약 여러분이 장소를 찾기 전에 그 사람이 여러분을 잡으려 한다면, 크게 소리 질러 도움을 청하세요. 호루라기를 부는 것도 도움이 될 수 있습니다. 그러나 다른 어떤 것도 효과가 없다면, 여러분은 싸워야 할지도 모릅니다. 가스총은 효과적인 무기입니다. 당신은 또한 전기 충격기를 사용할 수 있으며, 쏘기 어렵다면 최루 스프레이 역시 자기방어에 좋습니다. 이것은 공격자를 멈추게 하고 일시적으로 눈을 안 보이게 하는 데 쓰일 수 있습니다. 이런 조언들을 따른다면, 밤에 혼자 걸어갈 때 여러분은 안전할 수 있습니다.

DICTATION Answers

01 share some important information / stop all regular deliveries / at all times
02 I prefer white bread / is processed more than / get used to eating
03 how much it costs / by express mail / come back this afternoon
04 That makes sense / put it somewhere else / the list of books
05 cook something for dinner / get something delivered / How about trying
06 sounds like a lot of fun / having a big party / on a business trip
07 have a special discount / at least two hours / want to stay longer
08 got a small role / would love to see it / who leaves the city
09 getting a start / lasts for two hours / the number of participants
10 the length of the cable / is enough for everyday use / pay for those
11 going to see a movie
12 When shall we meet
13 On your next visit / lose some weight / three balanced meals a day
14 miscalculated the price / for a free drink / was supposed to be iced
15 is very satisfied with / in front of his door / as soon as possible
16-17 find themselves walking home / get to a place / it is hard to shoot

26 영어듣기 모의고사

본문 ▲ p.181

01 ③	02 ④	03 ⑤	04 ③	05 ⑤	06 ③
07 ②	08 ④	09 ③	10 ⑤	11 ①	12 ①
13 ④	14 ④	15 ③	16 ⑤	17 ④	

01 ③

여: 신발에 관한 한, 여러분은 신발이 얼마나 잘 맞는지 세심한 주의를 기울여야 합니다. 맞지 않는 신발을 고르는 것은 고통과 부상으로도 이어질 수 있습니다. 보통 신발은 때때로 이러한 종류의 문제를 일으킵니다. 반면에, 주문 신발은 신는 사람을 위해서 특별히 디자인되어 여러분께 가장 편안한 착용감을 줄 수 있습니다. Johnson and Sons에서, 저희는 몇몇 세계 최고의 주문 신발을 만듭니다. 50년이 넘는 시간 동안, 저희 가족은 어떤 요구에도 잘 들어맞는 최고 수준의 특별한 신발을 만들어 왔습니다. 저희 신발은 고품질 재료로 만들어집니다. 저희 가게에 오셔서 40가지가 넘는 스타일 중에서 선택해보세요!

02 ④

남: 안녕, Amy. 오늘 무엇 때문에 여기 왔니?
여: 전 이가 아파요, Smith 선생님.
남: 어디 보자… *[잠시 후]* 충치가 있지만, 그다지 심각한 건 아니야.
여: 잘됐네요. 하지만 저한테 왜 충치가 있는지 이해를 못 하겠어요.
남: 음… 넌 제대로 양치하고 있니?
여: 네, 저는 하루에 적어도 세 번 3분간 양치해요.
남: 음, 양치가 언제나 충분한 것은 아니야. 너는 규칙적인 스케일링 치료도 받아야 해.
여: 그게 정말 필요한가요?
남: 응. 많은 플라크가 치아에 쌓이면, 항상 혼자서 제거할 수는 없어.
여: 아, 알겠어요. 얼마나 자주 와야 하나요?
남: 6개월마다 와야 해.
여: 알겠어요.

03 ⑤

남: 실례합니다. 저를 도와주실 수 있나 궁금해요.
여: 당연하죠. 무엇을 도와드릴까요?
남: 음, 전 「The History of the Wild West」라는 책을 찾고 있어요.
여: 저자의 이름을 아시나요?
남: 네, 알아요. 저자는 Benjamin Horne입니다.
여: *[타자치는 소리]* 음… 그 책은 이미 다른 사람에 의해 대출된 것 같아요.
남: 알겠어요. 언제 대출되었나요?
여: 바로 지난주에 대출되었네요. 그 책이 반납되면 저희가 연락을 드릴까요?
남: 그거 좋네요. 여기 제 휴대전화 번호가 있습니다.
여: 책이 반납되자마자 알려드리겠습니다.

04 ③

남: 여보, 나 집에 왔어요!
여: 당신을 기다리고 있었어요. 주방을 재배치했거든요.
남: 정말요?
여: 네! 와서 봐요. 양념 통을 가스레인지 오른쪽에 놓았어요.
남: 좋은 생각이에요. 가스레인지 위쪽 찬장에 그것들을 놓았을 때는 불편했어요.
여: 또 양념 통 위쪽 벽에 주방 도구 걸이도 달았어요.
남: 그렇네요. 아, 양념 통 앞에 있는 저건 뭐예요?
여: 그건 토스터예요. 바로 오늘 아침에 샀어요.
남: 좋아요. 우리는 하나 필요했잖아요. 그리고 당신은 커피 메이커를 정수기 옆으로 옮겼네요.
여: 네, 그렇게 하면 커피를 만드는 게 더 쉬워질 거예요.
남: 나도 그렇게 생각해요. 정말 잘했어요!

05 ⑤

여: 이번 여행은 대단했어. 거의 끝났다니 믿을 수가 없어.
남: 응. 하루만 더 머무를 수 있으면 좋을 텐데.
여: 나도 그래. 우리 계획을 바꿔서 오늘 저녁 대신 내일 떠나는 건 어때?
남: 좋다. 그러면, 우리는 오늘 밤 불꽃놀이를 볼 수 있겠다!
여: 좋아! 아, 잠깐만! 먼저 우리가 항공편을 바꿀 수 있는지 확인해야 해.
남: 네 말이 맞아. 우리가 내일로 항공편을 바꿀 수 있도록 내가 확인해 볼게.
여: 좋아. 지금 당장 항공사에 전화해보는 게 어때?
남: 그럴게. 우리는 또 하룻밤 더 방을 예약해야 해. 네가 그걸 해줄 수 있겠어?
여: 문제없어. 네가 항공편에 관해 전화하는 동안 내가 그걸 처리할게.

06 ③

남: 안녕, Kate. 여기서 뭘 하고 있니?
여: 안녕, Kevin. 난 지금 여기서 아르바이트를 하고 있어.
남: 정말? 왜 아르바이트 일자리를 구했니?
여: 약간의 여윳돈을 벌고 싶어서.
남: 알겠어. 그것은 이력서에 기재할 좋은 근무 경력이 될 거라고 생각해.
여: 나도 그렇게 생각하는데, 나는 졸업하고 나서 교사가 되고 싶어.
남: 좋은 목표구나. 그러면 무엇을 위해서 돈을 모으고 있니?
여: 난 이번 여름에 유럽을 여행하고 싶어.
남: 재미있을 것 같아. 하지만 틀림없이 비용도 꽤 많이 들 거야.
여: 맞아. 그래서 내가 이 일자리를 구한 거야.
남: 음, 나는 그것이 그만한 가치가 있을 거라고 확신해. 여행은 훌륭한 경험이야.
여: 나도 그러길 바라.

07 ②

여: Mint 장난감 박물관에 오신 걸 환영합니다. 무엇을 도와드릴까요?
남: 전 표 몇 장을 사고 싶어요. 가격이 얼마인가요?
여: 가격이 다양합니다. 성인 표가 필요하세요 아니면 어린이 표가 필요하세요?

남: 저희는 4명입니다. 성인 두 명과 어린이 두 명이에요.
여: 알겠습니다. 성인 표는 15달러이고 12세 미만 어린이 표는 10달러예요.
남: 그렇군요. 저는 4살짜리 딸과 11살인 아들이 있어요.
여: 아, 5세 미만 어린이는 무료입장입니다, 손님.
남: 좋군요! 그러면 딸의 티켓은 필요하지 않겠네요. 그리고 이 쿠폰을 사용할 수 있나요?
여: 확인해 보겠습니다. *[잠시 후]* 물론입니다. 이렇게 하면 총액에서 10퍼센트 할인이 될 거예요.
남: 잘됐네요! 그러면, 티켓 세 장 주세요.

문제풀이

남자는 15달러인 성인 표를 두 장, 10달러인 어린이 표를 한 장 구매해야 하는데 쿠폰으로 10퍼센트 할인을 받았으므로 총 36달러(= ($15×2+$10) ×0.9)를 지불할 것이다.

08 ④

[전화벨이 울린다.]
여: 안녕하세요, Mansfield 대학 행정실입니다.
남: 안녕하세요. 저는 장학금에 관해 전화 드렸습니다.
여: 네. 음, 자격을 갖추기 위해서는 현재 Mansfield 시에 거주하는 고등학교 졸업반 학생이어야 합니다.
남: 알겠습니다. 지원은 어떻게 하나요?
여: 저희 웹사이트에서 지원서를 다운받고, 그것을 작성해서 저희에게 이메일로 보내주시면 됩니다.
남: 언제 그것을 보내야 합니까?
여: 음, 저희가 6월 1일까지 받아야 합니다.
남: 알겠습니다. 제가 선발되었는지 어떻게 알 수 있나요?
여: 저희가 6월 15일에 학생에게 그 정보를 이메일로 보낼 겁니다.
남: 좋습니다. 그리고 질문이 하나 더 있습니다. 장학금은 얼마인가요?
여: 세 가지 종류의 장학금이 있는데, 각 3,000달러 정도입니다.

09 ③

남: 듀공은 바다 포유류입니다. 그것은 코끼리와 가까운 친척입니다. 코끼리처럼, 그것은 두껍고 주름진 피부를 가지고 있습니다. 그것은 또한 헤엄치려고 위아래로 움직이는 고래와 같은 꼬리를 가지고 있습니다. 듀공은 길이가 3미터까지 자랄 수 있고 무게가 500킬로그램까지 나갈 수 있습니다. 듀공은 새끼일 때는 모유를 먹고 삽니다. 그러나 약 18개월 정도 지나면, 그것은 해조류를 먹기 시작합니다. 듀공은 주로 해조류가 자라는 호주 근처의 연안 해역에서 큰 무리를 이루고 삽니다. 안타깝게도, 듀공은 수천 년 동안 고기와 기름을 위해 사냥당해 왔습니다. 듀공은 현재 보호되고 있지만, 그 개체 수가 계속해서 줄어들고 있습니다.

10 ⑤

남: Water World에 오신 걸 환영합니다. 무엇을 도와드릴까요?
여: 저는 정수기를 대여하고 싶어요.
남: 알겠습니다. 어떤 종류를 원하세요?
여: 음, 온수가 나오는 것이 있나요?
남: 물론입니다. 고객님께서는 또한 제빙기가 내장된 것을 원하시나요?
여: 아니요, 그건 필요 없어요. 저는 돈을 너무 많이 쓰고 싶지는 않아요.
남: 음, 가격이 비싼 것일수록 필터 교환이 덜 필요합니다. 필터는 매우 비쌀 수도 있어요.
여: 음… 저는 필터를 교환하는 걸 좋아하지 않아요. 한 달에 한 번은 너무 빈번하네요.
남: 그러면 고객님께는 오직 두 가지 선택 사항밖에 없습니다. 어떤 것이 더 좋으세요?
여: 물론, 더 저렴한 거죠.

11 ①

남: 전 두 명이 앉을 테이블을 원해요.
여: 죄송합니다만, 꽤 오래 기다리셔야 할 것 같습니다.
남: 아. 우린 좀 바쁜데요. 얼마나 기다려야 하나요?
여: 적어도 20분이 걸릴 것 같습니다.

문제풀이

② 고객님께서는 예약을 하셨어야 합니다.
③ 저희는 오전 11시에 개점합니다.
④ 유감스럽게도, 지금 두 명이 앉을 테이블밖에 없습니다.
⑤ 죄송합니다만, 곧 저희는 식당 문을 닫습니다.

12 ①

여: 프랑스어 동아리에 대해서 어떻게 생각해?
남: 좋아. 나는 가입한 이후로 프랑스어가 많이 나아졌어.
여: 나는 정말 동아리에 가입해서 프랑스어를 배우고 싶어.
남: 그렇다면 그 동아리가 너에게 꼭 알맞을 거야.

문제풀이

② 난 새 친구들을 좀 사귀고 싶어.
③ 너는 그 언어 동아리 회원이니?
④ 나는 언어를 배우는 데 관심이 없어.
⑤ 대신에 다른 것을 배우는 게 어때?

13 ④

남: 와! 볼 다양한 밴드들이 아주 다양하게 많이 있구나.
여: 맞아. 이것은 역대 최고의 록 페스티벌이 될 거야!
남: 첫 번째 공연은 5시야. 선택할 수 있는 무대가 세 개 있어.
여: 음, 나는 5시에 Red Rock의 공연을 보고 싶어. 그들은 Stage B에 있어.
남: 하지만 나는 오히려 Quiet Monkeys를 보고 싶어. 그들은 Stage C야.
여: 음… 우리는 누구든 우리가 좋아하는 것을 봐야 한다고 생각해.
남: 나도 그렇게 생각해. 그러면 우린 헤어져야겠다. 너 8시에 Stage A에서 Dexter's Shadow를 볼 거지, 그렇지?
여: 물론이지! 그들은 내가 제일 좋아하는 밴드야!
남: 좋아. 나도 그들의 공연을 보고 싶어.
여: 그러면 지금 헤어졌다가 8시 전에 어딘가에서 만나자.
남: 좋아. 우리 Stage A 앞에서 만나자.

문제풀이

① 우리가 나중에 만나면, 그 공연을 놓칠지도 몰라.
② 그 공연은 굉장했어. 나는 그걸 절대 잊지 못할 거야.
③ 우리 둘 다 좋아하는 밴드를 선택하는 게 어때?
⑤ 그들은 오늘 밤늦게 Stage C에서 공연하기로 되어 있어.

14 ④

여: 안녕, Ken. 주말 잘 보냈어?
남: 응. 나는 등산 갔다 왔어. 너는 어땠어, Brenda?
여: 나는 초를 몇 개 만들었어. 그건 내가 정말로 즐겨 하는 거야.
남: 흥미롭네. 너는 왜 초 만드는 것을 좋아하니?
여: 음… 그건 재미있고, 내가 느긋해지도록 도와줘.
남: 그거 좋다. 우리 삶은 스트레스로 가득 차 있으니까, 느긋해지는 것은 중요하지.
여: 맞아. 또 나는 선물로 사람들에게 초를 주는 것을 좋아해.
남: 이해가 간다. 나도 빵을 굽는 것에 대해서 같은 생각을 해.
여: 네가 빵을 굽는 걸 좋아하는지 몰랐네. 어떤 종류를 굽니?
남: 나는 케이크 만드는 것을 좋아해. 내가 만든 것을 친구들이 먹는 걸 볼 때마다, 나는 행복해.
여: 맞아, 즐길 수 있는 취미를 갖는 것은 정말 좋지.

문제풀이

① 초를 어떻게 만드는지 보여 줄 수 있니?
② 미안하지만, 난 케이크를 구울 시간이 없어.
③ 우리는 대신에 제과점에서 조금 살 수 있어.
⑤ 너는 내가 이 초를 만들기 전에 나에게 말했어야 했어.

15 ③

여: Joyce는 어제 Middleton 고등학교 연설 대회에서 우승을 했다. 이제 그녀는 지역 대회에 참가하여 다른 학교에서 온 학생들과 경쟁할 것이다. 그녀는 작년에도 교내 연설 대회에서 우승했다. 하지만 지역 결선에 진출했을 때, 그녀는 상위 3명 안에 드는 것에 실패했다. 지금 그녀는 다시 시도하는 것에 대해서 정말 초조해하고 있다. 그래서 그녀는 자신이 가장 좋아하는 선생님에게 조언을 얻으러 간다. 그녀의 선생님은 그녀가 교내 대회에서 했던 것처럼 연설을 하면, (지역 대회에서도) 우승할 수 있을 것이라 생각한다. 이런 상황에서, Joyce의 선생님이 Joyce에게 할 말로 가장 적절한 것은 무엇인가?
선생님: 네가 전에 했던 것만 하면, 넌 괜찮을 거야.

문제풀이

① 내가 심사위원으로 대회에 참가할 거야.
② 너는 작년보다 더 열심히 노력해야 했어.
④ 너는 내년에 또 시도할 수 있으니, 실망하지 마.
⑤ 너는 올해 대회에 참가하지 않는 것이 낫겠어.

16 ⑤ 17 ④

남: 당신이 전에 한 번도 만난 적 없는 사람의 집에 방문했다고 상상해보세요. 단지 (집을) 둘러보는 것만으로 당신이 그 사람의 성격에 대해 알 수 있다고 생각하세요? 한 사회 심리학자는 단지 집에 있는 물건을 보고 우리가 사람에 대해 많은 것을 알 수 있다고 생각합니다. 예를 들어, 어떤 사람의 선반이 장식품으로 가득 차 있으면, 그 사람은 아마도 외향적일 겁니다. 그리고 만약 그들이 많은 그림을 가지고 있다면, 그 사람은 창의적일 가능성이 큽니다. 벽에 자연에 관한 사진을 걸어 놓은 사람은 조용하고 수줍음을 타는 경향이 있습니다. 책꽂이 또한 큰 단서를 제공할 수 있습니다. 예를 들어, 많은 다양한 장르의 책을 가진 사람은 보통 융통성이 있습니다. 이러한 것들은 항상 사실이 아닐 수도 있습니다. 그러나 당신은 사람들이 선반에 놓거나 벽에 거는 것에 여전히 주의를 기울여야 합니다. 그것이 당신에게 그들의 성격에 대한 단서를 줄지도 모릅니다.

DICTATION Answers

01 When it comes to / On the other hand / to fit any needs
02 What brings you here / brushing your teeth properly / get it off by yourself
03 I'm wondering if / already been checked out / when it is returned
04 to the right of / above the spice jars / make it easier
05 I wish we could stay / change our flight / Would you mind doing
06 working here part-time / saving money for / it will be worth it
07 They vary in price / get in for free / use this coupon
08 I'm calling about / download the application form / if I was selected
09 a close relative of / moves up and down / has been hunted for
10 I need to rent / spend too much money / Once a month
11 wait for quite a while
12 has improved a lot
13 I'd rather see / whomever we like / let's split up
14 went hiking in the mountains / are full of stress / Whenever I see
15 compete against students / failed to finish / gives a speech
16-17 by looking around / it is likely that / pay attention to

27 영어듣기 모의고사

본문 ▲ p.188

01 ⑤	02 ②	03 ②	04 ④	05 ②	06 ①
07 ③	08 ③	09 ⑤	10 ④	11 ⑤	12 ⑤
13 ③	14 ②	15 ④	16 ④	17 ②	

01 ⑤

여: 사람들이 한 번에 두 가지 일을 하는 걸 발견하는 것은 흔합니다. 예를 들면, 사람들은 종종 공부나 일을 하면서 음악을 듣거나, 영화를 보면서 전화로 수다를 떱니다. 왜 사람들은 동시에 두 가지 일을 하기를 원할까요? 음, 많은 사람들은 그것이 한 번에 한 가지 일만 하는 것보다 더 효율적이라고 생각합니다. 그러나, 그건 사실이 아닙니다. 한 번에 한 가지 이상의 일을 하는 것은 실제로 그것들을 완료하는 데 더 오래 걸리게 합니다. 또한, 그것은 당신의 뇌를 과도하게 자극하고 단기 기억력에 부정적인 영향을 미칠 수 있습니다. 그래서 당신이 공부할 때, 그저 당신의 일에 집중하세요. 결과는 반드시 더 나을 것입니다.

02 ②

여: Green 선생님, 하루가 끝날 무렵이면 눈이 매우 피로해져요.
남: 컴퓨터 화면과 TV를 응시하면서 많은 시간을 보내시나요?
여: 그래요. 저는 종일 사무실에서 컴퓨터로 일을 해요.
남: 그렇군요. 안타깝게도, 컴퓨터 화면을 응시하는 것은 눈에 나쁩니다.
여: 제가 어떻게 해야 하나요?
남: 눈을 쉬게 하기 위해서 매시간 5분씩 휴식 시간을 가지세요.
여: 그게 효과가 없으면요?
남: 눈이 건조할 때 안약을 사용하고 너무 오랫동안 콘택트렌즈를 착용하지 않을 것을 제안합니다.
여: 알겠습니다. 그렇게 해볼게요.
남: 게다가 에어컨이나 난방기에 너무 가까이 있으면 안 됩니다.
여: 그러지 않겠습니다. 조언 감사합니다, 의사 선생님.

03 ②

남: 좋아요, Penelope. 오늘은 어떻게 하고 싶으세요?
여: 솔직히 말하면, Jonathan, 나는 마음이 열려 있어요. 제안할 게 있나요?
남: 음, 당신은 일 년이 넘게 이렇게 해 왔어요. 이번에는 짧게 하는 것이 어떨까요?
여: 그거 멋지겠어요. 얼마나 짧게요?
남: 여기, 이 사진들에 있는 모델들을 보세요. 어깨까지 오는 길이로 자를 수 있어요.
여: 음… 그것보다 더 짧은 건 어떨까요? 전 이 스타일이 마음에 들어요.
남: 와, 용감하시네요! 하지만 걱정 마세요. 제가 기막히게 멋져 보이게 해드릴게요.
여: 알았어요. 나는 머리를 금발로 염색도 하고 싶어요.
남: 하지만 불과 두 달 전에 머리를 염색했잖아요. 만약에 또 염색을 하면, 머리가 손상이 될 거예요.
여: 아, 그러면 그냥 자르고 스타일만 만들게요.

04 ④

남: 이 사진첩 멋지다! 네가 만들었니?
여: 응, 내가 남동생을 위해 만들었어!
남: 아, 왼쪽 페이지 위에 "생일 축하해!"라고 쓰여 있네.
여: 응, 이게 생일 선물이야.
남: 나는 왼쪽 페이지에 있는 세 개의 원형 모양의 사진이 마음에 든다. 근데 정사각형 모양의 사진이 가장 마음에 들어.
여: 나도 동의해. 또한 난 오른쪽 페이지에 있는 커다란 직사각형 모양의 우리 가족 사진이 마음에 들어.
남: 좋아 보여! 다른 사진에 있는 저건 너희 가족의 개니?
여: 응, 맞아. 저 개는 내 남동생의 가장 친한 친구야. 그게 내가 사진을 하트 모양으로 자른 이유야.
남: 알겠어. 너희 개의 사진 옆에 있는 저것은 편지니?
여: 그래. 내가 직접 썼어.

05 ②

남: 이봐, Mary. 뭘 하고 있어?
여: 나는 우리의 새 웹사이트에 대해 작업을 하고 있어. 초기 화면을 더 좋아 보이게 만들고 싶어.
남: 어려울 것 같아.
여: 쉽지 않지만, 즐기면서 하고 있어. 그런데 이제는 웹 디자이너를 찾아야 해.
남: 내가 정말 좋은 웹 디자이너들을 많이 알아. 내가 누구를 추천해줄까?
여: 실은, 나한테 이미 디자이너 명단이 있어. 그냥 한 명을 결정하기만 하면 돼.
남: 그건 쉬울 거야.
여: 아마도, 하지만 내가 오늘 회의가 4개 있어서 시간이 별로 없어. 내가 한 명을 선택하는 걸 도와줄 수 있니?
남: 물론이야. 나에게 그 명단을 이메일로 보내 주면 내가 추천해줄게.
여: 잘됐다! 정말 고마워!

06 ①

남: 이봐, Amy. 휴가는 어땠어?
여: 좋았지만, 돌아와서 기뻐.
남: 어디 갔었어?
여: 가족과 하와이에 갔어.
남: 멋지다. 날씨는 좋았니?
여: 그래. 날씨는 대체로 좋았어.
남: 좋은데! 그런데 너 꽤 탄 거 같아!
여: 맞아. 나는 밖에서 많은 시간을 보냈어. 하나만 빼면 완벽한 휴가였어.
남: 이런. 비행기에서 멀미를 했니?
여: 아니. 실은, 우리가 머물던 곳에 모기와 개미가 많았어. 그것들이 나를 미치게 만들었어.
남: 아! 그건 나도 역시 성가셨을 거야.
여: 아름다운 곳이었지만, 다시는 가고 싶지 않아.

07 ③

남: 무엇을 도와드릴까요?

여: 저는 물속에서 신을 수 있는 신발을 찾고 있어요.
남: 저희에게는 3가지 종류의 워터슈즈가 있습니다. 그것들은 80달러입니다.
여: 꽤 비싸지만, 그 신발이 정말 마음에 드네요.
남: 회원 카드를 갖고 계세요? 그러면, 25퍼센트를 절약할 수 있습니다.
여: 네. 50퍼센트 할인되는 쿠폰도 갖고 있어요. 여동생을 위해 같은 신발로 한 켤레 더 사고 싶어요.
남: 아, 이 쿠폰은 오직 한 켤레에만 적용됩니다.
여: 그러면 쿠폰을 다음에 써야겠네요.
남: 음, 한 켤레는 회원 카드로 구매하시고 다른 한 켤레는 쿠폰으로 구매하실 수 있어요.
여: 그게 좋겠네요!

문제풀이

여자는 80달러짜리 신발을 두 켤레 사면서 하나는 25퍼센트 할인을 받고, 다른 하나는 50퍼센트 할인을 받을 것이므로, 총 100달러(=(\$80×0.75)+(\$80×0.5))를 지불할 것이다.

08 ③

여: 무엇을 읽고 있니, Steve?
남: 드야 동물 보호 구역에 대한 블로그 게시글이야.
여: 아, 그게 뭐야?
남: 그곳은 카메룬에 있는 보호 열대 우림이야. 그 게시글에 그곳이 5,260제곱킬로미터라고 쓰여 있어.
여: 그러면 그곳에는 많은 다양한 동식물이 있겠구나.
남: 응. 그곳에 1,500개 이상의 식물 종과 107개의 포유류 종이 살고 있대.
여: 와, 그곳은 정말 놀라운 장소구나. 아, 봐. 블로거가 그곳은 1950년에 설립되었다고 썼어.
남: 그리고 그곳은 1987년 이래로 UNESCO 세계 문화유산 명단에 올라 있어.
여: 'Baka'가 무슨 의미야? 식물 이름이야?
남: 아니, 그곳에 사는 원주민 집단이야.
여: 음, 흥미로운 게시글인 것 같아.

09 ⑤

남: Anderson Cooper는 미국에서 가장 잘 알려진 기자들 중 한 명이다. 그는 부유하고 유명한 집안에서 태어났다. 그러나, 그가 아주 어렸을 때, 그의 가족에게 비극이 닥쳤다. 그가 겨우 10살이었을 때, 그의 아버지는 심장 수술 중 사망했다. 약 10년 후, 그의 형은 자살을 했다. 이런 사건에 깊게 영향을 받아서, Cooper는 삶과 죽음의 문제에 관심을 갖게 되었다. 그는 기자가 되어서 전쟁을 보도하였다. 미얀마와 아프리카 일부 지역의 분쟁을 보도한 후에, 그는 국제 특파원이 되었다. 그리고 그는 뛰어난 보도로 많은 상을 받았다.

10 ④

남: 무엇을 도와드릴까요?
여: 캐나다에 있는 제 친구에게 소포를 보내고 싶은데요.
남: 알겠습니다. 특급 배송과 일반 배송이라는 두 가지 옵션이 있어요.
여: 음… 급한 건 아니니까, 더 저렴한 것이 더 좋을 것 같아요.
남: 알겠습니다. 표준 규격 상자를 사용하실 건가요?
여: 제가 보내는 것은 깨지기 쉬운 것이라서 포장이 잘 되어야 해요.
남: 그런 경우라면, 기포 포장재를 추천합니다.
여: 좋습니다. 소포가 어디에 있는지 제가 추적할 수 있나요?
남: 만약에 소포가 어디에 있는지 추적하고 싶으시면, 소포를 등록하실 수 있습니다. 하지만 그것은 또한 추가 요금이 듭니다.
여: 좋습니다. 저는 꼭 추적을 하고 싶어요. 총 가격이 얼마인가요?

11 ⑤

남: 다음 주 월요일에 학교 현장 학습에 빨리 가고 싶어요.
여: 아, 어디로 가니?
남: 동물원에 갈 거예요! 현장 학습이 정말 취소되지 않았음 좋겠어요.
여: 날씨만 좋다면, 아무 문제 없을 거야.

문제풀이

① 너는 동물원에 전화해서 현장 학습을 취소할 수 있어.
② 반드시 모든 규칙을 잘 따르도록 해라.
③ 현장 학습은 학생들에게 매우 좋은 경험이야.
④ 동물원은 다양한 동물을 보기에 가장 좋은 장소야.

12 ⑤

여: 내 침실로 이 책꽂이를 옮기는 걸 도와줄래?
남: 음… 책꽂이가 너무 커서 거기에 들어갈 수 없을 것 같아.
여: 그러면 우리가 그것을 어디에 둘 수 있을 것 같아?
남: 거실에 충분한 공간이 있어.

문제풀이

① 그건 너무 큰 것이 확실해.
② 내가 이 책들을 책꽂이에 꽂는 걸 도와줘.
③ 나는 그걸 그 새 가구점에서 샀어.
④ 그게 네 침실에 들어맞을지 보자.

13 ③

남: Karen. 기분이 안 좋아 보인다.
여: 아, 내 여동생하고 크게 싸웠어.
남: 정말 안됐다. 무슨 일이야?
여: 그 애가 허락도 없이 내 원피스 중 하나를 빌려 갔어.
남: 그렇게 큰일은 아닌 것 같은데.
여: 보통 때는 신경 쓰지 않았을 테지만, 그 애가 얼룩을 묻히고 옷을 가져간 것에 대해서 거짓말을 했어.
남: 그 애가 옷을 가져간 걸 어떻게 알았어?
여: 난 몇 주 동안 그 옷을 입은 적이 없는데, 세탁물 바구니에서 그 옷을 발견했어.
남: 네 여동생이 그 옷을 가져간 게 확실해?
여: 응. 그 애는 전에도 그랬어. 게다가, 그 애가 그걸 입고 있는 걸 엄마가 보셨어.
남: 그렇구나. 이제부터 너는 그 애에게 네 물건을 빌려주는 것에 대해 명확한 규칙을 정하는 것이 나을 것 같아.
여: 그게 싸우는 것보다 더 도움이 되겠다.

문제풀이

① 나는 이미 그녀에게 그것을 빌려주겠다고 약속했어.
② 내일 아침에 그녀에게 사과할 거야.
④ 네가 나를 믿지 않는다니 정말 실망했어.
⑤ 나는 절대 여동생의 원피스에서 얼룩을 빼지 못할 거야!

14 ②

[휴대전화벨이 울린다.]
여: 여보세요?
남: 여보세요, Johnson 교수네.
여: 아, 교수님! 오늘 오전에 수업에 가지 못해서 죄송합니다.
남: 그래. 왜 자네가 수업에 출석하지 않았는지 궁금하네.
여: 실은, 오늘 오전에 자전거에서 떨어져서 발이 부러졌습니다. 몇 시간 동안 병원에 있었어요.
남: 아, 안됐구나. 지금은 괜찮은가?
여: 훨씬 좋아졌습니다. 수업에 빠지지 않았으면 좋았을 텐데요.
남: 그건 걱정하지 말게. 전에는 수업을 한 번도 빠진 적이 없었잖아.
여: 그런데 오늘까지 내기로 한 제 보고서는 어쩌죠? 누군가에게 오늘 밤에 교수님께 가져다 드리게 할까요?
남: 그냥 내일 아침에 내 사무실에 갖다 놓으면 돼.
여: 정말이요? 하지만 저는 교수님께서 제가 제시간에 보고서를 끝내지 못했다고 생각하시는 걸 원하지 않습니다.
남: 나는 자네를 믿어. 내일도 괜찮아.

문제풀이
① 제시간에 끝내지 못해서 미안해.
③ 자네 발은 몇 주 후에 완치가 될 거야.
④ 자네는 지금 당장 병원에 가야 해.
⑤ 괜찮아. 내 친구가 곧 그곳에 갈 거야.

15 ④

여: Megan은 온라인 쇼핑 회사의 고객 서비스 직원이다. 어느 날 오후, 그녀는 화가 난 고객으로부터 전화를 받는다. 그 고객은 자신이 주문한 것이 도착하기를 3주 동안이나 기다렸다고 말한다. 그녀는 배송 물품이 제대로 발송되었으나, 물건 발송 주소가 부정확했다는 것을 발견한다. 그녀가 이것을 설명했을 때, 그 고객은 최근에 새로운 곳으로 이사를 가서 웹사이트에 자신의 주소를 바꾸는 것을 잊어버렸다고 말한다. 그 고객은 그녀에게 자신의 새 주소로 소포를 다시 보내달라고 요청한다. 이는 고객의 실수이기 때문에, 그 고객은 배송료를 지불해야 한다. 이런 상황에서, Megan이 그 고객에게 할 말로 가장 적절한 것은 무엇인가?
Megan: 추가 배송료가 발생할 것입니다.

문제풀이
① 고객님의 주문 번호를 알 수 있을까요?
② 저도 그러고 싶지만, 고객님의 주소는 부정확합니다.
③ 가능합니다만, 저는 무엇을 보내야 할지 모르겠습니다.
⑤ 고객님은 잘못된 번호를 알려주시지 말았어야 합니다.

16 ④ 17 ②

남: 안녕하세요, 여러분. 제 이름은 Miriam Jordan이고, 저는 영양 전문가입니다. 오늘날 많은 사람들이 자신들의 건강에 관심이 있습니다. 그들은 건강을 유지하기 위해서 시금치, 사과, 그리고 마늘을 포함해서 다양한 종류의 건강에 좋은 음식을 섭취합니다. 건강에 좋은 이런 음식은 몸에 유익한 영향을 주기 때문에 '슈퍼푸드'라고 불립니다. 여기 여러분이 알아야 하는 슈퍼푸드가 하나 더 있습니다. 바로 블루베리입니다! 블루베리는 여러분의 면역 체계를 강화하도록 돕는 산화방지제의 함유량이 높습니다. 블루베리는 또한 우리가 나이가 들수록 좋은 시력과 기억력을 유지하는 것을 돕는다고 알려졌습니다. 블루베리는 심지어 심장병과 암과 싸우는 것을 돕습니다. 게다가, 블루베리는 85퍼센트가 수분으로 이루어져 있어서 살을 빼고 복부 지방을 감소시키는 것을 돕습니다. 이 모든 건강상의 이점이 있는 블루베리는 세계에서 가장 건강에 좋은 음식 중 하나입니다. 여러분의 하루를 건강하게 시작하기 위해서 아침 식사 시리얼이나 요구르트에 블루베리를 첨가하는 건 어떨까요?

문제풀이
16 ① 건강식품의 부작용
② 다양한 종류의 슈퍼푸드
③ 심장병을 예방하는 음식
④ 블루베리 섭취의 이점
⑤ 면역 체계를 강화시키는 방법

DICTATION Answers

01 doing two things at once / take longer to complete / concentrate on your work
02 get very tired / is bad for your eyes / give that a try
03 have any suggestions / something shorter than that / have it cut and styled
04 at the top of / on the left page / the shape of a heart
05 working on our new website / a list of designers / make a recommendation
06 happy to be back / except for one thing / That would bother me
07 wear in the water / have a coupon for / apply to one pair
08 a protected rainforest / it was founded in / a group of native people
09 He was born into / became interested in / won many awards
10 the cheaper option / needs to be packaged well / an additional fee
11 the trip doesn't get canceled
12 too big to go
13 be in a bad mood / got a stain on it / set clear rules
14 fell off my bike / feel much better / finish it on time
15 gets a call from / forgot to change / to his new address
16-17 are concerned with / maintain good eyesight / reduce belly fat

28 영어듣기 모의고사

본문 p.195

01 ①	02 ②	03 ②	04 ⑤	05 ④	06 ③
07 ②	08 ④	09 ④	10 ②	11 ①	12 ⑤
13 ②	14 ③	15 ③	16 ④	17 ③	

01 ①

여: 안녕하세요, 여러분. 우선, 오늘 직원회의에 참석해 주셔서 여러분 모두에게 감사드립니다. 저는 특별한 발표로 이 회의를 시작하고 싶군요. 이 분은 Scott Brady 씨입니다. 우리의 새 재정 고문이 되실 겁니다. 그는 회계학 학위가 있고 10년 이상의 근무 경험이 있습니다. 저는 Brady 씨가 우리 팀을 다방면으로 도와줄 것으로 믿습니다. 그의 성실함과 지식 또한 장차 회사 전체가 성공하고 성장할 수 있게 도와줄 것입니다. Brady 씨가 우리 기업 가족의 일원이 되는 것에 적응할 때 편하게 느낄 수 있도록 도와주세요.

02 ②

남: 그거 새 원피스니, Hailey?
여: 응. 온라인에서 샀는데, 옷에 커다란 얼룩이 있어.
남: 아, 세상에. 그게 내가 매장에서 옷을 사는 것을 선호하는 이유야.
여: 무슨 뜻이야?
남: 그렇게 하면, 옷을 입어 보고 네가 사려는 것을 정확하게 볼 수 있어.
여: 그렇지만 온라인 쇼핑은 훨씬 더 저렴해. 실은, 난 이 원피스를 가게 가격보다 20퍼센트 싸게 구입했어.
남: 그렇지만 너는 그 옷을 반품하기 위해 다시 포장해서 우편으로 돌려보내야 하잖아.
여: 반품하는 건 쉬워.
남: 가게에서 그 원피스를 샀으면, 너는 그것을 새것으로 빨리 교환할 수 있잖아.
여: 사실이야. 이번엔 그냥 환불을 요청할까 봐.

03 ②

[휴대전화벨이 울린다.]
여: 여보세요.
남: 여보세요. Johnson 씨입니까?
여: 예, 접니다. 누구세요?
남: 제 이름은 Rob입니다. 고객님이 저희 서비스 센터에 전화를 주셨죠. 저는 지금 고객님의 아파트 밖에 있습니다.
여: 제가 오전 내내 기다렸는데, 지금은 슈퍼마켓에 있네요.
남: 그러면 제가 내일 다시 방문해도 괜찮을까요?
여: 저는 정말로 오늘 오후에 컴퓨터를 사용해야 해요. 컴퓨터가 작동을 멈춘 지 벌써 3일이나 되었어요. 잠시만 기다려 주실 수 있으세요?
남: 얼마나 오래 걸릴 것 같으세요?
여: 10분 후에 집에 도착할 거예요.
남: 알겠습니다, 그럼 기다리겠습니다.
여: 매우 감사합니다.
남: 천만에요.

04 ⑤

남: 우리 새 아파트 거실을 어떻게 배치해야 할까요?
여: 음, 우선, 세로줄 무늬가 있는 이 커튼을 창문에 달도록 해요.
남: 알겠어요. 이제, 커다란 에펠 탑 사진은요?
여: 창문 왼쪽 벽에 걸면 어떨까요?
남: 좋아요. 그리고 그 아래 직사각형 탁자를 놓을 수 있어요.
여: 아니에요, 그 아래에 소파를 놓아요.
남: 알았어요, 그게 좋을 것 같네요.
여: 그러면 우리는 탁자를 소파 옆에 놓을 수 있어요.
남: 알았어요. 내 생각에 우리는 그 위에 이 작은 액자를 놓아야 할 것 같아요.
여: 나는 동의하지 않아요. 내 생각에는, 실내용 화초가 더 나아 보일 것 같아요.
남: 음… 좋은 제안이에요, 여보!

05 ④

남: 아야!
여: 무슨 일이에요, 여보?
남: 이 상자를 옮기다가 목 근육을 접질렸어요. 정말 아프네요. 고개를 전혀 못 돌리겠어요.
여: 저런! 내가 병원에 데려다줄까요?
남: 나중에는 그래야 할지도 몰라요. 그런데 지금은 괜찮아요.
여: 통증이 있으니 약을 먹어야 할 거 같아요. 약국에 가서 약을 사 올까요?
남: 아니요. 서랍에 몇 개 있어요. 내가 지금 먹을게요.
여: 그러면 얼음은 어때요? 목에 댈 얼음팩을 만들어 줄게요.
남: 오, 좋은 생각이에요.
여: 당장 가서 만들어 올게요.
남: 고마워요, 여보. 당신이 최고예요.

06 ③

남: 미래 목표에 대한 작문 숙제는 어떻게 되어 가고 있어?
여: 며칠 전에 끝냈어. 나는 어떻게 내가 로스쿨 진학을 고려하고 있는지에 대해서 썼어.
남: 정말? 그게 네 부모님이 네가 공부하길 원하시는 것이니?
여: 아니야. 우리 부모님은 단지 무엇이든지 내 관심을 끄는 것을 공부하기를 원하셔.
남: 그러면 법학에 관심이 있니, 아니면 보수가 좋은 직업을 원하는 거니?
여: 편안하게 살려면 돈이 필요하지만, 나는 Jeannie Suk 때문에 법 공부를 고려하기 시작했어.
남: 그녀가 누구니? 네 역할 모델이니?
여: 그래. 그녀는 하버드 로스쿨에서 교수가 된 최초의 아시아계 미국인 여성이야.
남: 그래서 그녀의 발자취를 따라가고 싶은 거니?
여: 정확해.

07 ②

남: 집안일을 하는 것이 운동의 일종이 될 수 있다는 것을 알고 있어?
여: 정말? 어떻게?
남: 이 블로그를 봐. 접시를 문질러 닦을 때 한 시간에 대략 300칼로리를 소모해.
여: 그러면 너는 좀 전에 30분 동안 설거지를 할 때 칼로리를 좀 소모했겠구나.
남: 응, 그랬지. 게다가 내가 오늘 집 전체를 진공청소기로 청소했는데, 그건 한 시간이 걸렸어.
여: 어디 보자… 한 시간 동안 진공청소기로 청소하는 것은 대략 150칼로리를 소모한다고 쓰여 있네.
남: 나는 또 창을 닦느라고 30분을 썼어.
여: 그건 얼마나 많은 칼로리를 소모한 거야?
남: 이 블로그에 따르면, 한 시간에 대략 240이야.
여: 와! 너는 합쳐서 정말 많은 칼로리를 소모했구나.

문제풀이

남자는 30분 동안 설거지를 하는 데 약 150kcal, 진공청소기로 한 시간 동안 청소하는 데 약 150kcal, 그리고 30분 동안 창문을 닦는 데 약 120kcal를 소모했으므로, 총 약 420kcal(= 150kcal+150kcal+120kcal)를 소모했다.

08 ④

여: 안녕, Tom. 어디 가고 있니?
남: 안녕, Anne. 우리 동네에 최근에 지어진 새로운 공원에 가고 있어.
여: 아, 나는 그것에 대해서 들어본 적이 있어. 그곳이 정확히 어디니?
남: 그곳은 여기서 북쪽으로 네 블록 가서 시청 옆에 위치해 있어.
여: 알겠어. 얼마나 큰데?
남: 우리 학교 운동장의 약 두 배만큼 커. 공원을 가로질러서 걷는 데 대략 20분이 걸려.
여: 벌써 그 공원이 일반 사람들에게 개방되었는지 몰랐어. 아직 공사 중이라고 생각했는데.
남: 바로 지난주 월요일에 열었어.
여: 잘됐네. Roger's Park라고 불리는 곳이 맞지?
남: 맞아. 나중에 가고 싶으면 알려줘. 아마 우리는 함께 갈 수 있을 거야.
여: 알았어!

09 ④

남: 우리 시 최고 전자기기 소매상인 Circuit Center는 10월 10일에 연례 사이버 게임 토너먼트를 주최할 것입니다. 등록 마감은 9월 30일이니 서두르시기 바랍니다. Circuit Center 회원권이 있으시면 참가는 무료입니다! 그렇지 않더라도, 참가 비용은 선수당 3달러밖에 안 합니다. 여러분은 여러분의 키보드, 마우스, 그리고 헤드셋을 가지고 오는 것이 허용됩니다. 그러나, 속임수와 해킹을 방지하기 위해서 무선 장비는 허락되지 않습니다. 참가자들은 시합 중에 음료를 마시는 것이 허용되지만, 음식은 게임 부스 안에 허락되지 않습니다. 메달은 1등, 2등, 그리고 3등 선수에게 수여됩니다. 더 많은 정보를 원하시면, 저희 사이트인 www.circuitcenter.com에 방문해 주세요.

10 ②

여: 여보, 우리 내일 Peter를 Newtown 수족관에 데리고 가기로 약속했어요.
남: 기억해요. 여기 수족관 일일 프로그램 일정이 있어요.
여: 좋아요. Peter를 위해 하나를 선택해요.
남: 우리가 몇 시에 도착할 것 같아요?
여: 수족관은 여기에서 머니까, 우리는 아마 정오쯤에 거기에 도착할 거예요.
남: 맞아요. Peter는 바다표범을 좋아하니까, 이 프로그램 어때요?
여: 시간은 괜찮은데, Peter는 8살밖에 안 됐어요.
남: 그러면 이 두 가지 프로그램 중에서 하나를 선택해야 해요.
여: 그래요. 음… 이 프로그램이 80달러의 가치가 있다고 생각해요?
남: 아니요, 약간 비싼 것 같아요. 그리고 다른 것이 신날 것 같아요.
여: 저도 동의해요. 그 프로그램에 Peter를 등록시켜요. 그 애는 매우 좋아할 거예요.

11 ①

남: 다음 주 토요일 모금 행사에 참석할 거니?
여: 그러고 싶지만, 표가 이미 매진되었다고 들었어.
남: 걱정하지 마. 내게 여분의 표가 좀 있어.
여: 잘됐다. 내가 그중 두 장을 구입할 수 있니?

문제풀이

② 너는 아직 표 한 장을 구매할 수 있는 시간이 많이 있어.
③ 내일이 표를 구입할 수 있는 마지막 날이야.
④ 미안해, 그 파티에 대해서는 아무것도 몰라.
⑤ 네가 옳아. 그 행사는 언제 열리니?

12 ⑤

여: 너 걱정이 있어 보여. 무슨 일이야?
남: 쇼핑몰 어딘가에서 휴대전화를 분실했어. 내가 그것을 어디에 놓았는지 기억이 안 나.
여: 분실물 취급소에 가서 확인해 보는 게 어때?
남: 이미 확인해 봤는데, 갖고 있지 않다고 하더라고.

문제풀이

① 나는 네가 네 휴대전화를 곧 찾기를 바라.
② 내일 나랑 쇼핑하러 갈 수 있니?
③ 내 도움이 필요하면 언제든지 내게 전화해.
④ 내가 분실물 취급소에서 방금 내 전화기를 찾았어.

13 ②

남: 안녕하세요, 도와드릴까요?
여: 네, 부탁합니다. 다음 학기 장학금을 신청하고 싶어요.
남: 알겠습니다. 전에 신청한 적이 있나요?
여: 아니요, 없어요. 이번이 처음이 될 거예요.
남: 그렇군요. 음, 학생은 1학년이거나 2학년 학생이어야 해요.
여: 이번이 여기서 2년째입니다.
남: 잘됐네요. 또한 학생은 모든 강의에서 B학점이나 그 이상을 받았어

야 합니다.
여: 실은, 저는 매 학기에서 모두 A를 받았습니다.
남: 훌륭하네요. 마지막 요건은 이번 학기 완벽한 출석 기록입니다.
여: 아. 제가 이번 달 초에 수업을 몇 번 빠졌어요. 독감에 걸렸었거든요.
남: 그런 경우라면, 학생은 이번 학기에 지원할 수 없습니다.

문제풀이
① 당신은 내 수업 필기를 빌려 가도 됩니다.
③ 당신은 오늘 병원에 가는 게 좋을 것 같습니다.
④ 그 말을 들으니 안타깝네요. 곧 낫기를 바랍니다.
⑤ 성적이 향상되면, 다시 지원할 수 있습니다.

14 ③

남: 내가 빌려준 그 책 다 읽었어?
여: 음… 네가 어떤 책을 말하고 있는지 잘 모르겠어.
남: 내가 가장 좋아하는 책인 「A Tale of Two Cities」에 대해 말하고 있어. 네가 몇 달 전에 빌려 갔잖아.
여: 정말? 근데 내가 빌려 간 걸 전혀 기억 못 하겠어.
남: 뭐라고? 농담하는 거야?
여: 아, 기다려. 이제 기억나는데, 내가 어디에 두었는지 모르겠어.
남: 믿을 수 없어. 너는 내가 아는 가장 부주의한 사람이야!
여: 이 일에 대해서는 정말 미안해. 내가 그걸 다 읽었는지조차 기억이 안 나.
남: 어서 찾아줘. 가능한 한 빨리 돌려주면 좋겠어.
여: 알았어, 내가 그걸 어디에 두었는지 기억하려고 열심히 노력할게.

문제풀이
① 내일 내게 그걸 돌려줘.
② 내가 도와줄 수 있으면 좋겠지만, 이것은 도서관 책이야.
④ 미안하지만, 여전히 그걸 빌렸는지조차 기억을 못 하겠어.
⑤ 문제없어. 난 지난주에 그 책을 다 읽었어.

15 ③

여: George와 Amy는 학교 밴드에 속해있다. 다음 달에, 그들은 학교 강당에서 공연을 할 것이다. 공연을 광고하기 위해서, 그들은 이번 주에 함께 포스터를 만들 예정이다. 그들은 일을 그들 사이에서 나눈다. 그런데 Amy는 갑자기 심한 복통을 느껴서, 병원에 가야 한다. 그녀는 며칠 동안 입원해야 한다는 이야기를 듣게 된다. 이 시점에서, Amy는 George에게 그녀가 포스터 작업을 더는 할 수 없다고 말하기 위해 전화하고, 그에게 그녀의 부분을 마쳐 달라고 부탁한다. 이런 상황에서, Amy가 George에게 할 말로 가장 적절한 것은 무엇인가?
Amy: 나 없이 포스터 만드는 것을 끝내줄 수 있니?

문제풀이
① 너는 내게 아프다고 말했어야 했어.
② 너의 밴드는 언제 연주하니? 정말 가고 싶어.
④ 공연이 취소됐다는 소식을 들으니 슬프다.
⑤ 오늘 나를 병원에 데려다줘서 고마워.

16 ④ 17 ③

남: 많은 사람들에게, 남미로 여행하는 것이 꿈에 지나지 않습니다. 그곳은 너무 멀고, 거기에 가는 데 많은 비용이 듭니다. 하지만 Trans Atlantic 항공 덕분에 흥미진진한 도시가 있는 이 대륙이 그전 어느 때보다도 도달하기가 더 쉬워졌습니다. 내일부터 시작해서 Brasilia와 Lima로 가는 왕복 티켓이 모두 딱 정상가의 반값입니다. 게다가, 일반 티켓에서 20퍼센트 할인된 가격으로 Buenos Aires와 Santiago를 방문할 수 있습니다. 이 놀라운 세일은 일주일 동안만 지속되니 재빨리 행동하세요. 티켓은 올해 3월, 4월이나 5월에 예약되어야 합니다. 티켓은 Trans Atlantic 웹사이트에서 구매되어야 하며 변경이나 환불이 되지 않을 수도 있습니다. 더 많은 정보를 원하시면, 저희 웹사이트로 가세요. 저희는 여러분이 가고 싶은 곳은 어디든지 모시고 가길 고대하고 있습니다.

문제풀이
16 ① 남미 배낭여행을 제안하려고
② 남미 도시가 관광객을 끌어들이는 이유를 설명하려고
③ 남미 도시에 있는 호텔에 대한 할인을 제공하려고
④ 남미로 가는 항공 요금에 대한 할인 가격을 발표하려고
⑤ 남미 환경의 보존을 장려하려고

DICTATION Answers

01 begin the meeting with / has a degree in / being part of
02 bought it online / try things on / ask for a refund
03 Who is this / my computer stopped working / wait for you
04 with the vertical stripes / beside the sofa / In my opinion
05 pulled a muscle / take some medicine / make an ice pack
06 a few days ago / whatever interests me / follow in her footsteps
07 a type of exercise / which took an hour / How many calories
08 built in our neighborhood / twice as big as / Let me know
09 The deadline for registration / are allowed to bring / Medals will be awarded
10 Let's choose one for / arrive there around noon / choose one of these two
11 tickets are already sold out
12 where I put it
13 apply for a scholarship / This is my second year / missed several classes
14 Are you finished reading / I have no idea / as soon as possible
15 divide the work between them / for a couple of days / finish her part
16-17 nothing more than a dream / last for just one week / look forward to taking

29 영어듣기 모의고사

본문 ▲ p.202

01 ⑤	02 ①	03 ⑤	04 ③	05 ③	06 ⑤
07 ③	08 ③	09 ⑤	10 ③	11 ⑤	12 ②
13 ⑤	14 ⑤	15 ⑤	16 ②	17 ④	

01 ⑤

여: 안녕하세요. 이 메시지는 Worldcorp International의 모든 직원을 위한 것입니다. 여러분이 금요일 저녁에 퇴근할 때, 의자를 책상 위에 올려주시기 바랍니다. 또한, 컴퓨터를 포함한 모든 전자기기의 플러그를 뽑아 놓고 모든 것을 책상 위에 올려놓으십시오. 이것은 청소부가 바닥에 광을 내는 것을 훨씬 더 쉽게 해줄 것입니다. 덧붙여, 책상에 접근할 수 없을 것이기 때문에 주말에 사무실에 오지 마십시오. 월요일 오전에 사무실에 돌아오셨을 때, 사무실 바닥이 산뜻하게 광이 나 있을 겁니다. 협조해주셔서 감사드리며, 좋은 주말 보내십시오.

02 ①

남: 난 우리의 시험이 끝나서 기뻐.
여: 나도 그래. 난 일주일 내내 스트레스를 받았어. 재미있는 걸 하자.
남: 영화 보고 싶니?
여: 아니. 나는 좀 더 사교적인 것을 하고 싶어.
남: 그러면 십 대들을 위한 센터를 방문하는 게 어때?
여: 음, 그곳은 지난달부터 문을 닫았어.
남: 정말? 그럼 우리는 이 주위에서 무엇을 할 수 있지? 나는 모르겠어.
여: 정말 좌절스럽다! 이 인근의 모든 것이 어린이나 성인을 위해서 설계된 것 같아.
남: 그러게! 우리는 십 대만을 위한 장소가 필요해.
여: 맞아! 우리가 친구들과 어울릴 수 있는 장소가 있으면 좋을 텐데.
남: 나도 동의해.

03 ⑤

여: 카터를 볼 시간을 내주셔서 감사합니다.
남: 천만에요. 그에게 무슨 문제가 있나요?
여: 그는 어제부터 아팠어요.
남: 어제는 무엇을 먹였습니까?
여: 전 그에게 음식과 수박을 좀 주었어요.
남: 그게 문제네요. 강아지들은 많은 물을 소화하는 데 어려움을 겪기 때문에 수박이 카터에게 복통을 일으켰어요.
여: 와, 몰랐어요. 제가 그를 돕기 위해 무엇을 할 수 있나요?
남: 그에게 더 이상 수박을 주지 않도록 하세요.
여: 네, 안 그럴게요. 그밖에 제가 또 무엇을 할 수 있을까요?
남: 이 처방전을 약국으로 들고 가세요. 카터는 다음 3일 동안 하루에 알약 2개를 먹어야 합니다.
여: 감사합니다!

04 ③

여: 지금 뭘 하고 있어요, 여보?
남: 이건 우리 전원주택 설계도예요.
여: 나는 이 큰 직사각형 창문이 마음에 들어요. 이건 많은 빛이 들어오게 할 거예요.
남: 정문에서 집까지 연결하는 계단에 대해서는 어떻게 생각해요?
여: 멋져요.
남: 계단 왼쪽에 있는 정사각형 탁자도 괜찮아 보여요?
여: 네, 괜찮아 보여요.
남: 좋아요. 그 옆에 있는 나무가 그것을 햇빛으로부터 보호해줄 거라고 생각했어요.
여: 똑똑한 생각이었네요. 계단 오른쪽에 있는 건 농구 링이에요?
남: 그래요. 당신은 내가 얼마나 농구하는 걸 좋아하는지 알잖아요.
여: 네, 알아요. 이건 살기에 매우 멋진 집이 될 것 같아요!

05 ③

[휴대전화벨이 울린다.]
남: 여보세요, Anne. 오늘 어떠니?
여: 좋아, Hank. 나는 그냥 쉬고 있어. 어제 한라산 등산은 힘들었어.
남: 나도 피곤해. 하지만 재미있지 않았니?
여: 당연하지. 정상에서 보는 경치는 정말 그럴 만한 가치가 있었어.
남: 그래. 우리는 제주도를 거의 전부 볼 수 있었어.
여: 우리 조만간 또 다른 여행을 계획해야겠어.
남: 나도 동의해. 그런데, 나는 좋은 사진을 많이 찍었어.
여: 잘했어! 나에게 사진 몇 장을 보내줄 수 있어?
남: 물론이야. 그런데 아직 사진을 아무것도 인화하지 않았어.
여: 그럼 이메일로 사진을 보내주는 게 어때?
남: 좋아. 내가 지금 빨래를 하고 있어서, 끝나면 바로 보내줄게.
여: 고마워!

06 ⑤

[휴대전화벨이 울린다.]
남: 여보세요?
여: 안녕, Carl. 내가 회의에 조금 늦을 거 같아.
남: 무슨 일이야? 아프니?
여: 아니, 나는 괜찮아.
남: 넌 자명종을 맞춰 놓는 것을 잊어버렸니?
여: 음, 난 일찍 일어나서 30분 전에 집을 나왔어.
남: 그럼 뭐가 문제야?
여: 음, 내 발표 자료가 모두 USB 메모리 스틱에 있는데 그걸 가지고 나오는 것을 잊어버렸어.
남: 아, 너는 그게 꼭 필요하잖아. 지금은 그걸 가지고 있니?
여: 응. 내가 교통 체증에 갇히지 않는 한, 약 30분쯤 후에 회의에 도착할 거야.
남: 알았어. 모든 사람에게 우리가 회의를 약간 늦게 시작할 거라고 알릴게.

07 ③

여: 안녕하세요. 무엇을 도와드릴까요?
남: 네. 오늘 아침 일찍 여기 왔었어요.
여: 기억합니다. 뮤지컬 티켓을 4장 구입하셨어요.
남: 맞아요. 각각 20달러였어요. 그런데 제가 초과 지불한 것 같아요.
여: 아, 정말요?
남: 전 몇 가지 할인을 받아야 했어요. 티켓 한 장은 아버지를 위한 건데, 아버지는 65세가 넘으세요.
여: 그렇다면, 그분은 티켓에 20퍼센트의 고령자 할인을 받습니다.
남: 좋네요. 또한, 이 공연은 제 여동생의 생일에 해요.
여: 그러면, 생일에 사는 티켓은 반값입니다.
남: 완벽해요. 여기 그들의 신분증이 있어요.
여: 알겠습니다. *[잠시 후]* 그리고 여기 환불금입니다.
남: 도와주셔서 감사합니다. 정말 고맙게 생각해요.

문제풀이

티켓 한 장은 20달러인데, 남자의 아버지는 고령자 할인으로 20퍼센트를 돌려받고, 여동생은 생일 티켓 할인으로 반값을 받을 것이므로 남자가 환불받을 금액은 총 14달러(= ($20×0.2)+$10)이다.

08 ③

여: 와, Greg. 지난 학기 이후 네 중국어 어휘가 정말 늘었어.
남: 고마워, Sally. 난 여름 방학 동안 많이 공부했어.
여: 어떻게 공부했어? 넌 비결이 있는 게 틀림없어.
남: 음, 나는 스마트폰에 WordZone이라는 정말 유용한 애플리케이션을 다운로드했어.
여: 아, 난 그것에 대해 들어봤어. 그건 Lingua Limitless에서 개발된 거 아냐?
남: 맞아. 그 회사의 모든 애플리케이션은 중국어 단어를 암기하는 데 매우 좋아.
여: 아마 나도 다운받아야 할 것 같아. 얼마야?
남: 10달러야.
여: 아, 정말? 애플리케이션치고는 약간 비싼데.
남: 하지만 전적으로 그럴만한 가치가 있어. 그리고 모든 리뷰가 긍정적이야!
여: 와. 그러면 나도 시도해봐야겠어.

09 ⑤

남: 안녕하세요, 학생 여러분! 여러분이 아마도 알고 있듯이, 전 세계 수백만 명의 사람들이 매일 음식이 거의 없이 지내고 있습니다. 그래서 세계 기아에 대한 의식을 높이기 위해, 학생회는 특별한 행사를 계획 중입니다. 그것은 4월 10일에 학교 강당에서 개최될 것입니다. 총 24시간 동안, 참가자들은 아무것도 먹지 않을 것입니다. 그들은 단지 물만 마시도록 허락됩니다. 게다가, 우리는 전 세계적인 기아에 대한 영화를 보여 줄 것입니다. 소액인 5달러 참가 비용이 있는데, 이 돈은 굶주리는 아이들에게 기부될 것입니다. 관심이 있는 학생은 행사 당일 강당 밖에서 등록해야 합니다.

10 ③

남: 안녕, Alice. 이번 주말에 너희 부모님이 방문하실 거라고 들었어.
여: 맞아. 우리가 갈 좋은 식당을 추천해 줄 수 있어?
남: 물론이야. 난 이 주위에 좋은 곳을 많이 알고 있어.
여: 좋아. 난 채식주의자라는 것만 기억해 줘.
남: 알았어. 교외로 운전할 수 있니?
여: 아니, 나는 도시에 있고 싶어. 저녁을 먹은 후에, 우리는 명소를 구경하러 시내로 갈 거야.
남: 알겠어. 생각해 둔 요리 종류가 있니?
여: 아니. 그런데 우리 부모님은 중국 음식을 좋아하지 않으셔.
남: 알겠어. 그러면 난 굉장한 추천지가 있어.
여: 좋아! 어디야? 우리는 거기로 갈게.

11 ⑤

[휴대전화벨이 울린다.]
남: 여보세요, Linda. 영화관에 도착했어?
여: 응. 방금 여기에 왔어. 우리 오후 6시에 만나는 거지, 그렇지?
남: 음, 나는 약 20분 정도 늦을 거야.
여: 괜찮아. 우리는 영화 시작 전까지 충분한 시간이 있어.

문제풀이

① 그러면 극장이 어디 있는지 알려줄래?
② 그렇다면, 내가 도착하자마자 네게 전화할게.
③ 서두를 필요 없어. 나도 늦을 거야.
④ 오후 6시에 만나자. 로비에서 너를 기다릴게.

12 ②

여: 우리 많이 걸었는데, 아직도 지하철역이 보이지 않아.
남: 나는 약국을 지나서 바로 있을 거라고 생각했어.
여: 걱정이 되네. 우리가 길을 잘못 든 거면 어떡하지?
남: 우린 누군가에게 길을 물어보는 게 낫겠어.

문제풀이

① 우리 약국에 들르는 게 어때?
③ 나는 지하철을 타는 것보다 버스를 타는 걸 선호해.
④ 네가 약을 좀 먹으면, 나아질 거야.
⑤ 걱정하지 마. 내가 너를 제시간에 버스 정류장으로 데려다줄게.

13 ⑤

여: 그건 멋진 카메라구나. 어디서 그걸 샀니?
남: 고마워. 나는 그것을 지난주 시내에 있는 전자 제품 매장에서 샀어.
여: 난 그 모델을 전에 본 적이 없어. 신제품이니?
남: 응, 그건 신제품이야. 그리고 이게 얼마인지 너는 믿지 못할 거야.
여: 맞춰 볼게… 500달러?
남: 음, 정가는 550달러였어. 하지만 난 300달러만 지불했어.
여: 정말 좋다! 세일 중이었니?
남: 아니. 하지만 이건 전시용 모델이었어.
여: 카메라는 잘 작동하니?
남: 응, 이건 완벽하게 작동해. 사람들은 보통 전시용 상품을 사는 것을 원하지 않아서, 가게에서 그것의 가격을 낮춰.
여: 음, 너 정말 싸게 산 것 같아.
남: 응, 그리고 나는 다른 사람들이 이걸 만졌는지 아닌지는 신경 쓰지 않아.

문제풀이

① 나도 동의하지만, 너는 할인을 요청해야 해.
② 대부분의 가게는 예전 모델의 가격을 낮춰.
③ 너는 항상 온라인으로 가격을 비교해야 할 것 같아.
④ 너는 먼저 사용해 보지 않고 카메라를 사면 안 돼.

14 ⑤

여: 실례합니다, Stewart 선생님. 여기 제 과제물이 있습니다.
남: 음, Jenny, 이 과제물은 지난주까지였어.
여: 죄송해요, 하지만 제가 지난주에 정말 아팠거든요.
남: 아, 정말? 무슨 문제가 있었니?
여: 전 식중독에 걸렸었어요. 전 응급실에 가야 했고 며칠간 입원해야 했어요.
남: 아 이런. 그건 몰랐구나.
여: 그래서 전 제 과제물을 제시간에 제출하지 못했어요.
남: 그렇다면, 네 과제물을 받아 주마.
여: 정말 감사합니다, Stewart 선생님!
남: 하지만 네가 아팠다는 걸 증명할 의사의 진단서를 가지고 와야 해.
여: 내일 병원에 가서 선생님께 그것을 가져다 드릴게요.

문제풀이

① 제가 끝내는 대로 과제물을 드릴게요.
② 왜요? 저는 선생님이 감점을 하면 안 된다고 생각해요.
③ 선생님이 옳아요. 저는 지난주에 그걸 제출해야 했어요.
④ 너무 많이 걱정하지 마세요. 지금은 훨씬 더 나아졌어요.

15 ⑤

여: Vanessa는 주말에 그녀의 고향을 방문할 것이다. 그녀는 몇 달간 그녀의 가족을 보지 못했기 때문에 매우 신이 나 있다. 출발하는 날, 그녀는 택시를 타고 기사에게 기차역으로 데려다 달라고 말한다. 갑자기 그녀는 여동생의 생일이 이번 주말이라는 것을 깨닫는다. 그러나 그녀는 여동생의 선물을 사는 것을 잊어버렸다. 하지만 운이 좋게도, 기차역으로 가는 길에 쇼핑몰이 있고, 그녀는 조금의 여유 시간이 있다. 그녀는 쇼핑몰에서 여동생에게 선물을 사 줄 수 있다고 생각한다. 이런 상황에서, Vanessa가 택시 기사에게 할 말로 가장 적절한 것은 무엇인가?
Vanessa: 대신에 저를 쇼핑몰에 내려주시겠어요?

문제풀이

① 저를 제 아파트로 다시 데려다주시겠어요?
② 역에 도착하려면 얼마나 걸리나요?
③ 당신의 차에 제가 선물을 놔두고 왔는지 확인해주시겠어요?
④ 가능한 한 빨리 기차역에 가주세요.

16 ② 17 ④

남: 안녕하세요, 임신부님들! 저는 여러분 모두 아기가 튼튼하고 건강하게 자라길 바라는 걸 압니다. 여기 제 최고의 팁이 있습니다. 먼저 저는 모유를 먹이는 것을 정말 추천합니다. 모유는 아기들에게 최고의 음식입니다. 모유에는 아기의 면역 체계를 증진하는 다양한 영양소를 포함하고 있습니다. 다음으로, 집을 청결히 하도록 하세요. 아기들은 감염에 저항력이 거의 없고, 더러운 환경은 알레르기를 일으키는 위험을 증가시킵니다. 마지막으로, 피부를 맞대고 접촉하는 것이 아기에게 좋습니다. 캥거루식 돌보기에 대해 들어본 적이 있으신가요? 그것은 간단합니다. 아기를 맨가슴에 안고만 있으세요. 이 방법은 특히 조산아에게 효과적입니다. 캥거루식 돌보기를 통해서, 아기의 심장 박동은 안정되고 호흡이 일정해집니다. 아기는 잠을 더 잘 수 있고 심지어 몸무게도 증가할 수 있습니다. 또한, 아기의 체온이 따뜻하게 유지될 수 있습니다. 저는 이 정보가 도움이 되었기를 바랍니다. 다음에 봅시다!

문제풀이

16 ① 직접적인 신체 접촉의 유형
② 건강한 아기를 키우기 위한 조언
③ 모유 수유하는 올바른 방법
④ 어떻게 아동기의 환경이 지능에 영향을 주는지
⑤ 유아 교육이 매우 중요한 이유

DICTATION Answers

01 When you leave work / make it much easier / have access to
02 I've been stressed out / I have no idea / hang out with our friends
03 He has been sick / have trouble digesting / for the next three days
04 let in plenty of light / to the left of / how much I like
05 I'm just resting / The views from the top / doing my laundry
06 set your alarm clock / have it with you / let everyone know
07 earlier this morning / I may have overpaid / are half price
08 has really improved / memorizing Chinese words / It's totally worth it
09 millions of people / be allowed to drink water / will be donated to
10 for us to go to / drive to the suburbs / had in mind
11 arrived at the movie theater
12 I'm getting worried
13 how much it costs / was the display model / you got a great deal
14 stay at the hospital / turn in my essay / get a note from your doctor
15 visit her hometown / take her to the train station / on the way to
16-17 grow up strong and healthy / have little resistance to / put on weight

30 영어듣기 모의고사

본문 ▲ p.209

01 ①	02 ①	03 ②	04 ④	05 ⑤	06 ⑤
07 ②	08 ②	09 ④	10 ④	11 ①	12 ⑤
13 ⑤	14 ③	15 ⑤	16 ⑤	17 ①	

01 ①

여: 주목해주세요, 모든 탑승객 여러분. 여러분이 아셔야 할 항공편 변경 사항이 있습니다. 태풍 때문에, 샌디에이고행 West 항공사 90편 비행기가 2시간 지연될 예정입니다. 저희는 현재 그 비행기가 대략 저녁 8시 30분에 출발할 것이라고 예상합니다. 이는 불가피한데, 강풍과 폭우가 얼마간 지속될 예정이기 때문입니다. 그러나 폭풍우는 곧 갤 것이고, 더 이상의 지연은 없을 것으로 예상됩니다. 불편함에 대해 보상하기 위해서, 90편 비행기에 탑승하려고 기다리고 계신 탑승객들은 10달러짜리 식사 쿠폰을 받으실 것입니다. 그것은 공항의 어떤 식당에서도 이용될 수 있습니다. 여러분의 협조에 감사드립니다.

02 ①

남: 안녕, Judy. 너의 새집은 어때?
여: 정말 좋아. 그것은 최근에 지어져서 멋지고 깨끗해. 하지만 한 가지 문제가 있어.
남: 정말? 뭔데?
여: 그 집이 나를 아프게 하고 있어. 집에 있으면 머리가 아프고 기침을 많이 해. 하지만 이유를 모르겠어.
남: 그건 아마도 새집 증후군일 거야.
여: 아, 그게 뭐야?
남: 새 건물에 있는 화학 물질이 때때로 너를 아프게 만드는 거야.
여: 정말? 내가 할 수 있는 게 있을까?
남: 응. 신선한 공기가 더 많이 들어올 수 있도록 그저 창문을 이따금 열어 둬. 실내용 화초를 기르는 것도 공기가 깨끗해지게 도와줄 거야.
여: 와, 너는 이것에 대해서 많이 아는구나! 네 제안대로 해 볼게. 고마워!

03 ②

여: 안녕하세요, 저를 도와주시겠어요?
남: 네, 그런데 먼저 진정하세요. 다치셨나요?
여: 아니, 아니요. 저는 괜찮아요.
남: 알겠습니다. 문제가 뭔가요?
여: 지하철역으로 걸어가고 있었는데, 갑자기 어떤 남자가 저에게 달려와서 가방을 훔쳐 갔어요!
남: 알겠습니다. 그가 어떻게 생겼는지 보셨나요?
여: 아니요, 그는 너무 빨리 달아났어요. 저는 그가 검정 모자를 쓰고 청바지를 입고 있었다는 것만 기억나요.
남: 그렇군요. 가방에 값비싼 것들이 있었나요?
여: 네. 돈하고 휴대전화요.
남: 알겠습니다. 그 일이 발생한 장소로 다시 가봅시다. 우리는 그곳에 보안 카메라가 있었는지 확인할 수 있어요.
여: 정말 고맙습니다.

04 ④

여: 우리 마침내 놀이공원에 왔어!
남: 여기 지도가 있어. 보고 어디로 갈지 결정하자.
여: 음, 나는 입구의 오른편에 있는 꽃밭을 정말 보고 싶어.
남: 알았어. 롤러코스터가 정원 바로 뒤에 있어.
여: 우선 정원에 갔다가 그다음에 롤러코스터를 타자.
남: 그 후에 입구 왼편에 있는 카페에 가자.
여: 그래, 우린 거기서 음료수를 마시고 쉴 수 있어.
남: 알겠어. 롤러코스터 맞은 편에 있는 아이스 링크에 가는 건 어때?
여: 좋아. 그 후에, 우리는 공원 중앙에 있는 분수대에 들러서 함께 사진을 찍을 수 있어.
남: 좋은 것 같아. 그렇게 하자!

05 ⑤

남: 내 휴대전화가 젖어서 작동이 안 돼요.
여: 당신은 고객 서비스 센터에 가야 해요. 거기에서 수리를 받을 수 있을 거예요.
남: 하지만 그곳은 너무 멀어요. 솔직히, 새것을 사는 게 나을 거 같아요.
여: 이해가 되네요. 당신 전화는 아주 오래됐어요. 내일 새 것을 살 거예요?
남: 그러고 싶지만, 회의가 6시까지 끝나지 않을 거예요.
여: 매장은 7시에 문을 닫아요. 시간이 충분하지 않아요?
남: 음, 퇴근 후 누군가가 농구 연습을 한 Timmy를 태우러 가야 해요. 나를 위해서 당신이 그걸 해줄 수 있겠어요?
여: 물론이죠, 그렇게 할게요.
남: 정말요? 고마워요. 그러면 나는 집에 가는 길에 저녁으로 먹을 걸 사 갈게요.
여: 완벽하네요.

06 ⑤

[휴대전화벨이 울린다.]
여: 여보세요, 아빠.
남: 안녕, Amy. 오는 중이니?
여: 네. 실은, 지금 막 기차에 탔어요. 전 약간 늦을 거 같아요.
남: 무슨 일 있었어? 늦게 일어났니?
여: 아니요, 전 제시간에 일어났어요.
남: 아. 그러면 기차역까지 가는 길에 차가 많이 막혔니?
여: 아니요. 제가 기차표를 잘못 읽었어요. 전 기차가 10시 30분에 출발한다고 생각했는데, 실제로는 10시에 출발했어요.
남: 그랬구나.
여: 제가 10시 10분에 도착했었는데, 기차는 이미 떠났었어요. 그래서 11시 기차를 기다려야 했어요.
남: 괜찮아. 네가 도착할 때 우리가 역으로 태우러 갈게.
여: 고마워요, 아빠. 곧 봐요.

07 ②

여: 안녕하세요, 전 학교 댄스파티를 위한 드레스를 사고 싶어요.
남: 어느 학교에 다니세요?
여: Hatfield 고등학교요.
남: 좋네요! 이번 달 동안, Hatfield 학생은 어떤 구매품이든 10달러 할인을 받으십니다.
여: 정말요? 이 사진의 빨간 드레스 같은 것이 있나요?
남: 네. 이것은 어떠세요? 그것은 200달러입니다.
여: 입어볼게요. *[잠시 후]* 너무 크네요. 더 작은 사이즈가 있나요?
남: 애석하게도 없네요. 하지만 추가로 30달러를 내면 사이즈를 줄여 드릴 수 있어요.
여: 좋아요. 저는 이 30퍼센트 할인 쿠폰도 있어요.
남: 만약 그 쿠폰을 사용하면, 10달러 할인을 받지 못합니다. 그리고 그것을 수선비에도 사용할 수 없어요.
여: 알겠습니다. 그냥 쿠폰을 쓸게요.

문제풀이

여자는 200달러짜리 드레스에 30퍼센트 할인을 받고, 수선비로 30달러를 추가로 지불해야 하므로, 여자가 지불할 금액은 총 170달러(= (\$200×0.7)+\$30)이다.

08 ②

남: 우리가 내일 고등학교를 졸업한다는 게 믿어지니?
여: 아니! 바로 어제 우리가 신입생이었던 것 같아!
남: 시간이 쏜살같아. 졸업식은 학교 강당에서 개최되는 거지, 맞지?
여: 응. 거기에 정말 큰 무대가 있잖아.
남: 누가 연설을 하니?
여: 교장 선생님과 성적이 가장 좋은 두 명의 학생이 연설을 할 거라고 들었어.
남: 멋지다. 난 학교 밴드도 공연을 할 거라고 들었어.
여: 맞아. 그리고 공연 후에 우리는 졸업장을 받을 거야.
남: 좋다! 우리는 교복을 입어야 하니?
여: 응. 우리 선생님이 입어야 한다고 말씀하셨어.
남: 그게 우리가 교복을 입는 마지막 순간이 되겠네!

09 ④

남: 안녕하세요, 학생 여러분. 여러분에게 흥미진진한 발표가 있습니다! 연례 자연 사진 콘테스트가 다음 주에 개최될 것입니다. 참가하기 위해서, 여러분이 선택한 두 장의 사진만 보내 주세요. 주제가 자연이기 때문에, 호수, 산, 나무, 또는 동물과 같은 것이 사진에 있어야 합니다. Hearst 대학 웹사이트에 가서 배너를 클릭하세요. 이름과 학번을 입력하고 사진을 업로드하세요. 사진은 어떤 종류의 이미지 파일로도 저장될 수 있습니다. 마감일은 5월 21일입니다. 우리는 1등, 2등, 그리고 3등 수상자를 선정할 것입니다. 그들은 상금을 받을 것입니다. 행운을 빕니다!

10 ④

남: 오늘 무엇을 도와드릴까요?
여: 전 새 구두를 찾고 있습니다. 단순하지만 굽이 있는 것이 필요해요.
남: 알겠습니다. 이런 것들은 어떠세요? 이것들은 굽이 7센티미터입니다.
여: 저한테 너무 높아요. 전 6센티미터보다 높은 굽은 원하지 않아요.
남: 알겠습니다. 그럼 이것들은 어떠신가요? 발끝이 트인 것과 발끝이 막힌 것 중 어떤 것을 선호하세요?
여: 사실, 저는 발끝이 트인 구두가 좋아요.
남: 알겠습니다. 저희는 검은색, 빨간색, 그리고 갈색 구두가 있어요.
여: 음, 저는 검은색과 갈색이 좋지만, 구두에 60달러 이상은 지불할 수 없습니다.
남: 그렇다면, 이 구두가 최고의 선택일 것 같네요.
여: 저도 동의해요. 이걸 사겠습니다.

11 ①

남: 와, Sarah. 너 정말 날씬해 보인다. 비결이 뭐야?
여: 최근에 학교 체육관에서 운동을 많이 해왔어.
남: 정말? 체육관에서 얼마나 자주 운동하니?
여: <u>나는 매일 운동을 하려고 노력하고 있어.</u>

문제풀이

② 아니, 나는 보통 버스를 타고 거기에 가.
③ 나는 주로 체육관에서 달리거나 수영을 해.
④ 나는 살을 좀 빼려고 다이어트를 하고 있어.
⑤ 내일 같이 운동하는 게 어떠니?

12 ⑤

여: 엄마 생신이 다음 주 금요일이지 않아?
남: 응, 맞아. 난 이미 엄마를 위한 선물을 샀어.
여: 정말? 난 엄마한테 새 스카프를 사 드릴까 생각 중이야. 어떻게 생각해?
남: <u>좋아. 엄마가 지난번에 스카프가 필요하다고 말씀하셨어.</u>

문제풀이

① 응, 그 스카프는 너한테 정말 잘 어울려.
② 나도 엄마한테 드릴 선물을 구입하지 않았어.
③ 어쨌든 너는 파티에 일찍 와야 해.
④ 나도 그것이 좋아. 어떻게 고맙다고 해야 할지 모르겠다.

13 ⑤

남: 무슨 일이니? 넌 별로 좋아 보이지 않는구나.
여: 전 그냥 어제 본 제 과학 시험이 걱정돼요. 실수를 많이 한 거 같아요.
남: 너는 매우 열심히 공부했으니 나는 네가 잘했을 거라고 확신해.
여: 하지만 그것은 너무 어려웠어요. 전체 시험에서 쉬운 문제가 하나도 없었어요.
남: 음, 모든 반 친구들이 같은 상황에 있었잖아. 그러니 그것에 대해 너무 걱정하지 마.
여: 하지만 전 제 성적이 걱정돼요. 어제 영어 시험도 까다로웠어요.
남: 넌 아마 그 시험도 잘 봤을 거야. 어쨌든, 지나치게 걱정하는 것은 아무것도 도움이 되지 않아.
여: 걱정할 게 너무 많을 때는 어떻게 해야 할지 모르겠어요!
남: <u>네가 할 수 있는 모든 것은 기다리고 어떤 일이 일어날지 보는 거야.</u>

문제풀이

① 너는 시험 전에 휴식을 좀 취해야 해.

② 네가 나를 더 이상 실망시키지 않기를 바란다.
③ 다음번에 더 열심히 공부하겠다고 내게 약속해 줘.
④ 그건 사실이 아냐. 너는 실수를 거의 하지 않았어.

14 ③

남: 무엇을 읽고 있니, Rachael?
여: 그것은 내가 후원하고 있는 소녀가 나에게 보낸 편지야.
남: 후원? 네가 어려운 아이를 돕고 있다는 말이니?
여: 응. 나는 다른 나라에 있는 아이들을 돕는 단체에 돈을 좀 내고 있어.
남: 넌 정말 너그럽구나.
여: 나는 용돈을 조금씩 모아서 매달 20달러씩 보내. 이것 봐, 이건 내가 후원하는 여자아이의 사진이야.
남: 매우 귀여워 보이네. 이 아이는 어디에 살아?
여: 그 애는 에티오피아에 살아. 그 애가 내게 이 그림들도 보내줬어.
남: 좋다. 누군가의 삶이 향상되도록 돕는 건 틀림없이 네 기분을 좋게 만들 거야.
여: 정말 그래. 그게 내가 그 애를 돕고 있는 이유야.

문제풀이
① 아니, 별로. 나는 돈이 별로 없어.
② 괜찮아. 나는 지금 도움이 필요하지 않아.
④ 너는 그녀처럼 나에게 편지를 보내야 했어.
⑤ 나는 내 용돈의 대부분을 책을 사는 데 써.

15 ⑤

여: Brian은 그의 여동생과 좋은 식당에서 저녁을 먹고 있다. 그들은 나눠 먹을 몇 개의 맛있는 음식을 주문했고, 그 중 하나에는 굴이 들어 있다. 음식이 왔을 때, Brian은 굴 중 하나를 먹어 본다. 그것은 약간 맛이 이상해서 그는 다른 것을 집어 들어 냄새를 맡는다. 그것은 안 좋은 냄새가 난다. Brian은 굴이 상했다고 의심한다. 그는 식중독에 걸리는 것이 두려워서 웨이터를 부르기로 한다. 그는 웨이터에게 이 문제에 관해 알리고 요리를 새것으로 교환하기를 원한다. 이런 상황에서, Brian이 웨이터에게 할 말로 가장 적절한 것은 무엇인가?
Brian : 이 요리 맛이 이상합니다. 새것을 받을 수 있을까요?

문제풀이
① 당신이 추천하는 요리가 있나요?
② 전 지난주에 식중독으로 고생했습니다.
③ 전 굴에 알레르기가 있어서 이걸 먹을 수 없습니다.
④ 제게 이 요리의 조리법을 주시겠어요?

16 ⑤ 17 ①

남: 안녕하세요, 여러분. 저는 여러분과 오렌지에 관한 유용한 정보를 나누기 위해서 이 자리에 왔습니다. 오렌지는 세계에서 가장 인기 있는 과일 중 하나인데, 왜 그런지는 알기 쉽습니다. 오렌지는 맛있고 영양가가 높습니다. 하지만 대부분의 사람들이 오렌지의 가장 훌륭한 부분 중 하나인 껍질을 자주 버린다는 것을 깨닫지 못합니다. 만약 오렌지 껍질을 건조시켜서 태우면, 여러분은 모기를 쫓아 버릴 수 있습니다. 여러분은 또한 오렌지 껍질을 갈아서 목욕물에 그 가루를 첨가할 수 있습니다. 이것은 여러분의 피부가 특별히 깨끗하게 만들어줄 것입니다. 혹은, 여러분은 양치하기 전에 껍질 안쪽으로 치아를 문질러서 이를 더 하얗게 만들 수 있습니다. 마지막으로, 오렌지 껍질 차를 마시고 간 오렌지 껍질을 뿌린 음식을 먹는 것은 여러분의 콜레스테롤을 낮춰줍니다. 오렌지 껍질을 버리는 건 낭비처럼 보이지 않나요?

문제풀이
16 ① 사람들이 오렌지 껍질을 먹도록 장려하려고
② 오렌지 껍질을 쉽게 까는 방법에 대해 조언하려고
③ 건강을 위해 더 많은 오렌지를 먹도록 제안하려고
④ 오렌지를 신선하게 보관하는 방법을 소개하려고
⑤ 사람들에게 오렌지 껍질의 쓰임새를 알리려고

DICTATION Answers

01 be delayed two hours / make up for the inconvenience / for your cooperation
02 making me sick / from time to time / try your suggestions
03 calm down / stole my bag / the place where it happened
04 decide where to go / on the left side / in the middle of
05 get it repaired / won't end until six / on my way home
06 got on the train / misread my train ticket / pick you up
07 During this month / I'll try it on / reduce the size
08 graduating from high school / will be held at / is going to perform
09 two photos of your choice / click on the banner / as any type of
10 something simple but with heels / Which style do you prefer / pay more than
11 How often do you exercise
12 thinking of getting her
13 don't look so good / a single easy question / was also tricky
14 helping a child in need / generous of you / make you feel good
15 one of which has / the oysters went bad / exchange the dish
16-17 share some useful information / one of the best parts / feel extra clean

31 영어듣기 모의고사

본문 ☁ p.216

01 ①	02 ⑤	03 ②	04 ⑤	05 ③	06 ④
07 ④	08 ⑤	09 ④	10 ②	11 ①	12 ①
13 ①	14 ④	15 ④	16 ②	17 ⑤	

01 ①

여: 산에서 시간을 보내는 것을 좋아하세요? 편안하게 휴식을 취할 수 있는 장소를 찾고 있나요? 그렇다면 Cloudview 호텔에 예약하세요. Green Mountains에 위치해 있어서, 저희 호텔에는 바로 정문 밖에 여러 개의 하이킹 코스가 있습니다. 객실은 모두 편안한 침대와 훌륭한 경치를 갖고 있습니다. 저희는 무료 무선 인터넷과 24시간 룸 서비스를 제공합니다. 여러분은 또한 저희 식당에서 멋진 식사를 즐기실 수 있는데, 이곳은 일류 주방장에 의해 준비되는 신선한 현지 음식을 제공합니다. 여러분의 요구를 충족시키는 특별 패키지가 있는지 살펴보기 위해 저희 웹사이트를 확인해보세요. 저희 호텔이 여러분의 제2의 고향이 될 수 있기를 바랍니다.

02 ⑤

남: Anna, 우리 저 새로 생긴 스테이크 전문 식당에서 저녁을 먹는 게 어때?
여: 아냐, 괜찮아. 솔직히 말해서, 요즘 고기를 피하려고 노력 중이야.
남: 정말? 동물 학대에 대해서 걱정하는 거니?
여: 아니, 그런 게 아니야. 고기에 많은 호르몬이 있다고 들었어.
남: 호르몬? 무슨 말이야?
여: 일부 농부들이 동물을 더 빠르게 성장시키기 위해서 호르몬을 사용해.
남: 아, 알았다. 만약 우리가 그 고기를 먹으면, 그 호르몬들이 체내에 들어올 수 있겠다, 그렇지?
여: 응. 그리고 그것들은 시간이 흐르면서 해로워질 수 있어.
남: 하지만 적은 양은 위험하지 않잖아, 그렇지?
여: 아무도 확실히 몰라. 그런데 난 그런 위험을 감수하고 싶지 않아.
남: 어떤 말인지 알겠어.

03 ②

[휴대전화벨이 울린다.]
남: 여보세요?
여: 안녕하세요, Alicia Smith입니다. 오늘 아침에 당신의 이메일을 받았어요.
남: 아, 네. 질문이 있으십니까?
여: 실은, 수정을 요청하고 싶네요. 화장실이 너무 작은 것 같아요.
남: 알겠습니다. 그 부분을 좀 수정해 드리겠습니다.
여: 고맙습니다. 직원 수를 고려하면, 화장실은 반드시 더 클 필요가 있어요.
남: 문제없습니다. 그밖에 제가 바꿨으면 하는 게 있나요?
여: 그게 전부예요. 12월 20일까지 보수 작업을 끝낼 수 있을 거라 생각하세요?
남: 음, 확실하지 않습니다. 우선, 새 도면을 그려야 할 거예요.
여: 알겠습니다. 월요일까지 새 도면을 보여주시겠어요?
남: 물론이죠, 그렇게 하겠습니다.

04 ⑤

남: 여보, 뒤뜰 정리를 다 했어요.
여: 벌써요? 한번 봐요. *[잠시 후]* 와! 멋져요.
남: 난 중앙에 커다란 파라솔이 있는 직사각형 탁자를 사다 놨어요. 마음에 들어요?
여: 네. 그것은 앉아서 휴식을 취하기에 완벽할 거예요.
남: 나도 그렇게 생각해요. 그리고 아이들이 탁자 뒤의 미끄럼틀을 좋아할 거 같지 않아요?
여: 당연하지요. 그 애들은 미끄럼틀 옆의 벤치 그네도 좋아할 거예요.
남: 또, 난 탁자 오른쪽에 둥근 연못도 파고 그 안에 물고기 몇 마리를 넣었어요.
여: 좋은 생각이에요. 연못 오른쪽에 있는 나무가 좋아 보여요. 그것 주위의 저 꽃들도 새것이에요?
남: 네, 전 오늘 오후에 심었어요.
여: 아름답네요.

05 ③

[휴대전화벨이 울린다.]
여: 여보세요?
남: 안녕하세요. 저는 Express Delivery Services의 Steve Black입니다. Judy Kim 씨입니까?
여: 네. 뉴욕에서 온 제 소포가 벌써 도착했나요?
남: 네, 그렇습니다. 지금 고객님 집 앞에 있는데, 아무도 문을 열어 주지 않네요.
여: 아! 저는 지금 직장에 있어요. 옆집 이웃에게 그것을 받아 달라고 부탁해주시겠어요?
남: 제가 이미 해봤는데, 그곳에도 아무도 없습니다.
여: 알겠습니다.
남: 다른 유일한 선택 사항은 내일 배달하는 것입니다.
여: 아, 그런데 전 정말 오늘 밤에 그 소포가 필요해요.
남: 가까운 곳에 미용실이 있습니다. 전 그곳에 소포를 둘 수 있습니다.
여: 알겠습니다, 그것이 최선일 것 같네요. 전 그 주인을 알아요.

06 ④

남: Patricia, 그만 끝내자. 거의 7시야.
여: 벌써? 난 이렇게 늦었는지도 몰랐어.
남: 네가 월별 매출 보고서를 쓰고 있기 때문이니?
여: 응, 하지만 방금 끝냈어.
남: 좋다. 그나저나, 너 오늘 Julie와 나와 함께 저녁을 먹을래?
여: 그러고 싶지만, 난 남편하고 저녁을 먹기로 되어 있어.
남: 알았어. 그가 위장병으로 아팠다고 하지 않았니?
여: 응, 그런데 지금은 완전히 나았어. 그래서 내가 그에게 오늘 시내에서 맛있는 저녁을 사줄 거야.
남: 좋겠네. 남편과 즐거운 시간 보내.

여: 고마워. Julie와 저녁 맛있게 먹어!

07 ④

[휴대전화벨이 울린다.]

여: 안녕, 여보.

남: 안녕. 난 집에 가는 길에 슈퍼마켓에 잠시 들렀어요. 집들이에서 디저트로 대접할 과일이 좀 필요하지 않아요?

여: 맞아요! 하마터면 잊을 뻔했어요! 거기 있는 동안 좀 구입해줄래요?

남: 그래요. 무엇을 살까요?

여: 오렌지하고 사과가 어떨까요?

남: 좋은 생각이에요. 각각 2달러인데, 지금 오렌지는 50퍼센트 할인을 해요.

여: 좋아요! 좋은 가격이네요.

남: 우리는 파티에 8명을 초대했으니, 오렌지 5개와 사과 5개면 충분할 거예요.

여: 나도 그렇게 생각하지만, 오렌지 5개를 추가로 더 구입해줘요. 아이들도 오렌지를 좋아해요.

남: 좋은 생각이에요. 세일을 하는 동안에 구입하면 더 좋겠네요.

문제풀이

남자는 오렌지 10개와 사과 5개를 사야 하는데, 개당 2달러이나 오렌지는 50퍼센트 할인되므로 남자가 지불해야 할 금액은 총 20달러(=($2×10×0.5)+($2×5))이다.

08 ⑤

남: Olivia, Smithtown 공원에서 여는 대회에 대해 들어봤어?

여: 아니, 못 들어봤어. 뭐에 관한 거야?

남: 그들은 사람들이 공원에 관해 비디오를 제작하기를 원해. 수상한 비디오는 공원의 광고로 사용될 거야.

여: 멋있다! 누구나 참여할 수 있어?

남: 아니, 오직 Smithtown에 사는 사람들만 지원할 수 있어.

여: 우리 둘 다 Smithtown에 사니 잘됐다.

남: 맞아. 하지만 마감일이 지구의 날인데, 그날은 4월 22일이야. 5일 후야!

여: 우리는 그때까지는 끝낼 수 있어. 상이 뭐야?

남: 상위 세 개의 동영상은 지역 TV에 방영될 거야. 대상 수상자는 2,000달러를 받을 거야.

여: 그러면 우리는 둘 다 1,000달러를 받을 수 있겠다! 당장 작업을 시작하자!

09 ④

남: 신사 숙녀 여러분, 저는 새 자전거 전용 도로에 대한 시 의회의 계획을 발표하려고 합니다. 자전거를 타는 사람들에게 도로가 더 안전하도록 하기 위해 우리는 이 새 도로를 건설할 것입니다. 공사는 다음 달에 시작될 것입니다. 새로운 4개의 도로가 생길 것이므로, 시 전역의 사람들이 이 도로를 이용할 수 있을 것입니다. 또한, 시청과 기념 공원 밖에 자전거 보관대도 설치될 것입니다. 그러므로, 시로 오는 누구에게나 자전거 주차가 편리해질 것입니다. 이 도로를 건설하는 비용은 시 예산에서 나올 것이어서, 도로를 건설하기 위해 세금을 올릴 필요가 없을 것입니다. 공사는 올여름 초까지 끝날 것입니다.

10 ②

남: 난 중국어를 배우고 싶어서 온라인 강의를 듣기로 결정했어.

여: 잘했어. 어떤 강의를 수강할 거니?

남: 음, 전에 중국어를 배워 본 적이 없어서 중급 수업은 너무 어려울 것 같아.

여: 그렇구나. 예산은 어떻게 되니?

남: 난 80달러 이상은 쓸 수가 없어.

여: 네 가격대 내에 몇 개의 수업이 있네. 이 수업은 교재를 제공해.

남: 그건 나에게 중요하지 않아.

여: 그렇다면 나는 이 강좌를 추천해. 그것은 더 많은 강의를 제공해.

남: 응. 난 그것을 수강해야겠다.

여: 하지만 이게 다른 것보다 조금 더 비싸.

남: 괜찮아. 나는 여전히 지불할 여력이 돼. 도와줘서 고마워!

11 ①

여: 난 뉴욕 여행을 위해 선글라스가 필요한 거 같아.

남: 맞아. 뉴욕은 연중 이맘때 정말 화창하지.

여: 그래. 난 한 개 살 거야. 내가 고르는 것을 좀 도와줄래?

남: 물론이지. 우리가 갈 수 있는 좋은 상점을 알아.

문제풀이

② 난 네가 여행을 연기하는 게 나을 것 같아.
③ 좋아. 내가 여행을 위해 짐을 싸는 것을 네가 도와주길 원해.
④ 아니, 나는 그게 필요하지 않아. 뉴욕에는 비가 내리고 있어.
⑤ 그래, 내 것을 빌려 가도 돼. 언제든지 우리 집에 들러.

12 ①

남: 우리 여기서 피자를 좀 사는 게 어때?

여: 좋아. 하지만 너무 많은 사람들이 줄을 서 있어! 여기 피자가 그렇게 맛있니?

남: 그들은 버섯 피자를 반값에 팔고 있어.

여: 여기가 이렇게 붐비는 게 당연하네.

문제풀이

② 조심해. 피자가 매우 뜨거워.
③ 음, 그건 별로 인기 있어 보이지 않아.
④ 그건 내가 맛본 피자 중 최고였어.
⑤ 난 30분 동안 줄을 서서 기다리고 있었어.

13 ①

여: 오늘 밤에 영화 보러 가는 게 어때, Jason?

남: 그러고 싶지만, 난 완전히 빈털터리야.

여: 벌써? 그런데 넌 바로 지난주에 용돈을 받았잖아.

남: 맞아. 하지만 며칠 만에 다 써버렸어.

여: 왜 그랬어?

남: 그러려고 한 건 아니었어. 내가 주의를 기울이지 않았던 거 같아. 내가 좋아하는 물건 몇 개를 바로 사 버렸어.

여: 그건 정말 문제가 될 수 있어. 너는 돈에 대해서 좀 더 현명해져야 해.

남: 나도 전적으로 동의해. 하지만 어떻게 해야 하는지를 모르겠어.

여: 책임감을 가지는 건 어렵지 않아.
남: 음, 내가 뭘 해야 할까?
여: 내 생각엔 네가 미리 계획을 해야만 할 것 같아.

문제풀이
② 난 정말 어서 너와 영화를 보고 싶어.
③ 다음 주에 용돈을 더 많이 주세요.
④ 네가 그렇게 많은 돈을 저금한 것에 감명받았어.
⑤ 그래, 나도 그게 얼마나 비싼지 놀랐어.

14 ④

남: 난 커피숍에서 친구들을 좀 만날 거야. 너도 오고 싶니?
여: 아니, 괜찮아. 오늘 밤에는 그냥 집에 있을 거 같아.
남: 너 기분이 안 좋아 보인다. 아프니?
여: 아니, 난 괜찮아. 난 그저 잠시 동안 혼자 있고 싶어.
남: 음… 난 네가 향수병에 걸린 것 같아.
여: 네 말이 맞아. 난 고향에 있는 가족과 친구들이 정말 그리워지기 시작했어.
남: 안됐다.
여: 그리고 이 새 문화에 아직 익숙하지가 않아.
남: 걱정하지 마. 너는 여기 온 지 한 달밖에 안 됐잖아. 그건 완전히 정상이야. 내가 여기 처음 왔을 때 나도 그랬어.
여: 무슨 말이야?
남: 누구나 새로운 곳에 적응하는 데 힘든 시간을 보내.

문제풀이
① 너 정말 우울한 것 같아.
② 의사는 곧 네가 나아질 거라고 말했어.
③ 나는 아파서 영어 수업에 좀 빠졌어.
⑤ 너는 여기서 살면 영어를 훨씬 더 빨리 배울 거야.

15 ④

여: Mike의 친구인 Ellen은 최근에 새로운 일을 시작했다. 회사는 좋고, 그녀의 동료들도 친절하다. 그러나 그녀는 주말을 포함해서 거의 매일 밤늦게까지 일을 해 왔다. Mike가 그녀에게 그것이 괜찮은지 물어볼 때, 그녀는 개의치 않는다고 말한다. 그녀는 가장 신참 직원이기 때문에 그녀의 프로젝트를 열심히 해야 한다고 느낀다. Mike는 이해하지만, 그는 그녀가 언제나 피곤해 보인다는 것을 눈치챘다. 그녀는 또한 심각한 두통을 겪고 있다. 그는 그녀가 건강을 생각하고 휴식을 좀 취해야 한다고 생각한다. 이런 상황에서, Mike가 Ellen에게 할 말로 가장 적절한 것은 무엇인가?
Mike: 너는 네 건강에 좀 더 신경을 써야 할 거 같아.

문제풀이
① 네가 즐길 수 있는 일을 찾는 게 어때?
② 신참 직원으로서 너는 더 열심히 일해야 해.
③ 이 프로젝트는 중요하니까 그것에 집중하도록 해.
⑤ 네 약점을 개선하면 너는 성공할 거야.

16 ② 17 ⑤

남: 과학자 Harry Harlow는 어머니와 신생아 사이의 유대감에 관심이 있었다. 어떤 과학자들은 신생아들이 엄마를 그저 음식의 근원으로 여긴다고 말했다. 그러나 다른 과학자들은 동의하지 않았다. 1950년대에, Harlow는 새끼 원숭이들을 데리고 실험을 했다. 그는 그들이 태어난 직후 어미에게서 떼어 놓았다. 그러고 나서 그들에게 선택할 두 마리의 가짜 '어미'를 주었다. 첫 번째 어미는 차갑고 딱딱한 철사로 만들어졌고, 두 번째 어미는 부드럽고 따뜻한 천으로 덮여 있었다. 철사로 된 어미는 우유로 가득 찬 병을 들고 있었지만, 천으로 된 어미는 아무것도 제공하지 않았다. 흥미롭게도, 대부분의 새끼 원숭이들은 천으로 된 어미를 선택했다. 그들은 우유를 먹을 때만 철사로 된 어미에게 기어올랐고, 그러고 나서 천으로 된 어미에게 돌아갔다. 이는 신생아가 그들의 엄마에게 단지 음식 때문이 아니라 편안함 때문에 의존한다는 것을 증명했다.

문제풀이
16 ① 아기를 독립적으로 기르는 방법
② 엄마와 아이 사이의 접촉의 중요성
③ 아기에게 음식을 적게 주어 생기는 문제점
④ 인간과 동물의 감정 사이의 차이점
⑤ 유아기의 기억이 성격에 어떤 영향을 미치는지

DICTATION Answers

01 relax in comfort / offer free wireless Internet / home away from home
02 Are you worried about / grow faster / take that risk
03 request a change / needs to be larger / draw up new plans
04 finished setting up / in the middle / to the right of
05 answering the door / there's nobody there either / that would be best
06 call it a day / I'm supposed to / buy him a nice dinner
07 dropped by the supermarket / That's a good deal / they're on sale
08 will be used as / it's due on / start working on it
09 make our roads safer / from all over town / by the beginning of
10 take an online class / That doesn't matter / can still afford it
11 this time of year
12 standing in line
13 completely broke / I wasn't paying attention / not that hard
14 You look down / might be feeling homesick / I was the same
15 started a new job / the newest employee / get some rest
16-17 as a source of food / did an experiment / depend on their mothers

32 영어듣기 모의고사

본문 ▲ p.223

01 ⑤	02 ①	03 ④	04 ④	05 ②	06 ④
07 ③	08 ⑤	09 ⑤	10 ②	11 ②	12 ④
13 ①	14 ①	15 ②	16 ②	17 ④	

01 ⑤

여: 선물을 주는 것은 사람들에게 여러분이 그들을 생각하고 있음을 보여 주는 좋은 방법입니다. 보통, 선물이 무엇인지는 별로 중요하지 않습니다. 속담이 말하듯이, "중요한 것은 생각입니다." 하지만 다른 나라 사람들에게 선물을 줄 때, 여러분은 조심할 필요가 있습니다. 어떤 선물은 잘못된 메시지를 전달할 수 있습니다. 예를 들어, 중국에서 시계는 죽음과 관련이 있습니다. 따라서 시계는 나쁜 선물이 됩니다. 그리고 일본에서 누군가에게 가위나 칼을 주는 것은 친구 관계를 끊고 싶다는 의미입니다. 그러므로 외국인에게 선물을 주기 전에 항상 약간의 조사를 하세요. 문화적으로 알게 됨으로써 여러분은 잘못된 메시지를 전달하지 않을 것입니다.

02 ①

여: 우리 식당 개업이 단 한 달 남았어요!
남: 난 기다릴 수가 없어요! 실내 장식은 끝난 거죠?
여: 그건 어제 끝났어요.
남: 좋아요! 멋져 보일 거라 확신해요. 우리와 면접을 본 요리사에게 연락했어요?
여: 아뇨, 잊었어요. 지금 당장 그 요리사에게 전화할게요.
남: 난 그 요리사가 손님들을 끌어들일 거라고 생각해요. 요리사는 식당의 성공에 가장 중요한 요소에요.
여: 실은, 난 서비스가 가장 중요한 것이라 생각해요. 우리는 친절한 웨이터를 고용하도록 해야 해요.
남: 음, 음식이 형편없다면 누구도 좋은 웨이터를 기억하지 않을 텐데요.
여: 하지만 손님들은 잘 대접받지 않으면 우리 식당을 다시 방문하지 않을 거예요.
남: 맞아요. 둘 다 중요한 것 같아요.

03 ④

남: 요청하신 페이지 디자인 작업을 끝냈습니다. 한번 보세요.
여: 페이지 중앙에 블록을 가지고 놀고 있는 어린아이 두 명이 마음에 드네요.
남: 좋아요. 그리고 페이지 상단에 'Toy Land'라는 이름을 넣었어요.
여: 네, 좋아 보이네요.
남: 그리고 고객들이 '베스트 셀러' 버튼을 클릭하면, 회사에서 가장 잘 나가는 장난감들을 볼 수 있어요.
여: 알겠어요. 고객들이 로그인을 할 공간이 있나요?
남: 물론이죠. 곰 얼굴 모양처럼 생긴 로그인 버튼이 보이시나요?
여: 아. 정말 귀여워요!
남: 또한, 고객들은 메뉴 바에서 웹사이트의 모든 것에 접속할 수 있어요.
여: 모든 것이 아주 좋아 보이네요. 모두 열심히 일해 주셔서 정말 감사합니다.

04 ④

남: 난 우리 학교 뮤지컬의 무대 디자인을 작업하고 있어. 한번 볼래?
여: 물론이야. *[잠시 후]* 와, 정말 멋지다!
남: 고마워. 이야기가 크리스마스이브에 일어나. 그게 저기 큰 크리스마스 트리가 있는 이유야.
여: 그리고 트리 아래 선물이 보이네. 그것들은 아름답게 포장이 된 것 같아.
남: 고마워. 나는 또한 배경에 벽난로를 만들었어.
여: 멋지다. 그런데 크리스마스 양말은 어디에 있어?
남: 크리스마스트리에 그것들을 걸었어.
여: 이제 보여. 난 양말이 벽난로에 걸려 있는 게 더 좋아 보일 것 같아.
남: 생각해 볼게. 트리 바로 옆에 있는 안락의자에 대해서 어떻게 생각해?
여: 그건 배경과 완벽하게 어울려.

05 ②

여: 안녕, Gary. 너 최근에 작은 텐트를 샀지, 그렇지 않아?
남: 응, 지난달에 2인용 텐트를 샀어. 가격이 아주 적당했어.
여: 그게 바로 내가 필요한 거야. 나 다음 주에 캠핑 여행을 가거든.
남: 내 것을 빌리고 싶니?
여: 고맙지만, 난 내 것을 사고 싶어. 어디서 그걸 샀어?
남: Outdoor Equipment에서. 그건 우리 사무실 바로 옆에 있어.
여: 잘됐다. 내일 거기 가서 사야겠어.
남: 난 그 가게 회원이라서 30퍼센트 할인을 받을 수 있어.
여: 정말? 그러면 나를 위해서 그걸 사다 줄 수 있니?
남: 그럼, 문제없어. 내일 저녁에 우리 집에 들러서 가지고 가.
여: 고마워!

06 ④

남: 엄마, 잠시 이야기할 수 있어요?
여: 물론이야, Andy. 속상한 것 같아 보이는구나. 학교에서 나쁜 일이 있었니?
남: 아니요. 실은, 좋은 하루를 보냈어요. 수학 시험을 정말 잘 봤어요.
여: 그 말을 들으니 기쁘구나.
남: 하지만 집에 도착해서 제 휴대용 게임기 화면에 금이 가 있는 걸 발견했어요.
여: 아, 정말? 누가 그랬어?
남: Tara가 그랬어요. 그 애가 저한테 묻지도 않고 제 방에서 그것을 가져가서 깨뜨렸어요.
여: 그 애가 그랬어? 음, 지금 당장 네 여동생과 이야기를 하러 가야겠다.
남: 고마워요, 엄마. 그 애는 항상 제 물건을 사용해요. 제 물건이 자기 것인 양 행동해요.
여: 다시는 이런 일이 일어나지 않을 거야. 그 애가 네게 사과를 하도록 할게.

07 ③

여: 실례합니다. 이 빨간 수영복이 얼마인가요?
남: 그건 50달러입니다. 올여름에 매우 인기 있는 것입니다.
여: 네, 아주 멋지네요. 아, 그 파란 수영복은 얼마예요?
남: 그건 40달러입니다. 하지만 두 수영복 모두 이번 주에 20퍼센트 할인됩니다.
여: 잘됐네요. 저는 빨간 수영복을 살게요. 그리고 이 해변용 모자는 어떤가요?
남: 그건 20달러입니다. 그것도 하시겠어요?
여: 잘 모르겠네요. 이것도 이번 주에 세일하나요?
남: 아니요. 수영복만 세일합니다.
여: 음… 하지만 모자가 필요하긴 해요. 그리고 저에게 이 10퍼센트 할인 쿠폰이 있어요.
남: 죄송합니다만, 그 쿠폰은 세일되는 상품에는 사용할 수 없으세요.
여: 아, 알겠어요. 모자에만 그것을 사용할게요. 여기 제 카드 있습니다.

문제풀이

여자는 50달러짜리 빨간 수영복은 20퍼센트 할인 가격으로 사고, 20달러짜리 모자는 10퍼센트 할인 가격으로 살 것이므로, 총 58달러(=($50×0.8)+($20×0.9))를 지불할 것이다.

08 ⑤

여: 이봐, Sam! 다음 주 토요일에 뭘 할 거니?
남: 8월 30일? 아무 계획 없는데. 무슨 특별한 일이 있어?
여: 응, Harris Stadium에서 불꽃놀이가 있을 거래.
남: 정말? 난 불꽃놀이 보는 걸 좋아해. 그건 무료로 하는 쇼야?
여: 아니, 그런데 표가 한 장에 2달러밖에 안 해.
남: 그러면 우리 꼭 가야겠다. 그런데 기다려 봐… 너 토요일마다 일하지 않아?
여: 응, 맞아. 하지만 두 시간 동안만이야.
남: 아, 알았어. 그렇다면 언제 일이 끝나?
여: 7시에 끝나고, 쇼는 8시가 되어야 시작해.
남: 잘됐다. 그럼 네가 일하는 곳으로 데리러 갈게.
여: 완벽해! 그때 보자!

09 ⑤

남: Radio Seoul은 다음 주말에 있을 흥미진진한 콘서트를 발표하게 되어 자랑스럽게 생각합니다. 콘서트는 Radio Seoul 디제이들에 의해서 진행되며, 13명의 한국 가요 가수들이 특별 출연할 것입니다. 콘서트는 토요일 저녁 8시에 시작되어 11시까지 계속됩니다. 콘서트는 Riverside Park 야외무대에서 개최되며, 성인 표는 단 15달러, 학생 표는 10달러입니다. 표는 Radio Seoul 웹사이트에서만 구입할 수 있다는 것을 기억하세요. 좌석이 제한되어 있고 오랫동안 남아 있지 않을 것이기 때문에 여러분의 표를 빨리 예매하세요. 이 콘서트는 비가 와도 진행되며, 환불되지 않습니다. 더 많은 정보를 원하시면, 저희 웹사이트를 살펴보세요.

10 ②

여: 안녕하세요, 저는 새 아파트를 찾고 있어요.
남: 알겠습니다. 여기 몇몇 구할 수 있는 곳 목록이 있어요. 무엇을 찾으세요?
여: 저는 두 개의 침실이 있는 곳이 필요해요.
남: 알겠습니다. 두 개의 침실이 있는 곳이 몇 군데 있어요.
여: 아, 잊을 뻔했어요. 손님방으로 사용할 수 있는 여분의 침실도 필요해요.
남: 그렇군요. 그밖에 또 무엇이 필요하세요?
여: 발코니가 있으면 정말 좋겠어요.
남: 음, 여기 발코니가 있는 곳이 몇 군데 있습니다. 화장실 수는 어떻습니까?
여: 상관없어요.
남: 얼마나 돈을 쓰실 수 있나요?
여: 제 한도는 한 달에 1,000달러예요. 그 이상은 여유가 없어요.
남: 그러면 이 아파트가 당신에게 가장 좋은 곳이네요.

11 ②

여: 너 여행을 위한 특별 관광 패스를 샀니?
남: 아니, 그건 너무 비싸.
여: 음, 그 패스를 가지고 많은 관광 명소를 방문하면, 넌 돈을 절약할 거야.
남: 맞아. 그럼 그걸 구입해야겠어.

문제풀이

① 넌 왕복표를 사면 돼.
③ 왜 여행 전에 내게 그걸 말하지 않았니?
④ 여행은 즐거웠지만, 난 돈을 너무 많이 썼어.
⑤ 알았어, 하지만 우리는 내일 일찍 일어나야 할 거야.

12 ④

남: 실례합니다. Quick Way 슈퍼마켓이 어디에 있는지 아세요?
여: 네, 알아요. 세 블록을 곧장 간 다음 우회전하세요.
남: 좋습니다. 제가 찾아야 하는 랜드마크가 있나요?
여: 그 건너편에 큰 서점이 있어요.

문제풀이

① 한 블록 더 가서 다시 좌회전하세요.
② 네, 저는 정말 그 상점을 추천합니다.
③ 거기로 빨리 가는 지름길이 있어요.
⑤ 당신이 랜드마크를 좀 찾으면 쉬울 거예요.

13 ①

[휴대전화벨이 울린다.]
남: 여보세요.
여: 안녕하세요, Paul. 저 Jennifer예요.
남: 아, 안녕하세요. 당신이 오늘 뉴욕으로 떠난다고 들었어요. 공항에 있나요?
여: 네, 공항 대합실에 있어요. 그런데 제가 가져오는 것을 잊은 게 있어요.
남: 회의실에 태블릿 컴퓨터를 놓고 가지는 않았죠, 그렇죠?
여: 아니에요, 그건 바로 여기에 제가 가지고 있어요.
남: 그러면 뭔가요?

여: 당신 사무실의 탁자에 서류를 놓고 온 것을 방금 알았어요.
남: 아! 그런 것에 그렇게 부주의하면 안 돼요!
여: 알아요. 혹시 지금 사무실에 계신가요?
남: 네, 방금 도착했어요. 제가 어떻게든 도와줄까요?
여: 이 번호로 그 서류를 팩스로 보내주세요.

문제풀이

② 이메일을 자주 확인하도록 하세요.
③ 며칠 동안 태블릿 컴퓨터를 빌려주세요.
④ 세 시간 후에 공항으로 저를 데리러 와 주실래요?
⑤ 항공사에 전화해서 제가 비행기를 놓쳤다고 말해 주세요.

14 ①

남: 안녕하세요. 뭘 찾는 걸 도와드릴까요?
여: 네. 지난주에 여기서 아주 멋진 지갑을 봤어요. 그런데 오늘은 그게 안 보이네요.
남: 알겠습니다. 상표명이 기억나세요?
여: 죄송하지만, 기억이 안 나요. 하지만 저기 저 코너에 전시되어 있던 흰색 지갑이었어요.
남: 고객님이 어떤 걸 말씀하시는지 알 것 같네요. 금색 체인 줄이 있는 거죠, 그렇죠?
여: 네, 정확해요!
남: 그건 매우 인기 있는 상품입니다. 하지만 유감스럽게도 그건 일시적으로 재고가 없네요.
여: 아, 유감이네요.
남: 그밖에 또 관심 있는 것이 있으세요?
여: 음, 저는 특별히 그 지갑을 사러 여기에 왔어요. 나중에 그 상품이 들어오면 연락해주시겠어요?
남: 물론입니다, 고객님의 전화번호를 남겨만 주세요.

문제풀이

② 당신은 운이 좋은 고객입니다. 그것이 마지막 상품이에요.
③ 지난주에 그것을 어디서 봤는지 제게 알려주세요.
④ 죄송합니다만, 저희는 더 저렴한 게 없어요.
⑤ 그게 당신의 옷과 얼마나 어울리는지 보는 게 어떠세요?

15 ②

여: Edward는 문학 수업을 듣고 있고 몇 명의 반 친구들과 팀 프로젝트를 받는다. Edward와 그의 팀원들은 일을 나누기로 결정한다. 그러나 일주일 동안, 다른 팀원들은 너무 바빠서 자신의 부분을 못 한다고 말한다. 그래서, Edward는 그들을 위해 그들의 일을 하기 시작한다. 곧, 그는 거의 모든 일을 혼자서 했다는 것을 깨닫는다. 게다가, 이것 때문에 그는 다른 학업에는 집중을 하지 못했다. 그는 팀원들이 공정한 몫의 일을 해야 한다고 생각한다. 이런 상황에서, Edward가 팀원들에게 할 말로 가장 적절한 것은 무엇인가?
Edward: 좀 더 도와줄래?

문제풀이

① 너희는 도움을 요청해야 했어.
③ 내가 그냥 혼자 이걸 끝내는 게 더 나을 거야.
④ 왜 너 혼자서 모든 것을 했니?
⑤ 열심히 일해 줘서 너희 모두에게 고마워.

16 ② 17 ④

남: 요즘, 많은 사람들이 자신을 더 잘 표현하기 위해 머리 모양이나 색깔을 바꿉니다. 유감스럽게도, 점점 더 많은 사람들이 다양한 이유로 탈모를 경험하고 있습니다. 이 이유에는 스트레스, 오염, 모발 제품에 들어있는 화학 물질, 그리고 유전적인 요인이 포함됩니다. 이런 일이 발생하는 것을 방지하기 위해, 여러분이 따를 몇 가지 조언이 여기 있습니다. 너무 자주 머리를 염색하거나 파마를 하여 머리를 손상시키면 안 됩니다. 또한, 머리를 규칙적으로 감고 자연적으로 마르게 놔두어야 합니다. 그리고 반드시 항상 충분한 수면을 취하고 쉴 시간을 갖도록 하십시오. 마지막으로, 꼭 채소를 많이 먹도록 하십시오. 토마토와 당근은 탈모를 예방하는 데 도움이 되는 풍부한 양의 영양소를 함유하고 있습니다. 이런 조언들을 명심한다면, 걱정거리를 하나 덜게 될 것입니다.

DICTATION Answers

01 As the proverb says / make bad gifts / do some research
02 had an interview with / the most important thing / visit our restaurant again
03 playing with blocks / for customers to log in / can access everything
04 the gifts under the tree / hung them up / matches perfectly with
05 what I need / buy my own / Come by my house
06 did really well on / without asking me / have her apologize to you
07 I'll take the red one / Is it also on sale / can't be used
08 something special going on / we should definitely go / doesn't start until
09 is proud to / can only be purchased / even if it rains
10 Here's a list of / as a guest room / It doesn't matter
11 save money
12 I should look for
13 you're leaving for / shouldn't be so careless / help you out
14 on display / out of stock / when it comes in
15 is given a team project / too busy to do / almost all of the work
16-17 in order to express / a variety of / get enough sleep

33 영어듣기 모의고사

본문 ▲ p.230

01 ⑤	02 ①	03 ④	04 ④	05 ①	06 ④
07 ②	08 ③	09 ⑤	10 ③	11 ②	12 ①
13 ⑤	14 ④	15 ⑤	16 ②	17 ③	

01 ⑤

여: 멋진 휴가보다 더 편안한 것은 없습니다. 하지만 여러분이 사무실로 돌아왔을 때, 일이 쌓여있는 것을 발견하게 될지도 모릅니다. 그리고 여러분은 다시 집중하는 데 어려움을 겪을지도 모릅니다. 이는 휴가 후유증이라고 알려져 있습니다. 그것에 대처하는 가장 좋은 방법은 여러분의 바이오리듬을 맞추는 것입니다. 우선, 여러분이 잠들고 일어나는 시간을 조절하려고 노력하십시오. 또한, 깊은 수면을 취하는 것은 여러분이 쉬었다고 느끼도록 도움을 줄 것입니다. 마지막으로, 우선순위에 따라 일 더미를 처리할 수 있습니다. 그러면 휴가에서 돌아온 후 직장 일에 다시 익숙해지는 것이 훨씬 쉬워질 것입니다.

02 ①

여: 너 괜찮니, Michael? 좀 아파 보여.
남: 나는 아픈 게 아니라, 단지 정말 배가 불러.
여: 너 저녁 식사로 너무 많이 먹었니?
남: 응. 스트레스를 받아서 맛있는 음식이 좀 먹고 싶었어. 그런데 과식을 했어.
여: 음… 넌 스트레스성 섭취를 한 거 같아.
남: 스트레스성 섭취? 그게 뭐야?
여: 그건 스트레스를 풀기 위해 많이 먹는 거야. 하지만 그건 네 기분을 더 나쁘게 할 뿐이야.
남: 그렇구나. 그런데 어떻게 하면 내가 멈출 수 있을까?
여: 네가 먹기 전에 생각을 해야 해. 너 자신에게 정말 배가 고픈지 물어봐.
남: 그거 좋은 생각이다. 하지만 내가 먹지 않으면, 무엇을 할 수 있지?
여: 네 신경을 진정시킬 다른 활동을 시도해봐. 산책하거나 노래를 불러.

문제풀이

① 스트레스성 섭취를 줄이는 방법
② 아플 때 무엇을 해야 하는지
③ 스트레스를 푸는 최고의 방법
④ 스트레스를 받을 때 먹을 건강에 좋은 음식
⑤ 과식으로 발생하는 문제

03 ④

남: 안녕하세요.
여: 안녕하세요, 사장님. 오늘 기분이 어떠세요?
남: 매우 좋습니다.
여: 그 말을 들으니 기쁘네요. 내일 뉴욕에서 있는 세미나를 위한 비행기 표가 여기 있습니다.
남: 고마워요. 음… 더 이른 것이 있나요?
여: 원하시면 하나 찾아볼 수 있어요. 무슨 문제가 있나요?
남: 이건 내일 오전 10시에 도착하는데, 세미나는 오전 11시에 시작해요. 일정이 너무 빡빡할 거 같네요.
여: 죄송합니다. 표를 더 빠른 비행기로 변경하겠습니다. 또한 오늘 3시에 영업 회의가 있습니다.
남: 알았습니다. 상기시켜줘서 고마워요. 오늘 누가 발표하나요?
여: 영업부의 Nick입니다.
남: 알았어요. 그럼 회의 전에 나에게 자료를 가져다주세요.

04 ④

남: 새해 파티를 위해 사무실이 준비됐어?
여: 응. 내가 사무실 중앙에 큰 직사각형 테이블을 놓았어.
남: 아, 좋아. 그리고 케이크는?
여: 물론이야. 난 그것을 테이블 중앙에 놓았어.
남: 훌륭해. 나는 분위기가 재미있고 축제 같기를 바라.
여: 나도 그래. 그리고 벽에 큰 현수막도 있어.
남: 거기에 'Happy New Year'라고 쓰여 있니?
여: 응. 그리고 현수막 양옆에 하트 모양의 풍선들도 달았어.
남: 멋진 것 같네. 테이블에 샴페인도 좀 올려두는 것을 잊지 않았지, 그렇지?
여: 안 잊었어. 테이블 왼편에 음료 기계 두 대도 놓았어.
남: 훌륭해!

05 ①

여: 앞으로 며칠 동안 계획이 있니?
남: 특별한 건 없어. 무슨 일인데?
여: 음, 방금 내가 출장으로 LA에 가야 한다는 걸 알게 됐어.
남: 와! LA는 멋진 도시야. 언제 출발하니?
여: 내일 아침 비행기이고, 다음 주 목요일에 돌아와. 그래서 Sandy가 걱정돼.
남: Sandy가 누구야?
여: 내 새 고양이야. 만약 괜찮다면 나 대신 그녀를 돌봐 줄 수 있어?
남: 물론이지. 기꺼이 그렇게 할게. 나도 고양이가 있는 걸 알잖아, 그렇지?
여: 실은, 그게 내가 네게 부탁하는 이유야. 고마워, John! 내가 그 애랑 그 애의 물건을 너희 집으로 가져다줄게.
남: 응, 그녀를 오늘 밤에 데리고 와. 그녀를 보면 난 기쁠 거야.
여: 정말 고마워.

문제풀이

① 그녀의 애완동물을 돌봐주기
② 출장 가기
③ 그녀가 가방 싸는 것을 도와주기
④ 그녀의 고양이를 병원에 데려가기
⑤ 그녀에게 로스앤젤레스를 구경시켜 주기

06 ④

여: 안녕, Patrick. 어떻게 지냈어?
남: 잘 지내고 있어, Rebecca. 네 딸이 초등학교에 입학했다고 들었어.
여: 응. 그 애는 매우 신이 나 있어. 그나저나, 난 새집을 찾고 있어.
남: 아, 네 딸 학교 근처 어딘가로 이사하려는 거야?
여: 아니야, 그 애는 학교 버스를 탈 거야.

남: 그러면 왜 이사를 하니? 넌 네 집을 좋아했잖아, 특히 정원을.
여: 우리는 침실이 더 많이 있는 집이 필요해.
남: 왜 더 필요하니?
여: 내 쌍둥이 아들들이 지금 방을 같이 쓰고 있는데, 그 애들이 각자 자기만의 공간을 가져야 할 거 같아.
남: 그렇구나. 실은, 내 친구 중 하나가 부동산 중개인이야. 원한다면, 그 친구에게 물어볼게.
여: 그게 좋겠다. 고마워.

07 ②

여: Water Planet에 오신 것을 환영합니다. 표를 구매하시겠어요?
남: 네. 저는 두 아들과 함께 여기에 왔습니다. 표가 얼마인가요?
여: 성인 표는 장당 15달러이고, 어린이 표는 장당 10달러입니다.
남: 알겠습니다. 그 표에는 모든 워터 슬라이드 이용이 포함되나요?
여: Aqua Plunge를 제외한 모든 놀이 기구를 타실 수 있습니다.
남: Aqua Plunge는 얼마인가요?
여: 성인과 어린이 표는 3달러입니다.
남: 알겠습니다. 그러면 그것들도 3장 구매하겠습니다.
여: 알겠습니다. 회원 카드가 있으시면 5달러 할인을 받으실 수 있어요.
남: 잘됐네요. 여기 회원 카드와 신용 카드가 있습니다.

문제풀이

남자는 15달러인 성인 표 1장과 10달러인 어린이 표 2장, 3달러인 Aqua Plunge 이용권 3장을 사고, 회원 카드로 5달러를 할인받았으므로 총 39달러(= $15+($10×2)+($3×3)-$5)를 지불할 것이다.

08 ③

남: Molly! 오늘 저녁에 영화 보러 갈 시간 있어?
여: 잘 모르겠어. 난 오늘 밤에 늦게까지 일을 할 거야. 바로 지난주 화요일에 새 아르바이트를 시작했거든.
남: 정말? 무엇을 하고 있어?
여: 난 일주일에 3일 저녁을 웨이트리스로 일하고 있어.
남: 그렇구나. 저녁마다 얼마 동안 일하니?
여: 5시간 동안. 지금까지는 즐겁게 일하고 있지만, 힘든 일이야.
남: 정말 그럴 것 같아, 하지만 보수를 잘 받으면 괜찮지.
여: 맞아. 나는 지금 일주일에 200달러를 더 벌고 있어.
남: 멋지네. 그러면 오늘 밤 일을 마친 후에 계획이 있어?
여: 아니. 난 10시에 끝나. 10시 반에 영화 보러 갈까?
남: 물론이야. 일 마치면 전화해줘.

09 ⑤

남: 여러분은 fittonia에 대해서 들어본 적이 있습니까? 그것은 남아메리카 열대 우림이 원산지이고 주로 페루에서 발견되는 식물입니다. 그것은 극한의 기온을 좋아하지 않아서 매우 추운 장소, 사막, 또는 직사광선을 많이 받는 장소에서는 살 수 없습니다. 15종의 fittonia가 있지만, 가장 흔한 것은 잎에 정맥 같은 무늬가 있습니다. 이 선들은 잎의 중앙에서 끝으로 바깥쪽을 향해 뻗어 나갑니다. 모든 종의 색은 다양합니다. 잎은 거의 언제나 녹색이지만, 선은 흰색이나 심지어 분홍색일 수도 있습니다. 그것들은 모두 줄기에 털이 있고 작은 하얀 꽃을 피웁니다.

10 ③

남: 안녕하세요, 도와드릴까요?
여: 네. 저는 중고차를 찾고 있어요. 2013년 이후에 만들어진 SUV이면 가장 좋겠어요.
남: 저희는 이곳에 다양한 종류의 SUV를 보유하고 있습니다.
여: 잘됐네요. 저는 60,000킬로미터 미만을 주행한 차를 원해요.
남: 알겠습니다. 그러면 이 셋을 보시면 됩니다.
여: 그것들 중 사고를 당한 게 있나요?
남: 네, 그것들 중 한 대는 사고를 당했지만, 다른 두 대는 무사고입니다.
여: 아, 그건 중요해요. 저는 사고를 당하지 않은 것을 원해요.
남: 알겠습니다. 얼마만큼 돈을 쓰실 수 있습니까?
여: 제 예산은 13,000달러예요.
남: 그러면 손님께 완벽한 SUV가 있네요.

11 ②

여: 실례합니다. 제 주문에 잘못된 게 있는 것 같아요.
남: 아, 정말입니까? 문제가 뭔가요?
여: 저는 컵케이크 12개를 요청했는데, 이 상자에는 11개밖에 없어요.
남: 아, 죄송합니다. 하나를 더 가져다 드리겠습니다.

문제풀이

① 배달이 늦어서 죄송합니다.
③ 제가 예상했던 것보다 컵케이크가 더 많네요.
④ 그러면 12개 상자를 포장해 드릴까요?
⑤ 물론입니다, 저것들은 오늘 오전에 갓 구워진 겁니다.

12 ①

남: Lisa, 너무 추운 것 같지 않아?
여: 응. 사무실의 난방기가 금요일까지 제대로 작동하지 않을 거라고 들었어.
남: 우리가 한 주 내내 이 얼어붙는 추위를 겪어야 한다는 말이야?
여: 우리가 달리 할 수 있는 게 없어.

문제풀이

② 우리는 그냥 난방기를 꺼야 해.
③ 다음 주에 담요를 가지고 오는 게 낫겠어.
④ 우리는 겨울에 스키와 스노보드 타는 걸 즐겨.
⑤ 나는 여름에 그렇게 많은 전기를 써본 적이 없어.

13 ⑤

남: 네가 이번 주말에 해변에 갈 거라고 들었어.
여: 맞아. 어서 가고 싶어.
남: 정말 좋겠다! 하지만 자외선 차단제 바르는 걸 잊지 마.
여: 응. 나는 자외선 차단제를 좀 살 거야. 그런데 어떤 종류를 사야 할지 잘 모르겠어.
남: 햇빛이 매우 강할 테니, 자외선 차단 지수가 50인 것을 사용하는 걸 추천할게.
여: 아, 맞아. 그런데 물에 씻기면 어떡하지?
남: 방수가 되는 자외선 차단제를 꼭 사도록 해.
여: 알았어. 나는 온몸에 그걸 바르는 데 너무 오래 걸리지 않으면 좋겠어.
남: 스프레이 종류를 쓰는 게 어때?

여: 너는 자외선 차단제에 대해서 많이 아는구나! 그밖에 내가 명심해야 될 게 또 뭐가 있니?
남: 그저 두세 시간마다 그걸 바르는 것을 기억해.

문제풀이

① 네가 수영할 때 피부를 보호하려고 노력해.
② 스프레이 종류가 제일 효과가 좋을 것 같아.
③ 피부 보호제를 사는 데 돈을 너무 많이 쓰지 마.
④ 네 피부를 보호할 다른 방법을 찾아야 해.

14 ④

여: 멋진 캠핑 여행이었어. 그런데 이제 가야 할 시간이네.
남: 확실히 우리가 모든 것을 챙겼는지 보자.
여: 알았어. 이 테이블은 어떻게 해야 해?
남: 그 테이블은 캠프장에 속한 거야.
여: 알았어. 하지만 먼저 이걸 닦고 다시 놓아두자.
남: 쓰레기봉투 가져왔어? 우리가 쓰레기를 버리려면 몇 개 필요할 거야.
여: 물론이지, 그런데… 저 쓰레기 더미를 봐.
남: 끔찍하다. 병, 캔, 음식 포장지… 왜 저 사람들은 그들이 어지른 것을 치우지 않는 거지?
여: 바로 모퉁이만 돌면 공공 쓰레기통이 있어. 사람들이 어떻게 그렇게 게으를 수 있지?
남: 쓰레기봉투가 없다고 해도, 치울 수 있었을 텐데. 정말 부끄러운 일이야.
여: 사람들은 이곳에 왔을 때 책임감을 가져야 해.

문제풀이

① 우리가 도착하기 전에 그들이 치웠어.
② 이 근처에 또 다른 쓰레기통이 있을 것 같아.
③ 너는 이 쓰레기가 재활용되도록 분리해야 해.
⑤ 너는 환경을 보호하는 것에 신경 쓰지 않니?

15 ⑤

여: Eric과 Gina는 야외 마술 쇼를 준비해 왔다. 대부분의 표가 팔렸고, 많은 사람들이 올 것으로 예상된다. 그러나 일기예보가 갑자기 바뀌어 쇼 당일에 폭우와 강풍이 예상된다. 그래도 Eric은 관객을 위해서 마술 쇼가 계획대로 진행되어야 한다고 주장한다. 그러나 Gina는 그에게 동의하지 않는다. 그녀는 행사가 취소되어야 한다고 생각한다. 그래서 그녀는 Eric에게 약간의 안전 문제가 있을지도 모른다고 설득하기로 결심한다. 이런 상황에서, Gina가 Eric에게 할 말로 가장 적절한 것은 무엇인가?
Gina: 관객의 안전이 먼저 고려할 점이야.

문제풀이

① 나는 표 가격에 대해서 너에게 동의하지 않아.
② 나는 정말 오늘 밤 우리 친구들을 빨리 만나고 싶어.
③ 우리 마술 쇼는 분명히 큰 성공을 할 거야.
④ 나는 많은 사람들이 와서 쇼를 즐기길 바라.

16 ② 17 ③

남: 오늘 저는 첫인상에 대해 이야기하려 합니다. 일생 동안, 여러분은 많은 다양한 사람들을 만날 것입니다. 그들 대부분은 여러분을 처음으로 만나자마자 여러분에 대해 판단을 내릴 것입니다. 그것이 여러분이 그들의 첫 의견을 반드시 좋은 것으로 만들도록 해야 하는 이유입니다. 여러분은 가능한 한 최고의 방법으로 여러분 자신을 보여줌으로써 이를 조절할 수 있습니다. 예를 들어서, 지저분한 옷을 입는 것은 사람들이 여러분을 부주의하고 게으르다고 생각하게 만들지도 모릅니다. 그러니 언제나 단정하게 옷을 입으세요. 또한, 말을 할 때, 여러분의 어휘를 신중하게 선택하세요. 적절한 어휘를 사용하는 것은 다른 사람들이 여러분을 지적이고 사려 깊다고 생각하게 만들 것입니다. 여러분이 서거나 앉는 방법과 얼굴의 표정 또한 중요합니다. 여러분은 이 모든 것들에 각별한 주의를 기울여야 합니다. 사람들이 여러분을 만날 때 긍정적인 반응을 보일 것이라 확신합니다.

문제풀이

16 ① 다른 사람들과 의사소통을 잘하는 방법
② 좋은 첫인상을 만드는 방법
③ 부주의하고 게으른 사람들의 특징
④ 당신의 현재 이미지를 바꾸는 가장 좋은 방법
⑤ 어휘 선택과 성격 간의 관계

DICTATION Answers

01 might have trouble / getting some deep sleep / much easier to get back
02 look a little sick / makes you feel worse / calm your nerves
03 Here is the flight ticket / might be too tight / for reminding me
04 fun and festive / on both sides of / on the left of
05 for a business trip / watch her for me / bring her over tonight
06 started elementary school / a house with more bedrooms / a friend of mine
07 buy some tickets / have access to / get three of those
08 working late tonight / get paid well / when you're done
09 is native to / the most common one / vary in color
10 I'm looking for / a wide variety of / been in an accident
11 there's something wrong
12 won't work properly
13 can't wait to go / washes it away / keep in mind
14 belongs to the campground / clean up after themselves / such a shame
15 are expected to come / go on as planned / some safety issues
16-17 meet many different people / in the best way possible / pay close attention to

34 영어듣기 모의고사

본문 ▸ p.237

01 ①	02 ③	03 ②	04 ④	05 ⑤	06 ③
07 ③	08 ③	09 ⑤	10 ④	11 ③	12 ⑤
13 ④	14 ②	15 ②	16 ⑤	17 ⑤	

01 ①

여: 안녕하세요, 여러분. 저는 다가오는 학교 축제에 대해 발표를 하려고 합니다. 여러분이 아마도 알고 있듯이, 학교 축제는 오늘로부터 2주 뒤에 개최됩니다. 그러나, 노래 경연 대회 오디션은 다음 주 화요일에 개최될 것입니다. 경연 대회에 참가하고 싶은 사람은 누구든지 자유롭게 오디션을 볼 수 있습니다. 여러분은 개인이나 단체로 지원할 수 있습니다. 경연 대회를 위한 오디션에서 10명의 사람들이나 단체가 선발될 것입니다. 여러분의 이름과 여러분이 부를 노래의 제목을 늦어도 이번 주 금요일까지는 Swann 음악 선생님께 제출해 주세요. 오디션 장소와 시간은 곧 발표될 것입니다. 감사합니다.

02 ③

여: Jim, 새집에 들어갈 가전제품을 사는 것을 마쳤니?
남: 응. 냉장고와 TV가 곧 배달될 거야.
여: 그 제품들이 네 새 아파트와 잘 어울릴 것 같아?
남: 음, 난 그것들의 생김새에 대해 그렇게 많이 생각하지 않았어.
여: 정말? 디자인은 나에게 매우 중요해. 특별 기능도 그렇고.
남: 특별 기능도 나에게는 그렇게 많이 중요하지 않아.
여: 그러면 가전제품을 살 때 넌 무엇을 고려하니?
남: 난 에너지 효율에 초점을 맞추는데, 왜냐하면 나는 내 전기 요금 고지서 금액이 올라가는 걸 원하지 않거든.
여: 에너지 효율이 좋은 가전제품들은 보통 비싸지 않아?
남: 때때로 그렇지. 하지만 장차 돈을 절약하기 위해서, 나는 기꺼이 그것들을 사겠어.
여: 이해가 간다.

03 ②

남: 실례합니다.
여: 안녕하세요, 손님. 무엇을 도와드릴까요?
남: 「Carter의 꿈」이라는 제가 가장 좋아하는 만화책을 찾고 있는데요. 있나요?
여: 그것에 대해 들어본 적이 없어요. 누가 썼는지 아시나요?
남: 네. 그 책은 Tom Riley가 쓰고 그렸어요. 전 그걸 제 손주 생일 선물로 주고 싶어요.
여: 알겠습니다. 도서 목록을 확인해볼게요.
남: 천천히 하세요.
여: 책을 찾았어요! 이건 저희가 가진 가장 마지막 책이네요.
남: 아주 좋네요! 얼마인가요?
여: 양장본은 30달러이고 페이퍼백 책은 20달러입니다. 어느 것이 더 좋으세요?
남: 양장본으로 주세요.

04 ④

남: 안녕, Susan, 네가 출판사에서 일하기 시작했다고 들었어.
여: 응. 이제는 나만의 개인 사무실이 있어. 방 한가운데에 큰 책상이 있어.
남: 멋지다. 책꽂이는?
여: 응, 내 책상 뒤에 큰 책꽂이를 놓았어.
남: 잘했네. 넌 프린터도 필요할 것 같아.
여: 물론이지. 그건 내 책상 바로 옆에 있어.
남: 그거 정말 편리하겠다. 아, 공기를 신선하게 유지하기 위해 화분을 놓는 걸 추천해.
여: 난 이미 화분이 있어! 그건 내 프린터 옆에 있어.
남: 모든 게 완벽하게 마련된 것 같다. 사무실에 햇빛은 많이 들어오니?
여: 충분하지 않아. 그래서 책상 옆에 큰 스탠드를 놓았어.

05 ⑤

남: 아, 우리 건물 관리사무소로부터 주차 요금을 청구받았어요.
여: 뭐라고요? 그건 말도 안 돼요. 정확한 주차 자리에 주차했어요?
남: 네. 우리는 12번에서 20번 자리에 주차할 수 있잖아요, 그렇죠?
여: 맞아요. 그들이 실수를 했음이 틀림없어요.
남: 주차 혜택이 어제부터 시작하기로 되어 있지 않았나요?
여: 맞아요.
남: 그리고 당신은 관리사무소에 차량 등록증 사본을 제출했죠?
여: 아, 실은, 그걸 제출하는 것을 잊어버렸어요. 이 새 사무실로 물건을 옮기느라 너무 바빴어요.
남: 음, 그러면 그게 문제인 거네요. 즉시 그걸 제출할게요.
여: 알았어요. 그런다면, 그들이 주차 요금을 취소할 거예요.
남: 나도 꼭 그러길 바라요.

06 ③

[휴대전화벨이 울린다.]
남: 여보세요?
여: 안녕, 여보. 어디에 있어요?
남: 지금 집으로 가는 길이에요. 오늘 일찍 끝났어요.
여: 잘됐어요. 유감스럽게도, 나는 지금 회의에 가는 길이에요.
남: 아, 정말요? 그러면 당신 집에 늦게 오나요?
여: 네. 회의가 4시에 있을 예정이었는데 한 시간 지연됐어요.
남: 유감이네요. 당신이 체육관에서 나와 함께하지 못할 것 같네요.
여: 맞아요, 못할 거예요. Jenny를 학교에서 데리고 와 줄 수 있어요?
남: 물론이에요. 당신 저녁 식사 때 집에 올 수 있을 거 같아요?
여: 네. 오늘 밤에는 중국 요리를 주문해요.
남: 좋은 생각이에요. 집에서 봐요!

07 ③

여: 오늘 무엇을 도와드릴까요?
남: 아내를 위한 기념일 선물을 찾고 있어요.
여: 그러면 저는 이 금목걸이를 추천합니다. 700달러였는데, 지금은 특별

가인 550달러에 구입하실 수 있어요.
남: 음… 좀 비싸네요. 팔찌는 어떤가요?
여: 좋습니다. 이 금팔찌도 세일 중이에요. 550달러였는데, 지금은 325달러입니다.
남: 완벽한 것 같아요. 그걸로 할게요.
여: 그리고 300달러 이상 구매하시면, 귀걸이 한 쌍을 20퍼센트 할인받으실 수 있어요. 이 귀걸이의 원래 가격은 150달러예요.
남: 그것도 좋네요. 그것도 살게요. 모두 선물용으로 포장해주시겠습니까?
여: 물론이죠. 일반 선물 포장은 5달러이고, 특별 선물 포장은 10달러입니다.
남: 일반 포장으로 해주세요.

문제풀이
남자는 325달러짜리 팔찌를 구매하고, 추가로 150달러짜리 귀걸이를 20퍼센트 할인된 가격으로 구매하고, 5달러짜리 선물 포장을 하기로 했으므로, 총 450달러(= $325+($150×0.8)+$5)를 지불할 것이다.

08 ③

여: 와! 저게 네 새 차니? 난 전에 이 모델을 본 적이 없어.
남: 그래. 바로 어제 차를 샀어. Modern Motors에서 나온 최신 모델이야.
여: 나는 색깔이 마음에 들어.
남: 고마워. 빨간색을 사려고 했는데, 결국에는 짙은 파란색으로 하기로 결정했어.
여: 좋은 선택이었어. 그런데 틀림없이 비쌌겠네.
남: 대략 23,000달러였지만, 그만큼의 가치가 있다고 생각해.
여: 이 차는 연비가 좋니?
남: 1갤런당 대략 30마일을 가.
여: 내가 예상했었던 것보다 더 좋네.
남: 나도 그랬어. 나는 (이 차를) 구매해서 정말 기뻐. 드라이브하고 싶니?
여: 당연하지!

09 ⑤

남: 안녕하세요, 여러분. 오늘 저는 놀라운 소금 평지에 대해서 이야기할 것입니다. Salar de Uyuni라고 불리는 세계에서 가장 큰 소금 평지는 볼리비아의 남서부에 있습니다. 이곳은 안데스 산맥에 위치해 있어서, 매우 높은 고도에 있습니다. 수천 년 전, 이곳은 사실 거대한 호수의 일부였습니다. 시간이 지나면서, 호수가 말라버렸고 소금 평지가 형성되었습니다. 흥미롭게도, 그곳은 엄청난 양의 리튬을 가지고 있는데, 이것은 배터리를 만드는 데 쓰입니다. 그곳의 사막 기후 때문에, 거기에는 식물이나 동물이 거의 없습니다. 이런 흥미로운 장소이기 때문에, Salar de Uyuni는 볼리비아의 가장 유명한 관광지 중 하나가 되었습니다.

10 ④

여: 안녕하세요, 손님. 무엇을 찾고 계세요?
남: 안녕하세요, 전 태블릿 컴퓨터를 사려고 여기 왔습니다.
여: 알겠습니다. 얼마나 많은 저장 용량이 필요하세요?
남: 음, 저는 영화를 많이 다운로드해서 적어도 32기가바이트의 저장 용량을 가진 것이 필요해요.
여: 이것은 어떠세요? 이 14인치의 화면이 영화를 보는 데 아주 좋을 거예요.
남: 저도 그렇게 생각해요.
여: 손님께서 생각하시는 가격대가 어떤지 여쭤봐도 될까요?
남: 음, 저는 그저 450달러 이내에서 지출하고 싶습니다.
여: 그렇군요. 마음에 두신 다른 특정한 특징이 있습니까?
남: 저는 배터리 수명이 긴 것을 원해요.
여: 그렇다면, 이 모델이 손님에게 가장 좋을 것 같습니다.
남: 좋네요.

11 ③

여: 아이스크림 가게 밖의 저 긴 줄을 봐!
남: 저기에 무슨 일이 있는 거지?
여: 저 표지판에 아이스크림 하나를 사면 하나를 더 무료로 받을 수 있다고 쓰여 있어.
남: 그렇다면, 기다릴 만한 가치가 있네.

문제풀이
① 그러면 우리는 초콜릿을 사야겠다.
② 그건 내가 사기에 너무 비싸.
④ 그렇지만 너는 새치기를 하면 안 돼.
⑤ 나는 가게가 10시까지 문을 연다고 생각했어.

12 ⑤

남: 내 컴퓨터가 나를 미치게 하고 있어. 너무 느려!
여: 바이러스 방어 프로그램이 있니?
남: 응, 하지만 그건 어떤 바이러스도 감지하지 않고 있어.
여: 그러면 네가 사용하지 않는 프로그램을 삭제해봐.

문제풀이
① 나는 방금 새 컴퓨터를 샀어.
② 컴퓨터가 작동하는지 확인해 보자.
③ 그러면 병원에 가는 게 어때?
④ 미안하지만, 내일 프로젝트 때문에 그게 필요해.

13 ④

남: 이런, Anna. 너 정말 피곤해 보여.
여: 그래. 최근에 전혀 잠을 잘 자지 못했어.
남: 아마 네가 스트레스를 받나 보다.
여: 음, 난 별로 스트레스를 받지 않는데. 실은, 큰 프로젝트를 막 끝내서 별로 바쁘지 않아.
남: 내 경우에는, 카페인을 많이 섭취한 후에는 잠이 들 수 없어. 너는 커피를 많이 마시니?
여: 커피는 안 마셔. 하지만 에너지 드링크 마시는 것은 좋아해.
남: 그게 네 문제인 게 틀림없어.
여: 왜? 에너지 드링크에는 아무 문제가 없어.
남: 음, 그것들은 많은 양의 카페인을 함유하고 있어. 그중 어떤 것들은 심지어 커피보다 더 많이 함유하고 있어.

여: 난 너무 많은 에너지 드링크를 마시지 않는 게 좋겠어.

문제풀이
① 나는 잠을 좀 자야 할 것 같아.
② 그러면 나는 커피 마시는 걸 멈춰야겠어.
③ 그런 경우라면, 나는 휴가를 가야겠어.
⑤ 나는 밤에 잘 자고 나면 나아질 거야.

14 ②

남: 지난 주말에 즐거운 걸 했니, Kathy?
여: 응. 나는 내 딸과 시골에 있는 채소밭에 갔어. 우리는 당근을 좀 뽑았지.
남: 너한테 밭이 있는지 몰랐어.
여: 음, 그건 그냥 작은 거야. 우리 가족과 내가 함께 그것을 돌보고 있어.
남: 정말 좋구나. 딸이 밭에서 일하는 것을 즐거워하니?
여: 물론이지. 그 애는 채소를 먹는 것도 좋아해.
남: 와! 나는 내 아들이 채소를 먹게 할 수 있으면 좋겠는데.
여: 우리가 밭을 갖기 전에, 내 딸도 채소 먹는 걸 거부했어.
남: 그래서 너는 채소를 재배하는 것이 그 애의 마음을 바꿨다고 생각하니?
여: 분명해! 너도 네 아들과 함께 시도해봐.
남: 그래. 나도 채소를 재배해볼게.

문제풀이
① 그 애는 모든 것이 맛있다고 말했어.
③ 나에게 조리법을 보내주면 오늘 밤에 해볼게.
④ 미안해. 우리는 저녁을 요리할 시간이 없어.
⑤ 채소는 건강에 좋은 식단을 위해서 필수적이야.

15 ②

여: Jennifer는 사회학을 공부하는 것을 좋아하는 고등학생이다. 그녀는 대학에서 사회학을 전공하고 싶어 한다. 반면에, 그녀의 부모님은 그녀가 의사가 되기를 원한다. 그들은 그녀의 성적이 좋은 의과 대학에 입학하기에 충분히 좋다고 믿는다. 어떻게 해야 할지 몰라서, 그들은 조언을 얻기 위해 그녀의 담임 선생님을 찾아간다. 하지만 그녀의 담임 선생님은 Jennifer의 사회학에 대한 열정을 알고 있다. 그는 그녀가 좋아하는 것을 계속하게 하도록 Jennifer의 부모님을 설득하고 싶어 한다. 이런 상황에서, 선생님이 Jennifer의 부모님에게 할 말로 가장 적절한 것은 무엇인가?
Teacher: Jennifer에게 그녀의 꿈을 좇을 수 있는 기회를 주세요.

문제풀이
① Jennifer는 자신이 공부하고 싶어 하는 것을 모릅니다.
③ Jennifer는 훌륭한 의사가 될 잠재력이 있습니다.
④ 저는 Jennifer가 대회에서 1등을 차지할 것을 믿습니다.
⑤ 저는 그녀에게 좋은 대학에 입학하기 위해서 더 열심히 공부하라고 조언했습니다.

16 ⑤ 17 ⑤

남: 사람들은 고양이가 아주 독립적이기 때문에 돌보기 쉽다고 생각합니다. 그래서 점점 더 많은 가정에서 그들을 애완동물로 기릅니다. 그러나 그들의 독립성에도 불구하고, 그들은 여전히 사랑과 관심을 필요로 합니다. 고양이는 그들의 방식으로 감정을 표현해서 사람들은 그들이 무엇을 말하는지를 모를 수 있습니다. 고양이를 이해하기 위해서, 사람들은 고양이의 행동을 자세하게 살펴봐야 합니다. 예를 들어, 고양이가 화가 나면, 그들의 등은 둥글어지고 꼬리는 빠르게 앞뒤로 움직입니다. 하지만 그들이 행복하면, 꼬리는 천천히 움직입니다. 눈을 반쯤 감는 것도 같은 메시지를 보냅니다. 하지만 그들의 귀가 뒤로 향하고 소리를 내면, 그들은 공격할 준비가 되어 있는 것입니다. 마지막으로, 고양이가 여러분의 다리에 대고 앞뒤로 문지르기 시작하면, 이는 그들이 관심을 원한다는 것을 의미합니다. 고양이는 처음에는 이해하기 어려울 수도 있지만, 여러분이 이해만 한다면, 여러분은 그들의 평생 친구가 될 수 있습니다.

문제풀이
16 ① 고양이가 소리를 내는 이유
② 고양이를 좋은 애완동물로 만드는 것
③ 고양이가 가끔 할퀴는 이유
④ 건강한 고양이를 고르는 방법
⑤ 고양이의 기분을 이해하는 방법

DICTATION Answers

01 As you may know / Anyone who wants / no later than
02 think that much about / focus on energy efficiency / in order to save
03 haven't heard of it / check the book list / our very last copy
04 started working for / right next to / keep the air fresh
05 been charged a parking fee / supposed to start / cancel the parking fee
06 on my way back home / was delayed for an hour / order Chinese food
07 at a special price / is also on sale / a pair of earrings
08 I haven't seen / go with dark blue / better than I expected
09 Located in / huge amounts of / most popular tourist destinations
10 How much storage / no more than / In that case
11 get another one free
12 detect any viruses
13 you're stressed out / can't fall asleep / There's nothing wrong with
14 take care of it / I wish I could / try it with your son
15 would love to major in / for her to enter / pursue what she likes
16-17 more and more households / move back and forth / want some attention

35 영어듣기 모의고사

본문 ▸ p.244

01 ②	02 ③	03 ⑤	04 ④	05 ⑤	06 ⑤
07 ①	08 ③	09 ③	10 ③	11 ④	12 ④
13 ②	14 ③	15 ④	16 ①	17 ④	

01 ②

여: 안녕하세요. 새로운 대학교 기숙사에 오신 걸 환영합니다. 저는 기숙사 관리인으로서, 건물과 건물 거주자들을 관리합니다. 무슨 문제가 있으면, 마음 놓고 저에게 말씀해 주세요. 이제, 전 몇 가지 규칙에 대해 말씀드리고자 합니다. 첫째, 여러분은 기숙사 내에서 취사를 할 수 없습니다. 이유는 그것이 화재를 일으킬 수 있기 때문입니다. 둘째, 여러분은 여기 거주하지 않는 누구에게도 절대 정문 비밀번호를 주어서는 안 됩니다. 그러는 것은 절도와 같은 문제를 일으킬 수도 있습니다. 마지막으로, 여러분이 일으킬 수도 있는 어떤 손상에 대해서 배상을 하셔야 합니다. 무언가가 고장이 나면, 즉시 저에게 알려주십시오.

02 ③

남: Liz, 너 화 나 보여. 무슨 일이야?
여: 지하철에서 어떤 사람이 음식을 먹고 쓰레기를 바닥에 버렸어.
남: 정말? 그거 정말 짜증 나잖아.
여: 맞아. 게다가, 어떤 여자는 이어폰을 쓰지 않고 영상 통화를 했어!
남: 아, 이런! 목소리가 컸어?
여: 응. 난 책에 집중할 수가 없었어.
남: 어떤 사람들은 자신의 행동에 대해 다른 사람들이 어떻게 생각하는지 신경 쓰지 않는 거 같아.
여: 네 말이 맞아. 요즘 사람들은 지하철에서 하고 싶은 것은 무엇이든 해.
남: 그곳은 공공장소야. 그들은 다른 사람들을 생각해야 해.
여: 맞아. 모든 사람이 자신들의 행동이 다른 사람에게 영향을 미친다는 것을 이해해야 해.
남: 만약에 사람들이 그걸 기억한다면, 지하철을 타는 것이 모두에게 좀 더 즐거운 경험이 될 거야.

03 ⑤

[전화벨이 울린다.]
남: 여보세요?
여: 여보세요. Brian Mraz 씨인가요?
남: 맞습니다. 누구시죠?
여: 전 Katie Wilson이고, Happy Mart 웹사이트에서 지원해주신 것 때문에 전화드렸습니다.
남: 아, 네. 전 지난달에 지원했어요. 여전히 자리가 있나요?
여: 네, 하지만 양식에 근무 경력에 관한 부분이 공란으로 있더라고요.
남: 아, 그걸 잊어버렸네요. 전 1년 동안 큰 슈퍼마켓에서 출납원으로 일했어요.
여: 좋습니다. 그리고 근무 시간은 월요일에서 토요일까지 오전 7시에서 오후 3시까지입니다.
남: 좋네요.
여: 내일 아침 많은 제품이 가게에 정렬되어야 합니다. 그때 와서 일을 시작하는 게 어떠세요?
남: 당연하죠! 좋습니다.

04 ④

남: 안녕, Christine. 네가 학생회장으로 출마한다고 들었어.
여: 아, 안녕, David. 맞아. 실은, 나는 지금 선거 포스터를 작업 중이야.
남: 아, 어떻게 생겼는지 궁금하다. 내가 볼 수 있어?
여: 당연하지. 나는 포스터에 내 사진을 넣었어. 그리고 내 이름은 아래쪽에 쓰여 있어.
남: 좋아 보인다. 너는 배경으로 우리 학교 사진을 사용했네.
여: 응. 그리고 난 사진 밑에 슬로건을 넣었어.
남: 난 네 슬로건이 좋아. 그것은 "우리는 변화시킬 수 있습니다!"네.
여: 고마워. 난 선거 운동 노래도 만들었어.
남: 포스터 좌측 상단 모서리에 있는 이 QR 코드가 너의 노래를 위한 거니?
여: 응, 넌 그것을 스캔해서 노래를 들을 수 있어.

05 ⑤

남: 인터넷을 사용할 때 광고를 보는 것에 너무 질렸어.
여: 어떤 종류의 광고를 말하는 거야, James?
남: 팝업 광고 말이야. 그것들은 인터넷 모든 곳에 있어. 그것들이 너무 짜증 나.
여: 네가 어떤 기분인지 알겠어. 그것들은 아주 짜증이 나지.
남: 정말 그래. 난 그것들을 없애 버리고 싶어.
여: 음, 팝업 광고를 중단시키는 광고 차단 프로그램이 있어. 그것을 설치한 후에, 나는 더 이상 그런 문제가 없어.
남: 그 프로그램의 이름이 뭐야?
여: 생각날 듯 말 듯 한데. 지금 당장은 기억나지 않아. 집에서 그것을 찾아봐야겠어.
남: 찾으면 나에게 메시지를 보내줄 수 있어?
여: 물론이지.

문제풀이

① 고장 난 노트북 컴퓨터 고치기
② 그의 홈페이지에 팝업 광고하기
③ 그에게 문자 메시지 보내는 법 보여주기
④ 그의 컴퓨터에 바이러스 퇴치 소프트웨어 설치하기
⑤ 그에게 광고 차단 프로그램의 이름을 말해주기

06 ⑤

남: 안녕, Susie! 오늘 오후에 Jason의 생일 파티에 올 수 있어?
여: 못 갈 것 같아. 방과 후에 조깅하러 갈 거거든.
남: 조깅? 마라톤에서 달리려고 훈련 중이니?
여: 비슷해. 나는 내일 10킬로미터 경주를 뛰어. 그것은 자선을 위한 거야.
남: 와. 재미있을 것 같아. 행운을 빌어!

여: 고마워. 이봐, 나랑 내일 같이 뛰는 게 어때? 넌 현장에서 등록할 수 있어.
남: 음… 언제 시작해?
여: 오전 9시 반에 시작해.
남: 난 할 수 없을 것 같아. 그룹 프로젝트 때문에 오전 8시 반에 반 친구들 몇 명을 만나야 해.
여: 그러면 끝나고 오는 게 어때? 대신에 나를 응원해 줄 수 있으니까.
남: 좋은 생각이야. 내일 보자.

07 ①

여: Book World에 오신 걸 환영합니다.
남: 안녕하세요. 저는 선물로 책 몇 권을 사고 싶어요.
여: 그러면 운이 좋으시네요. 저희는 이번 주에 세일을 크게 하고 있거든요.
남: 잘됐네요. 얼마나 절약할 수 있나요?
여: 손님이 어떤 종류의 책을 사는지에 따라 다릅니다.
남: 알겠습니다, 가서 둘러볼게요. *[잠시 후]* 이 소설책들은 얼마인가요?
여: 그것들은 한 권당 4달러예요.
남: 알겠습니다. 이 아동 도서들은 어떤가요? 모든 아동 도서의 가격표에는 6달러라고 쓰여 있어요.
여: 실은, 이번 주에 그 책들은 정가에서 50퍼센트 할인됩니다.
남: 그렇군요. 이것들을 다 살게요. 총 얼마인가요?
여: 손님은 소설책 4권과 아동 도서 3권을 고르셨네요. 제가 모두 더해 보겠습니다.

문제풀이

남자는 4달러짜리 소설책 4권, 6달러에서 50퍼센트 할인하는 아동 도서 3권을 샀으므로 총 25달러(= ($4×4)+($6×0.5×3))를 지불할 것이다.

08 ③

남: Megan, 너 요즘 정말 건강해 보여. 특별한 이유라도 있는 거야?
여: 실은, 몇 주 전에 몸이 안 좋아서 진찰을 받았어. 의사가 건강을 증진하는 법에 대한 조언을 해줬어.
남: 그가 뭐라고 했어?
여: 그는 내게 운동을 더 많이 하고 먹는 것에 대해 주의하라고 했어.
남: 그래서 그의 조언을 받아들였어?
여: 응. 나는 매일 아침 요가를 해.
남: 와. 그것은 네 유연성을 향상시킬 거야!
여: 나는 또한 지구력을 기르기 위해서 일주일에 두 번 수영도 해.
남: 훌륭하네. 건강을 유지하기 위해서 또 다른 어떤 걸 하고 있어?
여: 언제나 균형 잡힌 식사를 하려고 노력해. 또한 매일 비타민을 먹어.
남: 잘하고 있네!

09 ③

남: 여러분은 한국에서 최고의 요리사가 누구인지 알고 계신가요? Best Chef Korea가 찾아드리겠습니다! 이 쇼는 Food Channel에서 다음 주부터 시작해 12주 동안 방영될 것입니다. 매주, 요리사들은 다양한 도전 과제로 경쟁할 것입니다. 이 쇼는 25명의 요리사와 시작하지만, 매주 2명이 떠나게 될 것입니다. 그러고 나서 최종 3명이 마지막 에피소드에서 경쟁할 것입니다. 매주, 3명의 음식 전문가 패널과 50명의 방청객이 그 주의 탈락자를 선택하게 될 것입니다. 그리고 3명의 결승 진출자들 모두가 세계적으로 유명한 식당에서 일할 기회를 얻게 될 것입니다. 우승자는 또한 3억 원을 받을 것입니다.

10 ③

남: 마침내 Greg를 다시 보게 되다니 너무 기뻐.
여: 음, 지금 3시야. 그가 어느 게이트로 도착할지 알고 있어?
남: 실은, 잘 모르겠어. 그가 도착할 정확한 시간을 물어보는 걸 잊어버렸어.
여: 이 비행기 스케줄을 보자.
남: 좋은 생각이야. 우리가 함께하면 어디서 그를 만날지를 알아낼 수 있을 거라고 확신해.
여: 그래. 나는 그의 비행기 번호가 400번대였던 걸 기억해.
남: 좋아. 그리고 우리는 분명히 베이징은 고려할 필요가 없지.
여: 그러면 선택의 범위가 좁혀진다.
남: 맞아. 게다가, 그는 늦어도 오후 4시까지는 도착한다고 말했어.
남: 음, 우리가 알아낸 거 같아!
여: 그를 찾으러 가자!

11 ④

여: 안녕하세요, 고객님. 무엇을 도와드릴까요?
남: 저는 중간 크기의 튼튼한 배낭을 찾고 있어요.
여: 음, 이건 어떠세요? 그것은 요즘 매우 멋지고 인기가 있습니다.
남: 그건 좋아 보이지만, 저는 실용적인 것이 필요해요.

문제풀이

① 그곳은 여행하기 좋은 장소인 것 같아요.
② 작은 종이 가방을 주시겠어요?
③ 감사하지만, 제 남동생이 하나를 사주었어요.
⑤ 적당한 가격에 그것을 찾을 수 있는 곳을 알아요.

12 ④

남: Wendy, 월요일 학급 소풍에 참석할 거니?
여: 네, 강 선생님. 전 무척 설레요.
남: 좋아, 하지만 아직 부모님의 서명을 받은 허가서를 내게 주지 않았구나.
여: 그것을 내일 수업에 가지고 올게요.

문제풀이

① 그걸 하실 필요가 없어요.
② 당연하죠, 지금 바로 사인할게요.
③ 안됐네요. 재미있을 것 같은데.
⑤ 그들은 오는 데 관심이 없어요.

13 ②

남: 저기요, 일어나야 해요.
여: 아, 안 돼! 여기가 어디예요?
남: 여기는 종점이에요. 버스에서 내리셔야 해요.

여: 제가 버스에서 잠이 들다니 믿을 수가 없네요! 시청까지 가는 방법을 알려주시겠어요?
남: 길을 건너서 저기에 있는 저 버스 정류장을 이용하셔야 해요. 272번 버스가 그곳으로 데려다줄 거예요.
여: 감사합니다.
남: 아, 잠시만요. 아무래도 당신이 방금 마지막 버스를 놓친 것 같아요.
여: 아, 안돼요. 어떻게 해야 하죠?
남: 택시를 타야 할 거 같아요.
여: 하지만 전 택시 타기에 충분한 돈이 없어요.
남: 음… 부모님께 도움을 요청하는 게 좋겠네요.
여: 네, 그냥 저를 데리러 오라고 엄마한테 전화해야겠어요.

문제풀이
① 당신 말이 맞아요. 저는 택시를 탔어야 했어요.
③ 좋아요. 저에게 전화를 빌려주셔서 감사합니다
④ 시간이 있는 게 확실한가요? 너무 멀거든요.
⑤ 친절하시네요, 하지만 저를 집까지 태워다 주시지 않으셔도 돼요.

14 ③

남: 기말고사가 드디어 끝났어! 우리는 자유야!
여: 너는 그럴지 몰라도 난 아니야. 난 아직 할 일이 있어.
남: 무슨 뜻이야? 아직도 시험이 남았어?
여: 아니. 나도 시험은 다 끝났어. 하지만 끝내야 할 리포트가 있어.
남: 정말? 안됐다. 무엇에 관한 리포트야?
여: 기후 변화에 관한 거야.
남: 아직 그 리포트를 제출하지 않았어? 지난주 금요일까지였잖아!
여: 맞아. 운이 좋게도, 선생님이 나에게 기한을 연장해 주셨어.
남: 내가 그 리포트 쓰기 위해 사용했던 참고 도서가 있어. 네가 원하면, 그것들을 네게 빌려줄 수 있어.
여: 정말? 아, 고마워. 그게 많은 도움이 될 거야.
남: 괜찮아. 나는 친구를 도울 수 있어서 기뻐.

문제풀이
① 네게 비용이 얼마나 드는지 알려줄게.
② 너는 기후 변화에 대해 써야 해.
④ 미안해, 오늘 그 도서를 반납해야 해.
⑤ 너는 제시간에 리포트를 마쳤어야 했어.

15 ④

여: Eric과 Julie는 음악 축제에 관해서 이야기하고 있다. 그 축제는 학교 강당에서 토요일에 개최될 것이다. 그들의 많은 친구들이 참석할 것이다. Julie는 친구 중 한 명이 그녀에게 축제 표를 주었지만, 가지 못한다고 말한다. 그녀는 Burger Chef에서 아르바이트를 하고 토요일에 일하러 가야 한다. Eric은 그가 정말 음악을 좋아하고 (축제에) 갈 수 있기를 바란다고 말한다. 하지만 그는 표가 매진되었기 때문에 살 수 없었다. 그래서 Julie는 그에게 자기의 표를 주기로 결심한다. 이런 상황에서, Julie가 Eric에게 할 말로 가장 적절한 것은 무엇인가?
Julie: 네가 원하면 내 축제 표를 가져도 돼.

문제풀이
① 학교 식당에서 표를 사는 게 어때?
② 연주하는 밴드를 너는 아니?
③ 미안하지만, 너와 함께 축제에 갈 수 없어.
⑤ 그날 나 대신 식당에서 일해줄 수 있니?

16 ① 17 ④

남: 그랜드캐니언 국립 공원에 오신 걸 환영합니다. 오늘, 저는 Adventure Time 여행을 소개하고자 합니다. 이 이틀간의 캠핑 여행에서, 여러분은 협곡이 어떻게 형성되었는지를 배우면서 협곡의 아름다운 경치를 즐길 수 있습니다. 협곡의 꼭대기에서부터 바닥까지 말을 탈 것이며, 가는 길에 몇몇 특별한 장소에 들를 겁니다. 해가 강하므로 많은 물과 자외선 차단제를 가져오는 것을 기억하세요. 저는 또한 모자를 쓸 것을 추천합니다. 바닥에 도착하면 하룻밤 야영을 하고 별을 올려다보며 휴식을 취할 겁니다. 그러고 나서 협곡의 꼭대기로 다시 돌아올 겁니다. 모든 것이 무료이니 비용에 대해서는 걱정하지 마세요. 하지만 이 프로그램은 7월 중순부터 8월 중순까지만 제공됩니다. 관심이 있으시면, 서둘러서 지금 등록해 주세요.

문제풀이
16 ① 공원에서 제공되는 여행을 소개하려고
② 더운 날씨의 위험에 대해 이야기하려고
③ 그랜드캐니언의 역사를 설명하려고
④ 캠핑 여행에 등록하는 방법을 설명하려고
⑤ 도시 근처에 새로 연 공원을 광고하려고

DICTATION Answers

01 feel free to talk to / it could cause a fire / let me know
02 without using earphones / do whatever they please / a more enjoyable experience
03 I'm calling about / worked as a cashier / start your job
04 running for student president / at the bottom / in the top left corner
05 What kind of ads / You can say that again / look it up
06 run in a marathon / sign up on the spot / cheer me on
07 having a big sale / It depends on / the regular price
08 how to improve my health / doing yoga every morning / eat balanced meals
09 run for 12 weeks / compete in the last episode / win a chance to work
10 ask the exact time / figure out where / no later than
11 I'm looking for
12 given me a permission form
13 get off the bus / cross the street / don't have enough money
14 have a report to finish / due last Friday / lend them to you
15 Many of their friends / needs to go / were all sold out
16-17 how it was formed / along the way / free of charge

01 기출 영어듣기 모의고사

본문 ▲ p.253

01 ③	02 ②	03 ①	04 ④	05 ①	06 ④
07 ④	08 ③	09 ④	10 ④	11 ④	12 ②
13 ②	14 ④	15 ②	16 ⑤	17 ④	

01 ③ 2016년 3월 고1

여: 주목해주시기 바랍니다. Moonlight 호텔 투숙객을 위한 안내 방송입니다. 야외 수영장에서 깨진 유리 조각들이 발견된 것을 알려드리게 되어 죄송합니다. 수영장은 수영하기에 안전하지 않으므로 폐쇄될 것입니다. 만약 수영을 즐기기 원하시면, 7층의 실내 수영장을 이용하실 수 있습니다. 저희는 야외 수영장이 준비가 되는 대로 알려드리겠습니다. 불편을 끼쳐드리게 되어 죄송하며, 여러분의 협조에 감사드립니다.

02 ② 2016년 6월 고1

여: Daniel, 뭘 하고 있니?
남: E-폐기물에 대한 다큐멘터리를 보고 있어.
여: E-폐기물? 전자 폐기물을 말하는 거니?
남: 응. 다큐멘터리에서 휴대전화와 같은 버려진 전자기기들이 심각한 문제를 유발하고 있대.
여: 아, 수업 시간에 그것에 대해 배웠어. E-폐기물의 유해한 금속들이 식수와 토양을 오염시킨대, 맞지?
남: 정확해. 게다가, 선진국에서 나오는 E-폐기물이 불법적으로 가난한 나라로 수출되고 버려져.
여: 그것은 그런 나라들의 환경에 심각한 위협임이 틀림없어.
남: 맞아. 이 문제를 해결하기 위해 조치가 취해져야 한다고 생각해.
여: 네 의견에 동의해.

03 ① 2015년 9월 고2

남: 괜찮으세요?
여: 아니요. 춥고 발목이 너무 아파요.
남: 여기요, 따뜻해지도록 이 담요를 받으세요. *[잠시 후]* 걸을 수 있겠어요?
여: 전혀요. 발목이 부러진 것 같아요.
남: 무슨 일이 있었나요?
여: 이 산을 걸어 내려가고 있는데 갑자기 미끄러졌어요. 다리로 심하게 넘어졌어요.
남: 걱정 마세요, 부인. 가까운 병원으로 모셔다드릴게요.
여: 정말 안심되네요. 저는 여기서 혼자 꼼짝 못 하게 되는 줄 알았어요.
남: 우리 응급 전화 교환원에게 당신이 어디에 있는지를 아주 잘 설명해서 다행입니다.
여: 제 휴대전화가 이렇게 깊은 산 속에서 여전히 작동하고 있어서 운이 좋았어요.
남: 네, 그렇네요. 우리가 이동하기 전에 다리에 붕대를 감아 드릴게요.
여: 감사합니다. 그렇게 해주세요.

04 ④ 2016년 9월 고2

여: Morris 씨, 저희 뮤지컬을 위한 세트 디자인을 마무리했습니다. 여기 제 스케치입니다.
남: 한번 볼게요. *[잠시 후]* 중앙에 출입문이 마음에 드네요.
여: 감사합니다. 왼쪽에는, 요청하신 대로 벽난로를 넣었습니다.
남: 좋아요. 그리고 벽난로 위에 저 초상화를 거는 것은 아주 좋은 생각이에요. 그 초상화가 많은 장면에서 매우 중요해요.
여: 맞아요. 소파는 어떤가요?
남: 벽난로 앞에 있는 것이 좋아 보이네요.
여: 그리고 구석에 둥근 탁자를 확인해보세요. 마음에 드시나요?
남: 완벽해요. 꽃병도 마음에 드네요.
여: 한 가지 질문이 더 있어요. 창문 아래 흔들의자를 두는 것은 괜찮을까요?
남: 좋아요. 아주 잘하셨어요!

05 ① 2016년 9월 고2

여: Steve, 내일 출발할 준비 됐니?
남: 네, 엄마. 제가 교환학생으로 미국에 가게 되다니 믿을 수가 없어요.
여: 네가 정말 자랑스럽구나. 의료보험과 여행자 보험은 가입했니?
남: 네. 그리고 제 모든 짐을 쌌어요.
여: 잘했다. 휴대전화는 이제 해지했니?
남: 아직 안 했어요. 그건 내일 공항에서 할 수 있어요.
여: 그래. 그리고 혹시 모르니 네 여권을 복사하는 걸 잊지 마라.
남: 맞아요, 알려주셔서 감사해요. 그렇지만 제 국제 학생증을 먼저 찾아와야 해요.
여: 그러면 네가 학생증을 받아오는 동안 내가 그것을 복사하마.
남: 감사해요, 엄마. 집에 오는 길에 친구들을 좀 만날게요.
여: 그래. 늦지 마라.

06 ④ 2016년 9월 고1

여: 안녕하세요, 무엇을 도와드릴까요?
남: 안녕하세요, 제 강좌를 다른 것으로 바꾸고 싶어요.
여: 어떤 강좌를 신청하셨나요?
남: 영문법이요. 그런데 저는 그것을 영어 작문으로 바꾸고 싶어요. 바꾸기에 너무 늦었나요?
여: 아니요, 이번 주 금요일까지는 가능해요. 신분증 좀 주시겠어요?
남: 여기 있어요.
여: *[잠시 후]* 아, 죄송합니다. 학생은 이 강좌를 들을 수 없어요.
남: 문제가 뭐죠? 인원이 꽉 찼나요?
여: 아니요, 그렇지 않아요. 그렇지만 영어 작문은 3학년 학생들만 수강할 수 있어요.
남: 아, 저는 1학년 학생도 들을 수 있다고 생각했어요.
여: 죄송하지만 그럴 수 없어요. 다른 강좌를 찾아봐야 해요.

07 ④ 2016년 6월 고1

남: 안녕하세요. 무엇을 도와드릴까요?
여: 보디로션을 좀 사고 싶어요.
남: 네. 이 제품은 어떠세요? 유기농이고 향도 좋아요.
여: 얼마예요?

남: 한 병에 10달러예요. 하지만 회원권이 있으면 10퍼센트 할인을 받으실 수 있어요.
여: 좋아요. 그러면, 세 병을 살게요. 여기 제 회원 카드가 있습니다.
남: 네. 다른 것은 필요 없으세요?
여: 아, 핸드크림도 필요해요.
남: 이 새로 나온 제품은 요즘 잘 팔려요. 하나에 5달러예요. 하지만 이 제품은 할인이 되지 않아요.
여: 좋아요. 그러면 두 개를 살게요.
남: 그러면, 보디로션 세 개와 핸드크림 두 개 맞죠?
여: 네, 여기 제 신용카드요.

문제풀이

여자는 10달러짜리 보디로션 세 개와 5달러짜리 핸드크림 두 개를 구매하기로 했는데 보디로션은 10퍼센트 할인이 된다고 했으므로, 여자가 지불할 금액은 총 37달러(= ($10×3×0.9)+$5×2)이다.

08 ③ 2016년 9월 고1

[전화벨이 울린다.]
남: Greenlight 서점입니다. 무엇을 도와드릴까요?
여: 안녕하세요. 다가오는 책 사인 행사에 등록하려고요. 작가가 Cindy Wallace라고 들었는데요.
남: 이번 주 토요일 행사 말씀이세요?
여: 네.
남: 죄송해요. 등록이 한 시간 전에 마감되었어요.
여: 아, 이런! 제가 참석할 수 있는 다른 방법이 있을까요?
남: 그 행사는 저희 메인 로비에서 열릴 거예요. 그곳에서 줄을 서서 기다리시면 돼요.
여: 아, 정말요? 잘됐네요! 행사가 언제 시작되나요?
남: 오후 3시부터 오후 5시까지예요.
여: 그렇군요. 그녀의 사인을 받으려면 새 책을 구매해야 하나요?
남: 아니요, 그러실 필요 없어요. 그녀의 책 중 아무거나 가져오시면 돼요.
여: 네. 정말 감사합니다.
남: 뭘요.

09 ④ 2016년 6월 고2

남: 안녕하세요, Roseville 헬스클럽입니다. 오셔서 저희의 최신 홍보 행사를 즐겨보세요. 저희 헬스클럽은 첫 달에 50퍼센트 할인을 제공합니다. 또, 여러분은 락커를 무료로 사용하실 수 있습니다. 저희의 다양한 프로그램에는 웨이트 트레이닝뿐 아니라 수영, 요가, 라틴 댄스 수업도 포함되어 있습니다. 저희 개인 트레이너들과 최신 시설이 여러분이 건강을 유지하도록 도와드릴 것입니다. 저희 헬스클럽은 매일 오전 6시부터 오후 10시까지 운영됩니다. 또한 여러분이 간식을 필요로 하실 경우에 대비해 다양한 스포츠음료와 과일 주스가 있는 카페도 있습니다. 오늘 저희 헬스클럽을 방문하셔서 회원 등록을 해 보세요! 감사합니다.

10 ④ 2016년 6월 고2

남: 와! 마침내 우리가 시드니에 도착했어. 우리는 어디를 가야 할까?
여: 내가 방금 이 도시 관광 전단을 집어 왔어. 한번 봐.
남: 이 24시간 티켓은 어떨까? 그건 24시간 동안 무제한 버스 탑승을 제공해.
여: 하지만 우리는 여기 3일 동안 있을 거잖아. 그 대신 48시간 티켓을 사는 것이 낫지 않을까?
남: 그거 말이 되네. 오디오 가이드가 필요할까?
여: 당연하지. 그건 틀림없이 우리가 시드니의 명소에 대해 더 많이 알도록 도와줄 거야.
남: 그래. 시드니 하버 크루즈는 어떨까?
여: 어디 보자… 130달러를 도시 관광에 소비하는 것이 너무 과도하다고 생각하지 않니?
남: 응. 만약 우리가 여기에 돈을 절약한다면, 우리는 나중에 박물관에 갈 수 있어.
여: 그러면 크루즈가 없는 것으로 하자.
남: 좋아. 가자.

11 ④ 2016년 9월 고1

남: 어제 지역 문화 센터에서 하는 요가 수업에 갔니?
여: 응, 갔었어. 그런데 나는 그 수업이 나에게 맞는 것 같지 않아.
남: 왜 그렇게 생각하는데?
여: 그 수업은 따라가기가 너무 어려워.

문제풀이

① 너는 곧 그것을 더 잘하게 될 거야.
② 더 유연해지기 위해 더 열심히 노력해.
③ 나는 요가 강사였어.
⑤ 요가 수업을 제공하는 곳은 많지 않아.

12 ② 2016년 6월 고2

여: Kevin, 너 피곤해 보인다. 괜찮니?
남: 어젯밤에 잠을 충분히 못 잤어. 새벽 2시까지 TV로 야구를 봤거든.
여: 아, 네가 야구를 그렇게 좋아하는 줄 몰랐네.
남: 실은, 나는 대단한 야구 팬이야.

문제풀이

① 아니, 게임은 오후 7시에 시작해.
③ 음, 나는 보통 이 시간에 잠이 와.
④ 너는 다음 게임에 참가해야 해.
⑤ 수면 부족은 요즘 심각한 문제야.

13 ② 2015년 11월 고2

남: 기말고사 준비는 어떻게 되어 가니?
여: 온종일 책상에 앉아 있었는데, 스마트폰 때문에 집중할 수가 없었어.
남: 공부하는 동안 스마트폰을 쓰는 걸 참기가 힘들다는 걸 알아.
여: 맞아. 몹시 어렵지.
남: 실은 나도 너처럼 똑같은 문제가 있었는데, 그 문제를 다루는 방법을 알아냈어.
여: 정말? 어떻게 그 문제를 처리했니?
남: 내 방을 '스마트폰 금지' 구역으로 만들었어.
여: 그게 무슨 뜻이야?
남: 그건 내가 방에서 공부할 때, 내 전화기를 가져오지 않는다는 뜻이야.
여: 그러면 네 전화기를 어디에 두는데?
남: 내가 공부하는 동안은 보통 그것을 거실에 둬.

여: 스마트폰을 사용하지 않으면 불편하지 않니?
남: 꼭 그렇지는 않아. 그것에 익숙해지고 있는 것 같아.

문제풀이
① 전혀. 너를 보기를 기대하고 있어.
③ 그럴 필요 없어. 나는 전화번호를 바꿀 거야.
④ 신경 쓰지 마. 내가 네 전화기를 잘 보고 있을게.
⑤ 걱정하지 마. 너와 함께 일하는 게 편해.

14 ④ 2015년 11월 고2

남: 와, 네 테니스 솜씨가 매일 점점 더 좋아지는걸! 비결이 뭐니?
여: 나는 '이미지 트레이닝'이라는 기법을 사용해.
남: 이미지 트레이닝? 그게 뭔데?
여: 그건 네가 개선하기 원하는 동작을 머릿속에서 되풀이해서 그려보는 거야.
남: 음, 좀 더 자세히 설명해줄 수 있니?
여: 당연하지. 훌륭한 테니스 선수들의 경기를 보고 네가 그들처럼 움직이고 있다고 상상해봐.
남: 상상하는 동안 실력을 향상하기라! 굉장한데!
여: 네가 그것을 계속하면, 네 몸이 결국에는 따라갈 거야.
남: 그러면, 그것이 내 테니스 문제에도 효과가 있을까?
여: 당연하지! 나한테 말해봐, 그러면 내가 이 기법으로 너를 도와줄게.
남: 내가 테니스공을 칠 때마다, (공이) 너무 멀리 나가. 코트 라인을 지나가 버려.
여: 코트 라인 안쪽으로 공을 치는 걸 계속해서 상상해봐.

문제풀이
① 내 테니스 훈련 시간은 이틀 후에 시작해.
② 네 행동은 학생으로서의 선을 넘고 있어.
③ 새로운 단어를 이미지와 함께 암기하려고 노력해봐.
⑤ 나는 테니스 라켓을 새것으로 교환할 거야.

15 ② 2016년 9월 고1

여: Julia는 영화를 좋아하는 고등학교 학생이다. 어느 날, Julia는 그녀가 가장 좋아하는 배우가 새로 개봉한 영화에서 주연을 맡은 것을 알게 된다. 그녀는 친구인 Paul과 함께 그 영화를 보기 원한다. 그녀가 Paul에게 자신과 함께 영화를 보기 원하는지 물어보았을 때, 그는 이미 그것을 보았으며 결말이 매우 좋았다고 말한다. Julia는 그가 자신에게 영화에 대해 모두 말하려고 한다는 것을 알아챈다. 그녀는 Paul이 그 영화의 줄거리를 말해버리는 것을 원하지 않는다. 이 상황에서, Julia가 Paul에게 할 말로 가장 적절한 것은 무엇인가?
Julia: 그것에 대해 더 이상 말하지 말아줘.

문제풀이
① 오늘 밤에 영화 보지 않을래?
③ 이 영화를 놓치면, 너는 후회하게 될 거야.
④ 어차피 나는 그 주연 배우를 그다지 좋아하지 않아.
⑤ 결말이 내가 예상했던 것과 달라.

16 ⑤ 17 ④ 2016년 9월 고1

남: 안녕하세요, 저는 「Five Minutes for Health」의 Jason입니다. 요즘 푸른색을 갖고 계신가요? 저는 여러분의 기분이 아니라 여러분의 음식에 대해 말씀드리는 겁니다! 형형색색의 과일과 채소를 섭취함으로써 여러분의 몸이 필요로 하는 것을 얻을 수 있다는 것을 알고 계셨습니까? 서로 다른 영양소들은 사실 그것들이 속해 있는 음식에 서로 다른 색깔을 부여합니다. 예를 들어, 블루베리를 푸른색으로 만드는 영양소는 여러분의 정신을 예리하게 하는 데 도움이 됩니다. 수박과 토마토를 붉게 만드는 영양소는 특정 암으로부터 보호하는 데 도움이 됩니다. 또한, 당근을 주황색으로 만드는 영양소는 여러분의 뼈를 튼튼하게 하고 여러분의 눈을 건강하게 유지하는 데 도움이 됩니다. 마지막으로, 브로콜리와 같은 녹색 채소에 들어 있는 영양소는 혈압을 낮추는 데 도움이 됩니다. 그러므로 만약 여러분이 건강해지고 싶으시다면, 반드시 여러분의 접시에 무지개의 선명한 색깔을 담으세요.

문제풀이
16 ① 십 대 사이에서의 원푸드 다이어트의 위험성
② 음식의 영양소에 대한 오해
③ 집에서 과일과 채소를 재배하는 법
④ 색칠하기 책이 정신 건강에 좋은 이유
⑤ 다양한 색깔의 과일과 채소를 섭취하는 것의 장점

DICTATION Answers

01 are sorry to inform / is not safe for / the outdoor pool is ready
02 cause serious problems / be a serious threat to / action should be taken
03 fell hard on / gotten stuck out here / before we move on
04 as you requested / in the corner / under the window
05 packed all my stuff / just in case / on my way home
06 register for / not allowed to take / only available for
07 smells good / Here's my membership card / buy two of them
08 The registration closed / wait in line / to get her signature
09 use lockers for free / help you to stay healthy / a variety of
10 provides unlimited bus rides / help us get / save some money on this
11 is right for me
12 enough sleep last night
13 hard to resist / used to have / without using a smart phone
14 get better and better / picturing the movements / work for my tennis problem
15 who loves movies / already watched it / give away the story
16-17 but about your food / keep your mind sharp / lower blood pressure

02 기출 영어듣기 모의고사

본문 ▲ p.260

01 ①	02 ⑤	03 ⑤	04 ④	05 ②	06 ③
07 ④	08 ⑤	09 ⑤	10 ③	11 ⑤	12 ③
13 ⑤	14 ①	15 ①	16 ①	17 ③	

01 ① 2016년 9월 고2

여: 안녕하세요, 학생 여러분. 주목해주시겠습니까? 이 안내 방송은 졸업반 학생들을 위한 것입니다. County 은행 재단에서 학과나 체육 성적뿐만 아니라 시민권에 근거하여 5,000달러의 장학금을 세 명의 졸업반 학생들에게 수여하고 있습니다. 여러분이 장래의 리더가 될 잠재력이 있고 평균 B학점 이상인 학생이라면, 이 장학금을 받을 수 있습니다. 여러분의 이야기 같은가요? 그러면 www.countybank.com에 접속하시거나 여러분의 지도 교사에게 Richard Citizenship Award 신청에 대해 문의하세요. 지원 마감일은 2016년 11월 30일입니다. 많은 학생 여러분들이 이 기회를 활용하기를 바랍니다. 들어주셔서 감사합니다.

02 ⑤ 2016년 3월 고1

남: 오늘 Alington 가에서 자동차사고를 목격했어.
여: 정말? 무슨 일이 있었어?
남: 트럭이 갑자기 멈췄는데 택시가 트럭을 뒤에서 들이받았어.
여: 정말 끔찍하다! 누구 다친 사람이 있어?
남: 택시 운전기사가 다쳤어. 그가 좀 더 조심했어야 했다고 생각해.
여: 무슨 뜻이니?
남: 그가 트럭에 너무 가깝게 운전했거든.
여: 트럭과 택시 사이의 공간이 충분하지 않았다는 뜻이구나, 그렇지?
남: 응. 앞차와 안전거리를 유지하는 것이 중요한데, 그는 그러지 않았어.
여: 그렇구나.

03 ⑤ 2016년 6월 고1

남: 어서 오세요. 무엇을 도와드릴까요?
여: 안녕하세요. 어디서 환전을 할 수 있나요?
남: 모퉁이를 돌아가면 은행이 있어요.
여: 감사합니다. 그리고 관광객용 지하철 노선도를 받을 수 있나요?
남: 그럼요. 저희는 영어, 일본어, 중국어로 된 노선도가 있어요.
여: 좋아요. 영어로 된 것으로 가져갈게요.
남: 네. 그밖에 제가 도와드릴 것이 더 있나요?
여: 아, 호텔에 대한 정보도 필요해요. 어젯밤 묵었던 호텔은 형편없었거든요.
남: 안됐군요. 여기 인근 호텔과 연락 전화번호 목록이 있어요.
여: 도와주셔서 정말 감사합니다.
남: 별말씀을요. 관광객을 돕는 것이 제 일인걸요.

04 ④ 2016년 3월 고1

여: Jason, 이것 좀 봐.
남: 뭔데?
여: 어떤 블로거가 그녀의 방을 꾸민 다음에 사진을 게시했어.
남: 아, 멋져 보인다. 바닥에 둥그런 양탄자가 마음에 들어.
여: 그건 줄무늬 커튼과 잘 어울리는 것 같아.
남: 맞아. 그리고 침대 옆에 있는 전기스탠드도 딱 내가 사고 싶은 종류야.
여: 그 블로거에게 어디서 그것을 샀는지 물어보면 되겠다. 의자 위에 있는 하트 모양 쿠션을 좀 봐.
남: 아주 편안해 보인다.
여: 응. 꽃무늬 담요도 좋아 보여.
남: 맞아. 우리가 방을 꾸밀 때 이 블로그가 도움이 될 것 같아.

05 ② 2016년 6월 고1

남: 안녕하세요, Jenny. 바빠 보이네요. 무슨 일 있어요?
여: 안녕하세요, Nick. 중국인 바이어들이 오늘 우리 회사를 방문해요. 전 그들의 방문을 맞을 준비를 하고 있어요.
남: 아, 그렇군요. 어떻게 되어 가고 있나요?
여: 거의 다 끝났어요. 호텔 방을 예약하고 그들을 위한 선물을 좀 샀어요.
남: 그들은 한국어를 이해하지 못할 수도 있어요. 통역사를 구했나요?
여: 네. 그녀가 곧 올 거예요. 이제 저는 그들을 위한 명찰을 만들 거예요.
남: 제가 도울 일이 있나요?
여: 실은, 공항에 바이어들을 마중 나갈 사람이 필요해요. 그걸 해줄 수 있을까요?
남: 그럼요, 문제없어요. 제가 그곳에 몇 시에 가면 될까요?
여: 5시까지요. 정말 고마워요, Nick.

06 ③ 2016년 6월 고2

남: Amy, 이 옷과 가방은 다 뭐야?
여: 아, 나 뉴욕에 가기 위해 짐을 싸야 해.
남: 뉴욕? 어쩐 일로?
여: 음… 뉴욕에 있는 현대 미술관에서 다음 달에 내 그림들을 전시할 예정이거든!
남: 정말? 축하해! 이건 네가 기다려 왔던 기회잖아.
여: 고마워. 정말 설레. 많은 방문객이 와서 내 그림을 구경할 거야.
남: 잘됐다. 어떻게 그런 기회를 얻었니?
여: 지난달에 그 미술관에 내 작품집을 보냈거든.
남: 그랬더니?
여: 오늘 아침에 그들에게 초대장을 받았어! 내게 비행기 표도 보내줬어.
남: 네 노력이 드디어 성과를 보는구나.
여: 난 개막식에 그곳에 있기를 기대하고 있어.

07 ④ 2016년 9월 고2

남: 뉴욕 시 관광에 오신 것을 환영합니다. 무엇을 도와드릴까요?
여: 안녕하세요. 오늘 사용할 도시 관광 패키지 티켓을 구매하려고 왔는데요.
남: 네. 종일과 반일 패키지 관광이 있어요. 어떤 것을 원하시나요?
여: 차이가 뭐죠?

남: 종일 투어는 세 가지 경로와 다섯 가지 관광지를 포함하고요, 반일 투어는 단 한 가지 경로와 두 가지 관광지를 포함해요.
여: 음. 종일 투어가 제 가족에게 더 나을 것 같네요. 얼마예요?
남: 성인은 60달러이고 어린이는 40달러예요.
여: 그렇군요. 성인 티켓 두 장과 어린이 티켓 두 장 주세요. Metropolitan 회원 카드로 할인을 받을 수 있나요?
남: 네. 전체 금액의 10퍼센트를 할인받으실 수 있어요.
여: 좋네요. 여기 제 신용카드가 있어요.

문제풀이

여자는 60달러짜리 성인 티켓 두 장과 40달러짜리 어린이 티켓 두 장을 사려고 하는데 전체 금액에서 10퍼센트 할인이 된다고 했으므로, 여자가 지불할 금액은 총 180달러(= ($60×2+$40×2)×0.9)이다.

08 ⑤ 2016년 6월 고2

여: 안녕하세요. 무엇을 도와드릴까요?
남: 제가 등에 피부 질환이 있어서요.
여: 제게 증상을 말씀해주시겠어요?
남: 등이 밤새 가려웠어요. 긁었더니 이제 등 전체에 작은 빨간 반점이 생겼어요.
여: 언제 증상이 시작됐죠?
남: 어제저녁에요. 어젯밤에 전혀 잘 수가 없었어요.
여: 최근에 무언가 색다른 것을 먹거나 하지 않으셨어요? 이런 질환들은 사람들이 일상에서 뭔가를 바꿀 때 자주 발생해요.
남: 새 비누에 대한 알레르기 반응일지도 모르겠네요.
여: 그렇다면 저는 이 가려움 방지 크림을 권해드릴게요.
남: 네. 하지만 효과가 없으면 어쩌죠?
여: 그런 경우에는, 병원에 가셔야 해요. 아마 심각한 것은 아닐 테지만, 나중에 후회하는 것보다 미리 조심하는 편이 나으니까요.
남: 맞아요! 감사합니다.

09 ⑤ 2016년 6월 고1

남: 마침내, 5월 17일에 Gainesville 주민 센터가 문을 열었습니다. 이곳은 모든 연령대와 다양한 관심사를 가진 사람들을 위한 곳입니다. 이곳은 컴퓨터실과 춤 연습실, 도서관, 그리고 놀이터를 제공합니다. 센터의 시설을 이용하기 전에 등록이 필요합니다. 등록하시려면, 여러분은 신분증을 가지고 주민 센터를 방문하셔야 합니다. 센터는 평일에는 오전 9시부터 오후 9시까지, 그리고 주말에는 오전 9시부터 오후 5시까지 개방됩니다. 더 많은 정보를 원하시면, 저희 웹사이트에 방문하시거나 정보 센터에 전화하시기 바랍니다. 감사합니다.

10 ③ 2016년 9월 고2

여: 여보, Jimmy가 탈 자전거 결정했어요?
남: 아직이요. 이 다섯 가지 모델들을 보세요. 어떤 것이 좋은 것 같나요?
여: 음, Jimmy의 키가 145센티미터이니까, 이것은 그 애한테 너무 작을 거예요.
남: 맞아요. 그리고 그게 10킬로그램보다는 가벼웠으면 좋겠어요.
여: 저도요. 무거운 자전거는 Jimmy가 타기 더 힘들 거예요.
남: 네. 그리고 우리 차에 싣고 다니려면 접이식 자전거가 더 좋을 것 같아요.
여: 당신 말이 맞아요. 우리는 이 두 가지 중에서 하나를 고르는 편이 좋겠네요. 그런데 저는 300달러 이상은 쓰고 싶지 않아요.
남: 그러면 이것이 우리에게 가장 좋은 선택인 것 같네요.
여: 좋아요. 저것을 사도록 해요.

11 ⑤ 2016년 6월 고2

남: Jane, 그 소설책 다 읽었니?
여: 응, 난 책 전체를 단 이틀 만에 읽었어. 정말 흥미롭더라.
남: 나도 그 책을 읽고 싶어. 내가 네게 빌릴 수 있을까?
여: 미안하지만 오늘 책을 도서관에 반납해야 해.

문제풀이

① 응, 나 영화 보는 것을 좋아해.
② 그럼, 난 네게 그 책을 빌릴 거야.
③ 아니, 나는 그 책의 등장인물들이 마음에 들지 않아.
④ 그래서 사람들이 너를 걸어 다니는 사전이라고 부르는 거야.

12 ③ 2016년 6월 고1

여: 어제 제 컴퓨터 일에 도움을 주셔서 감사합니다.
남: 아, 별일 아니었어요. 10분밖에 걸리지 않은걸요.
여: 아니요, 제게는 정말 큰 일이었어요. 저녁이나 다른 걸 대접하고 싶어요.
남: 아니에요. 도와드릴 수 있어서 저도 기뻤어요.

문제풀이

① 말도 안 돼요. 전혀 같지 않아요.
② 맞아요. 그 식당은 굉장히 좋았어요.
④ 감사합니다. 당신이 우리 집에 오셔서 기뻐요.
⑤ 죄송합니다. 그걸 도와드릴 시간이 없어요.

13 ⑤ 2016년 6월 고1

여: Tom, 오늘 학교에서 어땠니?
남: 힘든 하루였어요, 엄마.
여: 무슨 일 있었니?
남: Jessie가 저한테 화가 났어요.
여: 왜? 너희 둘은 가장 친한 친구잖니.
남: 목요일마다 우리는 함께 수학 공부를 해요. 그런데 제가 항상 늦어요.
여: 그러니? 늦는 건 좋은 습관이 아니야.
남: 알아요. 그래서 지난주에 늦지 않겠다고 약속했어요. 그런데 오늘 또 30분 늦었어요.
여: Jessie가 화난 것도 당연하구나. 그 애한테 미안하다고 말했니?
남: 네. 그렇지만 그 애가 너무 화가 나서 제 사과를 받지도 않고 집에 가버렸어요. 어떻게 해야 하죠?
여: 그 애한테 사과 편지를 써보는 게 어떠니?

문제풀이

① 적어도 넌 미안하다고 했어야 해.
② 그 애가 늦은 것을 용서해주는 것이 어떠니?
③ 네가 왜 그렇게 느끼는지 이해할 수 없어.
④ 때로는 화를 표출하는 것이 좋아.

14 ① 2016년 6월 고1

여: 안으로 들어가자. 영화가 곧 시작할 거야.
남: 그래. 이 영화를 드디어 보게 돼서 정말 신나.
여: 나도야. 재미있으면 좋겠다.
남: 그럴 거야. 주연 배우는 우리를 실망시킨 법이 없잖아.
여: 맞아. 나는 그가 정말 재능 있다고 생각해.
남: 나도 동의해. *[잠시 후]* 와, 오늘 여기 사람이 많네.
여: 응. 이 영화관은 주말에는 항상 붐벼.
남: 저기를 봐. 아주 많은 사람들이 영화 표를 사기 위해 줄 서서 기다리고 있어.
여: 우리가 미리 인터넷으로 표를 예매해서 기뻐.
남: 맞아. 그래서 우리는 오래 줄을 서지 않아도 돼.

문제풀이

② 미안해. 나는 온라인으로 표를 구매하는 법을 몰라.
③ 그렇지 않아. 예매는 필요 없어.
④ 좋아. 영화를 먼저 고르자.
⑤ 괜찮아. 네 잘못이 아니야.

15 ① 2016년 3월 고2

여: Daniel은 전망이 좋은 아파트로 이사를 온다. 그의 친구인 Sarah는 옆집에 산다. 어느 날, 그는 집에 와서 우체통에 작은 소포를 발견한다. 그는 그것을 자신의 아파트로 가져와서 열어본다. 그는 소포 안에서 두 개의 머리핀을 발견한다. 그는 혼란스러워 주소를 주의 깊게 읽어본다. Daniel은 그것들이 Sarah에게 온 것임을 알게 된다. 그 소포는 실수로 그의 우편함에 넣어진 것이었다. 그는 Sarah의 아파트로 간다. Daniel은 소포를 Sarah에게 건네주며 그가 왜 그것을 가지고 있는지 설명하려고 한다. 이런 상황에서, Daniel이 Sarah에게 할 말로 가장 적절한 것은 무엇인가?
Daniel: 이것은 네 거야. 내 우편함으로 배송됐어.

문제풀이

② 집들이가 훌륭했어. 고마워.
③ 물론이야. 이삿짐 회사를 고용하는 편이 더 좋아.
④ 맞아. 이 머리핀들을 환불하고 싶어.
⑤ 이 아파트는 전망이 좋아. 이사 오고 싶어.

16 ① 17 ③ 2016년 9월 고2

남: 안녕하세요, 여러분. 저는 Healthy Talk의 Benjamin Brown입니다. 사람들은 요즘 가정 치료의 편리함뿐만 아니라 모기 물린 곳과 같은 것들에 주는 건강상의 이로움을 발견하고 있습니다. 모기에 잘 물리는 철인데요, 그래서 오늘 그것을 치료하는, 제가 가장 선호하는 가정 치료법들 중 몇 가지에 대해 말씀드리겠습니다. 첫째로, 거의 모든 부엌에서 발견되는 베이킹소다는 좋은 치료제입니다. 베이킹소다와 물을 섞은 것을 환부에 문지르면 완화될 겁니다. 양파는 어떨까요? 양파 또한 물린 곳의 따가움을 없애는 데 도움이 될 수 있습니다. 신선한 양파 조각을 모기 물린 곳에 몇 분간 두기만 하면 가려움이 없어질 겁니다. 레몬 또한 여러분의 친구입니다. 레몬즙을 물린 부위에 바르면 감염이 생길 가능성을 낮추는 데 도움이 될 수 있습니다. 마지막으로, 꿀은 항균성을 많이 가지고 있기 때문에 도움이 됩니다. 이번 여름에 여러분이 이 치료법들의 효과를 보시기를 바랍니다.

문제풀이

16 ① 모기 물린 곳을 위한 가정 치료법
② 의료 행위에 대한 문화적 영향
③ 모기 관련 질병의 건강상 위험성
④ 커져 가는 자연 치료법의 인기
⑤ 벌레 물린 곳의 치료법에 대한 오해

DICTATION Answers

01 have the potential / sound like you / take advantage of
02 hit it from behind / should have been more careful / not enough space
03 around the corner / I can help you with / Here's a list of
04 decorated her room / where she got it / with flower patterns
05 visiting our company / made reservations / someone to pick up
06 exhibit my paintings / get the chance / paying off
07 What's the difference / sounds better for / off the total
08 have a skin problem / all over it / couldn't sleep at all
09 people of all ages / In order to register / is open from
10 decided on / lighter than 10 kg / spend more than
11 borrow it from you
12 treat you to dinner
13 got angry with / study math together / promised not to be late
14 get inside / never disappointed us / we booked tickets
15 with a nice view / a couple of / hands the package to
16-17 for treating them / take the sting out of / applying lemon juice to

03 기출 영어듣기 모의고사

본문 ▲ p.267

01 ②	02 ②	03 ②	04 ⑤	05 ④	06 ④
07 ②	08 ②	09 ④	10 ③	11 ⑤	12 ①
13 ①	14 ③	15 ①	16 ④	17 ④	

01 ② 2016년 3월 고2

여: 안녕하세요, 여러분. Jennifer의 Green Life에 오신 것을 환영합니다. 오늘 밤, 저는 여러분께 몇 가지 질문을 드리고 싶습니다. 여러분은 자연을 사랑하는 분인가요? 여러분은 어두워진 후 숲속에서 무슨 일이 일어나는지 궁금해하신 적이 있으신가요? 만약 여러분의 대답이 "그렇다"라면, 여러분께 꼭 알맞은 프로그램이 있습니다. 시에서 4월, 5월, 그리고 6월 동안 매주 토요일에 숲속 야간 산책을 제공하고 있습니다. 여러분은 숙련된 가이드와 함께 하이킹 코스를 따라 산책하며 밤에 숲속의 모든 경이로움을 즐기실 수 있습니다. 이 프로그램은 무료이지만, 온라인 사전 등록이 필요합니다. 여러분의 가족과 친구를 데려가세요! 이제, 광고 시간입니다. 채널 고정하세요!

02 ② 2015년 9월 고1

남: 고등학교 영웅들에 관한 기사 읽었어?
여: 고등학교 영웅? 무슨 말이야?
남: 몇몇 고등학생들이 그들의 반 친구 중 하나가 학교에서 심장마비를 일으켰을 때 구조했대.
여: 어떻게 그랬대?
남: 구급차가 도착할 때까지 차례로 돌아가면서 인공호흡을 하고 심장 마사지를 했대.
여: 말도 안 돼! 그들이 어떻게 무엇을 할지 알았지?
남: 신문에서는 그 학생들이 정규 응급 처치 훈련 수업을 들었대.
여: 그러면 모두 정기적으로 응급 처치를 실습한 덕분이네?
남: 그런 것 같아. 그래서 그들은 그런 응급 상황에서도 침착하고 그들의 친구를 구조할 수 있었지.
여: 정기적으로 응급 처치를 실습하는 것이 필요한 이유를 이제야 알겠어.
남: 정말 그런 것 같아.

03 ② 2016년 9월 고2

여: 안녕하세요, Brown 씨.
남: 안녕하세요, Duncan 씨. 제 주문이 어떻게 되어가고 있는지 확인하려고 잠깐 들렀어요.
여: 몇 가지 세부 사항들에 대해 여쭤보려고 당신에게 전화하려던 참이었어요.
남: 그렇군요. 무엇인가요?
여: 이 샘플을 보세요. 당신의 안내 책자를 위한 전반적인 콘셉트에 대해서 당신의 의견이 필요해요.
남: 음, 좋긴 한데, 제목을 더 크게 하고 사진을 더 작게 만들어주셨으면 해요.
여: 알겠습니다. 배경 색과 폰트는 어때요?
남: 폰트는 좋긴 한데, 색깔을 약간 더 밝게 하고 싶어요.
여: 네. 디자이너가 그것을 바꾸게 할게요. 1,000부를 프린트해 달라고 주문하셨는데, 맞죠?
남: 맞아요. 기한을 넘기지 말아주세요.
여: 당연하죠, 그러지 않을게요.

04 ⑤ 2016년 6월 고2

여: 어젯밤 마술 쇼 어땠니?
남: 환상적이었어! 사진 보여줄게.
여: 모자를 쓰고 있는 남자가 틀림없이 마술사겠구나.
남: 맞아. 나뭇가지에 앉아 있는 새를 봐. 쇼가 시작할 때, 새가 마술사의 모자에서 나왔어.
여: 멋지다! 그리고 마술사 옆에 있는 안경을 쓴 여자는 누구니?
남: 그녀는 관객 중 한 명이었어.
여: 그녀가 무엇을 했는데?
남: 그녀는 상자가 비었는지 확인했고 그것을 테이블 위에 올려놓았어.
여: 테이블 위의 저 상자 말이니?
남: 응, 믿을 수 없게도, 마술사가 상자에서 꽃을 잡아당겨 꺼냈어. 그래서 꽃이 바닥에 놓여 있는 거야.
여: 와, 틀림없이 멋졌겠구나!
남: 물론이지! 난 무대에서 눈을 뗄 수 없었어.

05 ④ 2015년 11월 고2

[휴대전화벨이 울린다.]
남: 여보세요.
여: 여보, 저예요. 집에 오는 길이에요?
남: 아니요. 아직 사무실인데, 10분 후에 출발할 수 있어요.
여: 잘됐네요. 그럼 이제 요리하기 시작할게요.
남: 오늘 저녁은 뭐예요?
여: 해산물 파스타로 할까 해요.
남: 맛있겠네요. 디저트로 아이스크림 사 갈까요?
여: 아니요, 장 볼 때 그걸 벌써 샀어요. *[잠시 후]* 아, 이런!
남: 무슨 일이에요?
여: 세탁소에서 제 파란 셔츠를 찾아오는 걸 잊었어요.
남: 걱정하지 마세요. 내가 집에 가는 길에 대신 찾아다 줄게요.
여: 고마워요, 여보. 이따 봐요.

06 ④ 2015년 9월 고1

남: 안녕하세요. 도와드릴까요?
여: 네. 최근에 제가 교내 게시판에 저희 음악 동아리 콘서트에 관한 포스터를 좀 붙여 놓았거든요.
남: 그것들에 문제가 있나요?
여: 네, 오늘 아침에 포스터가 모두 사라진 것을 발견했어요.
남: 아마 저희 직원 중 한 명이 그것들을 떼어냈을 거예요. 포스터에 허가 도장이 있었나요?
여: 네. 모든 포스터에 도장을 받았고, 동아리 전용 게시판에 붙였는걸요!
남: 그러면 적절한 곳에 붙여 놓으셨는데요. 언제 그것들을 게시했는지

기억하시나요?
여: 음… 열흘 전에 그것들을 게시했어요.
남: 그래서 그것들이 모두 사라진 거예요. 저희는 포스터가 일주일간 게시된 후에 떼어내거든요.
여: 아, 저런! 그건 몰랐네요.

07 ② 2016년 6월 고2

여: 도와드릴까요?
남: 저희 학교 운동회에 쓸 티셔츠와 모자가 필요해요.
여: 저희는 다양한 종류의 셔츠와 모자가 있어요. 천천히 둘러보세요.
남: 음… 15달러 미만의 티셔츠가 있나요?
여: 그럼요. 이 파란색은 어떠세요? 10달러밖에 안 해요.
남: 좋은데요. 선반 위의 빨간 모자는 얼마예요?
여: 그건 5달러예요. 셔츠와 모자가 몇 개나 필요하세요?
남: 티셔츠 20장과 모자 20개요.
여: 그 정도로 많이 구매하시면, 전체 금액의 10 퍼센트를 할인해드릴 수 있어요.
남: 좋네요. 티셔츠에 "잘했어!" 같은 문구를 새겨주시나요?
여: 네. 저희는 학생들에게 무료로 문구를 새겨드려요.
남: 아주 좋은데요! 여기 제 학생증이에요. 현금으로 결제할게요.
여: 네.

문제풀이

남자는 10달러짜리 티셔츠 20장과 5달러짜리 모자 20개를 구매하기로 했는데 전체 금액에서 10퍼센트 할인이 된다고 했으므로, 남자가 지불할 금액은 총 270달러(= ($10+$5)×20×0.9)이다.

08 ② 2016년 3월 고2

남: Katie, 네 스탠드 귀엽다. 노트북에 연결되어 있니?
여: 이 USB 스탠드 말하는 거니? 응. 밤에 일할 때 쓰는 거야.
남: 나 그런 거 하나 사고 싶어. 어디서 샀니?
여: ABC 온라인 매장에서 샀어. 그건 세일 중이었어.
남: 얼마였는데?
여: 정가는 20달러인데, 나는 12달러만 지불했어.
남: 좋다. 꽤 밝은데. 그건 어떤 종류의 전구를 사용하니?
여: LED 전구가 들어 있어. 그건 에너지 효율이 높고 오랫동안 지속돼.
남: 디자인도 맘에 들어. 현대적이고 단순해.
여: 또 불빛 방향도 손쉽게 조절할 수 있어.
남: 그건 정확히 내가 찾고 있던 것 같아.

09 ④ 2016년 9월 고1

여: 안녕하세요, Kennedy 고등학교 학생 여러분. 저는 여러분께 저희 Kennedy 의류 운동에 대해 말씀드리려고 합니다. 저희는 어려운 이웃을 돕기 위해 매년 이 행사를 개최합니다. 여러분은 옷장을 정리하고 지역 사회를 도울 수 있습니다. 행사는 9월 5일부터 9월 9일까지 5일간 열릴 것입니다. 여러분의 기증품들을 학교 주차장으로 가져오세요. 저희가 그곳에서 오전 8시와 오후 3시 사이에 여러분의 물품을 수집한다는 것을 기억하세요. 저희는 입을 수 있고 사용 가능한 남성용, 여성용, 아동용 의류를 수거하고 있습니다. 신발과 벨트도 받을 것입니다. 커튼이나 담요는 수거하지 않을 것입니다. 여러분의 물품을 비닐 봉투에 담아 가져와주세요. 여러분의 참여를 기대합니다.

10 ③ 2016년 3월 고1

남: 컴퓨터로 뭘 하고 있어?
여: 여름 방학 동안 수영 강습을 들을까 생각 중이야.
남: 강습은 몇 시에 있는데?
여: 오전 7시는 내게 너무 이른 것 같아. 오전 8시에 시작하는 강습을 받고 싶어.
남: 얼마나 자주 강습을 받고 싶어?
여: 일주일에 세 번이 내게 더 좋을 것 같아.
남: 그렇구나. 넌 수영을 할 줄 아니까 아마 중급자 레벨을 원할 거야, 맞지?
여: 난 수영을 할 수 있지만, 기본기를 배우고 싶어.
남: 그러면 초급자 레벨부터 시작하기를 원하니?
여: 응. 난 이 강습을 신청할 거야.

11 ⑤ 2016년 6월 고1

남: 이 사진에서 네 옆에 있는 여자아이는 누구니?
여: 그 애는 내 친구 중 한 명인 Sophie야.
남: 너희 둘은 아주 친해 보인다. 너희는 어떻게 처음 만났니?
여: 우리는 함께 같은 학교에 다녔어.

문제풀이

① 나는 이 사진을 파리에서 찍었어.
② 너도 그 애를 좋아할 거라고 확신해.
③ 그 애는 항상 수학을 잘했어.
④ 너는 내 생일 파티에서 그 애를 만나게 될 거야.

12 ① 2015년 9월 고1

여: Jack, 너 「위대한 개츠비」라는 책 읽어 본 적 있니?
남: 당연하지. 나는 그 책을 작년 문학 수업에서 읽었어.
여: 그 책을 읽는 건 어땠니?
남: 그 책은 내게 정말 감명 깊었어.

문제풀이

② 나는 어제 이미 그 책을 다 읽었어.
③ 나는 올해 많은 책을 읽었어.
④ 문학 수업은 금요일에 있었어.
⑤ 너는 먼저 숙제를 해야 해.

13 ① 2015년 6월 고2

여: 여보, 저 왔어요. 와! 여기 왜 이렇게 더워요?
남: 에어컨을 틀지 않았어요.
여: 왜요? 제가 더위를 견디지 못하는 걸 알잖아요.
남: 네, 하지만 이걸 봐요. 지난달 우리 전기요금 고지서예요.
여: 왜 이렇게 높아요?
남: 분명히, 그건 우리가 한 달 내내 에어컨을 틀어 놓았기 때문이죠.
여: 음, 그렇지만 정말 덥고 습해요. 돈을 약간 아끼자고 여름 내내 땀을

흘리고 싶지는 않아요.
남: 이해해요. 그렇지만 여보, 그건 이번 달 우리 예산을 훨씬 초과해요.
여: 그래도 저는 더운 게 싫어요.
남: 생각해 봐요. 우리는 겨울 휴가를 위해 돈을 모아야 해요.
여: 음 그러면 어떻게 하죠?
남: 대신에 선풍기를 사용하는 것부터 시작해봐요.

문제풀이
② 공기가 너무 습한 것 같지 않나요?
③ 우리는 여행사에 연락해야 해요.
④ 에어컨이 잘 작동하는지 봐요.
⑤ 우리 여름 휴가가 어떨지 상상해봐요.

14 ③ 2015년 6월 고2

남: 지하철이 붐비네. 아! 저기 빈 자리가 있다. Lilly, 앉아.
여: 고마워. 실은, 나 오늘 너무 피곤해.
남: 아, 저쪽에 나이 든 여자분이 서 계시네. 저분께 자리를 양보해드리는 게 어때?
여: 하지만 나는 지쳤어. 다른 누군가가 자리를 양보해줄 거야.
남: 봐, 아무도 저분을 위해 자발적으로 일어나지 않고 있어.
여: 나는 저분을 몰라. 그리고 내가 지하철에 먼저 타 있었어.
남: Lilly, 저분이 네 할머니라고 생각해봐.
여: 음… 할머니는 내게 천사이기 때문에 나는 할머니를 위해 자리를 양보해드렸을 거야.
남: 음, 저쪽에 계신 여자분도 다른 누군가에게 소중할 수 있어.
여: 너는 내가 죄책감을 느끼게 만드는구나.
남: 어서. 그냥 양보해드려! 어차피 우리는 세 정거장 후에 내리잖아.
여: 그래. 저 여자분을 이쪽으로 모셔와 줄래?

문제풀이
① 저분이 네 어머니였으면 좋겠다.
② 나 늦었어. 어서 내리자.
④ 우리 부모님은 내게 교통규칙을 지키라고 가르쳐주셨어.
⑤ 다음 정거장에서 노란 노선으로 갈아타.

15 ① 2016년 6월 고1

남: 서점에서, Ally는 읽기를 기대하고 있던 소설을 산다. 그러나, 그녀가 집에 돌아와 그 책을 짧게 훑어보았을 때, 그녀는 몇 장이 거꾸로 인쇄되어 있는 것을 발견한다. 그녀는 서점으로 돌아가 책을 새것으로 교환해달라고 요청한다. 그러나 점원은 그 책은 지금 매진됐고 새 책이 도착하려면 며칠이 걸릴 거라고 말한다. Ally는 그녀는 돈을 돌려받고 그 소설을 사러 다른 서점으로 가고 싶어 한다. 이런 상황에서, Ally가 점원에게 할 말로 가장 적절한 것은 무엇인가?
Ally: 이 책을 환불할 수 있을까요?

문제풀이
② 이것을 다른 것으로 교환해주시겠어요?
③ 그건 잊어버려요. 이 책을 가져갈게요.
④ 당신이 좋은 책을 추천해주었으면 좋겠어요.
⑤ 새 책을 받으려면 얼마나 오래 걸릴까요?

16 ④ 17 ④ 2016년 6월 고1

여: 안녕하세요, 학생 여러분. 여러분을 위한 건강 관련 조언이 몇 가지 있습니다. 너무 오랫동안 책을 읽거나 컴퓨터를 사용하는 것은 눈의 피로를 유발할 수 있습니다. 그러나, 이러한 간단한 조언을 따름으로써 눈의 피로를 효과적으로 예방하고 경감시킬 수 있습니다. 먼저, 3에서 4초마다 눈을 깜빡이세요. 눈을 깜빡이는 것은 눈이 건조해지는 것을 막는 데 도움이 됩니다. 두 번째, 눈에 휴식을 주세요. 눈에 피로감을 느낀다면 책이나 컴퓨터 화면으로부터 눈을 돌리세요. 세 번째, 눈에 좋은 음식을 드세요. 아몬드와 아보카도와 같이 비타민 B가 풍부한 음식은 좋은 선택입니다. 브로콜리와 베리도 비타민 C를 많이 함유하고 있기 때문에 권장됩니다. 바나나와 감자처럼 비타민 E가 풍부한 음식을 먹는 것도 도움이 됩니다. 건강한 눈을 유지하기 위해 이러한 간단한 조언들을 명심하세요.

문제풀이
16 ① 비타민이 신체에 미치는 영향
② 눈 상태를 확인하는 방법
③ 건강한 다이어트 계획의 중요성
④ 피로한 눈을 다루는 법에 대한 조언
⑤ 스트레스받은 마음을 편안하게 하는 것의 필요성

DICTATION Answers

01 I'd like to ask / walk along the hiking trails / free of charge
02 took turns doing / is it all thanks to / You can say that again
03 about to call you / make the title bigger / have the designer change
04 came out of / made sure that / couldn't take my eyes off
05 leave in 10 minutes / want me to get / forgot to pick up
06 put up some posters / took them down / That's why
07 different types of / on the shelf / pay in cash
08 It was on sale / lasts for a long time / what I'm looking for
09 hold this event / collect your items / will be accepted
10 I'm considering taking / too early for me / learn basic skills
11 look very close
12 like reading it
13 can't stand the heat / left our air conditioner on / way over our budget
14 an old lady standing / give up their seat / making me feel guilty
15 looks through the book / exchange the book / get her money back
16-17 can lead to / keep your eyes from getting dry / maintain healthy eyes

04 기출 영어듣기 모의고사

본문 ▸ p.274

01 ①	02 ①	03 ④	04 ⑤	05 ④	06 ②
07 ④	08 ⑤	09 ③	10 ①	11 ②	12 ⑤
13 ①	14 ③	15 ③	16 ②	17 ②	

01 ① 2015년 9월 고1

남: 오늘 와주신 것에 감사드립니다. 이 학부모 회의를 마치기 전에, 여러분께 말씀드릴 것이 있습니다. 아시다시피, 우리 학교는 작년부터 베이징 중등학교와 제휴를 맺고 있습니다. 그 학교에서 다섯 명의 중국인 교사들이 다음 학기에 우리 학생들을 가르치기 위해 오실 것입니다. 그래서 우리는 방문자들에게 숙식을 제공할 가족들을 찾고 있습니다. 그들은 1월에 저희에게 합류하여 학기 말까지 머무를 것입니다. 여러분의 집에 그들이 머무르게 하는 것은 여러분의 가족이 새로운 문화에 대해 배울 좋은 기회가 될 것입니다. 관심이 있으시면, 교무실의 Gilmore 씨에게 연락주시기 바랍니다.

02 ① 2015년 11월 고1

남: 여보, 여기 흥미로운 기사가 있어요.
여: 뭐에 관한 거예요?
남: 그건 학교 숙제에 관한 거예요. 학교 숙제가 금지되어야 한다고 쓰여 있어요.
여: 이해가 안 되네요. 작성자는 왜 그렇게 생각하는 거죠?
남: 그는 학생들이 하루 종일 학교에서 공부를 해서 숙제를 내주는 것은 그들이 스트레스를 받게 한다고 하네요.
여: 하지만 숙제를 하는 것은 학생들이 학교에서 배운 것을 복습할 좋은 방법이에요.
남: 기사에 의하면, 학생들은 방과 후에 휴식을 취하고 친구들과 놀 시간이 필요하대요.
여: 그건 말이 되네요. 하지만 저는 학생들이 할 숙제가 없으면 온종일 컴퓨터 게임을 할까 봐 걱정되네요.
남: 저도 그게 걱정돼요.
여: 저는 학생들에게 숙제를 내주는 것이 필요하다고 생각해요.
남: 저도 동의해요. 그것은 학생들에게 도움이 될 거예요.

03 ④ 2016년 9월 고1

남: 안녕하세요. 무엇을 도와드릴까요?
여: 안녕하세요. 제가 최근에 이것을 샀는데, 이게 계속 저절로 꺼지네요.
남: 제가 봐도 될까요?
여: 네, 여기요.
남: *[잠시 후]* 바이러스에 감염돼서, 그게 당신의 휴대전화를 멈추게 만들고 있네요.
여: 그렇군요. 수리가 가능할까요?
남: 네, 그런데 만약 바이러스가 제거되지 않으면, 당신의 휴대전화를 초기화시켜야 할 거예요.
여: 초기화되면, 제 휴대전화에 있는 모든 애플리케이션과 파일은 어떻게 되나요?
남: 걱정하지 마세요. 휴대폰을 수리하기 전에 제가 모든 앱과 파일을 백업해 놓을게요.
여: 감사해요. 언제 찾으러 오면 될까요?
남: 오후 4시까지는 끝날 거예요. 그 이후에 서비스 센터로 다시 오시면 됩니다.

04 ⑤ 2016년 3월 고2

남: Amy, 그 가구 카탈로그에서 뭔가 살 거니?
여: 그럴 계획이야. 내 서재에 놓을 가구를 좀 사야 하거든.
남: 음… 벽에 걸린 책꽂이가 좋아 보이는걸.
여: 난 저런 걸 원했어. 이 책꽂이를 벽에 걸면 완벽할 것 같아.
남: 책꽂이 밑에 있는 이 게시판은 어떠니? 넌 그 위에 중요한 메모를 붙일 수 있어.
여: 마음에 들어! 그리고 책상 위의 스탠드도 책을 읽는 데 좋을 것 같아.
남: 그리고 책상 밑의 서랍도 유용해 보여.
여: 응, 나도 그렇게 생각해. 저 안에 많은 물건을 보관할 수 있을 거야.
남: 바퀴가 네 개 달린 의자도 마음에 들어.
여: 나도야. 편안하고 앉아서 이리저리 움직이기 쉬울 것 같아.
남: 너 이 페이지에 있는 모든 것이 마음에 드는 것 같은데.
여: 실은, 그래.

05 ④ 2015년 9월 고1

[전화벨이 울린다.]
남: Lanson 아파트 관리사무실입니다. 도와드릴까요?
여: 네, 저는 14호에 사는데요. 제 부엌 싱크대에 문제가 있어서요.
남: 좀 더 구체적으로 말씀해주시겠어요?
여: 방금 부엌 싱크대에서 물을 틀었는데, 물이 배수관으로 내려가지 않아요.
남: 알겠습니다. 오늘 오후에 댁으로 수리공을 보내겠습니다.
여: 그 시간에 제가 집에 있을지 잘 모르겠네요. 그분께 오시기 전에 제게 전화해 달라고 전해주시겠어요? 제 전화번호는 520-234-8500이에요.
남: 알겠습니다. 싱크대 아래 보관함에 들어 있는 것이 있나요?
여: 네. 조리 기구와 다른 것들을 그곳에 넣어 놓았어요.
남: 그러면, 수리공이 부엌 싱크대 아래 배수관을 확인할 수 있도록 그것들을 치워주세요.
여: 네, 그럴게요. 감사합니다.

문제풀이

① 싱크대에 뜨거운 물 틀기
② 관리사무실에 전화하기
③ 부엌 배수관 수리하기
④ 싱크대 아래 찬장 비우기
⑤ 배관공에게 그녀의 주소를 보내기

06 ② 2015년 9월 고2

남: 안녕, Olivia. 지난 주말에 자전거 탄 건 어땠니?
여: 음, 타지 못했어.

남: 왜? 자전거 타기에 완벽한 날씨였잖아.
여: 알아. 하지만 내가 막 출발하려고 했을 때, 우리 언니가 전화를 했어.
남: 중요한 일이었니?
여: 언니가 독감에 걸려서 내가 언니의 아기를 봐줄 수 있는지 물어봤어.
남: 그러면 자전거 타는 대신에 네 조카를 돌봐줘야 했던 거니?
여: 응. 그래도 조카와 아주 즐거운 시간을 보냈어.
남: 잘됐네. 하지만 너는 지난주에 시험공부 하느라 바빴고, 그래서 자전거 타기가 기분 전환하게 했을 텐데.
여: 항상 다음 기회가 있으니까. 다음 주 자원봉사가 끝날 때까지 기다려야 할 것 같아.

07 ④ 2015년 9월 고2

여: 안녕하세요, 저 좀 도와주시겠어요? 미니 컵케이크 팬을 사야 해요.
남: 알겠습니다. 저희는 금속과 실리콘 팬이 있어요. 금속 팬은 개당 20달러이고 실리콘 팬은 개당 15달러예요.
여: 음, 금속이 실리콘보다 더 튼튼하니까 금속 팬 두 개를 살게요.
남: 저희는 특별 행사를 진행 중이에요. 컵케이크 팬 두 개를 사시면 10퍼센트 할인을 받으실 수 있어요.
여: 좋은데요! 컵케이크용 선물 상자도 좀 살까 봐요.
남: 상자는 저쪽에 있어요.
여: 와, 이 빨간 상자 귀여운데요. 이것으로 네 개를 살게요.
남: 이것들은 개당 2달러예요. 더 필요한 것이 있으세요?
여: 이제 됐어요. 상자도 할인이 되나요?
남: 죄송하지만 안 됩니다.
여: 괜찮아요. 여기 제 신용카드요.

문제풀이

여자는 20달러짜리 금속 팬 2개와 2달러짜리 상자 4개를 구매했는데, 금속 팬은 10퍼센트 할인이 된다고 했으므로, 여자가 지불할 금액은 총 44달러(= (\$20×2×0.9)+(\$2×4))이다.

08 ⑤ 2015년 6월 고1

[전화벨이 울린다.]
남: 안녕하세요, Healing Spa 호텔입니다. 무엇을 도와드릴까요?
여: 예약 좀 하려고요. 귀하의 호텔에서 특가 행사를 한다는 이메일을 받았어요.
남: 네, 손님. 이번 달에 손님께서 2박을 하시면, 3번째 밤 숙박을 무료로 제공해드립니다.
여: 좋네요. 20일부터 23일까지 더블룸을 예약하고 싶어요.
남: 그러면 3박 맞으시죠?
여: 네. 바다 전망의 방이 있나요?
남: 한번 볼게요. *[잠시 후]* 네. 그런데 그 기간에는 방이 하나만 남아 있네요. 세금을 포함해서 하룻밤에 100달러예요.
여: 적당한 것 같네요. 그 방을 예약할게요. 언제 체크인할 수 있나요?
남: 오후 3시 이후에 체크인하실 수 있어요.
여: 좋아요! 그때 뵙겠습니다.

09 ③ 2016년 3월 고2

남: 바쁜 도시 생활로 인해 스트레스를 받으시나요? Annapurna Adventure Bike Ride는 히말라야의 심장부에서 일주일 동안의 멋진 모험을 제공합니다. 저희는 1년에 16번 출발합니다. 여러분은 아름다운 히말라야 계곡을 따라 자전거를 타실 수 있습니다. 그것이 너무 위험할까 봐 걱정되시나요? 걱정하지 마세요. 코스에서 가파르고 위험한 길은 차로 이동합니다. 저희는 여러분의 안전과 순조로운 여정을 위해 새 고급 산악용 자전거와 헬멧을 제공합니다. 또한, 자격을 갖춘 자전거 수리공과 여행 가이드가 각 팀과 함께 달립니다. 더 많은 정보를 원하시면, 저희 홈페이지 www.annapurnaadventure.com을 방문하세요.

10 ① 2015년 11월 고1

여: 여보, 이 웹사이트 좀 봐요! Mike에게 줄 비타민을 좀 살까 해요.
남: 그거 좋네요. 아이들에게 비타민이 아주 중요하다고 들었어요.
여: 저도 그렇게 들었어요. 그래서 제가 그 애를 위해 비타민을 사고 싶은 거예요.
남: 어떤 제품을 마음에 두고 있어요?
여: 비타민 C로 시작하는 게 좋을 것 같은데, 왜냐하면 가장 흔하니까요.
남: 맞아요. 그건 틀림없이 Mike에게 좋을 거예요. 아, 젤리와 알약, 두 종류의 비타민 C가 있네요.
여: Mike는 당연히 젤리 형태로 된 것을 먹고 싶어 할 거예요.
남: 저도 동의해요. 이제 우리에게 두 가지 선택이 남았네요.
여: 더 적은 양을 먼저 사보는 게 어때요? Mike가 좋아하지 않을 경우를 대비해서요.
남: 그래요. 또 이것은 20달러도 안 해요. 지금 이것을 사요.

11 ② 2015년 9월 고2

여: 와, 저기에 있는 저 분홍색 블라우스를 봐!
남: 아주 멋지다. 너에게 아주 잘 어울릴 것 같아.
여: 응, 마음에 들어. 내 사이즈가 있으면 좋겠다.
남: 가서 점원에게 물어보자.

문제풀이

① 더 큰 것으로 주실 수 있나요?
③ 나는 돈이 충분하지 않아.
④ 저희 가게에 들러주셔서 감사합니다.
⑤ 문제없어. 나도 그게 매우 마음에 들어.

12 ⑤ 2016년 9월 고2

남: 와, 네 식물들은 좋아 보인다! 내 것은 왜 이렇게 병든 것 같아 보이는지 모르겠어.
여: 얼마나 자주 네 식물에 물을 주니?
남: 나는 매일 몇 차례씩 꼭 물을 줘.
여: 그게 이유일 거야. 너무 많은 물은 뿌리를 상하게 할 수 있거든.

문제풀이

① 사실이야. 나는 그것들을 몇 년 동안 길러왔어.
② 나는 부모님께 식물 기르는 법을 배웠어.
③ 좋아. 너는 식물 기르는 데 재능이 있는 것이 틀림없어.
④ 방에 식물을 키우는 것은 네 기분을 좋게 하는 데 도움이 될 거야.

13 ① 2016년 3월 고1

남: Jessica, 너 몸이 안 좋아 보여.
여: 난 오늘 좀 피곤해.
남: 무슨 문제가 있니?
여: 난 어젯밤에 나쁜 꿈을 꿨어.
남: 나쁜 꿈? 내게 그것에 대해 말해줄 수 있니?
여: 괴물이 나를 쫓아오고 있었고 나는 도망쳐야 했어.
남: 그거 끔찍하다. 그다음에 무슨 일이 일어났어?
여: 괴물이 나를 붙잡기 바로 전에 나는 땀을 흘리며 깼어.
남: 그거 정말 무시무시하다.
여: 응. 오늘 내게 뭔가 나쁜 일이 일어날까 봐 걱정돼.
남: 걱정하지 마. 그저 꿈일 뿐이야.

문제풀이

② 맞아. 나는 괴물 영화를 좋아해.
③ 열심히 노력하면, 너는 꿈을 이룰 수 있을 거야.
④ 응. 내가 내일 아침에 널 깨워 줄게.
⑤ 그거 이상한데. 오늘 내게 아무 일도 일어나지 않았어.

14 ③ 2015년 11월 고1

남: 아, 이런! Sue, 우리 문제가 생겼어.
여: 뭐가 문제니, Kevin? 네 차에 무슨 문제가 있니?
남: 그런 것 같아. 시동이 걸리지 않아.
여: 정말? 다시 해봐.
남: 해보고 있는데, 작동이 안 돼. 실은, 며칠 전에 같은 일이 일어났었어.
여: 너는 자동차 정비소에 전화해서 바로 점검을 받아봐야 할 것 같은데.
남: 그러고 싶은데, 오늘은 일요일이야. 오늘 문을 연 정비소가 없을 것 같아.
여: 맞아. 아, 잠깐만! 우리 오빠가 차에 관해 많이 알아. 오빠가 뭐가 문제인지 알아낼 수 있을지도 몰라.
남: 정말? 지금 당장 시간이 있으실까?
여: 오빠에게 우리를 도와주러 올 수 있는지 물어볼게.

문제풀이

① 나는 엔진의 시동을 거는 법을 알아.
② 너는 이번 일요일에 내 차를 사용할 수 없어.
④ 우리 집 근처에 자동차 정비소가 하나 있어.
⑤ 우리 오빠는 자동차에 관해 아무것도 몰라.

15 ③ 2016년 9월 고2

여: Bill은 학교 연극 동아리의 회원이다. 어느 날, 동아리 회원들은 다음 달에 열리는 지역 학생 연극 경연대회에 출전하기로 결정한다. 그래서 동아리의 회장인 Rachel이 회원들에게 내일부터 일주일에 두 번 연습 시간을 가질 것이라고 말한다. 그러나, 그들은 일주일 후에 시험이 있고, Bill은 일정 때문에 걱정하고 있다. 그는 다가오는 시험 때문에 많은 회원들이 연습을 좋아하지 않을 것이라고 생각한다. 이제, 그는 Rachel에게 그들이 공부할 충분한 시간을 가질 수 있도록 시험이 끝난 후에 연습을 시작하자고 제안하고 싶어 한다. 이런 상황에서, Bill이 Rachel에게 할 말로 가장 적절한 것은 무엇인가?
Bill: 시험이 끝날 때까지 연습을 미루자.

문제풀이

① 우리는 시험에 늦지 말아야 한다고 생각해.
② 우리 학생 연극 경연대회에 출전하는 것이 어때?
④ 공연이 언제 열릴지 내게 말해줘.
⑤ 우리는 네가 계획했던 것보다 더 자주 연습을 하는 것이 좋겠어.

16 ② 17 ② 2016년 3월 고2

여: 안녕하세요, 여러분. 봄이 와서 더 많은 사람들이 몸매를 가꾸는 데 관심을 보이고 있습니다. 그러나 체육관에 갈 시간을 내는 것은 쉽지 않습니다. 일상생활에서 운동할 수 있는 좋은 방법들이 몇 가지 있습니다. 사무실에서 매시간 일어날 수 있도록 알람을 맞춰 두세요. 다시 자리에 앉기 전에 간단한 운동을 하세요. 통근하실 때는 걷고, 걷고, 또 걸으세요. 몇 정거장 전에 버스에서 내려서 걸으세요. 지하철역에서는 열차를 기다리는 동안 승강장 주변을 돌아다니세요. 쇼핑몰에서는 결정을 내리기 전에 쇼핑몰 전체를 적어도 두 번 돌아보는 것을 습관화하세요. 쇼핑 두 시간은 300칼로리 정도를 소모합니다. 집에서는 거실에서 TV를 시청하는 동안 춤을 추거나 스트레칭 운동을 하세요. 기억하세요. 여러분이 몸을 더 많이 움직일수록 더 건강하고 더 행복해집니다!

문제풀이

16 ① 운동을 위한 안전 지침
② 일상생활에서 운동하는 방법
③ 체육관에서 운동하는 것의 장점
④ 스트레스에 대처하는 데 있어 운동의 역할
⑤ 운동하는 동안 음악 듣는 것의 효과

DICTATION Answers

01 had a partnership with / to host the visitors / to learn about
02 should be banned / what students learned / That makes sense
03 keeps turning itself off / cannot be removed / repair your phone
04 for my study / put important memos on / easy to move around
05 going down the pipe / I'm not sure if / remove them
06 I didn't get to / she asked me if / you were busy studying
07 more durable than / take four of these / on discount as well
08 has a special offer / book a double room / during that period
09 stressed out / covered by car / ride along with
10 important for children / have in mind / have two options left
11 over there
12 How often do you water
13 had a bad dream / woke up in a sweat / something bad might happen
14 Is there something wrong / get it checked / Is he available
15 decide to join / twice a week / enough time to study
16-17 getting into shape / a few stops ahead / make it a rule

05 기출 영어듣기 모의고사

본문 ▲ p.281

01 ④ 02 ② 03 ② 04 ⑤ 05 ① 06 ④
07 ④ 08 ④ 09 ③ 10 ② 11 ② 12 ②
13 ⑤ 14 ⑤ 15 ① 16 ② 17 ④

01 ④ 2015년 6월 고2

남: 안녕하세요, 여러분. 여러분과 이 소중한 시간을 함께할 수 있어서 정말 기쁩니다. 저는 20년 넘게 치과의사로 일해 왔습니다. 그리고 심각한 치아 문제가 있는 환자들을 만날 때마다, 저는 치아를 건강하게 유지하는 법을 그들에게 알려주고 싶었습니다. 대부분의 충치와 잇몸 질환은 이를 닦는 동안 나쁜 습관으로부터 발생합니다. 이를 닦을 때, 입안을 네 부분으로 나누고 각각에 30초씩 써야 합니다. 잇몸 선을 따라 치아 표면의 안과 밖을 꼼꼼히 닦으세요. 하루에 3번 이상 이를 닦는 것은 이상적이지 않은데, 왜냐하면 여러분이 잇몸에 손상을 줄 수 있기 때문입니다. 여러분께 올바른 과정을 만화로 보여드리겠습니다.

02 ② 2015년 11월 고2

여: Jake, 네 중요한 발표가 내일이구나! 준비 잘했니?
남: 응, 나는 준비가 된 것 같아. 행운을 빌어줘!
여: 그렇게. *[잠시 후]* 아! 가능하면, 발표 전에 하늘이나 바다 사진을 봐.
남: 무슨 사진? 네 말이 이해가 안 가.
여: 나는 색에 대해 말하는 거야. 파란색이 사람들이 느긋하고 편안하게 느끼도록 도와준다고 잘 알려져 있어.
남: 정말? 나는 색이 우리 감정에 영향을 줄 수 있다는 걸 몰랐어.
여: 응, 내가 읽은 책에 의하면 그렇다고 해.
남: 흥미로운데! 좀 더 이야기해줄 수 있니?
여: 그럼. 빨간색은 사람들을 활기차고 들뜨게 해.
남: 아, 그래서 빨간색이 스포츠 경기에서 응원하는 데 널리 쓰이는 거구나.
여: 응. 색은 우리 감정에 영향을 미칠 수 있어.
남: 놀라운데! 좋은 정보 고마워.

03 ② 2015년 6월 고2

남: 상 탄 것 축하해요, Liz.
여: 고마워요, John. 당신의 최신 영화도 인상적이었어요.
남: 감사합니다.
여: 그 영화가 큰 인기를 얻을 거라고 생각해요.
남: 저도 그러기를 바라요. 최근에 제 다음 영화를 위한 완벽한 시나리오를 찾았어요. 당신을 주역으로 생각하고 있어요.
여: 어떤 역할인데요?
남: 젊은 나이에 기억을 잃어가는 알츠하이머 환자예요.
여: 아, 절대 안 돼요. 제가 마지막으로 암 환자 역할을 했을 때 10킬로그램이나 감량해야 했거든요.
남: 하지만 이번에는 그러지 않아도 돼요. 당신이 시나리오를 읽으면 좋

아하게 될 거라고 장담해요.
여: 알았어요, 읽어볼게요.
남: 좋아요! 제가 시나리오를 내일 당신 매니저의 사무실로 배달시킬게요.
여: 좋아요.
남: 당신이 그 역할을 수락하면, 우리는 가능한 한 빨리 촬영을 시작할 거예요.

04 ⑤ 2015년 11월 고1

남: 와! 우리 집 근처에 이런 카페가 있는지 몰랐어.
여: 응. 나는 가끔 휴식을 취하러 여기에 와.
남: 이곳은 매우 편안해 보이는걸. 아, 메뉴판 좀 봐. 꽃으로 장식되어 있어.
여: 그리고 카운터에 있는 화분이 이곳을 아늑하게 만들어주고 있어.
남: 맞아. 우리 커피 주문하지 않을래?
여: 좋아. 내가 주문할 동안 가서 자리에 앉아.
남: 고마워. 벽에 붙어 있는 긴 테이블에 앉기 원하니?
여: 중앙에 있는 원탁에 앉는 것은 어때?
남: 그거 좋지. 아, 책꽂이에 책이 몇 권 있네.
여: 응, 커피를 마실 동안 우리는 저 책들을 읽을 수 있어.
남: 이곳은 쉬기에 완벽한 장소인 것 같아.

05 ① 2016년 3월 고2

남: 수민아, 안녕. 여기야! 헝가리에 온 것을 환영해.
여: 안녕, Dominik. 공항까지 마중 나와줘서 고마워.
남: 별거 아냐. 내가 한국에 있을 때 네가 나를 위해 많은 것을 해줬잖아.
여: 나도 한국에서 너를 구경시켜 주는 게 즐거웠어.
남: 우리가 본 한국의 궁들과 함께 먹은 길거리 음식들이 기억나.
여: 응. 너는 매운 음식을 먹는 것을 힘들어했지.
남: 아, 그런데, 너 이곳 부다페스트에서 사용할 전화기가 필요하니?
여: 나 벌써 휴대전화를 빌렸는데, 언어 설정을 한국어로 바꿔야 해.
남: 도움이 필요하니?
여: 응. 이 전화기는 내가 한국에서 쓰던 것과는 아주 달라.
남: 응. 나한테 줘봐.

06 ④ 2015년 6월 고1

여: 살았다! 중간고사가 끝났어.
남: 응. 하늘을 나는 기분이야. 이번 토요일에 계획 있니, Lisa?
여: 동물 보호소에서 자원봉사를 하려고.
남: 거기서 뭘 하기로 했는데?
여: 고양이와 개들에게 먹이 주는 것을 도울 거야. 재미있을 거야. 나랑 같이 갈래?
남: 정말 재미있을 것 같긴 한데, 나는 못 가.
여: 왜? 이번 토요일에 할 일이 있니?
남: 아니, 한가하긴 할 텐데, 나는 동물 털 알레르기가 있어서.
여: 정말 안됐다. 다음에는 대신에 도서관 같은 다른 곳에 가자.
남: 그거 좋다.

07 ④ 2015년 11월 고1

여: 새로운 머리 모양이 마음에 드세요, 손님?
남: 이번이 제가 처음으로 파마하는 거예요. 그런데, 마음에 드네요.
여: 머리를 파마하시니까 더 멋져 보이시네요.
남: 감사합니다. 얼마예요?
여: 손님은 머리를 자르시고 파마하셨네요, 그렇죠?
남: 맞아요.
여: 음, 머리 커트 가격은 20달러이고, 파마는 40달러예요.
남: 할인이 되나요?
여: 네. 정오 전에 방문하신 고객님들은 20퍼센트 할인해드려요.
남: 잘됐네요. 그러면 전체 금액에서 할인을 받을 수 있나요?
여: 네, 그러실 수 있어요. 어떻게 결제하고 싶으세요?
남: 현금으로 결제할게요.

문제풀이
남자는 20달러짜리 커트를 하고 40달러짜리 파마를 했는데 전체 금액에서 20퍼센트 할인이 된다고 하였으므로, 남자가 지불할 금액은 총 48달러(= (\$20+\$40)×0.8)이다.

08 ④ 2015년 9월 고1

남: Clare, 네 보고서를 위한 설문 조사 어떻게 되어 가니?
여: 거의 다 준비됐어. 시작하기 전에 몇 가지를 확인하는 중이야.
남: 네 설문 조사는 무엇에 관한 거니?
여: 스마트폰이 우리 일상생활에 어떠한 영향을 미치는가에 관한 거야.
남: 흥미로운데. 누구에게 설문 조사를 할 거니?
여: 한 무리의 대학생들에게 설문 조사를 할까 해.
남: 어떻게 그들에게 설문 조사를 할 거니?
여: 적어도 100명의 학생들을 직접 인터뷰할 계획이야.
남: 그거 좋은 생각이다. 그 학생들에게 선물 같은 것을 주는 게 어떨까?
여: 그것에 대해 벌써 생각해봤어. 나는 그들에게 스마트폰 액세서리를 줄 거야.
남: 좋은데. 너는 모든 걸 계획해 놓은 것 같구나. 설문 조사 잘하기를 바라.

09 ③ 2015년 9월 고2

여: 안녕하세요, 학생 여러분! 오늘 저는 여러분께 온타리오 주 대학 박람회인 OUF에 대해 알려드리고자 합니다. 온타리오 주에서 대학을 다니는 것을 고려하신다면, 이 기회를 놓치지 마세요. 온타리오 주 21개의 모든 대학들이 이 행사에 참여할 것입니다! OUF는 Metro Toronto Convention Center에서 9월 25일부터 27일까지 3일간 개최됩니다. OUF에서는 모든 방문객들을 환영합니다. 입장료나 사전 등록은 필요하지 않습니다. OUF에서 여러분은 프로그램, 입학 요건, 학교생활 등 더 많은 것들에 대한 정보를 얻기 위해 대학생들과 교수님들과 직접 대화를 할 수 있습니다. 캐나다에서 가장 큰 교육 박람회를 놓치지 마세요! 더 많은 정보를 원하시면, 저희 웹사이트를 방문하세요. 감사합니다.

10 ② 2015년 9월 고1

남: 여보, 우리 이곳 런던에서 무엇을 할 거예요?

여: 셜록 홈스 도보 투어는 어때요? 호텔 로비에서 팸플릿을 가져왔어요.
남: 좋은 생각이에요. 어디 봐요… 우리가 언제 런던을 떠나죠?
여: 이번 토요일 아침에요. 그러니 우리는 수요일이나 금요일에 가야 해요.
남: 그래요. 우리는 투어 길이도 선택해야 해요. 2시간이나 3시간의 옵션이 있네요.
여: 이 더운 날씨에 3시간은 우리에게 조금 힘들 것 같아요.
남: 저도 그렇게 생각해요. 2시간이 나을 것 같네요.
여: 좋아요. 캐릭터 의상을 입어보고 싶어요? 재미있고 신날 거예요.
남: 네! 저는 셜록 홈스처럼 변장할 수 있겠네요! 우리 캐릭터 변장 옵션을 골라요.
여: 좋아요! 음, 두 가지 옵션이 남았네요. 더 저렴한 것이 나을 것 같아요.
남: 저도 그렇게 생각해요. 우리 이것으로 골라요.

11 ② 2015년 6월 고1

여: 아, 이런. 또 교통 체증이라니! 우리 콘서트에 늦을지도 몰라.
남: 걱정하지 마. 이 모퉁이만 돌면 괜찮을 거야.
여: 그러기를 바라. 공연이 시작하기 전에 시간이 얼마나 있지?
남: 아직 40분 남았어.

문제풀이

① 나는 보통 버스를 타고 출근해.
③ 그럼, 콘서트는 재미있을 거야.
④ 다음 모퉁이에서 조심해.
⑤ 아니, 나는 콘서트에 가고 싶지 않아.

12 ② 2015년 9월 고2

남: 왜 갑자기 네 컴퓨터가 멈췄니?
여: 그걸 알아내려고 했는데, 뭐가 잘못됐는지 못 알아냈어.
남: 그러면, 수리공을 불러야 할 것 같아.
여: 알았어, 고객 서비스 센터에 전화할게.

문제풀이

① 문제없어. 내가 언제 너를 방문하면 될까?
③ 그럼, 수리공이 방금 컴퓨터를 고쳤어.
④ 음, 우리는 새 컴퓨터가 필요할 것 같지 않아.
⑤ 저기, 우리 함께 컴퓨터 게임을 하지 않을래?

13 ⑤ 2016년 9월 고2

남: 안녕하세요, 부인.
여: 안녕하세요, Taylor 씨. 제 프랑스어 시험 결과를 확인할 수 있을까요?
남: 그럼요. *[타이핑 소리]* 여기요. 당신은 발음을 제외한 대부분의 영역에서 좋은 점수를 받았어요.
여: 음… 발음을 좀 더 연습하려면 어떤 수업이 제게 좋을까요?
남: 음, 초급 말하기 수업이 당신에게 적합할 것 같네요.
여: 그러면 다음 달에 말하기 수업을 들을게요. 아침에 하는 수업이 있나요?
남: 화요일 오전 7시 수업과 목요일 오전 9시 수업이 있네요.
여: 화요일 수업을 들을게요.
남: 네. 강사는 Martin 씨예요.
여: 아, 그분 수업이 조금 어렵다고 들었어요. 제가 따라갈 수 있을 거라 생각하세요?
남: 그럼요. 그분은 대부분의 초급자들에게 좋은 평가를 받고 있어요.

문제풀이

① 아니요. 그분 수업에는 자리가 없어요.
② 알겠습니다. 이번에는 언어 수업을 들어볼게요.
③ 신경 쓰지 마세요. 당신은 좋은 언어 선생님이 될 수 있어요.
④ 좋아요. 그 수업을 저희 반 학생들에게 추천할게요.

14 ⑤ 2016년 3월 고2

남: Ally, 나 점심거리를 사러 간이 식당에 갈 거야 나랑 같이 갈래?
여: 나는 괜찮아. 나 샌드위치를 싸 왔어.
남: 그러면, 마실 것이 필요하니?
여: 아니. 실은, 나 오늘 아무것도 사지 않을 거야.
남: 아, 왜 그렇지?
여: 오늘은 국제 아무것도 사지 않기의 날이거든.
남: 아무것도 사지 않기의 날? 그게 뭔데?
여: 그날 아무것도 사지 않고, 대신에 네가 아낀 돈을 자선 단체에 기부하는 거야.
남: 그것참 뜻깊다.
여: 나는 2년 전부터 그날을 기념하기 시작했는데, 그건 나를 기분 좋게 해.
남: 나도 참여하고 싶은데, 점심거리를 싸 오지 않았어.
여: 내 점심을 나눠 먹고 네 점심값을 기부하도록 해.

문제풀이

① 그러면 내가 네게 먹을 것을 사줄게.
② 네 기부는 가난한 아이들을 위해 쓰였어.
③ 오늘 내게 점심을 대접하다니 넌 상냥하구나.
④ 오랫동안 기부를 해왔다니 감명 깊은걸.

15 ① 2015년 9월 고1

남: Bill과 Carrie는 둘 다 여행하는 것과 사진 찍는 것을 좋아한다. 오늘 그들은 아프리카 탄자니아의 사파리 자동차 투어를 할 것이다. 탄자니아는 야생동물, 특히 아름다운 사진을 찍을 수 있는 수천 마리의 버펄로 떼로 유명하다. Bill은 그 버펄로들의 근접 촬영 사진을 찍을 수 있어 신이 난다. 그래서 그가 버펄로 떼를 보자, 그것들을 더 가까이서 사진 찍기 위해 차에서 내리려고 한다. 그러나 Carrie는 차 밖으로 나가는 것의 위험성에 대해 걱정한다. 그래서 그녀는 그에게 사진을 찍을 때 차 안에 있으라고 말하고 싶다. 이런 상황에서 Carrie가 Bill에게 할 말로 가장 적절한 것은 무엇인가?
Carrie: 사진을 찍으려고 차에서 내리지 마.

문제풀이

② 운전할 때 동물들을 조심해.
③ 나는 야생동물 사진을 찍는 것을 좋아해.
④ 뒷좌석에 여분의 카메라가 있어.
⑤ 밤에 공원을 혼자 걸어 다니지 마.

16 ② 17 ④ 2016년 3월 고1

남: 안녕하세요, 여러분! 향초에 대해 들어보셨습니까? 향초란 좋은 향이 나는 초인데요. 오늘, 저는 여러분께 향초를 켜는 것의 장점 하나를 말씀드리고자 합니다. 방을 환하게 하는 것 이외에, 향초는 그 향기로 평범한 방을 특별하게 만들 수 있습니다. 연구에 의하면 초의 향이 단지 분위기를 개선하는 것 이상을 한다고 합니다. 그것은 또한 여러분의 기분에도 영향을 줍니다. 어떤 향들은 실제로 스트레스 지수를 낮출 수 있습니다. 예를 들어, 라벤더 향은 스트레스와 불안감을 완화시키는 데 도움이 된다고 합니다. 바닐라 향 또한 안정 효과로 스트레스를 줄인다고 알려져 있습니다. 어떤 향들은 긍정적인 감정을 조성하는 경향이 있습니다. 예를 들어, 로즈메리 향은 만족감을 줍니다. 재스민 향은 슬픔과 우울감을 극복하는 데 도움이 될 수 있습니다. 여러분도 활기를 되찾기 위해 향초를 사용해보시는 것이 어떠세요?

문제풀이

16 ① 왜 보디 케어를 위해 오일을 사용해야 하는지
② 어떻게 향초가 감정에 영향을 주는지
③ 어떻게 향이 음식의 풍미에 영향을 주는지
④ 왜 사람들은 달콤한 향을 선호하는지
⑤ 향초를 만드는 방법

DICTATION Answers

01 been working as / keep their teeth healthy / along your gum lines
02 well prepared / is well known for / is widely used for
03 winning the prize / is the role like / won't have to
04 decorated with flowers / against the wall / place to rest
05 to pick me up / showing you around / what I use
06 I'm walking on air / supposed to do / allergic to animal hair
07 perming my hair / had your hair cut / who visit us
08 a couple of things / a group of college students / have everything planned
09 attending a university / participate in this event / Don't miss out on
10 When are we leaving / a little hard / want to try on
11 before the show starts
12 figure it out
13 You scored well / to work on / I can keep up
14 anything to drink / the money you saved / makes me feel good
15 famous for its wildlife / more closely / stay in the car
16-17 that smell good / how you feel / is said to help

MEMO

MEMO

MEMO

MEMO

MEMO

영어듣기
35+5회

1. 고1, 2 학생들의 수능 영어듣기 학습을 위한 기본 훈련서
2. 최신 수능 및 학력평가를 철저히 분석하여 반영
3. 모의고사 35회 + 학력평가 기출 모의고사 5회로 구성
4. 어려운 연음, 핵심 내용, 관용 표현 등을 중심으로 한 Dictation 수록
5. 매 회 Word & Expressions로 중요 어휘 및 학습 정리